ENGLAND

& WALES GUIDE

BE A TRAVELER - NOT A TOURIST!

**OPEN ROAD TRAVEL GUIDES SHOW YOU
HOW TO BE A TRAVELER – NOT A TOURIST!**

Whether you're going abroad or planning a trip in the United States, take Open Road along on your journey. Our books have been praised by **Travel & Leisure, The Los Angeles Times, Newsday, Booklist, US News & World Report, Endless Vacation, American Bookseller, Coast to Coast,** *and many other magazines and newspapers!*

Don't just see the world – experience it with Open Road!

ABOUT THE AUTHOR

Paul Tarrant was born at Barton-on-Sea, on the south coast of England. He has traveled extensively throughout Europe, North America, the Middle East and, of course, the United Kingdom, and is the co-author of books on New England, Scotland and Britain. He currently lives in Weymouth, Dorset, where he enjoys taking his highly energetic golden retriever, Tess, for long walks along the beach.

BE A TRAVELER, NOT A TOURIST - WITH OPEN ROAD TRAVEL GUIDES!

Open Road Publishing has guide books to exciting, fun destinations on four continents. As veteran travelers, our goal is to bring you the best travel guides available anywhere!

No small task, but here's what we offer:

• All Open Road travel guides are written by authors with a distinct, opinionated point of view – not some sterile committee or team of writers. Our authors are experts in the areas covered and are polished writers.

• Our guides are geared to people who want to make their own travel choices. We'll show you how to discover the real destination – not just see some place from a tour bus window.

• We're strong on the basics, but we also provide terrific choices for those looking to get off the beaten path and experience the country or city – not just see it or pass through it.

• We give you the best, but we also tell you about the worst and what to avoid. Nobody should waste their time and money on their hard-earned vacation because of bad or inadequate travel advice.

• Our guides assume nothing. We tell you everything you need to know to have the trip of a lifetime – presented in a fun, literate, no-nonsense style.

• And, above all, we welcome your input, ideas, and suggestions to help us put out the best travel guides possible.

ENGLAND

& WALES GUIDE

BE A TRAVELER - NOT A TOURIST!

Paul Tarrant

OPEN ROAD PUBLISHING

1st Edition

Copyright ©2001 by Paul Tarrant
- All Rights Reserved -
Library of Congress Control No. 00-134136
ISBN 1-892975-41-6

TABLE OF CONTENTS

MAPS

SIDEBARS

SIDEBARS

1. INTRODUCTION

One of the best things about visiting England and Wales is that you don't have to travel very far to sample some of Europe's most stunning scenery or some of its most glorious architecture. Whether you choose to rent a car, hop on a train or ride the bus, within a few hours of your arrival you will feast your eyes on a landscape of Suffolk that Constable so adored, or absorbing the green rolling countryside of southern England, home of attractions as far apart as mystical Stonehenge and the domes of Brighton's Royal Pavilion; going weak at the knees at the sight of one of England's great cathedrals – York or Durham, Winchester or Salisbury – or being totally overawed by the majestic landscape of mountains and lakes in Snowdonia, in north Wales, Britain's most majestic national park.

And let's not forget London! Noisy, bustling, crowded she may be – but you'll never forget your visit. There simply isn't enough space to mention all the historical attractions, museums, cultural and entertainment venues in what is one of the world's greatest, most fascinating cities. It's impossible to list every single attraction, every sight worth seeing, in a book like this, so in a way, all I can do is whet your appetite. To help you understand and appreciate this wonderful country, there are chapters on the nation's history, culture, geography and of course its people – be prepared to be surprised by the friendliness, politeness, gentleness, good humor and tolerance of the people here.

There are extensive hotel and restaurant listings to make your stay more enjoyable, and I've included helpful information ranging from attractions for children to the best places in London to take afternoon tea – and some of the best places to enjoy a pint or two of the stronger stuff!

Whether you're interested in nature, architecture, culture, history, nightclubbing, shopping, theater, family entertainment or a bit of each, England and Wales have it all in abundance.

2. OVERVIEW

There'll always be an England
While there's a country lane.
Wherever there's a cottage small
Beside a field of grain.
- **Ross Parker & Hugh Charles**, *"There'll always be an England"*

LONDON

I love London! This vibrant, cosmopolitan metropolis of 650 square miles and 7 million residents – Europe's largest – is truly one of the world's great cities, and one which just oozes history and culture. "There is in London all that life can afford," said diarist Dr. Johnson, and what rang true for him 200 years ago still rings true for residents and visitors today. Within its boundaries you'll find some of the world's greatest museums and galleries, historical monuments that will blow your mind, fantastic shopping, exciting nightlife, literally scores of theaters and concert venues, and, with gorgeous, beautifully manicured parks and gardens, it's also one of the world's greenest cities.

No longer is London a dead-end when it comes to high quality hotels and cuisine. It's rich in lavish hotels (though hotel prices in London tend to be among the most expensive in the world) and – according to many – has now surpassed Paris as the place to dine out.

High on the list of priorities for many visitors is the **Tower of London**, the fortress William the Conqueror built to keep the Saxons – and future claimants to the throne – at bay. As well as being the site of many of the most important – and grisliest – events in British history, it's home of the Crown Jewels, the Queen's mind-boggling collection of household gold and silver. Second on the list of priorities for many visitors is **Westminster Abbey**, a great barn of a place, built by Edward the Confessor in 1065, where British monarchs have been crowned for centuries and where many of them are buried.

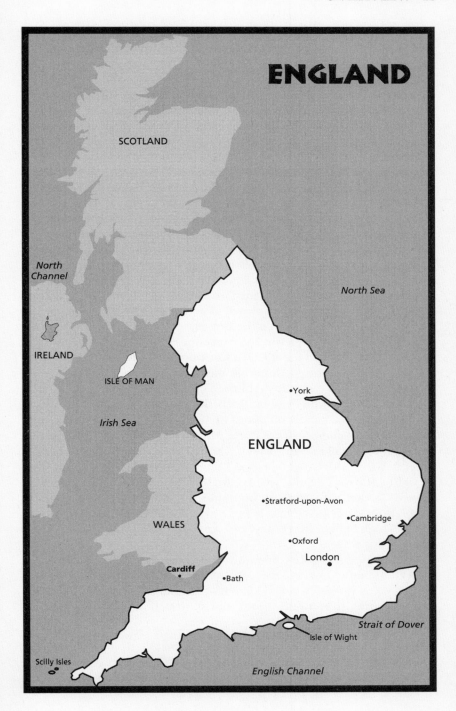

Within a stone's throw of the Abbey are the **Houses of Parliament** and St. Stephen's Tower, more commonly known as **Big Ben**, while a couple of miles – and a short Tube ride – to the east you'll marvel at **St. Paul's Cathedral** with its tall dome, scene of the 1981 wedding of Prince Charles to the late Princess Diana. Royal watchers will want to see **Buckingham Palace**, where you can watch the Changing of the Guard ceremony, and who knows? You may catch a glimpse of the Queen or her centenarian mother! Whatever you do, don't miss the superb **British Museum**, with one of the most extensive collections of art and artifacts in the world; the **Victoria and Albert Museum**, the planet's best fine arts museum, and, especially for children, the **Natural History Museum**, with an 80-foot long Diplodocus to greet you as you enter.

The most famous square in central London, **Trafalgar Square**, is flanked by the excellent **National Gallery**, with some of the world's most famous paintings. A mile further along the Thames, in the converted Bankside power station, is the newly-opened **Tate Modern Gallery** (just a stroll from the rebuilt Shakespeare Globe Theatre) – though the pedestrian bridge that was designed to bring visitors from the north bank of the Thames to the Gallery closed after its first day after it started to wobble from side to side! See the preserved Roman lady and a recon-structed Roman city street in the **Museum of London**, take a stroll in beautiful **Hyde Park** or the adjacent **Kensington Gardens**, where you can see the recently restored, stunning memorial to Prince Albert, Queen Victoria's husband – as well as a children's playground memorial to Diana, Princess of Wales, who lived in nearby **Kensington Palace**.

Walk past the stately buildings of Whitehall, the center of govern-ment, to catch a glimpse of the Prime Minister's residence at **10 Downing Street**, or for retail therapy head to **Oxford Street**, the busiest shopping street in the world; **Knightsbridge**, home of **Harrods** department store (as well as **Harvey Nichols**, well-known to viewers of *Absolutely Fabulous*), **Covent Garden**, with its trendy boutiques, or, if you really have money to spend, Bond Street. And take a bird's eye view of the whole lot from the 500-foot high **Millennium Wheel** (also known as London Eye), the world's largest ferris wheel.

If it's blood and gore you want you've come to the right place. Apart from attending an England soccer game, the **London Dungeon** is for you, though you'll probably get a kick out of **Madame Tussaud's**, London's most enduring (if not endearing) tourist attraction, with its gruesome Chamber of Horrors.

Take in a play or musical at one of London's 50 mainstream theaters or be a bit more daring and book a seat at one of the fringe venues. Follow that up with a visit to a lively pub, complete with warm beer and bartenders you don't have to tip. Rather than visit one of the tourist-trap taverns in the center, why not ride out a few stops on the Underground and sample the ambience of a pub with real Londoners in the suburbs?

London, outside of the West End and City, is made up of countless "villages," each with its own distinctive character and style; places like Hampstead in north London and Chelsea, to the southwest.

There's even more to see on the outskirts of the metropolis: **Windsor Castle**, west of London, the Queen's favorite residence; **Hampton Court Palace**, built by Henry VII for Cardinal Wolsey and then usurped by him; **St. Alban's**, with its magnificent Abbey.

Remember: there is just so much that you can see in London on one visit. Don't try to squeeze in everything on one trip. As Dr. Johnson reminds us, you won't even be able to fit all that London has to offer into a lifetime. Instead, plan to come again. I'm sure you'll want to!

THE SOUTHEAST

Although it's close to London, a fact that brings both advantages and disadvantages, England's wealthy southeast region has an identity all of its own, with vast stretches of idyllic countryside - a patchwork quilt landscape of gently rolling hills, orchards (**Kent** is known as the "Garden of England" on account of its fruit-producing industry), heath and woodland bisected by a host of streams and rivers leading down to the towering white cliffs of its southern coastline, or to the massive Thames estuary to the north.

Here are some of the nation's most historic small cities – places like **Canterbury**, with one of England's finest cathedrals and mother church of the Anglican/Episcopal community; **Rochester**, also in Kent, with another fine cathedral and strong associations with the author Charles Dickens; the smaller, beguiling towns of **Lewes**, **Arundel** and **Chichester** in Sussex, and numerous stately homes and castles speckled throughout the region.

The southeast coast is also a seaside playground for millions of Londoners, whose *piece de resistance* is the flamboyant, good-time Regency town of **Brighton**, sometimes known as "London by the Sea," and a host of smaller resorts, plus gorgeous historic towns like **Rye** and **Winchelsea**, and the great port of **Dover**, little more than 20 miles from the coast of France. Ferry services depart from Dover, Folkestone and half a dozen ports along the southeast coast to their counterparts in France, Belgium and Holland, while the high-speed Eurostar train whizzes through the green landscape before it dips below the Channel near Folkestone on its high-speed journey to Paris and Brussels.

WEST COUNTRY

The West Country is the term given to the counties of southwest England; the lush pastureland of **Somerset**, largely rural and dotted with the kind of picturesque villages that feature in picture books; the great Roman city of **Bath**, with its elegant honey stone Georgian terraces; and the regional capital of **Bristol**, with a fine cathedral and a great maritime history. To the west, the long, craggy wave-lashed peninsula that juts out into the Atlantic Ocean comprises the counties of **Devon** with its tall cliffs, wide estuaries, historic cities like **Plymouth** and **Exeter**, sophisticated resorts and large open tracts of moorland – and **Cornwall** with its whitewashed fishing villages, sandy coves, all steeped in Arthurian legend. It's no surprise that these two latter counties are the best-loved domestic holiday destinations for Britons, so if you're traveling there in the summer, expect long delays.

Cornwall retains a strong Celtic identity – though the ancient Cornish language fizzled out centuries ago and many locals claim that it's not England at all. Cross the **River Tamar** from Devon and you're in a different nation, they say – a statement that's certainly borne out by the many unusual traditions and customs – including unusual, distinctive place names – that make this place feel different from the rest of England.

CENTRAL SOUTHERN ENGLAND

Central southern England corresponds largely to Thomas Hardy's **Wessex**, comprising the counties of Hampshire, Dorset and Wiltshire, and is an area of gentle rolling hills, heath and moorlands. Here you'll find the **New Forest**, a 145 square mile tract of woodland and heath that offers some of the best walking and horse riding in England, and the Dorset's **Purbeck Hills** where spectacular chalk and granite cliffs meet the sea. Other features of this region's impressive coastline include salty **Portsmouth**, with a range of maritime attractions, including Nelson's flagship, *HMS Victory*, the large commercial port of **Southampton** and the sprawling seaside resort of **Bournemouth**, with miles of soft, sandy beaches. Further west is the virtually landlocked **Poole Harbour**, while just offshore and readily accessible by ferry is the **Isle of Wight**, England in miniature, and the favorite holiday destination for Queen Victoria, who built a summer residence at Osborne House.

The whole area, the heartland of King Arthur's Wessex, oozes history – from dozens of prehistoric remains, including the world's most famous – **Stonehenge** – to the magnificent cathedral cities of **Winchester** and

Salisbury, to the grand stately homes at **Longleat** and **Wilton**, and the stunning Capability Brown-designed gardens at **Stourhead** in Wiltshire. All around the region are pretty picture-postcard villages, complete with church, pond, village green, and a smattering of rose or ivy-covered thatched cottages. The region is rich in literary associations, too: as well as Thomas Hardy, who spent most of his life in and around the Dorset county town of **Dorchester**. And for you Jane Austen fans, she hails from Chawton, near Winchester.

THE MIDLANDS

The English midlands is a region of stark contrasts, a land of large and generally ugly industrial cities separated by some of the loveliest countryside in the nation. This lush landscape is speckled with old market towns and attractive villages – some of which have changed little in centuries – and some grand stately homes.

For most American visitors, the chief draws here are the market town of **Stratford-upon-Avon**, Shakespeare's home town, with a clutch of Bard-related attractions, including the National Shakespeare Theatre; the glorious **Cotswold Hills** with villages that seem to grow out of the landscape, and of course **Oxford**, university city of dreaming spires, nightmarish traffic, *Brideshead Revisted* and *Inspector Morse*. Just a few miles away from Stratford, **Warwick**, with its medieval castle, and **Coventry**, whose modern cathedral replaced one that was destroyed during World War II, are both eminently visitable, while further north, Britain's second largest city, **Birmingham**, has a wealth of artistic and cultural attractions, despite its bland reputation.

Further west, the cathedral city of **Worcester** and the nearby **Malvern Hills**, the home territory of the composer Edward Elgar, are the epitome of how every North American thinks England should be: cricket in the shadow of the cathedral tower, the River Severn lazily flowing by – and all surrounded by lush patchwork-quilt countryside, which reaches towards Hereford and the Welsh border country. Further north, **Stoke-on-Trent** is the hub of the **Potteries** region, while the county of Shropshire with its beguiling capital, **Shrewsbury**, attracts millions of visitors to its industrial theme park, **Ironbridge**.

EAST ANGLIA

East Anglia, the large protrusion that juts out into the North Sea just north of the Thames estuary, is a place where you can really feel you're off-the-beaten-path. Because it's on the way to nowhere, many visitors – like the Industrial Revolution a few centuries back – pass it by. In doing so, they're missing out on one of England's most attractive, unspoilt rural regions. Made up of the counties of Essex, Suffolk, Norfolk and Cambridgeshire, it contains some of the nation's most endearing, if unspectacular, countryside, as well as dozens of pretty towns and villages, and some of the nation's grandest village churches, evidence of the region's enormous wealth when the wool industry was flourishing.

Then there's the area known as **The Broads**, a series of lakes linked by canals and rivers that are a favorite holiday destination for many thousands of Britons every summer. The region is rich in stately homes, as evidenced by the wonderful **Holkham Hall** and the royal residence of **Sandringham**. The semi-circular coastline ranges from broody marshes in the south to some fine sandy, often isolated, beaches and small seaside resorts – as well as a couple of larger ones – further north.

This is not a region of large cities; its only large city, **Norwich**, with its ancient Norman cathedral and a host of other historical attractions, is a real gem, as is tiny **Ely**, whose cathedral looms high above the "fens" (the flat low-lying landscape that's similar to parts of Holland). More famous still is the spacious, elegant university city of **Cambridge**, where many of England's most illustrious personages – such as Milton, Bacon, Newton and Byron – received their education. This region also produced Oliver Cromwell, the Puritan leader who ousted King Charles I from the throne, John Wesley as well as many of the original *Mayflower* passengers.

THE NORTHWEST

Stretching in the south from the Roman city of **Chester**, with a host of well-preserved half-timbered medieval buildings, to the hilly **Scottish border** in the north, England's northwest is one of its most diverse but engrossing regions. Two of the nation's largest cities are here: **Manchester**, an industrial metropolis which has undergone something of a resurgence in recent years and now has a vibrant arts and cultural life – as well as the world's most successful soccer club; and the great port of **Liverpool**, for many years England's busiest commercial port and home town of the "**Fab Four**" – John, Paul, George and Ringo.

On the eastern side of the region, the Derbyshire **Peak District** is an area of dramatic landscapes, pretty villages and towns and magnificent stately homes, while on the Lancashire coast, England's most visited resort, brash and bawdy **Blackpool** offers a unique chance to see Brits letting their collective hair down. Between Blackpool and the Scottish border lies England's most stunning landscapes in the area much beloved by Bryron, Keats and Wordsworth – the **Lake District**, while further north the 75-mile long **Hadrian's Wall**, built by the Romans in the second century AD to fend off invasion by the Pict tribes from southern Scotland, offers a wealth of walking opportunities and, in its several museums, a chance to see how the Roman invaders spent their time at Europe's most remote outpost.

YORKSHIRE

England's largest county is also home to its proudest, most opinionated people – as well as to some of the nation's most attractive countryside and some of its most enthralling historical attractions. In fact, many Yorkshire folk say that the best thing to come out of neighboring Lancashire is the M62, the main motorway that leads into Yorkshire – and they're deadly serious! As you'd expect with a county of this size, Yorkshire offers a tremendous variety of scenery, from the rugged **coast** between Whitby and Scarborough, to the windswept **North York Moors**, just a few miles inland.

To the west, the rolling **Yorkshire Dales** offer endless opportunities for walking and exploring, while further south the gentle rolling landscape of the **Vale of York** is closer to the kind of countryside you'd find in the south of England. Yorkshire's *piece de resistance* and its greatest treasure is the wonderful, intriguing, ancient city of **York**, with one of Europe's largest and most beautiful cathedrals and a fascinating history that goes back to Roman times when it was an important trading and military center.

Yorkshire is also home to several large, industrial cities, several of which have experienced regeneration in recent years. Bustling **Leeds** and **Bradford** with their large ethnic populations offer a real contrast to the rural destinations; a different cultural experience; and a wealth of excellent restaurants, museums and parks. The mixture of large and lively urban areas, and Yorkshire's myriad picturesque towns and villages, stunning churches and peaceful ruined abbeys evokes a real sense of pride among its people: "Ee bah gum," as a Yorkie might put it, "there's nowt like it."

THE NORTHEAST

England's most remote region is in many ways its most attractive, a land of gloriously beguiling historical buildings, including some of the nation's most spectacular castles and one of its most inspiring cathedrals, the great Norman edifice at **Durham**. Attractive though the man-made sights are, it's the countryside here that truly captures the imagination; a magical, moody landscape that ranges from lonely windswept moors of the **Northumbria National Park**, speckled by isolated stone villages and crossed by the ancient Roman **Hadrian's Wall**, to a long **coastline** alternating between rocky promontories topped by historic ruined fortresses and long sandy stretches backed by acres of dunes. There's a raw beauty here that reaches deep into the spirit. No surprise, then, that this was the cradle of Christianity in northern England, begetting a host of saints, drawn and inspired by its power. There's no better place to get a feel for this than **Lindisfarne**, or Holy Island, accessible only by crossing a causeway that's only passable at low tide.

On the flip side, much of the southern half of this region formed part of one of the world's largest coal mining areas. Though the demise of the coal industry is well documented, many of the associated manufacturing and chemical industries continue to this day, so that, particularly in the area around the sprawling city of **Newcastle**, the landscape can vary tremendously. Further north along the coast and inland it's a different story; the industrial revolution hardly reached here, and the legacy is an unspoilt, dramatic, atmospheric and utterly beautiful landscape that, perhaps more than any other in England, can still truly claim to be "far from the madding crowd."

WALES

Wales is a land of myths and legends with a rich and distinctive culture that sets it apart from England, like the lilting Welsh language that sounds so different from the Anglo-Saxon tongue. **Cardiff**, the capital, is only two hours from London, a cosmopolitan city with an array of cultural and historical attractions, including a flamboyantly restored castle, while to the west, **Swansea**, the second city, is the gateway to the dramatic coastline of **The Mumbles** and the **Gower Peninsula**.

North of here, the **Pembrokeshire coast** offers some of the most engaging coastal scenery in Britain (and some of the most glorious sandy beaches anywhere in Europe). Visit **St. David's**, Britain's smallest city, with its fine cathedral; the lively seaside town of **Aberystwyth**, home of the National Library of Wales; the **Brecon Beacons National Park**, a land of moorland, lakes and mountains, and, in north Wales, the majestic landscapes of the **Snowdonia National Park** with its jagged mountains – including **Snowdon**, the tallest in England and Wales, from whose summit, on a clear day, you can see three nations: Wales, England and Ireland. Throughout the land, the many castles, ruined and intact, are for the most part strongholds built by the Normans to quell the Welsh tribes; **Carnarvon** and **Harlech** stand out in particular for their splendid locations.

And let's not forget the Welsh people; dominated by the English for centuries (and for many of them quite happily so), the establishment of the new **Welsh Assembly** in 1999 means that for the first time in 700 years, they can exercise at least a degree of self-determination. A warm-hearted, friendly people, you can be sure of that "welcome in the hillsides" when you visit Wales.

3. SUGGESTED ITINERARIES

Here are a few suggested itineraries for varying lengths of stay in England and Wales. Although it's not a big country, the massive volume of places to visit, combined with the frequency of traffic delays, means that you will inevitably miss out. The best thing is to try and plan what you want to see ahead of your trip – though even then there will be places that particularly take your fancy and where you will want to linger and, as a result, perhaps you'll miss another intended sight. Be flexible! The regional tourist boards listed in Chapter 6, *Planning Your Trip*, will be more than happy to offer advice and local information.

The best tip is to take things easy (especially in the first few days when you will be jet lagged) and don't try to do too much.

If you're planning to stay in London, don't bother to rent a car while you're there: the traffic is horrendous, there's nowhere to park (and where there is, it's prohibitively expensive) and the public transport system is very efficient. Even though picking up a car at the airport on your arrival sounds very attractive, the truth will soon prove otherwise.

Many attractions close between 5:30pm and 7pm in the summer, even earlier at other times of the year. Maximize your touring time by seeing all that you can in an area during the day, and traveling late evening (remembering that it's still light at 9:30pm in June and July). If you do this, ensure that you call ahead to confirm your hotel or B&B reservation, telling them that you will be late.

THREE DAYS IN LONDON

Note: many flights from London arrive in the early morning, and you may not be able to check into your hotel room until 1pm or even later, in which case my advice would be to leave your luggage with the concierge, then take a brief walk around the neighborhood, noting banks, etc. In the afternoon, I suggest a tour of the city in one of the sightseeing buses. The following suggested itinerary is based on three full days in the capital.

Day 1
Sightseeing Tour of London or Visit the London Eye for overview of the
  city
Visit Westminster Abbey, see Big Ben and the Houses of Parliament
Pub lunch at the Albert, Victoria Street
Walk up Whitehall to Trafalgar Square
Tour the National Gallery
Early dinner
Theater

Day 2
Visit the Tower of London (early, to avoid crowds)
Tour St. Paul's Cathedral
Lunch at Covent Garden
Tour the British Museum
Dinner

Day 3
Visit the Victoria and Albert Museum and/or the Natural History
  Museum (they are adjacent)
Lunch
Visit Knightsbridge for shopping (Harrod's, Harvey Nichols) or Oxford
  Street
Dinner

SEVEN DAYS IN ENGLAND & WALES
Day 1
Sightseeing Tour of London by bus
Visit Westminster Abbey, see Big Ben and Houses of Parliament
Lunch
Walk up Whitehall to Trafalgar Square
Tour the National Gallery
Early dinner
Theater

Day 2
Visit Tower of London
Lunch
Visit British Museum
See Buckingham Palace and take a walk through St. James or Hyde Park
Dinner

Day 3
Early start
Pick up car, drive to Cambridge
Visit King's College
Lunch
Drive to York
Dinner in York

Day 4
Tour York Minster
Walk the city walls
Lunch
Visit Jorvic Viking Centre
Shopping in the Shambles
Dinner
Stay in York

Day 5
Early start!
Drive to Stratford
See Shakespeare's Birthplace
Visit Ann Hathaway's Cottage
Lunch
Drive to Coventry
Visit the Cathedral
Drive to Warwick Castle for short tour
Return to Stratford
Dinner
Theater at RSC
Stay in Stratford

Day 6
Drive to Oxford
Take a Blue Guide Tour
Spend some time at Christ Church
Lunch
Drive to Blenheim Palace
Tour Blenheim
Drive to London
Dinner in London

Day 7
Time for Shopping

14 DAYS IN ENGLAND & WALES
Days 1-3 as in first itinerary above.

Day 4
Drive to Cambridge
Visit King's College
Lunch
Drive to York
Evening stroll around the city walls
Dinner
Stay in York

Day 5
Tour York Minster
Visit Jorvic Viking Centre
Lunch
Drive to Castle Howard
Dinner in York
Stay in York

Day 6
Early start!
Drive to Stratford
Visit Shakespeare's Birthplace
Visit Anne Hathaway's Cottage
Lunch
Visit Coventry Cathedral
Visit Warwick Castle
Dinner in Stratford
Theater at RSC

Day 7
Drive to Oxford
Guided Tour with Blue Badge guide (two hours)
Lunch
Stroll around the city
Shopping
Dinner
Stay in Oxford

Day 8
Drive to Winchester
Visit Cathedral

Visit Winchester College and Great Hall of Castle
Lunch
Drive to Salisbury
Visit Cathedral
Drive to Stonehenge
Dinner in Salisbury
Stay in Salisbury

Day 9
Drive to Exeter
Visit Cathedral
Lunch
Drive to Looe and begin exploring south Cornish coast
Dinner in Penzance
Stay in Penzance

Day 10
Drive up north Cornish coast to Somerset border then Bath
Visit the Roman baths
Visit the Abbey
Lunch
Shopping in Bath
Dinner in Bath
Stay in Bath

Day 11
Drive across Severn Bridge into Wales
Morning in Cardiff: Visit castle and shops
Lunch in Cardiff
Drive to St. David's
Visit cathedral
Drive north up Pembrokeshire coast
Dinner at Aberystwyth
Stay at Aberystwyth

Day 12
Drive to Snowdonia
Stop for lunch
Drive to Birmingham
Visit City Art Gallery, Barber Institute
Return to London
Dinner in London
Stay in London

Day 13
Day at leisure in London:
Visit new Tate Modern Gallery
Take a tour in the Millennium Wheel
Lunch
Shopping
Dinner
Theater

Day 14
Early start!
Book taxi to airport
Check out

4. LAND & PEOPLE

Great Britain is the name of the largest of several hundred islands off the northwestern coast of Europe, stretching from **Land's End** in the extreme southwest of England, around 868 miles to Scotland's most northerly mainland point, **John o'Groats**. Its width varies from almost 300 miles in the south and from the Welsh coast to England's east coast, to little more than 80 miles at the "neck." You are never more than 150 miles from the sea.

The climate is generally mild and temperate. Prevailing winds are southwesterly with few extremes of temperature: It is rarely above 90 degrees Farenheit or below 20 degrees. The average rainfall, more than 1,600mm (millimeters) in the mountainous areas of the west and north, falls to 800mm in central and eastern areas. Rain is fairly well distributed throughout the year, but on average March to June are the driest months and September to January the wettest. During May, June and July – the months of longest daylight – the mean daily duration of sunshine varies from five hours in the north to more than eight hours in the extreme south of England.

LAND

Draw a line from the mouth of the River Tees in northeast England to the mouth of the Exe in the southwest (**the Tees/Exe line**). Basically, to the north and west of this line you have the ancient mountain zones and highlands of Britain. This is an area of dramatic, rugged landscapes, deep valleys and generally poor soil. To the south and east are the lowlands of England, a gentler, lush landscape of hills, valleys and plains.

Britain's varied scenery is largely due to the influence of the underlying rocks, some of which date back more than 3.4 billion years, and are among the oldest in the world. Meanwhile, in the south and east of England, new landscapes are still being formed. The oldest of the rocks from the pre-Cambrian era were formed when there was no life on earth, long before even the earliest fossils were discovered. These rocks tend to be the hardest and therefore to stand out as highlands, evidenced in the mountains that form the northwest fringe of the Scottish Highlands and the Outer Hebrides, down to parts of Anglesey in North Wales, and in the Malvern Hills of England.

The first evidence of life appears in fossils dating from the Cambrian period, about 570 million years ago, when a great ocean trough lay between Norway and Ireland, with ancient land masses to its northwest in north Scotland, and to the southeast, where the English midlands now exist. Great thicknesses of mud developed in this sea, compressed under the weight of later sediments, while from time to time volcanoes poured ash and lava into the sea, and pushed up a high mountain range from the deposits of the Great Basin – the Caledonian mountains, with high, often rocky and bare peaks.

Around 300 million years ago, the Caledonian mountains were worn down, and much of Britain became a desert. Old Red Sandstone was laid down in inland basins and lakes. Exmoor and the Brecon Beacons in Wales were formed in this way, as were parts of Caithness in Scotland and the Orkney isles.

During the Carboniferous period (345-320 million years ago) the sea slowly drowned the deserts. Thick layers of limestone formed, then covered by the deltas of large rivers, which silted up allowing dense forests to flourish. The remains of these forests, when compressed by more mud, formed Britain's coalfields, while the Pennine mountains and the south Wales mountains were also formed from these sediments.

Limestone formed during the Jurassic period (195-136 million years ago) created a long ridge between the North York Moors through the Cotswolds right down to the Purbeck Hills in Dorset, on the south coast of England. To the east of this line, chalk uplands, composed by the vast numbers of miniscule sea creatures, was formed at a rate of one foot every 30,000 years during the Cretaceous period (136-65 million years ago). Flints in the chalk provided human beings with their first tools and later on with building materials.

During the Tertiary era of 65-1 million years ago, southern England was on the edge of the Great Earth Storm which raised the Alps, the limestone and chalk being folded up against the more durable massifs to the north and west, while rivers formed deep valleys. In the broader valleys, a new incursion by the sea deposited large amounts of sand which later formed the heathland so typical of areas like the New Forest and some of the heathland around London.

The most recent moulding of their landscape was caused by the Ice Age, which started about a million years ago. At one stage, most of Britain north of a line from the mouth of the Thames to the Severn was covered in a great ice sheet, leaving deep valleys in the Scottish Highlands, England's Lake District and Snowdonia in North Wales. The ice sheets deposited huge amounts of sand and gravel and as sheets of clay, rich in important minerals, that resulted in such fertile soil in much of southern and eastern England.

As the ice melted, the resultant rise in sea levels meant that Britain, which had once been linked to continental Europe by a land bridge, was separated. This took place only about 8,000 years ago.

Britain is constantly changing, even today. As global warming continues, and sea levels rise, so the coast of eastern England is being eroded as frightening rates. In other places, sand and gravel deposited by rivers is leading to the formation of new tracts of land.

Today

It's quite remarkable, in such a densely populated land, how easy it is to get right away from the madding crowd and find total peace and beauty. Wales is a land of mountains, deep valleys, pretty villages and market towns, wide sandy beaches and rocky coves. Most of the industry here is in the south, where large-scale coal-mining and steel production led to the scarring of much of the landscape. Here, too, are the country's largest cities, all on the coast: Cardiff, the capital, with some fine civic buildings, a castle and a wealth of green spaces, and Swansea, close to the rugged coastline of the Mumbles.

Northern England was deeply affected by the Industrial Revolution, where large towns sprang up to tap the fast-flowing Pennine rivers and streams for cotton and wool manufacture. Among the largest cities here are Manchester, Leeds, and Sheffield. However, you're never far from idyllic countryside, whether it's the gentle landscapes that surround the ancient city of York, the Peak District, or England's most scenic corner, the Lake District. Further east, the wild landscapes of Northumberland, dotted with castles and abbeys, offer some of the best walking anywhere.

The Industrial Revolution also ravaged the midlands, leaving huge cities like Birmingham, Nottingham and Leicester that now sprawl across acres and acres of land. Just as in the north, though, there are vast tracts of unspoiled countryside with gorgeous market towns and wide open spaces; rural counties like Shropshire, with its half-timbered houses, Worcestershire and Warwickshire, home of Shakespeare. Further east, the even more rural East Anglia is noted for its off-the-beaten-path towns and villages, long stretches of unspoiled coast and stunning churches and cathedrals. Here too is Cambridge, one of England's must-sees.

In the southeast, the London sprawl dominates the whole region, though it's still possible to find peace and quiet in the highways and byways of Kent, the "Garden of England," and Sussex, and in the Channel coastal resorts. London itself is one of the greatest showpieces on earth, a magical city. Dr. Johnson said that if you're tired of London, you're tired of life, and it's not difficult to see why: there's just no end of things to do and sights to see. The central south is notable for more gentle country-side, including the New Forest, with excellent walking, the spectacular Dorset coastline and some fine cathedral cities. Further west, the West Country is England's holiday playground – its long coastline dotted with fine sandy beaches and sheltered coves, pretty fishing villages and larger resorts – not to mention both Dartmoor and Exmoor National Parks, and some of the wildest landscapes you'll find in England.

FACTS ON ENGLAND & WALES

Total population: England 47 million, Wales 3 million

Largest city: London, 6.9 million

Longest river: Severn, 215 miles

Highest mountain: in England, Scafell Pike 3,210 feet; in Wales, Snowdon 3,560 feet

Largest lake: Lake Windermere

Unemployment: 6.5%

Birth rate: 13.9

Total area: England 130,000 square kilometers Wales 21,000 square kilometers

Population density: England, 367 per square kilometer; Wales, 139 per square kilometer

---

PEOPLE

Background

For years, Americans and Canadians have seen their pre-existing stereotypical views of the English affirmed by the appearance on televi-sion of a variety of costume dramas, the conclusion being that all older English women walk, talk and behave just like Miss Marple, while older English men all walk, talk and look like Alistair Cooke. For younger people, the British pop culture, which has produced such wayward (and now aging) characters as Boy George and David Bowie seems to have given rise to the idea that most English young people are a bit wayward, too.

While Miss Marple look-alikes can be seen nibbling cucumber sand-wiches at church garden parties the length and breadth of the nation, and a thousand genteel Alistair Cooke clones can be witnessed all summer long dressed in white flanels and playing bowls at a host of Costa Geriatrica seaside resorts, such stereotypes are far from reality.

To understand something about the people of England, it's first necessary to know something of her (recent) history. Such stereotypes are largely the product of Empire, when Britannia ruled most of the world's waves, and, as the cliche goes, waived the rules. Domestically, Britain was the powerhouse of the world, her manufacturing industries in particular providing a high percentage of the world's needs – and all fueled by an apparently abundant supply of coal.

Both World War I and World War II resulted in virtual bankruptcy for England, as the manufacturing base began to erode and industrial disputes prompted a growth in the labor movement, just at the same time as the Empire was beginning to collapse, beginning with India in 1947.

Yet even amid the gloom, there were some bright sports:

• The founding of a National Health Service, aiming to provide free medical care for every citizen
• Social welfare programs that would virtually eradicate the extreme poverty so redolent during the so-called prosperous Victorian years
• Economic booms (inevitably followed by busts) which prompted Prime Minister Harold MacMillan to tell the people in 1957 that they had "never had it so good."

Britain in the 1940s and '50s was a peaceful, generally law-abiding nation, where it was possible for **George Orwell** to say, "An imaginary foreigner would be struck by the gentleness, by the orderly behavior of the British crowds, and the lack of pushing and quarreling."

The 1960s were a different matter. Rampant inflation took hold and industrial conflicts and strikes were in abundance. Britain struggled to find a new world role and became a member of the European Community or "Common Market," yet was still unclear as to where exactly she was headed.

Margaret Thatcher's election success in 1979 brought about some major changes, not only in the way things were done, but in the way the nation began to view itself. A popular war against Argentina in the Falklands bolstered her popularity and set the stage for a number of reforms. Private enterprise was encouraged, and tough new legislation weakened the power of the unions. Home ownership was encouraged, and people were sold the benefits of share ownership. The old, rather innocent, unassuming Britain of the past was fast disappearing.

By the early 1990s, a serious recession led people to question the kind of society England was becoming. The murder of two-year-old James Bulger by two boys only slightly older in 1993, brought about a period of intense national navel-gazing. Increasing crime – some racially motivated, sometimes violence for violence's sake – brought calls for immediate action from some, but led others to question the values of a society where the rich/poor divide was growing and where public services were increasingly being curtailed in order to save costs (and, one assumes, bring shareholders a better return).

Today, some of the questions have been answered. Tony Blair's "caring capitalism" may not have endeared him to some of the more dogmatic members of his Labour Party, but the concept seems to go down well with the bulk of public opinion. And while there is still something of the traditional "fair play" element in the national psyche, people are happy to be making money, but easing their social conscience with some of the most generous charitable giving in the world, and by getting involved as volunteers (25%).

Britain continues to evolve. An attempt by the government to bring about a ban on the tradition of fox hunting, plus the demise of many agricultural industries, initiated with the BSE scare when millions of cattle were slaughtered, has exacerbated some of the pre-existing tensions between urban and rural areas. In the cities, growing incidences of racist attacks indicate that there is still plenty of work to be done. And a debate on entrance to England's two main universities, Oxford and Cambridge, has brought up the whole class issue.

There are signs that William Hague's Conservative Party is beginning to claw its way back into public affection by successfully exploiting the xenophobic "Little Englander" attitude that appeals to many people, by latching on to the general anti-European sentiment that exists in England, symbolized by the proposed replacement of the pound sterling with the European ecu. It's been called the new "Battle for Britain," and its outcome will determine what kind of nation Britain becomes in the future, as well as indicating what kind of nation Britain is now.

A Melting Pot

What strikes many first-time North American visitors to England is how complex and cosmopolitan so many of its major cities are. In the post-war period, huge numbers of immigrants, predominantly from the Caribbean and from Asia settled here, and began an exciting new dimension to the English way of life.

But England has been a melting pot for centuries. First it was the **Celts**, who arrived here from France and southern regions of Europe before 1000 BC. Subsequent invasions have included the **Romans**, who arrived here in 43 BC and immediately set about pushing the Celt tribes back into the inhospitable, hilly terrain of Wales, Scotland, Ireland and Cornwall – explaining the fiercely independent traits found in many of the people who live in these areas today.

The next to arrive were **Angles**, **Saxons** and **Jutes** from Germany. Essentially farmers, it was the language they brought with them that was to form the basis of the English language spoken today. Perhaps the best tangible evidence for their presence is the abundance of place names ending in *ham* and *ton*. The Anglo-Saxons had a lot of trouble keeping the Vikings at bay, but failed dismally to repel the **Normans**. The year 1066, perhaps the most famous date in English history, is remembered for the defeat of Harold, King of the Saxons, at the **Battle of Hastings**, by William, Duke of Normandy, who soon set about replacing Saxon structures with feudal Norman ones. For many years, ethnic tensions existed between conquerors and conquered, but the lack of any further major invasion over the next 1,000 years allowed a gradual fusion of the cultures.

Until the thirteenth century, England and Wales had remained **separate kingdoms**. This changed in 1381, when **Edward I** of England conquered Wales, and established rule from London. Meanwhile, Scotland and England did not come together until the **Act of Union** in 1707. Bowing to increasing demand from the Welsh for greater autonomy, in 1998 certain powers were devolved from Westminster to a new **Welsh Assembly**, meeting in Cardiff. For a long time, Scots had resented being governed from London, so it was almost inevitable that at some point Scotland should get its own devolved **Parliament**, with autonomy from the rest of Britain on all but a handful of matters. Many Scots, however, still advocate total **independence** from the "auld enemy." Never refer to the monarch as **Queen of England** to a Scot or Welshman.

The reaction to all this in England has been a growth in English nationalism. This has manifested itself primarily in demands for greater autonomy for the **English regions**, many of which, such as Yorkshire, have a highly distinctive character.

There's no doubt that of all the nations that constitute the United Kingdom, England is by far the most **cosmopolitan**. This century, waves of immigration have brought **Jews** fleeing the carnage of continental Europe, and **Irish**, **Greek** and **Cypriot** refugees. In the 1950s, large numbers of **Afro-Caribbeans** arrived, taking on jobs the indigenous English did not want – bus conductors, garbage collectors and the like. More devoted to the Queen than many of her own family, and as devoutly Anglican as many a Bishop, they were soon shocked – not by the gloomy skies, but by the discrimination and social rejection they found. Even the Church they espoused rejected them. This led to an explosive growth in black churches throughout London and the larger cities. Added to these are **Bangladeshis** fleeing the poverty of their native land; **Sikhs** from the Punjab, **Gujeratis** and **African Asians** who escaped from Idi Amin's regime in Uganda, **Indians** and **Pakistanis**.

In an increasingly pluralistic England, many of these have become successful entrepreneurs; all have brought their own distinctive cultural and religious identity and practice, to the point where there are now, for example, more practising members of the Islamic faith in England than active members of the Church of England.

Many people of ethnic origins feel that the system is stacked heavily against them, with employment and educational opportunities favoring Caucasians. A **National Campaign for Racial Equality** promotes fair play and equal opportunities for all ethnic minorities (even English feeling discriminated against in Scotland), and there are policies actively promoting **positive discrimination** (affirmative action).

Tensions sometimes exist when ethnic cultures, particularly those with strong religious beliefs, conflict with the culture or law of the land. When live animals were slaughtered in the street in a religious ceremony in London, there was a public outcry, as there was when books were burnt following the publication of Salman Rushdie's *Satanic Verses*. For many of Britain's ethnic groups, it's a more domestic issue, recently-arrived families having to contend with the "westernization" of their children – especially over issues such as marriage – and the resulting clashes and conflicts. Relations between the black communities and the police reached an all-time low in the late 1980s, with a series of riots throughout the country. New policies encouraging affirmative action in getting more ethnic officers in the police service is slowly beginning to pay dividends.

However, the influence of television, radio and newspapers means that most people, even across ethnic and social divides, seem to respect certain general traits and behavioral characteristics, values, customs and style welded together by one common denominator – the **English language**.

How It Is

Most English are envious of their North American cousins' lifestyle but have a tendency to take things at home for granted. After all, Britain still has one of the highest standards of living in the world; the English just hate it if the French have a better one!

Perhaps the best place to observe the English is when they are living overseas. English expatriates living in the US desperately miss the BBC, real pubs, the British sense of humor, driving on the left, decent public transport and electric kettles. Despite surveys showing that many English would love to emigrate, there's a real sense of loyalty. While Americans swear allegiance to the flag and all it represents, the English don't swear allegiance at all, except, when called for, to the Queen, the symbol of the nation. The English wouldn't mind too much if you burned their flag (whether the Union Jack or England's St. George's flag) but they would mind very much if you tried to burn the Queen– just like in 1605 when a certain Guy Fawkes plotted to blow up James I.

Expect the English to be pleasant, polite and helpful to you. They are generally proud of their heritage and very keen to show you that they have something special to share. The English are approachable, and in most cases will gladly help you find your way if you get lost or need directions. But, as opposed to the Irish, who think nothing of inviting a new acquaintance to their home, don't expect such favors from the English. Jeremy Paxman, author of *The English*, explains, "What the English see as no more than respect for privacy look to others like disdain."

They may resent your assumed financial superiority (don't flaunt it too much), and they'll hate those bright red check pants Chuck is wearing, but they will treat you with great respect and warmth – even more so out of London, where you will be treated like a lord. (If you really want to feel like a lord, you can buy your own title.)

Make a real effort to mix with English people, whether in a pub, restaurant or hotel. Some weird and wonderful traits will baffle you completely, but keep a 'stiff upper lip' and you'll be fine. If you're in a pub, don't announce "Hi, I'm Brad from Providence and I really want to know all about you." They'll run a mile. Instead, break the ice by talking about the weather (don't be *too* critical, even if it's been raining for days), ask questions about cricket or who they think will win the Premiership (national soccer league, not the prime minister's office) this season – even if you haven't a clue about it yourself. If the person is not interested in talking to you, you'll get a very polite smile but little else; otherwise, you'll have a friend for life. Allow too for some regional variations: people in London may have a lot less time to talk to a stranger, while in rural areas they may have all day. But for goodness' sake, however friendly you get, don't give an Englishman a hug; the English hate to be touched – even in bed.

Despite the stereotypes, you'll be pleasantly surprised at how warm the English people can be, once they have overcome their initial shyness and suspicion. Just remember, you'll likely have to make the first move.

THE ENGLISH FLAG

England's flag, the flag of St. George, is a simple red cross on a plain white background. St. George, England's patron saint, was not an Englishman but a legendary local from a place called Lod, near modern Tel Aviv, who slaughtered the dragon. English Crusaders fighting to protect the Christian holy places from the Ottoman Turks liked the legend and adopted George and his flag for the nation.

THE CLASS SYSTEM

Ever watched *Keeping Up Appearances* on PBS? It's all about Hyacinth Bucket, a pretentious English homemaker who pronounces her name Bouquet, and the inherent snobbery that motivates her to behave in all kinds of ways – keeping up with the Joneses being her forte. It's all a bit of a spoof on the class system in Britain – a system that, many feel, still hampers the nation from fulfilling what it could be.

If, in the US, money talks, then in Britain, breeding positively screams. Top of the list is of course the **Royal Family**, followed by an aristocratic assemblage of earls, dukes, barons and others, all of whom (until recently) had the automatic right to sit in **the House of Lords**. Many of these are the descendants of families who supported the monarchy at some crucial stage in its history and were rewarded with titles, and sometimes vast estates. Alongside them comes a bevy of **life peers** – non-hereditary lords created by successive governments, often in appreciation of their service in political or public office, who can sit in the House of Lords.

Next down the line are the **professional and senior managerial** classes, including lawyers, doctors, media barons, and showbiz personalities whose sole purpose in life, it is argued, is not even vast material wealth but to be awarded one of the knighthoods which are doled out at regular intervals by the monarch, at the behest of the government of the day. All of the above categorized are likely to send their children to public schools - the ultimate evidence of social status in Britain is to send your child to the famous public (which means private in Britain) schools such as Eton (where Prince William was a student), Harrow or Winchester, followed by a stint at Oxford or Cambridge Universities.

Next come the **middle classes**, into which category comes small business owners, middle management, teachers and other professionals. Their children by and large attend local state schools, and are expected to win a place at university.

Finally come the **lower middle classes**, formerly known as the working class. Here we have factory workers, shop and office assistants, mechanics and so on. Children are sent to the local state school, and are encouraged to continue the same trade as their parents, or to aspire to the next rung up the ladder. Having a bright child who wins a place at university (which in Britain is all down to academic achievement, not the ability to fund the student) is all rather embarrassing, really.

WALES' FLAG

The flag of Wales is a red dragon on a white and green background.
*The **red dragon** is the heraldic symbol for Wales. According to tradition,*
the red dragon appeared on a crest borne by Arthur, whose father had seen
a dragon in the sky predicting he would be king.

Despite the radical changes that have taken place in Britain over the past 20 years, the **establishment** elite are very much still in control. Shopping in Harrod's; attending Eton or Harrow, Oxford or Cambridge; being invited to a garden party by the Queen; owning a few hundred inherited acres; living off unearned income; taking holidays in Mustique and owning a cottage or two in the country are all unmistakable statements of prestige – but no longer, necessarily, of power.

Surveys show that, despite the discrepancies between the classes, most people are fairly content with their lot. Many millions still dream of becoming instant millionaires with a lottery win, or by 'doing the pools' – betting on the outcome of soccer games – or with a successful run on the hit TV show *Who Wants to Be A Millionaire?* But even if they win a fortune, it does not in itself guarantee social acceptance and respect: Accent, education and social background continue to be the major criteria by which people are measured for important work – hence most of the national institutions; civil service, government, the army, the church, are still dominated by Oxford and Cambridge.

"Game plans" and "goal setting" is not something the English do readily. The game plan is already set out, and they know their place in it. Well, sort of.

National Traits
- Politeness. Expect the English to apologize even when the fault is not theirs.
- Warmth. But not the huggy type.
- Love of the countryside, the garden, the sun.
- A self-deprecating sense of humor, with the emphasis on self. They do the deprecating, don't you even think about it!
- Pride in their history
- Dissatisfaction with marriage, the family, the government, the health service, the church, the royal family, Europe (not necessarily in that order!)
- A love of animals, especially the underdog – like the fox
- A degree of formality, at least to start with.
- Envy of others' success – individuals or nations

For a profound, yet readable insight into what makes the English tick, you can do no better than pick up a copy of *The English*, by the BBC's Jeremy Paxman (Overlook Press, £29.95).

LANGUAGE DIFFERENCES

American	English
Ballpoint pen	Biro
Bathroom	Loo, lavatory, toilet
Busy (telephone)	Engaged
Cookie	Biscuit
The check	The bill
Crib	Cot
Dessert	Pudding, Sweet
Diaper	Nappy
Highway	Motorway
Jello	Jelly
Jumper	Pullover
Mail	Post
Newsstand	Newsagent
Orchestra (theater)	Stalls
Pacifier (baby's)	Dummy
Pants	Trousers
Phonebooth	Phonebox
Rotary	Roundabout
Running shoes	Trainers
Santa Claus	Father Christmas
Scotch	Whisky
Sidewalk	Pavement
Soccer	Football
Store	Shop
Stroller	Pushchair/pram
Subway	Underground, Tube
Sweater	Jumper, jersey
Truck	Lorry
Tylenol	Paracetemol
Undershirt	Vest
Vest	Waistcoat

*From Open Road's **London Guide**, by Meg Rosoff & Caren Acker.*

POLITICAL ARRANGEMENTS

The largest of the three nations that comprise Great Britain (i.e., excluding Northern Ireland, which is part of the United Kingdom but is physically located on Ireland), is **England**, with a land area of some 130,000 square kilometres, and a population of 47million. **Scotland** covers 77,000 square kilometres, with a small population of 5 million, while **Wales** is smaller still; just over 3 million people living in 26,000 square kilometres.

Great Britain has not always been united; until 1707, largely Celtic Scotland was a completely separate kingdom, and Wales, also with a strong Celtic culture was independent until subjugated by England's King Edward I in 1307.

Great Britain is a **constitutional monarchy**, governed by Parliament from **Westminster** in London. However, in recent years the **devolutionary process** has meant that both Scotland has its own **Parliament** and Wales its own **Assembly**, giving both a degree of self-determination, though some powers, such as defense and immigration, remain at Westminster.

5. A SHORT HISTORY

The history of England and Wales goes back a lot further than Big Ben or Westminster Abbey. Evidence of human life as far back as 250,000 BC has been found in east London, indicating that even at the earliest stages of human development, this was very much a place for migrants, though the ability of the migrant communities to settle here depended on the fluctuations of the various Ice Ages. It's important to remember that up until 6,000 BC Britain had not been an island at all – but connected to continental Europe by a land bridge.

After the thawing of the most recent Ice Age, the waters rose and the British Isles were separated permanently from the European mainland. The new moat around Britain did not curb the arrival of new immigrant groups however: around 3,500 BC the arrival of **neolithic settlers** from the continent had a major impact. With them came the new farming methods - including clearing woodlands and enclosing fields, making tools and weapons from the flint and stone they mined – that paved the way for the future development of the land.

THE BRONZE AGE

The Bronze Age began around 2,000 BC, with the arrival from Iberia, via northern Europe, of the **Beaker Folk** – so-called because of the implements found at their burial sites. With their distinctive social structure and their ability to intermix with existing cultures, they had a distinctive view on life, and were responsible for some of the **stone circles** – like **Stonehenge** – still visible today.

Warriors too, they dotted the landscape with **fortresses** – mainly earthworks with wooden stockades. But these were insufficient to stand up against the hordes of **Celtic invaders** from central Europe, who started arriving here around 2,500 years ago. The Celts established a sophisticated farming economy and a social hierarchy led by the high priests or **Druids**, used iron instead of bronze and began minting coins. Just like their Bronze Age precursors, the mighty fortresses the Celts were able to build – such as the massive **Maiden Castle** in Dorset – were insufficient to withstand invasion by the next invaders – the Romans.

THE ROMAN INVASION

The Romans had already launched two unsuccessful invasions of England before forces led by **Julius Caesar** arrived on the south coast near Dover in 43 AD. Their weapons and building skills were no match for the hapless Celts, who retreated into the hill country of Cornwall, Wales, Scotland and Ireland, as England became the most distant outpost of the Roman Empire. The language of the Celts still survives in Irish Gaelic, Scots Gaelic and Welsh – all of which are living languages spoken by significant numbers of people in those areas today; a fourth variant, Cornish, disappeared centuries ago.

The Romans established **commercial** and **political centers** – such as London and York – and built networks of **fine roads** – traces of which can still be seen today – and **forts**. They also constructed the 70 mile-long **Hadrian's Wall** stretching from the Solway Forth to the Tyne, and later the **Antonine Wall**, further north, which they operated for only 40 years due to the inhospitable terrain, designed to keep out Pict raiders from the north of England. The Romans integrated fairly well into the existing culture: Roman and Celtic gods were often worshiped side by side (as with Aquae Sulis, the Celt's water goddess and her Roman equivalent, Minerva, at Bath). It was also during the Roman period that **Christianity** was first introduced to England – a move that would change the shape and destiny of the nation forever.

ANGLES & SAXONS

When the Roman legions finally left in 410 AD, **Angles**, **Saxons** and **Jutes** – already frequent raiders – vied with **Danish** raiders for control of the country. The Anglo-Saxons, highly capable farmers, establishing the **rotational field system** that is still in existence today. Although Christianity was already well-established in other parts of Britain, it was in 597 that Pope Gregory dispatched the missionary **Augustine** to convert the Anglo-Saxon tribes. Arriving in Kent, he was befriended by Edgar, the local Saxon king, who was converted. **Canterbury** became the focal point for Christianity in Britain.

VIKING INCURSIONS

During this period, the coasts of Britain, particularly the North Sea and Channel coasts, were regularly attacked by **Danish Viking** incursions, which became a major invasion in 865 when a large Danish army landed on the coast of East Anglia, soon conquering the Anglo-Saxon kingdoms of Northumbria, Mercia and Anglia. It was left to the leader of another Anglo-Saxon kingdom, **Alfred the Great** of Wessex (the kingdom of the west Saxons), to sort things out, manifestly by establishing a border separating his kingdom from the northern **Danelaw** – the area of England where the Danish rule of law was in operation.

Alfred's successor, **Edward the Elder**, established supremacy over Danelaw and thus became overlord of all England. But the first ruler to be crowned king of all England was **Edgar**, King of Mercia and Northumberland. It was his successor Ethelred the Unready who fled to Normandy, allowing a Danish dynastic to become established, the first king of which was the eccentric **Canute** – famous according to legend for trying to turn back the waves. Canute's two sons proved to be such awful rulers that soon a Saxon dynasty was re-established, led by Ethelred's son, Edward, later known – on account of his apparent godliness – as **Edward the Confessor**. He it was who established **Westminster Abbey**.

THE NORMAN CONQUEST

When Edward died, **Harold** was proclaimed king, a decision disputed by **William, Duke of Normandy**, who claimed that Edward had earlier promised him the throne. Harold was defeated at the **Battle of Hastings** in 1066, and William became king. William, who detested the Saxons, ruled England with an iron rod, building the **Tower of London**, the most advanced military fortress of its kind, which dominated the London skyline and put fear into all his subjects.

One of his outstanding achievements was the **Domesday** (pronounced "Doomsday") **Book**, a compendium listing all the nation's landowners; the value of their holdings; the number of villagers and tenants; the number of animals and so on – thus providing a framework for administering the country.

PLANTAGENETS & MURDER

Tensions between the Normans and Saxons was prevalent for centuries, through the reigns of the Conqueror's two sons, **William Rufus** and **Henry I**, who at least did make some attempt at bringing the communities together by marrying a Saxon princess. When **Henry** died in 1135, the accession of Matilda (Henry's daughter) was contested by **Stephen**, William I's grandson. Eventually Matilda's son was recognized as rightful heir and in 1154 he (**Henry II**) became king, establishing the **Plantagenet** dynasty.

Among the many reforms that Henry introduced were trial by jury. But things went wrong when he attempted to restrain the power of the Church by having the Archbishop of Canterbury, **Thomas a Becket**, murdered in his own cathedral. Before long Thomas Becket became Saint Thomas of Canterbury, and among many thousands of pilgrims arriving at Canterbury to pay respects at his shrine was a sorrowful Henry himself.

RIGHTS & WRONGS

Henry was succeeded by his son **Richard the Lionheart** who spent a good deal of time fighting overseas in the Crusades. His brother, often known as **"bad King John"** was the monarch responsible for the **Magna Carta**, signed at Runnymede in 1215, which guaranteed the rights of the already powerful barons.

The struggle with the barons continued through the reign of **Henry III**, defeated by the barons' leader **Simon de Montfort** in 1265. Henry and his younger brother **Edward** were captured, Edward eventually escaping to defeat the baronial army at the battle of Evesham in 1265.

SUBJUGATION OF SCOTLAND & WALES

Edward, who became **Edward I**, was another great law-maker, presiding over the so-called **Model Parliament** and imposing English rule first over **Wales** and later **Scotland**. Edward's subjugation of Scotland led to fierce resistance. In 1306 **Robert the Bruce** had himself crowned King of Scotland, explicitly defying Edward. In 1307 Edward died, but the English were determined to wrest the crown from the Bruce. Ultimately, it was the defeat of a large English army under Edward II at **Bannockburn** in 1314 that finally determined **Scotland's independence**, a move consolidated by the **Arbroath Declaration**, which added the Church's support to Scottish independence. During this period, thousands of knights traveled to Palestine in another series of **Crusades** to defend the Christian holy places again the Ottomans.

REVOLTING PEASANTS, WAR & PLAGUE

Edward II suffered a terrible death at Berkeley Castle, Gloucester, and was succeeded by **Edward III**, who laid claim to large chunks of France, resulting in the **Hundred Years' War**, which, despite early English victories, ultimately ended in the loss of French possessions. At the same time, hundreds of thousands of English – almost a third of the population – fell victim to the so-called **Black Death**, a vicious plague brought to the country by infested rats arriving on ships.

With the population decimated, there was an urgent need to raise taxes –including a **poll tax** which has had clear resonances 600 years later. A **Peasants' Revolt** in 1381 resulted in the death of the rebel leader, **Wat Tyler**, soon after meeting the boy king **Richard II**. Despite the turmoil, at long last a distinctive English civilization was beginning to take shape, given extra focus by **John Wycliffe's** translation of the Bible into English in 1380, and by Geoffrey Chaucer's *Canterbury Tales*.

TROUBLE WITH FRANCE

Richard II was little more than a puppet to **John of Gaunt**, Duke of Lancaster and Edward III's son. In 1399 Richard was replaced by John of Gaunt's own son, **Henry IV**, who founded the Lancastrian dynasty. His son, **Henry V**, renewed the war with France, defeating them at the **Battle of Agincourt**. In 1420 a treaty ensured that the English king would be heir to the French throne, but when Henry died in 1422 his own son and heir was just two years old, leaving England governed weakly by regents and allowing the French under **Joan of Arc** to defeat the English forces.

BATTLE OF FLOWERS & THE TUDORS

Henry VI, whose reign saw the construction of such masterpieces as King's College Chapel, Cambridge, had begun to go insane, leaving a power vacuum. The strongest of the claimants for the throne was **Richard, Duke of York**, a direct descendant of **Edward III**. The battle between the rival Lancaster and York dynasties became known as the **War of the Roses** – a red rose being the symbol of Lancashire, a white rose the symbol of York. Even today, cricket games between the two counties of Yorkshire and Lancashire are known as the Roses games.

As the Duke of York began to exert more influence over Henry VI, Henry's wife **Margaret** sprang into action, routing Richard's forces at the **Battle of Wakefield** in 1460, resulting in Richard's death. She in turn was overcome by Richard's son who became **Edward IV** in 1460, establishing the **York** dynasty. In 1483, Edward was succeeded by his 12 year-old son who became king in 1483 – but only for two months – he and his younger brother were murdered in the Tower of London, most probably by their uncle, the **Duke of Gloucester**, who then became **Richard III**, who was himself defeated in 1485 at the **Battle of Bosworth Field** by **Henry, Earl of Richmond**. This Henry became **Henry VII**, establishing the powerful **Tudor** line.

Lancastrian Henry was no fool. Seeing the advantages of forging links with the York clan, he married **Elizabeth**, Edward IV's daughter. A period of relative calm and prosperity ensued, and England began to emerge as a major European power.

A DIVORCE BRINGS RELIGIOUS STRIFE

Henry VIII, perhaps the most famous of all English monarchs – for his libido if nothing else – succeeded his father in 1509. A Catholic by birth and by nature, Henry established cordial relations with the papacy, even writing a book in which he castigated the doctrine of Protestant reformer **Martin Luther**. For his efforts, Henry was awarded the title "**Defender of the Faith**" – a title which all subsequent monarchs have retained, and which can be seen on all British coins – abbreviated as "F.D." Henry's problem was that he wanted a male heir – female just wouldn't do. When first wife **Catherine of Aragon** gave birth to a girl, Mary, Henry applied to the pope for a **divorce**. The Pope refused, but Henry went ahead anyway, against the advice of his Catholic chancellor, **Thomas More**, giving himself the title of **Supreme Head of the Church of England**.

One of Henry's first acts in this role was the **Dissolution of the Monasteries**, from 1536-1539, when monastic foundations were sacked and left in ruins. Henry's subsequent behavior, and in particular the manner in which he treated his wives, is well documented elsewhere. Ironically, Henry did eventually have a son, **Edward**, a sickly child who came to the throne at the age of nine as **Edward VI** and was cleverly manipulated by the senior advisers around him. He died aged just 16.

SOME IMPORTANT DATES IN ENGLISH HISTORY

circa 2800 BC Building of Stonehenge
43AD Roman invasion
circa 123 Building of Hadrian's Wall
597 St. Augustine arrives in Canterbury
871 England unified under Alfred the Great
1066 Battle of Hastings
1086 Completion of Domesday Book
1167 Oxford University founded
1170 Thomas a Becket murdered in Canterbury cathedral
1209 Cambridge University founded
1215 Signing of the Magna Carta
1272 Edward I conquers Wales
1337 Start of Hundred Years' War with France
1348 Arrival of the Black Death
1402 Welsh rebellion against English rule
1455 Start of the Wars of the Roses
1477 William Caxton prints first book
1485 Battle of Bosworth establishes Tudor dynasty
1530s The Reformation begins
1549 Publishing of first Prayer Book in English
1555 Anglican bishops Latimer and Ridley burned at stake
1556 Archbishop Cranmer burned
1558 Elizabeth I comes to throne
1564 Birth of William Shakespeare

SOME IMPORTANT DATES IN ENGLISH HISTORY

1587 Mary, Queen of Scots executed
1588 Spanish Armada defeated
1603 Scotland's James VI becomes James I of England
1605 Guy Fawkes' plot to blow up Parliament fails
1611 Authorized version of Bible published
1620 The Pilgrims depart for America
1649-49 Civil War beween Royalists and Parliamentarians
1649 Charles I executed; England a republic
1660 Restoration of the monarchy: Charles II
1665 Great Plague decimates London's population
1666 Great Fire of London
1688 The Glorious Revolution brings William and Mary to throne
1697 Foundation of the bank of England
1714 George I establishes Hanoverian dynasty
1775 Start of American War of Independence
1801 Union with Ireland
1805 Britain defeats France at Battle of Trafalgar by Nelson
1815 France defeated by Wellington at Waterloo
1825 World's first passenger railway established
1832 The Great Reform Bill is passed
1834 Slavery abolished
1837 Victoria comes to the throne
1851 Great Exhibition
1901 Death of Victoria
1914-1918 First World War
1919 Ireland declares independence
1926 General Strike
1936 Edward VIII abdicates to marry Wallis Simpson
1939-1945 Second World War
1945 Labour election victory establishes welfare state
1952 Accession of Elizabeth II
1972 Britain joins the Common Market
1981 Marriage of Prince Charles to Lady Diana Spencer
1982 Falklands War
1991 The Gulf War
1993 European Union established
1994 Channel Tunnel opened
1996 Charles and Diana divorce
1997 Death of Princess Diana in Paris
1997 Labour win landslide victory
1999 Good Friday Agreement paves way for peace in Ireland; Welsh
Assembly established

TURBULENT TIMES

During this period, the new Church began to establish its own doctrines, formulated in the **Book of Common Prayer** of 1549. Edward was succeeded by **Mary I**, his half-sister and the daughter of Henry's first wife, **Catherine of Aragon**. Mary was a staunch Catholic and set about re-establishing Catholicism in England, marrying the future Philip II of Spain, and setting about an uncompromising persecution of the leaders of the new Church, including the Archbishop of Canterbury, **Thomas Cranmer**.

In 1558, after Mary's death, her half-sister Elizabeth (daughter of Anne Boleyn) became **Elizabeth I**. With the support of her team of highly competent ministers, Elizabeth was able to foster, for the first time, a real sense of English **nationhood** which reached its zenith in the defeat of the **Spanish Armada** in 1588. She was also able to broker some agreement between the rival factions within the church. It was during Elizabeth's 45-year reign that English seafaring prowess was established, with explorers like **Sir Walter Raleigh** and **Sir Francis Drake** leading the pack. This was also the time when English culture began to flower, helped on by a young chap by the name of **Will Shakespeare**.

THE STUARTS

The childless Elizabeth died in 1603, and the throne passed to her cousin Mary's son, James VI of Scotland, who now became **James I** of England, thereby uniting the two crowns and establishing the **Stuart** (Stewart) dynasty.

Although not a Roman Catholic, James had Catholic sympathies and set about trying to restore peace with Spain, much against the wishes of the growing **Puritan** movement, whose cause was aided in 1605 when the Roman Catholic conspirator **Guy Fawkes** was discovered attempting to blow up Parliament on **November 5** – a day still marked throughout England by the lighting of bonfires and fireworks. It was during James' reign that the first English settlements were established in **North America**, in Virginia (named after Elizabeth, the "Virgin Queen") and at Plymouth, Massachusetts.

CIVIL WAR & COMMONWEALTH

James's son **Charles** came to the throne in 1625. An Episcopalian of the High Church brand, he supported the enforcement of a new prayer book (like the one in England) on the ultra-Protestant Presbyterian Church in Scotland. Those opposed to the prayer book were regarded as rebels. Charles wished to put the rebellion down, but lacked finance and summoned the English Parliament which he hoped would provide the necessary cash. But Charles severely misjudged the mood of the increasingly Puritan assembly, which vociferously criticized him.

Charles initiated the **English Civil War**. Although at first the Royalist forces had some notable victories, the reorganization of the Puritan forces under **Oliver Cromwell** proved too much and Charles was imprisoned, and eventually beheaded outside the Banqueting House, Westminster, on January 30, 1649. For the next eleven years the nation was known as the **Commonwealth** – not exactly a republic, as Cromwell, was just as impatient of parliament as Charles had been – pronounced himself **Lord Protector**. The Commonwealth was short-lived; Cromwell's son and successor **Richard** proved a disaster, and parliament invited Charles I's son to return from exile as **Charles II**.

MONARCHY RESTORED

The **Restoration of the Monarchy** in 1660 also led to a restoration of many other things: the replacement of the sombre Puritan heritage with greater freedom of thought, and a golden period for the arts. Two national disasters overshadowed Charles' otherwise happy reign: the **Great Plague**, which decimated the population of London in 1665, and the **Great Fire of London** in 1666, which razed much of the medieval city to the ground. The rebuilding that ensued included a magnificent new **St. Paul's Cathedral**, designed by **Sir Christopher Wren**, and grandiose new public buildings and elegant brick homes on wider streets less prone to fire and disease. Thatch was banned from all subsequent construction in London (with one notable exception – the new Globe Theatre in the 1990s).

Charles was succeeded on his death by his brother, the Catholic **James II**, but the country was too war-weary to take much notice. However, when James' son was born, many began to sit up and take note, fearing that England would become permanently Catholic again. **William of Orange**, who was married to James II's Protestant daughter, **Mary**, was invited to take up the crown, and so in 1688, he and Mary became joint sovereigns in what has become known as the **"Glorious Revolution"** because it was bloodless.

TWO FOR THE PRICE OF ONE

The **William and Mary** period saw a number of significant events, most notably the introduction of a **Bill of Rights** which laid down rules regarding the limitations of the crown's power – and the **Act of Settlement** of 1701 which effectively barred Catholics from the English throne. Mary died in 1694, William continuing as sole monarch until his own death in 1702, when Mary's sister **Anne** became queen.

It was during Anne's reign that the **Act of Union** was passed by the Scottish parliament, which, as well as establishing a **pan-British parliament in London**, also guaranteed the retention of a distinct Scottish legal system, and a national Church, **the Kirk**. Thus the monarch would be supreme governor of two separate, unrelated churches – the Church of England and the Church of Scotland – a situation which continues to this day.

THE HANOVERIANS

The death of childless Anne in 1714 saw the throne pass to a German, George of Hanover, who became **George I**. George, who spoke no English and showed little inclination to learn it, was immediately faced with the **Jacobite Uprising** – an unsuccessful attempt to restore the Stuart lineage in the person of **James Edward Stuart** – known as "the Old Pretender."

It was during **George II's** reign – in 1745 – that the Old Pretender's son, **Charles Edward Stuart** (known affectionately as Bonnie Prince Charlie) launched another invasion to claim the throne. His army reached as far south as Derby, just a hundred miles from London, but was driven back by the Hanoverian forces led by the **Duke of Cumberland**. The Jacobites retreated as far as **Culloden Moor**, where they were decisively beaten by Cumberland, who was later nicknamed "Butcher Cumberland" on account of the atrocities committed against many of the opposing forces. During this period Britain was extending its power overseas, with explorers like **Captain James Cook** leading the way.

BRITAIN OUSTED FROM NORTH AMERICA

The most significant point in George II's 60-year reign was Britain's defeat by the colonial forces in the **American Revolutionary War**. Revolutionary fever had also reached France, focused on **Napoleon**, who was seen as a major threat to British national security. Two decisive victories by British forces – a sea battle in 1805 at **Trafalgar**, led by **Admiral Horatio Nelson**, and a land victory ten years later by the **Duke of Wellington** at **Waterloo** ensured that Britain remained secure.

BRITAIN BECOMES THE WORKSHOP OF THE WORLD

It was during this period that the **Industrial Revolution** got under way, as people moved from the countryside to the new mill towns, mainly in the midlands and north of England. Coal mining became big business, with a **canal network** and **railroad network** constructed to carry coal and other manufactured goods around the nation. The population almost doubled during this period, as scientific and medical advances increased longevity, and large numbers of **immigrants**, particularly Jews from Eastern Europe and Irish, arrived.

CRY FOR DEMOCRACY

With the growth of manufacturing industry came a new desire for greater democracy and a greater say by workers in the affairs of their business. Many men did not have the vote (women were not to get the vote until 1922), and some ridiculous anomalies in the parliamentary system meant that some constituencies returned an MP (Member of Parliament) to office without anyone living in them! Reform came in 1832 during the reign of **William IV**, when the **Great Reform Bill** went some way (but not all the way) in addressing the concerns – possibly averting a similar kind of revolution as had been witnessed in continental Europe). Public sympathy for the plight of the **Tolpuddle Martyrs** – six Dorset farm laborers deported to Australia for daring to set up a trade union – led to their being pardoned, while the **Chartism** movement pushed for universal male suffrage. The nation's conscience was pricked by the novels of **Charles Dickens**, whose own parents had been imprisoned for a minor crime. Christian social action, prompted by **John Wesley** and the Methodist movement, and later by the **Oxford Movement** within the Anglican Church, led to the **abolition of slavery** in Britain – in 1772.

THE VICTORIANS

Britain reached its peak of its industrial and colonial power during the long reign of **Victoria** (1837-1901), its industrial strength symbolized by the massive **Great Exhibition** of 1851, organized by Victoria's husband, **Albert**, and a burgeoning of artistic and cultural organizations. London was the largest city in the world, and the hub of the largest Empire the world had ever seen. However, extreme poverty was still a feature of inner city as well as rural life. Two prime ministers, the Conservative **Benjamin Disraeli** and the Liberal **William Ewart Gladstone**, great rivals, set about making major changes that would change the country forever. These included the introduction of **compulsory education** for all, and further enfranchisement in a second **Reform Bill** in 1867. Meanwhile, Britain was feeling the effects of administering such a large empire – most particularly in the **Boer War** that led to self-government for South Africa.

THE FUTILITY OF WAR

Victoria was replaced on her death in 1901 by her son, who became **Edward VII** – as well known for his liaisons with his mistresses – including the most famous, Lily Langtry – as anything else. Then, in 1914, Britain and France declared war on Germany. Countless lives were lost on all sides in the trenches of Belgium and northern France in what became known as the **First World War**. And November 11, 1918, became etched on everyone's heart as **Armistice Day**. In 1918, **voting rights** were extended to all males over 21 and women over 30 – largely after pressures from the Suffragette Movement, although women were not to achieve equality with men until 1929.

A DAMAGED NATION

Britain had suffered badly as a result of World War I. Not only had her economy deteriorated, but severe psychological damage had been done, especially when men returning from the battlefield relayed the truth as to how their compatriots had been killed. The disillusionment with the ruling classes and the way in which many young men had been treated as little more than cannon fodder and general dissatisfaction with the existing political parties led to the formation and rapid growth of the **Labour Party**, which formed its first government in 1923. But even the pro-worker government was unable to prevent a massive **General Strike** in 1926, the result of rapid industrial decline and widescale **unemployment**.

Things were no better by 1936, when workers marched in their thousands from Jarrow, in the northeast, on London. Britain's national unhappiness was reflected in the gradual **decline of the Empire** and by the establishment of the **Irish Free State** in 1922 – with the exception of the six largely Protestant counties which were to form **Northern Ireland**, a part of the United Kingdom.

ABDICATION & ANOTHER WAR

The nation was shaken further by the **abdication of Edward VIII** in 1936 in order for him to marry a twice-divorced American, **Wallis Simpson**. Edward's position as king was taken over by his brother, who became **George VI** – the father of the present queen. Meanwhile, relations with Adolf Hilter's **Nazi Germany** were deteriorating, despite assurances given to British Prime Minister **Neville Chamberlain** in 1938 that Germany posed no threat to Britain. Germany's **invasion of Poland** in 1939 prompted Britain's **declaration of war** against Hitler.

Britain, though unprepared, managed to stand fast – though virtually isolated – for a couple of years. With the inspirational **Winston Churchill** as Prime Minister, a new spirit of defiant patriotism prevailed, despite the **severe bombing of London** and other major cities – and, most symbolically – the destruction of **Coventry Cathedral**. Even Buckingham Palace took a direct hit, enabling King George VI and Queen Elizabeth (the present Queen Mother) to claim that at last they could "look the people of the East End in the eye." Japan's attack against **Pearl Harbor** in 1941 prompted American entry into the conflict and swung the balance firmly Britain's way, although it would be another four years before the end of a war that claimed more than 300,000 British lives.

POSTWAR OPTIMISM

There was tremendous hunger for change after the end of World War II as the electorate returned a new Labour government under the leadership of **Clement Attlee**. Among the radical new policies was the **nationalization of key industries** such as coal, gas, steel and the railroad system; the establishment of a **National Health Service** (NHS) offering free health services to all; and a social security system funded by national insurance. Meanwhile, overseas, the result of Britain's forces pulling out of Palestine led to the establishment of the State of Israel, while Britain, the US and several other nations formed the **North Atlantic Treaty Organisation** (NATO) to counteract the perceived threat from the Soviet Union.

THE NEW ELIZABETHAN ERA

In 1952, George VI died after a battle with cancer and was succeeded by his daughter, who became **Queen Elizabeth II**. By the late 1950s, Britain was regaining some economic strength, prompting Prime Minister **Harold Macmillan** to tell the British public, "You've never had it so good."

The 1960s saw England, and particularly London, become the trendiest place on earth, prompting songs like "England swings like a pendulum do." During the '70s, Britain became a member of the **European Economic Community**, but the decade was dominated by **industrial strife**, epitomized by the "**Winter of Discontent**" in 1978, which led to a general election the following year, won by **Margaret Thatcher** and the Conservative Party.

The Thatcher years were characterized by an increasing **polarization** in British society. The power of trades unions was curbed, tax cuts benefited the wealthy, and the process of privatizing many of the industries nationalized after World War II began. This was also a period in which welfare was cut back and poor funding of the health service resulted in a serious deterioration of services. A war with **Argentina** over the sovereignty of the **Falkland Islands** boosted her popularity. Thatcher almost lost her life in 1984, when an IRA bomb blasted the hotel in which she and members of her cabinet were staying while attending a party conference. The "Iron Lady" was twice re-elected, but was ditched by her party before the next election as she was seen increasingly as an electoral liability – especially after the introduction of the so-called **poll tax**.

Her successor, **John Major**, presided over a Conservative Party divided over what to do about membership of the European Community, and particularly whether Britain should become more integrated. Major's government held back as most of the member states plunged into a new currency, the **Euro**.

TRAGEDY IN PARIS

The 1990s saw a rapid drop in popularity for the Royal Family, as the marriages of three of the Queen's children hit the rocks, and anger over the queen's alleged reluctance to pay income tax mounted. A general election in 1997 saw Labour, under the dynamic leadership of **Tony Blair**, take control of Parliament with a huge majority. The initial euphoria that accompanied the victory was dampened by the sudden death in 1997 of **Diana**, **Princess of Wales**, in a car crash in Paris. In an uncharacteristic display of emotion, millions of people took to the streets, many weeping openly. The Royal Family's popularity plummeted further as public anger at their apparent nonchalant attitude mounted.

MODERNIZING THE NATION

Blair set about a number of important domestic reforms and a new, more positive attitude to Europe. The domestic reforms included devolved government for both Scotland and Wales. A **Scottish Parliament** and a **Welsh Assembly** were both established in 1999, as many English MPs called for a similar arrangement for England. Changes were also under way in the **House of Lords**, Britain's second, unelected chamber, where many life peers lost their seats.

In 1998, a bomb planted by the so-called "**Real IRA**" killed more than 30 people in **Omagh** in Northern Ireland, causing widespread anger and revulsion. In 1998, the **Good Friday Agreement** between the British and Irish governments and the various parties in Northern Ireland paved the way for an IRA ceasefire and the establishment of an **Assembly for Northern Ireland**. The Assembly was suspended early in 2000 following differences over the implementation of the agreement, but an IRA statement in May 2000 promising to put their weapons "beyond reach" appeared to allay many Protestant fears and led to the re-establishment of the assembly and the hope of a lasting peace.

WELSH NATIONALISM

Wales, originally a separate kingdom from England, was subjugated by England's King Edward I as far back as 1307. Unlike Scotland, which had only been linked with England since 1707 and had managed to retain its own legal, educational and ecclesiastical systems, the English legal and educational systems were adopted in Wales, and the Church of England – known here as the Church of Wales – became the largest religious denomination. In other words, for the 700 years in which Wales has been inextricably linked with England, it has been governed from London.

However, Wales has always retained a strong cultural identity (if not as strong as Scotland's), particularly through the Welsh language, which is spoken by well over a million people today. Many Welsh have long had separatist longings but failed to make much impact on the majority, who seemed more than satisfied with the strong link with Westminster. A Welsh **Nationalist Party** (**Plaid Cymru**) was founded in 1925, but has never really been able to muster the support of the masses.

However, things began to change in the 1980s and 1990s, as many people in Wales and Scotland found themselves governed by a Conservative government which, by and large, they had failed to support. As support for the Nationalist Party began to grow, the Labour and Conservative parties looked on nervously.

The Labour Party, sensing that limited self-government would appease the majority constituencies in both countries, set forth its election manifesto in 1996 promising, if elected, to hold a referendum to give the Welsh people the right to determine whether they wished to allow some of the powers hitherto held by Westminster to be devolved to a new Welsh Assembly.

Labour's resounding victory in the 1997 election paved the way for a referendum in September of the same year, in which approval for a new devolved assembly was given – if only by a small majority. The **Assembly**, based in Cardiff, was finally set up in 1999 and the Welsh (along with the Scottish, and most recently, the people of Northern Ireland) can now look forward to a greater say in their own affairs.

6. PLANNING YOUR TRIP

More and more Americans and Canadians are visiting England and Wales than ever before. But there's much more to a trip than simply grabbing your passport and jumping on a plane to London or Manchester. Planning ahead means that you will get the most out of your trip.

BEFORE YOU GO

WHEN TO VISIT - CLIMATE & WEATHER

Dr. Samuel Johnson once said that, "When two Englishmen meet, their first talk is of the weather." By and large, that holds true today. Brits are obsessed by the weather, and when you've spent a few weeks here it's easy to see why: Britain's weather is an endless pageant of blue skies, menacing clouds, blue skies with menacing clouds, frost and dew, balmy heat wave, ice and snow, fog drizzle, pouring rain and gale force winds – and all on one summer's day.

The reason for this fickle climate is the **Gulf Stream**, which brings warm currents to the west coast, so that, even as far north as Scotland, palm trees can grow because the winters are so mild. Much of the moisture in these prevailing 'westerlies' is trapped when it reaches the curved spine of mountains and hills that extends the length of Britain, so that the west gets considerably more rainfall than the east. London, in southeastern England, gets less rain per year than Boston or New York. Trouble is, it's more evenly spread out, so that even in mid-summer you can get a series of gray drizzly days and cool temperatures. So when you ooh and aah at the patchwork quilt English and Welsh landscapes, where there are more shades of green than you knew existed, remember that the reason for this is the frequency of rain, which can come at any time, anywhere throughout the year. Despite the unpredictability of the weather (weather forecasters are widely regarded as a joke in Britain) it rarely rains hard enough to dampen the enjoyment of the many sights there are to see.

One result of the British climate's Piscean indecisiveness is the preponderance in many homes, hotels and businesses of equally indecisive, antiquated heating systems – air conditioning, for example is rarely found except in the most modern office complexes, a few department stores and the more expensive hotels. So, if you want to see a West End play during high summer, try to avoid seats in "the gods" where rising hot air means it's more like Hades.

Neither does it get particularly cold in England, except on some northern hills, where heavy snowfall in not uncommon. In the south, just one inch of snow means that everything comes to a halt; while temperatures over 90° in the summer are virtually unheard of. Twenty-mile traffic jams caused by melting motorways are not unknown when the temperature rises above 80° in the north.

In winter, early spring and late fall, bring a raincoat and a supply of sweaters, and the rest of the year, a lightweight raincoat and a lightweight sweater (mainly for the evenings) and you should be fine. And, of course, a 'brollley' (umbrella) at any time of year.

July and August are the peak tourist months, though any time after Easter and before October you may find yourself waiting in long lines to see the Crown Jewels or other similar attractions. Early spring is quiet, but a number of attractions won't be open yet – and in late fall many will have closed for the season. The winter can be a gloomy time to visit, but great if you're here for the theater or on a shopping trip. London and the main centers of population get very crowded in the run up to Christmas, when everyone seems to be out shopping.

As you'd expect, hotel and B&B rates are seasonal, so you'll pay significantly more during the high season. You'll pay the lowest rates from November to February, and something in between for the rest of the year.

If you want to check out what the weather's likely to be during your stay, call the **Weather Channel** *(Tel. 900/932-8437)*, which includes detailed forecasts for a number of UK cities, at 95c per minute, or, on the web, *www.CNN.com* or *www.BBC.co.uk/weather* will give you up-to-date five day forecasts.

WHAT TO PACK

I'm one of those people who tends to overpack, wherever I'm headed. The advantage is, of course, that I'm covered for just about every feasible occasion. The disadvantage: having to trudge around with a case that weighs a ton, and sweating buckets at the end of the trip trying to pack everything, including all the stuff I've bought. Of course, when it comes to packing, much depends on the season and the geography; it can get quite steamy in London in August, but a couple of hundred miles north you may find the east coast shrouded and mist and shivering in 50° temperatures.

So, for visiting the UK my best advice for men visiting in the summer is take a real mixture; some lightweight, casual shirts, T-shirts; casual pants and a pair or two of shorts; maybe a jacket and tie for one of the more formal restaurants or hotels; and of course plenty of socks and underwear. For women, a nice dress, skirt, blouses and maybe shorts. For both sexes, a pair of comfortable shoes is essential – there's no escaping the walking and a light sweater or cardigan for those chilly (but comfortable) summer evenings. For children, pack clothes comparable to what you're packing for yourself, but more of them; children go through clothes much more quickly! As it rains frequently in England (though not much more than east coast of the US), take a lightweight 'mac' (mackintosh, a light raincoat) or alternatively purchase a cheapie in England. You may need an umbrella, but I suggest buying a cheap one in England; they can really be a pain to pack.

In winter, forget the shorts and pack some heavier garments, including a couple of heavy sweaters and heavyweight shoes and a heavy coat.

You can get just about all the toiletries you'll need in England, but if you insist on a particular brand, bring it with you. If you take prescription drugs, make sure you have plenty to last the trip; bring a note from your doctor just in case you run out and need to get some more (or if you get questioned at Customs) – most US prescription drugs are available in the UK, but with different names. You may want to bring a packet of Advil or Tylenol, but English pharmacies will be very helpful to you in selecting an equivalent UK brand.

Hairdryers and the like are often available in hotels; if you want to bring your own, make sure you have a **converter** and **plug adapter** (the voltage is 220c). Many hotels have facilities for washing clothes, or you may prefer to go to a local launderette where you'll meet some of the locals. Hotels almost always provide irons.

If you have children, bring a selection of games – these especially come in useful when you're driving long distances between towns. Bring some good road maps; large **AA** (UK Automobile Association) **road maps** are available in places like Borders and Barnes & Noble, and see if you can't also find local maps of the area you're visiting. The best are the **Ordnance Survey** series, again available in US and Canadian stores.

ENTRY REQUIREMENTS

To enter the UK, you'll need **a current passport**. US passports are valid for five years for children and ten years for adults, so, well before you travel, make sure you passport hasn't expired or isn't about to expire. Canadian passports, by contrast, are valid for just five years. For Canadian citizens, children under 16 can be included on their parents' passports, but if traveling alone they'll need their own.

If you do need a new passport, make sure you apply at least six weeks before you are due to travel – just to be safe. Application forms are available at US and Canadian passport offices, and some post offices. Some Canadian travel agencies also stock passport applications.

You don't need a visa to enter the UK, so long as your visit is for less than 180 days. If you plan to stay longer than that, you will have to prove that you have sufficient funds and a return airline ticket.

If you are getting a new passport, you will require:
• a notarized copy of your birth certificate – a hospital copy won't suffice
• two identical passport photos taken within the past six months
• a picture ID, such as a driver's license

If this is your first passport, you will need to apply in person. For first passports, the cost is $65 for people aged 18 and over, $40 for under-18s. For passport renewals, the costs are $55 (if you are over 18 and your last name is still the same).

CUSTOMS REGULATIONS

Britain operates import restrictions on a variety of goods and substances, from firearms to furs derived from an endangered species, as well as pets. However, you may bring in up to 200 cigarettes **or** 100 cigarillos **or** 50 cigars **or** 250 grams of loose tobacco; up to two litres of still wine plus one litre of alcoholic drinks not over 22% proof; 60ml of perfume plus 250ml of toilet water; other goods to the value of £145.

US citizens returning to the US after 48 hours out of the country are allowed one liter of liquor, 200 cigarettes and $400 worth of purchases. Up to an additional $1,000 of purchases you will be charged 10% duty. You must be at least 21 years old to bring liquor back to the US.

Canadian citizens are permitted to bring back $300 worth of foreign goods annually without paying duty, but you must have been out of the country for at least seven days. If you've been out of the country more than 48 hours but less than seven days, you can bring back $100 worth of good duty-free each trip – with no limit as to how many trips this involves. You can also bring home 1.14 liters of wine or liquor or twenty-four 12oz. bottles of beer or ale. If you're over 16, you can also bring home 200 cigarettes, 50 cigars **or** cigarillos and 400 tobacco sticks **or** 400 grams of manufactured tobacco duty-free.

Citizens of both countries may mail gifts to the value of US$50 or C$60 duty-free – but only one package per day per address. Packages need to be marked "unsolicited gift."

On your flight home, you will be required to fill out customs forms, declaring the total value of all goods you have brought back with you.

For more information about British import regulations, contact **HM Customs and Excise**, *Dorset House, Stamford Street, London SE1 9PY, Tel. 020 7 202 4227.*

BRITISH REPRESENTATIVES IN THE STATES & CANADA

The following organizations can be very helpful in helping you plan your vacation, whether you are looking for advice, brochures, or travel information:

US
- **British Tourist Authority**, *551 5th Ave, Suite 701, New York, NY 10176. Tel. 800/GOBRITAIN*
- **British Tourist Authority**, *World Trade Center, Suite 450, 350 S Figuera St, Los Angeles CA. Tel. 213/628-3525*
- **British Tourist Authority**, *625 N Michigan Ave, Suite 1510, Chicago, IL (no telephone enquiries)*
- **British Tourist Authority**, *2580 Cumberland Pkwy, Suite 470, Atlanta, GA. Tel. 404/432-9641*
- **BritRail Travel International**, *1500 Broadway, New York NY 10036. Tel. 800/677-8585* – for all rail passes, Eurostar tickets, Channel ferry tickets etc.

Canada
- **British Tourist Authority**, *111 Avenue Rd, Toronto, Ontario M5R 3J8. Tel. 416/961-8124*
- **Canadian Reservations Centre**, *2087 Dundas East, Suite 105, Mississauga, Ontario L4X 1M2. Tel. 800/361-7245*

REGIONAL TOURIST BOARDS IN ENGLAND & WALES
- **British Travel Centre**, *12 Regent St, London SW1Y 4PQ (no telephone enquiries); www.visitbritain.com*
- **Cumbria Tourist Board**, *Ashleigh, Holly Rd, Windermere, Cumbria LA23 2AQ. Tel. 01539/444444; www.cumbria-the-lake-district.co.uk*

- **East of England Tourist Board**, *Toppesfield Hall, Hadleigh, Suffolk IP7 5DN. Tel. 01473/822922; www.visitbritain.com*
- **Heart of England Tourist Board**, *Woodside, Larkhill Rd, Worcester WR5 2EF. Tel. 01905/763436; www.visitbritain.com*
- **London Tourist Board**, *26 Grosvenor Gardens, Victoria, London SW1W 0DU (no telephone enquiries); www.LondonTown.com*
- **North West Tourist Board**, *Swan House, Swan Meadow Rd, Wigan WN3 5BB. Tel. 01942/821222; www.visitbritain.com*
- **Northumbria Tourist Board**, *Aykley Heads, Durham DH1 5UX. Tel. 0191/ 384-6905; www.ntb.org.uk*
- **Southeast England Tourist Board**, *Old Brewhouse, Warwick Park, Tunbridge Wells TN2 5TU. Tel. 01892/540766; www.visitbritain.com*
- **Southern Tourist Board**, *40 Chamberlayne Rd, Eastleigh, Hampshire SO50 5JH. Tel. 02380 625400; www.visitbritain.com*
- **West Country Tourist Board**, *60 St David's Hill, Exeter EX4 4SY. Tel. 01392/276351; www.wctb.co.uk*
- **Yorkshire & Humberside Tourist Board**, *312 Tadcaster Rd, York YO2 2HF. Tel. 01904/707961*
- **Wales Tourist Board**, *Dept RJ3, PO Box 1, Cardiff CF1 2XN. Tel. 029 2049 9909; www.ytb.co.uk*
- **North Wales Tourism**, *77 Conway Rd, Colwyn Bay LL29 7LN. Tel. 01492/ 531731 or 0800/834-820; www.nwt.co.uk*
- **Mid-Wales Tourism**, *The Station, Machynlleth SY20 8TG. Tel. 01654/ 702653 or 0800/273747; www.mid-wales-tourism.co.uk*
- **Tourism South & West Wales**, *Charter Court, Phoenix Way, Enterprise Park, Swansea SA7 9DB. Tel. 01792/781212 or 0800/243-731*

BOOKING TICKETS FROM NORTH AMERICA

If you're traveling to Britain in the high season, it makes a lot of sense to book your hotel, rental car and even theater tickets well in advance. This can be done by phone – transatlantic calls can cost from as a little as 10¢ per minute these days – or through a travel agent or a web site. Doing it this way will spare you all kinds of hassle and wasted time after you arrive, and may make the difference between seeing a particular play or missing it completely, and/or save you a fortune, as ticket agencies tend to add obscene surcharges during the peak season.

For theater, you can find out what shows are on in advance by calling booking agents **Edwards and Edwards** (in the US, *Tel. 800/223-6106*), who take a commission for all tickets sold, or write to the **London Theatre Guide**, *32 Rose Street, London WC2, Tel. 0207 836 0971*, asking for their current broadsheet and future booking information.

GETTING TO ENGLAND

No fewer than 14 major airlines fly direct from the US to London, with another couple flying to Manchester. London flights land at either **Gatwick**, about 30 miles south of the city, with frequent rail services into central London from the adjacent station, as well as bus services; and **Heathrow**, the larger and busier of the two, 15 miles west of the city, on a direct Tube line into central London (see London chapter, *Arrivals & Departures*, for more information).

Such is the intensity of the competition between the major carriers (BA, American, Virgin Atlantic, Northwest, Continental and United) over the past few years, that economy fares are lower than they've ever been, especially in low and mid-season, though you may feel something like a sardine. Of the airlines I've used, Virgin has offered the best deal: reasonable food, attentive young cabin staff, individual TVs, and "luxuries" such as Dove bars. Other airlines offering cheap fares includes Air India, Kuwait Air and Japan Air. Fares are cheapest of all during the winter months, which, although likely to be damp and gloomy, has its compensations.

TOLL-FREE AIRLINE NUMBERS

Air Canada, in US Tel. 800/776-3000
Air India, Tel. 212/751-6200
American Airlines, Tel. 800/433-7300
British Airways, Tel. 800/247-9297
Canadian Airlines, in Canada Tel. 800/665-1177; in US, Tel. 800/426-7000
Continental, Tel. 800/231-0856
Delta, Tel. 800/221-1212
Kuwait Airlines, Tel. 800/458-9248
Northwest Airlines, Tel. 800/447-4747
TWA, Tel. 800/221-2000
United, Tel. 800/538-2929or 800/241-6522
Virgin, Tel. 800/862-8621

From the US east coast, it usually takes about six hours to London or Manchester, sometimes less when there's a strong tailwind – but an hour longer on the return flight due to headwinds. From the US west coast, it's closer to eleven hours. Due to British noise regulations, most are overnight flights, arriving in London or Manchester at some unearthly hour the following morning – although daytime flights are available.

GETTING AROUND ENGLAND & WALES

There are a variety of ways to get around England and Wales, depending entirely on what kind of adventure you're seeking:

BY BUS

The word "bus" in Britain usually means a local or regional service operated by private companies, or, occasionally, by local authorities. Bus services are generally comprehensive, with frequent runs of single or double-decker buses along main urban routes. Local buses are numbered for identification both back and rear. You normally pay as you enter, though some of the older London buses still have conductors who come round to collect your fare. Fares are usually calculated on the basis of distance traveled, though some routes operate on a flat-fare basis. Bus stops are usually clearly marked. You may be required to hold out your hand as a signal for the bus to stop. Local bus rides are good places to meet local people. Show interest in the things you see and you'll soon have someone telling you all about them.

Long-distance buses are usually called **coaches** in England and Wales. A national network of coaches is operated by **National Express**, which has become increasingly popular in recent years due to the high train fares – so – especially if you're traveling at the weekend or on certain busy routes, it makes sense to buy a **reserved journey ticket** that guarantees you a seat. The main drawback, of course, is that coaches take a lot longer; the train journey from London to Bournemouth, for example, can take less than two hours, while the coach takes around three.

US and Canadian travelers can also purchase a **Tourist Trail Pass**, offering unlimited use of the National Express network; unlimited travel on any 8 days within a 16-day period costs £90 for students and under-23s, £119 for others; unlimited travel on any 15 days within 30 days costs £145 and £179 respectively. You can obtain these passes at Gatwick, Heathrow, Birmingham and Manchester airports, at the British Travel Centre in London, or at the main **National Express office**, *Victoria Coach Station, Buckingham Palace Road, London SW1, Tel. 0990 808080*. Coaches are rarely as comfortable as trains, though the newer models have toilets, refreshments and even television.

BY CAR

England and Wales, away from their clogged-up conurbations, is ideal for a driving vacation for a number of reasons:
• you can explore off-the-beaten path locations not covered by train or bus
• you can pull up at a roadside restaurant or a meal or to use the loo (bathroom)
• you have the freedom to stop at whim to photograph a stunning Lakeside landscape or a herd of grazing New Forest ponies

Many Americans and Canadians visiting Britain set out to "do" the whole country in a week or two. On paper, that doesn't seem to be outside the realm of possibility. After all, the whole country is less than a third the size of Texas and about the same size as New York. Visitors soon find, however, that Britain's population is three times that of Texas, and four times New York's – and at certain times of the day, all 60 million inhabitants (plus visitors) seem to be on the road at the same time. Rather, it makes more sense to concentrate on one or two regions, and save up the rest for your next visit. Don't even think of renting a car if you're intending to spend most of your vacation in London. There's an excellent public transport system, the roads are impossibly congested, parking is incredibly expensive, and Londoners' driving habits leave a lot to be desired.

Car Rental

Car rental in Britain can be a very expensive business, so the secret is to shop around – that is, unless your airline is able to offer a special fly-drive deal. Your travel agent will certainly be eager to help, or you can do it for yourself. Check out any discounts you might be entitled to through membership of clubs, organizations or the company you work for. Be aware that car rental charges vary greatly from season to season, reaching a peak during the months of July and August, and plummeting during the winter (although they rise over the Christmas, New Year and Easter holidays). And the longer you rent the car, the cheaper it works out per day.

The major US car rental agencies like **Alamo**, **Budget**, **Dollar** (known as **Eurodolla**r in the UK) all operate in Britain too. But if you have time on your hands, there is an alternative; check out local companies in British newspapers or over the Internet. These can often work out considerably cheaper than the larger companies. If you're really starved of cash, there are a number of companies in and around London and the major cities where you can rent older cars at considerably lower cost – in which case, make sure you're properly insured.

When booking a car, specify exactly what you want: a British rental company will, for example, give you a car with manual transmission unless you specify otherwise. And in Britain, an economy car means *really* small with little leg room, let alone space for all those suitcases! When checking the rates, see if they include mileage charges, service charges and taxes – and don't forget that **VAT** in Britain is a massive 17.5%! Most agencies include unlimited mileage in their rates, but make absolutely sure before you agree to anything. Some will give you a full tank of gas, requiring a deposit to cover the cost. If you return the car with a full tank, the deposit is refunded.

As far as insurance goes, check what coverage you already have before you rent. Your own domestic insurance policy will not cover you for driving in the UK, but some credit cards will cover your car rental insurance, so that you need not take out Collision Damage Waiver.

Here are the US and UK phone numbers of the major car rental agencies:

- **Alamo**
  US: Tel. 800/522-9696   UK: Tel. 0800 272 2000
- **Avis**
  US: Tel. 800/331-1084   UK: Tel. 800 879 2847
- **Budget**
  US: Tel. 800/472-3325   UK: Tel. 0800 181181
- **Dollar**
  US: Tel. 800/800-4000;   UK (Eurodollar): Tel. 0990 565656
- **Hertz**
  US: Tel. 800/654-3001   UK: Tel. 0345 555888

For those who do want to travel by car from one end of the country to the other (over 800 miles from the tip of Scotland to Land's End in southwest England), use the fairly reliable system of **motorways** – only "fairly" because many of these Interstate-type roads seem to be in a constant state of repair. These motorways are indicated in blue on maps, and with the prefix "M" – hence **M1**, M2, etc. The speed limit on these roads is 70 mph unless specified otherwise.

If you want to concentrate on a smaller area, the "**A**" roads (the main roads before the motorways were built) which connect major towns and cities are universally well-surfaced and marked. The speed limit here is generally 60 mph – 30 mph in built-up areas. "**B**" roads are the next step down, but again are in generally good condition. Even unclassified roads – often no more than narrow country lanes – are usually well-surfaced. Here you may encounter different hazards – herds of cows or sheep blocking the way, or octogenarians cruising along at 80 mph.

ENGLISH DRIVING TERMS

ENGLISH TERM	AMERICAN TERM
Bonnet	hood
Boot	trunk
Caravan	trailer (one that travels)
Car park	parking lot
Central reservation	median
Dip	dim (as in headlights)
Diversion	detour
Dual carriageway	divided highway
Give way	yield
Lay by	rest area
Hard shoulder	shoulder
Motorway	interstate
Petrol	gas
Way out	exit
Windscreen	windshield

Road markings indicating rights of way are clearly indicated on British roads, but they don't always correspond to markings in the US and Canada. The same goes for traffic signs. Most of them are pretty easy to understand, but it makes a lot of sense to buy a copy of the **Highway Code** from most newsstands and bookstores, which will explain what they are.

Americans are shocked by the high cost of **petrol** in Britain, where Government taxes make it as much as $6 a gallon. To make it more confusing, gas stations indicate prices in liters (UK spelling: litres) only, so keep a calculator handy. Another difference is that at British gas stations you simply draw up, unlock the gas cap (most have keys, because petrol is such a valuable commodity) and insert the nozzle without pressing any buttons or lifting levers. Just squeeze the trigger and the gas comes out. Pay by cash or credit card at the counter (British fuel companies have yet to latch on to pay-at-the-pump).

British cars – apart from the right hand drive – operate in much the same way as their US counterparts – foot controls are in the same place, and so on...

On the whole, Americans have few problems driving in England. These tend only to materialize when panic sets in: the car stalls, and in a split second you look up to the right for the mirror and it's not there; you reach to the right for the shift and it's not there. You eventually get started and drive off, only to discover a thirty-ton truck coming straight at you.

You're driving on the wrong side – again. For most drivers, it takes two or three days to get used to driving on the left, for some considerably longer, especially if you're driving a car with manual shift (most rental cars in England are manuals; to avoid the unthinkable, **specify automatic** when you book).

DRIVING TIPS FOR ENGLAND

• Don't drink or use drugs and drive.
• Drivers and front seat passengers are required by law to wear seat belts. Rear seat passengers must too, where belts are included.
• Read the Highway Code before setting out.
• Overtake (pass) only on the right.
• On motorways and dual carriageways, keep to the left unless passing.
• Turning right on red is not allowed.
• Always stop for pedestrians at a zebra (striped black and white) crossing.
• Do not drive when tired or suffering from jet lag. Early in your vacation, short leisurely drives will ease you into your new routine.
• Never park on a double yellow line.
• Stay within the speed limits, even if other drivers are visibly irritated with you.
• Beware of the temptation to drift to the right on empty roads. It's very easily done.

HITCHHIKING

Hitchhiking is legal in Britain, and it's still popular among many young people. However, in recent years there have been a number of highly publicized cases where hitchhikers have been murdered, so there is something of a risk factor. The golden rule is to be cautious, travel in pairs and trust your own instincts.

BY TRAIN

The self-deprecating English had always regarded poking fun of **British Railways** as a national pastime. Jokes abounded about the dubious nature of its timekeeping, the quality of its rolling stock, and the flavor of its tea. But when the unthinkable happened six years ago, nobody was laughing. The nationalized British Rail network was sold off, divided up and replaced by a mishmash of smaller companies, each company owning and operating a specific part of the system, such as rolling stock, track, catering and so on.

Six years on, things have generally deteriorated rather than improved, though there have been improvements in some areas where much-needed new rolling stock has replaced medieval carriages and a number of train stations have been spruced up beyond recognition – some rivaling the Chelsea Flower show for their floral displays. Thousands of pounds were spent by the new companies teaching rail staff how to smile and say, "please" and "thank you" – though they drew the line at saying, "Have a nice day." The reality is many suburban and inter-city trains are dirty, crowded, frequently late, and the tea in most cases still tastes awful. More seriously, in the last couple of years, a series of train crashes, most recently at Paddington, have resulted in widespread public anger that not enough money has been spent on improving safety standards.

However, traveling the country by train is still a good option. Even if it is overpriced, it means that you can get from the center of one city to another without the hassle of parking.

You can buy tickets for most journeys at stations or from travel agents. For the major inter-city routes, it makes sense to reserve a seat, though this isn't technically necessary. Ordinary second-class fares are high, and first class seats cost 33% more. What's more, there's a mind-boggling array of reduced-fare tickets that confuses all but those with a doctorate in rail travel. Basically, these are **Savers**, round-trip (return) tickets that you can use on all trains on weekends and Bank Holidays, most weekday trains outside rush hour for the outward journey and all trains for the return leg. Supersavers cannot be used on Fridays or on certain other specified days during the year and are not valid for any peak-time service in, to or through London. Outward travel must be completed within two days of the date on the ticket.

Apex tickets are available on some inter-city journeys of 150 miles or more, and must be booked at least seven days before traveling. Finally, **Superapex** tickets work in a similar way to Apex tickets, but must be booked fourteen days before outward travel. Children from 5-15 pay half the adult fare on most journeys – but there's no discount on the Apex or Superapex tickets.

Avoid this bewildering system by purchasing a rail pass in the US or Canada. These are available from **British Rail International**, *1500 Broadway, New York, NY 10036, Tel. 800/677-8585*, or in Canada from the **Canadian Reservations Centre**, *2087 Dundas East, Suite 105, Missassauga, Ontario L4X 1M2, Tel. 800/361-7245*, and from various specialist tour operators outside the UK. It gives unlimited travel in England, Wales and Scotland for eight days ($230), 15 days ($355), 22 days ($445) or a month $520. The **BritRail Flexipass** allows you to travel on four days out of one month for $195, eight days out of one month for $275, fifteen days ($405).

In addition, there are discounts for travelers aged under 26 or over 60. An **England/Wales Flexipass** means that you can't travel into Scotland, but it's a bit cheaper at $155 for four days out of a month.

BY BICYCLE

Many towns and larger villages in England and Wales have bicycle shops where you can rent a bike for a day, week or month. These usually work out at about £7 a day, £30 a week, or £115 a month. Bikes are an ideal way of exploring some of the less arduous regions, but make sure you have appropriate clothing, including a safety helmet.

HOTELS, GUEST HOUSES & B&Bs

Many hotels and B&Bs in Britain still work on a **per-person sharing basis**, which means this: the "norm" is that two people will share a double room. If a hotel lists its rate as £20 per person sharing, this means the room will cost £40 for two people. If only one person rents the double room, instead of charging the full £40, a single supplement is added to the per person rate, normally between £5-10. If the hotel or B&B has single rooms available, these normally come at a special rate that is generally just a few pounds short of the double room.

However, the good news is that more and more hotels, especially in London and the larger cities, are beginning to work on a per room basis, like most hotels in the US and Canada. Until fairly recently, smaller hotels and B&Bs in Britain were advertising "hot and cold running water" in their rooms as if it were some kind of luxury. Bathrooms were out in the corridor and shared with several other rooms. Thankfully, this is largely a thing of the past: most hotel rooms these days are **en suite**, which means they have their own bathroom, but when booking, check just to be sure.

In this book, the single room price I've given for each hotel refers to actual single rooms, and double rooms used as singles. The great thing about B&Bs is that, first, it often means you're more likely to get to meet British people, and secondly, you're in a good position to strike up a friendship with the hosts, who will go out of their way to make you feel welcome, give suggestions (and directions) for local places to visit – and tell you all about their family history!

7. BASIC INFORMATION

BANK HOLIDAYS

Brits love their **Bank Holidays** – the term used for national holidays. Normally, there are eight in England and Wales each year but occasionally, such as at the Millennium, an extra day may be granted by the government, who immediately surge ahead in the poll ratings. Gone are the days when absolutely everything closed on Bank Holidays, but even today many businesses, including banks, stores and restaurants, will be shut. Most tourist attractions, however, remain open (with the exception of Christmas Day and Boxing Day) – Bank Holidays are good for business!

The late spring and late summer Bank Holidays are perhaps the best time to see the English and Welsh at play – although the fickle weather means that, more often than not, a keenly-anticipated day at the seaside becomes a "washout."

The eight holidays you can count on are: New Years' Day (the closest Monday to it); Good Friday; Easter Monday; May Bank Holiday (the closest Monday to May 1); Spring Bank Holiday (last Monday in May); Summer Bank Holiday (last Monday in August); Christmas Day (25 December) and Boxing Day (26 December). **Boxing Day**, by the way, is the day when Christmas presents were traditionally boxed and exchanged.

BUSINESS HOURS

Shops & Businesses

Many High Street stores retain the traditional opening hours of 9am to 5:30pm, but this is gradually changing, especially in areas where there are large numbers of tourists. Out-of-town supermarkets and stores tend to stay open much later, with some supermarkets – especially the larger ones – staying open 24 hours. In some areas, some smaller shops and businesses still operate "**half day closing**" – normally from 1pm, on either Wednesday or Saturday; others may close down for lunch between 1-2pm.

Pubs

Britain's archaic opening hours mean that pubs are generally open from 11am to 11pm, Monday through Saturday and noon to 10:30pm on Sundays, though a radical overhaul of these opening hours is due. Liquor stores (known as Off-Licences or "Offies"), tend to keep similar hours to pubs, but often close a bit earlier. Many supermarkets now sell alcoholic drinks, so that may be the best place to buy your booze late at night.

Theaters

Standard performances time ranges from 7:30 to 8pm, and anything in between. Matinees start around 2:30pm.

Restaurants

While fast-food restaurants stay open from 9am until 5:30pm or later, many restaurants in Britain still open from noon to 2pm or 3pm for lunch and from 6pm to about 11pm at night, though habits are changing. The exceptions are ethnic restaurants – particularly Indian ones – which often stay open until the small hours.

You only need to book for lunch, which starts around 1pm, in the most exceptional restaurants, while dinner reservations are made for around 8pm or 8:30 in London, around an hour earlier in the provinces. Some restaurants offer special low-price pre-theater meals from 5pm or 6pm.

COST OF LIVING & TRAVEL

London is one of the most expensive cities in Europe. Although Brits don't notice it much – inflation has been pegged down to around 2% – the high value of the pound means that, for foreigners, everything seems exorbitant – eating out, hotel rooms, clothing, transportation (especially gas, which works out at around $6 per gallon). However, it is possible to find bargains. Go for a neighborhood ethnic restaurant instead of a West End one, or check out the local pub where, in many cases, you can get a good meal for less than £10.

Spending a lot of time in both the UK and US has shown me that, as a rule of thumb, **what costs you $10 in the US will cost about £10 in Britain** – in other words, in real terms, prices in England are about half as much again as they are in the US.

DOLLAR-POUND EXCHANGE RATE

*One pound is roughly $1.50, so for a quick calculation of pounds to dollars, **multiply the pound amount by 1.5** and you have a good idea of the dollar price.*

CRIME

Britain is generally a safe country, and as long as common sense prevails you should be fine. You're asking for trouble if you go out for a walk **alone late at night** through one of the sleaziest areas of town, or if you insist on wearing that jangly solid gold necklace, tiara or diamond ring that is crying out, "Steal me, steal me!" Instead, lock them in the **hotel safe**. Artful Dodger-type **pickpockets** are rife in some of the more crowded tourist areas, and on the Underground. And don't keep your ample wallet tucked in the back pocket of your pants, especially when you're packed like a sardine on an Underground train.

Keep your **car doors locked and windows shut** at all times when you're not using the auto, and don't encourage thieves by leaving expensive goods, such as cameras, hi-fi equipment or mobile phones on the back (or front) seat.

DISABILITIES (TRAVELERS WITH)

The general situation for travelers with disabilities visiting Britain has much improved over the past few years, but still lags far behind the US and Canada. While access to many cinemas and theaters is better, public transport still leaves a lot to be desired, and getting around on a train or bus is extremely stressful. The one major concession is that wheelchair users and blind or visually-impaired people are given a 30-50% reduction on train fares, while disabled people are also eligible for the **Disabled Person's Railcard**, which slashes the price of standard rail tickets by a third, and costs £14 for a year.

Specially modified accommodations for people with disabilities are few and far between, and are found normally only in the top range hotels and some of the more visionary smaller hotels and B&Bs. The **Royal Association for Disability and Rehabilitation** (RADAR), *12 City Forum, 250 City Road, London EC1V 8AF (Tel. 020 7250 3222; www.radar.org.uk)* offers advice on holidays and travel and produces an annual UK holiday guide. In the US, a number of tour operators specialize in tours for people with disabilities, including **Directions Unlimited**, *720 N. Bedford Road, Bedford Hills, NY 10507 (Tel. 800/533-5343)*, while general travel information for people with disabilities is provided by the **Society for the Advancement of Travel for the Handicapped** (SATH), with offices at *347 Fifth Avenue, #310, New York NY 10016 (Tel. 212/447-7284)*.

ELECTRICITY

The voltage in England (and most of Europe) is 220/240, more than twice the American current. In addition, the plugs and sockets in Britain are quite different from their American counterparts – large things with three square prongs, their own built-in fuses and separate on/off switches, making them, as they stand, totally incompatible with your favorite electric curlers or laptop computer. Step-up converters are available – enormously heavy things, costing around £30 each. It's probably cheaper to buy a new set of curlers. If you do crave one of these converters, try the High Street Dixons chain.

If you want to take back, say, an antique electric lamp or chandelier, most can be easily converted to American wiring back home. As far as most elaborate electrical goods, such as power tools, televisions, computers etc. go – forget it! You'll get most things cheaper in the US anyway.

EMBASSIES

In England
• **US Embassy**, *5 Upper Grosvenor Street, London W1, Tel. 020 7 499 9000*
• **Canadian High Commission**, *1 Grosvenor Square, London W1, Tel. 020 7 258 6000*

In the US & Canada
• **British Embassy**, *3100 Massachusetts Avenue, Washington DC 20008, Tel. 202/462-1340*
• **British High Commission**, *80 Elgin Street, Ottawa, ONK1P 5K7, Tel. 613/237-1530*

EMERGENCIES

For the emergency services – police, fire, ambulance and coastguard throughout Britain – dial **999**.

FLOORS

When I first arrived in the States I visited the Kennedy Center in Boston and immediately asked the concierge for the "**lift**" – when I should have said "**elevator**." When I got into the lift (sorry, elevator), I pressed #1, thinking it would take me up to the first floor, the next floor up from street level. I had forgotten that in the US, #1 *is* the ground floor, so I should have pressed #2. And so the lift didn't move, much to the amusement of the other passengers. Remember that in Britain, the **US second floor is the first floor**, the third floor the second floor and so on.

GAY & LESBIAN TRAVELERS

Homosexual acts between consenting males were legalized in Britain in 1967, but it was only in 1994 that the age of consent was lowered from 21 to 18. The Blair Government has been seeking to bring the UK in line with other European nations by lowering the age still further to 16, but has come up against fierce opposition from the House of Lords. Lesbianism has never been outlawed, Queen Victoria insisting that there was no such thing!

Attitudes in Britain vary; in the larger cities, like London and Manchester, they tend to be very liberal, while in the remoter rural areas this may not be the case, though you are unlikely to encounter antagonism.

Most medium- to large-sized towns in England and Wales have some kind of organized gay scene – maybe a pub or club, and a social group. The bigger cities, especially London, Manchester and Birmingham have many, as does Brighton, the self-styled "gay capital" of the south coast.

You can find out more about the gay scene in England and Wales by buying a copy of *Gay Times*, available at most newsagents. It comes with a detailed guide to gay pubs, clubs, hotels and local information lines. If you prefer, check out the website *at www.gaytimes.co.uk.*

HEALTH CONCERNS

Make sure you check with your health insurance company before leaving whether you are covered in the event of emergency, illness or injury during your travels in Britain. If you are covered, ensure that you know the procedures you need to follow in order to get the required treatment.

If you don't have adequate insurance, Britain's government-run **National Health Service** (NHS) will offer treatment in the case of **emergency only**. Depending on the severity of your illness/accident, dial **999** for an ambulance, or drop in at the **casualty department** (emergency room) of the local hospital – if it has one. In the case of minor ailments, your hotel (or the local library or police station) will be able to provide you with the names of local GPs.

If you're taking **medication**, make sure you have enough to cover your trip. American and Canadian prescriptions are not honored at British pharmacies (often referred to as "**chemists**"). If you do run short, arrange to see a local doctor and if you lose medication, **report it to the police straight away**. British pharmacies usually close at around 5:30pm, but most operate a **rotational system** with other pharmacies in the neighborhood, so that at least one local pharmacy stays open much later. If you arrive at a pharmacy after it has closed, look in the window for a list of pharmacies which are open late. Increasingly, some of the larger supermarkets have pharmacies which will stay open late – Safeway, Asda, Tesco and Sainsbury's being the major examples.

If you're in London with a medical problem and don't know where to turn, you could call **Medical Express** (*117a Harley Street, London W1,*

Tel. 020·7499 1991, Monday to Friday 9am to 6pm; Saturday 9:30 to 2:30pm), staffed by a rotation of local doctors who charge between £55 and £65 for a consultation, or £65 to £75 for an emergency call out in central London, when you must call *0800 136 106.*

LAUNDRY

Unless you're staying in self-catering accommodations where a washing machine is provided, there will come a point in your stay where you may have to do a **wash**. There are a variety of options: many of the larger hotels operate **valet laundering services**, but expect to pay exorbitant prices for this service. Some Bed & Breakfasts and guest houses may allow you to use their washing facilities, but this is by no means a foregone conclusion and you should check when you make your booking. Your best (and cheapest) bet is to take your laundry to the local **launderette** or **washeteria** (laundromat) which are all self-service – where you'll also have a chance to meet the locals. **Dry cleaning shops** are plentiful in most towns and cities.

LOOS

The **loo** is the British expression for what Americans call the bathroom, or what Europeans call the water closet. There's no better country in the world to get caught short! England and Wales are liberally sprinkled, so to speak, with **public conveniences**, commonly known as "the gents" or "the ladies." They certainly vary in cleanliness and hygiene (there's one I discovered in northern England where the attendant provides fresh flowers and bowls of fruit every day). It usually costs 10p to enter a cubicle (not long ago it was just a penny – hence the expression "spend a penny"). If there is no public convenience nearby, try a local pub, department store or train station.

As in the US, many restaurants in the UK frown upon people walking in off the street and using the facilities.

MONEY & BANKING

Most English and Welsh people do their banking at the "**big four**" High Street banks – **Barclays**, **HSFC**, **Lloyds TSB** and **National Westminster** (Natwest) – which are generally open from 9:30am to 5pm and have branches in just about every town throughout the nation. But the best place to exchange **travelers' checks** is **American Express** – though their branches are few and far between, confined mostly to the main tourist areas. American Express cardholders can cash a personal check drawn on a US bank free of charge ($1,000 for green cardholders; $5,000 for gold; $10,000 for platinum). Branches are open from 9am to

5:30pm Monday through Friday, and on Saturday from 9am to 4pm. American Express also offers an Emergency Service from 9am to 4pm weekdays and 24 hours at weekends. *Call 020 8667 1111 for more information.*

Other options for changing money are **Thomas Cook** branches, more common than American Express – and, if you're in dire straits, the numerous **Bureaux de Change** which are found in the main tourist areas. But beware: these bureaux, and your hotel, if you end up changing money there, are likely to charge you much higher rates of commission.

The increasing use of **credit cards** in Britain means that most restaurants, shops and hotels will take the major ones (Visa, MasterCard, American Express, but not Discover). In more remote areas, businesses often only take cash or personal (UK) checks, so find out when you make your reservation. In Britain, the word 'check' is spelled 'cheque.'

However, it's easier and safer to get cash direct from your US or Canadian account now than it ever has been, if your credit or debit card is affiliated to the **Cirrus** or **Yankee 24** networks, to which most British ATMs are linked. The service usually comes with a small one-time charge, and you'd use the machine in exactly the same way as you'd use an ATM back home. Look for machines with the Cirrus or Yankee 24 symbol – most of the main banks and building societies have them.

A NOTE ON TRAVELERS CHECKS

Although technically speaking travelers' checks can be used as cash, in Britain this is rarely if ever done, and is usually more trouble than it's worth.

Currency

The British currency is the **pound sterling**. Although the nation has been under pressure to ditch the pound and replace it with the **Euro**, this is unlikely to happen for many years. Think yourselves lucky that you aren't visiting England pre-1971, when the pound was divided into 240 pennies, with twelve pennies making a shilling, and twenty shillings making a pound. 'Decimalisation' in 1971 divided the pound into **100 pennies or pence**.

The coins in use are: the penny, much the same size and color as a US cent; two pence, much larger; five pence, much like a nickel; ten pence, like a dime; fifty pence, seven sided, and like nothing you've ever seen; the pound coin, a small coin, yellowish in color and thick; and the much larger two-metal two-pound coin. In this book and throughout the UK, for example, when you see "10p", that means ten pence.

Bills, known as "**notes**" in Britain, come in denominations of £5, £10, £20 and £50, each a different color and graded in size.

QUEUING

For many Americans, the act of **queuing** (standing in line) is almost as ridiculous as the spelling of the word. The British obsession with queuing is said to have developed with the strict rationing during two world wars, but it likely predates even that. However, traditions are changing, and climbing aboard a bus may be a bit of a free-for-all. Still, Britons generally expect to queue and are likely to get very upset when someone breaks the queue by pushing in (especially if a foreigner).

THE NATIONAL TRUST & ENGLISH HERITAGE

*The **National Trust**, established in 1895 to safeguard Britain's places of historical interest and natural beauty, is today one of Britain's major landowners, holding its various properties in trust for the nation. Most of its thousands of historic houses, castles, gardens and tracts of land are open to the public. You can choose to pay an entrance fee for each individual property or, better still, become a member. For a flat free, you can enter all NT properties without having to pay the admission charge. It certainly works out cheaper this way. For more information, contact the National Trust at 36 Queen Anne's Gate, London SW1H 9AS, Tel. 020 7222 9251.*

*   ***English Heritage**, 23 Savile Row, London W1X 1AB, Tel. 020 7973 3000, www.english-heritage.co.uk, is a state-run organization with a similar aim, as well as a similar membership scheme. A similar organization, **Welsh Historic Monuments**, exists across the border. Contact them at Crown Building, Cathays Park, Cardiff CF1 3NQ, Tel. 029 2050 0200.*

NEWSPAPERS & MAGAZINES

In such a small country, **national papers**, instead of regional ones, dominate the scene. Around a dozen national dailies with southern, northern and Scottish editions are published in London, Manchester and Glasgow, offering a diversity of political opinion and of quality that seems to appeal to the world's most newspaper-friendly nation.

The once high-quality *Times*, the world's most famous newspaper, has, since its purchase by press baron Rupert Murdoch become far more populist and sensationalist. The right-wing *Daily Telegraph*, left-of-center *Guardian* and independent *Independent* have good reputations, but like the Times have fallen prey to the need to boost ratings, often at the expense of good journalism.

In the middle of the quality range, the popular Conservative-supporting *Daily Mail* and the Blairite *Express*, the majority of whose readers are women, are both printed in tabloid form, and are generally less controversial than the downmarket tabloids: the right-wing *Sun*, left-wing *Mirror* and *The Star*. These papers battle it out for numerical superiority by specializing in the reporting of the latest whiff of scandal from the Palace or the sexual exploits of some famous TV or football star – though they claim to be serious national newspapers. The *Sun's* topless page 3 girl has become something of a national institution and has been the butt, so to speak, of many a stand-up comedian.

Many of the national newspapers produce Sunday versions so thick they most likely had to demolish a rain forest to produce it. Most come with free magazines listing TV programs for the week ahead.

Local dailies are published Monday to Friday from late morning onwards in the larger towns and cities, concentrating mainly on local and regional news but with some national and international content. Many of them produce lively **"What's On"** guides on Fridays – such as the London Standard. If you're really feeling homesick, the *International Herald Tribune* is available from many newsstands – even if it's a European edition, published in Frankfurt, and the *Washington Post* and *New York Times* are widely available in the big cities.

For listings information in London, you just can't beat *Time Out*, where everything from gay cabaret to political demonstrations, not to mention theater, exhibitions and sales bargains are listed.

Brits don't go in for newsmagazines the way other nations do. There's *The Economist*, which provides some really serious reading, if that's what you need on vacation, plus a host of specialist magazines, from the zany, satirical *Private Eye*, which is always being sued, to upmarket publications like *Country Life*.

POSTAL SERVICES

Post Offices are generally open from 9am to 5:30pm Monday through Friday – though some smaller offices close for lunch and/or may be closed completely for one afternoon of the week. Larger branches may also open on Saturdays from 9am to 12:30pm.

Notorious for their long queues, if it's just **stamps** you're after, and unless you want to be really pedantic and have exactly the right stamp on your letter or card, you can purchase these at a variety of **shops** and **stores** (most have a sticker on their window indicating this). You can buy books of four or ten, first-class (26p) or second-class (20p) stamps, or a £1 or £2 book which will give you a mixture. Postcards to the US cost 35p each, and letters (under 50mg) 64p.

Note: First and second class stamps come marked either "1st class" or "2nd class" without indicating their monetary value. I've discovered that sending the former to the US results in their being returned by the confused US Mail Service, so try and ensure that you have stamps with the exact denomination required. Mail to the US usually takes about five to seven days to arrive. Domestic first-class mail within the UK costs 26p and normally arrives next morning. Now how about that!

THE IMPORTANCE OF THE POSTCODE

Adding the rather odd-looking postcode to the address when writing a letter to Britain will guarantee its arrival at the right place! The first letters designate the town or area the letter's being sent to, and the number following that the area within that town/area where the address is located. The remaining half of the code allows the local postal services to pinpoint the property.

RELIGION

Britain's religious **diversity** is such that there is something for everyone; all the major **Christian denominations** – and then some – many of which originated here; **Jewish synagogues**, **Hindu temples** and **Muslim mosques** – today there are more practising Muslims in Britain than Anglicans. If you're in London or one of the great cathedral cities like Winchester or York, attending a service in such an inspiring building is enhanced by the musical accompaniment of some of the finest choirs in the world. The best time to catch a choir singing is at **Evensong**, the late afternoon/evening service, which begins anytime between 3:30 to 6:30pm.

Local tourist information offices should have information about service times of all local services, or check the local paper the night before. The *Times* publishes the service times of some of London's and the nation's best-known churches in its Saturday edition.

ROAD SAFETY

Despite the crazy speed at which the British seem to drive, the roads, though very crowded, especially in the southeast, are generally safe. I've found that there are three areas where Americans get particularly nervous: **roundabouts** (rotaries), a very common feature on British roads, where you need to remember that the traffic moves **clockwise**; very **narrow country lanes**, where even if you see octogenarian old ladies in half-timbered Austin 1100s tearing along at 70 mph, don't attempt to emulate them; and finally **zebra** (pronounced zeb-rah) **crossings**, crosswalks with black and white stripes. **Pedestrians have right of way** on these crossings, and British drivers will stop for a pedestrian even as they're approaching the crossing.

Road rage has certainly been a problem in Britain in recent years, with some well-publicized attacks, so if you're involved in a 'conflab' (conflabulation or conflict) with another driver, keep cool.

And finally, as a pedestrian, remember to **look to the right, then left, then right again** before crossing.

SMOKING

Just as in the US and Canada there has been a concerted campaign in Britain to reduce smoking. It has been fairly successful, many people having given up the habit, and in many public places (such as the Underground and on buses) it is completely banned. However, not all businesses are smoke-free, so when you make a restaurant reservation, ask for a table in the no-smoking area. Pubs still tend to be smoky.

SUNDAYS

The once-sacrosanct "Great British Sunday" has been changing in character ever since the introduction of **Sunday trading** some ten years ago. Up to that point, virtually all shops and businesses (except newsagents and some local shops) were closed, pubs and off-licences (liquor stores) had limited opening hours and city centers were virtually desolate. Although there has been tremendous liberalization of the Sunday trading laws, stores are still only allowed to open for **five hours** on a Sunday, so if you want to go out Sunday shopping, it makes sense to check what is open ahead of time.

TAXES

Brits have been paying less and less income tax over the past twenty years, but a variety of other **indirect taxes** have kept the general burden of taxation high. Americans and Canadians are horrified at the cost of gas in Britain – around £6 a gallon – but more than 80% of that is tax!

The best-known indirect form of taxation is **VAT (Value Added Tax)** much like a sales tax. The 17.5% tax is added to goods before purchase, so when it comes to paying, you won't be in for a surprise. What VAT means is that many goods manufactured in Britain can be bought more cheaply elsewhere – such as whisky. Foreign tourists are technically exempt from this tax on all items they are taking back home with them, though claiming back the tax can sometimes be a complicated business.

So what can you claim back on? Well, you can't claim back VAT on hotels or other services or on any purchase below a certain minimum (usually £100, set by the individual retailer). However, you can claim it back on single or multiple purchases from any one store where the cost of the goods exceeds the stated minimum. The way it works is this: pick up **a VAT 707 form** at the store, making sure they're filled in and signed when you hand them in to the VAT booth at customs. You may well be asked to produce the goods there and then, so make sure you've packed them near the top. The form will then be stamped, and you send it back to the store.

The store will then send you a VAT refund (it can take up to a month, so be patient) on a British account in pounds, so you will need to take it to your US or Canadian bank who will convert it – for a fee.

TELEPHONES

Britain's telephone services are dominated by **British Telecom**, which, since privatization, has spend a fortune on modernizing and updating the service. The result is a system that is as close to the US/Canadian system as anywhere else in the world. Phone booths – called **phone boxes** here – once came in bright red livery, but few of these survived modernization, so look for glass booths with the BT (or Mercury, another operator) sign. Public phones can also be found in many pubs, stores, theatres and other public places.

First note that the dialing tones are different here. The busy signal is similar to US/Canada, but instead of one long ringing tone, in the UK there's a double ring. To call another number in Britain, dial the local code (usually a five-digit number listed in the directory or in the phone booth) followed by the person's number. If you're calling a local number, there's no need to use the local code, just dial the number. Numbers in London and five other major cities went through a major overhaul in early 2000, confusing just about everybody, and costing businesses millions of pounds. London numbers all start with 020 7 – for central London – or 020 8 for outer London, followed by a seven digit number.

To **call the US or Canada**, simply dial 001 followed by the area code and the seven-digit number, hence 001-508/123-9595. Many Americans carry phone cards from MCI, AT&T or some other company; in this case, simply follow the instructions on the back of the card.

Many of the more modern phone booths accept **credit cards** as well as **cash**, or you can purchase special phone cards in many post offices, newsagents and stores. If using cash, rather than use small denominations like the 10p, use 50p or £1 coins. 10p gives you very little time, even for a local call, and the quick succession of beeps means that you must insert another coin or lose the line. Using higher denominations is better because even if you're only making a short call, you will receive change when the call is over.

The **operator** can be reached by dialing 100, **internal directory enquiries** (directory assistance) is 192, **the international operator** is 152, and **directory assistance overseas** (including the US and Canada) is 153. Don't forget that for the **emergency services** you need to dial 999 – the call is free.

A word of caution: Many hotels mark up their room telephone charges by as much as 200%! Unless you *want* to pay such exorbitant fees, use the public phones in the lobby.

TIME

England and Wales are **five hours** ahead of New York and Toronto, **eight hours** ahead of Los Angeles and Vancouver, and an **hour behind** most of the rest of Europe (except Ireland and Portugal). Clocks normally go forward to BST – British Summer Time – one hour on the last weekend of March and return to GMT (Greenwich Mean Time) in late October. As the US and Canada change one week later, for one week only in the spring there's a six hour difference between London and New York, while in the fall for one week it's four hours.

TIPPING

It may be customary to leave a tip for the bartender in the US or Canada, but it's simply not the done thing in England and Wales. In **cafes**, where you've just ordered a cup of tea or coffee and a snack, and in basic **restaurants**, leave 10%, while in more upmarket restaurants, 10-15% is about right (unless the service has been appalling). Examine the bill (check) to see if a **service charge** has been included. If it is, then there's no need to tip – unless you feel the service has been particularly good. **Taxi drivers** usually expect 10%.

TV & RADIO

Most hotel rooms come with cable TV these days, so you can watch *Larry King Live* every night if you wish. Those who wish to dabble with British TV will find the two main BBC channels, commercial-free **BBC1** and **BBC2**, with a mixture of news and current affairs, documentaries, sport, films and –what the "Beeb" does best – costume drama; **ITV**, with a similar diet; arty **Channel 4** – and **Channel 5**, which doesn't quite know *what* it is. You'll also likely find some of Rupert Murdoch's **Sky** Channels, including **Sky News**, much like CNN, **Sky 1**, a downmarket mixture of quiz shows and cheap imports, and **Sky Sports**.

These days, most Brits own either satellite, cable or terrestrial digital packages, so gone are the days when there were only two or three channels available. See the chapter 12, *Culture*, for more information.

WATER

Brits don't go in for bottled water like their American counterparts, because they've had it drummed into their heads that the water is perfectly safe to drink. Generally speaking, it is, but if you want to play safe, most supermarkets carry a range of bottled water. In restaurants, don't expect water to be provided automatically; this may happen in the fancier establishments, but generally you'll have to ask. After a brief grunt from the waiter/waitress, he/she will come with a large jug, almost certainly without ice and lemon. If you do strike it lucky and get ice, it'll likely be only one cube!

WEIGHTS & MEASURES

Despite government attempts to move things along, most older Brits are reluctant to part with **imperial measurements**, regarding Europe's desire to replace them with the metric system as part of an attempt to take over the nation. So **distance and speed** are still measured in miles. With smaller lengths, there's a national divide. Younger people tend to think **metric**, while anyone over 40 is stuck in a yards, feet and inches mode. Petrol (gas) is measured in **liters** (litres), which confuses everybody, and weather in degrees **celsius** (or centigrade) – though many still think in **farenheit**.

Food is weighed in **kilograms** and **grams**, and liquid generally measured in **liters** (litres), though the precious **pint** of milk and pint of beer still remain – after a vigoruous campaign to preserve it. Meanwhile, most confusingly of all, bodyweight is given in **stones** – a stone equaling fourteen pounds.

8. SPORTS & RECREATION

The nation that gave the world soccer, rugby, possibly tennis and, most proudly, cricket, is justifiably proud of its sporting heritage.

BOWLS

Many young English people partake in the exciting game of ten-pin bowling, but older bowlers prefer the gentler outdoor delights of **Bowls**, which, along with archery, has been practised since ancient times.

Requirements are a "jack" – a small ball no less than 2 1/2 inches in diameter nor more than ten ounces in weight), a few sets of bowls (which must not exceed 16 1/2 inches in circumference and 34 1/2 pounds in weight). The most important ingredient is the **green** – a superb lawn 42 yards square, with six rinks and a ditch six inches wide all round.

Bowling clubs flourish especially in areas where there are large numbera of retirees, such as the south coast seaside resorts. It's common to see teams of flannel-clad seniors battling it out behind tall privet hedges on a warm summer's day. There are local leagues, and the game is also played at county and international level.

CRICKET

If you haven't a clue what they're up to in soccer, then you'll be even more perplexed by a game of **cricket** (50% of the English are). Quintessentially English, it's the **national summer game**, and has been successfully exported to many other nations. There is something oh-so-English about seeing two teams of white-flanneled players contrasted against the lush hue of an idyllic village green, overlooked by tall oaks and the tower of the local parish church; spectators sitting on picnic chairs patiently awaiting the thwack of the hard, leather-coated ball against the willow of a cricket bat, and the polite applause that greets the scoring of a run, or the fall of a wicket, with the cry "Owzat!" ("How's that?").

Today, cricket is played in schools and colleges, in local parks, and in local leagues comprising teams from pubs, factories and even clergy. Local league games may last just a few hours, but international games, called "**tests**," can last up to five days! Not the most exciting of games, it can certainly have its exciting moments – such as when the result of a five-day game depends on how many runs can be scored from the last ball of the game. Another reason for its lack of appeal in some quarters is the incredibly complicated scoring system – just look at a cricket scoreboard in the sports pages of national newspapers and you'll see what I mean.

Though not popular with everyone, cricket is such an integral part of the nation's culture that it has given the language a number of expressions such as "sticky wicket" and "knock for six" (meaning being taken aback) and, when rules are broken, "It just isn't cricket!"

Modern cricket is said to date from the formation of the Hambledon Cricket Club in Hampshire, who established official rules in 1750. However, it's likely that the game goes back much further. It became a national game after the foundation of the **Lord's Cricket Ground** in London in 1814, and the subsequent formation of the **Marylebone Cricket Club** (the MCC), now the world governing body of cricket. With the expansion of Britain's empire, cricket was relayed all round the world, so that today it is a popular game in Australia, Pakistan, New Zealand, South Africa and the West Indies.

England's main national cricket league is called the **county championship**, and dates from 1850. The cricket season starts in April and ends in September, overlapping for a few weeks with the soccer season. County matches are programmed to last three days – that is, unless rain stops play, or a side is bowled out (twice) before.

A separate Sunday league, also involving the county clubs, has been lambasted by the game's purists. It involves much shorter games, and consequently a different approach is demanded.

England's national side has been the cause of much consternation and embarrassment in recent years. English pride as the founder of cricket has been dented by a series of defeats at the hands of much smaller nations. The international game that gets most attention is the game against Australia. The **Ashes** is the title of a non-existent prize awarded to the winner of the best of five five-day tests between the two nations. The fact that Australia always seemed to get the better of England prompted the astronomer, Fred Hoyle, to say that he could not look up into the galaxy without feeling that somewhere out there, there must be a team that could beat the Australians.

Take some time – but not too much – to study the game. In the unlikely event that you get to attend one you certainly *will* have the time to study it. After all, the game does have some parallels with its young upstart nephew, baseball.

CROQUET

This is a summer game introduced to England from France in the mid-1800s. It's not particularly popular – you need a large flat **lawn** to play it. It's another genteel pastime that somehow seems to epitomize everyone's stereotype of the laid-back English way of life.

GOLF

Britain is the proud possessor of some of the best **golf courses** in the world, a sport where England in general has been able to hold its own. Not surprising, as the game had its roots here. Maybe this too explains why Britain, despite its size, is able to produce some of the world's finest golfers. In this case, the unpredictable weather can actually help.

It's not in England, but in **St. Andrew's**, **Scotland**, where the Royal and Ancient Golf Club claims to be "the home of golf," with roots going back as far as the fifteenth century and is a real place of pilgrimage for golf addicts, even if they're staying south of the border. The Old Course there is the main focus of attention, and no fewer than 24 **British Opens**, arguably the most prestigious tournament in world golf, have been held here.

There are many famous courses in Scotland, but England has some fine courses, too, such as **Royal Lytham**, **Wentworth** and **Sunningdale**. Golf courses are dotted all round the country, and it's possible to gain temporary membership in most of them.

At the large number of public golf courses in Britain, visitors need only show up and pay a fee; in many private clubs this is also the case, but many others require arranging a temporary membership in advance. The more exclusive ones may have a strict members and friends-of-members-only policy. For more information about golf clubs in Britain, contact **The Golf Club of Great Britain**, *3 Sage Yard, Douglas Road, Surbiton, Surrey KT6 7TS, Tel. 020 8390 3113.*

HOCKEY

Say the word hockey to an English person and they'll assume you are talking about the game played on grass – **"field hockey"** as it's known in most parts of the world. It's played in schools and universities, local and regional leagues and internationally. **Ice hockey** is generally confined to the larger towns and cities, wherever facilities are available, and has a relatively small following.

HORSE RACING

Horse racing has been practised in England since the twelfth century. Today the sport is still popular, and the most famous race, the **Grand National**, held at Aintree, near Liverpool, is one of the nation's most famous and prestigious sporting events, evoking the same kind of interest as the FA Cup Final or Wimbledon fortnight.

Races, which are held both on the **flat**, and over hurdles (known as **National Hunt** racing) are televised most afternoon on one or more of the national networks. All over the country, betters can "**have a flutter**" at bookmakers' shops (**bookies**) which can be found in virtually every High Street. Among the best known of these are **William Hill** and **Ladbrokes**.

Race tracks are always grass, with sufficient time allowed between each meeting for the grass to recover. Race meetings are frequently postponed due to damp or soggy conditions, and when a meeting does go ahead, the state of the race surface – categorized as soft, good or firm – plays a major part in the deliberations of both bookies and betters.

The most famous races, apart from the Grand National, include the **Derby**, held at Epsom in Surrey; the **St. Ledger**, which takes place at Doncaster, Yorkshire; and the **Cheltenham Gold Cup**.

In June, the course at **Ascot** hosts **Ascot Week**, considered a high point in the nation's calendar – at least by the rich and famous. The Week has enjoyed royal patronage for more than 250 years, and for that reason, attracts many hangers-on. In the Royal Enclosure, men wear top hats and women wear their latest designer outfit, topped by an outrageous hat. In all the social revelry, it's easy to forget that the race itself, the 2 1/2 mile **Ascot Gold Cup**, happens to be one of the high-spots of Britain's flat-racing season.

POLO

There are only about 500 regular polo players in England, but because of the kind of people who play it, predominantly aristocrats such as Prince Charles, it gets coverage out of all proportion to its size. Known as "the sport of kings," the game is said to have been imported into England by army officers stationed in India.

RUGBY

Rugby is a winter game that reached its current format in 1823 in the famous public school at Rugby, Warwickshire. According to the myth, a soccer-playing schoolboy picked up the ball and started running with it. The idea caught on, and had become so popular by the 1870s that a **Rugby Football Union** was formed. The game was exported to the United States, and evolved into what is known in Britain as American football.

Widely played in school and colleges, this is a fast-paced, frequently exciting game, though it has never enjoyed the almost-universal popularity of soccer. The season runs from September to April.

To complicate matters, there are **two versions** of the game: **rugby union**, played at the international level, and very strong at club level in the south and Wales, has teams composed of fifteen players; and **rugby league**, with its heartland in the industrial centers of the north, with teams of thirteen players and some differences in rules. In both versions, points are scored when the oval-shaped ball in touched down, called a **try**, with additional points available if the try is converted. In rugby union games, a common sight is the **scrum**, when the forwards of both teams push and shove each other for possession of the ball.

Rugby has been successfully exported throughout the British Isles (the Welsh, Scots and Irish all have strong teams), parts of Europe (especially France) and throughout the Commonwealth, where New Zealand (the "Kiwis") and South Africa (the "All Blacks") are among the strongest teams.

SOCCER

It will take a while to get used to English people referring to the nation's most popular spectator sport, soccer, as "**football**." Despite a number of setbacks in recent years, including two major disasters that resulted in the death of dozens of people, football is still the game you'll see being played by little boys and girls kicking a ball against a wall in an inner city street; and by countless teams in local leagues in parks all over the country.

The games' popularity reached its peak in 1966, when the English national team reached the **World Cup Final**, the most prestigious football event in the world, and still the world's largest sporting event. Not only that, but they beat arch-rivals West Germany 3-2, as the nation came to a virtual standstill. The story was almost repeated in 1990, when England again progressed to the semi-finals of the World Cup, facing Italy. Such was public interest in the game that during the half-time break, the National Electricity Grid was barely able to keep up with the power surge created by the switching on of ten million electric kettles at the same time, while the water authorities were pressed with the sudden demand for enough water to flush 25 million loos.

Today, England's national soccer team continues to have mixed fortunes after a poor spell. Despite the optimism that accompanied the appointment of a new young coach, Kevin Keegan, to the national team, England's disastrous early exit from the Euro 2000 Tournament dashed hopes that the national team was set for a major revival. A string of further poor results prompted Keegan's resignation. English people expect their team to do well and – spurred on by the tabloid press – become ultra-critical when things do not go according to expectations. Home games had always been played at **Wembley Stadium**, north London, built for the Olympic Games of 1948. But the historic stadium with its famous twin towers was demolished in 2000 to make way for a new state-of-the-art facility accommodating 90,000.

The name "soccer" derives from the **Football Association**, the sport's governing body in England and Wales. Teams from the two nations compete in a **national league**. The most prestigious clubs, like world-renowned **Manchester United**, the largest club in the world, and London-based **Arsenal** slog it out over 38 games in a season that stretches from August to May in the top-level division known as the **Premiership**. Three lower divisions cater for smaller clubs. Each game lasts for 90 minutes, with most games taking place on Saturday afternoons at 3pm. In addition to the league, all English and Welsh clubs (and a limited number of non-league clubs who've made it through the qualifying rounds) contend for the **F.A. Cup**, a knockout competition that concludes with the F.A. Cup Final, with much the same status in England as the Superbowl has in the US.

The reputation of English soccer has been tainted in recent years by the appalling behavior of some of its so-called "supporters." In one of the most serious examples, fans of Liverpool's football team attacked fans of the Italian team Juventus at an international match being played at the Heysel Stadium in Brussels. Scores died in the tragedy, with the result that English clubs were banned from European competitions for several years. Much of the violence on this and other occasions was linked to infiltration of soccer supporters by extreme right-wing groups. Another tragedy took place on June 1, 1997, in Sheffield, when, ironically, dozens of Liverpool supporters were crushed to death when the crowd surged forward. This, along with a fire during an earlier game at the stadium in Bradford, where scores died, led to major changes in ground safety requirements, and the rebuilding or total replacement of many football stadia, so that today England and Wales have some of the best-equipped safest stadia in the world. League football is gradually becoming a **family game** once again, and numbers attending matches are increasing, despite the virtual saturation coverage of TV.

Attending a game between two Premiership clubs can be an exciting, thrilling experience – even for the uninitiated and even if there are no goals. You'll inevitably get caught up in the atmosphere, discover a vocabulary you never knew existed, and see the normally tranquil English at their most passionate. Soon you'll be shouting and screaming for the local team – even though you haven't a clue what they're doing.

SNOOKER

Closely related to **pool** (which is also popular in England), snooker has its origins in pubs and "workingmen's" clubs. In recent years it has reached new heights of popularity, thanks mainly to the fact that it translates so well on to television – especially since the advent of color TV. The game is played locally at thousands of snooker halls and venues throughout the nation; millions of people stay up to the small hours of the morning to watch the **World Championships** on TV. Its leading protagonists are household names.

TENNIS

Tennis is a popular summer game in Britain. Municipally and privately-owned grass and clay courts can be found throughout the land.

By far the most famous and important event in the English tennis calendar is **Wimbledon**, where the **All England Championships** take place annually in June. There's saturation coverage of the event on TV.

Despite the popularity of the sport in Britain, it's a source of great irritation and frustration to many English people that they haven't produced a Wimbledon champion since **Virginia Wade** won the ladies' singles title in 1976 or a male champion since 1935, when **Fred Perry** won the men's event. Currently two British men, Tim Henman and Canadian-born Greg Rusedski, flit in and out of the world top ten, raising hopes of a British title winner in the near future. Inevitably, the damp gray climate and poor funding for the sport is blamed for the poor showing.

OTHER SPORTS

Other popular sports in England include **boxing** (though after a recent spate of deaths there have been calls to have the sport banned), **motor racing** (Britain has produced an impressive number of Formula 1 champions, including most recently Nigel Mansell and Damon Hill) and **swimming**. **Basketball** and its cousin, **netball**, are played in schools and colleges. Popular North American sports, such as **baseball** and **football**, have a small but loyal following.

BEACHES

Perhaps you wouldn't normally associate a visit to England and Wales with a beach holiday, but because of the nation's long coastline, there are plenty of choices, many of which are easily accessible by public transport

– very few indeed are private. And if it's warm water you want – forget it! Despite the influence of the Gulf Stream, **sea temperatures**, even in the extreme southwest, rarely reach the upper 60s, even at the height of the summer season, while on the North Sea coast they're often 10 degrees lower. Most of the major resorts offer extensive **beach facilities**; places to eat, half-decent toilets and lifeguards.

Bear in mind that many of the beaches – especially those around river mouths and estuaries – are prone to **dangerous currents and undertows**; a **red flag** flying means don't enter the water on any account. Although there are sharks in British waters, they pose very little risk to bathers; you're far more likely to encounter jellyfish, which invade southern waters during warmer spells. A far greater hazard is the water itself; many English and Welsh beaches fail to come up to the minimum European standards for cleanliness and hygiene.

The most popular region for a beach holiday is **Devon** and **Cornwall**, with a multitude of sandy bays and inlets, many of which are exposed to the **Atlantic** and consequently popular with surfers. Further east, the shoreline becomes rather pebbly, except for some long stretches of sand around **Bournemouth**, and possibly the best beach in southern England, the dune-backed **Studland Bay** in **Dorset**. Further east again, you'll find some of England's brashest resorts, like **Brighton** and **Margate**.

The North Sea coast of **East Anglia** is a mixture of sand and pebbles, very exposed to chilly easterly winds and often the victim of sea frets (fog) even in mid-summer. Further north, **Yorkshire** has some good sandy beaches and attractive coves as well as some garish resorts, while **Northumberland**, with some long stretches of white sand, is the place to really get away from it all (even if the water is cold). On the other side of the country, you'll find some long wide sandy beaches on the **south Wales** coast up through **Pembrokeshire**. North of the Mersey estuary is Britain's brashest resort, **Blackpool**, but nobody goes there for the beach, while northern **Lancashire** and **Cumbria** offer hills and mountains, but little in the way of decent beaches.

For more beach information, check out the *Good Beach Guide*, published annually by David and Charles, while surfers may want to check out *Surf UK* by Wayne Alderson (Fernhurst Books, £13.95).

BIRD WATCHING

Britain is a bird watcher's paradise. As well as the 130 resident species, such as the **nightingale**, with its beautiful song, found only in the south of England; rare species such as the **Dartford Warbler**, and the **red kite**, usually only seen in Wales. England and Wales are visited by many hundreds of **migrant** species – up to 500 species have been recorded here.

Some, like the **chiffchaff**, flying north in the spring, while others, like the **brent goose** and **whooper swan**, fly to spend the winter here, avoiding the much harsher Arctic climate.

The country is speckled with **bird reserves**, many of which contain a large part of the breeding population of resident birds. Some of these are owned and maintained by the **Royal Society for the Protection of Birds**, *The Lodge, Sandy, Bedfordshire SG19 2BR (Tel. 01767 680551)*, who can provide more information. For a basic guide to Britain's birds, there's nothing better than the *Field Guide to the Birds of Britain* (Reader's Digest Association).

BOATING

As a maritime nation, Britain is full of sailors (or would-be sailors), and coastal waters tend to get very crowded in the summer. Boats can be rented from a variety of sources. If you are more interested in the calmer waters of Britain's inland waterways, including several hundred miles of canals, contact the **Association of Pleasure Craft Operators**, *35a High Street, Newport, Shropshire TF10 7AT, (Tel. 01952 813572)*, who will be happy to send you relevant information.

CAMPING

Summer traffic in Britain is frequently slowed down by family cars pulling hefty "**caravans**" – the name Brits give to mobile trailers – to the hundreds of camping sites dotted around the country. Most of these sites have trailers for **rent** as well as **touring pitches**. For more information about campsites in Britain, contact the **Camping and Caravanning Club**, *Greenfields House, Westwood Way, Coventry, CV4 8JH, Tel. 01203 694995*.

CYCLING

Every year, many thousands of Britons take cycling holidays, many choosing to transport their own bicycles by car, others to **rent** them from the increasing number of bicycle rental companies throughout the land. Some areas, such as the **New Forest**, or the relatively flat, undemanding coast of **East Anglia** make wonderful destinations for cycling holidays. For a £25 fee (£12.50 for students, £16.50 for Over-65s and £42 for families of three or more) you can join the **Cyclists' Touring Club**, *Cotterall House, 69 Meadrow, Godalming, Surrey GU7 3HS*, which promotes touring by bicycle and provides information about destinations, routes, general advice and accommodation for members.

FISHING

Fishing is immensely popular in England, not surprisingly in a nation with such a long shoreline and countless harbors and estuaries. But this favorite English pastime is not confined to the coast. Inland, ponds, lakes canals and above all, **streams** and **rivers** provide a teeming variety of freshwater fish, and whole stretches of once badly-polluted rivers and streams that were once void of fish are now being cleaned up. Salmon have even been spotted near Westminster Bridge on the Thames. Rod licenses are available from post offices throughout England and Wales; fishing tackle shops are usually very good places to make enquiries about fishing locally.

There are three main categories of fishing. **Sea fishing**, or **angling**, requires no permit. Many coastal resorts and towns operate special sea fishing trips, or you can often rent a boat yourself. **Coarse fishing** includes all fish except trout or salmon in freshwater rivers or lakes. Some stretches of water require no license, while others demand a permit paid for by a fee. Check the local yellow pages, fishing tackle shop or tourist information center for details, and for general information and advice about local conditions. Equipment, such as rod and line, portable stools and umbrellas, can often be rented from fishing tackle shops.

Finally, there's **game fishing**, which is freshwater fishing (in rivers and lakes) for salmon and trout. Most game fishing in England is private and therefore out-of-bounds to outsiders, unless you're on a specialist game-fishing vacation. Some clubs and associations do issue permits, usually at sky-high prices. On the web, go to *www.fisheries.co.uk* for useful links to many fisheries and fishing authorities in Britain, or contact the local tourist office.

RIDING

Horseback riding is a popular pastime in England and Wales, opening up a new perspective of the countryside. **Riding schools** can be found the length and breadth of the country. The most popular areas, naturally, tend to be those far from the madding crowd; like **Dartmoor;** the **New Forest;** the **Yorkshire Dales;** and the **Northumberland National Park.**

WALKING

The Brits take their walking very seriously. The nation is criss-crossed with protected public **rights of way**, some of which have been thus for centuries, many of which cross private land. As a statement of how seriously Brits take their public rights of way, a recent housing development was halted when it was discovered that a home had been built over one. When the builders realized that walkers would have a legal right to walk through the house (this would mean the new owners of the house would have walkers streaming through their hallway), they demolished the house! It's essential that you keep to the path, making sure you close any gates behind you.

There are also literally thousands of miles of specially-designated **long distance footpaths** (LDPs). LDPs are scattered all over the nation and are designated at regular intervals by an **acorn** sign. For more information about these, consult the **Ramblers Association**, *(1-5 Wandsworth Road, London SW8 2XX, Tel. 020 7582 6878)*, who provide an annual walkers' guide which includes information on accommodations close to the main long distance walks. In addition, **The Long Distance Walker's Association**, *(9 Tainter's Brook, Uckfield, East Sussex TN22 1UQ)* provides information on LDPs. For less serious walkers, buy a copy of the local *Ordnance Survey Map*, which indicates the public rights of way in the area.

Among the most popular areas for walkers are the coastline from **Dorset to Devon** and **Cornwall**; the **New Forest**; **Dartmoor**; the **Peak District**; the **Yorkshire Dales**; the **North York Moors**; the **Lake District**; the **Northumberland National Park**; and the **Pembrokeshire coast** and **Snowdonia** in Wales.

9. SHOPPING

England may no longer be Napoleon's "nation of shopkeepers," but even the most shop-phobic visitors to the country are amazed by the sheer variety and quality of the merchandise that's available. When it's time to return home, you may end up having to sit on your suitcases to get them shut.

Many of the main tourist meccas abound in tacky souvenir and gift shops, selling such delights as Union Jack underwear, Camilla Parker Bowles souvenir mugs and plastic policemen's helmets. Avoid them, and concentrate instead on the myriad of quality stores where you can find the classic items for which Britain is renowned – china and porcelain, crystal and glass, designer fashion, rainwear (naturally), tartans from Scotland, woolens and shoes.

Despite the growing number of out-of-town shopping centers, whose expansion was fueled by the efforts of successive governments to put the emphasis on private transport, and add to the equation the plain and simple fact that a large proportion of the English populace does not drive, most shopping in England is still focused on **downtown**, easily accessed in most cases by public transport. Many towns have purpose-built malls in their downtown areas, like Manchester with its Arndale Centre, and Birmingham with its Pallisades. In many towns and cities, the downtown shopping environment has been made more comfortable by the "pedestrianisation" of once heavily trafficked, formerly fume-filled streets, and by importing trees and hanging baskets of geraniums to brighten things up.

As a general rule, most stores in England are open from 9am until 5:30pm, though increasingly many of them are staying open later, especially in the summer. The stormy debate over Sunday opening has now settled down, with about half the nation's stores open, most commonly supermarkets and some of the larger chain stores.

SHOPPING IN THE CAPITAL

London is the hub of the nation's retail life. The main shopping drag, **Oxford Street**, runs east to west for about two miles from Marble Arch to Tottenham Court Road and contains branches (sometimes more than one) of just about all of England's **chain stores** with names that will soon become familiar to the visitor, such as Marks & Spencer's, Boots, British Home Stores and C&A, as well as multi-story **department stores** like Selfridge's and John Lewis. The more upmarket **Regent Street** bisects Oxford Street at Cambridge Circus, and is the home of world-famous stores such as fabric specialists Liberty's and Hamley's, reputedly the biggest toy store in the world and a must, as the cliche goes, for children of all ages. Both Regent and Oxford Streets are especially busy in the run-up to Christmas, when frustrations and irritation of shopping sardine-like among unbelievable hoards are offset by some spectacular Christmas illuminations.

Knightsbridge, on the other side of Hyde Park from Oxford Street's western end, is another fine upmarket shopping center that is distinguished by the presence of **Harrod's**, the world's most famous department store. Harrod's boasts of being able to sell you anything from an elephant to a pin. Explore the **food hall**, one of the wonders of London, and see the tacky "shrine" dedicated to **Princess Diana** and **Dodi Al-fayed** by the latter's father, the store's owner.

Central London also boasts a number of speciality shopping areas, ranging from the antiques, fine art and upscale fashion stores around **New Bond Street** to **Tottenham Court Road**, littered with hi-fi and computer stores and Savile Row for that perfect made-to-measure suit. Many of the nation's finest book stores are to be found in **Charing Cross Road**. If shopping is your thing, make sure you pick up a copy of one of the guides to London shopping; one of the best of these is published by *Time Out*.

Two important factors are worth bearing in mind when shopping in England. First, English people are surprisingly docile when it comes to making a purchase. Timid English people hate to be approached by a sales assistant or associate when they enter a store, and are more content wasting hours searching for the object of their desire before "bothering" a member of staff. When they do approach an associate, they tend to come over all shy and apologetic, as if *they* are doing the assistant a favor. And when the assistant admits to having the required item in stock, the prospective purchaser is completely aghast.

CLOTHING SIZES*

Women's Dresses & Skirts

American	6	8	10	12	14
English	8	10	12	14	16

Women's Shoes

American	6	7	8	9	10
English	4	5	6	7	8
European	37	38	39	40	41

Women's Underwear

American	5	6	7
English	7	8	9

(note: bra sizes are the same)

Men's Shoes

American	6	7	8	9	10	11	12
English	5	6	7	8	9	10	11

Men's suits, shirts and trousers are the same sizes in England as in America, but beware of shirt cuffs which are often designed for cufflinks rather than buttons.

Chart taken from Open Road's **London Guide, by Meg Rosoff & Caren Acker.*

QUEUING

Queuing, as English as a game of cricket or a cream tea on the Vicarage lawn, is said to have its roots in the English obsession with fair play (though, in reality, it was always the wealthy who got in first). The orderly act of queuing for rations during successive world wars stamped the idea firmly in the English psyche, so today, "First come, first served," is as popular a principle for most English people as it has always been – even thugs about to run riot inside a soccer ground will first queue in orderly fashion in order to enter the stadium.

The practice of queuing is taken to extraordinary lengths at the start of the January and summer **sales**, when, for a set period that's usually well advertized in the local and national press, many stores drop their prices drastically to dispose of old stock. People frequently camp in line outside stores for days in advance in order to get the reduced item they want, relying on friends to bring them regular cups of tea and meals.

NEIGHBORHOOD SHOPPING

Shopping in local stores in smaller towns, villages or suburbs can be a real pleasure. You may pay slightly more for your purchase, but you'll have the experience of dealing with usually friendly, helpful staff and a chance to meet some of the locals and catch up on the gossip.

In most medium-sized villages in England you'll find, in addition to a **bank** and **post office**, a **butcher**, **chemist** (pharmacy), **baker**, **fruiterer**, **grocer**, **fishmonger** and **ironmonger** (hardware store). In the cities, an increasing number of neighborhood stores are owned and run by members of various ethnic communities, so that in addition to the regular stock, you may find some more exotic items not normally found elsewhere. In addition, many of these stores stay open far later than their High Street counterparts.

MARKETS

Bustling, noisy, colorful and fun, markets – many of whose origins can be traced back centuries – are scattered the length and breadth of England and Wales, both in the historic market towns that speckle the countryside, and in the suburbs of large cities – sometimes indoors in specially-built halls, or out in the street. Here you can find all manner of inexpensive goods, from fresh fish to frilly underwear and everything in between. Charismatic **stallholders** ply their wares in a cacophony of sights, sounds and smells – like a scene from *Oliver Twist*.

In London, and some large cities, **specialist markets** are increasingly popular. London's **Portobello Road** and **Camden Lock** markets are, for example, two that deal predominantly with antique and second-hand goods, where it's always possible to find a major bargain.

JUMBLE SALES & CHARITY SHOPS

Yard sales as such do not exist in Britain; very few people have yards large enough to display their goods. Still popular, however, are **jumble sales**, more akin to rummage sales than anything else. These usually take place in local community or church halls, on Friday evenings or Saturday mornings, and benefit local or national charities. The main focus is usually on secondhand clothes, but there are usually bric-a-brac stalls and you may even find a priceless treasure. You can usually find out what jumble sales are on in the area you're staying by checking in the Friday night edition of the local paper, where there will likely be a whole page of jumble sale advertisements. It's also a great way to see the English at play and – who knows? – you might pick up a priceless Rembrandt!

In recent years, **car boot sales** have also become popular. Vendors pay a fee to an organizer, who then allows the vendor to sell goods – new and secondhand – from the boot (trunk) of their car. These, too, are often advertized in the Friday night edition of the local paper.

Many English shopping streets are the focus for **charity shops**, much the same as thrift shops in North America, but usually benefiting national charities. Some of these, such as **Oxfam**, are the place where young professionals turn to purchase, for next to nothing, some designer-label throw-off that's been cluttering up someone's closet for years, while easing their social conscience at the same time. Other well-known stores are run by **Help the Aged** and **Christian Aid**.

FOOD SHOPPING

Supermarkets are an essential port-of-call for travelers staying in self-catering accommodations, and even in smaller towns, you'll find at least one branch of the half-dozen or so of England's major supermarket chains: **Sainsbury's**, **Tesco**, **Asda** and **Safeway,** most of which have their own vast car parks.

At first sight, there's little to distinguish them from their North American cousins. They're clean, well laid-out and retail a vast range of goods. Many of the larger branches come with in-house pharmacies, delicatessens and bakeries, so there's often a delightful aroma around the place. Most have cash machines (ATMs). Be prepared to be run off the road by determined old ladies wheeling their own shopping trolleys, like appendages, behind them.

But don't be lulled into a false sense of security by these familiar surroundings; it's the little things that will catch you out. When you enter the store, you'll need to pick up a shopping basket (usually wire, not plastic) or a trolley (cart). As you begin your tour, you'll likely be impressed by the range of merchandise, but not by the absence of many of your favorites from back home. After all, Twinkies means no more to the English than Marmite does to you.

Among the staggering array of fresh produce, meat, fish and veg-etables, you're sure to spy some unfamiliar sights like **chidlings, tripe** and **winkles**. Other, more familiar-looking items are labeled with different names, especially vegetables like **courgettes** (zucchini), **mange-tout** (snow peas) and **swede** (rutabaga). There's even a different vocabulary to describe cuts of meat.

By law, all perishable items must have an expiration date, and labels indicate the content. Weights are now given in **kilos** and **pounds,** so it may be worthwhile taking a small calculator with you. Even the English are struggling to cope with the introduction of the metric system, which many blame wholeheartedly on Brussels (city, not sprouts).

The major chains all cater to **vegetarians** and **vegans**, and there are plenty of low-fat, low-calorie and low-cholesterol items to keep the punters happy. Many of the supermarkets also produce a range of excellent **ready-to-cook** meals, ideal if you're self-catering. If you're near a larger branch of Marks & Spencers, check out their range of ready-to-cook dishes – they're superb.

Supermarket checkouts in England are lined with the same kind of titillating trash as you'll find in North America, you know, the "My wife is an alien" type of tabloids. Queue up, then be ready to pack the items in the bag yourself; British supermarkets rarely if ever produce spotty, pre-pubescent juniors to do your packing for you. Doing this and juggling with your wallet or purse at the same time can be a nightmare. Payment is made in cash, credit or debit card, but **not travelers' checks** – despite their propaganda, they're simply not used in the UK for this type of purchase, and you're likely to incur the wrath, not only of the cashier, but everyone else in the line, if you start fiddling around with them at this point.

10. TAKING THE KIDS

England and Wales are great places to visit with kids. Many of the main tourist attractions offer discounted rates for children, as do many B&Bs and hotels. Even pubs very often have "beer gardens" with play areas for children. Kids are fascinated by ruined castles, and to some extent by museums (especially places like the Natural History Museum with its dinosaurs), but you can have too much of a good thing, and you can bet your bottom dollar they'll want to do something a little more energetic. You might be grateful for it, too, at the end of the day. I've listed below some of the main attractions for London, followed by some ideas for places further afield.

SUGGESTIONS IN LONDON

Once you've arrived and settled in to your accommodations, the kids will want to start exploring. A great way to get your bearings is to take a **boat trip** on the **Thames**, for centuries London's main highway. Most Thames cruises depart from **Charing Cross Pier**, near the Houses of Parliament. **Catamaran Cruisers** offer return trips to Greenwich, with commentary, at £7 per adult return, £3.80 for children under 16 – or check out the Thames barrier for £10 adults, £5.50 children. A Catamaran Discover Pass allows unlimited use of all scheduled sightseeing cruises with discounts to six major attractions – all for £8.50 (£4.25). *Call 020 7925 2215. Nearest Tube: Westminster or Embankment.*

The **London Eye**, also known as the **Millennium Wheel**, is a huge ferris wheel – the largest of its kind in the world. Since opening, the 500-foot high wheel, with its 32 glass capsules, has become one of London's most popular tourist attractions. The wheel moves round extremely slowly – one revolution takes around 20 minutes – affording passengers spectacular views over the whole city and beyond. It's a great place to start your London visit. *Millennium Wheel, Jubilee Gardens, South Bank, London SE1. Open daily April to mid-September 9am to 10pm (last entry 9:30pm); mid-September to March 10am to 6pm (last entry 5:30pm). Fees: Adult £8.50,* *children £5, seniors £5.95, students £7.95. For tickets, call 0870 5000 600. Nearest Tube: Waterloo.*

You will get a meal with a difference at Europe's first **Rainforest Café** in Shaftesbury Avenue. Spanning three floors, the Café includes a massive 340-seat restaurant and a retail village set against the backdrop of a tropical rainforest. The special effects are dazzling: tropical rain showers; thunderstorms; cascading waterfalls and wild animal sounds. The resident live parrots and tropical fish co-star with a cast of fantastic animatronic inhabitants – chattering gorillas, a splashing life-size crocodile and a slithering boa constrictor. Watch mum cringe! Tour guides lead adventurers to their tables and orders are taken by "safari guides." The jungle theme extends to the menu with exotically named dishes like "China Island Chicken Salad" and "Rumble in the Jungle." *Rainforest Café, located at 20 Shaftesbury Avenue, is open 12noon to 11pm Sunday to Thursday, 12noon to midnight Friday and 11.30am to midnight Saturday. Nearest Tube: Piccadilly Circus.*

Just around the corner, the **Trocadero Centre** in Piccadilly Circus is home to **Segaworld**, the world's largest indoor futuristic entertainment park. When you enter, a 50-meter Rocket escalator whisks you from the ground floor to the upper levels where you can explore six themed zones covering an area the size of 10 Wimbledon Centre Courts. Each zone has its own interactive ride attractions offering up to seven minutes of real action-packed entertainment. Try Aqua Planet with its 3-D effects, or take out your frustrations by shooting at fellow competitors from an armored dodgem car! The Combat Zone includes the latest fighting arcade games, and in the Race Track you can take on up to eight challengers in exciting racing games like Daytona USA and the Manx TT. Flight Deck features a real Harrier Jump Jet suspended from the ceiling, and younger members of the family will be in their element in the Carnival and the Sega Kids zones. There is even a Sports Arena with sporting challenges for all ages. *Segaworld is open daily from 10am until midnight Sunday to Thursdays, and until 1am Fridays and Saturdays. Entrance is free, and prices for games and attractions vary from 20p to £3. Nearest Tube: Piccadilly Circus.*

A royal palace and fortress for 900 years, the **Tower of London** is Britain's most visited tourist attraction. It has also been a prison and place of execution, an arsenal, a royal mint, menagerie and jewel house. Inside, pick up the free "What to See" leaflet – plan your own itinerary, or take one of the tours led by Yeoman Warders (wrongly known as "Beefeaters") which set off from the front entrance every half-hour. Families can explore the free children's trail: Yeoman Warder Mick Casson will take you all round the Tower following clues before bringing you back (hopefully) to a host of different prizes when you complete the quiz. Who knows? You may see the headless ghost of **Anne Boleyn** or even the Little Princes, murdered (probably) in 1483. Gawp at the Crown Jewels (but expect long lines), and do not forget to check out the famous ravens – legend says if they ever escape the monarchy will collapse – that's why their wings are clipped! *A special family ticket for up to three adults and two children costs £31. Nearest Tube: Tower Hill.*

For a fascinating insight into life in wartime Britain, visit the **Cabinet War Rooms** in Whitehall. These dingy basement rooms, just behind Admiralty Arch, were Britain's wartime nerve center. During the worst air raids of the Second World War, Winston Churchill, his Cabinet and his most senior staff lived and worked here, planning the war effort. A new exhibition, "Churchill: The War Years" is currently showing. Touring the site is made easy with new interactive audio guides with separate versions for primary age children and adults. *Admission charges are £1.60 for students up to and including 18 years and £3.30 for adults. Tel. 020 7930 6961.*

One of London's newest attractions is the **London Aquarium**, located in the old County Hall building, on the opposite bank of the Thames from the Houses of Parliament. Visitors are submerged in a stunning display of hundreds of varieties of fish and sea life from around the world, including piranhas and sharks. *Aquarium, Westminster Bridge Road, London SE1. Admission is £7 for adults, £5 for children aged 3-14. Nearest Tube: Waterloo/Westminster.*

Children of all ages love the **London Transport Museum** in Covent Garden. There are fifteen giant hands-on KidZones with things to push and pull, lights to switch on and off, feely boxes, sliders, magnifiers and more. You'll see live actors in period costume, spectacular displays of old trams, trains and buses and even bus and tube train simulators. Special events include the Covent Garden Flower Festival at the end of June, when the Museum, once home of the Covent Garden Flower Market, is decked in flowers and running special family fun workshops. There's a café, and a shop selling a range of classic transport posters, books, models and gifts. *The Museum is open daily 10am-6pm (Friday 11am-6pm). Under 5s are admitted free and there are concessions for children aged 5-15. Nearest Tube: Covent Garden or Leicester Square. Tel. 020 7379 6344.*

Another favorite for kids is the **London Dungeon**, a macabre medieval horror museum with bloodcurdling exhibits like martyrs at the stake, Great Plague displays and the Jack the Ripper Experience. *Open Monday to Wednesday 10:30am to 9pm, Thursday to Sunday 10.30am to 5:30pm. Admission adults £8.95, children £6.50. Tel. 020 7403 7221. The Museum is located in Tooley Street. Nearest Tube: London Bridge.*

After all this, you'll definitely need to take it easy for a few days. One of the great things about British cities, including London, is that the lush British countryside is only minutes away.

For more information about *What's On for Children* in London, and for general information about Britain, write the **British Tourist Authority**, *2580 Cumberland Parkway, Suite 450, 350 S. Figueroa Street, Los Angeles CA 90071*, or call them toll-free, *Tel. 800/GO BRITAIN*. In London, call *09068 505 456* for "What's On for Children" or *09068 505 460* for "Places to Visit for Children."

SUGGESTIONS FOR KIDS OUTSIDE LONDON

- *A visit to **Alton Towers** in Staffordshire – Britain's largest theme park*
- ***Blackpool Pleasure Beach**, with dozens of exciting rides*
- *A day at the **beach** in **Bournemouth** or **Brighton***
- *A **boat ride** on the **River Dart** in Devon*
- *A visit to the amazing ruins of **Corfe Castle**, Dorset*
- *A day of hiking in the **New Forest***
- *A visit to **Hadrian's Wall***

11. FOOD & DRINK

A BIG IMPROVEMENT

Foreigners tend to be very rude about British food, like Calvin Trillin, who said "Even today, well brought-up English girls are taught by their mothers to boil all veggies for at least a month and a half, just in case one of the dinner guests comes without his teeth." But there has been a massive sea change in the British attitude to food over the past 20 years. While Britain may still not be most people's automatic choice for a gourmet vacation, it can no longer be said that the fog in Britain is due to overboiling the potatoes.

Britain's reputation for dull, unadventurous cooking is becoming increasingly irrelevant. Culinary standards throughout Britain have risen dramatically over the past twenty years, partly due to her membership in the European Community and to the growing number of immigrant groups importing their own indigenous dishes, to the point where today, curry, not roast beef and Yorkshire pudding, is Britain's favorite dish. Another reason for the change has been a shift in shopping patterns. For many years, Britons relied on small, local food stores and markets for just about everything. Today, huge supermarket chains like Tesco, Sainsbury's, Safeway and Asda (recently purchased by Walmart) with their fast transportation links mean that fresh produce is available from virtually anywhere in the world.

And finally, television has played a major role in the transformation. Fanny and Johnny, the original TV chefs of the '60s, have been replaced by a plethora of gourmets, ranging from *The Naked Chef* to *Two Fat Ladies*.

VARIETY

Today's Britain offers as wide a **variety of culinary choices** as anywhere in the world, particularly in the larger cities where Indian, Chinese, Malaysian and Japanese restaurants rub shoulders with French, Italian, Spanish and even American establishments. Meanwhile a new generation of British chefs vie for creative flair with the French as the number of gastronomic restaurants increases daily. And even in the home, the simplest cook today dabbles with herbs and spices, garlic and olive oil – unthinkable in the past. Even motorway restaurants, long the target of stand-up comedians' jokes for the blandness of their food, have improved beyond recognition.

THE ENGLISH DIET

A **traditional English breakfast** is a special treat that all visitors should try. In most hotels and restaurants, breakfast will start with a glass of fruit juice and a bowl of cereal. This is followed by a main course of bacon (considerably leaner than the American variety), sausages, eggs (usually fried, scrambled or poached), often accompanied by mushrooms, grilled tomatoes and fried bread (terribly fattening but a real treat). Slices of **blood pudding** (known in Britain as **black pudding**) may also be available. As an alternative to bacon and eggs, some hotels and restaurants offer kippers (smoked herring), lamb chops or even kidneys as the main course. Look out for delicious **Arbroath Smokies** – small haddock smoked over oak, served with a dab of butter. The breakfast main course is usually followed by toast, transported to your table in a "toast rack" (it's meant to be eaten cold), marmalade and jelly, known as jam. Tea and coffee will be provided, but, unlike America, don't expect a refill unless you ask for one (and then you may have to pay extra). The alternative to all this gorgeous stuff is a **continental breakfast** – usually a roll or croissant, preserves and a beverage of your choice.

Much of Britain stops for a mid-morning coffee or tea break known as "**elevenses**," which may include biscuits (cookies), a doughnut (though don't expect much variety here – you'll be lucky if you get one filled with jam) or other confection such as a **Chelsea bun** (a raisin-infested bun topped with icing sugar) or a slice of **lardey cake** – greasy (but very tasty) layers of cake embedded with raisins.

In the old days, when people worked near to their home and would come home for a midday break, **lunch**, often known as dinner, was the main meal of the day. This is rarely the case nowadays, and most Brits are content to get by with a sandwich or filled roll. The exception is on Sunday, traditionally the time when families and friends get together to eat – though this tradition is also dying fast. Then, main course is likely to be either lamb with mint sauce, pork with apple sauce, beef (sliced thinly) with Yorkshire pudding, or poultry with stuffing – usually accompanied by crispy roast potatoes, and another vegetable or two, with lashings of gravy drowning the meat. Many pubs and hotels serve very inexpensive Sunday lunches, or you may want to try a **carvery** – a self-service restaurant where the roast dinner is arranged buffet-style, with a main course sandwiched in between starters (first course) and a choice of traditional, often stodgy puddings such as **spotted dick** (a traditional dessert, consisting of a steamed suet pudding "spotted" with sultanas, a kind of raisin), jam roly poly or bread and butter pudding. Carveries rarely require reservations.

Perhaps England's most famous dish is **fish and chips**, traditionally heavily battered cod, haddock or plaice (a kind of flatfish) accompanied by soggy French fries, barely recognizable from the crispy American variety you're accustomed to. If purchased at a **take-away** (take-out) the meal is usually liberally doused with malt vinegar and showered with salt. Wrapping fish and chips in newspaper is a thing of the past.

England's **roast beef and Yorkshire pudding** is about as close as you get to a national dish, though steak and kidney pie, **bangers** (sausage) and **mash** (mashed potatoes) come a close equal second. **Bubble and squeak** (leftover cabbage and potatoes fried together in a pan) and **toad-in-the hole** (sausages buried in soft batter) are other dishes to consider. Or if you're really adventurous you may wish to try every East Enders' favorite: **jellied eel and mash**.

EATING OUT

Generally speaking, the British eat out less frequently than their North American counterparts, for one important reason: eating out in Britain is considerably **more expensive** than it is in North America: in even moderately priced restaurants you're talking around about £20 per head without wine for a three course meal, while in London you can add another 50%. And if you're in the enviable position of being able to afford a meal at one of the top-notch establishments, here we're talking upwards of £100 per head. Having said that, it can often be very difficult to find an empty table in central London, even on a weekday, so to be safe make a **reservation** – for some of the more pretentious London restaurants there may even be a waiting list several weeks long.

Of course, it is possible to eat more cheaply; many **pubs** offer pretty good "bar food" at around £8 for two courses, while those who take their food really seriously often have separate dining areas where the food can compete with at least the better of the middle-range restaurants. Then there are, of course, if you're really desperate, the **greasy spoons**, where you can usually get an all-day breakfast or a meat-and-two-veg type meal for under a fiver.

Recent developments have included a growing number of **vegetarian** restaurants, especially in the larger towns and cities, while non-vegetarian restaurants will usually provide at least two or three veggie options – and French style **bistro-brasseries**, like the Cafe Rouge or Cafe Flo chains, where you can get reasonably good food in an informal setting, for around £15 per head.

Eating out in England differs from eating out in the States in a variety of other ways. Brits, almost universally, will use **knife and fork** (except with the soup). While no one will object to your fork-only tradition, it will firmly identify you as a North American, which may be a very good thing. Strangely, Brits have not yet been entirely persuaded of the benefits of consuming a **salad** with their meal, so if you want one, you'll have to order it separately – and unless you specify otherwise, it will likely come with or after your main course, not before it. When you order it, don't expect a list of salad dressings as long as the President's Valentine's list. Most likely, it will come with a simple vinaigrette dressing.

Service in English restaurants is by comparison to the US, quite simply, terrible. I've been in a restaurant where I've ordered champagne and discovered there's no one on the staff who knows how to open the bottle! But it's not really their fault. Waiting in England has never been seen as a career; and there is little prospect of promotion and no proper training given. Combine this with the fact that waiting staff are among the poorest paid workers in the nation, and you have a good reason for the glum faces, if not the sloppy service. The waiting staff may look terribly offended if you complain about the burnt fries or the raw chicken breast. This is partly due to the English reluctance to complain – they're as shy in restaurants as they are in shops. I've even heard Brits apologizing to the waiter when they can't eat everything on the plate.

After the main course an appealing (or appalling) array of **desserts** (puddings) will be wheeled to your table on a trolley. Or you may prefer to indulge in the venerable and totally wonderful British habit of concluding your meal with a slab of **Stilton** cheese and a glass of **port wine**.

Tipping has long been a source of controversy in England. Many **bills** (checks) include a **service charge**, but many more do not – make sure you read the bill carefully. Any tip over and above the service charge is entirely discretionary, and payable only if the waiting staff have been particularly courteous, efficient and attentive – which is highly unlikely. Otherwise 10% is expected – make it 15% if the service is *really* good.

ETHNIC CUISINE

The waves of immigration from the Caribbean and New Commonwealth (India and Pakistan) in the 1950s and '60s, combined with Britain's membership in the **European Community** meant that the quantity and quality of Britain's ethnic food scene has expanded rapidly. For a long time, **Chinese** and **Indian** restaurants were just about the only non-

English restaurants on the High Street, but now dozens of exotic and not-so-exotic ethnic cuisine are available, reflecting the multi-ethnic culture that now exists in Britain.

More than 2.5 million Indian meals are consumed in over 8,000 Indian and Asian restaurants every week in what has been described as a "tidal wave of curry." Heat-and-serve Indian meals are also big business, generating over £100 million in profits annually, and takeaway Indian meals are even bigger business. However, with the spicier dishes there is a definite tendency to anglicize many dishes to suit the more temperate British taste buds.

French and Italian restaurants are popular, with Italian restaurants lending themselves to the take-away market. Additional popular ethnic foods include Greek, Afro-Caribbean, Thai, Malaysian, Japanese and Lebanese.

FAST FOODS

The growth in fast food restaurants in Britain has been phenomenal. Burger joints such as McDonald's, Burger King and Britain's own Wimpy vie with Pizza Hut, Taco Bell and many other American franchises for the ever-expanding market.

TEA

The famous playwright Noel Coward wrote that "everything stops for tea," and his words still ring true.

Tea drinking in England became popular in the early 1700s, when tea houses, mainly for ladies, sprouted up in London to rival the male-dominated coffee houses. Tea drinking grew enormously in popularity as Empire expanded.

Today, the average English person consumes **eleven cups of tea** a day, often accompanied by biscuits, crumpets or buttered toast and jam. On several occasions recently, there has been a problem with the national electricity supply, when, during halftime in an important England foot-ball game, millions of homes switched on their electric kettles at the same time to make a cup of tea. Though tea is drunk at any time of the day, generally around **4pm** is the time. Some old-fashioned establishments still serve **high tea**, which includes a light snack, often something like scrambled egg on toast.

But despite having stomachs permanently coated with tannin, British people are not the great experts on tea you might expect them to be. Ask Brits if they like Lapsang Soochong or Oolong and most of them will say, "I've never met them." People tend to rely on mass-produced "safe" blends than bother with all that foreign stuff, with popular brands like

Typhoo, Brooke Bond PG Tips and other supermarket brands cornering the massive market. But although they may not be tea experts, tea is something of an obsession in Britain. A "nice cuppa tea" – at any time, and usually doused with milk – is sure to make any Brit feel better .

But why tea? What's in the stuff that makes it have such a hold over the nation? Is it the long association with the "tea break" – an opportunity for British workers to down their tools for a few minutes each day? Is it the association with Britain's glory days of Empire, when she ruled the waves and most of the world's tea plantations? I offer no answers. For whatever reason, tea is a panacea for all ills, bringing a smile to the face of the burliest bricklayer or a frail nonagenarian. Whether served in an elegant antique cup or a cracked World Cup souvenir mug, tea is as British as steak and kidney pie.

For a special treat, take **afternoon tea** at one of the top London hotels, such as **The Ritz** or **Brown's**. You'll have an enormous variety of blends to choose from, and you'll be able to choose from many finger sandwiches with dozens of fillings. It may be expensive, and you may need to book in advance, but it's an experience you'll never forget. See the chapter on London for more information.

Similarly, if you're visiting the West Country, try a **clotted cream tea**. The pot of tea comes with scones, jam, and thick, locally made clotted cream. It may not do your cholesterol or calorie count much good, but it's so yummy!

HOW TO MAKE A "NICE" CUP OF TEA

The key to making a "nice" cup of tea is to make sure the inside of the tea pot is tannin-stain-free. Warm the pot with some hot water. When the water is boiling (nearly all English use electric kettles these days) empty the water from the tea pot. Add fresh tea leaves (one spoonful for each person and one "for the pot" is the general rule) or tea bags, and then pour in the boiling water. Allow the tea to steep for about five minutes, covering the pot with a tea cosy to keep it hot. Your tea is then ready to pour. You can add the milk after pouring the tea or before – there are endless debates on which is best – but what is certain is that milk is nearly always added to tea in Britain.

Should you visit an English home, expect to be offered a cup of tea even before you've crossed the threshold. Chances are, once you've finished, you'll be offered another – then another, until your host says, "I think I can squeeze a little more out of the pot? Would you like some more?"

Coffee is growing in popularity in Britain, especially since the influx of a wider variety of blends, and the machinery to make better-tasting brews. However, nothing, it seems, can break the stranglehold of tea.

PUBS & BARS

The best known British institution – after the Royal Family – is surely the pub. Short for "**public house**," they have been imitated all over the world, but none quite seem to catch the unique atmosphere of their British forebears. Even Britain's two most popular TV soaps – *Coronation Street* and *Eastenders* – focus on local pubs – the Rover's Return and the Queen Vic.

Pubs can be found everywhere in Britain – from remote villages to inner cities and everything in between. Pubs cover every mood, occasion, and personality. There are pre-theater pubs, gay pubs, old people's pubs, gay old people's pubs, pubs for shoppers, pubs for journalists, pubs for car workers – but nothing as yet for travel writers, as far as I know. They vary from being places so quiet you can hear a mouse shriek to noisy, rowdy places where the juke box or worse still – live music – reigns supreme. And pubs are a great place to meet the often-reserved Brits over a warm pint of beer.

Pubs have their roots in the **ancient hosteries** and **taverns** used by pilgrims and merchants during the Middle Ages, when, both en route to their destination and at the end of their journey, they would need somewhere to stay. Market towns attracted many people from outlying districts for their regular market days, and thus pubs became a focus for city life, too. When the population rose dramatically during the Industrial Revolution, pubs began to appear in the suburbs and the "**local**" was born. Pubs had become such an essential part of the British social fabric that during World War I when road signs were removed, people would give directions to (non-German) strangers in terms of the local pubs.

During the 1960s and '70s, brewery conglomerates took over more and more of the smaller, independent breweries, and a good deal of streamlining took place. Long oak-mirrored bars and original brass fittings were replaced by wood veneer, formica and other cheap materials, provoking a movement to preserve the more historic establishments. At the same time, more and more people grew upset by the large breweries' aptitude to mass-produce beers and lagers; consequently **CAMRA** (the **Campaign for Real Ale**) was inaugurated to try and reverse the trend and encourage the production of beer by traditional methods. Check out both the CAMRA *Good Beer Guide* and Vermilion's *Good Pub Guide* – both essential reading if you want to know what's what.

Whatever the furnishings may be like, the most important feature of any pub – except for the beer – is the **people**. In Britain, the pub is a center of community social life unlike any other – an extension of your own living room. Neighborhood locals usually mirror the people who live in the vicinity, downtown pubs at lunchtimes attracting people who work or shop in the vicinity, while at night a completely different set of customers may drink there. Americans accustomed to the bar scene will be amazed at the variety of customers. Singles, couples, whole soccer teams and elderly women gossiping over a gin & tonic can all be found. And most pubs possess their very own special "characters."

Pubs are usually divided into two or three bars. Generally speaking, the **public bar** is the place to enjoy a sport of snooker or darts in a smoky, noisy environment with basic furnishings. The **lounge bar** will be a bit more luxurious and a little quieter, though you may still be able to cut the smoke in the air with a pair of scissors. Many country and some city pubs have **beer gardens** equipped with children's rides and even live animals to pet – great on a summer's day.

Opening Hours

This is one of the most confusing aspects of the British pub/bar scene for American visitors. Pub opening times were curtailed enormously during WWI because of concerns over night light during the blackout, as well as the risk of military personnel getting "sloshed." Pubs were closed afternoons, then reopened in the evening and closed at about 11pm. Sunday opening hours were even more restrictive, largely due to the powerful influence of the established Church. It was only in 1988 that anything was done to change the law. For the first time since 1918, pubs were given permission to stay open during the afternoon. However, nothing was done at that time to extend the 11pm closing time. Things look set to change with government proposals to allow pubs to stay open much later a night, in line with European opening hours.

At present, closing time is indicated with the traditional cry of "Time, gentlemen, please," followed by the loud clanging of a bell, and ten minutes "drinking up" time. There are certainly plenty of ways of continuing drinking after 11pm, including joining a club (where you will likely be asked for a temporary membership fee with some ID), a wine bar – or, of course, your hotel.

PUB ETIQUETTE

• *Find a place to sit or stand. Standing for several hours is considered quite normal.*

• *Pubs virtually never have waiter/waitress service. Don't fall into the trap of sitting at the table waiting for the bartender to come over and serve you. Go to the bar. Although it may appear a bit of a frenzy, the bartenders usually know which pecking order to follow. If you're being ignored, wave a £10 note or call out.*

• *If you're in a group (unless it's the whole cast of Les Miserables) it's considered polite to buy a round of drinks for everyone in that group – on the understanding that the future rounds will be bought by somebody else!*

• *Never ask for a beer – it's a bit like asking for a drink. Beer is a very broad term. (See below)*

• *Don't tip the bar staff.*

• *You must be 18 to drink alcohol.*

• *Under-14s must not enter a pub unless accompanied by an adult*

• *Don't drink and drive.*

DRINKS

The yellow potion that most Americans and Canadians call **beer** is known as **lager** in Britain. As in the US, it's served cooled, and available on draft, bottled or canned. Among the most popular brands are Heineken and Foster's. Budweiser, Coors and Labatt's are also widely available if you're feeling homesick.

Darker beers are generally known as **ales**. **Bitter**, served on draft, refers to a darkish, froth-crowned liquid with a strong sharp taste. When applied to bitter, the terms **special** and **best** refer to strength, not quality. **Pale** and **light** brews are the bottled versions of bitter. A refreshing drink that many American friends of mind go crazy about is the concoction of half-bitter, half lemonade, known as **shandy**.

Mild, another brew, contains more sugar and is sweeter than pale or light. **Stouts** are made from well-roasted, unmalted barley. Guinness, Ireland's most famous concoction, popular in Britain too, is thick and rich like stout, but not sweet.

Many Americans are horrified to discover that most of the darker brews are consumed **warm**. Actually, not "warm" but room temperature, which, like a good red wine, means that you get the best taste.

All beers and lagers, when on draft, are available as half pints or pints. Just ask for "Half o' bitter" or "A pint of lager". You may also be puzzled to be asked what kind of glass you require – with or without a handle. It's simply a matter of personal preference, and bears no relation to the taste of the beer.

Another popular drink, served on draft, or bottled or canned, is **cider**. Beware – unlike its harmless American counterpart, British cider is alcoholic, and often potently so. As a general rule, the murkier it is, the stronger it is. If you happen to visit the West Country – Gloucestershire or Herefordshire in particular – the local cider, or "**scrumpy**" is very powerful.

Cocktails are not the big deal in Britain that they are in America, referring usually to a pre-dinner drinks party. Even then, it's almost always a glass or two of wine or gin and tonic, scotch and dry or a remarkably crude Bloody Mary. The best place to get the unpronounceable potions Americans adore is at the hotel bar – but don't be surprised if it tastes nothing like what you're accustomed to back home.

Popular pub **shorts** include gin, usually served with tonic – and whisky, one of Scotland's top exports, whose standard measure in Britain is a measly one sixth of a **gill** – so you may want to order a double. Note: A 'short' refers to certain basic alcoholic drinks, usually measured as one-sixth of a gill; for example, whisky, gin, rum are shorts. Beer and lager are not. A gill is an old-fashioned measurement, equal to a quarter of a pint.

Outside of pubs and bars, alcohol is available at most **supermarkets** and at **off-licences** (liquor stores).

When a Brit lives in America, the aspect of life missed the most – I know – (apart from the BBC) is the pub. Pubs are wonderful places for meeting or making friends and no other place gives you a better glimpse into the everyday lives of the locals.

12. CULTURE

While London, the focus of much of England's cultural activity, is one of the world's leading centers for music, theater, opera and dance, many other towns and cities are cultural centers of considerable achievement and diversity.

THEATER

While the English are apt to take the brilliance of their **theater** (spelled theatre over here) for granted – all part of the very English tendency to undervalue anything they do well – for most foreigners, a visit to England is incomplete without a visit to a stage play or musical.

There are about three hundred theaters in England, about one hundred of which are in London. Here, theater life is focused – but by no means confined – to the famous **West End**, where top-notch productions feature well-known national and international names: **plays** by British playwrights like John Mortimer, Alan Ayckborn and Tom Stoppard, **bawdy romps** inspired by popular TV sitcoms, and **variety shows** featuring international celebrities – the most famous variety theater being the legendary **London Palladium**. Or maybe you'd like to see the world's longest-running play, Agatha Christie's *The Mousetrap*, now in its 39th year as of press time.

Away from the main theater district, just across the Thames from the Houses of Parliament, the **National Theatre** is located in the **South Bank** complex (I'd thoroughly recommend one of their backstage tours – a terrific insight into what makes a great theater work), while a mile to the east, the reconstructed Shakespeare **Globe Theatre** offers a full summer season of productions. In the city of London, not far from St. Paul's Cathedral, the relatively new **Barbican Centre** is, along with the **Theatre Royal** in Stratford-upon-Avon, home to the prestigious **Royal Shakespeare Company**. London is arguably today the world capital for musicals, with shows like *Cats, Les Miserables* and *Phantom of the Opera* still packing 'em in.

But that's not all. And if the West End is London's equivalent of Broadway, then the London **fringe** theaters correspond to Off-Broadway. Here, budding new bards get a chance to strut their stuff in a host of theaters, large and small, dotted around the capital.

So extensive is the selection, it's important to choose carefully. I've known groups of foreign tourists come away from a production disappointed, baffled and bored, because they've had problems with the accents, terminology and cultural references so integral to understanding the plot that the whole point of the play is lost to anyone but the English in the audience.

Most of London's theaters are relatively small – around 500 seats – often laid out in tiers with the **stalls** occupying the main floor and various **circles** above. Playbills are known as **programs**, and are available before performances and during the **interval** (intermission), when it's also possible to purchase drinks at the bar. You can even order your drinks in advance before the performance begins, thus avoiding queues later on. The quaint British habit of selling ices during the interval continues.

The **Pantomime** is a uniquely British theater phenomenon, ideal for families. Pantomimes are costumed musical comedies with a good deal of slapstick, audience participation and corny jokes. They usually star well-known domestic TV personalities and are built around the theme of children's stories like Jack in the Beanstalk or Cinderella. Pantomimes are primarily intended for children but seem just as popular with adults. The pantomime season starts just before Christmas and extends into the New Year – in much the same way as performances of the Nutcracker do in North America.

Check the weekly magazine *Time Out*, or the Thursday edition of the London *Evening Standard* for current listings. Theater tickets are available at **ticket agencies** all over London, but beware inflated prices. There's also a **ticket booth** in **Leicester Square** where it's possible to pick up tickets for same-day performances, often at reduced rates, though you may have to stand in line here for some considerable time, especially in the peak summer months.

DRESS CODE

At one time, going to the theater, opera or ballet in England demanded some degree of formality when it came to dress codes. In ultra-prestigious halls like Covent Garden Opera House, many people still dress fairly formally. However, by and large, the invasion of London, Stratford and other major theater centers by casually-dressed tourists has led to a more informal approach. When you also take into account the fact that many British theaters are not air-conditioned, this is not such a bad thing. On a hot summer's day, a seat "in the gods" can be more like a seat in Hades if you're wearing a jacket and tie.

OPERA

London is home to two major opera houses, The **English National Opera**, situated in St Martin's Lane just off Trafalgar Square, which specializes in new productions in English, and the restored **Covent Garden Opera House**. Various regional operatic companies operate in leading centers as **Birmingham** and **Manchester** and at **Glyndebourne**, in Sussex. The **Welsh National Opera**, based in Cardiff, has an international reputation.

FILM

The English have been in love with films for a long time. At one time going to the **pictures** (movies) was more popular here than anywhere else in the world. Cinema attendance peaked in 1946 with a total attendance of 1,600 million, then plummeted to a little over 50 million visits by 1985. In more recent years, there has been a reversal of this trend. New, multi-screen cinemas have been opening the length and breadth of the nation, including several IMAX complexes. While many movie theaters are found in downtown districts, more and more of the larger complexes are being built in out-of-town shopping centers.

England's hard-up industry has seen better days, yet English films, actors and creative and technical services seem to achieve wide acclaim at international film festivals.

TELEVISION

The **BBC** – the British Broadcasting Corporation – was founded in 1927 and is one of the largest broadcasting companies in the world. Regarded primarily as a **public service** (although this is continually being called into question), the BBC is obliged by its charter to provide **impartial news** and current affairs coverage, as well as sports and drama. For this reason, its coverage of international news is in general considerably more extensive than that of the American TV networks.

The BBC is funded not by commercial advertising, but by a **license fee** – essentially a tax, costing around £110 a year – which every household owning a TV must pay – whether or not they watch the BBC. The government dispatches hundreds of "detector" vans that prowl the streets seeking out homes where people are watching TV to check if their license has been paid. A hefty **fine** is imposed on those who have not paid the fee. The BBC has been known to go to ridiculous lengths to avoid any semblance of commercial bias. In one popular children's show, for example, bandaids were used to cover brand names on items being used for handicrafts.

The question facing the BBC now is whether its policy of producing quality programming can survive in an era when huge global players like Time/Warner or ABC/Disney increasingly call the tune. Can the BBC survive as a public sector organization barred by regulation and its own culture from acting independently?

Although the BBC (known affectionately as **"Auntie"**) exerts tremendous influence, long gone are the days when she dominated the airwaves. Since 1950 she has had to contend with a major rival, **ITV** (Independent Television), which exposed the public to **commercials** for the first time. Despite being regarded as down-market from the BBC, ITV has managed, in addition to a staple diet of soaps, sitcoms, quiz shows, children's programs, current affairs and variety, to produce some excellent television in its own right, particularly fine costume drama and crime series. American imports also make up a hefty slice of ITV's programming. Both BBC1 and ITV show regional programs.

These two national channels were joined by a second BBC channel, **BBC2**, in 1967; by **Channel 4,** noted for its generally radical programming in the 1980s; and, most recently, **Channel 5** in 1997.

The main channels are also available, along with a host of new channels, including the **Sky** network, on Britain's burgeoning cable network and digital terrestrial services as well as via satellite dishes. **Digital TV** came to England in 1999, introducing still more channels and online services.

Among the most popular TV programs in England are two soaps: the BBC's *EastEnders*, based on life in a suburb of east London, and rival ITV's *Coronation Street*, set in the northern city of Manchester.

RADIO

The BBC enjoyed a virtual monopoly of Britain's radio waves until the 1970s, when broadcasting laws were liberalized, resulting in the establishment of hundreds of new national, local and specialist commercial stations, catering to many of the nation's ethnic and religious tastes.

The main national BBC stations are **Radio 1**, specializing in pop and rock; **Radio 2**, for light music; **Radio 3**, classical; **Radio 4** for news and current affairs (as well as some excellent radio drama) and **Radio 5**, much of whose programming comes directly from the famous **BBC World Service**, which broadcasts in about 40 languages all over the world from studios in Bush House, the Strand. Among the better-known commercial stations are Virgin Radio, Classic FM and Jazz FM.

MUSIC

Classical

Among the leading centers for classical music in London is the **South Bank** complex, which contains three concert halls: the Royal Festival Hall, Queen Elizabeth Hall and the Purcell Room. The London Symphony Orchestra is based at the **Barbican Centre**, near St Paul's, north of the Thames, while other important venues are **St. John's Smith Square**, Westminster, a former church with superb acoustics; and **St. Martin-in-the-Fields**, where the famous Academy of St. Martin-in-the-Fields is based. There are a host of other halls and churches throughout the capital where concerts of all kinds are held regularly.

For a special free treat, attend a service of Evensong at **Westminster Abbey**, **St. Paul's Cathedral**, or one of England's other great cathedrals. These late afternoon services are normally sung by the resident choirs, which happen to be some of the best in the world. You'll be transported to another world by the celestial quality of the singing, in glorious surroundings. Check with the individual church for service times – and note that you don't have to be a Christian to attend. If choral music appeals to you, in July you should head for the **Three Choirs Festival**, sung by the combined choirs of Worcester, Gloucester and Hereford Cathedrals at a different venue each year; or the **Southern Cathedrals Festival**, where the choirs of Winchester, Salisbury and Chichester do more or less the same thing.

A series of **Promenade Concerts** held throughout the summer at the **Royal Albert Hall**, organized by the BBC and featuring famous orchestras and artists from the world over, culminates in November with **The Last Night of the Proms**, one of the leading musical events in the British calendar.

In the provinces, some of the leading orchestras are: the **City of Birmingham Symphony**, with its new Symphony Hall; the **Halle** (Manchester) which plays at the brand-new Bridgewater Hall in the city; the **Bournemouth Symphony** and the **Royal Liverpool Philharmonic**.

Jazz & Pop

Don't forget Britain's massive contribution to contemporary music and jazz. The **British Invasion** was led by the Beatles in the 1960s and continued with such bands as the Rolling Stones, The Who, Pink Floyd and individuals like Elton John, Rod Stewart, David Bowie and George Michael. The survivors from this list and American performers are frequently on stage at venues throughout the nation; the real mega-stars appearing at **Wembley Stadium** and other major facilities throughout the country, and sometimes at the annual festivals, like the **Glastonbury**

Festival held at the end of June. There are a number of jazz venues throughout the country, the best known being **Ronnie Scott's** in London's Soho.

LITERATURE

The most dominant figure in British literature is of course the Bard, **William Shakespeare**, who was born in Stratford-upon-Avon in the midlands and whose plays were watched by thousands at his Globe Theatre on the South Bank. The theater has been reconstructed using original methods and, along with the Royal Shakespeare Theatre in Stratford, is a must for all Shakespeare fans.

Take away Shakespeare, and English literature would still be the richest in the world. The English language, with the largest vocabulary of any world tongue, can produce more nuances of meaning and mood than any other.

The *Anglo-Saxon Chronicles* were written in Old English during the time of King Alfred the Great, while **Geoffrey Chaucer's** masterpiece, *The Canterbury Tales*, was written in Middle English two centuries later. The development of **William Caxton's** printing press and the growth of universities like Oxford and Cambridge led to a burgeoning of English literature, epitomized in the work of **Christopher Marlowe** and **Sir Thomas More** during the Tudor period; **Ben Jonson** with his satirical comedies during the Jacobean period; the metaphysical poets, like **George Herbert** and **John Donne**, Dean of St. Paul's Cathedral, whose work appeared in the seventeenth century, along with the **King James** (the 'authorized') version of the Bible. Even during the somber Commonwealth period, serious literature did not dry up. How could it, with the likes of **John Bunyan's** *Pilgrim's Progress* **and John Milton's** *Paradise Lost*? After the Restoration of the Monarchy in 1660, the glum mood gave way to the exuberance of writers like **Sheridan,** and Great Fire of London diarist **Samuel Pepys**, while in the eighteenth century, diarist and wit **Dr. Samuel Johnson** also produced his *Dictionary of the English Language*. Other great writers of the period were **Daniel Defoe**, **Henry Fielding** and **Oliver Goldsmith**.

Some of the nation's greatest poets were to emerge in the nineteenth century – the likes of **Blake**, **Shelley**, **Wordsworth**, **Coleridge**, **Byron** and **Keats**, while the early to mid-1800s saw even more great names in English literature – **Charles Dickens**, **The Brontes**, **Jane Austen**, **Lewis Carroll**,and **Matthew Arnold**, while in the late 19th and early 20th centuries writers like **Rudyard Kipling**, **Thomas Hardy**, **Somerset Maugham** and **Dylan Thomas** led the way.

TAKE A LITERARY TOUR

A number of tour operators feature special tours covering the life and times of some of England and Wales' best-known literary figures, many of whom are associated with a particular region of the country: Thomas Hardy and his beloved Wessex, The Bronte's Yorkshire, Jane Austen's Hampshire and Dylan Thomas' Wales. One such US operator is **Lord Addison Travel**, *PO Box 3307, Peterborough, NH 03458, Tel. 800/326-0170; www.lordaddison.com.*

MUSEUMS

England and Wales have more than 2,000 museums and art galleries, some of which are among the finest in the world.

In London, world-class institutions such as the **British Museum**, the **National Gallery, Victoria and Albert Museum, Natural History Museum** and **Tate Galleries** are legendary for the quality and quantity of the work they possess – what you see on display is frequently a mere portion of what the museum or gallery owns, the majority of items being hidden from public view. All the time, new museums and galleries are opening – like the fantastic new **Tate Modern**, which opened in 2000 at Bankside in London, where an old electricity generating station has been converted into one of the world's finest galleries of modern art.

Many large and not-so-large cities have important museums and art collections, such as Birmingham's **City Art Gallery**, with its extensive collection of pre-Raphaelites, Oxford's **Ashmolean**, the **Fitzwilliam** in Cambridge, and the **Tates** in Liverpool and St. Ives, Cornwall. Vast new galleries have just opened in **Walsall**, in the West Midlands, **Salford**, near Manchester – with a huge collection of Lowries – and in a vast restored warehouse at **Gateshead**, on the River Tyne near Newcastle.

Many of England and Wales' **stately homes** are treasure troves of art, displayed in opulent surroundings. You can even see some of the Queen's art collection in the **Queen's Gallery** adjacent to Buckingham Palace.

Admission charges can vary, but more often than not entry is free of charge – Britain's museums and art galleries are seen as part of the overall educative process.

Finally, another place to check out if you're in London is the new **British Library**, near King's Cross Station. This new state-of-the-art building was completed recently and, as well as being one of the three largest libraries in the world, also contains important historical documents, such as a copy of the *Magna Carta*, ancient manuscripts, and even musical scores.

13. ENGLAND'S & WALES' BEST PLACES TO STAY

All kinds of ingredients make a hotel special – the location, the decor, the food, the history, the service. What makes a hotel extra special is hard to define, and of course varies from person to person. The following are some of the places I've stayed in over the years that have lingered in my memory, and that, for me at least, have that special something. I hope you enjoy them too.

LONDON - CHAPTER 14

THE CADOGAN, *75 Sloane Street, London SW1X 9SG. Tel. 020 7235 7141, Fax 020 7245 0994. Rooms: 52, plus 13 suites. Rates: singles from £194, doubles from £217, suites from £364. Restaurant, drawing room, bar, leisure facilities nearby with reduced rates for guests. All major credit cards accepted. Nearest Tube: Knightsbridge or Sloane Square.*

This, for me, is one of London's great hotels, a place that seems in some ways to be in a time warp, yet has all the possible conveniences that you could imagine. The Cadogan is a quiet, traditional hotel that holds on to the old values many similar grand hotels seem to have relinquished. For one thing, the service is first-class; staff will go out of their way to help you and make your stay more pleasant. The hotel's ambience is relaxed, unhurried and friendly, so you never feel rushed.

The location is good, too: half-way between Knightsbridge and Chelsea, within easy reach of Harrods store and the museums of South Kensington. Staying here is, in some ways a bit like stepping back fifty years; the wonderful drawing room is the perfect place to read your newspaper in peace – a sign on the door expressly forbids the use of mobile phones and laptops here and the only noise you'll hear is the clock ticking on the mantelpiece. The rooms are simply but pleasantly and individually furnished, and show that the hotel is not totally averse to modernity, as the modem points and bathroom telephones indicate.

The hotel has quite a history, too. Oscar Wilde was a frequent guest here (the turret room where he used to stay still bears his name and is decked out with period William Morris wallpaper and fabrics), and Edward VIII's mistress, Lily Langtry, occupied part of the building for a period. You can even rent her drawing room and dining room for business meetings! The restaurant, all in pink, offers excellent traditional English fare cooked imaginatively and with flair.

THE PEMBRIDGE COURT, *34 Pembridge Gardens, London W2 4DX. Tel. 020 7229 9977, from US 800/709-9882. Fax 020 7287 4982. Rooms: 20. Rates: singles from £110, doubles from £150. Restaurant. All major credit cards accepted. Nearest Tube: Notting Hill Gate.*

From being one of London's least salubrious suburbs, Notting Hill has become one of its most fashionable, thanks in part to the movie *Notting Hill* – though the gentrification process was already well under way when the film came out. The Pembridge Court owned by entrepreneur Derek Mapp who stayed here 12 years on the trot and liked it so much that he bought it – is located on a quiet – yes, quiet – tree-lined street.

Major pluses include stylishly decorated rooms equipped with all the usual modern conveniences, 24-hour room service, and discounted access to an exclusive local health club, with pool, gym and spa. The whole place is brimming with the antiques the owners' wife Merete has assembled over the years; she will happily point you in the right direction if you want to expand your own collection – the hotel is just a short walk from Portobello Road Market.

The public rooms are full of character – like the Darling Bar, where photographs from bygone parties adorn the walls, while the next door Caps Restaurant is decorated with various paraphernalia such as schoolboy's headwear (hence "caps") and oddities like framed corkscrews. Breakfast is served here, along with Asian influenced dinners that can be taken in your room. Step outside the front door and who knows? You might just bump into one of the many celebrities – such as Tina Turner, John Cleese, Madonna and Tom Cruise – who have homes around here.

SOUTHEAST - CHAPTER 15

GRAND HOTEL, *King's Road, Brighton. Tel. 01273 321188, Fax 01273 202694. Rooms: 200. Rates: singles from £155, doubles/twins from £195, suites from £600. Restaurants, bars. 24-hour room service. Health suite, pool. All major credit cards accepted*

Brighton's most famous hotel became even more famous in 1987 when a terrorist bomb caused widespread damage and several deaths.

The target was Prime Minister Margaret Thatcher and her cabinet, staying in the hotel while attending a Conservative Party Conference in the nearby Brighton Conference Centre. Since then, the seafront hotel has been extensively modernized to spectacular effect. The public rooms, with their chandeliers and marble trimmings and intricate moldings, are stunning. The guest rooms, too, many of which have sea views, have been beautifully and skillfully renovated, and include a full range of facilities. There's a full-service restaurant and exercise center, including a heated indoor swimming pool. This is a truly exceptional place, in a truly exceptional town.

CENTRAL SOUTHERN - CHAPTER 16

CHEWTON GLEN, *Christchurch Road, New Milton, Dorset BH25 6QS. Tel. 01425 275341, Fax 01425 273310; www.chewtonglen.com. 33 rooms, 19 suites. Rates: single occupancy/double/twin £230 to £530, suite £430 to £530. Restaurant (see below), outdoor and indoor pools, health club, golf course.*

One of the most remarkable hotels in England, the Chewton Glen has received numerous accolades, and has been consistently voted one of the top twenty hotels in the world by travel publications.

Located on the edge of the New Forest, all the rooms in this old country house that was owned by the brother of author Captain Marryat – remembered for *The Children of the New Forest* - have balconies or terraces overlooking lush parkland. The rooms themselves are elegant and come with a range of trimmings, from bathrobes to sherry and lots of fresh flowers. The hotel's facilities include both outdoor and indoor swimming pools, croquet lawn and health club. Of course it's not cheap, but then, there are few hotels around of this quality and standard.

WEST COUNTRY - CHAPTER 17

THE IMPERIAL, *Park Hill Road, Torquay TQ1 2DG. Tel. 01803 294301, Fax 01803 298293. Rooms: 153. Rates: singles from £95, doubles from £170. Restaurants, bars, Indoor and outdoor pools, tennis courts, squash courts, pool room, leisure suite, beauty salon All major credit cards accepted.*

I've always enjoyed Torquay, the heart of the "English Riviera," but never more so than when I've stayed at the Imperial. This magnificent, luxurious hotel located atop the cliffs comes with wonderful views over the bay and all the facilities you'd expect from a first-class hotel.

Many of the beautifully furnished bedrooms have balconies with sea views, and the public rooms are the height of elegance, with marble floors and chandeliers all over the place. In addition, the extensive grounds are luxuriously planted, with sub-tropical plantings and wide lawns; a wonderful place to relax in the sunshine. There are two excellent places to eat: the

Regatta Restaurant, with, as you'd expect, a wide range of seafood dishes, and the Sundeck Brasserie.

MIDLANDS – CHAPTER 18

LYGON ARMS, *High Street, Broadway WR12 7DU. Tel. 01386 852255, fax 01386 858611. Rooms: 63. Rates: singles from £143, doubles from £175, four-poster from £235. Restaurants, bar, lounges, games room, garden, indoor pool, tennis croquet, gym, sauna. All major credit cards accepted.*

This delightful, 16th century former coaching inn makes a number of plausible historical claims: it's said to have accommodated King Charles I and Oliver Cromwell (but not, one assumes, at the same time). It's no surprise, then, then that one of the rooms is known as the Charles I suite, and comes with four-poster bed and dark wood paneling. If you're a bit spooked by such historic surroundings, like certain members of my family, you can opt instead for the 1970s wings. They're every bit as comfortable but without the creaky floorboards – and the character.

Spooked or not, you'll enjoy a meal in the barrel-vaulted Great Hall, or you can opt (again) for something simpler in the brasserie. The hotel comes with an array of leisure facilities – including a galleried pool and comprehensive fitness center – but then that's probably what you'd expect at these prices.

NORTHWEST – CHAPTER 20

STORRS HALL HOTEL, *Storrs Park, Bowness-on-Windermere LA23 3LG. Tel. 015394 47111, Fax 015394 47555. Rooms: 18. Rates: singles from £125, doubles from £215 (both include full breakfast). Four-poster beds available. Restaurant, bars, private fishing, sailing, water-skiing. All major credit cards accepted.*

This beautifully restored Georgian mansion is located in pleasant grounds on a peninsula of Lake Windermere, with fantastic views to three sides. The revamped bedrooms are stunning, and are lavishly furnished with fine arts and antiques. The public areas are luxurious, too, with wonderful, deep-cushioned sofas that you won't want to get out of. The staff is helpful and friendly and the atmosphere, encouraged by the peaceful surroundings, is very relaxed.

It's not exactly the cheapest place to stay around here, but if you really fancy a splurge there's nowhere better to relax and unwind, read a book, or enjoy a spot of fishing and sailing, especially if you've just spent a few days in the hustle and bustle of London.

YORKSHIRE - CHAPTER 21

MIDDLETHORPE HALL, *Bishopthorpe Road YO23 2GB. Tel. 01904 641241, Fax 01904 620176. Rooms: 31. Rates: singles from £99; double/twin from £145; deluxe double/twin from £160; four-poster from £225; suites from £185. English breakfast: £12.50. Restaurants, health spa, gardens, free parking. Credit cards: MC, Visa.*

Right on the outskirts of York, near the famous racecourse, and set in nearly 30 acres of beautifully maintained grounds is this stately William and Mary house built in 1699. Once the home of diarist Lady Mary Wortley Montagu, it had fallen into a very poor state of repair until it was bought by Historic House Hotels and completely refurbished.

The place definitely has a feel of country manor house (which indeed it was), with lots of antiques, an elegant drawing room and even a library – though it's only minutes from York city center and all its attractions. Some of the rooms are located in a gorgeous courtyard setting. Another very nice touch is the fresh flowers that adorn the rooms and public places. There's also a fine, wood-paneled restaurant which serves classic Anglo-French cuisine, including fresh vegetables grown in the hotel garden and, to cap it all, they've just added a new health and fitness suite with pool and steam room.

NORTHEAST - CHAPTER 22

LANGLEY CASTLE HOTEL, *Langley on Tyne, Hexham NE47 5LU. Tel. 01434 688888. Rooms: 14. Rates: singles from £75, doubles from £105, four-posters from £155. Restaurants, bars, garden. All major credit cards accepted.*

This is a fantastic place to stay! It's actually a Grade-I listed 14th century castle, built by Sir Thomas de Lucy, a veteran of the Battle of Crecy. Later on, after years of neglect, the castle fell into ruin, until Victorian Cadwaller Bates lovingly restored it. There's so much to admire about this place it would be easy to write pages about it, but best of all are the lavishly-decorated bedrooms, replete with original Gothic arches, mullioned windows set in walls seven feet thick, open fireplaces and an amazing range of modern conveniences including, in some cases, four poster beds and personal saunas.

The public rooms, such as the drawing room and the dining room, are the height of elegance, with original features mingling with luxuriant decor to stunning effect. When you take all this into account, it's really not expensive at all! If you do decide to stay here, ask for a room in the main building, rather than the coach house; it's not that the rooms there are perfectly acceptable – but you'll miss out on the real fun – which is staying in such an ancient, historic establishment.

WALES - CHAPTER 23

HOTEL PORTMEIRION, *Portmeirion, Penrhyndeudraeth LL48 6ET. Tel. 01766 770000, Fax 01766 771331. Rooms: 29, suites 11. Rates: singles from £85, doubles from £105, suite from £125. Restaurant, bar, lounges, library, gardens, outdoor pool, tennis. All major credit cards accepted.*

There are many fine hotels in Wales, but for somewhere that's a bit unusual – and uncompromisingly luxurious – you can't beat the Hotel Portmeirion. For one thing, there's the magnificent location: the beautifully appointed accommodations are part of an Italianate village, allegedly modeled on Portofino, with narrow lanes, whitewashed and pastel-shaded cottages, cupolas and bell tower – all overlooking the sandy Traeth Bach estuary, with Snowdonia in the distance. Sound familiar? Well, the village was once used as the location for the cult 1960s TV series *The Prisoner*, with Patrick MacGoohan (remember that giant bubble that used to chase him across the sand?).

The main villa, a Victorian construction converted into a hotel in 1926, contains some lovely public rooms, including an elegant, highly-acclaimed restaurant with marble pillars. Most people choose to stay in the various apartments and cottages scattered throughout the landscaped grounds – all luxuriously furnished, some with private sitting rooms, some with balconies offering magical views – some with both. If you want somewhere different to stay, and don't mind hordes of day-trippers and *Prisoner* fans gaping at you, this is just the place.

14. LONDON

By seeing London, I have seen as much of life as the world can show.
– Dr. Samuel Johnson

London, England's capital, is one of the world's great cities. It just oozes history and culture. With about seven million inhabitants, and covering around 650 square miles, it's the largest city in Europe, full of fascinating places to visit: some of the world's greatest museums and galleries, historical monuments, fantastic shopping, exciting nightlife, literally scores of theaters and concert venues, and gorgeous parks and gardens – it's one of the world's greenest cities. It's rich in wonderful hotels and – according to many – has now surpassed Paris as a culinary center.

High on the list of priorities for many visitors is the **Tower of London**, the ancient fortress built by William the Conqueror, site of many of the most important – and grisliest – events in British history, and home of the Crown Jewels. Then there's **Westminster Abbey**, built by Edward the Confessor in 1065, where British monarchs have been crowned for centuries and, close by, the **Houses of Parliament** and St. Stephen's Tower, more commonly known as **Big Ben**. Listen to the choir of **St. Paul's Cathedral**, scene of the wedding of Prince Charles to the late Princess Diana in 1981, singing evensong.

Don't miss the mind-blowing **British Museum**, with one of the most extensive collections of historical artifacts in the world; the **Victoria and Albert Museum**, the best fine arts museum on the planet, and the **Natural History Museum**, where you'll be greeted by an 80-foot long Diplodocus as you enter. The world-famous **National Gallery**, with some of the world's most famous paintings, the newly opened **Tate Modern Gallery** at Bankside (close to the rebuilt **Shakespeare Globe Theatre**) and the **Museum of London** are all unmissable. If it's blood and gore you want, then the **London Dungeon** is for you, though you'll probably get a kick out of **Madame Tussaud's**, London's most enduring (if not endearing) tourist attraction, with the famous Chamber of Horrors.

Take a stroll in beautiful **Hyde Park** or the adjacent **Kensington Gardens** where you can see the recently restored, stunning memorial to Prince Albert, Queen Victoria's husband, glittering with lashings of gold leaf. Walk past the stately buildings of **Whitehall**, the political heart of the nation, to **Trafalgar Square**, overlooked by the 17-foot statue of Lord Nelson atop a 170-foot plinth. For retail therapy, head to **Oxford Street**, the busiest shopping street in the world; **Knightsbridge**, home of **Harrods** (as well as Harvey Nicholls, well known to viewers of *Absolutely Fabulous*); **Covent Garden**, with its designer boutiques; or, if you really have money to spend, **Bond Street** and the warren of chic shopping streets between Oxford Street and Piccadilly. And finally (or perhaps first of all) take a bird's eye view of the whole lot from the 500-foot high **Millennium Wheel** (London Eye), the world's largest ferris wheel. And I haven't even mentioned the pomp and pageantry on show in this city – from **Buckingham Palace**, just one of the places where you can watch the Changing of the Guard ceremony – to the grand parades and processions of the **City of London**, to the outrageous hats worn by the ladies during Ascot Week.

Outside of the **West End** (the theater district) and **City** (the name given to the main business district), London is made up of countless "villages" each with its own distinctive character and style: places like **Hampstead** and **Highgate** in north London, **Fulham** and **Chelsea** to the southwest, **Stoke Newington** or **Bethnal Green** to the east and **Brixton** and **Clapham** in the south. There's even more to see on the outskirts of the metropolis: **Windsor Castle**, west of London, is the Queen's favorite residence; **Hampton Court Palace**, built by Henry VIII for Cardinal Wolsey and then usurped by him; **St. Alban's**, to the north of London, with its magnificent Norman Abbey.

This is a truly great city; whether you're here for just a few days or a few weeks you won't fail to be captivated by it. You may get tired *by* it, but you'll never be tired *of* it. And maybe, just maybe, you'll end up agreeing with Dr. Johnson.

ARRIVALS & DEPARTURES
By Air
Most transatlantic flights arrive at either **Heathrow** or **Gatwick** airports, about 14 and 25 miles from central London respectively. Once you've cleared customs and immigration (be prepared for your first experience of a British queue coming through immigration) and you've picked up your baggage, there are a number of options for getting into downtown London.

By Taxi

Easily the most expensive way to travel, it's also the most exciting; an encounter with that rare and very special breed, the London taxi driver, or "cabbie." Drivers of the famous black cabs (though some of them are now maroon) have to undergo extensive tests over a period of four years before they qualify and can claim to have "**the Knowledge**" – you just tell them the address you want, and they're supposed to know exactly where it is. It usually works. They're generally a friendly bunch, too, extremely knowledgeable, it seems, about every subject under the sun – especially their beloved London. The ride from Heathrow will cost somewhere in the region of £30; from Gatwick it will be £40 and up.

The black cabs are by no means the only taxis in London, which hosts hundreds of **minicabs**, many of which operate a fixed rate – usually about £20 – for travel into central London. The cabs are usually regular cars, but large and comfortable enough to accommodate two or three passengers and their luggage. A list of these "mini cab" companies is available from Tourism offices, and if you can make arrangements in advance, they will happily arrange to meet your flight. A number of companies offer shuttle bus services from the airports direct to your hotel. Among the best are **Airport Transfers**, *Tel. 020 7403 2228,* and **Hotelink**, *Tel. 01293 532244,* who charge £12 per person to the West End from Heathrow and £18 from Gatwick. Tipping for all taxi drivers is customarily 10%.

By Express Train from the Airports

There's a train station adjacent to the main terminal building at Gatwick, from which **Gatwick Express** trains leave every fifteen minutes for **Victoria Station** in London's West End. As the night progresses, the service becomes less frequent (one an hour after 2am) but it is reliable and takes about half an hour. At Victoria, there are plenty of cabs to take you to your final destination. Train tickets cost around £9. Follow the signs in the terminal building.

A new frequent service train from Heathrow Airport to **Paddington Station** in central London started in 1998, whisking you into town in only fifteen minutes. The cost is £10.

By Buses

Regular bus services operate from both major airports. From Gatwick, **Flightline 777**, *Tel. 0990 747 777,* buses will get you to Victoria, but because of the traffic it's hard to predict how long it will take, though it's inevitably longer than the train. The service is less frequent than the train service, too, and only slightly less expensive

From Heathrow, you can get London Transport **Airbus A1**, which terminates at Victoria, stopping at various strategic points along the way, such as Earl's Court and Knightsbridge, while bus **A2** takes a more northerly route, terminating at Euston Station and Russell Square. These buses operate at regular twenty minute intervals throughout the day until 8:30pm and cost around £6. *Call 0171 222 1234 for more information.*

By The Underground (Tube)

London Underground's **Piccadilly line** extends west to Heathrow, connecting the airport with such central destinations as Piccadilly Circus and Leicester Square (and around 20 other stops on the way). The ride into central London usually takes around 45 minutes and costs £3.50, although if you're going to be using the Underground later on in the day, it makes sense to buy a **One Day Travelcard, zones 1-6**, which will get you around most of the System for £3.90.

Working the system can be confusing at first: you must first insert the ticket into the slot at the barrier. The machine will register it and it will very quickly appear on top of the barrier. You must pick it up in order for the barrier to open. At the end of your journey, the same happens, except that the machine knows if your ticket is still valid for further journeys. If not, it will not release the ticket, the barrier opens anyway, and you just move on (quickly).

By Rental Car

Renting a car to drive around central London is one of the craziest things you can do. Not only do the Brits drive on the wrong side of the road, they have a totally different driving culture too. On top of that, due to government taxes, petrol (gas) works out at least five times as expensive as it does in the US. Instead, take advantage of the capital's excellent and efficient **public transport system**, which will also give you the opportunity to meet some of the locals. If you're heading out of the city for any length of time, it's a different matter, but save money by not renting a car when you're actually in London. If you do insist on renting a car, arrange it with your travel agent, if possible, when booking your flights.

CAR RENTAL PHONE NUMBERS AT THE AIRPORT

HEATHROW:	GATWICK:
Avis, Tel. 020 8899 1000	*Avis*, Tel. 01293 29721
Budget, Tel. 0800 626 030	*Budget*, Tel. 0800 626 030
Eurodollar, Tel. 020 8897 3232	*Eurodollar*, Tel. 01293 67790
Europcar, Tel. 020 8897 0811	*Europcar*, Tel. 01293 531062
Hertz, Tel. 020 8897 2060	*Hertz*, Tel. 01293 530555

By Train

It may be that you're arriving in London after some time in another part of Britain. What's confusing here is that central London has no fewer than eight major train stations, each of which operates services to different regions of the country. These are **Waterloo Station**, with suburban and long distance services to the south, **Charing Cross Station**, with mainly commuter services to the southern suburbs, but also longer distance journeys to places like Canterbury; **King's Cross Station**, which follows the east coast line to York, Newcastle and Edinburgh; **St. Pancras Station** for services to Leeds and Sheffield; **Euston Station** to Birmingham, Manchester and Glasgow, the west coast line; **Liverpool Street Station** to Cambridge, Norwich and the east; **Paddington Station** to the West Country and Wales; and **Victoria Station** to the southeast, including Brighton.

Euro Express trains from continental Europe arrive at and depart from a newly-constructed annex to Waterloo Station.

GETTING AROUND TOWN

Maps

London's layout is, to say the least, complicated, so please don't try to navigate London without a decent map. The maps they give you at the tourist center are all well and good for getting to the basic sights, but for just £5 you can buy an *A to Z* (the Z in England is pronounced "Zed"), which even Londoners use to get around. These maps come in a variety of shapes and sizes, cover the whole city and list a reference for every street. There's a blown-up map of the central area and an underground map. They're updated frequently, so you can't go wrong.

Boats

Yes, boats! In olden days, the Thames was London's main thoroughfare, and on a sunny spring or summer's day there's nothing better than to take a trip on the Thames, whether it's with a specific destination in mind (like Greenwich, Richmond or the Thames Barrier), just for the fun of it, or perhaps you would like to enjoy an evening supper cruise with your partner.

For information about river trips, call the London Tourist Board's **River Trips Phoneline**, *Tel. 0839 123 432*, or just show up at Westminster Pier, just below Big Ben.

Buses

London's red **double-decker buses** are familiar to everyone, and a great way of getting round the city, and, occasionally, striking up conversation with the locals. Maps of London's bus routes are available from

London Transport, *Tel. 020 7222 1234*, and at most Underground stations, but if you have a particular destination in mind, don't hesitate to phone them and ask for the best way of getting there.

The older buses come complete with conductors, who have an amazing knack of knowing who hasn't paid their fare. They'll often (but not always, they sometimes forget) point out your destination stop to you if you ask nicely. Newer buses tend to be one-person operated, so make sure you have your fare ready (and bus drivers hate to be given large bills for small fares; you might not even be able to get on the bus if you don't have any change). Most bus stops have lists of the buses which stop there, along with a printed schedule of destinations. If you see the bus you want approaching, put at your arm as if hailing a taxi; otherwise the bus might whizz by.

Buses are not always the fastest way of getting around London – though the introduction of bus-only lanes has helped a great deal – but you can enjoy a wonderful view (especially from the top deck).

Night buses are a useful way of getting home late at night, after the Tube has shut down, though there are disadvantages: they don't accept travelcards, and you might end up singing rugby songs with a load of drunks. Most night buses run hourly through the night; Trafalgar Square tends to be a good place to catch one.

SIGHTSEEING TOURS OF LONDON & ENVIRONS BY BUS

The Original London Sighseeing Tour, *Tel. 020 8877 1722* *www.theoriginaltour.com*
Evan Evans Tours, *Tel. 020 7950 1777; www.evanevans.co.uk*
Back-Roads Touring Company, *Tel. 020 8566 5312; www.backroadstouring.co.uk*
Green Line, *Tel. 020 8688 7261*
London Pride, *Tel. 020 7520 2050*

Driving

One word – don't! But if you must, see the car rental section above under *Arrivals & Departures*.

Taxis

Taxis are a great way to get around if you've got the money to spare; if you're in a rush, of course, or have lots of luggage there may be no alternative. London taxis are spacious, the drivers are usually real characters, and you can count on getting to your destination in the shortest possible time (you find yourself being whisked through all manner of back streets – drivers are short-cut experts).

If you're hailing a cab, look for one with an **illuminated amber light** on top; that means they're available for hire. Put out your arm, and tell the driver the destination you want. At the end of the journey, get out to pay, and don't forget the 10% (at least) tip. Minicabs are also available throughout London, and are generally slightly cheaper than the traditional black cabs, but I wouldn't recommend picking one out of a list in yellow pages or on an advertisement. Ask your hotel if they can recommend a company.

Travelcards & Tickets

London's transport system is the most extensive – and expensive – in Europe, but bear a few things in mind and you can significantly cut your losses. A one-day **travelcard** can be used on all buses and Underground trains in the zones specified (except night buses) for a flat fare. If you're going to be making two or more bus/Underground journeys on any one day, it makes a great deal of sense to purchase one. Weekly and monthly travelcards are also available; for the latter, two photo booth-size snaps are necessary. Family travel cards can work out even more cheaply – but check your sums first.

A one-day travelcard costs £3.90; weekly £15.30. Available from Tube ticket offices and selected newsagents throughout the city

Children under five travel free; 5-15s travel at reduced cost (until 10pm, when they are charged as adults on buses). Kids 14 and 15 years old will need to carry a Child-Rate Photocard as proof of their age, available at post offices.

If you're traveling without a travelcard, you'll need a **single ticket**. Check the cost of your journey to your destination at the station. Purchase the ticket at one of the automated machines or from the ticket office. Make absolutely sure you have the right ticket – if you travel one stop too far, you may not be able to get through the exit barrier and you could be charged an excess fare of £10. And, for goodness sake, don't lose your ticket – again, you won't be able to exit the system without a substantial surcharge.

Trains to Suburban Attractions

Since the demise of British Rail, a host of smaller companies have become responsible for ferrying London's commuters and tourists in and out of the city. While it's likely that you're staying at a fairly central location and won't need the train, they can come in very handy for getting to some of the suburban attractions such as Windsor and Hampton Court. *For rail information, call 0345 484950.*

Maybe you're considering popping over to Paris for a day or two on the Eurostar train, which can whisk you from capital to capital in around 3 1/2 hours! If you know your plans in advance, I strongly urge you to make the arrangements in the US by calling *888/EUROSTAR*. In the UK, call *0990 848 848*.

The Underground (Tube)

This is by far the quickest way to get around London (unless there are track, signaling or staffing problems, in which case London Transport is usually very good at posting information at the entrance to the stations). Each of the 12 underground lines is **color-coded**.

Look for your destination on an Underground map, then figure out the most logical way to get there, remembering that you'll need to know the final destination on your chosen line (which is marked on the front of the train and on the overhead illuminated display) and the general direction (north, south, east or west) that the train is traveling. It may sound complicated, but it won't take long to get the hang of it. The trains themselves, with their padded seats, are pretty luxurious by US (if not Canadian) standards, but they can get very busy, so the chances are you'll have to stand for a good portion of your journey anyway.

Trains normally run from around 5am to midnight, but don't take any chances – check before you travel. Remember too to hold on to your ticket – losing it could mean you have to pay a fine, even if you're the Prime Minister's wife, as Cherie Booth, Tony Blair's wife, found out recently.

Walking

Of course this is by far the best way to get a feel for the city, and it's inevitable that you'll be doing quite a bit of walking on your visit. Make sure you bring good walking shoes, an umbrella (just in case) and a lightweight mac (or coat in the winter). Don't be afraid to ask directions, but make it clear where you want to go; don't fall into the trap of asking, US-style, the way to Oxford, when you actually mean Oxford Street! It's a long walk to Oxford!

Note that traffic in central London is very heavy just about all the time, so try and plan your walks though parks and smaller side streets (though at night it's advisable to stay to the main thoroughfares).

Walking Tours

A number of companies offer excellent **themed walking tours** of London, covering subjects like The London of Shakespeare, a Knightsbridge Pub Walk, The Beatles "In My Life" Walk and Jack the Ripper Haunts, to name but a few. The best known company in this field is **The Original London Walks**, *PO Box 1708, London NW6 4LW, Tel. 020*

7624 3978; www.walks.com. Walks cost £5 (£3.50 for seniors and students under 26, free for children under 15 if accompanied by an adult). You can also check the listings in *Time Out*.

HELPFUL TOURIST INFORMATION LINES

The London Tourist Board, who have a website at www.londontown.com, operate the following tourist helplines:
What's On information: *Dial 09068 505 then 440*
Changing the Guard information: *Dial 8-digit number above then add: 452*
Rock and pop concert information: *Dial 8-digit number above then add 447*
Pageantry: *Dial 8-digit number above then add 453*
Museums and galleries: *Dial 8-digit number above then add 462*
Palaces: *Dial 8-digit number above then add 466*
Famous houses and gardens: *Dial 8-digit number above then add 468*
Day trips from London: *Dial 8-digit number above then add 469*
West End shows: *Dial 8-digit number above then add 473*
Non-West End shows: *Dial 8-digit number above then add 476*
What's on for children: *Dial 8-digit number above then add 456*
Places to visit with children: *Dial 8-digit number above then add 460*
Guided tours and walks: *Dial 8-digit number above then add 470*
River trips/boat hire: *Dial 8-digit number above then add 471*
Shops and stores: *Dial 8-digit number above then add 478*
Street markets: *Dial 8-digit number above then add 463*
Getting around in London: *Dial 8-digit number above then add 488*
Getting to the airports: *Dial 8-digit number above then add 489*
Eating out: *Dial 8-digit number above then add 464*
Accommodation service: *Dial 8-digit number above then add 487*
Gay and Lesbian London: *Tel. 09068 141 120*

WHERE TO STAY

Accommodations in London can be very expensive, unless you want to go so low down the market you'd be better off sleeping in a cardboard box on the street. Having said that, there is a huge variety of quality hotels available in the city, many of which are very reasonably priced. It makes a lot of sense to book your hotel with your travel agent – it can often work out cheaper than making your own reservations.

When you arrive at your hotel remember that facilities North Americans often take for granted – such as orthopaedic mattresses and fast-flowing showers – may not be at the top of the list here. Put it down to cultural difference and don't make a fuss; you won't change anything. What you can almost always be assured of, however, and which in many ways compensates for the missing amenities, is warmth and charm.

West End
   1. REGENT'S PARK HOTEL, *156 Gloucester Place, London NW1 6DT. Tel. 020 7258 1911, Fax 020 7258 0288. Rooms: 29 Rates: singles from £60, doubles from £90, family room from £100. Restaurant. All major credit cards accepted. Nearest Tube: Baker Street.*

   This white stone building is situated – as the name implies – close to Regent's Park, home of London Zoo, and just a fifteen minute walk to Oxford Street. The Regent's Park offers comfortable and functional accommodations at extremely competitive rates; the decor and furnishings may be nothing to write home about but are perfectly adequate, with modern facilities including cable TV, tea and coffee-making machines and phone. Hairdryers, irons and dry cleaning services are also available. Excellent value for such a central location.

   2. DURRANT'S, *George Street, London W1H 6BJ. Tel. 020 7935 8131, Fax 020 7487 3510. Rooms: 88 Rates: singles from £90, doubles from £140. Bar, lounges. All major credit cards accepted. Nearest Tube: Bond Street.*

   This perfectly acceptable hotel may not have the high chic quality of some of its rivals, but it makes up for that by offering extremely good value for central London. Another major plus is that it's located in a very quiet area, just around the corner from the famous Wallace Collection. A hotel for 200 years, it's especially attractive if you like lots of dark wood, dark red carpets and a clubby atmosphere. The rooms are comfortable and fairly spacious. The bathrooms are modern – and there are a couple of bedrooms with no bathroom for which you pay around £10 per night less.

   3. DORSET SQUARE HOTEL, *39 Dorset Square, London NW1 6QN. Tel. 020 7723 7874, Fax 020 7724 3328. Rooms: 37. Rates: singles from £116, doubles from £153. Restaurant, garden. All major credit cards accepted. Nearest Tube: Baker Street.*

   Lovely Georgian townhouse hotel built on what was the site of the original Lord's Cricket ground (the present Lord's ground in St. John's Wood is the world cricket headquarters), so don't be surprised to see cricket bats and other cricketing relics among the more traditional antiques here. This is a classy place, with nice touches including lots of fresh flowers, pleasant furnishings and cheerful bold colors. Many of the bedrooms have a country house feel about them, and the marble and mahogany bathrooms are particularly attractive. The Potting Shed Restaurant serves morning coffee, good value lunches and evening meals where jazz is sometimes on the menu.

4. BLOOM'S, *7 Montague Street WC1 5BP. Tel. 020 7323 1717, Fax 020 7636 6498. Rooms:27 Rates: Singles from £130, doubles from £195. Restaurant. All major credit cards accepted. Nearest Tube: Goodge Street or Russell Square.*

Just yards from the British Museum, this elegant 18th century house has tremendous charm and a real sense of civilization. Regency portraits and equestrian paintings adorn the walls, there's an extensive library, and the sitting room is so civilized! There are 27 rooms, all of which are comfortably furnished and come with hostess tray, TV, radio and 24-hour room service. A small walled garden makes a lovely space for afternoon tea in the summer.

5. MYHOTEL BLOOMSBURY, *11-13 Bayley Street, London SW1W 9QQ. Tel. 020 7667 6000, Fax 020 7667 6001. Rooms: 77. Rates: singles from £155, doubles from £195, suite from £395. Restaurant, bar, library, lounge, fitness center, playroom. All major credit cards accepted. Nearest Tube: Tottenham Court Road.*

Myhotel (no, it's not a typo) is the result of a new concept in hotels, designed on feng shui principles with the aim of "radiating calmness and tranquillity," and to some degree it succeeds. A relaxed, comfortable lobby, complete with fish tank lies adjacent to a bar and restaurant, with an eastern-influenced menu that is as you'd expect liberally sprinkled with vegetarian options. Other public areas include the library, down in the basement, a former wine cellar now painted white, with computer terminals, comfortable seating and self-service tea and coffee.

The bedrooms are large, with simple, pale wood furnishings, CD players and TVs, not to mention mineral water and energy bars in paper bags. The main drawback is the noise from the traffic rumbling past on Tottenham Court Road, though the secondary glazing goes some way towards solving the problem.

6. THE MARLBOROUGH, *Bloomsbury Street, London WC1B 3QD. Tel. 020 7636 5601, from US 800/333-3333, Fax 020 7636 0532. Rates: singles from £160, doubles from £220. Restaurants. All major credit cards accepted. Nearest Tube: Tottenham Court Road.*

This splendid, grand Edwardian hotel is conveniently located for the British Museum and all the attractions of Covent Garden and Bloomsbury, including shops and restaurants. There's a pleasant lobby with period furniture and an elegant staircase, and a dark wood-paneled bar with lots of atmosphere. The rooms are good-sized, with a full range of conveniences, including cable TV; 24-hour room service is available.

7. DUKES, *35 St. Jame's Place, London SW1A 1NY. Tel. 020 7491 4840, Fax 020 7493 1264. Rooms: 62. Rates: singles from £180, doubles from £185. All major credit cards accepted. Nearest Tube: Green Park.*

This charming Edwardian hotel is tucked away in a quiet cul-de-sac just two minutes' walk from Buckingham Palace. With lots of wood

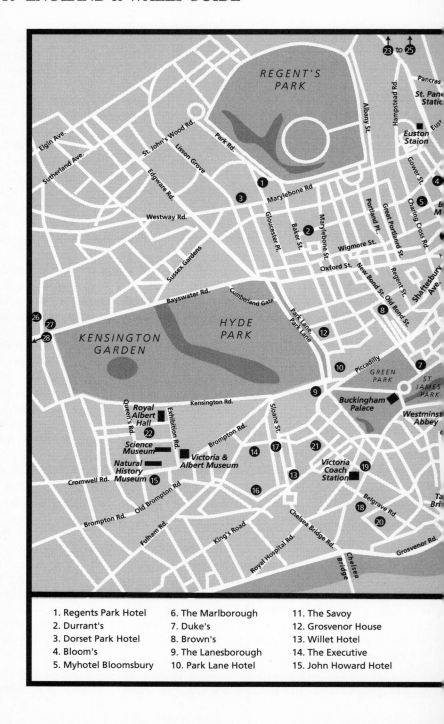

1. Regents Park Hotel
2. Durrant's
3. Dorset Park Hotel
4. Bloom's
5. Myhotel Bloomsbury
6. The Marlborough
7. Duke's
8. Brown's
9. The Lanesborough
10. Park Lane Hotel
11. The Savoy
12. Grosvenor House
13. Willet Hotel
14. The Executive
15. John Howard Hotel

CENTRAL LONDON HOTELS

6. The Sloane Hotel	21. The Diplomat	26. The Gate
7. The Cadogan	22. The Gore	27. Pembridge Court
8. The Elizabeth	23. Hampstead Village Guest House	28. The Portobello
9. James House	24. La Gaffe	
0. The Windermere	25. The Sandringham	

panelling and leather chairs it has, like many of its counterparts, a relaxed, clubby atmosphere, and each of the rooms is decorated with antiques and floral fabrics.

8. BROWN'S, *Albemarle & Dover Streets, London W1A 4SW. Tel. 020 7493 6020, Fax 020 7493 9381. Rooms: 118 Rates: singles from £294, doubles from £329, family rooms from £423. All major credit cards accepted. Nearest Tube: Green Park.*

The elegant Brown's Hotel first opened the year Victoria came to the throne (1837). Now occupying eleven Georgian houses, Brown's attracts large numbers of North American clientele, attracted by the sheer (perceived) Englishness of the place; brocade wallpapers, plush carpets, cozy public rooms with acres of wood paneling, and old-fashioned bathtubs. Among the famous guests who've stayed here are Napoleon III, Theodore Roosevelt; Franklin and Eleanor Roosevelt (who honeymooned here) and Rudyard Kipling. Brown's is also the place to come for an excellent afternoon tea, with a vast choice of brews, and dainty finger sandwiches in all kinds of fillings.

9. THE LANESBOROUGH, *Hyde Park Corner, London SW1X 7TA. Tel. 020 7259 5599, from US 800/999-1828, Fax 020 7259 5606. Rooms: 95 Rates: singles from £276, doubles from £364. Restaurant, gymnasium, air-conditioning. All major credit cards accepted. Nearest Tube: Hyde Park Corner.*

With a reputation as one of London's finest hotels, the newly restored Lanesborough offers superb views of Hyde Park and Buckingham Palace in the atmosphere of a refined Georgian manor house. Rooms are beautifully furnished with canopied beds, satin cushions and gilt-framed paintings, and come equipped with all the latest modern conveniences – fax machines, compact disc players and VCRs. The sumptuous Conservatory Restaurant, with ceiling-high palms, makes a delightful venue for afternoon tea.

10. PARK LANE HOTEL, *Piccadilly, London W1Y 8BX. Tel. 020 7499 6321, Fax 020 7499 1965. Rooms: 266. Rates: singles from £280, doubles from £280. Restaurants, hairdresser, fitness suite. All major credit cards accepted. Nearest Tube: Green Park.*

This centrally located, Sheraton-owned hotel has been one of London's greats ever since it opened in the 1920s as the only place in the country where each room had its own bathroom. The hotel is currently in the process of being modernized. As you'd expect, the rooms are superbly appointed and well-equipped, with TVs, hair dryers, trouser presses and the like, though not with tea and coffee-making facilities. However, it's the public rooms that really stand out: a Palm Court with oriental features, including cane chairs and silk wall panels; a stunning art deco ballroom, used mainly for social events, and an excellent restaurant, the Brasserie on the Park, with more art deco.

11. THE SAVOY, *The Strand, London WC2R 0EU. Tel. 020 7836 4343, Fax 020 7240 6040. Rooms: 202. Rates: singles from £275, doubles from £295, one-bedroom suite, £435, two-bedroom suite £870. 3 restaurants, bars. All major credit cards accepted. Nearest Tube: Covent Garden.*

One of London's most famous and historic hotels, the Savoy stands sentinel over the Strand, the main thoroughfare between Westminster and the City. Among its several claims to fame are that it hosted Elizabeth Taylor's first honeymoon, poured the world's first Martini in its American bar and has hosted such luminaries as Hemingway, Gershwin, Fitzgerald and so on. The rooms are large and elegant, furnished with antiques and serviced by attentive valets. The famous Savoy Grill is the place to enjoy that most English of meals, Roast Beef and Yorkshire Pudding.

12. GROSVENOR HOUSE, *Park Lane, London W1A 3AA. Tel. 020 7493 6363, Fax 020 7493 3341. Rooms: 360. Suites: 70. Rates: singles from £250, doubles from £295. All major credit cards accepted. Nearest Tube: Marble Arch.*

The "old lady of Park Lane" is one of London's poshest establishments, all the better for a recent refurbishment which has re-established her among London's top five. With marble floors, open fires, oil paintings and antiques in abundance, it's not surprising that you're paying top whack. Rooms are, as you'd expect spacious and beautifully decorated, and the marble bathrooms are sumptuous. On top of all the glitz and glamor, there's an excellent health club with full-sized pool. Pronunciation note: the 's' in Grosvenor is silent.

Kensington & Chelsea
13. WILLET HOTEL, *32 Sloane Gardens, London SW1W 8DJ. Tel. 020 7824 8415, Fax 020 7730 4830. Rooms: 18. Rates: singles from £65, doubles from £120. All major credit cards accepted. Nearest Tube: Sloane Square.*

Restored Victorian townhouse that's located in a fairly quiet side street just a couple of minutes' walk from Chelsea's trendy King's Road and the Sloane Square Tube Station. The comfortable rooms come with a range of facilities including cable TV, hairdryers and tea- and coffee-making facilities, and are all en suite. A substantial buffet breakfast is served daily in the dining room.

14. THE EXECUTIVE HOTEL, *57 Pont Street, London SW1X 0BD. Tel. 020 7581 2424, Fax 020 7589 9456. Rates: singles from £90, doubles from £120. All major credit cards accepted. Nearest Tube: Knightsbridge.*

Restored red brick Victorian townhouse in the posh Knightsbridge district, just around the corner from Harrods department store and just a short walk to the major museums. The Executive has "listed" status with English Heritage, which means it's the genuine article. When Heritage-listed buildings are restored, strict guidelines must be followed, so when you enter the 19th century lobby, you know it's as close to the original as it can possibly be, right down to the intricate wall carvings and staircase. The rooms are comfortable with TVs and some thoughtful touches, including bathrobes and daily complimentary newspapers. The bathrooms may be a bit on the small side but they're perfectly adequate and spotlessly clean.

15. JOHN HOWARD HOTEL, *4 Queen's Gate, London SW7 5EH. Tel. 020 7581, from US 800/448-8355, Fax 020 7589 8403. Rates: singles from £95, doubles from £125. All major credit cards accepted. Nearest Tube: Gloucester Road.*

Owned by the Best Western Chain, this John Howard offers exceptional value. It's located in a converted regency townhouse just minutes from the Royal Albert Hall, Hyde Park, Kensington Gardens and the museum district. The elegant exterior belies a more modern, hotel-like interior, with fairly unexciting color schemes and standard hotel furnishings. But don't let that put you off. The rooms are spacious, with king-size beds, bars and air conditioning, and there's even 24-hour room service. Also available for longer stays are studio and two-bedroom apartments with fully-equipped kitchens which start at around £250 per night. Overall, the John Howard offers exceptional value.

16. THE SLOANE HOTEL, *29 Draycott Place, London SW3 2SH. Tel. 020 7581 5757, from US 800/324 9960, Fax: 020 7584 1348. Rooms: 12. Rates: singles from £165, doubles from £165, suites from £265. Lounge, roof terrace. All major credit cards accepted. Nearest Tube: Sloane Square (Chelsea).*

This quiet, intimate Chelsea townhouse has the feel of a private home, a sense that's accentuated by the selection of hand-picked antiques and objets d'art that adorn each of the rooms. The standard doubles are smallish, but comfortable, the larger suites come with four poster beds and galleries with seating area – but no tea- or coffee-making facilities. There's air conditioning throughout, and 24-hour room service is provided. Another plus is the hotel's connection with a local health club; guests can access a swimming pool, fully equipped gym, and massage facilities.

17. THE CADOGAN, *75 Sloane Street, London SW1X 9SG. Tel. 020 7235 7141, Fax 020 7245 0994. Rooms: 52, plus 13 suites. Rates: singles from £194, doubles from £217, suites from £364. Restaurant, drawing room, bar, leisure facilities nearby with reduced rates for guests. All major credit cards accepted. Nearest Tube: Knightsbridge or Sloane Square.*

Quiet, traditional hotel with a relaxed friendly ambience that's conveniently located half-way between Knightsbridge and Chelsea, within easy reach of Harrods store and the museums of South Kensington. Staying here is in some ways a bit like stepping back fifty years; the wonderful drawing room is the perfect place to read the paper in peace

– a sign on the door expressly forbids the use of mobile phones and laptops here. The rooms are simply but pleasantly and individually furnished, and show that the hotel is not totally averse to modernity, as the modem points and bathroom telephones indicate. The hotel has quite a history, too. Oscar Wilde was a frequent guest here (the turret room where he used to stay still bears his name), and Edward VIII's mistress, Lily Langtry, occupied part of the building.

Selected as one of my Best Places to Stay – see Chapter 13 for more details.

Victoria

18. THE ELIZABETH, *37 Eccleston Square, London SW1V 1PB. Tel. 020 7828 6812, Fax 020 7828 6814. Rooms: 38. Rates: singles from £45, double room from £69, family room from £99. Access to garden, tennis courts. Credit cards: MC, Visa. Nearest Tube: Victoria.*

Eccleston Square is one of London's best addresses; a dignified square of neoclassical terraces overlooking a private garden and tennis courts used by residents of the square – and accessible to hotel guests. The Elizabeth has a lot of character; prints and cartoons of historic local figure adorn the walls, and there's a very pleasant, elegant lounge with TV, but the bedrooms themselves are unexciting – there aren't even the usual tea- and coffee-making facilities. It's also not the quietest of locations, but if you don't mind traffic noise it represents excellent value. There's a public parking lot nearby where the charge is £13.50 per day – but then, if you've taken my advice about not renting a car in London, this won't apply.

19. JAMES HOUSE, *108 Ebury Street, London SW1W 9QD. Tel. 020 7730 7338. Rooms: 6. Rates: single £45, double from £65. All major credit cards accepted. Nearest Tube: Victoria.*

This no-frills establishment offers exceptional value, given its proximity to some of London's major tourist sites: Buckingham Palace and Westminster Abbey included. The rooms are spotlessly clean, and come with tea- and coffee-making facilities and TV. You take breakfast in a wood-paneled room in the basement, complete with the owner's family photographs and mementoes.

20. THE WINDERMERE, *142 Warwick Way, London SW1V 4JE. Tel. 020 7834 5163, Fax 020 7630 8831. Rooms: 22. Rates: singles from £65, doubles from £75, family rooms from £125. Bar, restaurant. All major credit cards accepted. Nearest Tube: Victoria.*

This extremely pleasant small Victorian hotel offers a range of facilities normally associated with larger establishments: rooms with TVs, hairdryers, phones, even modem points. It's all part of owner Nicki Hambi's drive to keep the place as up-to-date as possible – some of the larger hotels could learn a great deal from him.

The rooms are all stylishly decorated and furnished – all but two are en suite – and public rooms include the Pimlico Room in the basement, which doubles up as a restaurant and bar, and a cozy lounge on the first floor. The place is child-friendly, even to the point of offering early suppers for the little ones, and the service is friendly and welcoming. The hotel is close to Victoria's main line train station, Tube station, and bus station, which means you have good access not only to city attractions, but to the coast and countryside as well. Great value.

21. THE DIPLOMAT, *2 Chesham Street, London SW1X 8DT. Tel. 020 7235 1544, Fax 020 7259 6153. Rooms: 27. Rates: singles from £90, doubles from £125. All major credit cards accepted. Nearest Tube: Sloane Square.*

Right in the heart of chic Belgravia, this is a comfortable, attractive hotel that doesn't cost an arm and a leg. Built as a "palazzo" terraced house by 19th century architect Thomas Cubitt, the hotel contains some interesting features, including a wonderful circular staircase that's lit by a Regency-style chandelier. The 27 rooms are all pleasantly furnished and decorated.

22. THE GORE, *189 Queen's Gate, London SW7 5EX. Tel. 020 7584 6601, Fax 020 7589 8127. Rooms: 54. Rates: singles from £110, doubles from £165. Restaurants, bar. All major credit cards accepted. Nearest Tube: Gloucester Road or South Kensington.*

Not far from the Royal Albert Hall, this is a small intimate hotel of immense character and charm, epitomized by the amazing and eclectic collection of prints, etchings and antiques in the foyer. There's even a shrine to Queen Victoria, complete with photographs, paintings and drawings. The thirty bedrooms contain mahogany four-poster beds, cable TV and hairdryers. Bistro 190, adjoining the hotel, serves British/ Mediterranean specialties, but you may want to explore the incredible diversity of restaurants in nearby Kensington and Knightsbridge.

North London

23. HAMPSTEAD VILLAGE GUESTHOUSE, *2 Kempley Road, London NW3 1SY. Tel. 020 7435 8679, Fax 020 7794 0254. Rooms: 6. Rates: single (there's only one): £40, doubles from £60, family room from £80. Garden, play area. Credit cards: MC, Visa. Nearest Tube: Hampstead.*

This little gem is located a just half a dozen tube stops from the West End in the affluent suburb of Hampstead, close to the wonderful Hampstead Heath and Kenwood House. It's a large Victorian house that owner Annemarie van der Meer has transformed into a cozy and characterful family hotel. The rooms are each named after a member of her family, and come with various personal possessions – such as toys and books – that the family member has left behind, along with some unusual antiques and up-to-date conveniences like TVs and hair dryers. Note that some of the bedrooms come with washbasin only, which means sharing a bathroom. If you don't mind that, and if you don't mind being just a little but out of central London, the place represents excellent value.

24. LA GAFFE, *107-111 Heath Street, London NW3 6SS. Tel. 020 7435 8965, Fax 020 7794 7592. Rooms: 18. Rates: singles from £60, doubles from 85. Restaurant, terrace, bar. All major credit cards accepted.*

The word gaffe in Cockney slang means "home." This particular home is an 18-room shepherd's cottage dating from 1737 when most of the land around here was open fields on which sheep roamed. The hotel is owned by an Italian poet and playwright whose typed work is framed and displayed about the place. The single rooms are small but comfortable, with canopied bed and TV; the double rooms much larger. The restaurant (through which you enter the hotel) serves home-made Italian food and is a favorite haunt of a number of Hampstead celebrities. Some rooms are located in a separate annex.

25. THE SANDRINGHAM, *3 Holford Road, London NW3 1AD. Tel. 020 7435 1569, Fax 020 7431 5932. Rooms: 18. Rates: singles from £75, doubles from £120. Lounge, garden. All major credit cards accepted.*

It's very small – just 19 rooms – but this beautifully maintained Hampstead hotel is perfect if you prefer to be a little bit away from the noise and bustle of central London. It's a large Victorian house, and there are superb views over London towards the south. The rooms have all recently been redecorated, several with working fireplaces, and each has a clean modern bathroom with shower. Hampstead Village, with all its attractions, is minutes away; if you don't want to venture the 100 yards or so to the Heath, perhaps London's most beautiful and natural open space, you can enjoy the pretty walled garden where afternoon tea is served in the summer months.

Notting Hill

26. THE GATE, *6 Portobello Road, London W11 3DG. Tel. 020 7221 2403, Fax 020 7221 9128. Rooms: 6. Rates: singles from £55, doubles from £85. All major credit cards accepted. Nearest Tube: Notting Hill Gate.*

It's really tiny – just six rooms – but this utterly charming hotel is a real gem. For a start, it's located on the Portobello Road, a busy thoroughfare that's famous for its open air market and a host of small family-owned shops and restaurants. The rooms are small but clean, and each has color TV, fridge, and tea- and coffee-making facilities. A continental breakfast is served in your room.

27. THE PEMBRIDGE COURT, *34 Pembridge Gardens, London W2 4DX. Tel. 020 7229 9977, from US 800/709-9882, Fax 020 7287 4982. Rooms: 20. Rates: singles from £110, doubles from £150. Restaurant. All major credit cards accepted. Nearest Tube: Notting Hill Gate.*

From being one of London's downbeat suburbs, Notting Hill has become one of its most fashionable, thanks in part to the movie *Notting Hill* – though the gentrification process was already well under way when the film came out. The Pembridge Court is located on a quiet tree-lined street. Advantages to staying here include stylishly decorated rooms equipped with all the usual modern conveniences, 24-hour room service, and discounted access to an exclusive local health club, with pool, gym and spa. The whole place is brimming with the antiques the owners' wife Merete has assembled over the years; she will happily tell you where to shop to expand your own collection; the hotel is just a short walk from Portobello Road Market. Breakfast is served in the basement Caps restaurant. Who knows? You might just bump into one of the celebrities – such as Tina Turner, John Cleese, Madonna and Tom Cruise – who have a home around here.

Selected as one of my Best Places to Stay – see Chapter 13 for more details.

28. THE PORTOBELLO, *22 Stanley Gardens, London W11 2NG. Tel. 020 7727 2777, Fax 020 7792 9341. Rooms: 16. Rates: singles from £125, doubles from £150, four-posters from £180, suite £250. Restaurant, drawing room, bar, access to health club. All major credit cards accepted. Nearest Tube: Notting Hill Gate.*

This wonderful little hotel close to the Portobello Road Market has undergone some major improvements recently, though it's hard to see how it could be improved. The hotel offers charming, comfortable accommodations, with friendly service and exceptionally good value. The drawing room, with French windows leading out to the garden, retains many of its original Victorian features. The bedrooms are all different, but utterly adorable – one of them boasting a circular bed, a Victorian bathing machine and Chinese wallpaper. Several of the singles, which are situated at the top of the house, are decked out as ships' cabins.

WHERE TO EAT

Prince Francesco Caracciolo once said that "There are in England sixty different religious sects, but only one sauce." He might well have been right, and it might also well have been true that London's fog was once caused by the over-boiling of potatoes, but neither of these are true today. While Britain may not be considered an automatic choice for a gourmet vacation, there is no doubt that British culinary standards, both in restaurants and domestically, have improved beyond belief over the

DINING COSTS

Inexpensive: under £15
Moderate: £15 to £30
Expensive: over £30 per person

last twenty years. London is very much the culinary capital of England, with a vast range of quality ethnic restaurants, as well as more traditional British and French fare and more than its fair share of fast food joints.

Eating out in London, as in any major world city, can be extraordinarily expensive, but you can also find good food at much lower prices. **Indian** restaurants are always a good bet in this respect, as are **pub meals**, often with a great variety of dishes to choose from, no longer something to sneer at.

Another way to eat more cheaply in London is to take your main meal at lunch time, when prices tend to be cheaper, and a snack in the evening. Or check out the many **pre-theater restaurants** in the West End, where you can get a good three-course meal at a much lower rate than it would be, say, an hour later – although you may find yourself rushed. Another good bet for inexpensive and tasty food is the **Soho** area, with a myriad of sandwich bars and cafes, many Italian-run.

Prices listed here cover a basic three course meal for two with a bottle of wine and coffee. Don't forget to make reservations – unless, of course, you've decided on that fast food joint across the road.

Of course, there's always fish and chips...

Chinatown

London's Chinatown is bounded by Shaftesbury Avenue and Charing Cross Road, close to all the main theaters, cinemas, museums and other attractions of the West End.

1. NEW WORLD, *1 Gerrard Place, London W1. Tel. 020 7734 0677. Inexpensive. Open daily 11am to midnight. All major credit cards accepted. Nearest Tube: Leicester Square.*

Dim Sum is one of London's cheapest epicurean thrills; one unpronounceable dish after another. Basically, this entails a wide variety of dumplings and snacks wheeled around the room in metal steam trolleys. When the trolley stops at your table, lids are lifted off individual dishes (usually containing 2 to 4 items) for your examination. Say no to things that make you feel squeamish; yes to prawns wrapped in paper, vegetarian peanut dumplings and the like. A tally of your meal is kept on a scorecard on the table; two hungry people would have a hard time spending more than £20 between them. It's a huge place – it seats 500 – but even so, this place can get packed, especially at lunchtimes.

2. CHINA CHINA, *3 Gerrard Street, London W1. Moderate. Tel. 020 7439 7502. Open daily noon to 11:45pm (12.45am Friday and Saturday) All major credit cards accepted. Nearest Tube: Leicester Square.*

This four-story Chinese restaurant is a compromise between the less salubrious establishments along Newport and Lisle Streets, and the more expensive, upmarket choices like Fung Shing (below). It stays open late, and the service is pretty good (though a smile wouldn't hurt here and there). Best of all, the Cantonese food is excellent. The Peking Duck is particularly good, and there are always lots of Chinese eating here – always a good sign.

3. FUNG SHING, *15 Lisle Street, London WC2. Tel. 020 7437 1539. Moderate. Open daily noon to 11:30pm. All major credit cards accepted. Nearest Tube: Leicester Square.*

Fung Shing's fascinating menu includes such delicacies as spicy jelly fish with chicken and pickles, and double boiled fluffy supreme shark's fin. Or enjoy stewed eel with roast pork or broccoli with fried scallops. There are lots of other, less challenging meals to choose from, as well as a fine wine list. The place can get crowded, so book in advance!

Covent Garden

The converted former vegetable market is now a major attraction in its own right, and a place where crowds of all ages congregate.

4. THE STOCKPOT, *40 Panton Street. W1. Tel. 020 7839 5142. Very inexpensive. Open all day. No credit cards. Nearest Tube: Leicester Square.*

One of a chain of inexpensive, lively, no-frills restaurants that serve good hearty fare at minimal cost. Typical dishes include Lancashire hotpot, lasagna, spaghetti bolognese and that sort of thing – with desserts like apple pie with custard. A meal rarely costs more than £10. Note: Other branches at 6 Basil Street, SW3; 18 Old Compton Street, Soho; 273 King's Road, Chelsea.

5. PIZZA EXPRESS, *9-12 Bow Street, Covent Garden, London WC2. Tel. 020 7240 3443. Inexpensive. Daily 11:30am to midnight. All major credit cards accepted. Nearest Tube: Covent Garden.*

This chain of pizza restaurants has a strong following in London. More upmarket than their Pizza Hut and Pizzaland rivals, these are by and large set in elegant, modern surroundings, fresh flowers on each table, and gentle, unhurried service – perhaps the best example of which is the branch at Kentish Town. The pizzas and pasta are good, too, and there's usually a lively, if not raucous atmosphere, sometimes soothed by piano playing or a small jazz ensemble. Even if you don't try this branch, don't leave London without sampling one of the others.

6. LE PALAIS DU JARDIN, *136 Long Acre, London WC2. Tel. 020 7379 5353. Moderate. Open daily noon to 3:30pm, 5:30pm to midnight. All major credit cards accepted. Nearest Tube: Covent Garden.*

Noisy, trendy brasserie and seafood bar located in the heart of Covent Garden. The elegant, mirrored restaurant is located at the back which means you have to navigate your way through the hordes of early evening drinkers first. But it's worth the effort: the all-French menu includes lots of seafood, with lobster a particular favorite here; venison, confit of duck, and confoundingly, bangers and mash. The choice of desserts is limited – only three or four choices – but after a delicious lobster thermidor – and a few glasses of house wine (which starts at £9.50 a bottle) – who cares?

7. PORTERS, *17 Henrietta Street, W1. Tel. 020 7836 6466. Moderate. Open daily noon to 11:30pm. All major credit cards accepted. Nearest Tube: Covent Garden.*

Porters makes a good place to visit on your first night in town as English cuisine is the thing here. You can sample the delights of steak and kidney pie or pudding, try jellied eels with mash, a staple diet for Londoners for centuries (but much less so today), the ubiquitous roast beef and Yorkshire pudding and a variety of thick, gungy puddings like spotted dick (a suet sponge smothered in jam and occasionnally topped with custard).

8. IVY, *1 West Street, London WC2. Tel. 020 7836 4751. Expensive. Open daily noon to 3pm (3:30pm Sunday), 5:30pm to midnight. All major credit cards accepted. Nearest Tube: Leicester Square.*

The Ivy has been around for quite a long time and has become one of London's best-loved restaurants, on account of its pleasant unassuming atmosphere, excellent service, and wide range of dishes available. Although it changed hands in 1999, the new owners have obviously realized they're on to a good thing, and have decided to make few, if any changes, so thankfully the dark wood paneling and stained glass have remained, as have most of the customers, an interesting mixture of theater people, media and advertising types, and travel writers...

There's a wide range of dishes on the menu, including some classic British favorites like braised beef in stout, haddock and chips with mushy peas for main courses, spotted dick, bread and butter pudding and the like for dessert, and some more contemporary choices – pork tenderloin on lemon polenta for example. The extensive wine list opens with house red at £11.25.

9. RULES, *35 Maiden Lane, Covent Garden , London WC2. Tel. 020 7836 5314. Expensive. Open daily noon to 11:30pm. All major credit cards accepted. Nearest Tube: Covent Garden.*

This plush 200-year-old institution has welcomed everyone from Charles Dickens to Charlie Chaplin, and including royalty, like the Prince

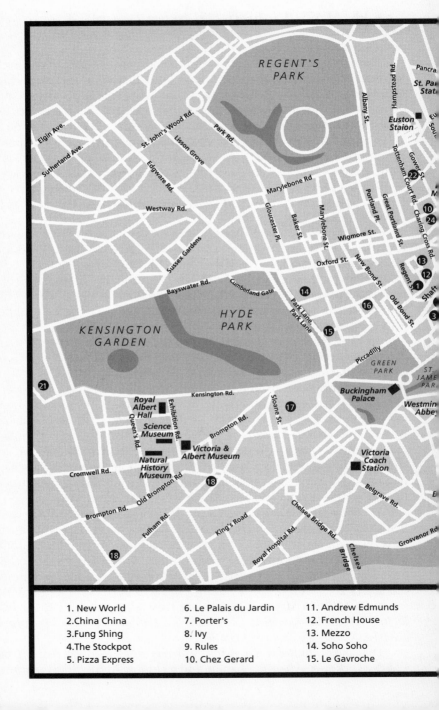

1. New World	6. Le Palais du Jardin	11. Andrew Edmunds
2.China China	7. Porter's	12. French House
3.Fung Shing	8. Ivy	13. Mezzo
4.The Stockpot	9. Rules	14. Soho Soho
5. Pizza Express	10. Chez Gerard	15. Le Gavroche

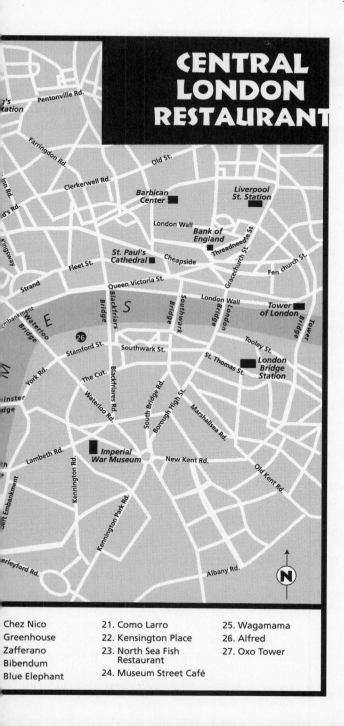

CENTRAL LONDON RESTAURANT

Pentonville Rd.

Farringdon Rd.

Old St.

Clerkenwell Rd.

Inn Rd.

d's Rd.

Kingsway

Barbican Center

Liverpool St. Station

London Wall

Bank of England

Threadneedle St.

St. Paul's Cathedral

Cheapside

Fleet St.

Fen church St.

Gracechurch St.

Strand

Queen Victoria St.

Blackfriars Bridge

Southwark Bridge

London Wall

London Bridge

Tower of London

Tower Bridge

Embankment

Waterloo Bridge

E

S

26

Stamford St.

Southwark St.

Tooley St.

St. Thomas St.

London Bridge Station

York Rd.

The Cut.

Blackfriars Rd.

Waterloo Rd.

South Bridge Rd.

Borough High St.

Marshallsea Rd.

inster dge

Lambeth Rd.

Kennington Rd.

Imperial War Museum

New Kent Rd.

Old Kent Rd.

Kennington Park Rd.

erleyford Rd.

Albany Rd.

N

Chez Nico	21. Como Larro	25. Wagamama
Greenhouse	22. Kensington Place	26. Alfred
Zafferano	23. North Sea Fish Restaurant	27. Oxo Tower
Bibendum		
Blue Elephant	24. Museum Street Café	

of Wales, later Edward VII, who frequently brought his mistress, Lily Langtry, here. The menu is very English, with its steak, kidney and mushroom pudding one of the highlights. But it's worth eating here just for the decor; plush red banquettes and lacquered yellow walls, adorned with 19th century oil paintings, prints and engravings. In the height of summer it can be a little touristy, but that's a small price to pay for one of the great dining experiences London has to offer. Count on spending £60 and up.

Soho

Soho abounds in eating places of all shapes and sizes – from tiny hole-in-the-wall establishments to elegant, sophisticated restaurants where you can pay an arm and a leg.

10. CHEZ GERARD, *8 Charlotte Street, W1. Tel. 020 7636 4975. Moderate. Open Monday to Friday noon to 3pm, 6pm to 11:30pm, Saturday 6pm to 11:30pm, Sunday noon to 3pm, 6pm to 10:30pm. All major credit cards accepted. Nearest Tube: Goodge Street.*

Recently renovated, Chez Gerard serves good unpretentious food in a pleasant, uncluttered, though lively environment. The speciality of the house is cote de boeuf (for two) with sauce bearnaise, while other courses include lamb brochette, duck confit, escalope of veal and salade nicoise. Every evening after 6pm and at Sunday lunch time there a £15 prix fixe menu – one of the best deals in town. Dinner for two with wine can come to around £50-60.

11. ANDREW EDMUNDS, *46 Lexington Street, W1. Tel. 020 7437 5708. Moderate. Open daily 12:30pm to 3pm and 5:30pm to 11pm. All major credit cards accepted. Nearest Tube: Piccadilly Circus or Oxford Circus.*

Andrew Edmunds occupies the ground and basement floors of a rather rundown looking 18th century house in Soho. The restaurant is popular with artsy types, travel writers and others who enjoy the cluttered, intimate French bistro-type ambiance. The food's good too, and depends largely on what's available at the local market. So you might end up with Moroccan buttternut squash soup followed by swordfish steak with warm potato salad.

12. FRENCH HOUSE DINING ROOM, *63-64 Frith Street, London W1. Moderate. Open Monday to Saturday noon to 3:15pm, 6pm to 11:15pm. All major credit cards accepted. Nearest Tube: Leicester Square.*

The name here is deceptive; it refers to the French former owner of the downstairs pub, which was a meeting place for the Free French during WWII. In fact, this restaurant has a distinctly English feel, with its bare floorboards, dark red wallpaper and wood paneling. The menu includes a mixture of traditional dishes – ox tongue, braised duck with carrots and the like – with some more unusual choices – grilled ox heart with chicory salad to name but one. The desserts are traditional too: pear and almond tart, bread and butter pudding and a selection of cheese. Best of all, most of the main courses come in at under £15. The wine list starts with house French at £10.

13. MEZZO, *100 Wardour Street, W1. Tel. 020 7314 4000. Moderate. Open daily noon to 2:50pm and 6pm to 12:30am. All major credit cards accepted. Nearest Tube: Piccadilly Circus.*

Owned by fashion guru Sir Terence Conran, this 700-seat restaurant complex contains all you'd expect: art on the walls, waiters in Armani suits, and a bustling atmosphere. The food is good, too: on the ground floor, lots of Asian-British cuisine – peanut sauces and healthy noodle and vegetable compilations. Prices here are about £15 for an average meal. Downstairs it's more expensive, though you can get a three course lunch for a set price of £19.50, but if you're eating a la carte, expect to pay in the region of £75 for two.

14. SOHO SOHO, *11-13 Frith Street, London W1. Tel. 020 7494 3491. Moderate. Open Monday to Friday noon to 2:30pm, 5:30pm to 11:30pm; Saturday 5:30pm to 11:30pm. All major credit cards accepted. Nearest Tube: Leicester Square.*

Lively, noisy and crowded, Soho Soho draws a generally young crowd, attracted by the social atmosphere (though the upstairs room is a lot calmer) and by a comprehensive, broadly Mediterranean menu that ranges from salade nicoise to steamed sea bream on linguine. The desserts include a wonderful passion fruit brulee and a baby pavlova. Wines on the list are mainly French, house red or white starting at £9.95.

Mayfair

15. LE GAVROCHE, *43 Upper Brook Street, W1. Tel. 020 7408 0881. Expensive. Open Monday to Saturday noon to 11:45pm (midnight Friday and Saturday); Sunday 11am to 11pm. All major credit cards accepted. Nearest Tube: Leicester Square.*

Once known as London's finest restaurant, things may not be quite the same as they were, but you can still be assured of a memorable meal. The establishment, formerly owned by master chef Albert Roux has handed the torch to his son Michel, who has retained many of his father's capital-C classic dishes under the heading *homage a mon pere*. It's expensive – expect to pay £80 and up – but lunch is a little more affordable at £40.

16. CHEZ NICO AT NINETY PARK LANE, *Grosvenor House, 90 Park Lane, W1. Tel. 020 7409 1290. Expensive. Open Monday to Friday, noon to 2pm, 7pm to 11pm; Saturday dinner only 7pm to 11pm. All major credit cards accepted. Nearest Tube: Marble Arch.*

If you really want somewhere to splash out on a special occasion, this is the place! Nico Ladenis, one of the world's great chefs, owns this plush

Louis XV dining room next to the Grosvenor House Hotel and offers a menu that's remarkably straightforward, yet cooked to a first-class standard. It's even been said that so tender is the lamb you can cut it with a fork! The wine list is extensive, but there are no house wines, so nothing under £20.

17. GREENHOUSE, *27A Hays Mews, London W1. Tel. 020 7499 3331. Expensive. Open Sunday to Friday noon to 2:30pm, 6:30pm to 11pm (10pm Sunday); Saturday 6:30pm to 11pm only. All major credit cards accepted. Nearest Tube: Green Park.*

Set back from the street in a quiet Mayfair mews, The Greenhouse made a lot of news when it opened in the early '90s for its emphasis on British ingredients and recipes. Fortunately, the tradition that made the news then continues today, and on a typical menu you'll find dishes like Cornish crab in a tomato vinaigrette and grilled tuna with a relish of cockles and chili. The Brit influence is maintained in the dessert menu, which contains lots of traditional favorites like rice pudding and bread and butter pudding. The house wines start at around £12.

Kensington & Knightsbridge

18. ZAFFERANO, *15 Lowndes Street, SW1. Tel. 020 7235 5800. Moderate to expensive. Open Monday to Saturday noon to 2:30pm, 7pm to 11pm. All major credit cards accepted. Nearest Tube: Knightsbridge.*

Customers (clients might be a better word) of this Lowndes Street establishment include Princess Margaret, Joan Collins, Eric Clapton and many other celebrities. This restaurant is the greatest exponent of cucina nova. Try such delights as pumpkin ravioli, minced pork wrapped in Savoy cabbage leaves and monkfish with walnuts. The desserts are excellent too, especially the Sardinian pecorino pastries served with unsweetened vanilla ice cream. Be sure to book early.

19. BIBENDUM, *Michelin House, 81 Fulham Road, SW3. Tel. 020 7581 5817. Moderate. Open daily noon to 2:30pm, 7pm to 11:30pm. All major credit cards accepted. Nearest Tube: South Kensington.*

Many people regard this as one of London's finest dining rooms, converted as it was from an Edwardian garage. The food is excellent, with a mixture of British, French and Italian dependable dishes, and some more creative offerings, like smoked eel on a thin pancake. There's a vast wine list, with house wines starting from £12.

20. BLUE ELEPHANT, *4-6 Fulham Broadway, London SW6. Tel. 020 7385 6595. Moderate. Open Sunday to Friday noon to 2:30pm, 7pm to 12:30am; Saturday dinner only 7pm to 12:30am. All major credit cards accepted. Nearest Tube: Fulham Broadway.*

It's worth taking the ride out to Fulham for the experience of dining in this Thai restaurant, in what amounts to a stage set from the film *The*

King and I. Why? There are real fishponds (with live carp – any on the menu?), lots of thatch, bamboo, waterfalls and palm trees. The waitresses, who greet you on arrival with a bow, are all dolled out David Beckham-style in silk sarongs – Mr. Beckham is a famous soccer player (and husband of Posh Spice of Spice Girl fame) who is frequently seen around town in his silk sarong – in keeping with the theme.

And the food? Well, it's good. There's a full range of classic Thai dishes, or you can really go over the top (and that would be fitting here) and try the 17-dish Royal Thai banquet. It's great value when you consifer the entertainment you're getting, too.

21. COMO LARIO, *22 Holbein Place, London SW1. Tel. 020 7730 9046. Moderate. Open Monday to Saturday 12:30pm to 2:45pm, 6:30pm to 11:30pm. All major credit cards accepted. Nearest Tube: Sloane Square.*

This lively north Italian trattoria draws a young neighborhood crowd to its premises in a Chelsea back street. The authentic Italian feel of the place is validated by the tiled floor, venetian blinds, and of course the food itself; lots of good pasta dishes as well as some classic Lombardian main dishes, like breast of chicken in lemon and cream or polenta with mushrooms and sausages. There's an extensive (Italian, what do you expect?) wine list, with house red starting at £10 a bottle.

Notting Hill
22. KENSINGTON PLACE, *201-207 Kensington Church Street, London W8. Expensive. Tel. 020 7727 3184. Open daily noon to 3pm, 6:30pm to 11:45pm. All major credit cards accepted. Nearest Tube: Notting Hill Gate.*

Brash, noisy, glass-fronted restaurant in fashionable Notting Hill, where you come as much for the people-watching as for the food. That doesn't mean that the food's not good, though – it is, with a range of old favorites to choose from, roast cod with anchovy gravy, veal kidneys on leek and potato cake and confit of duck in gooseberry sauce to name but a few. Because the place is so busy, don't expect top-notch service. At least, if you're waiting for your meal there's plenty to keep your eyes occupied.

Bloomsbury
23. NORTH SEA FISH RESTAURANT, *7 Leigh Street, WC1. Tel. 020 7387 5892. Inexpensive. Open Monday to Saturday, noon to 11pm. All major credit cards accepted. Nearest Tube: Russell Square,*

This is where to partake of that national institution – the fish and chip supper – or lunch! Battered, deep-fried cod (or plaice, a flatfish) with greasy chips and all smothered with vinegar and smattered with salt. There's nothing quite like it. If you prefer to have your fish grilled, they can deal with that, too, but what's the point? The whole raison d'etre here, it seems, is to allow foreigners to sample the delights of the British national dish, which they'll enjoy so much, they'll want to take it back home. You can eat in or take away.

24. MUSEUM STREET CAFE, *47 Museum Street, WC1. Tel. 020 7405 3211. Inexpensive. Open Monday to Friday, 9am to 10pm. Credit cards: MC, Visa. Nearest Tube: Tottenham Court Road.*

This small, intimate cafe close to the British Museum serves a selection of salads and sandwiches at lunchtime, and a more extensive menu in the evenings, when you might try chicken with pesto.

25. WAGAMAMA, *4 Streatham Street, London WC1. Tel. 020 7323 9223. Inexpensive. Open daily noon to 11pm. All major credit cards accepted. Nearest Tube: Tottenham Court Road.*

London's first Japanese noodle bar is still probably the best. Located in a stark basement just around the corner from the British Museum, it's a magnet for students from the nearby University of London, on account of the quality and of the price – main courses range from between £5 to £7.50. Inside, you sit at long communal tables where the waiter, armed with electronic notepad, will take your order: noodle dishes with chicken, pork, seafood or beef; fried dishes and curries. Green tea is free, and there are Japanese beers and sake. Wine starts at about £9.50. This is a great place to go if you want to eat well on a strict budget; even if you're not, it's worth a visit anyway.

26. ALFRED, *245 Shaftesbury Avenue, London WC2. Tel. 020 7240 2566. Moderate. Open Monday to Friday noon to 3:30pm, 6pm to 11pm, Saturday dinner only 6pm to 11pm. All major credit cards accepted. Nearest Tube: Tottenham Court Road.*

Alfred, just around the corner from the British Museum, is one of the new breed of restaurants offering authentic British food. Unlike the pricier outfits, Alfred manages to succeed in maintaining reasonable, if not low, prices. Expect to find choices like Welsh lamb shank with garlic mash, braised knuckle of bacon with pease pudding, bubble and squeak (leftover cabbage and potatoes fried together in a pan), wild boar sausages and the like. Desserts like chocolate tart and gingerbread complete the picture. The bulk of the wine list is English, with prices starting at £12 a bottle.

South Of The River

27. OXO TOWER RESTAURANT, *Oxo Tower Wharf, Barge House Street, London SE1. Tel. 020 7803 3888. Expensive. Open daily noon to 3pm (3:30pm Sunday), 6pm to 11:30pm (6:30pm to 11pm Sunday). All major credit cards accepted. Nearest Tube: Blackfriars (you'll need to walk across Blackfriars Bridge).*

For those of you who don't know, Oxo was (and still is) Britain's favorite beef and chicken stock – a little brown cube you crumble into a jug and add hot water to – so popular that it's said Brits not only have blood in their veins, but Oxo too. The Oxo tower, on London's South Bank, is the converted former Oxo headquarters, now offering one of the most spectacular dining spots in the city – an eighth floor room from which you can look across the Thames to the famous city skyline, the dome of St. Paul's at the center.

If the view isn't enough for you, just wait 'till you've sampled the food, which includes a number of fish options as well as year-round and seasonal meat specialties. There's an extensive choice of desserts, and an equally extensive wine list. It is on the expensive side, but remember that you're paying for the view as well as what you're eating.

SEEING THE SIGHTS

London is such a vast city, that it's impossible to see everything in one trip for, as Dr. Johnson said, "When a man is tired of London, he is tired of life." It's best to concentrate on some of the main visitor attractions before exploring some of the nooks and crannies that make London one of the most fascinating cities in the world.

THE TOWER OF LONDON

London's top visitor attraction is best known for its gory associations with many of the nation's most famous historical figures, such as **Anne Boleyn** and **Sir Thomas More**, and for its famous **"Beefeaters"** or yeomen of the guard – honorary members of the Queen's bodyguard, who double up as very informative and helpful tour guides.

There has been a fortress on the site since Roman times, though little of the original fortress, save a few walls, remains. It was **William the Conqueror**, seeking to consolidate his new power base in London, who built the **White Tower** in 1078. With walls up to 15 feet thick and at 90 feet in height, the Tower stands sentinel over the rest of the fortress. Inside, there has been a collection of armor since the time of Henry VII (though the national collection is now kept in Leeds) and in the basement (where else?) there's also an exhibition of implements used in various methods of torture.

A more reflective atmosphere pervades in the **Chapel of St. John**, on the second floor, pure and simple Norman in style. Close to the White Tower is another spiritual oasis; the **Chapel of St. Peter ad Vincula**, now fully restored to its Tudor glory, with a fine ceiling made from Spanish chestnut, and the tombs of Anne Boleyn, Catherine Howard and Sir Thomas More, now officially a saint. The chapel can only be entered as part of an official tour.

Other parts of the Tower to note are the **Bloody Tower**, where the Little Princes (Edwards V and the Duke of York) are said to have been

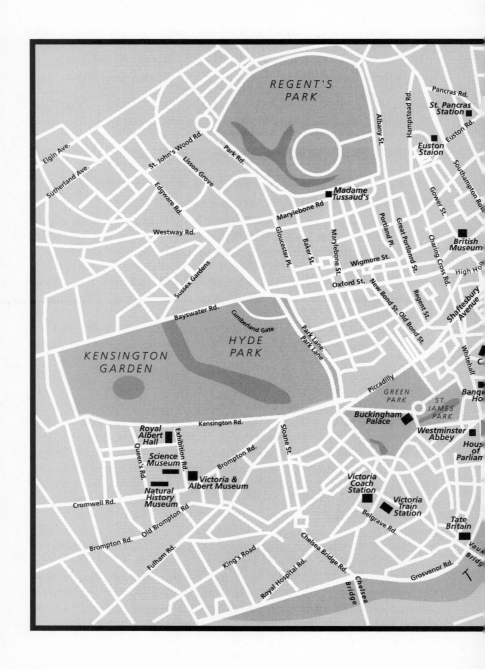

REGENT'S PARK

Pancras Rd.

Hampstead Rd.

St. Pancras Station

Albany St.

Euston Rd.

Elgin Ave.

Euston Staion

St. John's Wood Rd.

Park Rd.

Southampton Row

Lisson Grove

Gower St.

Sutherland Ave.

Edgware Rd.

Westway Rd.

Madame Tussaud's

Marylebone Rd

Portland Pl.

Charing Cross Rd.

British Museum

Gloucester Pl.

Baker St.

Marylebone St.

Great Portland St.

High Ho

Sussex Gardens

Wigmore St.

New Bond St.

Old Bond St.

Regent St.

Oxford St.

Shaftesbury Avenue

Bayswater Rd.

Cumberland Gate

Park Lane

Whitehall

HYDE PARK

Park Lane

KENSINGTON GARDEN

Piccadilly

GREEN PARK

Banq Ho

ST. JAMES PARK

Buckingham Palace

Kensington Rd.

Royal Albert Hall

Exhibition Rd.

Sloane St.

Westminster Abbey

Hous of Parliam

Queen's Rd.

Science Museum

Brompton Rd.

Victoria & Albert Museum

Natural History Museum

Cromwell Rd.

Victoria Coach Station

Old Brompton Rd

Victoria Train Station

Tate Britain

Brompton Rd.

Belgrave Rd.

Fulham Rd.

King's Road

Chelsea Bridge Rd.

Vaux Bridg

Royal Hospital Rd.

Chelsea Bridge

Grosvenor Rd.

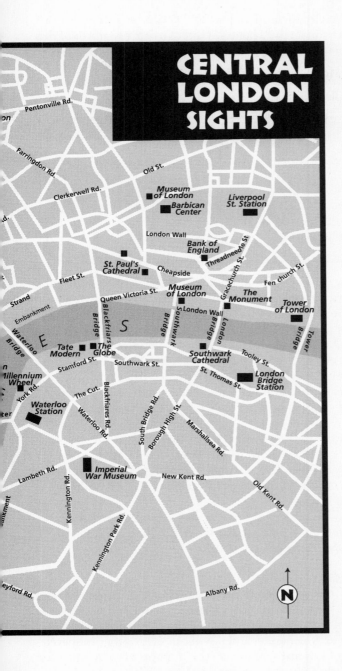

murdered by their uncle, Richard II, and the **Traitor's Gate**, once the Tower's main entrance from the Thames. Tower Green, just north of the Tower, and outside its walls was the main **mass execution** site, while privileged prisoners like Anne Boleyn, and Katherine Howard (two of Henry VIII's wives) Lady Jane Grey and Sir Thomas More met their grisly end inside the complex.

THE TOWER RAVENS

Six large ravens are kept in the Tower and are listed as official Tower residents. They're all extremely well-looked after, receiving special rations every day. They have to be: Legend says that as long as the birds remain in the Tower, the monarchy will survive. No wonder they had their wings clipped – although everyone had a scare when one was ravaged by a bull terrier (it managed to survive).

There's a happier atmosphere in the **Jewel House**, the main attraction within the Tower complex, though not, perhaps, when there's a vast queue as there can be for much of the summer season. Among the most spectacular pieces of jewelry are the **Imperial State Crown**, worn by the Queen when she opens Parliament, and made for Victoria's coronation in 1838. It contains nearly 3,000 stones, mainly diamonds, including a priceless ruby worn by Henry V at the Battle of Agincourt in 1415, and the **Second Star of Africa**, a 320-carat diamond. Even bigger is the **First Star of Africa**, the largest cut diamond in the world that's part of the **Sceptre with the Cross**.

If you're here at the right time, you might catch one of the Tower's ancient ceremonies – the **Ceremony of the Keys**, which goes back more than 700 years. Every night at 9:40, a sentry is challenged at the gate. His response, "Who goes there?" is followed by an identification of the keys and the presenting of arms.

Open Monday to Saturday 9am to 6pm, Sunday 10am to 6pm. Admission adults £10.50, children £6.90, family ticket (2 adults, 2 children) £31. Tel. 0171 709 0765. Nearest Tube: Tower Hill.

WESTMINSTER ABBEY

Founded by Saxon **King Edward** (later venerated and known as "The Confessor") in 1065, Westminster Abbey was once part of a Benedictine monastic foundation. Harold was crowned king here in 1066, as was his vanquisher, **William of Normandy**, and just about every other monarch (except Edward V and Edward VIII) since. It's an impressive building in its own right, especially following the major clean up it received in the

1980s and 1990s, and very much the "**national church**," for which reason it can seem rather cluttered with tombs and monuments to hundreds of Britain's most worthy citizens. It's also the last resting place of dozens of royal personages, so that sometimes it can seem more like a museum than a place of worship. It has also been the setting for countless **national events** –the weddings and funerals of kings and queens, and of course, more recently the moving funeral service for Diana, Princess of Wales.

The present building dates largely from the 13th and 14th centuries, a rebuild of Edward's original 11th century edifice, though the twin towers at the west end are much later; they were designed by **Sir Christopher Wren**, and added in the 17th century.

Entering by the west door, the **nave**, with its fine fan-vaulting, spreads out before you as far as the intricately gilded choir screen, beyond which lies one of the highlights of the Abbey, the **Henry VII Chapel**. Close to the west door is the **Tomb of the Unknown Warrior**, an anonymous World War I soldier, whose grave symbolises the tragedy of war, while just a few paces away is the marble slab memorial to **Sir Winston Churchill**, whose funeral service took place here in 1965.

Pass through into the **choir** area, with its 19th century stalls, and into the **North Transept**, whose **Rose Window** is one of the largest of its kind in Britain. To proceed further, into the Henry VII Chapel and beyond, it's necessary to pay a further admission charge, but it's worth it. The Chapel, with its fine rib-vaulting, carvings and sculptures, has often been described as "the finest in Christendom." Here, you can see the white marble tomb of **Elizabeth I**, buried with her half-sister **Mary I**.

Further on is the **Chapel of Edward the Confessor**, where, next to the saints' shrine, stands the **Coronation Chair**, on which most coronations have taken place. The Stone of Scone, which had graced the chair for centuries, was recently returned to Scotland from whence it originally came.

Another focal point for visitors is **Poets' Corner**, which contains monuments to just about every luminary of British literature, starting with Chaucer, and including Shakespeare, Tennyson, Hardy and the poet Dylan Thomas.

Other Abbey attractions worth at least a peep are the 13th century **Chapter House**, and the **Museum**, located in the Norman undercroft with a motley collection of artifacts, including wax effigies, old religious vestments and ancient documents.

Open Monday to Friday 9:20am to 3:45pm, Saturday 9am to 1:45pm. Admission Royal Chapels, nave and cloisters adults £5, children £2; Abbey Museum, Pyx Chamber and Chapter House £1 extra. Tel. 0171 222 5152. www.westminster-abbey.org Nearest Tube: Westminster.

THE HOUSES OF PARLIAMENT

Just across the road from Westminster Abbey, the Victorian Gothic Houses of Parliament are dwarfed by the 363-foot high **St. Stephen's Tower**, containing **Big Ben** – which is not the name of the clock but of the **bell** that strikes the hour. This was the site of the **Royal Palace of Westminster**, where kings and queens lived until they moved to Whitehall. The present building, designed by the architect Pugin, dates from 1840, replacing an earlier building that was burned down in the 1830s, though enemy bombing during World War II also wreaked considerable destruction.

The two Houses, the **House of Commons**, where 650 **MPs** (members of Parliament) sit, is built in the shape of a chapel, with the two major political parties facing each other in a confrontational way. Debates can often be very lively and noisy, with constant heckling, provoking the **Speaker** to cry "Order, order!" The **House of Lords**, which has undergone considerable constitutional reforms in recent years, meaning that hereditary peers no longer have an automatic right to a seat, is generally a more sedate affair.

The two Houses of Parliament are in general closed to the public, but it is possible to watch a debate from the **Strangers' Gallery**, though it may involve a long wait in line. US or Canadian citizens might expedite things by getting a special pass from the US Embassy or Canadian High Commission; though both can only issue four tickets a day. *Information: Tel. 020 7219 4272. Nearest Tube: Westminster.*

SOME SUGGESTIONS FOR AFTERNOON TEA

Brown's Hotel, *Albermarle Street W1, Tel. 020 7493 6020. Need to book. Price £19.95.*

Capital Hotel, *Basil Street SW3, Tel. 020 7589 5171. Pleasant small hotel. £15.50.*

Connaught Hotel, *Carlos Place W1, Tel. 020 7499 7070. £14.45.*

Fortnum & Masons, *Poccadilly W1, Tel. 020 7734 8040. Tea in the St. Jame's Restaurant. Price £16.50.*

Lanesborough Hotel, *1 Lanesborough Place W1, Tel. 020 7259 5599. Magnificent setting. Price £19.50. Booking recommended.*

The Ritz, *Piccadilly W1, Tel. 020 7493 8181. THE place for tea. Book well in advance. Full tea £24.50.*

BUCKINGHAM PALACE

The Queen's central London residence was originally built in red brick for the **Duke of Buckingham**, then purchased in 1762 by George III who needed space for his 15 children and courtiers. The palace was expanded and remodeled so that today it stands 360 feet long and contains 600 rooms. Visitors can tell if the Queen is in residence by the presence (or not) of the **Royal Standard** flying from above the central portico. Much public anger was vented during the period after the death of Diana, Princess of Wales, by the Crown's initial refusal to lower the flag to half-mast – for reasons of protocol. The Queen finally relented, but it was a public relations disaster.

The Palace is not generally open to the public, but a small number of rooms may be open in the summer. However, just round the corner from the palace, in a former chapel accessed from Buckingham Palace Road, is the **Queen's Gallery**, offering samples from what is recognized as the finest private art collection in the world. This includes famous works like Vermeer's *The Music Lesson* and others by Rubens, Rembrandt and Canaletto.

Many tourists come to the building to watch the **Changing of the Guard**, an impressive ceremony that takes place every morning from early April to mid-August and every other morning the rest of the year, at 11:30am precisely. The ceremony lasts about half an hour, and involves a new guard, preceded by a marching band, coming from the Wellington or Chelsea barracks to take over from the old guard. A similar ceremony takes place yards away at **Horse Guards Parade**, just off Whitehall, starting at 11am Mondays through Fridays and 10am on Sunday. Both ceremonies are curtailed in winter, from October 1 to March 31, when it officially takes place on even calendar days in October, December and February. *Nearest Tube: St. James's.*

MADAME TUSSAUD'S

You can see the Queen again at one of London's most enduring tourist attractions, Madame Tussaud's, on Marylebone Road. Tussaud's owes its existence to a certain **Dr. Curtius**, who in 1770 opened an exhibition of life-size wax models in Paris. His niece, Marie Tussaud, learned the secret of making lifelike replicas of famous people, and the Madame Tussaud's concept was born.

While some of the older figures on display come from molds taken by Madame Tussaud herself, most of the models are much later. They include effigies of kings and queen through the ages, past and current world leaders, and of course rock, pop and sports stars – a real who's who.

Most popular, especially with younger visitors, is the **Chamber of Horrors**, where some of the world's most grisly murder and torture scenes have been captured in real life; there's even a Victorian London Street with a figure of Jack the Ripper lurking in the shadows!

New technologies have been adopted to bring some of the models "to life." There's also a garden party where you can mix with the rich and famous and a new attraction which explores Madame Tussaud's 200-year history.

Marylebone Road. Open Monday to Friday 10am to 5.30pm, Saturday and Sunday from 9.30am. Admission, adults £9.50, children £6.25, under 5s free. Tel. 0207 935 6861. Nearest Tube: Baker Street.

ST. PAUL'S CATHEDRAL

Completed in 1710 and replacing an even larger medieval cathedral, St. Paul's still manages to dominate the City skyline, despite the encroaching skyscrapers. **Old St. Paul's** was ravaged by the **Great Fire of London**, and had such a terrible reputation for sleaze anyway that rather than rebuild, a whole new design was sought. This was provided by **Sir Christopher Wren**, whose new Renaissance-style structure stretches just over 500 feet in length and 365 feet from ground level to the top of the dome – a fitting scene for the royal wedding of Prince Charles to Diana.

St. Paul's classical **dome** dominates the building. You can climb to the level of the **Whispering Gallery** (so-called because a visitor whispering into the wall on one side can be heard by another on the other side) and higher still to the **Stone Gallery**, for a spectacular 360 degree view of London.

The cathedral is made out in the shape of a Latin cross, but contains few art treasures (Grinling Gibbon's exceptional **choir stalls** being an exception), but there are a host of monuments, including one to the **Duke of Wellington**, and a very fine memorial chapel to the American servicemen and women who lost their lives while stationed in the UK during WWII.

Below the nave, the crypt contains tombs and monuments to a number of statesmen and military leaders such as **Admiral Nelson**, and there's a fascinating scale model of the old cathedral, with its 500-foot spire, 100 feet higher than Salisbury Cathedral's, England's tallest.

One of highlights of this and of many other English cathedrals is the opportunity to listen to the **choir**. The service of **Evensong** is performed here daily at 5pm on weekdays and 3:15pm Sundays, by the men's and boy's choir of St. Paul's – one of the finest in the world.

Open Monday to Saturday 8:30am to 4pm. Admission free, but charge to crypt: adults £4, children £2. Tel. 0207 236 4128. Nearest Tube: St. Paul's.

THE BRITISH MUSEUM

The mind-blowing British Museum, on Great Russell Street in Bloomsbury, contains one of the most extensive collections of art and artifacts in the world, including world-famous collections of **antiquities** from Egypt, Western Asia, Greece and Rome, as well as Prehistoric and Romano-British, Medieval renaissance, Modern and Oriental collections; prints and drawings; coins, medals and banknotes – some six and a half million objects, ranging from fragments of ancient manuscripts to colossal statues and all spread out over 13 acres. Although it may sound overwhelming, the great thing about this vast collection is that it's so well laid out that you can easily call it quits one day and resume your tour another.

As you enter the front hall, you may want to check out the **Assyrian Transept**. Here, the winged and human-headed bulls and lions that once guarded the gateways to the palaces of Assyrian kings. Nearby is the **Black Obelisk of Shalmaneser III**, depicting Jehu, King of Israel, paying tribute. From here you can access the hall of Egyptian sculpture and see the famous **Rosetta Stone**, whose discovery paved the way to the decoding of heiroglyphics. Also on the ground floor is the **Duveen gallery**, where the renowned **Elgin Marbles** – still the cause of much friction between Britain and Greece, who desire their return – are located.

Also on the ground floor is the **Manuscripts Room**, where you can see an amazing range of manuscripts of every kind – Dickens' hand-written draft of *Nicholas Nickelby*, the original manuscripts of several Beatles' songs, Handel's *Messiah*, an original **Magna Carta**, a 15th century edition of Chaucer's *Canterbury Tales* and the famous **Gutenburg Bible** of 1455.

On the second floor are the galleries of **Medieval and Later Antiquities**. One of the most interesting exhibits here is the remains of an **Anglo-Saxon burial ship**, discovered at Sutton Hoo in Suffolk, which contains gold jewelry, armor, weapons, silverware and other implements.

The main attractions of the **upper floor** are the **Egyptian Antiquities**, the largest and most comprehensive collection of its kind outside Cairo. **Room 63** is magnificent, looking like something from a Hollywood epic, including **mummies**. The collection illustrates every aspect of ancient Egyptian culture from pre-dynastic times (circa 4000 BC) to the Coptic period (12th century AD) including a large amount of material from Nubia and the Sudan. The recently installed Japanese galleries on the top floor are softly lit, uncrowded and well worth a visit.

If you need a break, there's a pleasant **cafe** on the ground floor, just past the bookshop, where you can get tea, coffee and sandwiches. For something more substantial, try the **restaurant** (hot meals from about £5).

Great Russell Street. Open Monday to Saturday 10am to 5pm, Sunday noon to 6pm. Admission free. Tel. 0207 636 1555. Nearest stations: Holborn, Tottenham Court Road.

THE VICTORIA AND ALBERT MUSEUM

This museum prides itself on being the largest and most influential **decorative arts** museum in the world. Located on Cromwell Road in South Kensington, its 146 galleries reflect centuries of achievement in such varied fields as ceramics, sculpture, furniture, jewelry and textiles.

This visually stunning Gothic building also contains the National Collections of sculpture, glass, ceramics, watercolors, portrait miniatures and photographs, and also houses the National Art Library.

Founded in 1852 as a Museum of Manufacturers, its aim was to educate British manufacturers by building on the success of the previous year's **Great Exhibition**. It moved from Marlborough House, where it became known as the Victoria and South Kensington Museum, later renamed the Victoria and Albert Museum in honor of the widowed Victoria's husband, whose brainchild it had been.

Among the museum's many treasures are the 12th century **Eltinberg Reliquary**, the early English **Gloucester candlestick** and the **Syon cope**, a priceless vestment woven in England in the 14th century.

Cromwell Road. Open daily 10am to 5:45pm. Admission adults £5, seniors £3, students and under 18s free. Tel. 0207 938 8441. Nearest Tube: South Kensington.

THE NATURAL HISTORY MUSEUM

This massive Victorian cathedral of natural history is located next door to the Victoria and Albert (the V&A) in Cromwell Road and is the most visited of all the London museums. On entrance, you'll be met by a huge 80 feet long, 150 million year-old **Diplodocus** dinosaur, surrounded by glass cases containing **fossils** of various creatures – such as lions, elephants and bears – associated with Africa and Asia today but which millions of years ago roamed free in the area where you're now standing.

Kids (but maybe not mom) will love the **Creepy Crawlies Gallery**, with its gigantic enlarged scorpion and a host of cuddly tarantulas, and everyone will be thrilled by the **Earth Galleries**, where, among other things, you can see a mock-up of a shop damaged during the 1995 earthquake at Kobe, Japan. As with its neighbor, the V&A, your biggest problem will be where to start.

Cromwell Road. Open Monday to Saturday 10am to 5:50pm, Sunday 11am to 5:50pm. Admission adults £6, children £3, under 5s free. Tel. 0207 942 5000. Nearest Tube: South Kensington.

THE NATIONAL PORTRAIT GALLERY

Many of the most famous faces from English history can be found at the National Portrait Gallery, just behind the National Gallery off Trafalgar

Square. Gaze into the lecherous eyes of **Henry VIII**, exchange doleful looks with **D.H Lawrence**, and try to amuse **Queen Victoria**. Most of the portraits are by famous artists, such as Sir Joshua Reynolds, Holbein right through to Andy Warhol. There's a wonderful painting of **Sir Winston Churchill** by Walter Sickert, and the famous George Beresford photograph of **Virginia Woolf**.

On the next landing, you'll find a roomful of portraits of the current royal family, including several of the Queen, one of which, reportedly, particularly upset her.

Then on the next floor, there's Boldini's portrait of **Lady Colin Campbell**, a Rodin bust and a portrait of the **Bronte sisters** painted by their artist brother Brangwen. On level four, a roomful of **English kings** is on display, all painted in the 16th century on board in the style of Holbein, while on **level 5** there are some wonderful Gainsboroughs and Reynolds. The main problem with the gallery is that in order to see some its best pieces, you have to wade through scores of (mostly) insignificant characters to get to the really good ones!

St. Martin's Place. Open Monday to Saturday 10am to 6pm, Sunday noon to 6pm. Admission free. Tel. 020 7306 0055. Nearest Tube: Leicester Square.

THE TATE GALLERIES

The Tate Gallery on Millbank has been a repository of post-1500 British art and international modern art for well over a century, but never more than a small fraction of the collection was ever on display because of its size. In the 1990s, work started on converting a disused power station on Bankside, south of the River, into a massive new gallery to house the modern art collection – to be known as the **Tate Modern**, while the collection of British art remained at the old Tate, now called the **Tate Britain**. Amazingly, admission to both galleries is free (though donations are requested), During the summer, a special free **ArtBus** links the two galleries between 10am and 6pm.

Tate Britain

The Tate Britain holds the largest collection of British art in the world, with works by Blake, Constable, Epstein, Hockney, Hogarth and Rossetti. Like the National Gallery, the volume of works on show is staggering, and more than one visit may be required. Among the Tate's highlights are William Hogarth's *O The Roast Beef of Old England* and *Satan, Sin and Death*, several works by famous 18th century British artists Sir Joshua Reynolds and Sir Thomas Gainsborough, and a collection of works by J.M. Turner, left to the nation by the artist himself and displayed in the new Clore Gallery. There's a room dedicated to another great British landscape artist, John Constable. The Tate Gallery Restaurant is almost a work of art in itself; an elegant dining room decorated with murals by Rex Whistler, while the adjacent cafe serves cakes, croissants, sandwiches and salads at reasonable prices.

Located at Millbank, London SW1. Open year-round daily 10am to 5:30pm. Admission free (but donations welcome). Tel. 020 7887 8000. Nearest Tube: Pimlico.

Tate Modern

This breathtaking new gallery displays the Tate's collection of modern art from 1900 to the present in a converted power station that had been an eyesore for years. The former Turbine Hall, which runs the length of the building, is now an awe-inspiring entrance hall. From here, you're swept up by escalator through two floors, featuring a café, shops and auditorium to three levels of galleries. At the top of the building is a two-story glass roof that provides natural light for the galleries as well as the location for a café, which provides stunning views over London. And the art? Well, among the amazing collection of pieces on display are works by Bacon, Dali, Matisee, Picasso and Warhol, to name but a few. This truly is one of London's greatest attractions and is a must-see for anyone who is even remotely interested in art.

Located at Bankside, SE1. Open Sunday to Thursday 10am to 6pm, Friday and Saturday 10am to 10pm. Admission free, but donation welcome. Tel. 020 7887 8000. Nearest Tune: Blackfriars or Southwark.

THE NATIONAL GALLERY

Occupying one side of Trafalgar Square, the neoclassical National Gallery houses one of the most comprehensive collections of **western paintings** in the world, the largest part of which is dedicated to Italian works, now housed in the controversial new **Sainsbury Wing**. Given the number of works on display, it's remarkably uncluttered.

The collection spans the history of art from the 13th to the 20th century. Among the earliest works, the **Wilton Diptych** (French School, late 14th century) is the greatest treasure. It shows Richard II being introduced to the Madonna and Child by John the Baptist and Saxon King Edward the Confessor (founder of Westminster Abbey).

Italian art is represented by Masaccio, della Francesca, da Vinci, Michelangelo, a roomful of Raphaels, with the breathtaking *Crucifixion* as a centerpiece, and notable works by Titian, Tintoretto and Veronese. Northern European painters are well represented; Breughel's *Adoration*, Vermeer's *Young Woman at a Virginal* and de Hooch's *Patio in a House in Delft* being three of the most memorable.

There's a roomful of Rembrandts, including four stunning portraits, a roomful of Rubens, Van Dyke's massive and famous painting of an equestrian Charles I, and paintings by some of the greatest home-grown artists – Constable, Turner, Reynolds, Gainsborough and Hogarth, as well as three giants of Spanish art – Velesquez, El Greco, and Goya.

Other rooms are dedicated to **French** painters, such as Delacroix and Ingres, 19th century impressionists like Manet, Monet and Renoir, and post-impressionists like Cezanne and Van Gogh.

If you need refreshment here, the Brasserie restaurant on the first floor of the Sainsbury Wing has an Italian-style coffee bar, which includes sandwiches and salads and more exotic fare (Lincolnshire sausages, grilled vegetables, etc.) at lunchtime.

Trafalgar Square. Open daily 10am to 6pm. Admission free. Tel. 020 7747 2885. Nearest Tube: Charing Cross.

THE MUSEUM OF LONDON

This modern concrete and glass building traces the history of London from the Ice Age through to the present in a combination of ancient antiquities, costume, furniture, war posters, ration books and all kinds of memorabilia.

While the Ice Age exhibition is a must for kids, it's best to breeze through here to **Roman London**, where you can see a mammoth tooth found near Downing Street, a chopping tool found near the Bloomsbury YMCA and a pair of bone tweezers, and an new addition – a reconstruction of a London street in Roman times, complete with sounds – and smells!

Don't forget that London was an important city in Roman times. This section contains a reconstructed Roman kitchen, dining room and dressing table with elaborate jewelry and cosmetics from the period. Further on, a Viking battle ax is a reminder of a ninth century invasion of London by 300 Viking ships.

Further displays include the construction of the original **London Bridge** in about 1200, maps of medieval England, and building of a **Tudor house**, **Oliver Cromwell's** death mask, and the original **Mortality Broadsheet** listing the names of all the London plague deaths between November 1602 and November 1603 – all 37,000 of them. There's a display about the **Great Fire of London** in 1666, complete with a narration from Samuel Pepys' diary.

You can also see the Lord Mayor of London's Coach, still used once a year on Lord Mayor's Day, an 1890 hansom cab, an art deco elevator from Selfridge's store on Oxford Street, and a reconstructed 19th century High Street. There's a large costume department where the stars are various Roman vestments and a 19th century dandy's outfit.

150 London Wall, near Barbican Centre. Open Monday to Saturday 10am to 5:50pm, Sunday noon to 5:50pm. Admission adults £5, children £3. Tel. 020 7730 0717. Nearest Tube: Barbican.

LESSER KNOWN SIGHTS

THE BANQUETING HOUSE

Inigo Jones (1573-1652) created this banqueting hall in 1622 out of an old remnant of the Tudor **Palace of Whitehall**. Influenced by the Italian Palladio's work, Jones restructured the palace with Palladian sophistication. Charles I later employed the Flemish painter Rubens to paint the ceiling; the allegorical paintings, depicting a wise king being received into heaven, were ironically the last thing Charles saw before being beheaded on a scaffold outside the building on January 30, 1649.

Whitehall. Open Monday to Saturday 10am to 5pm. Admission £3.50. Nearest Tube: Charing Cross.

IMPERIAL WAR MUSEUM

It sounds stuffy, as if it should be full of retired white-moustached colonels, but in reality this old museum that occupies the former bedlam asylum offers a well-put-together, child-friendly museum that avoids glamorizing its subject. Of course, there's all the stuff you'd expect to find in a war museum: **Spitfires**, a Polaris missile, part of the Messerschmidt flown by **Rudolph Hess**. You can even look through the eyepiece of a German mast periscope, first used in 1917, and now, surprisingly perhaps, offering a bird's eye view of London.

It's the **lower level** that's the more stimulating, with dozens of interactive exhibits, German propaganda films on the invasion of Europe, a moving account of life in London during the WWII Blitz taken with a home movie camera, and an even more moving film of the liberation of **Belsen Camp**. For most people, the highlight of the museum is the **Blitz Experience** – a recreation of life in London during an enemy air raid that starts in a cramped bunker with all the associated sounds effects. When the siren gives the all-clear, you can wander out and witness the devastation of a London suburb. **The Trench Experience**, depicting life in a World War I trench and **Operation Jericho**, a simulated RAF (Royal Air Force) flight across occupied Europe, are also powerful. Upstairs there are galleries, a self-service cafe and a gift shop.

Lambeth Road, SE1. Open daily 10am to 6pm. Admission adults £5.20 (free after 4:30pm), children free. Tel. 020 7416 5320. Nearest Tube: Lambeth North.

THE LONDON EYE (MILLENNIUM WHEEL)

This huge ferris wheel – the largest of its kind in the world – was finally hauled upright a few weeks after schedule – New Year's Eve 1999/2000.

Since opening, the 500-feet high wheel with its 32 glass capsules has become one of London's most popular tourist attractions. The wheel moves 'round extremely slowly – one revolution takes around 20 minutes – affording passengers spectacular views over the whole city and beyond. It's a great place to start your London visit.

Jubilee Gardens, South Bank, London SE1. Open daily April to mid-September 9am to 10pm (last entry 9:30pm); mid-September to March 10am to 6pm (last entry 5:30pm). Fees: Adult £8.50, children £5, seniors £5.95, students £7.95. For tickets, call 0870 5000 600. Nearest Tube: Waterloo.

LONDON ZOO

This well-kept zoo opened in 1828 with a collection of gifts to the royal family: a hippo, two giraffes, a chimp and a number of thylacines (marsupials, known as Tasmanian wolves, sadly now extinct). The zoo's collection has expanded greatly since then, and along with all the expected residents you can see: an anoa, a pudu, a leadbetter's possum, a bird-eating spider and a herd of oyrx – and an excellent reptile house, just as frightening as any Chamber of Horrors! There's also a Children's Zoo with goats, sheep, ponies and rabbits for petting, and a selection of cafes and restaurants serving hot and cold food at reasonable prices.

Regent's Park. Open daily 10am to 5:30pm (last admission 4pm). Admission adults £9, children £7 (under 4s free). Family ticket £28. Tel. 020 7722 3333. Nearest Tube: Regent's Park.

DOWNING STREET

This unassuming street of row houses has contained, at **Number 10**, the official London home of the **Prime Minister**. Access to the residence is limited for obvious reasons. The **cabinet office**, where important decisions of state are taken, is on the ground floor, while the prime minister resides in an apartment on the top floor. **Number 11** is official residence of the **Chancellor of the Exchequer**, the British finance minister.

Nearest Tube: Westminster.

LAMBETH PALACE

Since the 13th century Lambeth Palace has been the London residence of the **Archbishop of Canterbury**, spiritual head of the Anglican Communion. Located on the south bank almost opposite St. Thomas Hospital, the Palace is rarely open to the public, but you can admire the fine Tudor gateway from the outside.

Nearest Tube: Westminster.

HYDE PARK

Hyde Park, central London's largest green space, bounded by Park Lane to the east, started life as one of Henry VIII's hunting grounds. Today, its 350 acres is mostly laid to grass, with fine trees, shrubs, and a lake – the **Serpentine** – where Londoners take a dip on hot days in the summer (and even on cold days in the winter). The Park's southern boundary, **Rotten Row**, is used by the Household Cavalry, who are based at the nearby Knightsbridge Barracks. With its wide open expanses, Hyde Park is just perfect for flying that kite, or as a venue for Luciano Pavarotti and others when they feel moved to sing in the park.

Several Tube lines serve the Park. The most convenient is Hyde Park Corner.

TOURS & GUIDED WALKS

Here are just a handful of the literally hundreds of guided walking tours around London. Call for full tour itineraries;

Architectural Dialogue, *Tel. 020 8341 1371*
Historical Walks of London, *Tel. 020 8668 4019*
The Londoner Pub Walks, *Tel. 020 8883 2656*
The London Walking Forum, *Tel. 01992 717711*
The Original London Walks, *Tel. 020 7624 3978*
Pied Piper Walks, *Tel. 020 7435 4782*
Stepping Out Walking Tours, *Tel. 020 8881 2933*
Walk the Millennium Mile, *Tel. 020 7261 9211*

ST. JAMES'S PARK

More ornate than Hyde Park, St. James's Park is a pretty space, where hundreds of ducks congregate and generations of Londoners have sat and basked in the sun. The view from the bridge on the lake over to Westminster, with its spires and turrets, is particularly enchanting – like something from a fairy tale. The northern side of the Park is bounded by **The Mall**, a wide tree-lined thoroughfare that leads from Trafalgar Square to Buckingham Palace. This is an excellent vantage point for many of the more elaborate state occasions, particularly when there is a visiting head of state.

Nearest Tube: St. James's Park.

TRAFALGAR SQUARE

London's main square is the geographical center of the city – all distances are measured from here. The wide open space, flanked by such buildings as the **National Gallery** and **St. Martin-in-the-Fields** (see below), has become a focal point for political demonstrations over the years, as well as for the capital's main New Year's party when the fountains come in very handy. Center stage is **Nelson's Column**, a 170-foot high granite plinth with a 17-foot, often pigeon-encrusted Lord Nelson standing sentinel on top. The reliefs round the base depict scenes from his life and were made from cannons he captured. Feeding the pigeons in Trafalgar Square does little to enhance the beauty of the place, but it's what every little boy and girl – and some bigger ones – want to do.

Nearest Tube: Charing Cross.

ST MARTIN-IN-THE-FIELDS

Probably London's most famous church after the cathedrals and abbey, St. Martin's was built in 1726 by the architect James Gibbs, whose classic design became the inspiration for countless colonial churches in the US. The church is popular with music lovers – the **Academy of St. Martin-in-the-Fields** was formed here – and concerts take place frequently throughout the year. The church has a fine reputation for caring for London's homeless, work that is partly funded by the excellent restaurant in the crypt. Here also is the **London Brass Rubbing Centre**, where you can find all the bits and pieces needed to make your own souvenir knight from replica tomb brasses.

Trafalgar Square. Nearest Tube: Charing Cross.

ST. PAUL'S COVENT GARDEN

This interesting and elegant church was built during the reign of Charles II, and has become known as the "Actors' Church" on account of all the tombs and monuments to British actors. Check out the memorial to Lawrence Olivier.

St. Paul's Church, Bedford Street, Covent Garden. Nearest Tube: Covent Garden.

THE SCIENCE MUSEUM

Geared primarily to schoolchildren, the Science Museum hardly inspires awe like its neighbor the Natural History Museum. But it's a fascinating place, full of hands-on exhibits and treasures, including the **Puffing Billy**, the oldest train in the world, and the **Exploration of Space Exhibition**, with the original **Apollo 10** capsule on view. Better still is the **Land Transport** exhibit, loaded with trains, cars (including a **1909 Silver Ghost Rolls Royce**), buses, bicycles and motorcycles, a 1910 horse-drawn coal trolley that still whiffs strongly of coal, and a huge 1923 Express locomotive. With sections on telecommunications, computing, nuclear physics and chemistry and a **History of Medicine** Exhibit, this is the place for all would-be scientists – and anyone else who can't resist pressing buttons.

Exhibition Road, South Kensington. Open daily 10am to 6pm. Admission adults £6.50, children £3.50. Tel. 020 7938 8080. Nearest Tube: South Kensington.

THE MONUMENT

This strange-looking column topped by a golden ball is the work of Sir Christopher Wren. Built to commemorate the Great Fire of London, and close to the spot in Pudding Lane where the Fire is said to have started, you can walk up the 311 steps to a viewing platform.

The Monument, Monument Street, The City. Nearest Tube: Bank.

THE GLOBE THEATRE

Shakespeare's original Globe Theatre was about 200 yards away from its replacement, which was opened in 1996 in New Globe Walk, thanks to the unstinting efforts of American actor Sam Wanamaker, who was shocked to find on a visit to London that there was no permanent memorial to the Bard in the city. Authentic Elizabethan methods were used to build the theater, and the first thatched roof in London since the Great Fire was a popular finishing touch. Plays are presented in natural light to up to 1,000 people on wooden benches and a further 500 groundlings standing on a carpet of shells, as they did 400 years ago. The theater is open for performance only in the summer, but guided tours are available year round from the Globe Exhibition Centre next door.

New Globe Walk, Bankside. Open May to September daily 9am to noon; October to April 10am to 5pm. Admission adults £6.50, seniors and students £5, children £4.50. Tel. 020 7902 1500. Theater performance information: Tel. 020 7401 9919. Nearest Tube: It's a bit of a walk from Blackfriars Tube Station, but that's the nearest!

SOUTHWARK CATHEDRAL

South London's main Anglican cathedral, Southwark is the second-oldest Gothic church in London after Westminster Abbey. Inside, there's a fine **nave** and medieval screen. The 1408 tomb of poet John Gower, a friend of Chaucer, is here too, as is a chapel dedicated to **John Harvard**, founder of Harvard University, who was baptized here in 1608. Another slab marks the last resting place of **Edmund Shakespeare**, brother of William, while a more evocative recent memorial commemorates the victims of the 1988 *Marchioness* disaster, when a pleasure craft hit a bridge nearby and sank in the Thames.

Borough High Street. Open daily from 8:30am to 4pm. Admission donation. Tel. 020 7367 6700. Nearest Tube: London Bridge.

NIGHTLIFE & ENTERTAINMENT

Theater

London, the focus of Britain's cultural life, is one of the world's leading centers for drama, music, opera and dance, even though the English, who have a quaint custom of undervaluing everything they do well, tend to take it for granted. Of England's approximately 300 professional theaters, about 100 are in London, many of them centered around the **Shaftesbury Avenue/Leicester Square** area.

Theater life is centered – but by no means confined – to the famous **West End**, where the byword is choice, and you can revel in jolly musicals by Andrew Lloyd-Webber and Steven Sondheim; plays by British writers like John Mortimore and Alan Ayckbourn; bawdy romps inspired by popular TV sitcoms; and variety shows starring popular celebrities – they're all here. And further afield you can enjoy productions by the prestigious **Royal Shakespeare Company** at the Barbican Centre and the equally-famous **National Theatre Company** at the South Bank Complex.

If the West End is London's equivalent of Broadway, then the London "fringe" theatres are the equivalent to off-Broadway. Here, budding new bards get a chance to strut their stuff. Talk of Bards, don't

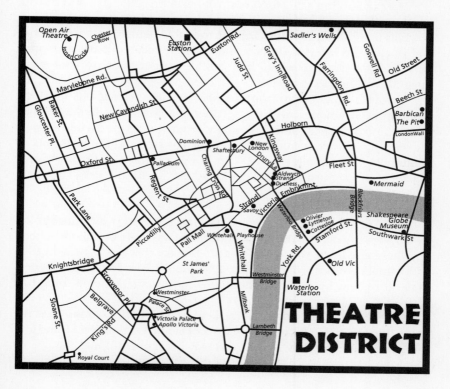

THEATRE DISTRICT

forget that the new **Globe Theatre** – a faithful reproduction of Shakespeare's Elizabethan original – is now open for performances during the summer and for tours only during the winter (see above listing). Like its illustrious predecessor, the Globe is open to the elements, so, even if the weather looks set fair, take precautions.

Such is the choice available, it's important to choose carefully. I've known whole groups of Americans come away from a successful play disappointed, baffled and bored. The accents and terminology are so integral to understanding the plot in some cases, that on occasion the whole point can be lost to all but Brits in the audience.

Theater tickets are available at **agencies** all over the city, but it may work out cheaper for you if you're able to book your tickets before leaving home. At **Leicester Square ticket booth** you can buy last-minute, same-day tickets at half prices. The *Official London Theatre Guide* produces a comprehensive, up-to-date theatre guide regularly throughout the year. You can access this online at *www.OfficialLondonTheatre.co.uk* or you may prefer to contact one of the major ticket agencies direct, like **Ticketmaster** *(Tel. 020 7413 1442 in UK, 800/775-2525 in US or www.ticketmaster.co.uk)* or **First Call** *(Tel. 020 7497 9977)*. Make sure you have a credit card handy.

Most of London's theaters are small – around 500 seats – and laid out in tiers with the **stalls** occupying the main floor and various circles above. Playbills are called **programs** and are available before the performance and during the **interval** (intermission). Many theaters have bars open before a performance where you can also order your drinks for the interval, avoiding long queues.

If you're in London around Christmastime, check out the local **pantomime** – a unique British theater phenomenon. Pantomimes (pantos) are costumed musical comedies usually based around the theme of a well-known child's story or nursery rhyme such as Jack and the Beanstalk or Cinderella. They usually star well-known TV personalities, involve a lot of slapstick, and are just as popular with adults as with the kids.

Film

The English have been in love with films for a long time but gone are the days when a night at the **pictures** (movies) was more popular here than anywhere else in the world. Cinema attendance reached its peak in 1946 with a total attendance of more than 1.6 billion, but had plummeted to less than 50 million by 1985. By the mid-'90s, however, cinema-going had recovered.

Many of the films arriving in England have already been shown in the States. On top of that, ticket prices are exorbitantly expensive (£6 and up), though on certain nights deductions may be in operation.

The pluses about going to the cinema in London is the sheer variety of films on show (more than 300 per week) and the plethora of **arts cinemas** where you may catch something you've always wanted to see but knew it would never come to Cheyenne. One of the best places to find out what films are on, including artsy flicks, is *Time Out* magazine.

Opera, Music & Dance

The English love their music, not surprising in a nation that has given the world such luminaries as Handel, Britten, and the Beatles. London's main music venues are as follows:

THE BARBICAN CENTRE, *Silk Street, WC2. Tel. 020 7638 8891. Nearest Tube: Barbican.*

This vast new complex houses the Royal Shakespeare Company, cinemas, theaters and a concert hall for the London Symphony.

ENGLISH NATIONAL OPERA, *The Coliseum, St Martin's Lane, WC2. Tel. 020 7632 8300. Nearest Tube: Leicester Square.*

Just off Trafalgar Square, the National, as its known, puts on excellent, innovative productions in a less stuffy atmosphere – and at much lower prices. Productions are entirely in English.

COVENT GARDEN OPERA HOUSE, *Covent Garden, London WC1. Nearest Tube: Covent Garden.*

Just reopened after major refurbishment and extension, this is one of the world's great opera houses, and regularly sees the greatest names in the opera world. Prices are exorbitantly high, and tickets sell like hot cakes, so it makes sense to try and purchase your ticket in advance – back home, if possible.

ROYAL ALBERT HALL, *Kensington Gore, SW7. Tel. 020 7589 8212. Nearest Tube: South Kensington.*

The Royal Albert Hall, named after Queen Victoria's husband, has a capacity of around 10,000 and hosts pop and classical concerts as well as sporting events, and – at the end of the summer, the world's greatest musical festival – the famous **Promenade Concerts**, sponsored by the BBC, which extend into November. The **Last Night of the Proms** is a national institution.

THE SOUTH BANK CENTRE, *The South Bank, SE1. Tel. 020 7960 4242. Nearest Tube: Embankment, then walk across the Hungerford pedestrain bridge to the South Bank.*

Ugly concrete and glass edifice that houses three concert halls – the Royal Festival Hall, Queen Elizabeth Hall and Purcell Room – and three theaters – the Lyttleton, Cottesloe and Olivier. This is the home base of the London Philharmonic.

Churches and small halls all over London – such as St. Paul's Cathedral – offer a wealth of musical events throughout the year, but especially in the summer. Check *Time Out* or one of the other listings magazines for more information.

Here are a few of them:

ST. JOHN'S, *Smith Square, SW1. Tel. 020 7222 1061.*

This 1728 former church is a major venue for chamber music and a weekly Monday and alternate Thursday lunchtime series of classical music from the BBC Radio Orchestra.

ST. MARTIN-IN-THE-FIELDS, *Trafalgar Square. Tel. 020 7839 1930. Nearest Tube: Charing Cross.*

Famous landmark church in Trafalgar Square that puts on lunchtime concerts two or three times a week, as well as candlelit evening concerts that may feature the celebrated Academy of St. Martin-in-the-Fields.

WIGMORE HALL, *36 Wigmore Street, W1. Tel. 020 7486 1907.*

One of London's leading venues for early and medieval music. Concerts are held every evening and Sunday mornings.

SADLER'S WELLS, *Rosebery Avenue, EC1. Tel. 020 7863 8000. Nearest Tube: Angel.*

An important venue for contemporary dance, opera and performance art that has been on this site for more than 300 years.

ATTEND AN EVENSONG CONCERT

*For ethereal singing of the highest quality, attend an **evensong service** at **Westminster Abbey, St. Paul's Cathedral** or **Southwark Cathedral**, where you can hear world-class men's and boy's choirs for free. You don't have to be an Episcopalian – or even a Christian – to attend, but you'll be sure of an uplifting experience whatever your persuasion. Check the times in the Sunday papers.*

Pubs

One of England's greatest assets is its **pubs** – a British institution that's even more popular (certainly with the natives) than the royal family. And while pubs may have appeared all over the world, including North America, nowhere do they quite capture the unique atmosphere of their British forebears. These days, more liberal licensing laws mean that pubs are generally open during the daytime (they used to close between lunchtime and early evening), and though further liberalization of the law is promised, many of them are closed by 11pm – with a further ten minutes' **"drinking up time."**

Pubs come in all shapes and sizes, and there's a pub for just about every mood and occasion. And they come with the most amazing names, such as The King and Tinker and The Scarlet Pig many of which have some historical reasoning. Some pubs have wonderful architecture – such as the **Salisbury** in St. Martin's Lane, with its wonderfully ornate wooden carvings and mirrors. See Chapter 11, *Food & Drink*, for more details on pubs in general.

London has literally thousands of pubs, many of which are effectively franchises of a handful of large brewery concerns and sell that brewery's products. However, there is an increasing number of **free houses** that stock a wider variety of beers and wines – and often serve excellent and inexpensive food. While there are some excellent pubs in the **West End** and the **City**, many of London's best pubs are to be found in the **suburbs** and along the River.

Half the fun of going to a pub in London is finding one that suits you. If you like really loud heavy metal, there's a pub for you; if you're into leather, there's a pub for you (several, actually); if you want a quiet evening watching the world go by, there's a pub for you. No one will bat an eyelid if you walk into a bar, and then walk straight out again because you don't feel it's right for you or if you feel uncomfortable for any reason; this happens all the time. The great thing is there's another pub just a few yards away.

North Americans tend to gravitate towards some of the **older pubs** with historical connections, such as the **Cheshire Cheese** in the Strand, where Dickens and Pepys used to drink, or the **Sherlock Holmes** on Northumberland Avenue, which is full of memorabilia relating to the great detective. Atmospheric these may be, but watch out because they tend to push up the prices.

Don't forget that you must be **over 18** to partake of alcohol in Britain; children under-14 are often tolerated in pubs, and always if they're eating, but it really is at the discretion of the landlord. Outdoor areas, such as **beer gardens**, are also child-friendly.

Just a word of warning about **drinking and driving**. Britain has some of the strictest laws on drinking and driving in the world, and even your feigned naivete and strong Texan drawl will not draw any sympathy. You have been warned!

London has more than 100 gay bars and pubs and many of them can be found in and around Soho. Check *Gay Times* or call Gay Switchboard for details, *Tel. 020 7837 7324.*

West End Pubs

SHERLOCK HOLMES, *10 Northumberland Street, WC2. Tel. 020 7930 2644. Nearest Tube: Charing Cross.*

Formerly known as the Northumberland Arms, this neighborhood pub behind Charing Cross Station was a frequent haunt of Sir Arthur Conan Doyle and is featured in his most famous book, *The Hound of the Baskervilles*. It's popular with tourists, who are drawn by the literary association, and the various Holmes memorabilia about the place – including the hound's head and plaster casts of its gigantic paws.

THE LAMB AND FLAG, *33 Rose Street, WC2. Tel. 020 7836 4108. Nearest Tube: Covent Garden.*

A 17th century pub with a violent history – the upstairs room was used for bare-knuckle boxing, giving it the nickname "the Bucket of Blood." Today the only thing that's bare are three floors, adding to the atmosphere. Things have quietened down a bit since then, though, and these days you can enjoy excellent lunches and real ale.

THE SALISBURY, *90 St Martin's Lane, WC2. Tel. 020 7836 5863. Nearest Tube: Leicester Square.*

Once one of London's prime gay pubs, the pub's ethos changed significantly around ten years ago with a change of management. Many of the gay patrons turned to Brief Encounter just across the road. The unremarkable exterior belies an interior that's another art nouveau gem – intricately carved woodwork, acres of mirrors, bronze sculptures of scantily clad ladies, bunches of grapes and that sort of thing. The best time to come in here is mid-afternoon, between the peak lunch and early evening pre-theater periods.

City Pubs

THE BLACK FRIAR, *174 Queen Victoria Street, EC4. Tel. 0171 236 5650. Nearest Tube: Blackfriars.*

Just yards from Blackfriars Station, this amazing art nouveau pub is a real gem. Located on the site of a former Dominican monastery, the Black Friar's decor – inlaid mother-of-pearl, gold mosaic ceilings, bronze reliefs of monks, etc. – make it worth a visit for the architecture alone. By the way, there are six beers on tap, and a real mix of customers – City gents, professional beer drinkers, and the like, make drinking here a really pleasurable experience.

YE OLDE CHESHIRE CHEESE, *145 Fleet Street, EC4. Tel. 020 7353 6170. Nearest Tube: Holborn.*

It's a real tourist trap, but worth a visit for its intriguing history and unique atmosphere. Dating from 1667, but built over the earlier remains of Whitefriars' monastery surviving under the crypt, it has sawdust-sprinkled floors, beamed ceilings, working fireplaces and dark wood paneling spread throughout six bars and three restaurants – though the food is not primary reason for coming here. Samuel Johnson, Oliver Goldsmith and Charles Dickens were regulars here.

South Of The River Pubs

MAYFLOWER, *117 Rotherhithe Street, SE16. Tel. 020 7237 4088. Nearest Tube: Rotherhithe (East London line).*

It's a bit of a trek to Rotherhithe, but worth a visit for this attractive, 17th century waterside inn with exposed beams and a delightful terrace. The pub is so-named because it's the place where the pilgrims originally set out in 1620 for Plymouth Rock, though they stopped off at Southampton and Plymouth on the way. The American connection is celebrated by the fact that the inn is licensed to sell US postage stamps.

GEORGE INN, *77 Borough High Street, Southwark SE1. Tel. 020 7407 2056. Nearest Tube: Borough.*

Located just a few yards from Southwark Cathedral, the George, a beautiful galleried building that dates from the late 17th century, overlooks a courtyard where Shakespeare plays were once performed. Indeed, legend holds that the Bard actually drank here – it's certainly not far from the Globe Theatre. Dickens was another regular, and it features in drawings by Hogarth and Rowlandson. Inside, it's an intricate maze of rooms, passageways, hidden bars and a restaurant.

THE PROSPECT OF WHITBY, *57 Wapping Wall, E1. Tel. 020 7481 1095. Nearest Tube: Wapping.*

One of London's most famous pubs, the Prospect of Whitby is a little ways out of central London, but if you get here you'll be the latest in an esteemed line of visitors including Whistler, Turner and – guess who? – Dickens. It straddles the edge of the Thames in an area, now gentrified, that was once the haunt of cut-throats, rogues and scoundrels – no wonder the original tavern on the site was called the Devil's Tavern. Hangings were held here, including that of notorious Captain Kidd. A choice of food is available, from traditional English fare such as shepherd's pie and, of course, fish and chips, to more elegant fare upstairs. With the gentle breezes wafting off the Thames, there's no better place to spend a warm summer's evening.

West London Pubs

DOVE INN, *19 Upper Mall, W6. Tel. 020 7748 5405. Nearest Tube: Hammersmith.*

This is a 16th century riverside pub close by Hammersmith Bridge that is immersed in history. Charles II and his lover Nell Gwynne are reputed to have been regulars here, as was the writer Ernest Hemingway. It's a busy place, and you'll likely have to practise your queuing. If it's all too much, there are several other interesting pubs just a few hundred yards up river.

North London Pubs

THE FLASK, *77 Highgate West Hill, N6. Tel. 020 8340 7260. Nearest Tube: Highgate.*

The leafy north London suburbs of Hampstead and Highgate, independent villages in their own right until subjugated by the sprawling metropolis, both have a number of interesting pubs. Highgate's The Flask, with its meandering irregular rooms, low beams and old photographs and books, makes a very pleasant place for lunch – though it gets very crowded in the evenings.

THE SPANIARDS, *Spaniard's Road, Hampstead, NW3. Tel. 020 8455 3276. Nearest Tube: Hampstead.*

It's a bit of a walk from the top of Hampstead High Street to the Spaniards but worth the effort – this is everyone's idea of how a pub should be. Originally built in 1585, tradition says it was once the residence of the Spanish ambassador to James I. Later on, it became the Inn at the Old Gate, guarding the toll gate into London. Among its many visitors have been Charles Lamb, Dickens (of course), Keats, Shelley, Sir Joshua Reynolds and legendary highwayman Dick Turpin. Order your drinks from the large downstairs bar (where you can also get reasonable food) and make your way outside to the garden, where kids will be mesmerized by the aviary and you will be soothed by the sweet-smelling roses.

SHOPPING

London is a paradise for shoppers because of the sheer volume and diversity of goods available. However, the strong pound and generally high prices in London have combined to make a shopping spree in London a far more expensive proposition than it might have been, say, twenty years ago.

London's main shopping drag is **Oxford Street**, which stretches about a mile and a half west to east through the West End from **Marble Arch** to **Tottenham Court Road**. A mixture of chain stores, such as Marks and Spencer, British Homes Stores and Boots, and large department stores like Selfridges, John Lewis and Debenhams rubs shoulders with smaller designer stores and tacky souvenir shops.

About half-way along, Oxford Street is punctuated by the more upmarket **Regent Street,** where you'll find the excellent Tudor-style Liberty's store, Hamley's toy shop (said to be the largest toy store in the world), Burberry's and other clothing stores. Just behind Regent Street, on its eastern side, lies **Carnaby Street**, made famous by rock stars in the

'60s but lacking its once avant garde feel and catering these days mainly to tourists. In the corner between Regent and Oxford Streets, you'll find such classy shopping drags as **Jermyn Street**, **Bond Street** and **New Bond Street**, great for antiques, designer wear and fine arts, not to mention the **Burlington Arcade**, built in 1819 to provide a retreat for the gentry from the mud-splashing thoroughfares of Piccadilly.

Regent Street's southern end meets **Piccadilly Circus**, with a vast Tower Records store and the street called **Piccadilly**, where, a few hundred yards along on the left, you'll find Fortnum and Mason's, London's most famous food store, where the staff still wear morning dress, and lots of wealthy Londoners do their daily shopping.

Other shopping areas to explore are **Knightsbridge**, home to what is claimed to be the world's largest and certainly most exclusive department store, **Harrod's,** where you can buy anything from an elephant to a pin (who'd want to buy a pin?). The food halls are particularly lavish, and you can also see a tacky "shrine" to Princess Diana and Dodi Al Fayed built by the stores owner, Dodi's father, Mohammed. Another upmarket department store to look out for here is Harvey Nichols, though it lacks the cache of Harrods.

Both **Kensington High Street**, with Barkers department store, and **Chelsea High Street**, with the Peter Jones store and countless more designer boutiques are well worth a visit. For a different experience, where you can rub shoulders with real Londoners doing their shopping, head out for one of the suburban centers like **Wood Green** or **Clapham**.

Specialist Shopping Areas

Tottenham Court Road, at the far eastern end of Oxford Street, is the place to go for hi-fi equipment, computers, cameras and the like. It's also the home of one of London's best contemporary furniture stores, Heals.

For books, check out the **Charing Cross Road**, made famous in the film of the same name. Foyles, claiming to be the largest bookstore in the world, but incredibly cluttered and run-down, is here, as is the main branch of Waterstones, Borders, and some fine antiquarian bookshops that you could have sworn you saw Anthony Hopkins just pop into.

Avoid the high-priced fine arts and antiques emporia around New Bond Street and head instead for **Camden Market**, now London's fifth most popular tourist spot. You can get just about anything here, prints, furniture, china, jewelry, but expect to pay more in the shops than you would in the market stalls. You'll have a similar fun time at **Portobello Road Market**, where everyone seems to be looking for that hidden treasure that will make them their fortune.

EXCURSIONS & DAY TRIPS

KEW GARDENS

The **Royal Botanical Gardens** at Kew, in west London, are a major botanical research institute, containing more than 38,000 plant species in over 300 acres of public parkland. The Gardens were founded by Queen Caroline and Princess Augusta in the eighteen century. Rapid expansion took place in the next century, when some of the huge glasshouses were built, containing all kinds of exotic species from all over the world. A major disaster hit Kew in October 1987 when a major storm uprooted most of the trees, the same year as the Institute received a major boost with the opening of the ultra-modern **Prince of Wales Conservatory**. Kew is a fascinating place, easily reachable by Tube (it has its own station) from central London.

Kew Road, Richomond, Surrey. Open daily 9.30am to 6:30pm. Admission adults £5, children £2.50. Tel. 020 8940 1171. Nearest Tube: Kew.

WINDSOR CASTLE

Windsor Castle was built 900 years ago by William the Conqueror to guard the western approaches to London. The site was chosen very carefully; high above the Thames, on the edge of a Saxon hunting ground and just a day's march from the Tower of London.

Today Windsor Castle is still a working palace, and the **State Apartments** contain some of the finest works of art, armor, paintings and decor in the world. Large sections of the Castle that were razed to the ground during the disastrous fire of 1992 have now been completely rebuilt and refurbished to the highest standards. The work, which cost more than £37 million (and caused a major furor when at first it was believed that all of the funds were to come out of the public purse), includes the restoration of the **Grand Reception Rooms**, **The Green and Crimson Drawing Rooms** and **the State and Octagonal Dining Rooms**. **St George's Hall**, where the Queen gives lavish banquets, had its ancient roof completely destroyed; today a brand new roof, built in the hammer-beam style like the old one, watches over the 600-year-old hall.

Winsdor Castle is so vast, it's only possible to touch on just a few of its major attractions here. As you enter, you can miss **St. George's Chapel**, where the queen invests new knights and where various other important events take place – the wedding of the Queen's youngest son, Edward, to Sophie Rhys-Jones to name but one. Dating from the 15th and 16th centuries, when the Perpendicular style was in vogue, it contains beautiful **fan vaulting** and beautifully carved choir stalls.

From the **North Terrace**, you can enjoy magnificent views across the Thames to the famous **Eton College** (Eton is the 'public' school –

remember, in England a public school is like an American private school); this is where Prince William was a student until summer 2000. From here, you enter the **State Apartments**, lavish beyond belief, with priceless antiques, Gobelin tapestries, old master paintings and even a Louis XVI bed. Also here are the **Throne Room** and the **Waterloo Chamber**, where you can examine the set of paintings of Napoleon's foes which hang on the walls. Several items of armor are on show, and you can take a look at the superb **Queen's Collection of Master Drawings**, with works by Leonardo, and 87 Holbein portraits.

You should also take a look at **Queen Mary's Dolls' House**, left of the entrance to the State Apartments. Sir Edward Lutyens won the commission to create the Dolls' House in 1921, and it was completed in 1924. His goal was to "enable future generations to see how a King and Queen lived in the 20th century, and what authors, artists and craftsmen of note there were during their reign." The house was built on a scale of one to twelve and involved over 1,500 craftsmen.

At Windsor you can also see (another) **Changing of the Guard** ceremony. This takes place daily (except Sundays) at 11am from April to the end of June, and on alternate days at other times of the year. Call *01753 868286* to confirm the times.

Open November to February 9:45am to 4:15pm (last admission 3pm); March to October 9:45am to 5:15pm (last admission 4pm). Admission adults £10.50, seniors £8, Under-17s £5, under 5s free. Tel. 01753 831118; www.royal.gov.uk. Windsor is best accessed by train from London Waterloo (about 35 minutes to Windsor-Eton Riverside station).

HAMPTON COURT PALACE

This is another beautiful (some would say the most beautiful) **royal palace**, this time about 20 miles west of central London, just upstream from Richmond. The magnificent red-brick Tudor house was begun in 1514 under the auspices of the powerful **Cardinal Wolsey**, the nations' Lord Chancellor (which amounts to prime minister today), as well as being Archbishop of York. His desire to create the most lavish palace in the land upset Henry VIII so much that Wolsey felt obliged to give it to the king, and Henry moved there in 1525.

Henry made some additions, including the **Great Hall,** but much greater expansion took place during the reign of William and Mary, with work by Sir Christopher Wren. The location adjacent to the Thames is glorious, and allowed the monarch to get into central London very quickly by boat. The palace is full of priceless paintings, original furniture and – it is said – the ghost of **Catherine Howard**, protesting her innocence of the adultery that had her beheaded. Outside, exquisite ornamental gardens are the perfect place to while away a few hours – while if you want to while away a little bit longer, you can explore the famous **Hampton Court Maze**.

State Apartments open April to October Tuesday to Sunday 9:30am to 6pm; November to march Tuesday to Sunday 9:30am to 4:30pm, Monday 10:15 to 4:30pm. Admission adults £10, children £6.60. Grounds open 8am to dusk daily (free, but maze £3) To get there: Take a train from waterloo to Hampton Court Station. Journey time: about 35 minutes.

PRACTICAL INFORMATION

American Express operates several branches in London. One of the most central is the office at *6, Haymarket (near Piccadilly Circus), Tel. 020 7930 4411*. **Thomas Cook** also has a large number of branches throughout the city if you want to change money. International **money transfer** is available from **Western Union**, *Tel. 0800 833833*.

Banks are generally open from 9:30am to 4:30pm, Monday to Friday, with some opening on Saturday mornings too. Most ATM machines are open 24 hours a day and accept overseas cards with a Yankee 24 or Cirrus symbol. If you use one of the myriad bureaux de change throughout the city, make sure you check their commission rates before parting with your dollars; some of them charge extortionate fees.

Emergency **dental treatment** is available at **Guy's Hospital Dental School**, *St. Thomas's Street, SE1, Tel. 020 7955 5000*. It's a walk-in facility and is open Monday to Friday, 9am to 3:30pm, weekends 9am to 5pm. The service is free. You can get emergency **medical information** by calling **Doctorcall**, *Tel. 07000 372255, Medcall, Tel. 0800 136106,* or **Opticall**, *Tel. 020 7495 4915*.

The **US Embassy** in London is located at *Grosvenor Square, Tel. 020 7499 9000*, as is the **Canadian High Commission**, *Tel. 020 7258 6600*.

Lost Property offices are located at **Heathrow Airport**, *Tel. 020 8745 7727, Gatwick, Tel. 01293 535353*. For lost credit cards, call **American Express**, *Tel. 01273 696933*, **Diners Club**, *Tel. 01252 513500*, **MasterCard & Visa**, *Tel. 01268 298178*. London transport lost property office: *Tel. 020 7486 2496*.

Late opening **pharmacists** are located at *5 Marble Arch* (**Bliss** – open to midnight, *Tel. 020 7723 6116*), and at *Piccadilly Circus* (**Boots** – open till 8pm, *Tel. 020 7734 6125*.

Tourist Information offices are located at:
- **Britain Visitor Centre**, *1 Regent Street (no telephone), www.visitbritain.com*
- **City of London**, *St. Paul's Churchyard, EC4, Tel. 020 7332 1456*
- **Greenwich**, *46 Greenwich Church Street, SE10, Tel. 020 88858 6376*
- **London Tourist Board**, *Victoria Station Forecourt (no telephone)*

15. SOUTHEAST ENGLAND

Although the **southeast** is England's most densely populated region, large tracts of it remain unspoilt – a patchwork quilt landscape of gently rolling hills, orchards (Kent is known as the "Garden of England" on account of its fruit-producing industry), heath and woodland bisected by a host of streams and rivers leading down to the chalky white cliffs of its southern coastline or to the massive **Thames estuary** to the north. As well as home to some of England's most historic cities – such as **Canterbury** and **Rochester** in Kent, **Lewes**, **Arundel** and **Chichester** in Sussex, numerous stately homes and castles, the southeast coast is also a seaside playground for millions of Londoners; it's not for nothing that **Brighton** is sometimes known as "**London by the Sea**."

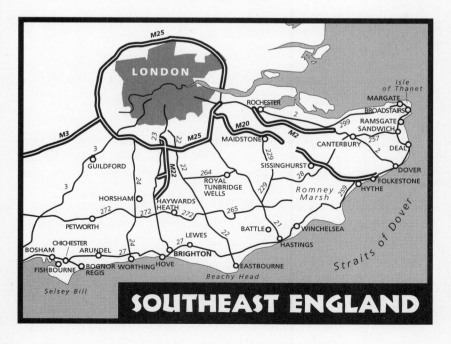

SOUTHEAST ENGLAND

This is also the closest part of Britain to continental Europe, and regular ferry services depart from half a dozen ports along the southeast coast to their counterparts in France, Belgium and Holland, while the high-speed Eurostar train whizzes through the green landscape before it dips below the Channel near Folkestone on its way to Paris and Brussels.

In order to explore this region, it makes a lot of sense to start in **Kent**, which borders the unsalubrious southeast outskirts of London, with the cathedral cities of **Rochester** and **Canterbury**, then on to the Channel ports and the main **East Sussex** seaside resorts, including Brighton, whose hinterland offers a number of exciting attractions to explore. Finally, there's **West Sussex**, with the handsome cathedral city of **Chichester**.

ROCHESTER

A Roman city about 28 miles southeast of central London on the River Medway, Rochester was the home – at Gad's Hill Place, just outside of town – for a number of years of **Charles Dickens**, a fact which has not been lost on the local tourism department.

ARRIVALS & DEPARTURES

By Car

From London follow the M2 southeast, and follow the signs for Rochester, about 28 miles southeast of central London.

By Bus

Buses for Rochester and the Medway towns leave London Victoria bus station regularly. *Call 0990 808080 for information.*

By Train

Rochester has a main line train station that's served every half-hour by trains from London's Victoria and Charing Cross stations. It's located at the eastern end of the High Street. *Call 0345 484950 for rail information.*

GETTING AROUND TOWN

The compactness of Rochester's town center means that everything can be seen on foot.

WHERE TO STAY

THE ROYAL VICTORIA AND BULL HOTEL, *16-18 High Street, Rochester ME1 1PX. Tel. 01634 846266, Fax 01634 832312. Rooms: 28. Rates: singles from £45, doubles from £57. Bar, restaurant, jacuzzi. All major credit cards accepted.*

This historic coaching inn in the center of Rochester was a frequent haunt of none other than Charles Dickens himself. There's a large downstairs bar – a great place to meet and engage in conversation with the locals – and an Italian restaurant. The bedrooms are generally large and come with tea- and coffee-making facilities and TV; some have four poster beds. In the unlikely event that you do decide to stay in Rochester overnight, this is the place.

SEEING THE SIGHTS

Dickens fans will want to visit Rochester. Take a walk along the High Street, and take a look at the gray Tudor, half-timbered building that was the legendary dwelling-place of Uncle Pumblechook in Charles Dickens' *Great Expectations*; other buildings which featured in his writings including the **Blue Boar** and **Bull Hotel** – the Bull in *Pickwick Papers* and the Blue Boar in *Great Expectations*. Opposite is the **Charles Dickens Centre**, featuring life-size models of many characters from Dickens' works, some of which might be more suited to Madame Tussaud's Chamber of Horrors, so parents be warned! *Eastgate House, High Street, Open daily 10am to 5:30pm. Admission £3.50. Tel. 01634 844176.*

Nearby is **Rochester Cathedral**, the second oldest in England, where the first English bishop was consecrated in 604 AD. The Cathedral may not be the most attractive of the English cathedrals, but the mixture of architectural styles and the various additions made over the centuries make it an appealing kind of place. Of the original Norman work that remains, the most striking feature is the intricately carved west front doorway. Before the Dissolution of the Monasteries, the Cathedral had its own shrine – dedicated to William of Perth, a humble Scottish baker who set out on a pilgrimage to the Holy Land in 1201, only to get as far as Rochester, where he was robbed and murdered. The Rochester monks, envious of the success of nearby Canterbury, and realizing they might be on to a good thing, built an elaborate shrine that attracted thousands of pilgrims until it was destroyed by Henry VIII's men.

Also worth checking out in Rochester is the **castle**, a Norman construction built on the site of an earlier Roman fortress. The architect, Gundulf, had earlier designed the great White Tower of the Tower of London, and on its completion was asked to beef up the southeastern approaches of the Medway. The impressive structure, with its 100-foot high walls, is generally well-preserved, with three square towers and a circular one, which was destroyed during a siege of the castle in 1215 by King John. There's an interesting model of the siege in the nearby **Rochester Guildhall Museum**. *Castle, Boley Hill. Open daily, Easter to September. Admission £3. Tel. 01634 402276.*

PRACTICAL INFORMATION

Rochester's **tourism office** can be found at *Eastgate Cottage, High Street, Tel. 01634 843666.* They produce an excellent guide-yourself leaflet to the city, as well as information about guided walks.

Rochester's banks are located mainly along High Street.

CANTERBURY

Although **Canterbury's** roots go way back to the Iron Age, the city came into its own in 597, when the Pope's Emissary, **Augustine**, landed on English shores for the first time. Augustine headed inland towards London, but was given such a warm welcome by the local king, Ethelbert, that he set up a monastery here, and Canterbury became a focal point for Christianity in England – a position it maintains today as the headquarters of the **Anglican Church**.

A visit to historic Canterbury is a must. This small (population 35,000) Kent city is home to one of the most stunningly beautiful cathedrals on earth, in which once stood one of the most magnificent shrines in Christendom – the shrine of **Thomas a Becket**. During the middle ages countless pilgrims from all over Europe thronged to the shrine – as evidenced in Geoffrey Chaucer's *Canterbury Tales* – before the Reformation and its desecration by Henry VIII. Although some damage was caused to the city by enemy bombs during World War II, a myriad of other important historical buildings remain intact.

ARRIVALS & DEPARTURES

By Car

From London take the A2 as far as the junction with the M2. Get on the M2 and follow signs for Canterbury. The distance is approximately 60 miles.

By Bus

National Express buses for Canterbury West leave from London's Victoria Bus Station. *For information, call 0990 808080.* The bus station is situated at the east end of High Street.

By Train

Trains for Canterbury leave frequently from two London stations: Victoria (hourly, journey time 1 1/2 hours) and Charing Cross (half-hourly, journey time 1 hour and 45 minutes). *Call 0345 484950 to see which service is more convenient for you.*

ORIENTATION

Canterbury's city center is surrounded by the ancient city walls, and these in turn are enclosed by a horrendous ring road, so once you're in, there's no escape!

GETTING AROUND TOWN

Nearly all of Canterbury's attractions are located within the old city walls, and within easy walking distance of each other. If you're heading into the countryside around Canterbury, renting a bike makes sense; **Downland Cycles**, *located at Canterbury West Station*, rent them for about £10 a day. If you need a taxi, call **Langport Taxis**, *Tel. 01227 458885.* Meanwhile, car rentals are available from **Avis**, *Tel. 01223 768339,* and **Hertz**, *Tel. 01227 470864.*

THOMAS BECKET, 1118-1170

*Born in London, **Becket** was well educated, studying for a time in Paris. In 1154 he was appointed Archdeacon of Canterbury, and in the following year was made England's chancellor by Henry II. On the death of Theobald, Archbishop of Canterbury, Henry nominated him for the see of Canterbury. Becket resigned the chancellorship and began devoting himself to religious duties, becoming a rigorous opponent of Henry's policy of anti-clericalism. In 1164 there was a major rift with the king over the Constitutions of Clarendon. A reconciliation was effected by the intervention of the Pope, and Becket returned to England. A month later he was brutally murdered in his own cathedral, apparently by members of the royal household.*

*There was certainly a quarrel between the two men, Thomas consistently defending the Church's authority and power against the king. Whether or not the much-quoted question, "Who will rid me of this turbulent priest?," was ever spoken, or if it was whether Henry had really intended to have Becket killed, is open to debate. What is certain is that Becket was savagely murdered by four of the king's knights in a side chapel. Two years later, in 1172, the **canonization** of Thomas a Becket and the apparently genuine contrition by the king meant that Canterbury became a focal point for pilgrims from all over Europe.*

WHERE TO STAY

CATHEDRAL GATE HOTEL, *38 Burgate, Canterbury CT1 2HA. Tel. 01227 464381. Rooms: 23. Rates: singles from £22, doubles from £40, family from £87. All major credit cards accepted.*

Traditional hotel located close to the Cathedral gatehouse and overlooking the Buttermarket. The hotel's origins go back to 1438 as a pilgrims' hospice. Later on, in 1588, it became licensed as a hotel and became one of England's leading coffee houses. The hotel's rooms are all adequately – but certainly not lavishly – furnished, some with four poster beds. Not all the rooms are en suite, so check when booking. Having said that, this is a wonderful, rambling old building that will give you a feel for medieval Canterbury like no other – and it's one of the cheapest places to stay in the city.

COUNTY HOTEL, *High Street, Canterbury CT1 2RX. Tel. 01227 766266. Rooms: 73. Rates: singles from £86, doubles from £100. English breakfast £9.50. Restaurant. All major credit cards accepted.*

Although this traditional provincial hotel has only been in operation since the 1890s, parts of the building date back to the 12th century. The spacious rooms are comfortable, some with four poster beds, and each comes with bath or shower, TV, tea- and coffee-making facilities. One of the hotel's best features is its restaurant, Sully's, which has an excellent reputation locally. If it's a snack you want, the coffee shop just to the right of the entrance is a good place. Centrally located, within easy reach of all the main attractions, it's a very pleasant place to stay.

FALSTAFF HOTEL, *St Dunstan's Street, Westgate, Canterbury CT2 8AF. Tel 01227 462138, Fax 01227 463525. Rooms: 48. Rates: singles from £91, doubles from £100. Bar, restaurant. All major credit cards accepted.*

This charming hotel was once a coaching inn, dates way back to the fifteenth century and retains many of the original features, including paneled corridors and creaking floorboards! It's conveniently located for the downtown Canterbury attractions and shopping facilities, next to the Westgate Tower, the ancient western entrance to the walled city. The rooms were refurbished and redecorated just recently, and there's a particularly lovely courtyard that's overlooked by the hotel's excellent restaurant. Plans are afoot to extend the hotel with an additional 15 rooms.

PILGRIMS HOTEL, *18 the Friars, Canterbury CT1 2AS. Tel 01227 464531, fax 01227 762514. Rooms: 15. Rates: singles from £45, doubles from £65. Restaurant. All major credit cards accepted.*

The Pilgrims Hotel is another ancient establishment, parts of which go back about 350 years. It's right in the center of the city, opposite the Marlowe Theatre, so convenient for all attractions. Among the public rooms is an atmospheric bar and a restaurant which has an a la carte menu as well as a selection of daily specials. The rooms are well-equipped and cozy, though the ones at the front overlooking the street can be a bit noisy.

TRAVELODGE, *A2 Gate Services, Dunkirk, Canterbury ME13 9LN. Tel and Fax: 01227 752781. Rooms: 40. Rates: Rooms rate (single or double use): from £45.95. All major credit cards accepted.*

Situated five miles west of Canterbury on the A2 highway, with easy access to Dover and London, the Travelodge is hardly the most sophisticated of places to stay, but it does offer good, clean basic accommodations at a price that's much lower than most of the city center hotels. The rooms are well-equipped with all the usual beverage-making facilities (so essential for the English) and televisions. There's no restaurant; to eat you'll either have to slum it at one of the nearby motorway services, or drive into Canterbury city, where there's an abundance of eating choices.

WHERE TO EAT

LA BONNE CUISINE, *Canterbury Hotel, 71 New Dover Rd. Tel. 01223 351880. Open daily noon to 1:45pm, 7pm to 9:45pm. Main courses around £12-16. All major credit cards accepted.*

Located in the imposing, rather grand Canterbury Hotel, this is a nice place to come for a special occasion. The restaurant's cuisine is essentially French, with a variety of Mediterranean-style dishes to choose from, and an excellent (mainly French, of course) wine list to boot.

CAFE DES AMIS DE MEXIQUE, *95 St Dunstan's Street, Cnterbury. Tel. 01227 464390. Open daily noon to 10pm. Main courses around £8-10. All major credit cards accepted.*

Bright, cheerful and atmospheric Mexican eatery that has become one of Canterbury's favorite places to eat. Try the pate con mole – a crispy duck burger with mole sauce, mango salsa and sour cream, and chive mash – for just £8.95. The chicken in a spicy almond sauce is a favorite, too.

MARLOWE'S, *55 St Peter's Street, Canterbury. Tel. 01227462194. Open daily 11am to 10:30pm. All major credit cards accepted.*

Bright and cheerful restaurant with a relaxed atmosphere enhanced by the oak beams and candle-lit tables. There's a wide-ranging choice of meals, with a particularly good selection of vegetarian dishes, more traditional English/French food, and some Mexican specialities (maybe that's why the walls are painted yellow). It's good value, too, all the better for being a bring-your-own bottle establishment.

TUO E MIO, *16 the Borough, Canterbury. Tel. 01227 761471. Open Tuesday 7pm to 10:45pm; Wednesday to Saturday noon to 2:30pm, 7pm to 10:45pm; Sunday noon to 2:30pm, 7pm to 10pm. Main courses around £13-15. All major credit cards accepted.*

Smart, stylish restaurant that has become very popular, thanks to the high quality of its food and the pleasant, comfortable surroundings and attentive staff. Try their house special: filetto tuo e mio, which means beef with cream brandy and mushrooms. The sweets trolley can be described in one word – magnificent!

SEEING THE SIGHTS

Canterbury is a **walled city**, with a main thoroughfare running from northwest to southeast. It's essentially along this route that most of the sites of interest are to be found. Standing at the northeast corner of the old city on St. Peter's Street is the fourteenth century **West Gate**, the only surviving city gate, which now houses a **Museum of Medieval Armaments**. It's certainly worth a peek inside, not only for the weaponry on display, but for a glimpse of the prison cells and the view from atop the roof. *Open Monday to Saturday, 11am to 12.30pm, 1:30pm to 3:30pm. Admission adults £1, children 5-18, 50pm, seniors and students 65p. Tel. 01227 452747.*

Heading southeast along St. Peter's Street you'll soon notice a row of half-timbered houses on the left that were once used by **Huguenot weavers** fleeing from religious persecution in nearby France. Just across the River Stour, on the opposite side of the road (which has now become High Street) is the **Eastbridge Hospital** of St. Thomas, where poorer pilgrims stayed on their visit to the shrine of St. Thomas a Becket. You can take a peek inside at the original refectory and crypt and the chapel with a thirteenth century mural and crown-post roof. It's all very musty, and for that reason atmospheric, so you can almost sense the babbling conversation of medieval pilgrims around you. It certainly beats the modern-day babbling of throngs of tourists! *Open Monday to Saturday 10am to 4:45pm. Admission adults £1, children 5-16 50p, seniors and students 75p. Tel. 01227 471688.*

The next street on the right is **Stour Street**, where a short walk will take you to the busy **Canterbury Heritage Museum**. It's busy for a good reason – it offers an excellent synopsis of the city's history and development. Starting with the Romans, the museum traces the city's development as the focal point of English Christianity. There's a particularly good video on Becket's life and death, but the piece de resistance is the building itself; it was formerly a **Poor Priests' Hospital** and the surviving vaulted hall is worth a visit on its own merit. Children (and some adults) will enjoy the Rupert Bear room – Mary Tourtel, Rupert's creator, was born in Canterbury. *Open November to May, Monday to Saturday 10:30am to 5pm; June to October Monday to Saturday 10:30am to 5pm and Sunday 1:30pm to 4pm. Admission adults £2.30, children 5-18 £1.15, students and seniors £1.50. Tel. 01227 452747.*

Further along High Street, **St. Margaret's Street** is the location of a very well-produced exhibit entitled **The Canterbury Tales**, depicting life in Chaucer's England in a series of tableaux, complete with sounds and (apparently authentic) smells. *Open mid-February to June daily 9:30am to 5:30pm; July to October daily 9am to 5:30pm; November to mid-February daily 9:30am to 4pm. Admission adults £5.25, 5-15 £4.25, students and seniors £4.50. Tel. 01227 479227.*

Back on High Street, before heading off to the cathedral, check out the **Canterbury Roman Museum**, on Butchery Lane below the Longmarket Shopping Centre. The museum, which is constructed some 20 feet below ground on the level of the old Roman town of Durnovernum, contains an original Roman mosaic floor and a hypocaust, along with interactive computer displays and exhibits depicting life in Roman Canterbury. *Open November to May Monday to Saturday 10am to 5pm; June to October Monday to Saturday 10am to 5pm, Sunday 1:30pm to 5pm. Admission adults £2.30, 5s-18s £1.15, seniors and students £1.50. tel 01227 785575.* Attractive **Mercery Lane**, with some lovely medieval houses, ends at the **Buttermarket**, where Christchurch Gate leads directly into the **cathedral close**.

Begun in 1070, then demolished and begun anew in 1096, Canterbury's **Christchurch Cathedral** is one of the glories of English cathedral architecture. Built over three centuries, and dominated by the 235-foot **Bell Harry Tower**, completed in 1505, its expansion was partly the result of the association with Archbishop **Thomas a Becket**, murdered in his own cathedral in 1170 by agents of King Henry II who believed, apparently erroneously, that they were carrying out the monarch's orders.

Becket's original **shrine**, destroyed by Henry VIII – a participant 400 years later in another major quarrel with the Church – was lavish beyond belief. It stood in **Trinity Chapel**, behind the high altar, where today 13th century stained glass windows depict some of the miracles attributed to the saint. Nearby, the tombs of **Henry IV** and his wife **Joan of Navarre**, and Edward II's son, the **Black Prince**, are further evidence of the importance of this site. In the **northwest transept**, the **Altar of Sword's Point**, with a simple sculpture of the assassins' weapons suspended above it – poignantly marks the spot where the archbishop died. It was here that the former Archbishop of Canterbury, the late Robert Runcie, and Pope John Paul II knelt together in prayer in 1982. From here you can descend down a flight of steps to the beautiful Norman **crypt**, its Romanesque arches a stark contrast to the later replacements on the main floor.

To the north of the nave, the **Great Cloister** leads to the 14th century **Chapter House**, with stained glass windows depicting more scenes from Becket's life. This was the venue for the first performance of T.S. Eliot's *Murder in the Cathedral* in 1935. For a special treat, try to attend a service of **Evensong** sung by the cathedral choir. The service is free, you don't have to be religious to attend, and you'll be treated to some of the finest choral singing in the world. *Cathedral open Easter to September Monday to*

Saturday 8:45am to 7pm, Sunday 12:30pm to 2:30pm and 4:30pm to 5:30pm; October to Easter Monday to Saturday 8:45am to 5pm, Sunday 12:30pm to 2:30pm and 4:30pm to 5:30pm. Crypt open Monday to Saturday 10am to 4:30pm, Sunday 12:30pm to 2:30pm and 4:30pm to 5:30pm. Admission (unless you're attending a service) adults £3, 5s-17s, seniors and students £2. Tel. 01227 762862.

To the east of the cathedral, through **Queningate**, are the remains of **St. Augustine's Abbey**, where the first church was established by Augustine in 598. Of the original Saxon edifice virtually nothing remains; it was replaced by a larger Norman construction built by Bishop Lanfranc in the eleventh century that itself was destroyed at the time of the Dissolution by Henry VIII and converted into lodgings for his then wife, Anne of Cleves. This is the site of Augustine's tomb, but no-one knows exactly where. *Open April to September daily 10am to 6pm; October daily 10am to 5pm; November to March daily 10am to 4pm. Admission adults £2.50, 5s-16s £1:30, students and seniors £1.90. Tel. 01227 767345.*

Just a short distance away, tiny **St. Martin's Church** on North Holmes Road, is believed to be the oldest parish church in continuous use in England with origins going right back to Queen Bertha, the Christian wife of Ethelbert, the local king who befriended Augustine in the late sixth century. The present church is largely medieval, but is still worth a visit for its lovely carved font, and, for Rupert Bear fans, the grave of Mary Tourtel in the churchyard. *Opening times vary. Call 01227 459482 for information.*

NIGHTLIFE & ENTERTAINMENT

Canterbury has two theaters, the **Gulbenkian**, *Giles Lane, Tel. 01227 769075*, maintained by the University of Kent, where serious plays are the thing, and the **Marlowe**, named after the playwright who was born in Canterbury. The Marlowe hosts touring drama productions and opera.

Canterbury has plenty of lively pubs, especially during term time when the university students are in residence. A couple of note are **Simple Simon's**, *St. Radigund's Street*, where folk music os often on the menu, and **Shakespeare's Inn**, *Butchery Lane, near the main entrance to the Cathedral.*

EXCURSIONS & DAY TRIPS

About 15 miles to the east of Canterbury is the **Isle Of Thanet**, not really an island at all, but the name given to the peninsula that juts out at the tip of Kent. Its main resorts, **Margate**, **Broadstairs** and **Ramsgate**, are a holiday playground for thousands of Londoners, and a much-sought-after retirement retreat. Unless you're in a beachy frame of mind, avoid this area, especially in high summer when thousands of day-trippers descend on this stretch of coast.

PRACTICAL INFORMATION

Canterbury's **main tourist office** is located at *34 St. Margaret's Street CT1 2TG, Tel. 01227 766567; www.canterbury.co.uk*. Most of the banks are located on High Street. **Thomas Cook** has an office at *Number 9, Tel. 01227 781199*. There's a post office *at the corner of St Peter's Street and Stour Street.*

DOVER

Dover is famous for the **white chalk cliffs** celebrated in the famous wartime song by British forces' sweetheart Vera Lynn: *There'll be blue birds over the white cliffs of Dover*. The gleaming white cliffs tower above the busy harbor area, one of the world's busiest passenger ports. Sadly, enemy bombing during World War II destroyed much of the old town and subsequent redevelopments have generally been hideously ugly. However, a number of attractions make it worthy of a short visit.

ARRIVALS & DEPARTURES

By Car

From London, take the A2 southeast out of the city. Come off the A2 at the junction with the M2, and continue on the M2 until it ends and becomes the A2. Dover is about seven miles south of Deal.

By Bus

There are frequent services to Dover from London Victoria, many of which stop at Canterbury

By Train

There are frequent services from two London train stations – Victoria and Charing Cross – to Dover Priory Station.

GETTING AROUND TOWN

Dover town center itself is quite compact and easily walkable, though there's a stiff climb to the Castle. If you're headed for the docks, there are special complimentary buses between them and the train station. **Britannia Taxis**, *Tel. 01304 204420*, offer a reliable service, or hail a cab in the street. If you need to rent a car, try **Avis**, *Eastern Docks, Tel. 01304 206265*.

WHERE TO STAY

CHURCHILL HOTEL, *The Waterfront, Dover CT17 9BP. Tel. 01304 203633. Rooms: 72. Rates: singles from £59, doubles/twins from £79, family room from £92. Breakfast £10. Restaurant All major credit cards accepted.*

Very comfortable hotel in a terrace of nicely-restored regency townhouses built in 1834 that resembles the Royal Terrace at Bath. The terrace was originally built for the wealthy, who wished to partake of the new fad of sea bathing. The houses and apartments were converted into hotels after WWI, but then closed at the outset of WWII. After the War, the place was re-opened and named in honor of the wartime Prime Minister. The rooms are comfortable, if somewhat insipid, but you can't complain at this price.

DOVER MOAT HOUSE, *Townwall Street, Dover CT16 1SZ. Tel. 01304 203270, Fax 01304 213230. Rooms: 79. Rates: singles from £55, doubles from £80. Restaurant, pool, carvery, coffee shop, bar, 24 hour room service. All major credit cards accepted.*

Part of a large chain of hotels, the Dover Moat House is right in the center of town, in close proximity to the ferry terminal and hoverport, as well as the train station and seafront. Although the decor is fairly standard, the hotel has a warm, friendly atmosphere, with 24-hour room service. Guest rooms are well-equipped with everything from TVs to hairdryers. An added bonus is the heated indoor swimming pool, and for lovers of English cuisine – both of you – there's a carvery restaurant on the premises.

WHERE TO EAT

DUNKERLEY'S, *Beach Street, Deal. Tel. 01304 375016. Bistro open daily 11am to 10:30pm, restaurant Tuesday to Sunday noon to 3pm, 6pm to 10:30pm. Main courses (restaurant) around £12-15. All credit cards accepted. Credit cards accepted: MC, Visa.*

You have a choice here: opt for the restaurant, with a tantalizing selection of mainly seafood dishes such as caramalized scallops with a vermouth butter sauce, or the bistro, with, as you'd expect less fancy dishes at lower prices. Both get very busy, especially at weekends, when it's advisable to book in advance.

PAUL'S, *2a Bouverie Road, Folkestone. Tel. 01303 226647. Open daily noon to 2.30pm, 7pm to 9:30pm. Set dinner £9.50. All major credit cards accepted.*

Long-established bistro with a relaxed, easy-going and friendly atmosphere much frequented by locals and by vacationers setting off for France. The extensive menu offers excellent value and includes specialities like venison sausage, sirloin steak with Stilton butter, and plenty of fresh fish caught locally from nearby Hythe. The wine list is extensive and in keeping with the general tone of the place again offers good value, house French starting at £8.65.

PARK INN, *1-2 Park Place, Dover. Tel. 01304 203300. Open Monday to Saturday 11am to 10pm, Sunday noon to 10pm. All major credit cards accepted.*

Rather lovely Victorian drawing room setting for this downtown Dover restaurant, where children are welcome, and where the wide range of main course dishes – including locally-caught seafood – are excellent value. The dessert trolley, too, is exceptional, with lots of gorgeous gooey things to tempt you.

SEEING THE SIGHTS

The most interesting of these by far is the spectacularly positioned **Dover Castle**, started in 1168 to protect the port from invasion. Here you can see the remains of the original hexagonal **lighthouse** built by the Romans to guide ships into the harbor they had constructed, and, standing next to it, a seventh-century Saxon church, **St. Mary in Castro** (St. Mary's in the camp) with original graffiti left there by soldiers embarking on the Crusades. The **Keep**, built by Henry II, is impressive in its size and grandeur, and contains a **Making of History** exhibit – climb the spiral staircase for views over to France, 21 miles away.

If you're interested in military matters, you might want to take one of two 40-minute **guided tours** of the **tunnels** beneath the castle – the highlight of a visit to the castle for most people – especially kids. These were originally constructed at the time of the Napoleonic Wars, but were extended during World War II, serving as a military hospital and communications center as well as the headquarters for planning the invasion of Dunkirk. *Open daily 10am to 6pm. Admission adults £6.90, 5s-15s £50p, students and seniors £5.20. Tel. 01304 211067; www.english-heritage.org.uk.*

Down below in the town itself, there's little to see, except for the **Roman Painted House**, on New Street, discovered in 1970 during the construction of a parking lot. It served as a hotel for official guests during Roman times, and has some well-preserved paintings, mosaics and a heating system from that era. *Open April to October Monday to Saturday 10am to 5pm; £1.50.*

If nostalgia's your thing, then it's worth getting into a boat to take a look at the white cliffs from out at sea – the last view of Blighty many young, departing soldiers ever saw (Blighty is an affectionate nickname given by Brits to Britain – e.g. 'dear old Blighty'). If you're prone to sea sickness, you might prefer to visit the **White Cliffs Experience**, Market Square, a rather engaging museum with animatronic dummies telling you all about Dover's history. There's a clever full-scale reconstruction of a local street during World War II, complete with air raid shelter and bombed-out homes, and lots of hands-on displays. *Open April to October daily 10am to 5pm; November to March daily 10am to 3pm. Admission adults £5.75, 4s-14s £3.95, seniors and students £4.60. Tel. 01304 214566.*

EXCURSIONS & DAY TRIPS

Folkestone, just eight miles southwest of Dover, once a small fishing port, became a fashionable seaside resort in Victorian times, but today is mainly known for its ferry links with Boulogne and Calais, France, and for the **Channel Tunnel**, which starts just west of the town, linking Britain with continental Europe by rail. There's little to see here, except for the **Eurotunnel Exhibition Centre**, Cheriton High Street, which gives a rather one-sided account of the history of the tunnel (it was first mooted as an idea nearly 200 years ago) and its development.

Just nine miles north of Dover is the seaside town of **Deal**, one of the so-called Cinque Ports, where Julius Caesar first landed in 55 BC and from which William Penn set out in 1682 on his first journey to America. **Deal Castle**, dating from 1540, was one of Henry VIII's most important coastal defenses, built in the shape of a Tudor rose. It's a grim kind of place, but there's an interesting museum with displays about prehistoric, Roman and Saxon England. *Located on Victoria Road. Open April to October daily 10am to 6pm; November to March Wednesday to Sunday 10am to 4pm. Admission adults £3, 5s-16s £1.50, students and seniors £2.30. Tel. 01304 3372762.*

Deal's other significant attraction is its **Maritime Museum**, in St. George's Road, with exhibits on the town's naval history, the life and times of local sailors, and the notoriously treacherous Goodwin sands, just off the coast, which have claimed many hundreds of lives over the centuries. *Open Easter to September daily 2pm to 5pm. Admission adults £1.50, students and seniors £1, 5s-15s £1. Tel. 01304 372679.*

About a mile south of Deal on Kingsdown Road is **Walmer Castle**, another of Henry's fortifications. This one, however, was converted in 1730 into domestic use, becoming the home of the Lord Warden of the Cinque Ports, an honorary title whose post holders have included such luminaries as the Duke of Wellington, and the present Queen Mother, whose drawing and dining rooms are open to the public. *Open April to October daily 10am to 6pm; November to March Wednesday to Sunday 10am to 4pm. Admission adults £4.50, 5s-16s £2.30, students and seniors £3.40. Tel. 01304 364288.*

THE CINQUE PORTS

It was during the reign of King Edward the Confessor (1042-1066) that this federation of ports was formed for the defense of the coast. They were given certain privileges by the monarch is return for supplying ships in time of war. The original five – Dover, Sandwich, Hastings, Romney and Hythe – were later joined by Winchelsea and Rye. The ports' prosperity reached a peak in the 12th to 14th centuries, but declined when they became silted up after the 14th century. Today, the only active port among them is Dover.

Sandwich, five miles north of Deal, was the first of the Cinque Ports, benefiting from a sheltered location and good access to London. For a while, this was also England's most important naval base, that is, until the harbor silted up – today, the town is more than two miles inland.

PRACTICAL INFORMATION

Dover's tourist information center is located at *Townwall Street,* close to the seafront, *Tel. 01304 205108*, and its main post office is on *Pencester Street*.

RYE & WINCHELSEA

Much more interesting and appealing than Folkestone is the town of **Rye**, reached by crossing the eerie **Romney Marshes**, a forty-square-mile area of wetlands that was submerged under the English Channel until sea levels dropped in the middle ages. With its cobbled streets and a cluster of original half-timbered houses, Rye has to be one of the most picturesque towns on the south coast. Formerly a thriving port, it is now at least two miles inland – with global warming, maybe someday it will become a port again.

ARRIVALS & DEPARTURES

By Car

Rye is approximately 30 miles southwest of Folkestone on the A259.

By Bus

There are regular buses from Folkestone and Hastings to Rye.

WHERE TO STAY

JEAKE'S HOUSE, *Mermaid Street, Rye TN31 7ET. Tel 01797 222828, Fax 01797 222623. Rooms: 12. Rates: singles from £27, doubles from £69. Credit cards: MC, Visa.*

This delightful small hotel was originally built in 1689 as a wool store and later became a Baptist school, complete with chapel! The rooms are outstanding, with a full range of modern facilities and elegant decor and furnishings, while the public rooms include a lovely lounge with original oak beams and a bar that's lined with books. There's no restaurant as such – breakfast is served in the former chapel of the Baptist school, with its original galleries and fittings. When you factor in the cost of staying here, it's a real bargain.

KING CHARLES II GUEST HOUSE, *4 High Street, Rye TN31 7JE. Tel 01797 224954. Rooms: 3. Rates from £75 per room. No credit cards.*

This small guest house just oozes with history! King Charles II was a frequent visitor here, and in the 1930s it was the home of novelist Radclyffe Hall. As for the building itself? Well, it dates back to 1420, has a wealth of period features, including ancient fireplaces and lots of original beams. The rooms are full of character and come with modern conveniences, such as TVs and tea- and coffee-making facilities. There's a small but very pretty patio that's filled with flowers. There's no restaurant, but the owners are happy to recommend places to eat in the locality.

MERMAID INN, *Mermaid Street, Rye TN31 7EY. Tel 01797 223065, Fax 01797 225069. Rooms: 31. Rates: singles from £68, doubles from £136. Bar, restaurant. All major credit cards accepted.*

This old, characterful hotel has a unique atmosphere; before becoming a hotel it was a smugglers' inn! So you can expect lots of low beamed ceilings, flagstone floors and smuggling memorabilia. The bedrooms are all different shapes and sizes (adding to the atmosphere) and come nicely furnished with antiques; four of them have four-poster beds. There's a bar where lunches are available and a fine restaurant.

WHERE TO EAT

LANDGATE BISTRO, *5-6 Landgate, Rye. Tel 01797 222829. Open Tuesday to Saturday 7pm to 9:30pm. Set dinner £15.90. All major credit cards accepted.*

Wonderful, charming, restaurant in a historic building with old beams and wooden wall paneling (as well as, apparently, a ghost or three). Despite the venerability of the building, the cooking is best described as modern British, using fresh local ingredients (including plenty of fish choices), poultry and game. There's an extensive wine list, including no fewer than seven house wines, starting at under £9. The fact that the chef has been here for more than 20 years is evidence of the bistro's popularity.

MERMAID INN, *Mermaid Street, Rye. Tel 01797 223065. Open daily noon to 2:15pm, 7pm to 9:15pm. Set lunch (3 courses) £16, dinner £30. All major credit cards accepted.*

Many people come to the Mermaid to sample its wonderful atmosphere, but eating in the bistro is also a pleasure, if a bit on the pricey side. Among the dishes on offer are a tasty onion and cider soup, and roast English lamb with a mint and tomato sauce. Being a hostelry, there's a good choice of wines, with the house red starting at around £9.

SEEING THE SIGHTS

Start your tour of the town with the **Rye Town Model Sound and Light Show** at the tourist information center on Strand Quay, which gives a very entertaining overview of the town's history. *Open year-round daily summer 9am to 5:30pm, winter 10am to 4pm; admission £2. Tel. 01797 226696.*

From here you can walk along the beautiful, cobbled **Mermaid Street**, with its timber framed houses, some of which date back to the 1300s.

Among the buildings of interest here are **Ypres Tower**, a stone construction built in 1249 to defend the town against invaders and subsequently used as a prison. *Open April to October daily 10:30am to 5:30pm; November to march Saturday and Sunday 10:30am to 4:30pm. Admission adults £2, 7s-a7s £75p, students and seniors £1.50.* The **Parish Church of St. Mary** contains what is said to be the oldest working pendulum clock in Britain, while **Lamb House**, on West Street, an attractive Georgian residence, has served as home to a variety of writers, including Henry James, who lived here from 1898 to 1916, and E. F. Benson, writer of the Lucia novels. You can see some of the furniture belonging to James on the ground floor. *Open April to October, Wednesdays and Saturdays only, 2pm to 5:30pm. Admission £3. Tel. 01797 224982.*

It's only two miles along the A259 to **Winchelsea**, another of the Cinque Ports, and much less of a tourist trap than Rye. The town, built on a grid pattern in 1283 after an earlier settlement had been destroyed by a storm, retains many attractive homes and a beautiful 14th century church dedicated to **St. Thomas a Becket**.

HASTINGS

Hastings will be eternally associated with the **Norman Invasion of 1066** and the ensuing battle which in which Saxon King Harold was defeated and replaced by **William of Normandy**. Today, Hastings is a large seaside resort with an interesting **Old Town** – the original fishing village – overlooked by a **castle** built by William the Conqueror in 1067.

ARRIVALS & DEPARTURES
By Car
Hastings is nine miles west of Rye on the A259. From London, take the A21 south.

By Bus
There are regular services to Hastings from London Victoria. Buses stop on the Queens Road as there is no proper bus station. Hastings is also a stop along the coastal route from Dover to Brighton operated by Stagecoach. *Call 01424 433711 for information.*

By Train
There are regular train services to Hastings from London Charing Cross via Battle, and from London Victoria via Gatwick. Hastings Station is located a ten minute walk north of the town center

GETTING AROUND TOWN
Hastings is certainly a walkable kind of place, but if you're trekking backwards and forwards from the town center to the Old Town, you might need a taxi. **Thomas Taxis**, *Tel. 01424 424216,* are a good bet.

Bicycles are inexpensive to rent here, most likely because of the vast numbers of foreign students who come to study English here. **Hastings Cycles**, *Tel. 01424 444013 in St. Andrew's Market,* offers rentals from about £2 a day.

WHERE TO STAY
CINQUE PORTS HOTEL, *Bohemia Road, Hastings TN34 1ET. Tel 01424 439222, Fax 01424 437277. Rooms: 40. Rates: singles from £50, doubles from £60. Restaurant, bar, leisure facilities (including pool) at leisure center next door. All major credit cards accepted.*

This medium-sized hotel is conveniently located for all Hastings attractions, including the seafront. The bedrooms are modern, with TV and tea- and coffee-making facilities; four of them have four-poster beds. The main public areas are comfortable, with real log fires in winter, wall tapestries and oriental rugs. Leisure facilities, including a heated indoor swimming pool, are available at the adjacent leisure center.

ROYAL VICTORIA HOTEL, *The Marina, St Leonards-on-Sea, Hastings TN38 0BD. Tel 01424 445544, fax 01424 721995. Rooms: 50. Rates: singles from £85, doubles from £95. Bar, restaurant. All major credit cards accepted.*

This grand hotel, right on the seafront just a couple of miles west of downtown Hastings, was purpose-built as such in 1828, and numbered among its many famous guests none other than Queen Victoria – hence the name. Though perhaps not as salubrious as in its heyday, the Royal Victoria is being refurbished throughout; the bedrooms, accessed by a fine marble staircase, are surprisingly large and a number of duplexes and family suites are available. Queen Victoria would surely be amused.

WHERE TO EAT

ROSER'S RESTAURANT, *64 Eversfield Place, St Leonards-on-Sea. Tel 01424 712218. Open Tuesday to Friday noon to 2pm, 7pm to 10pm, Saturday 7pm to 10pm. Set lunch £19.95, set dinner £22.95. All major credit cards accepted.*

Although the dining room itself is nothing to shout about – banquette seating, lots of stipped pine and the kind of frilly lampshades that I loathe, this small, unpretentious and friendly restaurant has built up an excellent reputation for the quality of its chef Gerard Roser's cooking, with splendid dishes like roast guinea fowl with shallots and wild boar bacon, and a number of fish choices. The desserts are more traditional, perhaps, but equally good.

SEEING THE SIGHTS

Accessed by the West Hill Cliff railway, the castle built by William the Conqueror should be your first stop here. Although little of the original fortifications remains, save for a few walls and dungeons, you can get a splendid view of the coast from it. Here also you can check out **The 1066 Story**, an audio-visual presentation outlining the events leading up to, and describing in detail the Norman invasion. *Castle Hill Road. Open April to September daily 10am to 5pm; October to March daily 11am to 3:30. Admission adults £3, 5s-15s £1.95, students and seniors £2.40. Tel. 01424 781112.*

Alternatively, in nearby **St. Clement's Caves**, a network of caves that have been used since pre-Christian times, you can visit the **Smugglers' Adventure**, a series of tableaux describing the town's association with the practice of smuggling contraband – tobacco and alcohol in particular – which reached a peak in the eighteenth century. *Open April to September daily 10am to 5:30pm; October to Easter daily 11am to 4.30pm. Admission adults £4.50, 5s-15s £2.95, students and seniors £3.75. Tel. 01424 422964.*

Although the battle is known as the Battle of Hastings, its actual site is some seven miles northwest of the town off the A2100 alongside which has grown a town with the not-too-original name of **Battle**. The site is marked by the ruins of **Battle Abbey**, a Benedictine monastery established by William after his victory. The abbey's high altar marked the spot – now indicated by a memorial stone – where King Harold was killed by being beaten about the head by a club – not by an arrow to the eye, as popular myth has suggested. The massive **abbey gatehouse**, built in 1338, contains an interesting audio-visual presentation on the battle that kids in particular will enjoy. *Open April to September daily 10am to 6pm; October daily 10am to 5pm; November to March daily 10am to 4pm. Admission adults £4, 5s-16s £2, students and seniors £3. Tel. 01424 773792; www.english-heritage.org.uk.*

THE BATTLE OF HASTINGS

*On October 14, 1066, **William, Duke of Normandy**, claimant to the English throne following the death of **Edward the Confessor**, landed at Pevensey. Having just defeated a Norwegian army at Stamford Bridge, Saxon **King Harold** hurried to meet him, taking up a position on a hill about six miles from Hastings. The battle was stubbornly contested, but after a time William tricked the Saxons into breaking rank. Shooting into the air, the Normans killed large numbers of Saxons, including Harold himself – though not in the eye, as long believed. Having lost their king, the Saxons retreated, leaving William to establish control over much of England. The event is commemorated in the famous Bayeux Tapestry, in Normandy.*

From Battle, take the A271 about eight miles west to the village of **Herstmonceux** and **Herstmonceux Castle**, originally built in 1444 by Sir Roger Fiennes, ancestor of *The English Patient* actor Ralph Fiennes, and surrounded by a wide moat. The castle had virtually disappeared under masses of ivy and brambles until it was reawakened, Cinderella-like, by new owners in 1911. They set about renovating it to such a degree that it was virtually unrecognizable from the pre-1911 version. The castle is currently owned by the Queen's University, Canada, and is open for guided tours only. Although the interior is relatively simple, there are some fine Elizabethan staircases and ceilings, and the 500-acre Elizabethan-style grounds are stunning. *Easter to October daily 10am to 6pm. Castle tours adults £2.50, 5s-14s £1, seniors and students 2.50. Grounds-only admission adults £3, 5s-15s £2, seniors and students £2; www.seetb.org.uk/herstmonceux.*

PRACTICAL INFORMATION

The Hastings **tourist information office** is at *Queen's Square, Priory Meadow, Tel. 01424 781111; www.hastings.gov.uk.*

LEWES

Lewes, the county town of East Sussex, stands on a steep hill overlooking the River Ouse. It's a fascinating place, full of interesting old buildings of all periods and styles, a Norman castle, and some excellent antiques and second-hand bookstores.

ARRIVALS & DEPARTURES

By Car

From Herstmonceux, take the A271 west to the town of Hailsham, then the A22 to Golden Cross, where you bear left on the B2124, following signs for Lewes. From London, take the A23 and M23 south to the A27, then follow the signs for Lewes.

By Bus

South Coast Buses, *Tel. 01272 474747*, operate a regular service from Lewes to Brighton, with connections to London

By Train

Lewes is on the main line from London Victoria to Eastbourne, and the coastal route from Brighton to Eastbourne. A trip into Brighton takes around 15 minutes. The station is on Station Road.

GETTING AROUND TOWN

Lewes is a compact little town of just 15,000; walking is by far the best way to see the place.

WHERE TO STAY

SHELLEYS, *137 High Street, Lewes BN7 1XS. Tel. 01273 472361, Fax 01273 483152. Rooms: 19. Rates: singles from £56, doubles from £116. Restaurant. All major credit cards accepted.*

Delightful hotel that started life in the sixteenth century as an inn. Later on it became the home of the Earls of Dorset and members of the Shelley family, of literary fame. Don't be put off by the slightly grubby exterior; inside is a treasure trove of antiques, with enough crooked ceilings and uneven floors to keep every Anglophile happy. The rooms are spacious and very comfortable. The hotel belongs to the large Thistle chain. This place really is special.

WHITE HART HOTEL, *55 High Street, Lewes BN7 1XE. Tel 01273 476694, Fax 01273 476695. Rooms: 52. Rates: singles from £58, doubles from £82. Bar, restaurant, indoor pool, sauna, gymnasium, jacuzzi. All major credit cards accepted.*

This historic hotel right in the center of Lewes is of particular interest to Americans, as it was the place where the first draft of the American constitution was written. Today, the hotel is a pleasant mixture of old and new; to the old Tudor bar, for example, has been added a patio and conservatory, and there's a leisure center with a full range of facilities, including a heated pool. The accommodations vary, too, between the characterful bedrooms in the older part of the hotel and the more modern but equally comfortable rooms in the annex. All in all, I'd say this hotel offers exceptional value, given what's on offer.

WHERE TO EAT

SHELLEY'S HOTEL, *High Street, Lewes. Tel 01273 472361. Open daily noon to 2:30pm, 7pm to 9:30pm. Three-course dinner from £28.50. All major credit cards accepted.*

The elegant restaurant in this charming hotel, which dates back to the 17th century, overlooks a beautiful walled garden with French windows so that in summer diners can sit al fresco. The cooking is international, but with a modern British slant, evidenced particularly in the dessert menu, which includes such scrumptious offerings as steamed lemon and ginger pudding. The main course menu includes fish dishes, such as pan-fried swordfish, and local game and poultry.

SEEING THE SIGHTS

The **Castle**, at the top of the High Street, was started in 1100, and retains its original Norman **keep**, from whose two towers excellent views of the surrounding countryside can be enjoyed. Meanwhile, at the **Barbican House Museum**, opposite the castle entrance, Lewes's history is unfolded in an audio-visual presentation, using a huge model of the town. *Open year-round Monday to Saturday 10am to 5:30pm, Sunday and Bank Holidays 11am to 5:30pm. Admission adults £3.50, 5s-15s £1.80, students and seniors £3. Tel. 01273 486290; www.sussexpast.co.uk.*

Also of interest in Lewes is the **Anne of Cleves House**, at 52 Southover High Street, given to Henry VIII's wife as part of her divorce settlement with the not-so-merry monarch – although Anne never actually lived here. Today it houses an excellent **Museum**, with original decor dating from the sixteenth century and with a Tudor bedroom – its 400-year-old Flemish bed is a must-see. *Open year-round Monday to Saturday 10am to 5pm, Sunday noon to 5pm. Admission adults £2.30, 5s-15s £1.10, students and seniors £2.10. Tel. 01273 474610; www.sussexpast.co.uk.*

GLYNDEBOURNE OPERA HOUSE

Britain's only unsubsidized opera house is located near the village of Glynde, just east of Lewes. Founded in 1934 by John Christie as a memorial to his wife, Audrey Mildmay, spending a night at the opera here is as upper-crust British as a day at Ascot races. Prices are extortionately high, which means that it's the privileged who benefit. At the same time, it must be said that the powers-that-be have deliberately pursued a policy of using young, often unknown talent instead of the kind of big names you'd only find at Covent Garden. Perhaps CG could take a leaf out of Glyndebourne's book in that respect. If you would like to get your hands on a ticket – and on a balmy summer's evening it really is a special place to be – call 01273 812231.

PRACTICAL INFORMATION

Lewes has its main **tourist information center** at *187 High Street, Tel. 01273 483448; www.lewes.gov.uk.*

BRIGHTON

Brighton, nine miles southwest of Lewes, is by far the largest town in Sussex, a cosmopolitan seaside city that's often dubbed "London by the sea." Brighton started life as an obscure fishing village called Brighthelmstone until Dr. Russell, a London physician, began sending patients there for the bracing air and for the curative sea water, which, he insisted, helped to prevent glandular diseases. Little did he know that he would be starting a trend that would continue to this day!

Brighton's popularity received an enormous boost when the **Prince Regent**, later **George IV**, began to visit regularly to bathe in the sea. The town expanded rapidly, and fashionable homes were built in elegant **terraces** overlooking the sea. Another home was built too – a fantastically eccentric seaside home for the Prince Regent, known as the **Royal Pavilion**, recently restored and looking more glamorous than ever, thanks to a National Lottery grant. The growth continued during the Victorian era, when two magnificent seaside "**pleasure piers**" were built, one recently restored, the other also looking to benefit from the Lottery.

Two centuries on, Brighton is still one of the most popular resorts in England, with a wealth of traditional seaside entertainments, such as amusement halls and parks and an abundance of fish and chip shops and seafood stalls. But it's more than that. Two universities and several colleges mean that the town has a lively, youthful atmosphere. The place abounds in pubs, clubs, theaters and concert halls, and it's also home to one of the largest gay communities in Britain. The elegant terraces remain largely intact, and some of the streets of the original fishing village have become "The Lanes," full of boutiques, restaurants and antique shops.

ARRIVALS & DEPARTURES

By Car

The worst part of the run to Brighton is getting through the south London suburbs, which can seem to take for ever. The best route is to take the A23 through Brixton and Streatham as far as the M23 junction. Get on to the M23 and follow the signs for Brighton. The last stretch of the journey takes you back on the A23 into central Brighton.

By Bus

National Express runs a frequent service from London Victoria Bus Station to Brighton, taking about two hours (depending on that south London traffic). *Call 0990 808080 for details*. The bus station is right in the center of town (Old Steine).

By Train

Trains leave London's Victoria Station every half hour, taking around 45 minutes to reach Brighton (though the line is often subject to delays, so be prepared). Trains also leave from King's Cross Station, calling at London Bridge and Blackfriars Stations. These normally take just over an hour. The Brighton train station is a 15 minute walk north of the beach. *For all rail enquiries, call 0345 484950.*

By Plane

London's Gatwick Airport is right on the edge of this region – about half way between London and Brighton. If you're spending most of your time in this area, it makes a lot of sense to book a flight to Gatwick rather than Heathrow, which is on the other side of London. Gatwick is also served by a rail station regular services to London Victoria train station.

GETTING AROUND TOWN

Despite its size, Brighton is a compact town, and most of the attractions are confined to a relatively small area, therefore walking is the best option. If you have a car, parking can be a major problem, especially on weekends, when the place gets choc-a-bloc with daytrippers. Car rental companies include **Avis**, *Tel. 01273 673738 at the Marina*, and **Hertz**, *Tel. 01273 738227 on Trafalgar Street, near the train station.*

If you need a taxi, **Radio Cabs**, *Tel. 01273 204060* will be able to help out, as will **Streamline Cabs**, *Tel. 01273 202020*. Cycling is a definite possibility here, although the traffic can be horrendous

WHERE TO STAY

GRAND HOTEL, *King's Road, Brighton. Tel. 01273 321188, Fax 01273 202694. Rooms: 200. Rates: singles from £155, doubles/twins from £195, suites from £600. Restaurants, bars. 24-hour room service. Health suite, pool. All major credit cards accepted*

Brighton's most famous hotel, subjected to a terrorist bomb blast in 1987 aimed at then-Prime Minister Margaret Thatcher, has since been extensively modernized to spectacular effect. The public rooms, with their chandeliers and marble trimmings and intricate moldings are stunning. The guest rooms, too, have been beautifully renovated, and include a full range of facilities. There's a full-service restaurant and exercise center, including a heated indoor swimming pool. This is a truly exceptional place.

Selected as one of my Best Places to Stay – see Chapter 13 for more details.

THE TWENTY ONE, *21 Charlotte Street, BN2 1AG. Tel. 01273 686450, Fax 01273 695560. Rooms: 7. Rates: singles from £35, doubles from £60. Credit cards: MC, Visa.*

Peacefully located in the Kemptown district, just a mile or so from Brighton center, this early Victorian house offers excellent value. Most rooms are furnished with period furniture, but all are cozy and very comfortable. Breakfast is a particular delight – as well as the a substantial traditional British offering of bacon and eggs, there are options for vegans and vegetarians.

THE REGENCY HOTEL, *28 Regency Square, Brighton BN1 2FH. Tel. 01273 202690, Fax 01273 220438. Rooms: 9. Rates: singles from £45, doubles from £68. Non-smoking. All major credit cards accepted.*

Elegant hotel at the top of Regency Square, with views to the sea and the wreck that is (at present) West Pier. Although some of the rooms at the top of the hotel leave a lot to be desired, the bulk of rooms are excellent. There's a lovely drawing room for relaxing in, and the dining room oozes sophistication and elegance.

PASKIN'S TOWN HOUSE, *18 Charlotte Street, Brighton BN2 1AG. Tel 01273 601203, Fax 01273 621973. Rooms: singles from £22.50, doubles from £45. All major credit cards accepted.*

This small hotel is located in a quiet neighborhood a little ways out of the central area, but within easy walking distance of all Brighton's main attractions. The nineteen bedrooms come in various shapes and sizes, but all are individually decorated and furnished. There's no restaurant, but cooked breakfast is available (with vegetarian options) in a pleasant dining room.

IMPERIAL, *First Avenue, Hove BN3 2GU. Tel 01273 777320, Fax 01273 777310. Rooms: 76. Rates: singles from £45, doubles from £70. Bar, restaurant. All major credit cards accepted.*

Hove, although a resort in its own right, is little more than an extension of Brighton, and within easy walking distance of Brighton's main attractions and downtown. The Imperial is close to the seafront, with seventy spacious rooms, many of which have been tastefully refurbished, with TV and tea- and coffee-making facilities. There's a pleasant, peaceful lounge, bar and restaurant. Being a little ways out of central Brighton, you'll pay just a bit less than a similar establishment right in the city center. If you don't mind a 20-minute walk, the Imperial is a good bet.

QUALITY HOTEL, *West Street, Brighton BN1 2RQ. Tel 01273 220033, Fax 01273 778000. Rooms: 138. Rates: singles from £76, doubles from £92. Bar, restaurant. All major credit cards accepted.*

Not everything in Brighton is regency. This modern, multi-story hotel was purpose-built and is located close to the seafront and the main attractions and shopping areas. The public areas include a spacious foyer and interesting staircase, and a restaurant that serves a wide range of international dishes. The rooms, as you'd expect, are all modern and come with the full range of facilities. If you're not desperate for regency atmosphere and charm, the Quality represents very good value.

QUEEN'S HOTEL, *1-5 Kings Road, Brighton BN1 1NS. Tel 01273 321222, Fax 01273 203059. Rooms: 90. Rates: singles from £70, doubles from £115. Bar, restaurant, indoor pool, sauna, gymnasium. All major credit cards accepted.*

This grand old hotel right on the seafront at Brighton was rapidly deteriorating until recently, when it underwent a complete refurbishment. The bedrooms, many of which have wonderful sea views, are all bright and airy and come well-equipped with a full range of facilities. More than half are reserved for non-smokers. As well as the comfortable bedrooms and public areas, guests can benefit from an excellent leisure suite with heated pool and sauna.

WHERE TO EAT

Brighton contains more eating places than anywhere in the southeast – an eclectic mixture of just about every kind of cuisine.

BLACK CHAPATI, *12 Circus Parade, New England Road, Brighton. Tel. 01273 699011. Open Tuesday to Saturday 7pm to 10pm. Main courses £10-12. All major credit cards accepted.*

Unassuming, even anonymous location for this highly popular restaurant that specializes in a range of dishes from across Asia, including Indian

– such as skewered chicken with leavened bread – and Thai. There's a limited but well-chosen wine list, where house wines start at around £10 per bottle. Well worth a visit.

ONE PASTON PLACE, *1 Paston Place, Brighton. Tel. 01273 606933. Open Tuesday to Saturday 12:30 to 2pm, 7:30 to 10pm. Set lunch (2 courses) £14.50, set dinner £38. Air conditioned. All major credit cards accepted.*

East of Palace Pier, set back from the waterfront on a gentle hill is this pleasant, relaxed restaurant, decorated with a trompe l'oeil country scene and a number of watercolors. The food is essentially French, with dishes like neatly trimmed rabbit served with "post modernist ratatouille" including crispy ratte potatoes. Desserts tend to be traditional but with a creative twist, and there's a good wine list, with, as you'd expect, the emphasis on French.

TERRE A TERRE, *71 East Street, Brighton. Tel. 01273 729051. Open Monday 6pm to 10pm, Tuesday to Sunday noon to 10:30pm. Main courses around £6-9. All major credit cards accepted.*

This lively, often noisy vegetarian restaurant with orange walls and blue central bar is something of a pace-setter. The creative menu includes dishes like scorched rice paper lumpia potsticker and walnut frisbee ravioli. It may sound a bit over the top, but in fact these and all the dishes, despite their often outlandish names, work extremely well. The same is true of the desserts. The wine list contains a selection of international organic wines.

QUENTIN'S, *42 Western Road, Hove BN3 1JD. Tel 01273 822734. Open Tuesday to Saturday, noon to 2pm, dinner 7pm to 9:30pm (no lunch Saturday), Set lunch from £7.95 for one course, set dinner from £17.95. All major credit cards accepted.*

First, don't confuse Western Road, Hove, with Western Road, Brighton. Quentin's is in Hove, a couple of miles west of downtown Brighton, and is probably the sister town's best restaurant. It's small, brightly decorated with orange walls, bedecked with lots of food magazine cuttings and pictures, worn floorboards and a motley collection of pine tables. As to the food itself? First, the ingredients are fresh – the chef even calls on a local fisherman for daily supplies. The menu is a bit of an idiosyncratic working over of some classic dishes; goat's cheese souffle with fig and walnut jelly, for example, and for dessert, apple pie with lavender (lavender?) ice cream. Actually, it's delicious! The house wine comes from a list that's mostly French, and starts at just under £10.

WHYTES, *33 Western Road, Brighton. Tel 01273 776618. Open Tuesday to Saturday, 7pm to 9:30pm. Set dinner from £17.50. All major credit cards accepted.*

Intimate restaurant just a short distance back from the seafront, with banquette seating and a convivial atmosphere. The menu is short, with a handful of starters, such as beef carpaccio with Parmesan and basil, main courses like Moroccan-spiced braised shank of lamb and traditional desserts like apple crumble. The wine list is similarly curt, but well-chosen; house wines start at just under a tenner (£10).

SEEING THE SIGHTS

Any visit to Brighton should start off with a stroll along the **seafront** – Brighton's pebbly **beach** is not itself its most endearing feature. The promenade, or boardwalk – particularly the stretch between the two piers – is particularly busy on Bank Holiday Weekends, when hordes of day trippers descend on the town from the capital and beyond. But even out of season there's no better place to savor the unique atmosphere of the British seaside, typified by seafront stores selling "kiss me quick" hats, saucy humorous postcards like stills from a Benny Hill show, candy floss (sugar candy) and whelk stalls. **West Pier** was recently awarded a Lottery grant which will enable it to be restored. *Guided tours run from April to October, Monday to Friday at 3pm, Saturday at 1:30pm and 3pm and Sunday at noon, 1:30pm and 3pm. From November to March, they run on Wednesdays at 3pm, and Saturdays and Sundays at 1:30pm and 3pm. Cost: £10 (no under-16s allowed). Tel. 01273 321499.*

Meanwhile the restoration of **Palace Pier** was recently completed at great cost, and hosts a variety of entertainments, including the **Pleasure Dome** with the latest video games and various funfair rides. On Marine Parade close to the pier entrance, there's a **Sea Life Center**, where you can observe sharks, stingrays and a host other sea creatures in a variety of displays, including a vast tank. *Open daily 10am to 6pm. Admission adults £5.95, 4s-14s £3.95, students and seniors £4.25. Tel. 01273 604233; www.sealife.co.uk.*

PIERS

Most British seaside resorts – and Brighton is no exception – have their piers, although many are in a poor state of repair. Piers originated from the jetties that were used to land ship passengers on an open shore – where there was no harbor. Later on, as visiting the seaside became the thing to do, attractions were added to the piers, so that visitors could enjoy the sea without having to get on a boat and being seasick. At Brighton, these attractions included a camera obscura, fairground rides, food stalls, clairvoyants, deck games, souvenir shops, and large areas simply to lounge in your deck chair.

From Palace Pier it's a short walk across the **Steine** (pronounced Steen) – a large open space that was the mouth of a river until drained by the Prince of Wales in 1793 – to the **Royal Pavilion**, the enormous oriental-style seaside palace built originally in a simple classical style in 1787, but transformed between 1815 and 1822 into the unique, extravagant, eccentric, exotic building seen today. That the palace is still here at all is a miracle. Queen Victoria hated the place so much that she intended to have it demolished, but died before she got the chance. The palace's acquisition by the local authority meant that it survived, though the lady in black did manage to ensure it had been stripped bare of all its furnishings and fittings. Recent restoration work, and the uncovering of designs long lost under layers of paint, plaster and wood, mean that the palace closely resembles how it must have looked when first built.

Of particular note, so to speak, is the **Music Room**, its vast dome lined with nearly 30,000 golden musical scales, and unusual umbrella-like lamps. Don't miss the **Banqueting Hall**, with its huge chandelier weighing more than a ton, the **kitchens** with columns designed as palm trees, and the **bedrooms**, where some unflattering caricatures of the Prince Regent can be seen. One of the rooms serves as a rather splendid, decadent tea room. *Open June to September daily 10am to 6pm; October to May daily 10am to 5pm. Admission adults £4.50, 5s-16s £2.75, seniors and students £3.25. Tel. 01273 290900.*

Across the restored regency-style gardens is the **Dome**, Brighton's main venue for concerts, pop and classical, and next to that, the **Brighton Museum and Art Gallery**, accessed by an entrance on Church Street. The museum contains a plenitude of Art Deco and Art Nouveau furniture, as well as Salvador Dali's famous sofa modelled on Mae West's lips. The Prince Regent would surely have approved. *Open Monday, Tuesday, Thursday to Saturday 10am to 5pm, Sunday 2pm to 5pm. Admission free. Tel. 01273 290900.*

To the southwest of the Pavilion is the maze of alleyways and streets that constitute **The Lanes**, once the heart of the old fishing village and now home to designer boutiques, restaurants and antique shops. Brighton's main shopping area, where you can find branches of all the main banks, is focused on Western Road and the Churchill Square precinct (see below under *Shopping*).

NIGHTLIFE & ENTERTAINMENT

The town has a staggering number of pubs, many of which are located in the maze of narrow streets around The Lanes. Brighton is also famous for its nightclubs, dotted all around the central area. Most of the gay bars, like **Zanzibar**, can be found in Kemp Town. There's a full range of concerts at **The Dome**, a fine theater, **The Theatre Royal**, and a range of other music and drama venues. To check out what's going on, get a copy of the town's monthly what's on guide, *The Latest*, which costs just 30p from most newsstands., or the very useful website produced by the local paper *The Argus: www.thisisbrighton.com.*

SHOPPING

Brighton is a shopper's paradise. The main chain stores can be found in the **Churchill Square** mall, and along **North Street** and **Western Road**. The jumble of narrow streets forming **The Lanes**, just south of The Pavilion, is home to dozens of boutiques, designer stores, antique shops and restaurants, and is a wonderful place to browse. Also worth a peep is the **Pavilion Shop**, *4-5 Pavilion Buildings, Tel. 01273 290900*, with souvenirs of regency Brighton, and various textiles and fabrics used in the Pavilion itself.

PRACTICAL INFORMATION

Brighton's **main tourist office** is at *10, Bartholomew Square, Tel. 01273 292599; www.brighton.co.uk.*

Banks are plentiful throughout the conurbation, and there's an **American Express** office at *82, North Street, Tel. 01273 321242.*

ARUNDEL & CHICHESTER

To the west of Brighton, the unexciting seaside resorts of Shoreham, Worthing, Littlehampton and Bognor Regis have little to commend them, apart from the usual attractions found at most British seaside resorts. Behind them tower the **South Downs**, a ridge of chalk hills which reach close to 1,000 feet in height, with a host of pretty villages. Twenty-three miles west of Brighton, on the A27, is the small hilltop town of **Arundel**, whose Norman castle has been home to the Dukes of Norfolk – Britain's leading Roman Catholic family – for over 700 years.

Chichester is an ancient Roman city with a fine cathedral and an important regional theater.

ARRIVALS & DEPARTURES

By Car

From London, take the A3. About six miles past Guildford, get on to the A286, which passes through Haslemere and Midhurst before reaching Chichester. Arundel is around 17 miles east of Chichester, on the A27.

By Bus

There's a regular service from Victoria to Chichester. *Call 0990 808080 for information.*

By Train

Rail services leave hourly for Chichester and Arundel from London Victoria, with a journey time of about 1 hour 45 minutes to Chichester, 1 hour 30 minutes to Arundel. *Call 0345 484950 for details.* If you're coming down from London to see a play at the Chichester Festival Theatre, make sure you book a hotel room for the night – the last train leaves for London at 9pm.

GETTING AROUND

Both Arundel and Chichester are small enough to get around comfortably on foot.

WHERE TO STAY

THE DOLPHIN & ANCHOR, *West Street, Chichester. Tel. 01243 785121. Rooms: 51. Rates: singles from £80, doubles from £100. Restaurant, coffee shop, bars. All major credit cards accepted.*

Located right opposite the Chichester Cathedral and adjacent to the Market Cross, The Dolphin and Anchor was originally two separate coaching inns that merged. You can stay in the older part of the hotel or opt for a more modern wing; in both cases, rooms are comfortable and come with a full range of amenities. The hotel restaurant, The Whig and Tory, offers a full a la carte menu, and there's a coffee shop for lighter meals and snacks.

THE SHIP, *North Street, Chichester. Tel. 01243 782028, Fax 01243 788000. Rooms 36. Rates: singles from £73, doubles/twins from £109, four-poster from £145. Restaurant, bar/pub. All major credit cards accepted.*

This elegant Georgian house was built in 1790 for Admiral Sir George Murray, a colleague of Admiral Nelson, of Trafalgar fame. Murray's wealth is evident in a number of features, including a Robert Adam staircase. The guest rooms, all named after historic ships, are comfortable, and the hotel is well-placed for all of Chichester's attractions, including the Festival Theatre, a fifteen minute walk away.

THE NORFOLK ARMS, *22 High Street, Arundel. Tel. 01903 882101, Fax 01903 884275. Rooms 34. Rates: singles from £60, doubles from £120. Restaurant. All major credit cards accepted.*

Centrally located close to Arundel Castle, the Norfolk Arms was formerly a coaching lodge, built by the Duke of Norfolk (hence the name). The hotel has a distinctively olde-worlde feel, most evident in the lounges and dining room, but comes with a full range of up-to-date facilities. The rooms in the older part of the hotel are a little on the small side, but comfortable nonetheless. If you want a bit more space, but less of an olde-world ambience, opt for a room in the modern annex. There's a fine restaurant, specializing in traditional English cuisine.

CROUCHER'S BOTTOM COUNTRY HOTEL, *Birdham Road, Chichester PO20 7EH. Tel 01243 784995, fax 01243 539797. Rooms: 15. Rates: singles from £52, doubles from £85. Lounge, bar, restaurant. All major credit cards accepted.*

Don't be put off by the name! Situated close to Chichester Harbour, and about a mile and a half from central Chichester, this family-run hotel offers fifteen pleasant coach house-style rooms with all modern facilities, including TV and tea- and coffee-making equipment. The public areas include a large cozy lounge and a beamed restaurant.

WHERE TO EAT

COMME CA, *67 Broyle Road, Chichester. Tel. 01243 788724. Open Tuesday to Saturday noon to 2pm, 6pm to 10:30pm; Sunday noon to 2pm. Set lunch £17.75 (3 courses). All major credit cards accepted.*

This French restaurant converted from a pub some years ago is close enough to the Festival Theatre to make it ideal for pre- and post-theater meals, which are available from Tuesday to Saturday. The dining room, decorated with antique toys and bunches of dried hops, is comfortable and the French dishes – cooked by a French chef – are outstanding – especially the grilled lamb with deep-fried leeks and an herb and garlic sauce. The service is friendly and helpful but not overpowering.

PLATTERS, *15 Southgate, Chichester. Tel. 01243 530430. Open Tuesday to Saturday noon to 1:45pm, 7pm to 9:30pm. Main courses around £13-15. Credit cards: MC, Visa.*

Relaxed ambience in this central Chichester restaurant, where the emphasis is on French, with a bit of an Asian influence. The portions are generous, and come with equally generous helpings of vegetables. With an extensive and reasonably-priced wine list, it's a good place for a post-Chichester Festival Theatre meal.

SEEING THE SIGHTS

Much of the original structure was destroyed during the Civil War, and rebuilt during the nineteenth century, though the **keep** itself is original, and the **Baron's Hall** and gatehouse date from the thirteenth century. Check out the **library**, where you can find paintings by VanDyck, Holbein and Gainsborough, and see the rosary and prayer book used by the catholic Mary, Queen of Scots before her execution. *Open April to October Monday to Friday and Sunday noon to 5pm. Admission adults £6.70, 5s-15s £4.20, students and seniors £5.70. Tel. 01963 882173.*

Arundel's other main attraction is its nineteenth century Roman Catholic **cathedral**, on Parson's Hill, built in 1873 by none other than Joseph Hansom of Hansom cabs fame. It's (loosely) based on the French Gothic style of around 1400, but somehow it doesn't quite work. Among the features inside are a lovely **rose window** over the west door, and the **shrine** of St. Philip Howard. Howard, a convert to Roman Catholicism during the Elizabethan period, was sentenced to death in 1589 for his religious views. More recently, the diocesan bishop, Cormack Murphy O'Connor, was sent to London to become Archbishop of Westminster, the leader of Roman Catholics in England and Wales. *Open year-round daily 9am to 6pm. Admission free. Tel. 01903 882297.*

It's only about twelve miles from here, via the A284, A29, B2138 and A283 to **Petworth**, with a cluster of timber-framed homes huddling close to the walls of **Petworth House**, a magnificent 17th century residence on 2000 acres landscaped by Capability Brown. The house itself is stunning, especially the **Carved Room** – where carvings by **Grinling Gibbons** can be seen, as well as the famous full-length portrait of Henry VIII. The **Great Staircase**, with murals by **Louis Laguerre**, is magnificent, and by contrast you can visit the humble servants' quarters, including the kitchen. Perhaps the most outstanding feature here, though, is the collection of art – paintings by Titian, Bosch, Reynolds and Turner are on display – Turner even had a studio here for a time. *Open April to October house Monday to Wednesday, Saturday and Sunday 1pm to 5:30pm; park daily 8am to dusk. Admission adults £5.50, 5s-17s £2.50. Tel. 01798 342207.*

Continue west on the A27 to **Chichester**, an ancient Roman city sandwiched between the downs and a large natural harbor. The city is laid out according to the original Roman plan; north, south, east and west streets radiating out from the attractive **Market Cross** (dating from 1501). Just a few yards along West Street is Chichester's Norman **cathedral**, built on Roman foundations, remnants of which are visible by looking through glass panels in the cathedral floor. The cathedral was begun in the 1070s, and is notable for its lofty **spire** added in the 1800s and which has served as an important marker for shipping out in the Channel. Also of note is the unusual fifteenth century **bell tower**, unusual among English churches in that it was constructed apart from the main building. Inside, the massive Norman pillars of the nave focus the eye on the **high altar** and the altar screen **tapestry** by John Piper behind it. Also worth a look is a pair of Saxon limestone **reliefs** in the choir depicting the *Raising of Christ* and *Christ Arriving in Bethany*. *Open Easter to October daily 7:30am to 7pm; November to Easter daily 7:30 to 5pm. Admission free, but donations welcome. Tel. 01243 782595.*

To the east of South Street, the quarter known as **The Pallants** is almost pure Georgian. Here, at Number 9, North Pallant, you'll find

Pallant House, built in 1712 for a local wine merchant. The house, with its intricate brickwork and wood carving, has been restored of late, and contains period antiques along with contemporary works of art by **Barbara Hepworth** and **Henry Moore**. *Open year-round Tuesday to Saturday 10am to 5pm, Sunday 12:30pm to 5pm. Admission adults £4, under-16s free, seniors and students £3. Tel. 01243 774557.*

To the north of the city, the **Chichester Festival Theatre**, built in 1962, is one of England's most important regional playhouses, with its own company which performs from May to September (with touring companies and various other offerings – orchestral concerts, opera, ballet and so on – for the rest of the year). *Should you wish to book tickets, call 01243 784437, or write to The Box Office, Chichester Festival Theatre, Oaklands Park, Chichester PO19 4AP. All major credit cards are accepted.*

A mile west of Chichester, on Salthill Road, are the remains of **Fishbourne Roman Palace**, the largest Roman palace in Britain, with more than 100 rooms. It likely belonged to Cogidubnus, a Romanized Celt aristocrat, who lived in the first century AD. You'll see mosaics and painted walls, along with bathing and heating systems, and there's a garden laid out as it would have been in the first century. *Open mid-February to March, November to mid-December daily 10am to 4pm; April to July, September and October daily 10am to 5pm; August 10am to 6pm; mid-December to mid-February 10am to 4pm. Admission adults £4.40, 5s-15s £2.30, seniors and students £3.70. Tel. 01243 785859.*

Four miles southwest of Fishbourne is the exquisite harborside village of **Bosham**, with its closely-packed thatched cottages, and a Saxon church dedicated to the **Holy Trinity**, with a copy of the panel from the Bayeux tapestry that depicts it; Harold is said to have prayed here before the Battle of Hastings in 1066. If you're driving, be careful where you park; at high tide the roadway near the church is submerged under several feet of water.

PRACTICAL INFORMATION

Chichester's **tourist information centre** is located at *29a South Street PO19 1AH, Tel. 01243 775888; www.chichester.gov.uk.*

Arundel has its own **tourist office** at *61 High Street, Arundel BN18 9AJ, Tel. 01903 882268; www.arun.gov.uk.*

All the main domestic banks have branches in both Arundel and Chichester.

TUNBRIDGE WELLS

Royal Tunbridge Wells (the prefix "Royal" was only added in 1909, and is very rarely used), is a spa town which, like Bath, owes its fame and fortune to the discovery of a **mineral spring** in 1606. As word spread about the spring and its medicinal qualities, so the number of visitors increased, including members of the royal family, and Tunbridge Wells became an important gathering-place for the well-heeled, with social events presided over by none other than that doyen of gentility, **Beau Nash**.

ARRIVALS & DEPARTURES

By Car

Take the A21 from London to the M25, at junction 4. Stay on the M25 until junction 5, then get back on to the A21, following the signs for Tunbridge Wells.

By Bus

There are regular services from London Victoria Bus Station to Tunbridge Wells. *Call 0990 808080 for information.*

By Train

There's a regular train service from London Charing Cross, passing through Waterloo East and London Bridge Stations. The journey time takes about an hour. *Call 0345 484950 for information.*

GETTING AROUND TOWN

Tunbridge Wells is best explored on foot. You'll need a car to get to the other destinations listed in this section.

WHERE TO STAY

HOTEL DU VIN & BISTRO, *Crescent Road, Tunbridge Wells TN1 2LY. Tel. 01892 526455, Fax 01892 512044. Rooms: 32. Rates: singles, doubles from £75. Bar, restaurant (see below), parking. All major credit cards accepted.*

This is a truly wonderful place to stay! The young Princess (later Queen) Victoria once spent the summer in this exquisite eighteenth century house. All the rooms are lavishly decorated and furnished – and named after a wine company, and come with hi fi systems, TV and mini-bars where fresh milk awaits you. The public rooms are equally attractive, and the restaurant has built up an excellent reputation (see below).

THE SPA HOTEL, *Mount Ephraim, Royal Tunbridge Wells. Tel. 01892 520331. Rooms: 71. Rates: singles from £82, doubles from £99. Restaurant, indoor pool, tennis courts, gymnasium, beauty salon. All major credit cards accepted.*

More like a resort than a conventional hotel, the Spa boasts an indoor swimming pool, sauna, solarium and tennis courts, as well as 15 acres of grounds offering superb views of the Kent countryside. The building is a Georgian country house dating back to 1766; it became a hotel in the 1880s. The nicely decorated guest rooms are equipped full a full range of amenities, and the Chandelier Restaurant has an excellent reputation.

ROYAL WELLS INN, *Mount Ephraim, Tunbridge Wells TN4 8BE. Tel 01892 511188, Fax 01892 511908. Rooms: 19. Rates: singles from £65, doubles from £85. Bar, restaurant. All major credit cards accepted.*

High above the town, with wonderful views over the town and surrounding countryside is this charming family-run hotel. The nineteen well-equipped rooms are all stylishly decorated and furnished, many affording beautiful views. Despite its size, the Royal Wells has two restaurants, the informal Brasserie, and the Conservatory Restaurant where a full a la carte menu is available.

WHERE TO EAT

HOTEL DU VIN & BISTRO, *Crescent Road, Tunbridge Wells. Tel. 01892 526455. Open daily noon to 12.45pm, 7pm to 9:45pm. Main courses from £10 to £14. All major credit cards accepted.*

Pleasantly informal bistro located in a Georgian townhouse, with bare floorboards, paneled walls covered by framed advertisements. The menu is eclectic with a tendency towards French; the grilled cod comes with the Portuguese delicacy chorico and in the dessert menu there's even chocolate brownie. Equally eclectic is the wine list, with selections from Israel and Morocco as well as France, Germany, Italy and the New World.

THACKERAY'S HOUSE, *85 London Road. Tel. 01892 511921. Open Tuesday to Saturday 12:30pm to 2pm, 7pm to 10pm, Sunday 12:30pm to 2pm. Set dinner from £13.50 to £23. Credit cards: MC, Visa.*

Yes, this three-story green-and-white house was the one-time residence of Victorian novelist William Makepeace Thackeray, who wrote *Tunbridge Toys* on the premises. Inside, the main restaurant's walls (there's a small bistro downstairs that serves a similar menu, but cheaper) are covered in paintings and you'll bounce up and down on the posh carpet. The creative menu includes grilled pigeon breasts with pea risotto, and a variety of duck dishes, and the dessert menu includes the host favorite – though not to my taste: a chocolate Armagnac loaf with coffee sauce.

SEEING THE SIGHTS

Among the places of interest in this prosperous little town are the **Pantiles**, a colonnaded arcade of shops dating from the seventeenth century, where you can also find the original **Chalybeate Spring** in the Bath House. Here, a "dipper" has been continuously serving the water since the eighteenth century (not the same one). Across the road, the **Church of King Charles the Martyr**, built in 1678 – after the Resoration of the Monarchy – is dedicated to King Charles I who was executed in 1649. Inside, a spectacular baroque ceiling is the dominant feature.

EXCURSIONS & DAY TRIPS

Royal Tunbridge Wells is a good base for exploring an area exceptionally rich in stately homes and castles. Just seven miles northwest of town on the B2188 is **Penshurst**, an exceedingly attractive village of fifteenth and sixteenth century houses centred round its own Leicester Square. Chief attraction here, though, is **Penshurst Palace**, one of the best-preserved medieval manor houses in England, and home of the Sidney family since 1552. The family's most famous son, Sir Philip, was born here. The oldest part of the house is the **Baron's Hall**, built in 1341, with a chestnut-wood roof, while outside is an outstanding 10-acre walled Tudor-style garden. *House open March Saturday and Sunday noon to 5:30pm; April to October daily noon to 5:30pm. Grounds open daily 10:30am to 6pm. Admission to house and grounds adults £6, children £4, seniors and students £5.50. Grounds only admission £4.50, £3.50, £4. Tel. 01892 870307.*

Just three miles west of Penshurst just off the B2027 is another exceptional building – **Hever Castle**, built in the 13th century. It's an exceptionally attractive pile, with turrets, battlements and drawbridge leading over a lily-dotted moat. **Anne Boleyn** was brought up here, and the castle was the scene of her courtship with Henry VIII. Upstairs, you can visit her room, and see the prayer books she took with her to her execution. Later on, Henry gave the castle to **Anne of Cleves**, in whose room hangs a beautiful **tapestry** depicting the wedding of Henry's sister to Louis XII of France. The castle was purchased in 1903 by American millionaire **William Waldorf Astor**, who painstakingly restored the interior and even built a Tudor-style village to house the staff – now used as a hotel. The gardens are exceptionally beautiful, particularly the Italian garden. *Open March to November daily noon to 6pm; December to February daily 11am to 4pm. Gardens open daily 11am to 6pm. Admission to castle and gardens adults £7.30, 5s-16s £4, seniors and students £6.20. Gardens only ££5.80, £3.80, £4.90. Tel. 01732 865224; www.hevercastle.co.uk.*

Nine miles north of Hever Castle is **Chartwell**, Sir Winston Churchill's home from 1924 to 1965. Chartwell is just off the B269, accessed by taking the B2027 west from Tunbridge. It is one of the most visited properties owned by the National Trust, so expect long lines. The unexceptional Tudor building was heavily restored during the Victorian period and contains, as you'd expect, lots of Churchill memorabilia – pictures, maps and so on – including a collection of his paintings. The house is set out in much the same way as it would have been in Churchill's time. There are lovely views over the Weald of Kent. *Open April to October Tuesday to Sunday 11am to 5:30pm; November and March Saturday, Sunday and Wednesday 11am to 4:30pm. Admission adults £5.50, children £2.75. Tel. 01732 866368.*

On the eastern side of Royal Tunbridge, just off the A262, is **Sissinghurst Castle and Garden**. The original Tudor castle, complete with moat, had fallen into such disrepair and the garden had become so overgrown by the 1920s that new purchaser, writer Vita Sackville-West and her husband Harold Nicholson, vowed to transform it into one of the finest gardens in England. This they did with some panache, and today Sissinghurst is one of the most popular gardens in England, created as a series of "outdoor rooms" around the gatehouse of the decayed Tudor edifice. *Open April to mid-October Tuesday to Friday 1pm to 6:30pm, Saturday and Sunday 10am to 5:30pm. Admission adults £6, 5s-15s £3. Tel. 01580 712850.*

Meanwhile, fifteen miles southeast of Tunbridge on the A262, you'll come to **Bodiam**, one of the most photogenic of all England's castles, with its rounded corner turrets, battlements, portcullis and dark green moat. Built in 1385 to thwart any French invasion, it was "slighted" (partially destroyed) during the Civil War to prevent its use by the forces of King Charles I. It subsequently fell into disrepair, until restored by Lord Curzon early in the last century. Enough of the interior survives to give a picture of castle life and an audio-visual presentation and small museum give some social and historical perspective. *Open mid-February to October daily 10am to 6pm; November to mid-February 10am to 4pm. Admission adults £3.60, 5s-15s £1.80. Tel. 01580 830436.*

Finally, don't miss **Leeds Castle** – which must surely rival Bodiam as one of the most beautiful castles in the country – located twenty miles northeast of Tunbridge just off the M20. Built partly on two islands in a lake, partly on the mainland, the castle dates back more than 1,000 years. It was rebuilt by the Normans in the twelfth century, and later became a favorite home-from-home for **Henry VIII**, who converted it from fortress to palace. Inside the much-restored castle you can see original period furniture and paintings and, bizarrely, a dog-collar museum, while outside attractions include a maze and a large aviary with some exotic species of feathered friends. *Open March to October daily 10am to 5pm; November to February daily 10am to 3pm. Admission adults £9:30, under 15s £6, seniors and students £7.30. Tel. 01622 765400; www.leeds-castle.co.uk.*

If you've been spending a day visiting stately homes and castles, there's no better place to spend a few relaxing hours than **Lamberhurst Vineyard**, just outside the village of Lamberhurst, just off the A21 about six miles east of Tunbridge. Wine growing was widely practised in Roman Britain, but only recently came back into prominence. The wines produced here are respected throughout the world. You can enjoy some wine tasting, a tour of the vineyard or enjoy a snack at the restaurant.

PRACTICAL INFORMATION

Tunbridge Wells' **tourist information** centre is at *The Old Fish Market, The Pantiles, Tunbridge Wells TN2 5TN, Tel. 01892 515675.* All the main banks are represented in the town.

16. CENTRAL SOUTHERN ENGLAND

This is a land full of contrasts and thus a great place for exploring – rich verdant pastureland, rolling hills and moorland, forests, large industrial cities, beaches and estuaries on a coast that becomes more and more dramatic the further west you go. It's also a region that abounds in history, with more prehistoric remains than anywhere else in the country, plenty of historic homes and two of the most beautiful cathedrals in the country – **Salisbury** and **Winchester** – not to mention a myriad of smaller churches, priories and abbeys.

Our first venerable port of call, Winchester, former capital of England, is contrasted with a visit to one of England's newest large cities, **Bournemouth**, a once genteel seaside resort that's finally put away her blue rinse and become a vibrant, young cosmopolitan place (and the beaches are good, too). There's the great passenger port of **Southampton**; **Portsmouth**, with more historical attractions to explore, mostly of a maritime nature; the 145 square-mile **New Forest**, which could have been made for walking or riding (except that it was actually made for hunting); and the lovely **Dorset coast**.

WINCHESTER

Winchester, framed by the rolling green hills of the Hampshire countryside, was Saxon England's capital long before the Normans established London as their chief commercial and political center. Check out the huge 1901 statue of Saxon England's most famous king, **Alfred the Great**, in the High Street.

But Winchester's history goes back even further. It was the **Romans** who first recognized the strategic potential of the site. They built a camp here and called it Venta Belgarum. Today's Winchester is a bustling,

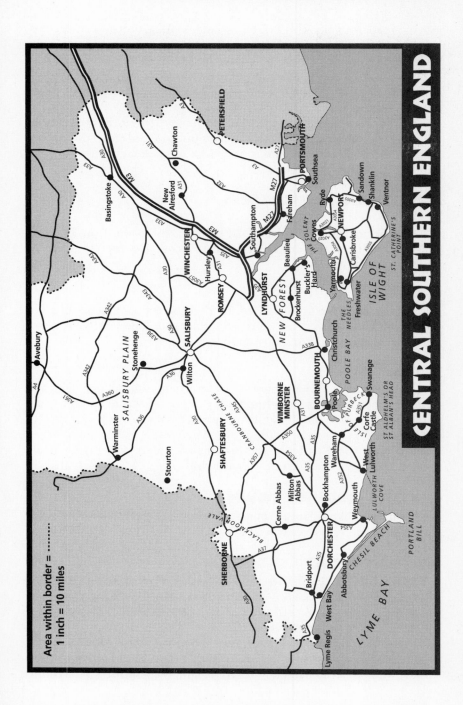

green, prosperous city with a vast range of historical sites and attractions, excellent shopping facilities and some fine pubs and restaurants. While the most famous sites, like the magnificent **Cathedral**, immortalized in famous song, and the **Castle** are not to be missed, the great thing about Winchester is that it's such a fun place to explore; there are surprises around every corner.

With dozens of places to eat and drink, many of them, like the famous Wykeham (pronounced "Wikkam") Arms pub and the Hotel du Vin and Bistro listed in good food guides, Winchester is a great place to use as a base for exploring the region.

ARRIVALS & DEPARTURES

By Car

Winchester is situated just off the main M3 motorway from London, which is just over an hour away. The A34 connects the city with the midlands and north.

By Bus

Almost opposite the Guildhall in High Street is Winchester's bus station, with frequent connections to Southampton, and service every two hours to London's Victoria bus station.

By Train

The city is on the main London to Bournemouth rail line, with two trains an hour running from London's Waterloo Station, and there are good connections to the midlands and north. *For rail information, call 0345 484950.* To get to the train station, from High Street follow Jewry Street, turning left at City Road. The station is set back about 200 yards – in all, about a ten minute walk from the cathedral.

GETTING AROUND TOWN

Winchester is a relatively small city, and all the attractions are easily manageable on foot.

WHERE TO STAY

ROYAL HOTEL, *St. Peter Street, Winchester SO23 9LQ. Tel. 01962 861611, US toll free number: 800/225-5843, Fax 01962 841503. Rates (including full English breakfast) for singles £80: doubles £115: suites from £140. All major credit cards accepted.*

Built at the end of the 17th century as a private house, for 50 years it was used by nuns from Brussels as a convent before being converted into a hotel, when it became one of the city's main social spots. All the rooms have traditional English decor, and particularly interesting is the secluded garden, hidden behind high gray walls. There's a small, formal restaurant, where fixed-priced meals start at £18.50 per person, and there's a 24-hour room service.

WESSEX HOTEL, *Paternoster Row, Winchester. Tel. 01962 861611. Rates for singles £45 to £65, doubles: £35 to £45 per person sharing. Rates include breakfast. Restaurant. All major credit cards accepted. Service charge.*

This modern low-rise structure stands just across the green from the Cathedral with many of the rooms boasting excellent cathedral views. The lounge and reception areas are built on several open levels, and there's a cocktail bar and restaurant – more traditional, with leather furniture, mahogany and brass. The well-equipped rooms contain TVs, radios and hairdryers, and 24-hour room service is available. The fine restaurant, which serves local delicacies like grilled trout caught in the famous Hampshire Avon, has traditional French and English dishes starting at £20.

WYKEHAM ARMS, *75 Kingsgate Street, Winchester SO23 9PE. Tel. 01962 853834. Rates for singles £50, doubles £40 to £50 per person sharing. Restaurant. All major credit cards accepted. Service charge.*

This ancient inn is very close to the cathedral and Winchester College, its proximity to the latter explaining the odd collection of old sports equipment and pewter mugs around the main bar. Handsomely furnished, antique-laden rooms are available, and there's an award-winning restaurant with a mixture of classic French and English dishes.

THE GUARD HOUSE, *Southgate Street, Winchester SO23 9EF. Tel 01962 861514. Rooms: 2. Rates: single occupancy from £50, twin from £60. No credit cards.*

Winchester has been a major regional military center since Roman times with, at one time, several barracks for the various regiments stationed here. One of these was the Peninsula Barracks, now converted into apartments. The Guard House was just that – the one-time guard house of the Peninsula Barracks, now tastefully converted into a small B&B. The bedrooms are bright and airy, nicely furnished and decorated and much larger than you'd find in most similar-sized establishments. Breakfast is served en famille in a large kitchen; choose from the traditional English variety of continental.

WHERE TO EAT

ELIZABETHAN RESTAURANT, *18 Jewry Street. Tel. 01962 853566. £16 to £25. Open daily from 7pm to 10pm. All major credit cards accepted. Service charge.*

This elegant restaurant, housed upstairs in a building that dates back to 1509, is an opportunity to dine in a romantic, candlelit environment under original hand-hewn beams. The food is good, too: English dishes with a flash of French inspiration. There's a special tourist menu for £10 per person, and a la carte dinners start from £20.

OLD CHESIL RECTORY, *1 Chesil Street, Winchester. Tel. 01962 851555. Open Tuesday to Thursday noon to 2pm, 7pm to 9pm; Fridays and Saturdays noon to 2pm, 7pm to 9:30pm. Set lunch around £16 (rwo course), set dinner £32 (three courses). Credit cards: MC, Visa.*

Wonderful old house that dates back to 1459 and is allegedly the oldest surviving house in the city of Winchester. It's particularly striking from the outside with enormous half-timbered gables making it look more like something you'd find in Stratford-upon-Avon than here. Inside the atmosphere is enhanced by candles, even at lunchtime. The food here is modern British; lots of fresh local produce, some of it organic, cooked to perfection. The desserts are generally light, and the wine list starts with house wines, a little on the steep side at £13.95.

HUNTER'S, *5 Jewry Street, Winchester. Tel 01962 860006. Open Monday to Saturday, noon to 2pm, 6:30pm to 10pm. Set dinner £9.95 to £12.95. All major credit cards accepted.*

This lively restaurant is right in the heart of Winchester. Casual in style, its walls are covered in murals and collages, its table tightly packed with lots of candles and fresh flowers. The cooking is essentially modern British, including some traditional dishes with a slight twist; there's also an Oriental influence in some of the choices. The desserts are drawn largely from old dependables like apple crumble and spotted dick. There's a good wine list, house wines coming in at £9.95 a bottle.

NINE THE SQUARE, *The Square, Winchester. Tel 01962 864004. Open Monday to Saturday noon to 2pm, 7pm to 10pm. All major credit cards accepted.*

This city center establishment is splendidly located in a little square just yards from the city's wonderful Norman cathedral. There are two eating areas: downstairs, the more informal of the two, with the atmosphere of a wine bar/bistro. Upstairs, which is only open in the evenings, is more formal, but not oppressively so. There's a strong Italian influence in the menu, with a variety of home-made pastas, which is reflected also in the wine list.

SEEING THE SIGHTS

If ever there was a building that makes you go weak at the knees, it's Winchester's magnificent Norman **Cathedral**, *The Close, Tel. 01962 853137. Open daily 7.15am-6:30pm; Expected donation: £2.50, students & seniors £2.* Started in 1079, it replaced an earlier Saxon minster, whose foundations can be traced just to the left of the main west door. After all the hype (including my own), you may find the Cathedral a bit disappointing from the outside – especially if you've just returned from a visit to its near neighbor, Salisbury – but once you're through the west door, the vast perpendicular **nave**, the longest in Europe, opens out in front of you and you're totally besotted by the place.

Take one of the regular guided tours, or pick up a leaflet from the stewards and guide yourself around. In a building of this size and importance – Winchester was and still is one of the leading ecclesiastical centers in England and one of the only five whose bishops automatically sits in the House of Lords – there are bound to be plenty of surprises: as you walk along the **north aisle**, among many other tombs in the floor, you can see the plain, simple slab that marks the resting place of **Jane Austen**, whose family lived at nearby Chawton.

Close to the **Lady Chapel**, behind the **High Altar** with its spectacular **rood screen**, a strange little statue of a man in a diving suit will inevitably catch your eye. This amazing building was built on a marsh, and at the end of the nineteenth century it looked as if the whole pile might collapse – it was a miracle it hadn't collapsed before! A diver, **William Walker**, was commissioned to plunge down into the watery foundations and prop up the building with bags of concrete. It took him 11 years, but he virtually single-handedly saved the Cathedral. To get an idea of how high the watertable is here, ask one of the stewards if you can take a peep at the crypt – for much of the year waist-deep in water.

THE LEGEND OF SWITHUN

Swithun *was one of Winchester's early bishops, a humble, saintly man who requested that, when he died, he should be buried outside of the Cathedral, not like most of his predecessors (and successors) in a place of honor inside. His request was carried out, but some years later, a group of zealous churchmen decided that he should, after all, be buried inside the building. When his body was exhumed, legend says that it rained for 40 days and nights. Locals will tell you to this day that if it rains on* **St. Swithun's day** *(July 15) it will continue to rain for 40 more. The only other miracle attributed to the saint is that he made whole some broken eggs dropped by a farmer's wife on her way to market. The magnificent medieval shrine of St. Swithun, located behind the High Altar, was destroyed during the Reformation. A triangular catafalque marks the spot where the saint's bones were originally housed.*

Moving from the ridiculous to the sublime, stay in the Cathedral for the service of **Evensong** which is sung every day (except Wednesday) by the world-famous choir at 5pm, a free musical treat. And don't forget to check out the **Cathedral Library**. Priceless books and manuscripts are on display, including the 12th century **Winchester Bible**.

If you're a **King Arthur** fan, you might want to check out the **Great Hall of Winchester Castle**. The only surviving part of what was once a much larger building, it was built in 1222 by King Henry III. The large **round table** that hangs on the wall inside is said by some to be the Round Table of Arthurian legend. Those with their feet firmly on the ground will tell you that it's of a much later vintage, probably 16th century. Look carefully and you'll note that the good king is wearing Tudor robes! *Castle Hill. Open April to October daily 10am to 6pm; November to March 10am to 4pm. Admission is 30p. Tel. 01962 846476.*

The public schools of Eton (where Prince William was educated) and Harrow may be more famous, but **Winchester College** predates them both. Founded by Bishop William of Wykeham in 1387 as a school for 70 scholars and up to 10 "commoners," it's the oldest school in use in the country (and one of the most expensive) and still uses many of its original buildings. You can take a peek at the chapel and Chamber Court, the focal point of school life here for more than 600 years. *College Street. Open April-September Mon-Sat 10am-1pm and 2-5pm, Sun 2-5pm only. Donation. Tel. 01962 621217.*

Winchester boasts several museums, including the **City Museum**, *The Square, open weekdays 10am-5pm Sat 10am-1pm and 2-5pm; free; Tel. 01962 848269,* which traces the archaeology and history of Winchester, and the **Westgate Museum**, used in the 17th century as a debtor's prison and now to display local artifacts. For military history buffs, there are no fewer than five military museums here – as the administrative center for the county of Hampshire, the city has been the home of many regiments. One of the barracks, Peninsular Barracks, has recently been converted into one of the most prestigious housing developments in Britain. *Westgate Museum open February to March and October Tuesday to Friday 10am to 1pm and 2pm to 5pm, weekends 2pm to 5pm only; April to September Monday to Friday, 10am to 5pm, Saturday 2pm to 5pm, weekends 2pm to 5pm. Admission is 30p.*

It's worth taking the mile-long walk from downtown Winchester across the River Itchen's water meadows to the ancient **Hospital of St. Cross**. Founded in 1136 by Bishop Henry de Blois for 13 poor men, not only is it the oldest charitable institution in England, it still maintains its ancient tradition of providing refreshment for weary travelers, even tourists. Just ask one of the brothers wearing the traditional black or red gowns for the **Wayfarer's Dole**, a beaker of ale and a morsel of bread, but make sure it's a weekday and that you're there before 11am. *Open Easter to September, Mondays to Saturdays from 9:30am to 12:30pm and 2pm to 5pm; October to Easter 10:30am to 12:30pm and 2pm to 3:30pm. Admission £2.*

NIGHTLIFE & ENTERTAINMENT

Winchester has a host of pubs, some of which date back for centuries. Among the most interesting are the **Wykeham Arms**, *75 Kingsgate Street*; the **Eclipse Inn**, *The Square*, a photogenic old pub facing the cathedral and serving good, inexpensive bar food. It can get rather crowded, especially on summer weekends); and the **Royal Oak**, *Royal Oak Passage, off High Street*. Pubs that claim to be the oldest in England come two a penny. This one's stake is the Saxon wall which forms part of the bar. Oldest or not, it's a good, atmospheric place to sample a pint of the local brew, or to partake of a tasty (and inexpensive) pub lunch.

Cultural attractions include an **Arts Festival** in the middle of July, and at the end of the same month, the **Southern Cathedrals Festival**, where the choirs of Winchester, Salisbury and Chichester get together to conjure up a world-class program of choral music, including specially commissioned works. The Festival works on a rotational basis and therefore takes place in Winchester once every three years.

SHOPPING

The **Antiques Market**, *King's Walk, Tel. 01962/862277,* sells craft and gift items in addition to antiques. For antiquarian books, it's hard to beat **H M Gilbert**, *19 The Square, Tel. 01962/852832.* A short walking distance from the cathedral, the books are housed in five medieval cottages.

EXCURSIONS & DAY TRIPS

If you're a devotee of steam trains, you might want to check out the **Watercress Line**, a ten-mile-long stretch of railroad that starts in **New Alresford** (pronounced "Allsford") eight miles north east of Winchester, and carries visitors on a nostalgic tour through nineteenth century England. It's called the Watercress Line because this is one of England's best watercress-producing areas; the fresh, clear water coming down from the surrounding chalk hills make it ideal. If you have time, spend a few minutes looking round the village itself, where some very pleasant Georgian cottages line a lovely village green, complete with gurgling stream. *Open March-October weekends and national holidays; daily from mid-July-early Sept; £7.50. Tel. 01962 733810; www.watercress.line.*

Meanwhile, in the village of **Chawton** about seven miles northeast of Alresford on the A31, you can see the house where **Jane Austen** lived for the last eight years of her life and where many of Jane's personal effects, manuscripts and letters can be seen. Here she worked on a number of her novels, including *Persuasion*, *Mansfield Park* and *Sense and Sensibility*. If you've ever read Jane Austen, the house is just what you'd expect; it's all a bit twee, really – an air of somewhat precocious gentility totally in keeping with the ordered lifestyle of the unmarried daughter of a parson. Among the bits and pieces of furniture that remain, you can see the piano that Jane would play every morning before taking to her mahogany writing desk in the sitting room, leaving her sister Cassandra to scrub the floors, do the washing and all the other tedious household chores that were not really Jane's cup of tea. The red brick house is located right in the center of the village. *March-December daily 11am-4:30pm; January-February weekends 11am-4:30pm; £2.50, students & seniors £2. Tel. 01420 83262.*

JANE AUSTEN

A flurry of lavish televised dramatizations and films of Jane Austen's best known works, such Pride and Prejudice, Sense and Sensibility and Emma, has brought the author back into the spotlight in recent years. Jane, the daughter of an Anglican clergyman, grew up in the village of Steventon, near Basingstoke. Between 1800 and 1817 Austen lived with her mother and sister Clarissa in Chawton, where she wrote **Mansfield Park**, **Emma** *and* **Persuasion***. She also spent a good deal of time in Kent, Bath and Lyme Regis where Bay Cottage can still be seen on the seafront. Jane spent the final years of her life is Winchester (where her simple grave, giving no indication of her "career," can be seen in the Cathedral's north aisle). It was deemed unseemly for women of her time to write novels, so Jane wrote her novels anonymously and the true identity of the author of her works was not made public until after her death.*

PRACTICAL INFORMATION

The **tourist information centre**, open from May to September, is located inside the vast, Victorian Guildhall building on High Street and offers details on attractions, activities and current events. *For tourist information and accommodations bookings, call 01983 840500 or visit the city website at www.winchester.gov.uk.* An excellent Visitor's Guide is available for £1. There is a range of very pleasant walks in the city, and the tourist office offers their own guided tours and walks.

The city is well served with banks, most of which are located on High Street, and post offices.

BOURNEMOUTH

Hanging flower baskets adorn the main shopping streets and lush ornamental gardens accompany the tiny Bourne Stream for almost two miles on its journey through the heart of **Bournemouth**, one of England's leading seaside resorts, set on a wide bay with soft yellow sandy beaches backed by 100-foot cliffs. An avenue of palm trees in the newly developed Central Square bears witness to the warming influence of the Gulf Stream, which results in mild winters, pleasant summers and a much longer seaside than many of England's more traditional resorts.

Described by **Thomas Hardy** as a "Mediterranean lounging place on the English Channel," Bournemouth is a relatively new town, at least by English standards. In the 18th century, the land on which the town stands was a wild heathland frequented only by smugglers. It was in 1810 that **Lewis Tregonwell** built the first house on what is now the site of the Exeter Hotel. By 1851, the population had climbed to 695, but it was the coming of the railroad in 1885 that heralded Bournemouth's meteoric rise. By 1900 the population had reached 60,000.

Today, along with the neighboring and much older towns of **Poole** and **Christchurch**, sprawling Bournemouth is at the center of a conurbation of more than 400,000, the largest non-industrial conurbation in Europe. Despite the urban sprawl, Bournemouth has managed to preserve about a sixth of its total area as **public parks and gardens**, employing more than 200 civic gardeners during the peak summer months. The quality of its floral displays earns it many accolades, including **Europe's Floral Champion**.

ARRIVALS & DEPARTURES

By Car

From central London, Bournemouth is about a two hour drive along the M3, M27 and A338, just over 100 miles in all.

By Bus

Twenty National Express buses a day leave London's Victoria Bus Station for Bournemouth. The number increases in the summer. The main bus station for regional services is located a mile east of town's main Square, next to the train station on Holdenhurst Road, while local Yellow Buses operate from various points around The Square.

By Train

Direct trains operate twice an hour from London's Waterloo Station, and there are direct links to stations in the midlands and north, including Birmingham, Manchester, Newcastle, Edinburgh and Glasgow. *The national train enquiry number is 0345 4849 50. South West Trains, who run the Waterloo to Bournemouth service, can also be reached on 023 8021 3600 or at www.swtrains.co.uk.*

GETTING AROUND TOWN

Bournemouth is a vast, sprawling kind of place, and although many of the main sites of interest are located downtown, many more are a good three or four miles away. The local Yellow Bus service covers the town, and neighboring Christchurch and Poole extensively. Local services in Bournemouth are operated by the distinctive **Yellow Buses**, *Tel. 01202 557272*, while the region in general is covered by the red **Wilts (Wiltshire) and Dorset** buses, *Tel. 01202 673555*, who operate multi-journey tickets as discounted rates during the summer, as well as a one-day Explorer ticket that allows you unrestricted access to bus services throughout the region for £5 (adults), £3.65 (seniors) and £2.50 (children).

Car rentals in Bournemouth are available from **Avis**, *400 Poole Road, Tel. 01202 751974*, and **Hertz**, *Hinton Road, Tel. 01202 291231*. The main taxi rank in town is just off the Square, but taxis can be hailed anywhere.

WHERE TO STAY

Because Bournemouth possesses more hotel beds than any other UK city apart from London, the choice of accommodations available varies from cozy B&Bs on the West Cliff starting at around £15 a night, to the sumptuous surroundings of the Carlton or Royal Bath.

LANGTRY MANOR, *26 Derby Road, Bournemouth BH2 5DU. Tel. 01202 557702, Fax 01202 292734. 27 rooms. Rates for singles: £49-£69, doubles: £79-129. Rates include breakfast. All major credit cards accepted.*

Situated in a tree-lined back street on Bournemouth's East Cliff, the historic Langtry Manor was built in 1877 by King Edward VII (then the Prince of Wales) for his favorite mistress, Lily Langtry or "Jersey Lily" as she was known, making it especially popular with honeymoon couples. The building contains many reminders of its royal past, including initials scratched on a windowpane and carvings on a beam in the entrance hall. On the half-landing is a peephole through which the prince could eye up his guests before coming down to dine. While all the rooms are beautifully furnished, two in particular stand out: the Langtry suite, with a four-poster bed and a heart-shaped bath, and the Edward VII suite, furnished exactly as it was when Edward was in residence here. There's an excellent restaurant, which includes dishes favored by the King himself. A three course meal starts at around £25.

THE SWALLOW HIGHCLIFF, *105 St Michael's Road, Bournemouth BH2 5DU. Tel. 01202 557702. Fax 01202 292734. 154 rooms. Rates for singles: £86, doubles: £120, suite: £180. Rates include English breakfast. All major credit cards accepted.*

Located atop the West Cliff, the Highcliff has long been one of Bournemouth's most popular hotels. In recent years it has been completely renovated, giving it a lighter, airier feel. Built in the 19th century, there are the kind of grand public rooms you'd expect from that period, and many of the bedrooms have stunning views of the sea. The hotels also boasts a wide range of sports facilities, including a heated indoor swimming pool, sauna and tennis court, and there's a restaurant and nightclub.

THE NORFOLK ROYALE, *Richmond Hill, Bournemouth, BH2 6EN. Tel. 01202 551521. Fax 01202 299729. 90 rooms. Rates for singles: £65-£95, doubles: £90-£150. Breakfast £8.75 extra. All major credit cards accepted.*

You can't get much more central than this four-story Victorian hotel, located on Richmond Hill, just fifty yards from Bournemouth's main Square and the main shopping district. Like several of its counterparts, the Norfolk Royale has been recently renovated and restored to its Edwardian grandeur. All the rooms are beautifully appointed. One of the Norfolk's greatest attractions is its lovely tree-shaded rear garden. There's a very pleasant swimming pool that's covered with a glass dome, and the Orangery restaurant must be one of the visually most attractive places to eat in Bournemouth.

THE ROYAL BATH, *Bath Road, Bournemouth, BH1 2EW. Tel.: 01202 555555. Fax 01202 554158. 124 rooms, 7 suites. Rates for singles: £95, doubles £200, suites from £215. Rates include English breakfast. All major credit cards accepted.*

The historic Royal Bath, whose guests have included Benjamin Disraeli, Oscar Wilde and Rudolph Nureyev, is located in a prime location on the East Cliff, close to Bournemouth Pier. This low-rise, sprawling Victorian hotel was opened in 1838 on the day Victoria became queen. The public rooms with their huge chandeliers and lavish furnishings exude turn-of-the-century elegance and a first-class restaurant, named Oscar's after one of the hotel's most famous guests, serving excellent English and French fare. The bedrooms, many of which have sea views, are luxuriously furnished. The three-acre grounds contain a heated swimming pool.

THE CUMBERLAND, *East Overcliff Drive, Bournemouth BH1 3AF. Tel 01202 290722, Fax 01202 311394. Rooms: 102. Rates: singles from £46, doubles from £92. Bars, restaurant, outdoor pool, temporary membership of leisure club. All major credit cards accepted.*

This lovely art-deco building is located atop Bournemouth's famous East Cliff, close to the Russell-Cotes Art Gallery and just steps (or a funicular ride) away from the sandy beach. The public rooms are spacious, and the bedrooms come with a full range of facilities; many have sea views and balconies. The hotel has a heated outdoor swimming pool, and guests are also entitled to free membership of a nearby leisure club, with a full range of facilities. The only slight drawback in summer is that live bands play most nights; not heavy rock or anything like that, but just enough to irritate a tad.

QUALITY HOTEL, *8 Poole Road, Bournemouth BH2 5QU. Tel 01202 763006, Fax 01202 766168. Rooms: 54. Rates: singles from £64, doubles from £76. Bar, restaurant. All major credit cards accepted.*

The Quality Hotel is located on Bournemouth's leafy West Cliff, just a few hundred yards from the main shopping center and public gardens and the same distance again to the beaches. The public rooms are not particularly large, but comfortable, and the bedrooms, though decorated in the standard fashion you'd expect in a medium-range chain, have a full range of facilities, including TV; some have four-poster beds. For a hotel so close to downtown, the Quality offers good value.

EAST CLIFF COURT, *East Overcliff Drive, Bournemouth BH1 3AN. Tel 0500 636943 (central reservations for the Menzies chain), Fax 01773 880321. Rooms: 70. Rates: singles from £95, doubles from £130. Bars, restaurant, outdoor heated pool, leisure facilities available at nearby hotels. All major credit cards accepted.*

The East Cliff Court offers high quality accommodations in a spectacular setting on Bournemouth's East Cliff, with views out to sea from the tastefull decorated and furnished public rooms and from many of the comfortable bedrooms, some of which have balconies. The rooms come with a full range of facilities and four-poster beds are available, if that's your thing. The hotel is just a stone's throw from soft sandy beaches, or if the English Channel's too cold for you, you can opt for the heated outdoor pool. Other leisure facilities are available at nearby establishments.

WHERE TO EAT

CORIANDER, *22 Richmond Hill, Bournemouth. Tel. 01202 552202. Open Monday to Thursday and Sunday noon to 10:30pm, weekends noon to 11pm. Set dinner £11.25 for two courses.*

This friendly Mexican restaurant was established 20 years ago and has recently undergone a major facelift. It's a great place for family dining, as kids are provided with pens and crayons to design their own placemats and adults can choose from a wide range of cocktails. Meals include what you'd expect – enchiladas, fajitas and that kind of stuff – and there's a wide range of Mexican beers and wines. The staff are really helpful – and patient!

HOT ROCKS, *Pier Approach, Bournemouth. Tel. 01202 555559. Open daily 10am to midnight. Two course meal with drinks about £25. All major credit cards accepted.*

Dubbing itself an "American Surf Restaurant Complex," this brand new establishment is spectacularly located right opposite the entrance to

Bournemouth Pier, with super water views. The restaurant is laid out on two floors, with a cafe-style area downstairs and the main dining area upstairs. The portions are extremely generous by British (if not American) standards, and you can enjoy such transatlantic delicacies as marinated chicken wings, steaks, beefburgers and fresh fish and pasta dishes. Maybe you want to avoid eating American, but it's fun to see how Brits *think* Americans eat!

THE MANSION HOUSE, *Thames Street, Poole. Tel. 01202 685666. Open Monday to Friday noon to 1:45pm, 7pm to 9:15pm; Saturday 7pm to 9:15pm; Sunday noon to 1:45pm. Set dinner (two courses) £17.25. All major credit cards accepted.*

This rather formal restaurant is located in a Georgian house close to the old Quay in the heart of old Poole. It's easy to see why diners want to dress up; with its fine wood paneling, original paintings and delicate table settings there's a real air of elegance about it. The ambience is equaled by the quality of the food: not surprisingly in this location, seafood abounds, with dishes such as red mullet with black olive and tomato couscous and some delicious sweets, including the house special (and my favorite) bread and butter pudding.

BISTRO ON THE BEACH, *Solent Promenade, Southbourne Coast Road, Bournemouth BH6 4BE. Tel 01202 431473. Open Wednesday to Saturday. Set dinner from £14.95.*

The Bistro on the Beach gets booked up weeks in advance, thanks mainly to its superb location on the promenade (boardwalk) at Southbourne, a suburb of Bournemouth about four miles east of the town center. That's not to say the food's not good though – it is. Among the main courses on offer is a variety of seafood dishes, including cod on roasted peppers, while desserts tend to be on the traditional side – to keep the Brit holidaymakers who come here happy. There's a small but engaging wine list; house wine starts at about £10 a bottle.

OSCARS AT THE ROYAL BATH, *Bath Road, Bournemouth BH1 2EW. Tel 01202 555555. Open Tuesday to Sunday 12:30pm to 2pm, 7:30pm to 10pm. A la carte. Three course dinner around £40. All major credit cards accepted.*

The reason for the restaurant's name and theme lies in the fact that Oscar Wilde stayed at the Royal Bath on a number of occasions; it was Bournemouth's best hotel even then. The elegant restaurant has recently undergone a facelift; the food can best be described as modern British, with a fair smattering of seafood choices appropriate to the location, including red mullet with saffron risotto. The dessert tray is impressive, with a mixture of traditional British fare with lighter, less calorific choices.

SEEING THE SIGHTS

The town's motto, "Beauty and Health," indicates that it originally earned its reputation, like Brighton, as a health resort. But Bournemouth has taken a lot longer than its south coast rival to shake off its sedate "bath chair" image. Today, the town is one of the leading centers of **English language tuition** among European, Middle Eastern and South American students – up to 32,000 of them a year – and in high summer resonates with Spanish, French, German, Italian and other languages less easy to discern. The result is lively pavement cafes and dozens of nightclubs which give the place a vibrancy that would make the town fathers turn in their graves.

Over the years the fortuitous combination of balmy sea breezes and the aroma of more than 100,000 pine trees has attracted such notables as Victorian Prime Minister **Benjamin Disraeli** who recuperated at the Royal Bath Hotel and Scottish writer **Robert Louis Stevenson**, who spent several years here "taking the air." That air was enough to inspite him to write *Dr. Jekyll and Mr Hyde* and *Kidnapped*. Stevenson's house was destroyed by bombs during World War II, but a memorial garden is preserved on the site in the suburb of Westbourne, on R.L. Stevenson Avenue, about a mile to the west of the downtown area.

TAKE A BALLOON RIDE OVER BOURNEMOUTH!

*For a good and novel overview of the town, you can take the **Vistarama** tethered balloon ride in the Lower Gardens. The balloon soars 500 feet, giving wonderful views for miles around. Tel. 01202 399939; www.vistarama.co.uk.*

The poet **Shelley's** heart is buried in the graveyard of **St. Peter's Church** which easily identifiable by its lofty 202-foot spire. Next to him is the tomb of his wife **Mary Shelley**, author of Frankenstein. A **museum** dedicated to the Shelleys can be found in aptly-named **Shelley Park**, a couple of miles east of the center of town. Close by, newly refurbished thanks to a Lottery grant, the **Russell Cotes Art Gallery and Museum** is one of the best small museums in England. Housed in a cliff-top mansion that was once the residence of a former mayor, the museum specializes in Victoriana, and objets d'art that Sir Merton Russell Cotes brought back from his world travels. *East Overcliff Drive. Tues-Sun 10am-5pm; free except Thursday. Tel. 01202 451800.* On the other side of the main Square, **St. Stephen's**, St. Stephen's Road, completed in 1901, is a stunningly beautiful church that is "worth traveling 100 miles and being sick in the coach" to see, according to the late Poet Laureate Sir John Betjeman. On the seafront are located the **Pier** – less tacky than most British seaside piers – and the new **Oceanarium**, Pier Approach, where cleverly designed displays recreate the world's water habitats, such as the Great Barrier Reef and the Antarctic Ice Shelf. Both are worth a visit. *Open mid-February to mid-October daily 10am to 5pm. Admission adults £4.95, children 3-16 £3.75, seniors and students £4.50. Tel. 01202 311993.*

Also worth a look are the **chines**, narrow valleys gouged out of the soft local soil that punctuate the cliffs. Most picturesque is **Alum Chine**, about a mile west of downtown. The chine is spanned by a suspension bridge, from which a young Winston Churchill fell during a visit here in 1881. His fall was halted by a pine tree. Bournemouth's eastern extremity is **Hengistbury Head**, which affords superb views towards the Isle of Wight and over Christchurch Harbour, and a pleasant and less developed beach. The headland is also the site of a neolithic trading community, whose protective earthworks, Double Dykes, can still be seen.

Bournemouth's main attraction, without doubt, is its six-plus miles of **beaches** of predominantly soft, gently shelving yellow sand, with the occasional patch of shingle. The resort has some of the best beachfront facilities in Britain, and the six-mile boardwalk – known here as the promenade – is liberally sprinkled with cafes, ice cream kiosks, fresh water showers – not to mention loos.

The peak summer season is the time when Bournemouth's main public park, the **Lower Gardens**, is illuminated by literally thousands of **candles** forming various topical and traditional images. The ceremony dates back more than 100 years, and only takes place on a few selected evenings. Check with the tourism department.

A five-mile **Yellow Bus** ride to the east of Bournemouth, takes you to the historic Saxon town of **Christchurch**, situated on a natural harbor at the confluence of the Rivers Avon and Stour. The town is dominated by its magnificent **Priory**, founded in 1000, and is one of the largest parish churches in England. It's particularly notable for its striking Norman nave, and some intricate medieval carvings, especially in the choir. *Open Monday to Saturday 9:30am to 5pm, Sundays 2:15 to 5pm. Donation.* Close by is the excellent **Red House Museum**, once the local workhouse. There are displays of local and natural history, geology and archaeology. *Opening hours: year-round Tuesday to Saturday, 10am to 4:30pm, Sundays 2pm to 5pm. Tel. 01202 482860.*

From Bridge Street, a picturesque riverside walk, the **Convent Walk**, passes the ruins of a **Castle** and a Norman constable's house towards the Town Quay, where **Place Mill**, a restored Anglo-Saxon water mill that even gets a mention in the Domesday Book, houses a collection of milling artifacts and local handicrafts. From the Quay, harbor cruises and boat hire is available. A boat ride to **Mudeford**, a tiny fishing village at the harbor entrance, is particularly enjoyable on a hot summer's day. There are some fine pubs in Christchurch, including **The George** *at the corner of Bridge Street at High Street.* Christchurch's **Information Centre** is located at *23 High Street, Tel. 01202 471780, or you can access the town's website at www.christchurch.gov.uk.*

THE LEGEND OF CHRISTCHURCH PRIORY

The original name of the settlement here was Twyneham, not Christchurch, but that changed when, in the 11th century, plans were drawn up for a Priory Church to be built on the top of St. Catherine's Hill, about a mile north of the present town center. First, for the workmen, there was the mystery of the stranger who showed up daily to work with them, but never claimed any wages and disappeared at the end of the day. However, when the workmen returned to the site each morning, they found that the building materials and tools had been moved to the church's present site. Finally it was decided to build the church there. According to tradition, one of the new church's most important beams was cut too short. The beam was left overnight, and when the workmen returned the following morning, they discovered it was exactly the right length. The workmen decided that the mysterious workman might be none other than Jesus the Carpenter. The beam in question can still be seen to this day just above the Priory's southern transept.

Five miles to the west of Bournemouth along the A35, **Poole** is an ancient port whose greatest asset is the vast, virtually landlocked **natural harbor** on which it is located. Though like its younger neighbor it sprawls well into the local landscape, the **Old Town** retains a salty maritime flavor, characterized by old quayside warehouses, salty pubs like the **Jolly Sailor** and elegant homes built by wealthy sea captains who made their money trading with Newfoundland. Right on the Quay is the famous **Poole Pottery**, which has been in operation for over 125 years. Here you can take a Factory Tour that will show you how 3,500 plates are made in a day, and kids can try to make a pot, model or plate for themselves. *Opening hours Monday to Saturday 9am to 5pm, Sunday 10am to 5pm. Admission Factory tour £2.50, children £1.50. Tel. 01202 666200; www.poolepottery.co.uk.*

Close by is the **Waterfront Museum**, which explores the area's history from Roman times and has a wonderful collection of smugglers' tales to delight the family. *Old High Street, Open April to October Monday to Saturday 10am to 5pm; November to march Monday to Saturday 10am to 3pm, Sunday noon to 3pm. Tel. 01202 683138.* Round the corner, **St. James's Church**, built in the 1820s on the site of an earlier building, has a nave with vast pillars made from Newfoundland timber. From the Quay you can take a boat trip, *Tel. 01202 680580*, to 500-acre **Brownsea Island**, owned and maintained by the National Trust, and one of the last bastions in the south of England of the red squirrel. **Brownsea Castle**, on the southern edge of the island, was built by Henry VIII to defend the port against invasion from France. The island is also the site of the world's first boy scout camp, established here by Lord Baden-Powell. *Island open April 1 to October 1, daily 10am to 5pm/6pm, depending on season. Landing fee: Adults £2.60, children £1.30.*

Poole's southern, ocean-facing suburbs, particularly pine-scented Canford Cliffs, are home to some of the most expensive real estate on the planet, according to a recent survey, as well as some of the south's best beaches. **Sandbanks**, a peninsula that protects the port from the worst storms, is particularly good. Among the trees are the celebrated **Compton Acres Gardens**, in Canford Cliffs Road, which actually comprises a series of several separate and distinct gardens, including a Japanese garden, Roman garden, Water gardens, and a Palm Court. There's a restaurant with brilliant views over the harbor. *Open March to November daily 10am-6pm. Admission adults £4.95, students and seniors £3.95, children £1. Tel. 01202 700778. www.comptonacres.co.uk.* Poole's **tourism office** is located on *Poole Quay, Tel. 01202 253253, www.poole.gov.uk.*

EXCURSIONS & DAY TRIPS

A **car ferry** (£2.30 per vehicle) from Sandbanks leads across the mouth of Poole Harbour to **Shell Bay and Studland**, unquestionably the best beach on England's south coast – backed by acres of sand dunes that are home to some of England's rarest animals, and an even rarer nudist area! The road leads on to the rolling green hills of the **Isle Of Purbeck**, which is not an island at all, but with enough of a different atmosphere from the rest of Dorset to make seem that it is. Purbeck is particularly notable for its superb coastal scenery.

Coming off the ferry, the B3351 road soon forks left to **Swanage**, an English seaside resort in miniature, with a sandy beach and some strangely out-of-context public buildings. The reason? A local builder who had grandiose plans had a number of buildings from London transported here, brick by brick – including the **Town Hall**. Continue straight on, through Swanage and on to the A351, for **Corfe Castle**, one of Dorset's prettiest villages, overlooked by the daunting, haunting and spectacular ruins of a 12th century **castle**, in a strategic position standing guard over a gap in the hills. The castle, now owned by the National Trust, owes its present, tumbledown status to **Oliver Cromwell**, who had it blown up in

1646. Villagers were grateful, though; many of them used stones from the ruined building to build new homes. *Open March 2-25, 10am to 4:30pm; March 26 to October 29 10am to 5:30pm; October 30 to March 11am to 3:30pm. Fee: Adults £4, child £2. Tel. 01929 481294.* The village has several attractive pubs, including **The Fox**, on West Street, with an ancient well that is visible through a glass panel in the floor of the lounge bar, and **The Greyhound**, right in the center opposite the market cross.

From Corfe, follow the signs to the small seaside village of **Kimmeridge**, with a tiny medieval church dedicated to St. Nicholas, a scattering of cottages, and impressive coastal views. The shingly, sometimes seaweedy beach is punctuated at low tide by long natural jetties known as the Kimmeridge Ledges. A walk along these at low tide on a calm day gives a fascinating glimpse of the sea life here, including a variety of species normally found in the Mediterranean – no wonder the place is popular with divers. The precarious gray cliffs are composed of shale, and the presence of a "nodding donkey" indicates the presence, deep below ground, of oil.

THE DORSET COAST PATH

*Part of the southwest coast path, the **Dorset Coast path** stretches virtually unbroken from Studland in the east, along the coast of the Isle of Purbeck to Weymouth and Portland, along Chesil Beach, past Abbotsbury with its swannery, until it rises dramatically,, reaching the tallest cliffs on the south coast of England at Golden Gap – before dropping 600 feet towards Charmouth and Lyme Regis. The 50-mile long path offers not only spectacular views, but all kinds of rare plants (some of which are only found in this part of England), animals and birds. You're never far from some excellent B&Bs and hotels, and of course, pubs, such as the amazing Ship and Compasses at Worth Matravers with its original flagstone floors, one room full of stuffed sea creatures and another choc-a-bloc with fossils and other antiquities. You can get more information about the Path from any of the local tourism offices; it's well marked on Ordnance Survey maps.*

Four miles north of Corfe on the A351 is one of my favorite small market towns. **Wareham** was an important port from Saxon times, but ceased to flourish when the River Frome silted up. The town's ancient walls can still be seen, as can the tiny Saxon church of **St. Martin**, at the northern end of the High Street. The church contains an effigy of Lawrence of Arabia, who lived not far away from here in a tiny, isolated cottage at **Cloud's Hill**, just north of Bovington. The austere rooms are much as he left them and reflect his complex personality and links with the Middle East. *Open April to end of October, Wednesday to Saturday 12noon to 5pm. Fee £2.30. Tel. 01929 405616.*

From Wareham, take the A352 passing through the village of **Wool**, where you turn left at the level crossing on to the B3071 to **Lulworth Cove**, Dorset's most famous beauty spot. Formed by erosion over millions of years, the Cove is essentially a small natural harbor backed on three sides by steep cliffs. The Lulworth estate maintains a small **heritage center** here, *Tel. 01929 400587*, where you can see exhibits on how the Cove was formed, and about local sea life. There's no charge for the center, but you have to pay around £4 to park. A few miles inland, near the village of **East Lulworth** is **Lulworth Castle**, a huge 17th century hunting lodge that has been beautifully restored after a disastrous fire in 1929. Visitors can take a tour of the Castle and see the photographic record made before the 1929 fire, explore the cellars and climb the southeast tower for spectacular views of the surrounding countryside. *Open November to March daily 10am to 4pm, April to October daily 10am to 6pm. Tel. 01929 400352.*

About eight miles north west of Bournemouth lies the ancient market town of **Wimborne**. Although the Bournemouth suburbs are encroaching upon the old town at an alarming rate, it has managed to retain much of the character of bygone days. The town's greatest attraction is its **Minster of St. Cuthberga**, built on the site of an eight century monastery. It's a largely Norman affair, with two huge towers that dominate the whole town. *Open daily 9am to 5pm. Admission free.* The Minster is also famous for its **Chained Library**, located above the choir vestry. The Library, founded in 1686, is one of the oldest public libraries in England. *Open year round Monday to Friday 10:30am to 12:30pm and 2pm to 4pm. Admission 50p.*

Two miles north of Wimborne, just off the B3082, is one of England's finest seventeenth century houses. **Kingston Lacy** was built for the Bankes family, who owned Corfe Castle until they were turfed out by the Roundheads. The house was designed by Sir Roger Pratt in the red brick that was typical of the Queen Anne period, but was encased in gray stone by Sir Charles Barry in the nineteenth century. The house is best known for its magnificent collection of **paintings**, which includes works by Titian, Rembrandt and Velazquez – and for its **Spanish Room**, with walls hung in magnificent gilded leather. The 250-acre grounds are a great place for a peaceful walk – though the place can get extremely crowded on summer weekends, when open-air symphony concerts are sometimes held here. *House open April to October daily, 11am to 6pm; November & December Friday, Saturday and Sunday, 11am to 4pm. Admission £6, children £3. Tel. 01202 883402.*

NIGHTLIFE & ENTERTAINMENT

Bournemouth is not a "pubby" kind of place like rival resorts Weymouth or Brighton, but despite that it manages to have more bars per capita than any other place in the country. This is partly due to the vast numbers of hotels, many of which have their own bars that are open to the public. More recently though, especially since the arrival of a new university, a number of new bars have opened, many of which can be found along Old Christchurch Road.

The town boasts three theaters – which as well as being used for serious plays and symphony concert by the acclaimed **Bournemouth Symphony Orchestra**, are usually given over to gaudy summer shows during the peak holiday months. It's at this time of the year, too, when the nightclubs come into their own – among them **The Zoo** and **The Cage**, *both in Fir Vale Road*, seem to do best *(Tel. 01202 311187)*. A new **IMAX cinema** located next to the entrance to the Pier was due to open in 2000.

SHOPPING

Bournemouth has some of the best shopping facilities in the south, focusing mainly on the pedestrian precincts of Commercial Road and Old Christchurch Road, radiating from The Square, with four large department stores, including the seven-floor family-owned **Beales**. A huge new Borders bookstore opened recently on Bourne Avenue. For **antiques**, take a yellow bus ride to the suburb of **Pokesdown**, where the main Christchurch Road is lined with around 30 or so antique stores.

PRACTICAL INFORMATION

The main **tourist information** centre is located on *Westover Road, Tel. 0906 802 0234*. There's a sophisticated accommodations booking service. The tourism department also arranges guided walks around the town. The tourism department's website is*: www.Bournemouth.co.uk.*

The town's main banks are located downtown in Old Christchurch Road, but there are many more in the suburbs. The main post office is in the appropriately-named Post Office Road, just off Old Christchurch Road.

DORCHESTER

Dorchester is the archetypal English market town, with strong connections with the author **Thomas Hardy**, who was born nearby and lived in the area all his life. It also happens to be the administrative center for the county of Dorset. While not exactly abundant in places to visit itself, it's a good base for exploring some of the most beautiful countryside in southern England.

ARRIVALS & DEPARTURES
By Car
From London, take the M3, M27 and A31 as far as the junction with the A35 at Bere Regis. The A35 then leads directly into the center of Dorchester.

By Bus
There are a few direct services from London to Dorchester, but your best bet is to take the National Express bus to Bournemouth, then one of the red Wilts and Dorset buses from the Bournemouth travel Interchange (next to the train station) to Dorchester. Many local services (mostly Southern National) operate from Dorchester to Weymouth and other towns in central and western Dorset.

By Train
There are around ten direct trains a day to Dorchester South station, a five minute walk from the town center and to Weymouth from London's Waterloo Station. *Call 0845 7 48 49 50 for information or www.railtrack.co.uk.*

GETTING AROUND
Both Dorchester and Weymouth are easily explored on foot, but you'll need a car or bus to get to some of the outlying rural areas. *Call 01305 224535 for local bus information.* Cycling is another option, though the countryside round here is rather hilly; **Dorchester Cycles**, *31 Great Western Road, Tel. 01305 268787*, rents bicycles starting at around £10 a day.

WHERE TO STAY
KING'S ARMS, *30 High East Street, Dorchester DT1 1HF. Tel. 01305 265353, Fax 01305 260269. 33 rooms. Rates single £60, double £80. Restaurant. Major credit cards accepted.*

This 300-year-old former coaching inn was made famous by Thomas Hardy in his novel *The Mayor of Casterbridge*. The hotel may have seen better days, and its location on Dorchester's main street may make it a little noisy, but this is a charming hotel. The rooms have all been recently refurbished and are well-equipped with tea-making facilities, trouser press and the like.

CASTERBRIDGE HOTEL, *49 High East Street, Dorchester DT1 1HU. Tel. 01305 264043, Fax 01305 260884. 15 rooms. Rates: singles from £46, doubles from £68. Bar. Major credit cards accepted.*

Built in 1790, this elegant small hotel which has been in the same family since 1917 comes with period furnishings and bags of character, though like the King's Arms it's on Dorchester's main thoroughfare and can get a little noisy. Each room is tastefully decorated and furnished, if a little small (larger rooms are available in the annex). One of the highlights of staying here (and there are many) is the excellent full English breakfast, taken in a delightful plant-filled conservatory. The staff are pleasant yet unobtrusive, and particularly helpful with children.

WESSEX ROYALE, *32 High West Street, Dorchester DT1 1UP. Tel 01305 262660, Fax 01305 251941. Rooms: 25. Rates: singles from £49, doubles from £69. Bar, restaurant. All major credit cards accepted.*

This centrally located hotel was once the family home of the Earl of Ilchester, though you might not think it, given its proximity to other properties and businesses close by. Close to Dorchester's main attractions and its shopping center, it has 25 comfortable, well-equipped bedrooms which vary in size. In a town where parking is sometimes very difficult, it's good to know that the Wessex Royale has its own parking facilities. The one drawback, however, is that many of the rooms front the main road and can be a bit noisy; make it clear that you want something away from the High Street and you should be fine.

WHERE TO EAT

MOCK TURTLE, *34 High West Street, Dorchester. Tel. 01305 264011. Open Tuesday to Saturday lunch, Monday to Saturday dinner. Dinner around £23. All major credit cards accepted.*

A modern, sophisticated and relaxing restaurant spread out over three floors right in the center of town, the Mock Turtle has an excellent reputation locally for its freshly prepared English and French dishes, such as pan-fried pork tenderloin with lime and green peppercorn sauce.

PERRY'S, *4 Trinity Road, The Old Harbour, Weymouth. Tel. 01305 785799. Open Tuesday to Sunday for lunch, Monday to Saturday for dinner. Three course meal around £23. All major credit cards accepted.*

A small, simply decorated bistro-style restaurant right on the harborside at Weymouth, which specializes in fresh local seafood (you can see the boats that brought it in just outside the window), which are chalked up on a board outside every day – most days there are up to ten seafood choices. They do an excellent bouillabaisse, and the moules mariniere are out of this world – or how about roast medallions of monkfish with a fricasse of mussels?

YALBURY COTTAGE, *Lower Bockhampton, Dorchester DT2 8PZ. Tel 01305 262382. Open daily 7pm to 9pm. Three- course set dinner £26. All major credit cards accepted.*

This pretty thatched cottage is located just over two miles east of Dorchester in Thomas Hardy's birthplace village of Bockhampton. The 300-year-old cottage, with a preponderance of oak beams and inglenook fireplaces in both lounge and restaurant, is the perfect place for a romantic soiree. Among the specialties here are rack of lamb with a cassis sauce and medallions of local venison with a red currant and gin sauce. The cottage, or rather a more recent extension, also doubles up as a hotel, with eight rooms.

SEEING THE SIGHTS

Dorset's ancient county town is the focal point of many of **Thomas Hardy's** novels, who coined it "Casterbridge." Hardy was born in the village of **Higher Bockhampton**, about three miles away, and attended school in Dorchester and served as an architect's apprentice here. In Higher Bockhampton, you can visit Hardy's birthplace, the picture-postcard **Hardy's Cottage**, but only by appointment; inside you'll see the desk where the author penned *Far From the Madding Crowd* and many of his poems.

If the visiting times here thwart you, visit instead the intriguing **Dorset County Museum**, on High West Street. *Open daily, July-Aug 10am-5pm, rest of year Mon-Sat, 10am-5pm, Admission £3.50, concessions £1.50. Tel. 01305 262735; www.dorset.museum.clara.net.* Here you'll find a reconstruction of Hardy's study, as well as local artifacts including Celtic and Roman relics, and antique farming implements. Across the road, in Icen Way, there's a **Dinosaur Museum**, ever popular with kids; the local coastline, particularly around Lyme Regis, is a fossil hunter's paradise. *Open April to October daily 9:30am to 5:30pm, November to March daily 10am to 4:30pm. Admission adults £4.25, children £2.95. Tel. 01305 269880.*

High Street, with its mixture, shops and offices and pubs – including the **Red Lion**, mentioned in *The Mayor of Casterbridge* – is itself an interesting mixture of architectural styles. Opposite, the timber-framed Judge Jeffrey's restaurant is the former lodging of bloodthirsty Judge Jeffreys, who sent hundreds of people to the gallows during his time. Around the corner, the Antelope Hotel marks the site of the notorious judge's courtroom.

Dorchester was an important town from Roman times and various Roman remains can be seen. **West Walk** and **Colliton Walk** follow the line of the ancient Roman town walls, there's an excavated **Roman villa** with a well-preserved mosaic just to the north of Colliton Park, and south of the downtown area, grassy **Maumbury Rings** are all that's left of a Roman amphitheater.

EXCURSIONS & DAY TRIPS

Five miles to the east of Dorchester, clearly marked from the A35, is **Athelhampton House**, renamed Athelhall by Hardy, one of the best preserved medieval houses in England, despite a recent fire which ravaged it. Begun in the 14th century on the site of an even earlier house, Athelhampton's greatest glories are its 15th century Great Hall and the King's Room. The 10-acre formal gardens, with topiary, fountains, pavilions and rare plants are also worth a visit. *Open March to October open daily except Saturdays, 10:30am to 5pm; November to February Sundays only 10:30am to 5pm. Admission house and grounds adults £5.40, seniors £3.95, children £1.50. Tel. 01305 848363; www.athelhampton.co.uk.*

THOMAS HARDY

*The county of Dorset, which he especially loved, and the surrounding counties are the backdrop for most of Thomas Hardy's novels. Hardy was born at High Bockhampton, near Dorchester, in 1840, in a picturesque cottage open to the public by appointment only. Here he wrote **Far From the Madding Crowd** and **Under the Greenwood Tree**. An architect by trade, Hardy built himself a house on the edge of Dorchester, Max Gate, in the late 1800s, where his later novels and many of his poems were scribed. The County Museum in Dorchester (see above) has a reconstruction of the author's study along with other memorabilia, while a few yards down High East Street, the King's Arms, the setting for the Mayor of Casterbridge, is still functioning as a hotel and bar.*

In his novels, Hardy invented new names (or re-ordered existing ones) for the various places he refers to. Hence, Dorchester becomes Casterbridge, Bournemouth is Sandbourne, Weymouth is Budmouth and so on.

Take the A35 east of Dorchester, then the A354 to the village of Winterborne Whitchurch, where a left turn will take you to one of Dorset's most beautiful villages, **Milton Abbas**, named after a large medieval monastic complex that dominated this quiet corner of the Dorset countryside. Over the years, a thriving village grew up around the **Abbey**. The Abbey suffered under the dissolution of the monasteries by Henry VIII, and many of the monastic buildings became part of a private estate. The lord was upset that his views were poor. He had the existing medieval village destroyed and a lake excavated in its place. The new village, composed of white or cream-painted thatched cottages, a church and almshouses, was built higher up the hill and is today one of the most picturesque villages in the country.

The former monastic buildings now form part of a **public school**. All that's left of the abbey church is part of the chancel, although it's so large, it's clear that the original abbey must have been massive. You can park your car at the school for around 50p, and walk across lawns to the abbey, used by the school as its chapel. It's an attractive building, with a graceful nave, and interesting features, including an unusual 15th-century hanging pyx, used to contain consecrated communion wafers. The abbey's setting, surrounded by the lush Dorset countryside, is magical, especially on a hot summer's day when you may catch a glimpse of a cricket match – cream flannels against the green hue of the hills beyond. *Abbey Church open year-round. Check for times. Admission: free, but donation requested. Tel. 01258 880489.*

Six miles north of Dorchester, on the A352, surrounded by rolling chalk hills, is the pretty village of **Cerne Abbas**, which owes its existence to the great **Abbey** that once stood here. All that remains today is an old gatehouse and Abbey House. The village once had a reputation for licentiousness; hard to believe now as you stroll past half-timbered Tudor cottages along the picturesque Duck Street to St. Augustine's Well, created, according to local folklore, by the saint himself. Several pubs survive to this day, however, notably the **New Inn**, *14 Long Street*, which has good food and a lovely garden. Cerne Abbas is most famous, though, for the striking, 180-foot figure of a **giant** carved into the hillside just to the north of the village. Probably a fertility symbol he (and it's most definitely a "he") probably dates from pre-Roman times.

South of Dorchester at the end of the A354 lies the seaside resort of **Weymouth**, with its wide sandy beach and promenade backed by elegant Georgian facades. The town became fashionable when King George III came here to recuperate after illness. A gaudy statue of his majesty erected by the loyal citizens of Weymouth stands at the western end of the esplanade, where you can also find Weymouth's **tourist information center**, *Tel. 01305 785747; www.weymouth.gov.uk.* The resort, with its wide sandy beach speckled with seafood stalls and cotton candy stalls has become fashionable again after a long period in the doldrums.

The main shopping precincts, St. Thomas Street and St. Mary Street, lead to the charming **Old Harbour**, lined by pastel-colored Georgian houses, restaurants and pubs. Just behind the quay is **Hope Square**, where the huge, former Devenish brewery has been converted into a major tourist attraction, with specialist shops, and the award-winning **Weymouth Timewalk** which traces the 600-year history of the resort through 24 lifelike dioramas, seen through the eyes of a cat and her past lives! The complex also includes Weymouth's **Town Museum** and the **Devenish Story**, which tells the history of the brewery building in which the whole complex is now housed, with a Tastings area. *Open year-round 10am to 5:30pm (9:30pm in August); Admission for Timewalk: adults £4.25, students & seniors $3.75, children £3, museum and brewery free. Tel. 01305 777622; www.brewers-quay.co.uk.*

On the opposite side of harbor, **Deep Sea Adventure** depicts the origins of modern diving and explores Weymouth's connection with the Titanic disaster. *Open Easter to June, September and October 10am to 5:30pm; July and August 10am to 10pm. Admission £3.50. Tel. 01305 760690.* At the other end of town, just east of the esplanade at Lodmoor, is **Sea Life Park**, where themed marine displays reveal many of the habitats found beneath the waves. Also on display, of course, are sharks, puffer fish, eels and a collection of sea horses – the center is home to one of the world's leading seahorse breeding programs. A new seal sanctuary opened in 2000. *Lodmoor Country Park. Open daily 10am to 5pm. Admission adults £6.50, seniors £4.95, children £3.95. Tel. 01305 761070. www.sealife.co.uk.*

At the mouth of Weymouth Harbour is **Nothe Fort**, a castle built during between 1860 and 1872 as part of the defences for the new naval base at nearby Portland. It was designed and constructed to house a 12-gun battery of massive cannons. Today it contains 30 displays with eleven dioramas, ship, aircraft and tank models, and photographs. *Open mid-May to mid-September daily 10:30am to 5:30pm. Admission adults £3, students & seniors £2, children (accompanied) free.* You can take a walk from here through the pretty **Nothe Gardens**, an excellent vantage point for views over the harbor and the Isle of Portland.

FERRIES FROM WEYMOUTH

Weymouth is also an important passenger port, and ferries depart daily from April to October for the Channel Islands of Jersey and Guernsey and St. Malo, France. Prices start from £29.90 round-trip, with children at half price. For information, call **Condor Ferries***, Tel. 01305 761551; www.condorferries.co.uk.*

Linked to the mainland by a narrow neck of land, the **Isle Of Portland**, a huge mass of granite that has not surprisingly earned the nickname of Dorset's Gibraltar, extends from Weymouth's southern suburbs four miles into the English Channel. Until recently one of the Royal Navy's main bases, recent defense cutbacks have seen the Navy's withdrawal from the island, but after a period of economic decline,

Portland like its mainland neighbor is now bouncing back. New, predominantly maritime industries are moving into the former Navy buildings. A drive to the southern tip of the island, **Portland Bill**, where one of the country's most powerful lighthouses stands, is rewarded by some spectacular coastal views, especially at sunset.

To the west of Portland, the fascinating **Chesil Beach** is essentially a barrier beach built of pebbles that protects an 18-mile-long stretch of Dorset coast from the worst the English Channel can throw at it. At its eastern end, the beach looms as high as 30 feet above the sea. The pebbles are at their largest here; as you move further west, they become smaller until they appear to be more like pea-stone. It's said that local sailors can pinpoint their position along the beach during a fog by the size of the stones. The currents are extremely strong here, and swimming is dangerous; storms have even been known to toss ships over the top of the beach, while the sound of the grinding pebbles can be heard as far away as Dorchester, nine miles distant.

The best view of Chesil Beach can be had by taking the B3157 from Weymouth. The road climbs around 500 feet, affording some spectacular vistas, especially looking back towards Portland. Halfway along the beach, the honey-stone village of **Abbotsbury** is home to a **Swannery**, whose swans were first introduced here by local Benedictine monks more than 600 years ago, primarily as a source of meat, not as something to ooh and aah at. The Swannery attracts large numbers of visitors during the hatching season in May. The Swannery is located just off the village's main street. *Open Easter to October daily 10am-6pm, last admission 5pm. Admission adults £5, seniors £4.70, children 5-15 £3, under 5s free. Tel. 01305 871858; www.abbotsbury-tourism.co.uk.*

Also in Abbotsbury, and also just off the B3157, are the **Sub-Tropical Gardens**, established in 1765 by the Countess of Ilchester as a kitchen garden to her nearby castle. Since then, it has been developed into a 20-acre garden filled with rare and exotic plants from all over the world. *Open March to November daily 10am to 6pm, last admission 5pm, December to February daily 10am-4pm or dusk, last admission one hour before. Admission adults £4.50, seniors £4.20, children (5-15) £3, under 5s free. Tel. 01305 871387.* On the hills above Abbotsbury and the next village of Portesham stands the **Hardy Monument** – not, as many assume, a tribute to Thomas Hardy, but rather to Sir Thomas Masterman Hardy, Nelson's flag captain at the Battle of Trafalgar – he of the "Kiss me, Hardy" (or Kismet, Hardy?) Fame. The monument is distinctly unappealing; it looks more like a factory chimney than a memorial, but the countryside views are spectacular.

Further west, the road descends to the tiny fishing village of **West Bay**, featured recently in a prime time BBC drama series and therefore attracts hordes of (mainly elderly) Brits on warm summer days. The road continues on to one of the most intriguing towns on the south coast, **Lyme Regis**, whose harbor wall, known as **The Cobb**, was built by Edward I in the 13th century to provide shelter from storms and increase the port's capacity. More recently, The Cobb featured in the film *The French Lieutenant's Woman*, based on the book by Lyme resident John Fowles. Just west of The Cobb is the beach where the protestant **Duke of Monmouth** landed in 1685 in an attempt to bring down his uncle, the Catholic King James II. One of Lyme's greatest fans was Jane Austen, who used to stay in one of the thatched cottages on the seafront.

The cliffs around here are especially rich in **fossils**. It was in 1810 that 12-year-old Mary Anning discovered the remains of a complete **icthyosaurus**, causing consternation among the establishment, grappling to come to terms with new theories of evolution. Though that particular fossil has long gone (it's on show in the Natural History Museum in London), Lyme has its own **Philpott Museum** with an excellent collection of local fossil finds, as well as other historical items. There are also a number of fossil shops in town – but chiseling away at the cliffs is somewhat frowned on these days, due to some serious erosion. *Open April to October Monday to Saturday 10am to 5pm, Sunday 10am to noon and 2:30pm to 5pm. Admission £1.* To the west of the town, a huge landslip that occurred in 1839 is now a nature reserve, and contains rare flora as well as affording some stunning sea views.

NIGHTLIFE & ENTERTAINMENT

There's a lot more going on in Weymouth than in Dorchester. The **Weymouth Pavilion**, *Tel. 01305 783225*, puts on shows and reviews – and the occasional Bournemouth Symphony concert – throughout the year. Otherwise, it's off to the pubs; try **The Black Dog**, *on St. Mary's Street*, said to be the town's oldest, and the **Royal Oak**, *down by the harbor on Custom House Quay*.

PRACTICAL INFORMATION

Dorchester's banks and post office are located in South Street, Weymouth's banks and post office in St. Mary's Street. The **tourist information center** for Dorchester is at *Antelope Walk*, just behind South Street, *Tel. 01305267992*, where you can get the town *Historical Guide*, listing all kinds of interesting walks around town.

Weymouth's **information center** is on *The Esplanade, Tel. 01305785747.*

SALISBURY

Salisbury, sometimes known as **New Sarum**, dates mainly from the 13th century, when the original settlement of **Old Sarum**, along with its cathedral some two miles to the north, had fallen into such a state of disrepair that medieval planners decided to start over again with a completely new city. The new city was sited at the confluence of the rivers Nadder and Avon, and on the water meadows it was decided that a brand new **cathedral** would be built.

ARRIVALS & DEPARTURES

By Car

From London, take the M3 and M27 as far as the A303, and then the A30 which will take you directly to Salisbury.

By Bus

Three National Express buses a day (more in the summer) leave London's Victoria bus station for Salisbury. If you need more choice, aim for Southampton, then change on to a Hampshire Bus for Salisbury.

By Train

There is a regular train service from London Waterloo to Salisbury. Trains take about one hour 40 minutes; the train station is about ten minutes west of the city center. *Call National Rail Enquiries on 0345 484950.*

GETTING AROUND TOWN

All the main attractions in Salisbury are within ten to fifteen minutes' walk from the cathedral. Bicycles can be hired from **Hayball Cycle Shop**, *Winchester Street*, for about £10 a day. Car rental is available from **Europcar**, *Fisherton Street, Salisbury, Tel. 01722 335625.*

To get to **Stonehenge** by bus, take the Wilts and Dorset bus #3; the bus leaves from Salisbury Bus Station, *Endless Street, Tel 01722 336855.* Cost: £2.95. Wilts & Dorset also run buses to Wilton and Avebury.

WHERE TO STAY

THE OLD BELL, *St Ann's Street, Salisbury SP1 2DN. Tel. 01722 327958, Fax 01722 411485. 10 rooms. Rates: single £30, Double £50, four-poster £75. Credit cards: Mastercard, Visa.*

Modest, unpretentious small hotel located opposite St. Anne's Gate, with a fish restaurant downstairs and accommodations upstairs. It's not the most luxurious of places, but it's clean and comfortable, and who cares when you're staying in a building that's more than 600 years old – most of the rooms come with the original beams.

THE RED LION, *Milford Street, Salisbury SP1 2AN. Tel. 01722 323334, Fax 01722 325756. 53 rooms. Rates for singles: £81.50, doubles £101.50, four-poster £115. All major credit cards accepted.*

An ancient former coaching inn that dates back to the 13th century, the Red Lion is now part of the Best Western chain. A typical English market town hotel, its public rooms are dark and gloomy, but utterly charming and full of antiques and oddities. The rooms are all comfortable, those in the extension being somewhat larger. There's an atmospheric restaurant serving excellent fresh poultry, meat, game and fish. The hotel is located in the center of Salisbury, close to the main attractions.

CRICKET FIELD HOUSE HOTEL, *Skew Bridge, Wilton, Salisbury SP2 9NS. Tel and Fax 01722. Rooms: 14. Rates: singles from £35, doubles from £50. No credit cards.*

This pleasant guest house is located a mile or so west of Salisbury city center just off the A36 Wilton Road, and adjacent to the South Wiltshire Cricket ground. Most of the rooms, including one specifically for the use of people with disabilities, are located in an annex overlooking a courtyard. The rooms are all comfortable and cozy, and meals are available in the attractive conservatory. The city's main attractions, including the magnificent cathedral, are a short drive or walk away.

THE OLD HOUSE, *161 Wilton Road, Salisbury SP2 7JQ. Tel 01722 333433, Fax 01722 335551. Rooms: 7. Rates: singles from £26, doubles from £38. No credit cards.*

A B&B property on the main Wilton road, this one is a bit closer to the city center, a few minutes' walk away. The property, which dates back to at least the 17th century, is essentially a family home that has been thoughtfully adapted to cater for guests. In particular, there's a very cozy cellar bar. The bedrooms, all of which come with modern facilities, are nicely decorated and comfortably furnished.

WHERE TO EAT

THE HAUNCH OF VENISON, *1-5 Minster Street, Salisbury. Tel. 01722 322024. Open Monday to Saturday 11am to 11pm, Sunday noon to 10:30pm. All major credit cards accepted.*

Wonderful old establishment that has been in existence for more than 600 years, full of fascinating nooks and crannies. The wood-paneled restaurant has some very low beams, an open fire and antique leather settees. If the mummified arm of an eighteenth century card player – found by workmen in 1903 – hasn't put you off, you can enjoy the restaurant's pretty straightforward English fare – venison steaks, pork and lamb chops, lots of mashed potatoes, and the like. And you can drink at one of Britain's only two remaining pewter bars.

HOWARD'S HOUSE HOTEL, *Teffont Evias, Salisbury. Tel 01722 716392. Open 7:30pm to 9:30pm. Set menu (3 course) £19.95. All major credit cards accepted.*

This delightful country house hotel is home to one of the best restaurants in or around Salisbury. On arrival, you're taken into a bright yellow-decorated lounge, then it's on to the recently refurbished dining room, where the emphasis is on simplicity of presentation, thus allowing the ingredients to speak for themselves. Those ingredients include the best local produce, including a delicious breast of pheasant with cranberry pomme anna and honeyed cabbage; the venison is also outstanding. Classic desserts are the order of the day here; rum flan with vanilla custard being one of their most popular. Not surprisingly in a place of this caliber, there's a good wine list.

SEEING THE SIGHTS

Salisbury is totally dominated by the massive, soaring 404-foot spire of its 13th century **cathedral**, unique among English cathedrals in that it was designed and completed in one style – Early English. The spire, an amazing feat of medieval engineering that is today just 2 1/2 feet off vertical, was completed in 1320, some 62 years after the building was consecrated. But the spire has always presented problems; in the late 1600s, eminent architect **Sir Christopher Wren** was summoned to strengthen it, while in the mid-1800s, the famous Victorian architect **Gilbert Scott** began another program of work to reinforce the spire and restore the cathedral's interior.

To be honest, the interior does look a bit dull and uninspiring, unlike close neighbor Winchester. But there are some sights well worth seeing: the remarkable **flying buttresses**, the **lancet** windows and several well-preserved tombs of **crusader knights**, and in the north aisle a **medieval clock** dating from 1386 that some say is the oldest in the world. Another highlight of the cathedral is the **cloisters**, where the monks of this former Benedictine community once perambulated. The beauty of the cloisters is enhanced by the presence of a large and ancient cedar tree.

Meanwhile, the unusual octagonal **chapter house**, from which the cathedral was governed during medieval times, contains a 13th century **frieze** showing scenes from the Old Testament. It also holds one of only four original copies of the **Magna Carta**, drawn up by King John in 1215, in an attempt to placate angry barons. *Open May to August daily 8am to 8.15pm, September to April daily 8am to 6:30pm. Admission free, but donation of £3 is suggested. Tel. 01722 555120; www.salisburycathedral.org.uk.*

The **Cathedral Close**, characterized by wide lawns and pretty houses and cottages, is everyone's idea of an English cathedral setting. One of the houses, the elegant **Mompesson House**, built during the reign of Queen Anne, is open to the public and contains some fine wood paneling and plasterwork, and an interesting collection of glasses. The house was featured in the award-winning film *Sense and Sensibility*. Tea and refreshments are served in an attractive walled garden. *Open April to October daily Saturday to Wednesday noon to 5pm. Admission £3.40. Tel. 01722 335659.*

To the north of the cathedral is the High Street Gate, one of four gates built to allow entrance into the Close from the rest of the city. This leads into modern Salisbury, a busy shopping and commercial center, with a clutch of wonderful medieval buildings and monuments, such as the **Poultry Cross**, on Silver Street, where for centuries market traders have set up their stalls; and **St. Thomas of Canterbury Church** and the broad **Market Square**, where on Tuesdays and Saturdays a centuries-old market is held.

STONEHENGE - MYSTERY ON THE DOWNS

*Just eight miles north of Salisbury, on a lonely windswept plain close to the junction of the A345 and A303, stands the mysterious and intriguing Stone Circle at **Stonehenge**. Many visitors here are disappointed: in order to protect this, one of the world's foremost archaeological sites, direct access to the stones is no longer permitted, due to the massive crowds of tourists and religious fanatics, and visitors have to make do with a walk round the periphery armed with audio phones giving a commentary. However, even if the site isn't particular aesthetically exciting, it's a haunting kind of place, and you can't help wondering why it was that some of the larger stones were brought here – most likely from South Wales – all those years ago.*

The origin of Stonehenge, anywhere between 3,500 to 5,000 years old, remains a mystery to this day. The Victorians believed that the site was the work of the Druids, an ancient religious sect, but it's believed that the arrival of the stones here predates the arrival of the Druids in Britain by many years. Other theories range from the sublime to the downright ridiculous, with the most plausible maintaining that Stonehenge was an astronomical observatory.

To visit from Salisbury by bus, take the Wilts and Dorset bus #3 from Salisbury Bus Station, Endless Street, Tel 01722 336855. Stonehenge is open April to mid-July daily 10am to 6pm, mid-July to September 10am to 8pm, September to March 10am to 4pm. Admission £3. Tel. 01980 623106.

Salisbury has a lively cultural life, evidenced by the annual **Salisbury Festival**, held in May and June, with classical concerts, plays and recitals, and the excellent **Salisbury Playhouse** theater on Malthouse Lane, which presents first-rate productions year-round, *Tel. 01722 323883.*

Four miles west of the city is the ancient town of **Wilton**, from which the name Wiltshire derives. The main attraction here is **Wilton House**, home of the Earls of Pembroke. The original Tudor mansion burned down in the 17th century. Its replacement, designed by famous architect Inigo Jones, contains some fabulous artwork, with paintings by Van Dyck, Rembrandt and Breugel, a surviving Tudor kitchen and a Victorian laundry. In the 20-acre grounds are a picture-perfect palladian bridge crossing the River Nadder. *Open Easter to October daily 10:30am to 5:30pm. Admission house and grounds adults £6.75, students and seniors £5.75, children 5-15 £4. Tel. 01722 746720.*

EXCURSIONS & DAY TRIPS

Two stunning locations make a worthwhile day trip from Salisbury. The first of these, **Stourhead Gardens**, about 30 miles west of Salisbury just north of Mere on the A303, is one of the most splendid landscaped gardens in England, if not Europe. Designed by the renowned Capability Brown in the 1720s, it centers round a large artificial lake, whose periphery is dotted with ornamental grottoes, temples and bridges, as well as a colorful display of shrubs and trees, including acres of rhododendrons and azaleas which produce a riot of color, particularly in early summer. After you've been for a walk round the Gardens, **Stourhead House**, built by wealthy London banker Henry Hoare is a bit of a let-down, but still worth a visit for the displays of fine Chinese and French porcelain and a superb library. *Gardens open daily 9am to 7pm or sunset if earlier. House open April 1 to October 29, daily except Thursday and Friday, 12noon to 5:30pm or dusk. Admission to gardens and house: £8, children £3.80. Gardens or house march to October £4.60, child £2.60. Garden only, November to the end of February, Adults £3.60, children £1.50. Tel. 01747 841152.*

West of the market town of **Warminster**, just off the A36, is the equally famous **Longleat House**, home of the Marquess of Bath, and the even more aristocratic Lions of Longleat. Completed in 1580 in the Italian renaissance style, the four-story home contains some stunning rooms such as the **minstrels' room** and the **Great Hall**, and there are some priceless tapestries, paintings and sumptuous original furnishings. The grounds of Longleat are also home to England's oldest **safari park**, with a variety of animals on view including those lions, giraffes, zebras and rhinos, and a variety of additional attractions designed to keep the money flowing in: a maze, dollhouses and a butterfly garden. *House open Easter to September daily 10am to 6pm, October to Easter 10am to 4pm. Admission*

£4.50. Safari Park open March to October 10am to 6pm. Admission £6.50. Tel. 01985 844400.

Avebury, about 35 miles north of Salisbury on the A4361, is not as well known as Stonehenge, but it's an equally evocative prehistoric (and even older) monument that's all the more so for its lack of pretense. The main area is a wide circular ditch and bank, around 1,400 feet across and about half a mile in circumference. The perimeter is punctuated by four entrances that seem to correspond to the four points of the compass, and inside are the remains of three stone circles. The largest of these, with 27 stones, once had 98, but many of them were destroyed or removed many years ago, often by religious fundamentalists. The **Alexander Kieller Museum**, maintained by English Heritage, contains an interesting collection of artifacts collected from the site.

NIGHTLIFE & ENTERTAINMENT

The **Salisbury Playhouse**, *Malthouse Lane, Tel. 01722 320333*, offers first-class drama year-round.

In recent years a number of lively new pubs have sprung up in the city center, complementing the more traditional older establishments. Among them, try the bustling **Woody's Bar**, *12 Minster Street*; **Churchill's** *on Endless Street* features live music; while if it's a bit of peace and quiet you're after, head for **Bishop's Mill Tavern**, where you can enjoy views of the river.

PRACTICAL INFORMATION

Salisbury's **tourist office** *is located in Fish Row,* in the center of town, *Tel. 01722 334956*. The city is well served for banks and post offices – the post office is on Chipper Lane. In May and June, the **Salisbury Festival** includes first-rate classical concerts, recitals and plays. For information, contact the tourist office.

THE NEW FOREST

The **New Forest** is not as new as you may think. In fact, it was established by **William the Conqueror** as a royal hunting preserve in the eleventh century, when it is said the king razed to the ground 22 Saxon villages, none of which has ever been found. A mixture of moorland and dense woodland, it covers 90,000 acres and is a major habitat for a variety of flora and fauna, most conspicuous of which are the hardy and free-roaming New Forest **ponies**, which you particularly need to be aware of if you're driving: they tend to pop up, lie down, stop for conversation in unexpected places like the center of the highway as if they own the place – and in many ways they do. There are also several varieties of **deer**, including red deer and sika deer, and thousands of cows. In recent years, motor access to the Forest, particularly attractive in the fall, when the trees are turning color and when the moors take on a purple hue, has been limited in order to preserve the environment. There are dozens of well-posted parking lots, picnic areas and campgrounds, all of which are great places to embark on a wealth of hiking trails that criss-cross the forest. If you prefer **horse riding**, there are a number of stables where you can get one for the day. The Forest was recently awarded National Park status.

ARRIVALS & DEPARTURES
By Car
From London, the M3, M27 and A31 will take you to the A337 (it's clearly marked "New Forest") which leads to Lyndhurst, the Forest's administrative center.

By Train
The Forest's main train station is at Brockenhurst, with an excellent and frequent half-hourly service from London Waterloo. Trains take about one hour twenty minutes. There are smaller stations at Ashurst (Lyndhurst Road) and Beaulieu Road.

GETTING AROUND
Wilts and Dorset Explorer bus tickets give you unlimited travel on any one day for just under a fiver. A similar weekly ticket (Busabout) costs around £20. *Call 01962 846924 for more information.* As well as being a wonderful place for hiking, cycling and horseback riding are also great ways of exploring the 145-square-mile forest.

Cycling is a great way to see the Forest. There are some hilly parts, but it's not exactly mountainous terrain. You can hire a bike from the following operators:

- **New Forest Cycle Experience**, *2-4 Brookley Road, Brockenhurst. Tel. 01590 624204*
- **Burley Bike Hire**, *Burley Centre. Tel. 01425 403584*
- **Country Lanes Bicycle Hire**, *The Station, Brockenhurst. Tel. 01590 622627; www.countrylanes.co.uk*

WHERE TO STAY
CHEWTON GLEN, *Christchurch Road, New Milton, Dorset BH25 6QS. Tel. 01425 275341, Fax 01425 273310; www.chewtonglen.com 33 rooms, 19 suites. Rates: single occupancy/double/twin £230 to £530, suite £430 to £530. Restaurant (see below), outdoor and indoor pools, health club, golf course.*

One of the most remarkable hotels in England, the Chewton Glen has received numerous accolades, and has been consistently voted one of the top twenty hotels in the world by travel publications. Located on the edge of the New Forest, all the rooms in this old country house have balconies or terraces overlooking lush parkland. The rooms themselves are elegant, and come with a range of trimmings, from bathrobes to sherry and lots of fresh flowers. The hotel's facilities include both outdoor and indoor swimming pools, croquet lawn and health club. Of course it's not cheap, but then, there are few hotels around of this quality and standard.

BALMER LAWN, *Lyndhurst Road (A337), Brockenhurst, Hampshire SO42 7ZB. Tel. 01590 623116, Fax 01590 623864. 55 rooms. Rates for singles 65, doubles from £70 per person sharing. Restaurant, inddor and outdoor pools, sauna and jacuzzi, gymnasium, tennis courts. All major credit cards accepted. Maintained by Best Western.*

Originally a nineteenth century hunting lodge, the Balmer Lawn is located just outside Brockenhurst, and overlooks a cricket green with uninterrupted views over open forest and heathland. The rooms are comfortable, and the atmosphere welcoming. There's a fine and highly-recommended restaurant.

RHINEFIELD HOUSE HOTEL, *Rhinefield Road, Brockenhurst, Hampshire SO42 7QB. Tel. 01590 622922, Fax 01590 622800. 34 rooms. Rates: Double rooms from £75 per person per night sharing, suites from £175 per night. Restaurant. Leisure facilities. All major credit cards accepted.*

Owned by Virgin Airline's Richard Branson, Rhinefield House is stunningly located half-way along a drive of ornamental trees, including California redwoods. The house overlooks beautiful gardens recently restored to their original 1890s design, and inside the Grand Hall is a replica of Westminster Hall. The Alhambra Room is an authentic recreation of the Alhambra Palace in Grenada. There's an excellent restaurant, and the rooms are luxurious.

CAREY'S MANOR HOTEL, *Brockenhurst SO42 7RH. Tel 01590 623551, Fax 01790 622799. Rooms: 79. Rates: singles from £79, doubles from 3129. Cafe, bar, restaurant, indoor pool, sauna, gymnasium, beauty therapist. All major credit cards accepted.*

Although not its administrative center, Brockenhurst is the New Forest's most visited village, its main advantage being that it has its own rail station with regular services to London. Carey's Manor is one of the village's oldest buildings, and is full of character, including a lounge with a massive fireplace where log fires blaze in the winter. The rooms are spacious and nicely decorated and furnished; there's both an informal French-style cafe for dining, or a more formal dining room which has established a very good reputation locally. Carey's Manor also boasts a comprehensive leisure facility, which includes a good-sized pool and a steam room.

LYNDHURST PARK HOTEL, *High Street, Lyndhurst SO43 7NL. Tel 023 8028 3923, Fax 023 8028 3019. Rooms: 59. Rates: singles from £60, doubles from £120. Bars, restaurant, outdoor pool, tennis courts, sauna. All major credit cards accepted.*

This extended Georgian country house is located just a short walk from Lyndhurst's main street, in grounds of about five acres and include tennis courts and terrace. The bedrooms are individually furnished and decorated and come in a variety of sizes; some have four-poster beds. The hotel has two bars and a pleasant wood-paneled restaurant with a pleasant conservatory extension. Lyndhurst is the New Forest's administrative center and, with a number of main roads radiating from the village, the hotel is within easy reach of all the Forest's attractions, as well as its main visitor center which is just a few yards down the road.

WHERE TO EAT

The New Forest contains a number of excellent restaurants, though some of them are a bit on the pricey side. A good alternative are the pubs, many of them picturesque old buildings with gardens where you can sit out during the summer months – and where you can often get excellent meals relatively inexpensively. Among them, try the **Queen's Head** at Burley, the **Hare and Hounds** at Sway, near Brockenhurst, and the **Checkers** at Pennington, near Lymington.

MARRYAT RESTAURANT, *at the Chewton Glen Hotel, Christchurch Road, New Milton, BH25 6QS. Tel. 01425 275341. Open Mondays 7:30pm to 9:30pm, Tuesday to Sunday 12:30pm to 2:30pm, 7:30pm to 9:30pm. Set 3-course dinner: £45; 2-course lunch £18. All major credit cards accepted*

The Chewton Glen's restaurant has as many accolades as the hotel itself. The beautiful dining room overlooks the lovely grounds, the service is impeccable, and the wine list, as you'd expect, extensive and well-chosen. Take a good look around you if you dine here; you may be eating with the rich and famous. Margaret Thatcher is said to be a regular here, and the last time I visited, Peter Ustinov was sitting at the next table.

PROVENCE, *Silver Street, Hordle, near Lymington. Tel. 01590 682219. Open Sunday and Monday noon to 2pm, Tuesday to Saturday noon to 2pm, 7pm to 10pm. All major credit cards accepted.*

Wonderful restaurant housed in a seventeenth century watermill that's in five acres of garden. The main dining room is a bit formal – a jacket and tie affair. In summer the terrace is a better bet. The emphasis, of course, is French, and dishes include roast lamb cutlets with a souffle of Roquefort cheese and a hot and cold white and dark chocolate plate.

SIMPLY POUSSIN, *The Courtyard, Brookley Road, Brockenhurst SO42 7RB. Tel 01590 623063. Open Wednesday to Sunday noon to 1:30pm, 7pm to 9pm. Set lunch from £15 (2 courses), dinner from £22 (2 courses). All major credit cards accepted.*

Simply Poussin is hidden in a courtyard just behind a bookstore in the center of this pleasant New Forest village. The small, intimate dining room is decorated in cream and dark green, and, as the name implies, there's a strong "chicken" theme that extends beyond the menu – it's not a chicken-only restaurant! The chef uses fresh local produce, much of it organic, like the New Forest mushrooms that appear in a variety of dishes. The restaurant has built up an excellent reputation even beyond the locality. Look out especially for the local game, evident in dishes like roast game in Madeira jelly with foie gras. As for desserts, look no further than the passion fruit souffle, the house special. There's an extensive, well-chosen 30-page wine list; house wines certainly don't come cheap, but then you wouldn't expect them to in a place like this.

THE THREE LIONS, *Stuckton, Fordingbridge SP6 2HF. Tel 01425 652489. Open Tuesday to Saturday, noon to 2pm, 7pm to 9pm, open for dinner Sunday. Credit cards: MC, Visa.*

Fordingbridge is a small town in the northeastern corner of the New Forest, not many miles south of Salisbury. The Three Lions, once a farmhouse, was converted into a pub in 1901, and has never looked back! With its open fireplace and pine tables, it's an unpretentious kind of place, where dinner choices are written up on a blackboard. But don't let that fool you. The food here is superb, tremendous care and attention going into each dish's preparation. Try the fillet of brill with saffron sauce or one of the best lasagnas you're ever likely to come across. The desserts are stunning too, especially the treacle tart which comes with a slab of vanilla ice cream and just a hint of lemon.

SEEING THE SIGHTS

The Forest's administrative center is **Lyndhurst**, a large village that's dominated by the lofty Victorian spire of St. Michael's Church, whose churchyard is notable as being the burial site of **Alice Hargreaves** (Liddell) of *Alice in Wonderland* fame. The fairly unremarkable and very noisy main street is home to a variety of souvenir shops, restaurants and a butcher's store that specializes in New Forest venison sausages. The Forest authorities have built a brand new **Visitor Centre** in the main car park, just off High Street, where, as well as general information about the Forest, you can see interactive displays on forest life, a 25-foot long embroidery created to mark the 900th anniversary of the Forest, and a hide where you can learn about the Forest's great variety of rare plants and wildlife. *Open year-round daily from 10am to 5pm. Tel. 01703 283914.*

The main center for tourists, though, is **Brockenhurst**, if only because it has a train station on the main London to Bournemouth line. There's a pretty church here, dedicated to St. Nicholas with fine yew trees from which bows were fashioned for use at the Battle of Agincourt. Next to the station there's a bicycle hire business; as well as hiking and riding, cycling through the relatively gentle Forest landscapes can be very appealing.

On the southern fringes of the Forest, the villages of **Beaulieu** and **Buckler's Hard** are worth a glance. **Beaulieu** (pronounced Bewlee) **Abbey** was established by the notorious King John in 1204. A Cistercian foundation, it was dissolved as a religious institution by Henry VIII, who wreaked much havoc and destruction on the place. Consequently, only the cloister, a doorway, gate house and two other buildings remain. **Palace House**, home of Lord Montague of Beaulieu since 1538, contains drawings rooms, dining halls and some charming family portraits. The present Lord Montague established the **National Motor Museum** here, which traces the development of motor transport from 1895 to the present day. With more than 200 vehicles on display, it's a must for anyone interested in cars and transport generally. Among Beaulieu's other attractions are a monorail and rides on a 1912 London bus, as well as, in the village center, a pretty duck pond. *Open daily 10am to 5pm, last entry 4:20pm. Admission adults £9, seniors £7.50, children 4-16 £6.50. Tel. 01590 612123; www.beaulieu.co.uk.*

Just two miles south of Beaulieu, on the Beaulieu River, is the 18th-century village of **Buckler's Hard**, a shipbuilding community of 24 brick cottages. Among the Navy ships built here, of New Forest oak, was the *HMS Agamemnon*, reputedly Nelson's favorite battleship. One of the cottages houses a small **Maritime Museum**, where the history of local shipbuilding can be traced.

SPORTS & RECREATION
Horseback Riding
The New Forest is tailor-made for horseback riding, with hundreds of miles of tracks and trails to explore. Among the riding stables are:
• **New Park Manor Stables**, *New Park, Brockenhurst. Tel. 01590 623919*
• **Forest Park Stables**, *Rhinefield Road, Brockenhurst. Tel. 01590 623429*

PRACTICAL INFORMATION
Banks
The main centers of Lyndhurst and Brockenhurst have branches of the main UK banks, though their opening hours are restricted. The market town of Ringwood on the western fringes of the Forest offers better facilities.

SOUTHAMPTON & PORTSMOUTH

With a population well in excess of 200,000, **Southampton**, England's busiest passenger port, regards itself as the capital of the region. It has been an important trading and commercial center for centuries. There is evidence of its importance during Roman and Saxon times, its prosperity as a port aided and abetted by the strange phenomenon of double tides along this part of the coast, which allow deep water access to the port for much longer periods than most other ports.

Because of its strategic importance, Southampton, like its neighbor **Portsmouth**, suffered incalculable damage from enemy bombs during World War II, when many of the city's more characterful buildings were destroyed. Their replacements, dull, concrete and utterly charmless, dominate the modern city center.

ARRIVALS & DEPARTURES

By Car

Southampton is about 72 miles from central London. Take the M3 to Winchester, then the A33 from junction 14. For Portsmouth, take the A3 from London directly to the city.

By Bus

National Express, *Tel. 0990 808080*, runs an hourly service from Victoria Bus Station to Southampton. The journey takes about 2 1/2 hours. Buses also leave Victoria for Portsmouth, just as frequently, and with a similar journey time.

By Train

South West Trains operate half-hourly service to Southampton from London Waterloo. The journey takes about an hour and a quarter. SWT also runs a service to Portsmouth from Waterloo, though the train is pretty slow and the journey normally takes around 2 hours.

GETTING AROUND

Both Southampton and Portsmouth have compact city centers that can easily be explored on foot.

WHERE TO STAY

DOLPHIN HOTEL, *35 High Street, Southampton SO14 2HN. Tel. 02380 339955, Fax 02380 333650. 73 rooms. Rates: singles from £60, doubles from £80. Restaurant. All major credit cards accepted.*

The current Dolphin – as old as it is – is just the most recent in a line of lodging places that have stood on this site for more than 700 years. The present building was in fact a Georgian coaching inn, and the large, comfortable rooms reflect the elegance of the period. There's a fine restaurant.

POSTHOUSE, *Herbert Walker Avenue, Southampton SO15 1HJ. Tel 0870 400 9073, Fax 023 8033 2510. Rooms: 128. Rates: singles from £80, doubles from £120. Bar, restaurant, indoor pool, sauna, solarium. All major credit cards accepted.*

This modern multi-story hotel run by the Trusthouse Forte chain is located between the docks and Southampton's burgeoning shopping district. Popular with tourists and business travelers alike, it has 128 well-equipped rooms all with TV and tea- and coffee-making facilities, several public lounges, bars and a restaurant with an extensive a la carte menu. You can also benefit from a leisure suite with indoor pool, jacuzzi and beauty therapy room.

DE VERE GRAND HARBOUR, *West Quay Road, Southampton SO15 1AG. Tel 023 8063 3033, fax 023 8083 3066. Rooms: 172. Rates: singles from £150, doubles from £170. Bars, restaurants, indoor pool, sauna, solarium, steam room. All major credit cards accepted.*

The De Vere Grand Harbour is a wonderful new hotel located in Southampton's West Quay district, close to the main shopping area and visitor attractions. The public areas are spacious and elegant and, unusually for all but the most upmarket British hotels, air-conditioned. Many of the lavishly furnished bedrooms and suites have balconies. You can also make use of a state-of-the-art leisure center, with gymnasium and pool, as well as its own bar and restaurant. There are two further restaurants where snacks as well as full meals can be ordered.

WHERE TO EAT

LEMON SOLE, *123 High Street, Portsmouth, Tel. 02380 811303. Open daily noon to 2pm, 6pm to 10pm. Set dinner £7.95 for two courses. All major credit cards accepted.*

An unusual seafood restaurant, where you go up to a large ice cabinet and choose your own, which is then cooked in whichever style you request (within reason). There's a good choice first courses, which are a la carte, and keeping to the theme of choice, you pick your bottle of wine from a rack-lined wall. Downstairs there's a wine bar with simpler fare. Meat, vegetarian and poultry dishes are also available for those who can't abide seafood.

PORTER'S, *Town Quay, Southampton. Tel. 02380 221159. Open Monday to Saturday noon to 3pm, 7pm to midnight. Three-course fixed price menu £16. All major credit cards accepted.*

This former warehouse was once lapped by the waves of Southampton water, and boats could unload their goods straight into its 600-year-old cellars. Today's restaurant is an elegant affair, with French regency trimmings and a wonderful array of fresh seafood dishes, including such delicacies as fresh shellfish on a bed of seaweed, and grilled salmon with hollandaise sauce.

BOTLEIGH GRANGE HOTEL, *Hedge End, Southampton SO3 2GA. Tel 01489 787700. Open daily 12:30 to 2pm, 7pm to 10pm (except closed for lunch Saturday). Dinner about £22. All major credit cards accepted.*

Located in Hedge End, a few miles out on the edge of the city, in extensive grounds that include a small lake, the Botleigh Grange is a large mansion with a huge dining room that seats 150. The food can best be described as eclectic, with French-influenced delights such as roast pigeon with a celeriac puree rubbing shoulders with Asian choices. There's a wide choice of desserts and an equally extensive wine list.

SEEING THE SIGHTS

Some of Southampton's older buildings did manage to survive WWII, including the medieval **Church of St. Michael** and the excellent **Tudor House Museum** in Bugle Street, a fifteenth century building with exhibits on local history and a reconstruction of a Tudor garden. *Open year-round Tuesday to Friday 10am to 5pm, Saturday 10am to 4pm, Sunday 1pm to 5pm. Admission free. Tel. 02380 635904.* The **God's House Tower**, in nearby Winkle Street, was once a gunpowder factory, now a museum of archaeology (opening times same as Tudor House).

THE PILGRIMS

*Southampton vies with Plymouth (sometimes it gets nasty) for the honor of being the port of embarkation of the **Pilgrims**. In truth, both cities have a legitimate claim. The Pilgrims' journey in the tiny **Mayflower** did indeed start in Southampton, on August 15, 1620; unforeseen repairs deemed it necessary to stop in Plymouth before battling the Atlantic. In Southampton's **Mayflower Park**, on the Western Esplanade, there's a rather tacky pilgrims' **Memorial**. Incidentally, one of the Mayflower's passengers, John Alden, was a native of Southampton.*

Southampton's more recent maritime history has seen some of the world's greatest liners, including the *Queen Mary*, the *Queen Elizabeth* and the *QEII* based here. This was also the home port of the *Titanic*. The **Southampton Maritime Museum** in Bugle Street traces the port's history, with photographs, artifacts and models of many of the more illustrious ships that have sailed from here. *Open year-round Tuesday to Friday 10am* *to 1pm, 2pm to 5pm; Saturday 10am to 1pm, 2pm to 4pm, Sunday 2pm to 5pm. Admission free. Tel. 02380 632493.*

Meanwhile, the city of **Portsmouth**, twenty miles east of Southampton on the A27, once Britain's greatest naval port, is synonymous with *HMS Victory* and **Admiral Horatio Nelson**. The *Victory*, which has been lovingly restored to appear as she did at the **Battle of Trafalgar** in 1805. You can visit the spot where Nelson entertained his officers and visit the place where he was shot dead by a French sniper. Other famous ships such as the *Mary Rose* and the *HMS Warrior* can be seen at the vast naval base, also home to the **Royal Naval Museum**, with its fascinating collection of hand-painted figureheads, ship artifacts, cooking utensils and paintings outlining British naval history.

One of the city's major attractions is the *Mary Rose*, former flagship of the Tudor navy, which sank in 1545 and was raised again in 1982. The ship is in a special enclosure, where her timbers must be sprayed regularly to stop them from drying out. *1/7 College Road, HM Naval Base, Portsmouth. Open March to October daily 10am to 5:30pm, November to February daily 10am to 5pm. Admission per individual attraction adults £5.95, children (5-14) £4.45, students and seniors £5.20. All-ships ticket adults £11.90, children £8.90, students and seniors £10.40. Tel. 02392 861512; www.flagship.org.uk.* Portsmouth is the home town of the novelist Charles Dickens who was born here in 1812. His birthplace at 393 Commercial Road is a charming, well-preserved early nineteenth century home, with a number of artifacts relating to the author and his work. *Open April to October daily 10am to 5:30pm. Admission adults £2, children (14-18) £1.20, students and seniors £1.50. Tel. 02392 827261.*

Southsea, the seaside resort section of Portsmouth, has a couple of piers, and the usual amusement arcades and seafood stalls that you'd associate with most British seaside resorts – though the beach is pebbly and shelves quite quickly. Southsea Common is also home to a **D-Day Museum**, one of the area's most popular attractions. A series of exhibits trace the preliminary planning that went into the June 6, 1944 assault, as well as details from the actual invasion. The main attraction here is a 270-foot tapestry, the **Overlord Embroidery**, which in 34 panels follows the history of World War II from the Battle of Britain in May and June, 1940, to D-Day and the first days of the liberation of Europe. *Open April to October daily 10am to 5:30pm, November to March Monday 1pm to 5pm, Tuesday to Sunday 10am to 5pm. Admission adults £4.75.*

Portsmouth's **Old Town** contains a number of interesting medieval and Georgian buildings that escaped German bombing raids that so devastated the rest of the city. Of chief interest here is the **Cathedral of St. Thomas**, originally a simple parish church but which became a cathedral in the 1950s. The Cathedral, much extended in recent years since its elevation to higher things, was begun in Norman times, as is evident in its many round arches.

EXCURSIONS & DAY TRIPS

Just to the west of Portsea Island, on which Portsmouth stands, near the bustling town of Fareham is the remains of **Portchester Castle**, with the best-preserved set of Roman walls in northern Europe, more than 1,600 years old. There's also a Norman keep, from which excellent views over the harbor and towards Portsdown Hill are afforded. *Open April to September daily 10am to 6pm, October to March Tuesday to Sunday 10am to 4pm. Admission £2.50. Tel. 02392 378291.*

Just ten miles north west of Southampton, on the famous trout river, the Test, the ancient market town of **Romsey** is worth a visit for its huge, but simple well-preserved Norman **Abbey** that looms above the surrounding town like a great ocean liner. Just outside the town, on the A3057, is **Broadlands**, home of the late Lord Mountbatten, killed by an IRA bomb in 1981. This Palladian mansion, built in the 17th century, is one of the south's grandest homes, with ornate plasterwork, paintings, antiques and memorabilia relating to the late Lord Mountbatten, who was the present Queen's uncle – the Queen and Prince Philip spent their honeymoon here in 1947 – and in 1981 Prince Charles and Princess Diana spent the first few nights fo their honeymoon here. The gardens were laid out by Capability Brown, and sweep down in wide lawns to the River Test. *Open mid-June to September daily noon to 5:30pm. Admission £5. Tel. 01794 516878.*

PRACTICAL INFORMATION

Southampton's main **tourist office** is located at *Number 9, Civic Centre (the unmissable concrete building with the clock tower), Tel. 02380 221106*. The town is liberally served with banks and post offices, and there's a branch of **American Express** at *99, Above Bar, Tel. 02380 634722*.

Portsmouth operates **tourism offices** at *The Hard, Tel. 02392 826722*, and at *Clarence Esplanade, Southsea, Tel. 02392 832464*.

THE ISLE OF WIGHT

The **Isle of Wight**, separated from the county of Hampshire by the two mile wide channel of water known as The Solent, is a great place for a day trip. About fourteen miles long by seven miles wide – around 150 square miles in all – it has fascinating historical attractions, some beautiful, lush, archetypal English countryside and excellent beaches. The island became fashionable as a holiday destination in the 1800s, noted for its fresh air and balmy climate, and attracted luminaries from Lord Tennyson to none other than Queen Victoria herself.

ARRIVALS & DEPARTURES

A car-ferry service to the Isle of Wight operated by **Wightlink**, *Tel. 0990 827744*, runs from Lymington to Yarmouth and takes about 35 minutes, while another ferry from Portsmouth to Fishbourne, on the north coast, takes about 40 minutes. **Red Funnel Ferries**, *Tel. 02380 330333*, also run a car-ferry service between Southampton and Cowes. **Hovertravel**, *Tel. 01983 811000*, operates a passenger hovercraft from Southsea (Portsmouth) and Ryde.

GETTING AROUND

The island is easily explored by car. While many of the island roads are narrow country lanes, reasonably good 'A' classified roads link the main towns and villages. Bus services on the Island are operated by **Southern Vectis**, *Tel. 01983 827005*, including a round-island bus. They also offer a special Rover ticket which allows access for a week.

Cycling is a great option. Try **Autovogue**, *140 High Street, Ryde, Tel. 01983 812989*, just ten minutes from the ferry terminal, or **Isle Cycle**, *The Square, Yarmouth, Tel. 01983 760219*, just a couple of minutes from Yarmouth ferry terminal.

Tourism Offices
- **Ryde Tourist Office**, *Western Esplanade, Ryde PO33 2LW. Tel. 01983 562905; www.isle-of-wight-tourism.gov.uk*
- **Coastal Visitors' Centre**, *Dudley Road, Ventnor PO38 1EJ. Tel. 01983 855400*

WHERE TO STAY

ROYAL HOTEL, *Belgrave Road, Ventnor. Tel 01983 852186, Fax 01983 855395. Rooms: 55. Rates: singles from £50, doubles from £60. Bar, restaurant, garden, swimming pool. All major credit cards accepted.*

An elegant stone building recently refurbished to a high standard, the Royal is close to Ventnor's main attractions, including the beach. The spacious bedrooms – all with a full range of facilities – have views over the attractive gardens with its heated pool. One of the main points to note is that this is very much a family hotel, and children are well provided for, with early suppers, high chairs and baby listening devices. At the end of the day, you can pack the kids safely off to bed, and enjoy the Royal's excellent restaurant.

PRIORY BAY HOTEL, *Priory Drive, Seaview. Tel 01983 613146, fax 01983 616539. Rooms: 25 (including seven cottage suites). Rates: singles from £65, doubles from £90, suites from £125. Bar, two restaurants, leisure facilities including outdoor pool, golf course. All major credit cards accepted.*

The luxurious Priory Bay at Seaview, at the eastern end of the Island, was opened as recently as 1998 and has won great accolades. For a start, it's in a superb location, surrounded by trees and with views to the sea; you can walk down from the hotel through the woods to a lovely sandy beach. The public rooms are elegant and the bedrooms are all stylishly and individually decorated and come with the full range of facilities. If you want a bit more solitude, you can choose from self-catering cottages in the grounds. On top of all this, there are two excellent restaurants. It's just the place for a spot a relaxation by the sea, and is within easy reach of the Island's main attractions.

WHERE TO EAT

GEORGE HOTEL, *Quay Street, Yarmouth. Tel 01983 760331. Restaurant open Tuesday to Saturday 7pm to 9:45pm, Brasserie open daily noon to 3pm, 7pm to 10pm. Three-course set meal (restaurant) £36. All major credit cards accepted.*

As you'd expect on an island, fish abounds in the George's restaurants, although a full range of meat dishes (and vegetarian options) are available too. For simpler fare, try the Brasserie; it's more informal, and in the summer, weather permitting, you can sit outside and watch the boats coming and going. The George is an old inn with lots of character right in the heart of old Yarmouth – and the only Michelin-rated restaurant on the Isle of Wight. Perhaps that explains why the food is a bit on the pricey side.

PRIORY BAY RESTAURANT & OYSTER SEAFOOD CAFE, *Priory Drive, Seaview. Tel 01983 613146. Restaurant open daily 12:30pm to 2pm, 7:30pm to 9:30pm, cafe open daily 9am to 2pm, 3pm to 6pm, 6:30pm to 9:30pm. All major credit cards accepted.*

Part of the Priory bay complex, this restaurant/cafe is situated in a stunning location in woodlands overlooking the sea, with a lovely sandy beach below. The restaurant has established a reputation as one of the best places to eat on the island, with dishes like Bembridge (an island town) crab ravioli and rack of lamb with wild garlic. The cafe serves lighter but equally good food. The combination of excellent food and such a gorgeous location is quite an inspiration.

SEEING THE SIGHTS

The Island's western point is the lethal **Needles Rocks**, the powerful red and white striped Needles lighthouse warning ships to keep well clear. Just below here is **Alum Bay**, noted for the multi-colored sands of its cliffs. A little further east is **Freshwater**, where the poet **Alfred, Lord Tennyson**, built a home, Farringford, now a hotel, while a few miles to the north lies the pretty town of **Yarmouth**, its small harbor filled with pleasure craft in the summer.

Further east is the town of **Cowes** – divided by the River Medina into East and West Cowes. Cowes is a major sailing center, and Cowes Week in August is a mecca for sailors from all over Europe. Just to the east of East Cowes is **Osborne House**, summer residence of Queen Victoria, built in the style of an Italian villa. Victoria loved the Island, and Osborne has been preserved much as it was when she died here in 1901. *Open April to September daily 10am to 6pm, October daily 10am to 5pm, November to mid-December, February and March, Monday, Wednesday Thursday and Sunday 10am to 2:30pm (for pre-booked tours only. Admission adults £6.90, seniors and students £5.20, children aged 5 to 15, £3.50. Tel. 01983 200022; www.english-heritage.org.uk.*

Right in the center of the Island is the capital **Newport**, and adjacent **Carisbroke**, in whose **castle** King Charles I was held before being taken to London for execution in 1649. A museum tells the story of his imprisonment. *Open April to August daily 10am to 6pm, September to March daily 10am to 4pm. Admission adults £4.50, seniors and students £3.40, children 5-15 £2.30. Tel. 01983 522107.*

Southeast of here, the Isle of Wight's southern "sunshine coast" is home to three resorts, the rather tacky bucket and spadey **Sandown** and **Shanklin**, both with sandy beaches, and slightly more refined **Ventnor**.

17. THE WEST COUNTRY

The **West Country** is the term given to the counties of southwest England, from the lush pastureland and rolling hills of **Somerset** and **Wiltshire**, still both largely rural and dotted with the kind of picturesque villages that feature in picture books, to the elegant Roman spa city of **Bath** and the large, historic port of **Bristol**. To the west, it includes the vast, craggy, wave-lashed peninsula that juts out into the Atlantic Ocean that comprises the counties of **Cornwall** with its whitewashed fishing villages, sandy coves, Arthurian legends – and **Devon**, with its mighty cliffs, wide estuaries, sophisticated resorts and large open tracts of moorland – no wonder these two latter counties are the best-loved domestic holiday destinations for Britons.

I've set out the first part of this chapter as a tour of the Cornwall/Devon coast, so rather than giving separate arrivals and departures information for each town, I've given general directions to the region as a whole, with instructions as to which routes to then follow.

Cornwall is the most westerly of all the English counties – in fact many locals would say it's not England at all. Because Cornwall's main attraction is its superb coast, I've decided to tackle the county by following the coast westwards from the small seaside town of Looe, just west of Plymouth on the Devon/Cornwall border, working westwards along the south coast, then eastwards along Cornwall's northern coast.

Cross the **River Tamar** from Plymouth, Devon, and you're in a different nation, they say – a statement that's certainly borne out by Cornwall's many unusual traditions and customs – including the existence of the ancient Cornish language – that make this place feel quite different from the rest of Britain.

To tour Cornwall, it makes best sense to begin by exploring the **south coast**, drive west to **Lizard Point**, the most southerly point in England, then on to **Land's End**, then turning east, and following the northern coast northeast back to the border with Somerset county. For an unusual

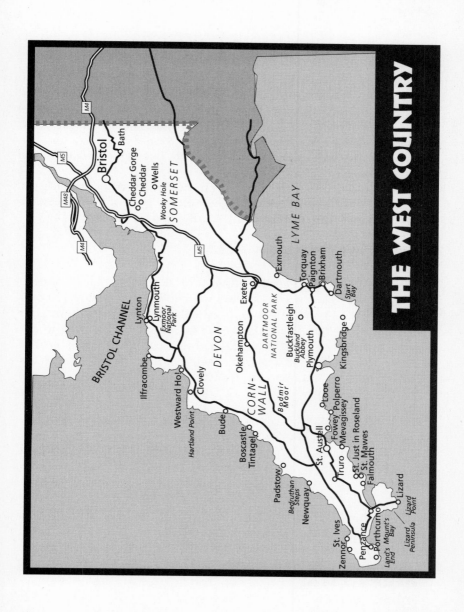

diversion, you might want to consider a day or two on the remote and incredibly peaceful Atlantic **Isles of Scilly**, with their sub-tropical plantings and lovely beaches.

THE SOUTH CORNWALL COAST

Traveling west from Devon, starting with **Looe**, the south Cornwall coast is a wonderful mixture of rocky headlands, sandy beaches and wide estuaries, punctuated with small seaside towns and fishing villages, like picturesque **Polperro**, with its terraced cottages rising steeply above a tiny harbor; **Mevagissey**, another tiny port that was once home to a thriving fishing industry; and, further west, **Falmouth**, one of Cornwall's larger towns, but none the less attractive for it.

Britain's southernmost point, the windswept **Lizard Peninsula**, leads the way to the **Penwith Peninsula**, the bustling port of **Penzance** and finally England's westernmost point, **Land's End**.

ARRIVALS & DEPARTURES

By Car

The quickest way to get to Cornwall is to take the M4 out of London. Bypass Bristol and join up with the M5 south to Exeter where you link up with either the A30 or A38 west to Cornwall. An alternative, slower, but more picturesque route is to take the M3 to just past Basingstoke, where you then link up with the A303 west. This eventually merges with the A30 to Exeter. Stay on the A30 west from Exeter, or link up with the A38. It's about 180 miles from London to Exeter.

By Bus

There are regular and frequent National Express services to Cornwall, leaving from London's Victoria Bus Station. The journey time to Plymouth, on the Devon/Cornwall border, is about 5 hours, and another 3 hours to Penzance. *Call 0990 808080 for information.*

By Train

The region is served by frequent fast trains from London Paddington. Trains to Exeter take just under 3 hours, an hour more to Plymouth and about 6 hours in total to Penzance. *Call 0345 484950 for train information.*

WHERE TO STAY

ABBEY HOTEL, *Abbey Street, Penzance TR18 4AR. Tel. 01736 366906, Fax 01736 351163. Rooms: 7. Rates: singles from £70, doubles from £100. Garden. All major credit cards accepted.*

Wonderful small hotel that's situated at the top of a slipway overlooking Penzance Harbour. Of the original abbey that dates from 1660, few traces remain, but this is more than compensated for in some delightful public rooms, like the lounge, which overlooks the stunning walled garden at the rear, and the various hallways and landings, furnished with fascinating artifacts such as Chinese tea chests and antiques. Some of the rooms have harbor views; all are decorated with flair and imagination – in all a great place to stay.

CAMILLA HOUSE HOTEL, *12 Regent Terrace, Penzance TR18 4DW. Tel./Fax 01736 363771. Rooms: 8. Rates: singles from £18, doubles from £36. Credit cards: MC, Visa.*

Small, attractive Georgian building set in a peaceful terrace parallel to the promenade. The hotel has recently been upgraded and all the rooms are comfortable, those at the front of the building benefiting from fine sea views. There's a pleasant lounge and a spacious dining room where breakfast is served. The owners, Rosemary and Bill Wooldridge, clearly take great pride in their hotel and offers a warm welcome.

THE COTTAGE, *The Coombes, Polperro PL13 2RQ. Tel. 01503 272217. Closed December to February. Rooms: 9. Rates: single from £32, double from £46. Restaurant, bar, garden.*

Delightful cottage B&B in one of the prettiest villages along this section of the coast. There's an attractive tea garden at the side, and the rooms are, in a nutshell, fairly small, well-equipped and cottagey. The two major big pluses here are the restaurant, where you can get superbly cooked locally caught seafood as well as meat dishes, and the staff – Pam and Dave Foster, who take enormous pride in their B&B – and rightly so.

PENMERE MANOR, *Mongleath Road, Falmouth TR11 4PM. Tel. 01326 211411, Fax 01326 317588. Rooms: 37. Rates: singles from £55, doubles from £60, family rooms from £100. Restaurant, bars, library, games rooms, indoor and outdoor pools, leisure suite. All major credit cards accepted.*

Set in five acres of grounds, complete with sub-tropical vegetation, the Penmere Manor is part of the Best Western chain, and offers superb value. The core of the hotel is Georgian, but much extended over the years, though some original features remain. The rooms are all extremely comfortable and well-equipped, but what makes this place special – particularly for the price – is the wealth of leisure facilities, including two pools and a leisure suite.

MARINA HOTEL, *The Esplanade, Fowey PL23 1HY. Tel. 01726 833315, Fax 01726 832779. Rooms: 11. Rates: singles from £48, doubles from £66. Restaurant, bar, lounges, garden. All major credit cards accepted.*

A superbly positioned four-story hotel with superb views over the Fowey estuary, the hotel almost looks as if it was built into the cliff side. Many of the rooms have this view; some even have balconies where you can while away those balmy British summer evenings (both of them). The bedrooms are all well-equipped and pleasantly decorated and furnished, and there's a fine restaurant where you can enjoy even more views over the Estuary. Note: the hotel's parking lot is around five minutes away; use the narrow one-way lane to drop off your luggage first.

IDLE ROCKS HOTEL, *1 Tredenham Road, St Mawes TR2 5AN. Tel 01326 270771, Fax 01326 270062. Rooms: 20. Rates: singles from £68, doubles from £136. Bar, restaurant, lounges. All major credit cards accepted.*

You can't get much closer to the briny than this harborside hotel in picturesque St. Mawes, with a wonderful terrace overlooking the water and a comfortable lounge with the kind of sofas you melt into and don't want to get up again. The bedrooms, all of which are fully equipped with TV, hairdryers and other modern conveniences, vary in size, those with sea views tending to be larger than the others (and for which you'll have to pay around £20-30 extra. There's a fine maritime-themed restaurant, where the emphasis is on but by no means confined to fresh seafood.

WHERE TO EAT

FOOD FOR THOUGHT, *The Quay, Fowey. Tel. 01726 832221. Open Monday to Saturday 7pm to 9:30pm. Set dinner Monday to Friday from £19.95, Saturday from £24.95. Credit cards: MC, Visa.*

Converted old customs house down by the Quay. The main emphasis, of course is on fresh seafood, though there are plenty of fish dishes too, and a particularly good bread-and-butter pudding. The house wine is a good option, coming in at £8.75 a bottle.

HARRIS'S, *46 New Street, Penzance. Tel. 01736 364408. Open Tuesday to Saturday noon to 2pm, 7pm to 9:30pm; Sunday 7pm to 9:30pm only. All major credit cards accepted.*

Long-established restaurant in a narrow side street in downtown Penzance. There's lots of fish, goujons of sole, scallops and the like, and a wide choice of meat dishes from traditional British favorites like Cumberland sausages with onion and mash to venison with beets. There's a good mixture of heavy and lighter desserts, and the wine list starts with house French at £11.50.

TRESANTON HOTEL, *27 Lower Castle Road, St Mawes. Tel. 01326 270055. Open daily 12:30pm to 2:30pm, 7pm to 10pm. Set lunch from £15, set dinner from £25. All major credit cards accepted.*

Lovely waterside restaurant with a terrace for eating al fresco. Seafood, as you'd expect, appears frequently on the menu, much of it coming straight off the boats at nearby Newlyn, but the meat is good here too, particularly the local lamb. There's a good wine list, with house Italian starting at £11.

SEEING THE SIGHTS

Leaving Devon's largest city, Plymouth (see below), it's about a twenty mile drive west on the A387 to the pretty seaside resort of **Looe**, which has been a popular tourist destination since the early 1880s, when the railroad arrived. Looe is in fact two communities, East and West Looe, linked by a seven-arch bridge across the river that divides them. Apart from sea bathing, the town also doubles up as a **shark fishing center**. From Looe, it's only a few minutes west on the same road to the pilchard fishing port of **Polperro**, at the mouth of the tiny Pol stream, its pretty harbor surrounded by two- or three-hundred year old tiny cottages rising up in terraces – giving it bags of charm. That charm is offset somewhat by the fact that on summer weekends its narrow streets get clogged up with cars and pedestrians – in fact drivers are not allowed to take cars into the town center unless they are booked in at a hotel.

From Polperro, it's certainly worth exploring the stunning coastal path towards **Polruan**, passing wonderful secluded sandy beaches on the way. Eventually you'll reach the Fowey (pronounced "Foy") estuary, the pretty port of **Fowey** sitting comfortably on the opposite bank as it has for centuries. Ferries ply the river crossing regularly during the summer, and it's worth it; there are plenty of interesting places to explore here, including the fifteenth century church of **St. Fimbarrus** and **Place House**, an extravagant edifice built by a wealthy local family. A Victorian tower has been stuck on to a sixteenth century fortified house. Close by is the Esplanade, from which you can access a spectacular coastal walk, passing **Readymoney Cove**, with a beach that was once, as the name implies, used by smugglers – and further on, the ruins of **St. Catherine's Castle**, built by a local dignitary on behalf on Henry VIII to protect the town against invasion from France.

A pleasant diversion here is to drive the ten or so miles inland on the B3269 to the ancient market town of **Lostwithiel**, with a charming mix of handsome Georgian houses and narrow cobbled alleyways, all over-looked by the remains of **Restormel Castle**, perched on a hill about a mile north of town. Despite its violent past – Royalist forces managed to wrest it from the control of the Parliamentarian army led by the Earl of Essex in 1644 – it's a quiet, tranquil spot today, perfect for a picnic. *Open April to September daily 10am to 6pm, October daily 10am to 4pm. Admission £1.30; www.english-heritage.co.uk.*

Just a few miles west of Fowey is the town of **St. Austell**, famed for its china clay producing industry, most of which is now exported overseas. Between St. Austell and **St. Mawes**, about 20 miles to the southwest, are a series of pretty coves backed by tall cliffs, and a string of small villages. To get to them, you need to take the B3273 south of St. Austell, then follow the jumble of country lanes along the coast. The first village of any size is **Mevagissey**, whose once-thriving pilchard fishing (and contraband) industry has now been replaced by tourism, though a few tattered lobster pots can still be seen. To the south is the sandy cove of **Portmellon**, and further south again, **Gorran**, formerly a crab fishing town but now largely residential. Just over two miles south of here is lethal **Dodman Point**, a striking promontory that has been the reason for many a shipwreck – atop of which is an ancient Iron Age fort.

From Dodman Point, the coast heads off to the west, passing some beautiful beaches such as **Hemmick Beach** and **Porthluney Cove** before reaching the village of Portloe and neighboring **Veryan**, just a few miles inland, with a lovely village green, pond, and a very odd-looking circular house built in the 1800s by an eccentric local clergyman. The coast continues southwest towards Zone Point, passing glorious **Pendower Beach**, backed by dunes, and **Carne Beach**.

St. Mawes is located at the end of the A3078 on the eastern side of the **Carrick Roads** – a flooded estuary – on the pretty **Roseland Peninsula**. It's an attractive town, with an unusual walled seafront, hillside villas and lush, sub-tropical gardens. It also possesses a castle, **St. Mawes Castle**, built during the reign of Henry VIII in the style of many of the fortifications along the southern coast which, though very small, is in excellent shape despite a siege by Cromwellian forces in 1646. It surrendered quickly, relieving itself of a good deal of potential damage. More recently, it featured in *Poldark*, the popular BBC TV series. *Open April to October daily 10am to 6pm; November to March 10am to 1pm, 2pm to 4pm. Admission adults £2.20, students and seniors £1.70, children £1.10. Tel. 01326 270526.* North of St. Mawes, the small village of **St. Just-in-Roseland** is worth a visit for its picture-postcard church next to a creek, with lots of palms and exotic shrubs.

Truro, fifteen miles north of St. Mawes, is Cornwall's county town, and main administrative and shopping center. Among the city's limited attractions are its **Cathedral**, designed by J. L. Pearson, one of the greatest church architects of the late Victorian period, and completed as recently as 1910, a bright, airy building that incorporated part of the original parish church. Among points of interest are the baptistry and the perpendicular-style south aisle which was part of the original church. Otherwise there's not much of tourist interest here, apart from some pleasant Georgian buildings, one of which now houses **The Royal Cornwall Museum**. The museum has exhibits relating to local industry and agriculture, displays by Cornish artists, a collection of antique toys, an exhibit on some of the minerals found in Cornwall (Cornwall was for centuries a major tin mining region) and other local artifacts. *Open year-round Monday to Saturday, 10am to 5pm. Admission adults £3, seniors and students £2, children 50p. Tel. 01872 272205; www.royalcornwallmuseum.org.uk.*

Now head back to the coast, where the A39 takes you south to the lively seaside town of **Falmouth**, a small unassuming fishing port until Pendennis Castle, on the southern tip of the Carrick Roads, was built in the sixteenth century. A century later, the deepwater harbor was constructed, ensuring better access for shipping and consequently prosperity and growth.

Today, Falmouth caters unashamedly to the tourist, with a High Street crammed with boring cafes and bars. The town's compensations, though, are many. In Arwenack Street, you can see the remains of **Arwenack House**, the Tudor home of the Killigrew family, who'd originally proposed the building of the harbor, while a climb up the 111 **Jacob's Steps** give wonderful views over the harbor. Jacob's Steps can be found in The Moor, the strangely-named main square of the old town. Then there's **Pendennis Castle**, spectacularly sited on a peninsula overlooking the Carrick Roads and out to the Channel. Under siege for five months by the forces of Oliver Cromwell during the English Civil War, it fell only after half the occupants had died and the other forces into starvation. *Open July and August 9am to 6pm; September and October 10am to 5pm; November to March 10am to 4pm. Admission adults £3.80, students and seniors £2.90, children 5-16 £1.90. Tel. 01326 316594; www.english-heritage.co.uk.*

South of Falmouth, a string of fine sandy beaches reach down to **Rosemullion Head**, in Mawnan, with a church dedicated to sixth century Welsh Saint Maunanus, and the lush countryside and prosperous villages either side of the Helford River estuary, heralding the start of the altogether different **Lizard Peninsula** (see sidebar on next page).

THE PENWITH PENINSULA & LAND'S END

The Lizard and Penwith peninsulas are separated by **Mount's Bay**, in whose northwest corner lies the bustling town of **Penzance**, long a major port and more recently a thriving tourist center. It's an elegant place; much of the old medieval heart of the town was destroyed in the sixteenth century by a Spanish raiding party and replaced with some fine Georgian homes, best seen at the top end of **Market Jew Street**, where you can see the green-domed **Market House**, fronted by a statue of Humphrey Davy, a local lad who invented the miner's safety lamp.

Chapel Street contains some fine buildings, including the slightly over-the-top 1835 **Egyptian House**, originally intended to house a geological museum, the seventeenth century **Union Hotel**, and the **Maritime Museum**, with a fascinating collection of artifacts, including items plundered from local wrecks. Penzance's neighboring town, **Newlyn**, was around the turn of the twentieth century the home of the famed Newlyn School of artists, and much of their work can be seen in the **Penlee House**

THE LIZARD PENINSULA

*The Lizard Peninsula, the most southerly part of England, is not the most inviting kind of place, though its is officially designated an area of outstanding natural beauty. The broad, windswept expanse of the **Goonhilly Downs**, with the strange saucer-shaped constructions of the Goonhilly Satellite Communications Earth Station, and remnant of various Iron Age communities that speckle the landscape. On the eastern side of the peninsula, the village of **Coverack** was once a thriving smuggling center, while at the extreme south of the promontory a white lighthouse marks **Lizard Point**, where the sea seems to churn endlessly. Half-way along the west coast of the peninsular, half a mile or so inland, is the attractive village of **Mullion**, with a fifteenth century church dedicated to **St. Mellane**, a Breton saint who known as St. Malo in France.*

*Back on the coast, **Mullion Cove** has a small harbor and some fascinating rock sculptures. There are some fine beaches here, especially if you're a surfer: **Polurrian, Poldhu**, and **Church** and **Dollar Coves** among the best. There's little to see at **Helston**, three miles inland from the coast at **Porthleven**. The place, however, is known for its seventeenth century **Furry Dance**, held annually on May 8 – lots of men in top hats and women dressed in summer frocks. Also here is **Flambards Theme Park**, an all-weather family theme park, with rides, playgrounds, exhibits, including "Britain in the Blitz" (though quite what it's doing on the Lizard Peninsula baffles me) and a reconstructed Victorian village. Open mid-April to mid-July 10:30am to 5pm, mid-July to August daily 10am to 6pm; September to October 10:30 to 5pm; rest of year: call for details. Admission adults £7.95, children 4-11 £6.95, seniors £5. Under 4s and over 80s free. Tel. 01326 564039.*

Gallery and Penzance Museum on Morrab Road. *Open year-round Monday to Saturday 10:30am to 4:30pm. Also open Sundays in July and August noon to 4.30pm. Admission adults £2, children £1.*

Penzance is also close to **St. Michael's Mount**, whose origins go back to the fifth century when a monk is said to have seen a vision of St. Michael who ordered him to build a church on this offshore granite outcrop. Later on, the church was replaced by a Celtic monastery, later still by an abbey constructed by **Edward the Confessor**, who handed it over to the monks of Mont St. Michel in Brittany. The abbey was used as a fortress by Henry V during the Hundred Years' War against France, was later dissolved by Henry VIII, and was used as a munitions store during the English Civil War, after which it became the home of the **St. Aubyn** family who still live here. The complex is definitely worth a visit, not only for a tour of the buildings, many of which date back more than 700 years, but for the **Chevy Chase Room**, once the refectory and now filled with seventeenth century decorations. It's certainly a spectacular site, smaller and less commercialized than its Breton counterpart. If you're traveling here from a distance make sure you leave plenty of time because of tides, etc. Also make sure you are wearing sensible shoes – many of the walking surfaces are uneven. *Open April to October Monday to Friday 10.30am to 5.30pm (last admission 4.45pm); rest of year: check with office as times vary. Admission £4, family £12. Tel. 01736 710507; www.stmichaelsmount.co.uk.*

From Penzance there's a regular (every 30 minutes in the summer) bus service to **Marazion**, the nearest community to St. Michael's Mount. From there, at low tide you can walk the cobbled causeway, or if it's high tide there are boats (£1). Alternatively, you could do the whole journey by boat from Penzance.

From Penzance, the B3351 leads to **Land's End**, Britain's most westerly point, passing the scenic fishing villages of **Mousehole** (pronounced "Muzzle") and **Porthcurno**, with its awesome 750-seat **Minack Theatre** hewn out of the solid rock hundreds of feet above the sea. The theater's summer season runs from May to September, when a variety of productions, including plays, operas and musicals are put on. *Call 01736 810181* for information.

Land's End itself is an awe-inspiring place, even if its potency is marred by the presence here of a tawdry theme park, the **Land's End Experience** that does nothing for the location, except bring in the bucks. *Open year-round daily from 10am. Car parking fee: £3. Tel. 01736 871220; www.landsend-landmark.co.uk.* The sixty-foot cliffs here provide far-reaching views towards the **Longships lighthouse**, and, on an exceptionally clear day, the Scilly Isles, 25 miles away.

THE NORTH CORNWALL COAST

Cornwall's north coast is perhaps a little more rugged than its southern counterpart, yet among the rocky Atlantic wave-lashed headlands and promontories are some of England's most glorious beaches and popular resorts; upmarket **St. Ives**, with its lively artists' colony; **Newquay**, a family resort that boasts some of the nation's best surf; magical **Tintagel**, legendary birthplace of King Arthur; and close to the Somerset border the sedate Victorian seaside town of **Bude**.

Again, refer to the first section of this chapter (South Cornwall Coast) for *Arrivals & Departures* information.

WHERE TO STAY

CARBIS BAY HOTEL, *Carbis Bay, St. Ives TR26 2NP. Tel. 01736 795311, Fax 01736 797677. Rooms: 35. Rates: singles from £45, doubles from £90. Restaurant, private beach, indoor pool, private fishing. All major credit cards accepted.*

Wonderfully located hotel overlooking its own sandy beach. The hotel has recently been refurbished and both the public rooms and individual rooms are decorated and furnished to a good standard. The hotel also benefits from a heated outdoor swimming pool, and among the facilities on offer to guests are private fishing

GARRACK HOTEL, *Burthallan Lane, Higher Ayr, St. Ives TR26 3AA. Tel. 01736 796199, Fax 01736 798955. Rooms: 16. Rates: singles from £62, doubles from £124. Restaurant, indoor pool, sauna, solarium. All major credit cards accepted.*

The Garrack stands in its own extensive grounds with lovely pan-oramic views over Porthmeor beach. The staff are friendly and courteous, and the rooms – both in the modern wing and the original building – are all well-equipped and nicely furnished. There's also a leisure suite with indoor pool and gymnasium. One of the Garrack's greatest strengths is its restaurant, particularly strong on local seafood dishes.

CORISANDE MANOR HOTEL, *Riverside Avenue, Pentire, Newquay TR7 1PL. Tel. 01637 872042, Fax 01637 874557. Rooms: 12. Rates: singles from £75, doubles from £130. Restaurant, croquet, putting green. All major credit cards accepted.*

Small, relaxing Victorian hotel located on the cliff top about ten minutes from the center of Newquay and in about three acres of grounds. The rooms are nicely furnished and decorated – several of them boasting wonderful ocean views – and the staff friendly and helpful. There's a nice terrace along the front of the hotel that's just perfect for relaxing.

HEADLAND HOTEL, *Fistral Beach, Newquay TR7 1EW. Tel. 01637 872211, Fax 01637 872212. Rooms: 108. Rates: singles from £55, doubles from £78. Restaurant, indoor and outdoor pools, tennis courts, putting green, sauna, gymnasium. All major credit cards accepted.*

This surely has to be one of the most spectacularly located hotels in the southwest of England. Located on a rocky headland and surrounded on three sides by water, many of the Headland's rooms benefit from stunning ocean views; all are comfortable and nicely furnished with modern facilities. As well as the formal restaurant, the Garden Room offers lighter meals during the day and in the evening.

STAMFORD HILL HOTEL, *Stratton, Bude EX23 9AY. Tel. and Fax 01288 352709. Rooms: 14. Rates: singles from £35, doubles from £50. Restaurant, outdoor pool, tennis courts (including grass), badminton court, sauna. All major credit cards accepted.*

The peaceful location of this hotel in glorious woodland and grounds belies a turbulent past – it was built on the site of the Battle of Stamford Hill, but don't let that put you off. It's a very pleasant place to stay, with many of the well-equipped rooms offering serene countryside views – and its only a mile from Bude's beaches. If you're into tennis, there's a rare opportunity to play on a grass court.

WELLINGTON HOTEL, *The Harbour, Boscastle, Cornwall PL35 0AQ. Tel. 01840 250202, Fax 01840 250621. Rooms: singles from £32, doubles from £58. Restaurant, pool room, games room. No children under 7. All major credit cards accepted.*

The imposing, turreted "Welly" as it is affectionately known, dates back at least 400 years and has connections with the writer Thomas Hardy, who stayed here. The ivy-clad stone building is full of character, with a beamed bar (where you can hear local folk singers on Mondays), pleasant public rooms and comfortable bedrooms of varying sizes. The restaurant has a good reputation locally.

ST. PETROC'S HOTEL, *Riverside, Padstow PL28 8BY. Tel 01841 532700, Fax 01841 532942. Rooms: 29 (in three different locations). Rates: singles from £40, doubles from £60. Bar, cafe, three restaurants, library, garden. All major credit cards accepted.*

This unusual set-up comprises three restaurants, each with accommodations attached. The luxurious bedrooms above the Seafood Restaurant are the best, with some nice touches including a bottle of wine ready for you in the fridge, and a private terrace overlooking the pretty harbor. The main hotel, up the hill from the Seafood Restaurant, is a Georgian building with an excellent bistro restaurant, and cozy, more homely (in Britain that's a compliment!) country-style rooms. There are plenty of nooks and crannies, including a library, where you can unwind. Finally, in the town center, there's Rick Stein's cafe, a bit more classy than your average run-of-the-mill affair, with three more very comfortable rooms above.

WHERE TO EAT

ALFRESCO, *Harbourside, Wharf Road, St Ives. Tel. 01736 793737. Open daily noon to 3pm, 7pm to 9:30pm. Closed January and February. Main courses (lunch) from £8, (dinner) from £11. Credit cards: MC, Visa.*

Modern, sophisticated restaurant whose glass front opens up in summer, hence the name "alfresco." Seafood is the thing here, fresh off local boats, but the meat dishes are perfectly respectable too. An imaginative dessert menu includes a mixture of lighter and heavier choices, while the extensive wine list includes house wines starting at just £9 a bottle.

TABBS, *Tregea Terrace, Portreath (on the B3301). Tel. 01209 842488. Open Wednesday to Monday, 7pm to 9pm, Sunday 12:15pm to 1:45pm. Set Sunday lunch £12, set dinner from £12 (2 courses). Credit cards: MC, Visa.*
This quaint former forge, just under the viaduct near the harbor, is decorated by paintings from local artists. The byword for owners Nigel and Melanie Tabb is clearly "do it yourself," as they select all produce from local markets personally and even produce their own, home-made chocolates and ice creams. There's definitely a French influence in the menu, which again, includes plenty of seafood; the wine list starts with house wine at just £8.95.

SEEING THE SIGHTS

Take the B3306 north from Land's End, passing by **Whitesand Bay** (which provides some of the best swimming in Cornwall), the grey stone village of **St. Just in Penwith**, once a thriving tin mining community, to the village of **Zennor**, a favorite haunt of author **D.H. Lawrence** and the place where he wrote *Women in Love*. Zennor's main attractions are the church of **St. Sennen**, with a 16th century pew carving of a mermaid, who according to local folklore, was so mesmerized by the singing of a (male) church chorister that she lured him down to the sea. Listen carefully and, locals say, you can still hear him warbling. Also in the village is the **Wayside Inn**, actually a small museum devoted to life in Cornwall from prehistoric times to the present.

It's about five miles northeast of Zennor to **St. Ives**, another former fishing port whose origins go way back to the arrival in the fifth century of a female Irish missionary, **St. Ia**, floating, according to legend, on a leaf. During its peak period in the mid-1800s, the town's fishing industry employed more than 90% of its population and it is said that over 16 million fish were caught in one day in 1868. Since the demise of fishing, mainly due to the reduction of stocks, St. Ives has managed successfully to reinvent itself as a major center for the arts and, of course, tourism. The establishment of an **artists' colony** led to the arrival here of such luminaries as **Dame Barbara Hepworth** – who resided here for 26 years – **Ben Nicolson** and **Terry Frost**. The town now hosts a dozen or so galleries, countless bars and restaurants, and two major arts attractions: the **Barbara Hepworth Museum**, located on Back Street, and the imposing **Tate Gallery**, an offshoot of the famous London art museum.

The Hepworth Museum, also maintained by the Tate, is located in the home where Hepworth lived from 1949 until her tragic death in a fire in 1975. As well as displaying a number of pieces by Hepworth, the museum also provides plenty of information on her background. The other main artistic focus is the **Tate Gallery**, a brilliant white modern building overlooking Porthmeor Beach, cleverly incorporating various stunning ocean views into its design. On show are works by artists who have lived and worked in St. Ives – most of which date from 1925 to 1975. There's a superb rooftop cafe with wonderful views. *Tate Gallery and Hepworth Museum open year-round Tuesday to Sunday (and Monday in July and August) 10am to 5:30pm. Admission adults £3.90, students and seniors £2.30; www.tate.org.uk/stives.*

There are plenty of places to enjoy a quick snack or a longer meal in St. Ives, among them the **Spinning Wheel**, *Street An Pol* and **Wilbur's Café**, *St. Andrew's Street*. St Ives' **tourist office** is located in the *Guildhall, Street An Pol, Tel. 01736 796297*. Surfing equipment is available from a number of stores on Fore Street.

North of St. Ives, beautiful sandy beaches reach as far as **Godrevy Point**, where the coastline becomes more rocky. The north Cornish coast from St. Ives to the border with Devon offers some of the most spectacular coastal scenery in England – rocky, windswept promontories give way to wide bays with glorious sandy beaches washed by the strong Atlantic surf. The coast's best known resort town is **Newquay**, another former fishing port that expanded with the coming of the railroad in the late nineteenth century and has never looked back. Newquay's greatest attraction is its location – a series of rocky headlands overlooking some fine sandy beaches, including Towan, the most central beach. The downtown area, with its shops, bars and restaurants is geared unashamedly to the holidaymaker, and is backed by residences with superb views. Newquay has a **tourist office** at *Marcus Hill, Tel. 01637 871345*.

Scenic route B3276 heads northeast of Newquay, paralleling the sandy beaches of **Watergate Bay**, then veers inland to the charming port of **Padstow**, located on the estuary of the Camel River, about 16 miles from Newquay. The busy harbor gets clogged up in summer with recreational boats and cruisers offering cruises along the coast and estuary. Among Padstow's attractions are the **church of St. Petroc**, built on a hill overlooking the town. Petroc was another Irish missionary who found his way here in the 500s. Inside the church is a fine 15th century font, a pulpit dating from Elizabethan times and a series of monuments dedicated to the Prideaux family, who still reside at nearby **Prideaux Place**, a rather lovely 16th century manor house and deer park with views over the Camel Estuary. *Open April to September Sunday to Thursday 1:30pm to 5:30pm. Admission to house and grounds £3.50. Tel 01841 532945.*

Again, there are many fine, sandy beaches in the vicinity, including **Bedruthan Steps**, about five miles south of the town on the Atlantic coast and one of the most spectacular in the county. Padstow is full of inexpensive cafes and pubs where in the summer months you can often sit outside. Many of these are located around the harbor quay, a hive of activity and a great place to watch the world go by. Padstow's **tourism office** is right on the harbor, Tel. 01841 533449, and you can rent bikes from Glyn Davies on the town's South Quay.

To continue up the coast, you'll need to take the A389 south to the A39, then the B3314 north to pretty **Port Isaac**, a tiny harbor village with a series of narrow lanes leading down to a pebbly beach backed by a couple of pubs. The B3314 continues northeast to the village of **Westdowns**, where you take a left towards the village of **Tintagel** and the legendary

---

THE SCILLY ISLES

*About thirty miles southwest of Land's End are the **Scilly Isles**, an archipelago of approximately 140 islands and islets in the Atlantic Ocean, located 40 kilometers (25 miles) off England's southwestern tip varying in size from little more than a rock to around three miles across. Only five of them – St. Mary's, Tresco, Bryher, St. Agnes and St. Martin's – are inhabited. The land area is 17 square kilometers (6.5 square miles), and the population is around 2,900. Only five islands are inhabited; the capital, **Hugh Town**, lies on St. Mary's, the largest island. Tourism and flower growing are the main sources of income. Landmarks include ruins of an abbey and of the 17th-century castle and its sub-tropical gardens on Tresco Island, laid out in 1834 with seeds from Kew Gardens in London. Once a haven for pirates, the Isles of Scilly came under English control in the 16th century.*

According to legend, the islands are all that's left of the mythical land of Lyonesse. The islands are not spectacular – rarely do they rise above 100 feet – but they have a wonderful salty, maritime feel, some super beaches and the sub-tropical vegetation – particularly the palm trees, plus the white-washed cottages give the place a unique atmosphere. The climate is very mild – influenced as it is by the passing Gulf Stream, which means that the island are famous for their flowers – in fact flower growing is the second most important industry here, after tourism. If you really want to get away from it all for a few days, there's no better place, though getting here might require some effort.

*The two most visited islands are **St. Mary's**, with the largest population, and **Tresco**. To get here, you can take the **Isles of Scilly Steamship Company's ferry** from the South Pier in Penzance, Tel. 01736 62009. Journey usually take three hours (depending on the weather – it can get very rough) and cost around £40 for a one-way ticket. Alternatively, you could fly from Exeter, with up to three flights a day, Tel. 01392 67433, or from Newquay, Tel. 01637 860551. There's a **tourism office** at Hugh Town, on Portcressa Beach, Tel. 01720 422536.*

birthplace of King Arthur, **Tintagel Castle**, perched precariously above the coast. In fact, the ruins you see today are the remains of a Norman stronghold once occupied by the Earls of Cornwall, who after several bouts of rebuilding, eventually ran out of money and allowed it to fall into disrepair. Much of it had already collapsed into the sea by the sixteenth century. Also visible on the headland are the remains of a Celtic monastery. In order to get to the castle, you'll need to park your car in the village and walk a half-mile along an uneven track. *Open daily 10am to 7pm. Admission adults £2.90, students and seniors £2.20, children £1.50. Tel. 01840 770328.*

Three miles east you'll come to the picturesque village of **Boscastle**, located in a narrow valley formed by the rivers Jordan and Valency and boasting cottages dating back to the thirteenth century. From the main village car park, you can walk a mile or so along the **Valency Valley** to **St. Juliot's** parish church, a medieval building that was falling into disrepair when restored by Thomas Hardy who had been working as an architect. Hardy's book, *A Pair of Blue Eyes,* is full of descriptions of the countryside around Boscastle.

North of Boscastle, the coast straightens out, characterized by spectacular cliffs that reach a height of 430 feet at **Crackington Haven**, and by the sandy beach of Widemouth Bay. Just north of here is the Victorian town of **Bude** – pronounced "Bood" locally – sitting on a small estuary. It's not the most attractive town, dominated as it is by holiday homes, hotels and camper parks, but it does have some lovely stretches of beach, most notably **Summerleaze**, close to the center. **Crooklets Beach** and **Sandy Mouth**, north of the town, are vast pristine expanses of sand popular with sun worshipers and surfers, extending as far as 450-foot **Henna Cliff** and the border with Devon.

SOUTH DEVON

EXETER

Exeter's roots go back to Celtic times, followed by the Romans who settled here and established an important trading outpost. The Saxon king, Alfred the Great, rebuilt the city, until the arrival of the Normans, who built the present cathedral. The city prospered during Elizabethan times, mainly from the wool trade and, as the county town, Exeter was also an important center for commerce in the region. The city suffered appallingly during WWII bombing raids, when many medieval buildings were damaged or destroyed. However, many more, including the cathedral, remained relatively intact, and are worthy of closer inspection.

ARRIVALS & DEPARTURES
By Car
From London, take the M3 west to the A30, which will take you all the way to Exeter.

By Bus
There's a regular National Express service from London Victoria to Exeter, with a journey time of around four hours. *Call 0990 808080 for information.*

By Train
There are direct trains to Exeter from both Paddington Station and Waterloo Station in London. Travel time is 2 3/4 hours. The Waterloo trains take up to half an hour longer. *Call 0345 484950 for information.* Exeter St. David's Station, where most trains arrive, is a twenty minute walk northwest of the city center.

ORIENTATION
The ancient core of Exeter is situated on a hill on a bend in the **River Exe** that's dominated by the cathedral. East of here is the main shopping and commercial district.

GETTING AROUND
Exeter is a walkable city. The city's own bus company offers a one-day Freedom ticket for £2.80, while the regional company **Stagecoach Devon**, *Tel. 01392 42771,* offers an explorer ticket which will take you anywhere in their region (including Torquay and Dartmouth) for £5.50.

WHERE TO STAY
ROYAL CLARENCE, *Cathedral Yard, Exeter EX1 1HB. Tel. 01392 319955, Fax 01392 439423. Rooms: 57. Rates: singles from £99, doubles from £125. Restaurant, cafe/bar. All major credit cards accepted.*
Situated right opposite the Cathedral, this lovely building has origins going back as far as the 14th century. The bedrooms, many of which have views of the Cathedral, are well-equipped, having been refurbished recently. There's an excellent restaurant, where in addition to lunch and dinner, Devon cream teas are served in the afternoon.

THE IMPERIAL, *Park Hill Road, Torquay TQ1 2DG. Tel. 01803 294301, Fax 01803 298293. Rooms: 153. Rates: singles from £95, doubles from £170. Restaurants, bars, Indoor and outdoor pools, tennis courts, squash courts, pool room, leisure suite, beauty salon All major credit cards accepted..*

Magnificent, luxurious hotel located atop the cliffs with wonderful ocean views. Many of the beautifully furnished bedrooms have balconies with sea views, and the public rooms are the height of elegance, with marble floors and chandeliers. In addition, the extensive grounds are luxuriously planted, with sub-tropical vegetation. There are two excellent places to eat: the Regatta Restaurant, with, as you'd expect, a wide range of seafood dishes, and the Sundeck Brasserie.

ROYAL SEVEN STARS HOTEL, *The Plains, Totnes, TQ9 5DD. Tel. 01803 862125, Fax 01803 867925. Rooms: 16. Rates: singles from £49, doubles from £62. Restaurant, bar.*

Very pleasant, comfortable hotel dating back to the 17th century and located right in the center of Totnes, not far away from Exeter. There's a lovely, lofty entrance hall with original flagstones floor and antique furnishings. The rooms are equally inviting, and the restaurant offers traditional cuisine (or you can choose to eat more informally in the bar).

THE WHITE HART, *66 South Street, Exeter EX1 1EE. Tel. 01392 279897, Fax 01392 250159. Rooms: 57. Rates: singles from£50 doubles from £80. Restaurants, bars, reduced cost leisure facilities at neighboring gym. All major credit cards accepted.*

Another ancient building that can trace its roots back at least 400 years, the White Hart has been a hostelry for most of that time. It's full of character – lots of beams, stone walls, and antiques in abundance. The rooms in the older part of the hotel are full of atmosphere or, if you want something a bit more modern, you can opt for the new wing. There's a fine restaurant and a bar where meals are also available.

THE EDWARDIAN, *30 Heavitree Road, Exeter EX1 2LQ. Tel 01392 276102, Fax 01392 253393. Rooms: 12. Rates: singles from £34, doubles from £48. All major credit cards accepted.*

This terraced guest house dates from Edwardian times, and the Edwardian theme is consistent throughout, from the comfortable lounge with its period ornaments to the bedrooms, some of which have four-posters – and all of which come with the full range of up-to-date facilities.

WHERE TO EAT

LAMBS, *15 Lower North Street, Exeter. Tel. 01392 254269. Open Tuesday to Friday noon to 2pm, Tuesday to Saturday 7pm to 10pm. Set lunch £15 and up, set dinner (Tuesday to Thursday) from £15, Friday and Saturday from £23. All major credit cards accepted.*

Just under the iron bridge in a historic five-story terraced house is this fine restaurant which makes the best use of local produce, from meat and poultry to local cheeses. The local influence extends to the desserts, where steamed Exeter pudding with local clotted cream is among the possibilities. There's a good wine list, with the house wines coming in at £10.

CARVED ANGEL, *2 South Embankment, Dartmouth. Tel. 01803 832465. Open Tuesday to Saturday 12:30pm to 2:30pm, 7pm to 9:30pm; Sunday lunch only 12:30pm to 2:30pm. Set lunch from £ 15, set dinner from £28. All major credit cards accepted.*

Very pleasant restaurant on Dartmouth's South Embankment with a good number of seafood specialities. There's a strong French or Italian influence in most of the choices, as well as the meat and poultry dishes. The house wine starts at £15 a bottle or a generous £3 a glass.

RAFFLES RESTAURANT, *Buckerell lodge Hotel, Topsham Road, Exeter EX2 4SQ. Tel 01392 221111. Open daily 12:30pm to 2pm, 7pm to 9:30pm (closed for lunch Saturday). Dinner around £30. All major credit cards accepted.*

Raffles Restaurant is located inside the Buskerell Lodge Hotel, on the outskirts of Exeter. There's an extensive menu, combining the best of traditional favorites with more ambitious offerings like red snapper on a bed of zucchini with lemon and ginger butter sauce. The desserts tend towards the traditional. Because this place tends to get booked up for wedding receptions at weekends, it's advisable to book up well in advance to check availability.

SEEING THE SIGHTS

The **Cathedral of St. Peter**, with its two Norman towers, dominates the city center. Externally, it's the west front that stands out; the three tiers of statues – which include kings of Wessex such as Alfred, Athelstan and Canute as well as William the Conqueror – were started in the 14th century when the original Norman construction of 1112 was rebuilt in the Decorated style, with the exception of the towers. Internally, the most striking feature is the **nave**, 300 feet long, again in the Decorated style, with the longest **vault** in the world. The vividly painted **ceiling bosses** are quite something; one shows the murder of Thomas Becket. The **Lady Chapel**, at the east end of the cathedral, contains two lovely wood carvings. One depicts the Virgin Mary being given an apple by her mother, while another shows the shepherds and sheep enjoying the first Christmas.

Right in the center of the cathedral are the massive **organ pipes**, while beyond them, in the choir, the **misericords**, decorated with weird and wonderful figures from mythology, are said to date from the mid-1200s, making them the oldest of their kind in England. Among the other items of interest in the cathedral is a memorial to *Lorna Doone* author **R.D. Blackmore**. *Open year-round Monday to Friday 7:30am to 6.30pm, Saturday*

7:30am to 5.30pm, Sunday 8am to 7:30pm. Guided tours are offered between April to October at 11am and 2:30pm on Mondays to Fridays, Saturday 11am. Admission free, but £2 donation expected. Tel. 01392 214219.

Much of Exeter's city center was rebuilt following the severe bombing of 1942, but some interesting older buildings remain: the **Guildhall** on High Street, built in the 14th century and still in use; **St. Petrock's**, one of the six medieval churches remaining in the central area; and **St. Nicholas Priory**, on The Mint just off Fore Street, a former Benedictine monastery that became a private home after the Dissolution of the Monasteries. Its interior has been restored to reflect what it might have looked like during the Tudor period. *Open Easter to October Monday, Wednesday and Saturday 3pm to 4:30pm. Admission adults £1.50, children 75p. Tel. 01392 265858.* Also worth a visit is the **Royal Albert Memorial Museum**, on Queen Street, with exhibits on the city's architecture, collections of silverware and clocks and a gallery specializing in West Country art. *Open year-round Monday to Saturday 10am to 5pm. Admission free. Tel. 01392 265858.*

The **River Exe**, close enough to the sea here to be tidal, was also deep enough to allow for fairly large ships to ply from here. Today, the riverfront area, especially around the **Quayside**, is devoted unashamedly to leisure, with a plethora of bars, shops and cafes, 19th century warehouses, and the lavish 1681 **Custom House**, reflecting Exeter's maritime importance. Next door, the **Quay House** offers visual displays of Exeter's history. *Open April to October daily 10am to 5pm. Admission free.* If you cross the river by the suspension bridge (or take the ferry if you prefer) you can visit the **Maritime Museum**, with displays on the area's maritime history.

EXCURSIONS & DAY TRIPS

Close by to Exeter are a number of places of interest. To the south, at the end of the A376, the resort of **Exmouth** has two miles of strand and some lovely Georgian terraces that once accommodated the wives of luminaries such as Nelson and Byron, while twelve miles to the east, **Sidmouth** has more than 500 buildings of special historical interest, including more elegant Georgian terraces.

Devon's chief vacationers' destination is the sprawling resort of **Torbay** – the name given to three once separate resorts – Torquay, Paignton and Brixham – which were united in local government reorganization in the 1970s. The largest of the three, **Torquay**, once a small fishing village, has a distinctive, almost Mediterranean feel, enhanced by a multitude of palm trees, promenades and harbor – no surprise, then, that the area likes to think of itself as the "**English Riviera**." The town boasts all the usual seaside attractions in a slightly refined air. This was also the home for many years of serial crime writer **Agatha Christie** – and of

Basil Fawlty, hotelier d'extraordinaire, whose fictional hotel, *Fawlty Towers*, was located in the town. Torquay's main beach is **Abbey Sands**, so-called because it is backed by **Torre Abbey**, the remains of a Norman foundation wrecked by Henry VIII at the Dissolution. However, the abbey's chapter house and tithe barn remain. You can visit the **Abbey Mansion**, built in the 17th century, with a collection of paintings, and a room given over to Agatha Christie. *Open Easter to October 9:30am to 6pm. Admission £2. Tel. 01803 293593.* There's a more in-depth exploration of the Agatha Christie's life and times at the **Torquay Museum** at 529 Babbbacombe Road, where there's also a natural history collection. *Open July to September Monday to Saturday 10am to 4:45pm, Sunday 1:30pm to 4:45pm; October to June closed Sunday. Admission £2.* Torquay's coastline is full of coves, several of which boast good, sandy beaches, including **Meadfoot**, while a few miles inland is the restored village of **Cockington**, complete with working blacksmith's shop and lots of thatch.

Neighboring **Paignton** is much more of the traditional English seaside resort. The town boasts a substantial main beach, with all the usual family attractions and diversions, and a **zoo**, one of the best in England, located about a mile out of town on the Totnes Road. *Open summer daily 10am to 6pm; winter daily 10am to 5pm. Admission adults £7.50, seniors £5.90, children 3-15 £5.40. Tel. 01803 527936; www.paigntonzoo.demon.co.uk.* A **Steam Railway** connects Queen Park Station with Goodrington Sands, a wide, mainly sandy beach, then goes on along the estuary of the River Dart to **Kingswear**.

Brixham, to the west of Paignton, is the smallest of the three towns, but in many ways the most attractive. The focal point here is most definitely the harbor, a working fishing port providing fish for dining tables throughout the region. You can always see plenty of trawlers in the harbor, as well as a full-size reconstruction of the *Golden Hind*, the ship in which Sir Francis Drake traveled the world.

All three Torbay towns have their own **tourist offices**, but one should suffice – the Torquay office is located at the Pavilion, on the front, *Tel. 01803 297428.* Torquay is choc-a-bloc with restaurants and cafes, as well as some good pubs and bars.

West of Torbay is the picturesque estuary of the **River Dart**. Two small towns here makes worthwhile diversions. **Totnes**, seven miles west of Paignton on the A385, is an ancient town that reached its peak of prosperity in the 16th century, from which period a number of interesting buildings remain. Today, Totnes is predominantly a market town, with a reputation as a center for New Age shops and stores. There's a lot of bustle, too, around the River Dart, where ships are constantly to-ing and fro-ing between here and European ports. You can also take river cruises from **Steamer Quay**, across the Dart. Among the town's attractions are its

Museum, a four story Elizabethan building on Fore Street, with a collection of domestic furniture, and a room devoted to local mathematician **Charles Babbage**, whose analytical engine is claimed to be the precursor of the computer. *Open April to October Monday to Friday 10:30am to 5pm; July and August open Saturday also 11am to 3pm. Admission £1.*

At East Gate, Fore Street changes to High Street. Take a look at **St. Mary's**, the 15th century parish church with its beautifully carved **rood screen**, and the 11th century **Guildhall**, that once served as refectory of a long-gone monastery. The building still houses the town council chamber. On Castle Street, **Totnes Castle**, built during Norman times, offers super views over the town and river estuary from its **keep**, perched on a mound. *Open April to October daily 10am to 6pm; November to March Wednesday to Sunday 10am to 1pm and 2pm to 4pm. Admission £1.50. Tel. 01803 864406.* The town's **tourism office** is at The Plains, at the bottom of Fore Street, *Tel. 01803 863168.*

Eight miles south of Totnes, on the western bank of the Dart, is the attractive naval town of **Dartmouth**. The place has been a thriving port since Norman times, and even today the deepwater harbor buzzes with commercial, leisure and naval craft – the town is home to the **Royal Naval College** which stands on a hill overlooking the town.

The center of Dartmouth is very much the 17th century **Butterwalk**, a timber framed four-story building notable for its fine wood carvings and granite columns that support it. The ground floor arcade contains a number of shops and the tiny **Museum**, which is given over to a motley collection of maritime artifacts, including models of ships and maps. Close by, **St. Saviour's Church**, remodeled in the 1600s from a 14th century original, is an important marker for boats sailing on the river. Other ancient buildings of note include the **Cherub Inn**, also at the top end of High Street, and the much-restored **Agincourt House** on Lower Street, built by a local merchant to celebrate the English victory against the French at Agincourt. The same street leads on to cobbled **Bayard's Cove** with a row of restored 18th century homes, and further on to **Dartmouth Castle**, built in the fifteenth century, and in excellent state of repair due to the fact that it never had to face the artillery that it had been built to withstand. *Open April to September daily 10am to 6pm; October daily 10am to 5pm; November to March Wednesday to Sunday 10am to 1pm, 2pm to 4pm. Admission adults £2.90, seniors and students £2.20, children £1.50. Tel. 01803 333588; www.english-heritage.co.uk.*

Carry further on down the **coastal path** and you'll eventually come to **Blackpool Sands**, one of the area's finest beaches, where a number of American servicemen lost their lives during a training exercise during WWII. From Dartmouth, you can get back across the river to Kingswear by ferry; in the summer, a number of companies offer river and sea cruises to such places as Totnes, and across the bay to Paignton. Dartmouth's **tourist information center** is located on Mayor's Avenue, *Tel. 01803 834224*. There are some good pubs and restaurants around the Quay area, as well as some great fish 'n' chip joints.

The triangular area bordered by the Dart estuary to the east, the A38 and A385 to the north and the rugged coastline, is often known as the **South Hams**, speckled with some of Devon's prettiest villages. Here also is **Kingsbridge**, the Hams' "capital," a busy market town, and, to the south at the mouth of the Kingsbridge estuary, the resort town of **Salcombe**.

NIGHTLIFE & ENTERTAINMENT

Exeter has a number of interesting pubs, several of them located around the cathedral. One of these, the **Ship Inn**, *St. Martin's Lane*, claims to be the "local" used by Sir Francis Drake. The **Well House**, close by, is another ancient pub that serves excellent bar food.

Exeter's main cultural draw is the **Arts Centre**, *Gandy Street, Tel. 01392 421111*, where films, plays and concerts are performed. In the early part of July there's a **Festival** featuring jazz and blues, and classical concerts at a variety of locations around the city. Plays are also performed at the **Northcott Theatre** *on the university campus, Tel. 01392 493493*.

PRACTICAL INFORMATION

Exeter's **tourism office** is located in the *Civic Centre, Parish Street, Tel. 01392 265700*. The main banks are well represented in the city.

PLYMOUTH

The South Hams lead to the western fringes of **Plymouth**, easily Devon's largest city, with a population in excess of 250,000. Although it had been an important naval port for centuries, it was in 1588 that the town really came into its own, when **Sir Francis Drake** sailed from its shores to defeat the **Spanish Armada**. In 1620, Plymouth became famous again as the last port of call for the **Pilgrims** before setting out for America – where, of course, they named their community "Plimoth."

During WWII, the city attracted the attention of the Luftwaffe, mainly because of its importance as a shipbuilding and military center. Subsequent rebuilding in the 1950s replaced the characterful buildings bombed by the Germans by ugly concrete-based monstrosities.

ARRIVALS & DEPARTURES

By Car

From Exeter, take the A38 west to Plymouth.

By Bus

National Express runs regular services to London Victoria Bus Station, *Tel. 0990 808080.* Stagecoach runs a regular hourly service to Exeter, taking about 45 minutes.

By Train

There are regular services to Plymouth from London Paddington. Plymouth Station is located north of the city center.

WHERE TO STAY

COPTHORNE HOTEL, *Armada Centre, Armada Way, Plymouth PL1 1AR. Tel. 01752 224161, Fax 01752 670688. Rooms: 135. Rates: double standard rate: £135. Restaurant, indoor pool, gymnasium, steam room. All major credit cards accepted.*

Large, modern hotel located in Plymouth city center. The public areas, spread out over two floors, include two restaurants – one decorated and furnished in the Edwardian style, the other a more informal brasserie – and a leisure complex. The rooms are spacious and comfortable, and parking is easy, as the hotel has an arrangement with the multi-story parking lot next door.

GIDLEIGH PARK, *Gidleigh Road, Chagford TQ13 8HH. Tel. 01647 432367, Fax 01647 432574. Single rooms at £250 include breakfast and dinner as do the double/twin rooms, which start from £300. All major credit cards are accepted.*

This sumptuous 1930s Tudor-style hotel is set in its own landscaped grounds, surrounded by the Dartmoor wilderness. There's a superb, award-winning restaurant, elegant public rooms, and a very helpful staff, all attired in the latest from Laura Ashley. The 14 rooms are all lavishly furnished, and outside activities include croquet, tennis and putting.

BOWLING GREEN HOTEL, *9-10 Osborne Place, Lockyer street, Plymouth PL1 2PU. Tel 01752 209090, Fax 01752 209092. Rooms: 12. Rates: singles from £38, doubles from £50. All major credit cards accepted.*

This Victorian B&B overlooks a small park and is within walking distance of most of Plymouth's attractions, including the Barbican. The comfortable bedrooms come with a full range of amenities, including satellite televisions and hairdryers; full English breakfasts (and lesser options) are served in the cheerful dining room.

DUKE OF CORNWALL HOTEL, *Millbay Road, Plymouth PL1 3LG. Tel 01752 275850, Fax 01752 275854. Rooms: 71. Rates: singles from £85, doubles from £99. Bar, restaurant, games room. All major credit cards accepted.*

This large Victorian landmark building was built in 1863 and is currently undergoing refurbishment. Some very grand public rooms complement the smart bedrooms, which come with modern facilities; a number have four-poster beds. It's within walking distance of most of Plymouth's attractions and as such represents very good value.

WHERE TO EAT

CHEZ NOUS, *13 Frankfort Gate, Plymouth. Tel. 01752 266793. Open Tuesday to Friday 12.30pm to 2pm, Tuesday to Saturday 7pm to 10.30pm. Set dinner £34. All major credit cards accepted.*

Chez Nous' location in an ugly concrete shopping center is far from idyllic, but that's more than compensated for by some delicious seafood dishes, such as scallops with ginger cream sauce, and more conventional meat dishes. The ambience is French too, right down to the red and white table cloths, the posters on the wall, and Gallic background music. The wine list is mainly – you guessed it – French, with house wines starting at around £10.50 a bottle.

DUKE OF CORNWALL HOTEL, *Millbay Road, Plymouth. Tel 01752 266256. Open daily 7pm to 10pm. Two course dinner from £19.95. All major credit cards accepted.*

The setting here is quite extravagant, but no more than you'd expect in a grand Victorian hotel; lots of chandeliers, pillars of marble, and long, rich drapes adorning the windows. The food is equally good; best described as modern British, it also has a strong hint of the Pacific Rim, with dishes like shellfish hotpot with lemongrass, ginger and chilies. Meat options include chargrilled wild boar. There's a good choice of desserts and an extensive wine list.

SEEING THE SIGHTS

Start your exploration of the city with a visit to **The Hoe**, a wide open space offering superb views of **Plymouth Sound**. Even better views are afforded from **Smeaton's Tower,** a lighthouse that was originally built in 1759 to stand atop the notorious Eddystone Rocks. When a larger lighthouse succeeded it in 1882, Smeaton's Tower was rebuilt here. *Open Easter to October daily 10am to 6pm; Admission £1.* Close by is the **Plymouth Dome**, a leisure complex where you can see audio-visual exhibits relating to Plymouth's history and some of the characters who influenced it. *Open winter 9am to sunset; summer 9am to 7:30pm. Admission £3.50. Tel 01752 600608.*

SIR FRANCIS DRAKE

Francis Drake was born into a Protestant farming family. He went to sea as a youth, taking part in a slave-trading expedition to the Cape Verde Islands and the West Indies in 1566. The next year he sailed on an expedition that was attacked by the Spanish at San Juan de Ulua (Vera Cruz, Mexico); only Drake's ship and one other escaped. Drake scouted the Panama region in 1570 and returned there the next year, when he bombarded several coastal cities and captured a lot of gold and silver.

The deterioration of relations with Spain led Queen Elizabeth I to back an expedition to sail around the world, a feat accomplished only once before, by a Spanish expedition under Ferdinand Magellan. Drake was placed in charge of five small ships and 160 men and left Plymouth in December 1577. The voyage was tough: Drake was forced to put down a mutiny off Patagonia and had to abandon two small storeships. It took 16 days to pass through the Strait of Magellan; one ship returned to England, another was lost in a storm. Eventually, Drake was left with only one, the **Golden Hind**. He traveled up the coasts of Chile and Peru raiding Spanish shipping and later landed in the San Francisco area which he claimed for England and named New Albion. He then set off across the Pacific, trading in the Spice Islands and signing treaties with local rulers. He returned to Plymouth on Sept. 20, 1580, laden with treasure and spices. For his achievements, he was knighted by Queen Elizabeth I.

Drake served as Mayor of Plymouth for several years. Then, in 1585, he was given command of a large fleet that sacked Vigo, in Spain, then crossed the Atlantic to capture and plunder Cartagena and Santo Domingo and to destroy St. Augustine, Florida. In 1587 he led a raid on Cadiz that destroyed the stores and many of the ships of the Spanish fleet. Drake played a major role in the successful English defense against the Spanish armada in 1588 and was acclaimed as a national hero. But his forces were defeated at Lisbon in 1589, and for some years he remained in Plymouth. A final voyage to the West Indies, begun in 1595, was totally unsuccessful; Drake died off the coast of Panama on January 28, 1596.

At the eastern end of the Hoe stands the **Royal Citadel**, built in 1666 and still serving as a military center, though two daily hour-long guided tours are offered from May to September. Check with the tourist office for details. Among its attractions are the **Royal Chapel of St. Catherine** and the **Governors House**, both of which may be visited as part of the guided tour. Outside there's a medium sized **Aquarium**, which should appeal to landlubbers of all ages. *Open April to October daily 10am to 6pm; November to march 10am to 5pm. Admission £2.*

The oldest part of Plymouth, known as the **Barbican**, is to the east of the Citadel, a maze of narrow streets lined with Tudor and Georgian homes and warehouses, many of which have been converted to antiques stores and bookstores. Down by the Harbor, you can see the **Mayflower Steps** where the pilgrims set off in 1620; a plaque lists the names of all 102 of them. This was also the point of departure for **Captain Cook** on his South Seas voyages, and for the convict ships that transported thousands of convicted felons to Australia's Botany Bay. At 33 St. Andrew Street, check out the **Merchant's House Museum**, with displays on local history. **St. Andrew's Church**, a post-WWII reconstruction of a 15th century building, contains the **font** where William Bligh of *Mutiny on the Bounty* fame, was baptized.

Two attractions within a short distance of Plymouth are well worth a visit; **Mount Edgecumbe**, acres of rolling parkland with fine views over Plymouth and the Sound, and landscaped gardens divided into French, English and Italian areas with a fine restored Tudor house with authentic furniture of the period. Another Tudor mansion, **Saltram House**, just off the A38 to the east of Plymouth, is Devon's largest country house. There's work by the eminent architect Robert Adam, but even more noteworthy are the 14 portraits painted by Sir Joshua Reynolds, who came from nearby Plympton. The piece de resistance is the **Saloon**, a bit ornate for modern tastes, but full of exquisite furnishings, including an original Axminster carpet made in 1770. *Open April to September Sunday to Thursday 12:30pm to 5:30pm; October Sunday to Thursday 12:30pm to 4:30pm. Admission house and garden £5.60, garden only £2.60. Tel. 01752 336546.*

EXCURSIONS & DAY TRIPS

Dartmoor

The 365-square-mile **Dartmoor National Park**, northeast of Plymouth, is best known to Americans for its association with *The Hound of the Baskervilles*, Sir Arthur Conan Doyle's masterpiece thriller about a beast that haunts the lonely moors hereabouts. It's easy to see why Conan Doyle chose this area for the book's location; the landscape consists largely of open heath and moorland with only a handful of roads daring to intrude. Just occasionally a granite outcrop – known locally as a **"tor"** – rises above the great expanse of moorland. No wonder they stuck one of the nation's high security prisons slap bang in the center of Dartmoor.

It was not always so desolate and forbidding; the area is speckled with a host of Stone Age settlements and relics of a thriving tin mining industry that reached its peak during Victorian times. Today, though, the only other life forms you're likely to see are grazing sheep and ponies – and occasionally, overhead, a buzzard, kestrel looking for its prey. Just be thankful it's not you.

Much of the land here is owned by the Duchy of Cornwall, and has done since 1307. However, generally speaking access is good, so long as visitors obey the rules and regulations – which are common sense anyway: for example, no vehicle can be taken more than fifteen yards from the road, and fires are forbidden.

There are two wonderful ways of exploring this region, both requiring a good deal of **preparation**: this is prime walking country, but for goodness sake make sure you have a decent map and a compass. Signposts and painted stones guide walkers in many cases, but it's very easy to get off the track and then you could be in real danger; the moor is prone to sudden changes of weather, particularly the thick, pea-soup fogs when you'll see little further than the end of your nose. Riding is popular here, but the same applies; use the marked bridleways, and make sure you have a map with you.

The central part of the moor is dominated by **Princetown**, a quite insignificant place but for the vast Dartmoor Prison that is located here. Originally constructed for prisoners of war captured during the Napoleonic Wars, it's a grim, eerie kind of place. However, Princetown is central, and it makes a lot of sense to call in on the **National Park Visitor Centre** here, located right on the central green in the village.

Okehampton, just off the A30, often regarded as the gateway to Dartmoor, has the very helpful **Museum of Dartmoor Life**, which, as its names suggests traces the history of human residence on the moor in a series of interactive models, photographs and the like. *Open Easter to June Monday to Saturday 10am to 5pm; July to September daily 10am to 5pm; October Monday to Saturday 10am to 5pm; November to Easter Monday to Friday 10am to 4pm. Admission £2. Tel. 01837 52295.* **Widecombe-in-the-Moor**, on the B3387, has an attractive Church of St. Pancras, known as "the Cathedral of the Moor," where the devil is said to have appeared. The unspoilt market town of **Moretonhampstead**, in the northeast corner of the Moor, and **Tavistock,** in the west, a largely Victorian town that expanded when copper deposits were discovered here in the 1840s, are other centers in this area.

Among the attractions on or around the moor are **Buckfast Abbey**, just off the A38 near Buckfastleigh, a modern monastery that occupies the site of a much earlier one established in the eleventh century by King Canute. The current complex, opened in 1932, was built by a small group of French Benedictine monks in the Anglo-Norman style. Apart from the building itself, you can see displays of the abbey's history and its treasures in the crypt – or you can load up on the honey, handicrafts and various wines produced by the current monks to help pay their way. *Open May to October daily 9am to 5pm; November 10am to 4pm. Admission free. Tel. 01364 645500.*

Not to be confused with Buckfast Abbey is **Buckland Abbey**, just off the A386,originally a Cistercian foundation, which became the home of Sir Francis Drake after the dissolution of the monasteries. It contains exhibits relating to the defeat of the Spanish Armada in 1588, and items relating to the great man himself. There's a newly decorated plasterwork ceiling in the Drake Chamber, and exhibitions on seven centuries of history at Buckland. *Open April to October daily except Thursday 10:30am to 5:30pm; November to March Saturday and Sunday 2pm to 5pm. Admission £4.50. Tel. 01822 853607.*

About five miles northwest of Buckland on the A3257 is **Morwellham Quay Open Air Museum**. In the nineteenth century, the Quay was England's most important copper-exporting port. The industry fizzled out over a period of time, but today the place has been restored as a working museum, complete with port workers and costumed coachmen, as well as a copper mine that you can explore. *Open Easter to October daily 10am to 5:30pm; November to March daily 10am to 4:30pm. Admission adults £8.50, seniors £7.40, children £5.80. Tel. 01822 833808.*

If you really want to pamper yourself during your time in Dartmoor you can stay at one of the West Country's poshest hotels – **Gidleigh Park**. For details, see above under Plymouth's *Where to Stay*.

NIGHTLIFE & ENTERTAINMENT

Among the pubs worth visiting here are **The Dolphin**, *South Street*, where you can get good snacks at lunchtime, and over in Devonport the **Brown Bear**, an old beamed pub with a mixed clientele and which serves excellent food.

Theaters include the **Theatre Royal**, *Royal Parade, Tel. 01752 267222*, for major touring productions, and **The Pavilions**, *Millbay Road, Tel. 01752 229922*, for rock, pop and ballet.

PRACTICAL INFORMATION

Plymouth's **tourist office** is at *9, The Barbican, Tel. 01752 264849*, where most of the city's best restaurants are to be found. There's a branch of **American Express** at *139 Armada Way, Tel. 01752 228708*. As a major regional center, all the main banks are to be found here.

NORTH DEVON

The spectacular **north Devon coast** is marked by towering cliffs, narrow valleys and long expanses of sand. In fact the local word for valley is "combe" – there is a host of towns and villages with the suffix combe around here. Along this coast and not far inland are some of the most photogenic towns and villages in England.

Top of the list is **Clovelly**, its pretty whitewashed cottages tumbling down a steep cobbled street towards the sea; further east is **Ilfracombe**, a pleasant family resort; and **Lynton**, little more than a cluster of cottages, shops and hotels at the foot of a steep wooded ravine. This last stretch of the coast before Somerset is backed by the **Exmoor National Park**, a hilly expanse of moorland, woods, speckled with some lovely villages.

WHERE TO STAY

THE RED LION, *The Quay, Clovelly EX39 5TF. Tel. 01237 431237, Fax 01237 431044. Rooms: 11. Rates: singles from £75, doubles from £123. Restaurant, bar. All major credit cards accepted.*

Location, location, location! It's fitting that one of England's most picturesque villages should have one of England's most wonderfully located hotels. The Red Lion, which dates back to the 18th century, is gloriously located right on the harbor, with sea views from all eleven rooms. A fixed price menu is offered in the restaurant each evening, with a strong emphasis on freshly caught seafood. Remember that Clovelly's main street is extremely steep; however, there is a back lane where guests can bring their cars right down to the hotel.

THE RISING SUN, *Harbourside, Lynmouth EX35 6EQ. Tel. 01598 753223, Fax 01598 753480. Rooms: 16. Rates: singles from £60, doubles from £98. Restaurant, bar, private fishing. All major credit cards accepted.*

This characterful hotel dates from the 14th century, when it was an inn. Later on it became the haunt of local smugglers, and later still the adjacent cottages were added to form the hotel. It's on the harborfront, and offers great views over Lynmouth. The rooms in the main part of the hotel are quaintly furnished with antique pine, or you can opt to stay in the separate detached cottage in the grounds. It also happens to be one of the places where Shelley is said to have spent his honeymoon – with his 16-year-old bride.

BONNICOTT HOUSE, *Watersmeet Road, Lynmouth EX35 6EP. Tel and Fax 01598 753346. Rooms: 8. Rates: singles from £32, doubles from £45. Bar, dining room. All major credit cards accepted.*

Bonnicott House, which stands in lovely grounds overlooking Lynmouth Bay, was originally built in 1820 as a church rectory. Though it's been much extended since then, it retains a good deal of character, enhanced by some nice antique furnishings. You can enjoy some spectacular views from some of the bedrooms and from the candlelit dining room.

ELMFIELD HOTEL, *Torrs Park, Ilfracombe EX34 8AZ. Tel 01271 863377, Fax 01271 866828. Rooms: 13. Rates: singles from £36, doubles from £72. Bar, restaurant, indoor pool, sauna, solarium, jacuzzi. All major credit cards accepted.*

Some British seaside hotels have to be seen to be believed in their state of genteel decay; the Elmfield, thankfully, doesn't fall into that category. Boasting wonderful views over Ilfracombe, and with lovely terraced gardens and an array of leisure facilities, the Elmfield represents excellent value with its well-equipped and spacious bedrooms. Add to this a pleasant bar and a restaurant specializing in good, traditional home cooking, and you have all the ingredients for a very pleasant stay.

WHERE TO EAT

THE RED LION, *The Quay, Clovelly. Tel 01237 431237. Open daily 7pm to 8:30pm. Three-course set meal from £25. All major credit cards accepted.*

The 18th century Red Lion is a lovely quayside inn accessed by walking down a cobbled street. The bar attracts a large crowd of locals and visitors alike, while the restaurant offers a wide selection of fresh local produce, including locally caught trout and seafood dishes. Desserts tend to be a bit on the traditional side.

SEEING THE SIGHTS

The north Devon coast, reached by taking the A377 from Exeter or the A388 from Plymouth, is dominated by rugged **Hartland Point**, a 350-foot headland that has seen more than its fair share of shipwrecks and other disasters over the years. Ten miles to the east of Hartland Point is the gorgeous picture-postcard village of **Clovelly**, which became famous after it was mentioned in two books – *A Message from the Sea*, by Charles Dickens, and *Westward Ho!* by Charles Kingsley.

Its pedestrianized, cobbled main street plunges steeply down towards the sea past pretty flower-covered cottages, whose deliveries must come by sledge – donkeys are no longer used. Make sure you're wearing good walking shoes if you decide to explore the village. At the foot of the village is a tiny harbor with a few herring boats and a pebbly beach. You can take a trip out on one of the boats to the remote offshore island of **Lundy**.

From Clovelly, the A39 follows the coast north east towards **Westward Ho!**, a small seaside resort established by local entrepreneurs who wanted to cash in on the success of Kingsley's book. It's not an attractive place, dominated as it is by amusement arcades, holiday homes and caravan parks, so you're better driving on to **Appledor**e, an old shipbuilding port pleasangly located at the confluence of the rivers Taw and Torridge. It's still a thriving boatbuilding center, and there are some lovely Georgian homes.

Across the water, accessible by ferry, the even tinier village of **Instow** has a nice sandy beach, while the much larger town of **Bideford**, five miles to the south, was built up round the ancient bridge which formed an important link between east and west Devon. The bridge, first constructed in the 14th century in wood, was replaced by a stone bridge a century later. The town grew prosperous during the 17th and 18th centuries when it became an important trading center with North America. Other historical associations in the town include **Richard Grenville**, a local man who commanded the ship carrying the first settlers

EXMOOR

*Broody, desolated **Exmoor National Park** occupies a sizeable chunk of north Somerset and north Devon. With wide open moors and acres of forest and pastureland it contains an enormous variety of wildlife, including the red deer, England's only wild population of such. East of **Challacombe Common**, there is an eerie pathless wilderness called **The Chains**, a string of quaking, bottomless bogs, just as sinister as those of Dartmoor. Exmoor's northern boundary, the sea, is characterized by rocky bays surrounded by some of Britain's highest cliffs, while in the valleys, tiny thatched cottages shelter in the green-wooded **combes** below the moor.*

*Among Exmoor's man-made attractions are **Porlock**, on the A39, a pretty old village surrounded by wooded hills offering spectacular views. The village has some interesting literary links: the delightful **Ship Inn**, on High Street, features in R.D. Blackmore's classic novel Lorna Doone, set on Exmoor, and is said to have provided shelter for Victorian poet Robert Southey after he got caught in a storm while walking. Also worth a visit is **Minehead**, a popular coastal resort since Victorian times, where you can catch the West Somerset railway train for the 20 miles journey to **Bishop's Lydeard**. The Higher Town contains some old houses, while lower down Quay Town, as its name suggests, contains the harbor area, and is full of the kind of seaside attractions you'd expect to find in most English resorts.*

***Dunster**, with its wide main street full of ancient houses and a 17th century **Yarn Market** is another fascinating village. It also boasts a packhorse bridge, an 11th century castle, heavily damaged after the Civil War but restored during the Victorian period, and a 1,000 year-old yew tree in the churchyard. South of Minehead, just off the A396, the village of **Winsford** is said to be the prettiest on Exmoor, with thatched cottages huddled round a village green, and no fewer than seven bridges – the result of its position at the confluence of several rivers, including the Exe itself.*

to Virginia, and Charles Kingsley, who wrote much of his acclaimed *Westward Ho!* in Bideford, and is commemorated with a statue on the quay.

There's no road across the Taw estuary, so the A39 turns inland from Bideford towards **Barnstaple**, the largest town in north Devon and an important market center. The town's mercantile tradition is evidenced by the large timber-framed **Pannier Hall**, just off the High Street, and the **Butchers' Row**, 33 stalls once run by butchers but now put to a variety of other uses. Down by the river is the elegant, colonnaded **Queen Anne's Walk**, where merchants once sealed deals, while on the High Street, **St. Anne's Chapel**, which became a grammar school in 1549, boasts among its former pupils John Gay, author of *The Beggar's Opera*. Barnstaple's **tourist office** is located next to the Library in Tuly Street, *Tel. 01271 388584*, with information not only about Barnstaple itself but the whole region.

The final stretch of coastline between the Taw estuary and the border with Somerset is characterized in the west by some fine sandy beaches, including **Saunton Sands**, near Braunton, and the two-mile long expanse of **Woolacombe Sands**, popular with families and with surfers, as it faces almost due west. Six miles to the east, the resort of **Ilfracombe** is the most popular on the north Devon coast. The town itself has little to commend it architecturally, although the medieval hilltop **Church of St. Nicholas**, whose light has guided mariners for centuries, is worth a visit, as is the **Ilfracombe Museum**, where exhibits range from a turtle to a turret clock. Outside of the town, on the B3230, 11th century **Chambercombe Manor** has a display of armor and period furniture.

Heading east, the cliffs become more precipitous as they near **Exmoor**, a series of deep valleys providing outlets to the sea. In these valleys you can visit picturesque villages such as **Coombe Martin** and the twin towns of **Lynton**, 500 feet above the sea, and **Lynmouth**, at the confluence of the East and West Lyn rivers. Although the area achieved fame in 1869 by featuring in R.D. Blackmore's melodrama *Lorna Doone*, in August 1952 notoriety was achieved when heavy rains coming off Exmoor virtually washed away Lynmouth, leaving dozens dead. It's a stunning spot that has won the affection of countless writers and artists over the years, inlcuding **Gainsborough**, who described it as "the most delightful place for a landscape painter this country can boast" and the poet **Shelley**, who spent his honeymoon here with 16 year-old Harriet Westbrook – though two different houses make claim to that honor.

BRISTOL

The West Country's biggest city by far, **Bristol**, with a population exceeding 400,000, is rare among English cities of its size in that despite WWII bombing, it has managed to preserve a large number of medieval buildings. That isn't to say that it doesn't have more than its fair share of ghastly modern office blocks and shops, but in parts of the city there's a real sense of being in a medieval market town rather than a large urban sprawl. The city is also something of a center for the arts, with a glut of excellent museums, galleries, concert hall and theater.

For American visitors, Bristol is of special interest in that it was from here that **John Cabot** sailed in 1497 to "discover" the American continent. It was also the home of **William Penn**, founder of Pennsylvania, and a major base for **John Wesley**. In its heyday, Bristol was the most important port in England for trade with North America.

ARRIVALS & DEPARTURES

By Car

The M4 from London leads directly to Bristol, a journey of around 120 miles.

By Bus

National Express operates regular services to the city from London Victoria, with a journey time of just under 3 hours. *Call 0990 808080.*

By Train

Paddington Station is the London departure point for services to Bristol Temple Meads Station. The journey takes less than 2 hours. *Call 0345 484950.*

GETTING AROUND

Bristol city center is walkable, but to get to Clifton you'll need transportation. Bus 8/9 from Colston Avenue will get you there. Alternatively, take a taxi from the rank at St. Augustine's Parade, or call **Premier Taxis**, *Tel. 0800 716777.*

WHERE TO STAY

BERKELEY SQUARE HOTEL, *15 Berkeley Square, Clifton, Bristol BS8 1HB. Tel. 0117 925 4000, Fax 0117 925 2970. Rooms: 39. Rates: singles from £49, doubles from £80. Restaurant, bar, nearby leisure facilities with reduced rates for guests. All major credit cards accepted.*

This medium-sized hotel benefits from a location on one of Bristol's most elegant squares, where Georgian terraces, now mainly given over to university offices, overlook a lush public garden. The hotel's bedrooms, named after famous Bristolians, are pleasant enough, many having views over the garden. There's a trendy modern restaurant and an even trendier basement bar – both of which are a private club to which guests have automatic membership.

BRISTOL MARRIOTT CITY CENTRE, *Lower Castle Street, Bristol BS1 3AD. Tel. 0117 929 4281, Fax 0117 927 6377. Rooms: 289. Rates: singles from £109, doubles from £119. Restaurants, bars, indoor pool, leisure suite. All major credit cards accepted.*

Large city center hotel offering everything you'd expect from this chain: large, spacious rooms with air conditioning, power showers and comfortable furnishings; a leisure suite, a large restaurant, **le Chateau**, which despite the name offers British cuisine – and the more informal **Brasserie**. There's also an executive floor with its own lounge and additional luxuries. Parking is available adjacent to the hotel

SEELEY'S HOTEL, *St Paul's Road, Clifton, Bristol BS8 1LX. Tel. 0117 9738544, Fax 0117 973 2406. Rooms: 55. Rates: singles from £65, doubles from £80. Restaurant, sauna, solarium, gymnasium. All major credit cards accepted.*

This privately owned hotel is close to fashionable Clifton Village and within easy reach of Bristol city center with all its attractions. The hotel is slightly unusual in that some of the rooms are in adjacent properties; all, however, are spacious and decorated to a high standard. The hotel has its own leisure suite, and you can choose to eat in either **Le Chasseur** restaurant, with a full a la carte menu, or opt for lighter fare in the bar.

DOWN'S EDGE, *Saville Road, Stoke Bishop, Bristol BS59 1JA. Tel and Fax 0117 968 3264. Rooms: 4. Rates: singles from £39, doubles from £59. All major credit cards accepted.*

This pleasant white-painted B&B establishment is situated, as the name implies, on the edge of the downs, in this case the Durdham Downs, just outside the city of Bristol. The hotel is within easy reach of downtown Bristol, yet far enough away for you to get some peace and quiet. The bedrooms are comfortable though not exciting, and breakfast, with a variety of hot and cold dishes to choose from, is served round a communal table.

WHERE TO EAT

BELL'S DINER, *1-3 York Street, Montpellier, Bristol. Tel. 0117 924 0357. Open Tuesday to Friday and Sunday noon to 2:30pm, Monday to Saturday 7pm to 10:30pm, Main courses from £7.50. All major credit cards accepted.*

Delightful converted grocer's shop in Bristol's Montpelier district with two rooms; an informal front room, where a real fire burns in the winter, and a more modern back room, which overlooks a courtyard garden. The menu shows influences from a variety of regions: Indian,

Spanish, Italian, French, but the key is the fresh local produce. There's a good selection of desserts and a well-balanced wine list starts with house wine at £9.95.

HARVEY'S, *12 Denmark Street, Bristol. Tel. 0117 927 5034. Open Monday to Friday noon to 2pm, Monday to Saturday 7pm to 10:45pm. Set lunch from £14.95, set dinner from £33.95 (both 2 courses). All major credit cards accepted.*

Set in converted medieval wine cellars in the center of Bristol, Harvey's plays on Bristol's role as England's main storage destination for sherry – Harvey's Bristol Cream being one of the most famous of all. This is a trendy place – lots of boldly colored artwork, elegant glassware and the like – and the trendiness is unfortunately reflected in the rather steep prices. However, the food is excellent, there's an attentive young French staff, and the (very) extensive wine list has soemthing for everyone. And don't forget the sherries and ports.

MARKWICK'S, *43 Corn Street, Bristol. Tel. 0117 926 2658. Open Monday to Friday noon to 2pm, Monday to Saturday 7pm to 10pm. Set lunch from £14.50, set dinner £25.50. All major credit cards accepted.*

There's a somewhat refined atmosphere in this restaurant, converted from an old bank vault, with oak-paneled walls and starched tablecloths. However, the appearance belies the reality, which is a welcoming and unstuffy. The food relies on classics like confit of duck with orange marmalade, and there's a choice of seafood specials, depending on the catch. With a wide range of desserts, ranging from the gooey to the light, and an international wine list that deliberately keeps prices low to encourage experimentation, this is a very pleasant place to spend an evening.

HUNT'S, *26 Broad Street, Bristol. Tel 0117 926 5580. Open Tuesday to Saturday noon to 2pm, 7pm to 10pm (closed Saturday lunch). Main courses (dinner) from £11. All major credit cards accepted.*

Well-established popular restaurant in downtown Bristol that has built up a strong reputation for the quality of its cooking. The dishes on offer are not overly ambitious – old favorites like leek and potato soup and Cornish hake with mushrooms rule the roost here, but all exquisitely treated. The theme continues with the desserts; creme brulee and treacle tart being two of the options. There's a long wine list, where house wines start at £9.95.

SEEING THE SIGHTS

The focus of the city is **The Centre**, a large traffic circle that has recently been the subject of traffic reorganization. The city's various attractions, with a couple of exceptions, are within walking distance.

Just a few hundred yards southwest of the Centre, on Deanery Road, is **Bristol Cathedral**, originally an abbey that did not receive cathedral status until the Dissolution of the Monasteries in the sixteenth century. Its most striking external features are the two towers at the west end, built in the late 1800s, and inside, some fine **choir stalls** and the **Elder Lady Chapel** with some wonderful thirteenth century carvings, including a monkey playing the bagpipes! Check out the **Eastern Lady Chapel** too – there's some of the best **heraldic glass** in England. *Open daily 8am to 6pm. Tel. 0117 920 4879.*

Cut across College Green, opposite the cathedral, to Park Street, at the top end of which stands the striking **Wills Tower**, part of the **University of Bristol**, and, adjacent, the **City Museum and Art Gallery**, with sections on local history, geology, archaeology and, surprisingly – the largest collection of Chinese glass on show outside China. Other treasures includes some 8th century BC Assyrian reliefs, and a third floor art gallery strong on work by the pre-Raphaelites and French Impressionists. *Open year-round daily 10am to 5pm. Admission free. Tel. 0117 922 3571.* Heading back along Park Row on the right is the **Red Lodge**, a sixteenth century merchant's house that later served as a finishing school for young women. The main attraction here is a beautifully carved **Great Oak Room**. *Open April to October Saturday to Wednesday 10am to 5pm. Admission free. Tel. 0117 921 1360.* Head northwest up Frogmore Street and Trenchard Street towards **Christmas Steps**, a steep, shop-lined pathway with **Foster's Almhouse**, a former merchant's house that dates back to 1481, adjacent to which is the **Chapel of the Three Kings of Cologne**.

Immediately to the east of The Centre, a warren of narrow streets is dissected by Corn Street, with its Georgian Corn exchange, in which are located the covered **St. Nicholas Markets**. Just round the corner, **St. Stephen's** is one of the city's oldest churches dating from the thirteenth century. Nearby Wine Street passes the site of the old **Bristol Castle**, completely destroyed after the English Civil War, and the shell of **St. Peter's Church**, a medieval structure that was virtually destroyed by enemy bombing during WWII.

To the north lies the city's main **shopping area** – in an area that was virtually wiped out by bombing raids. The replacement, low-rise concrete buildings, may not be aesthetically pleasing, but you can expect to find just about anything here. In among the concrete a couple of older buildings survived the destruction. The **New Rooms**, at 36, the Horsefair, was the first **Methodist chapel** in the country, visited and established by none other than John Wesley himself in 1739. *Open Monday to Saturday 10am to 4pm. Admission £2. Tel. 0117 926 4740.* Another survivor, off Broadway, **Quakers' Friars** is a thirteenth century building that was originally a Dominican friary, then later a Quaker meeting house, hence the name.

Head back to Wine Street, crossing the River Avon into Victoria Street, then on the right, Redcliffe Street, which leads to Bristol's most famous landmark, the thirteenth century **Church of St. Mary Redcliffe**. The sumptuous building, built in the 1300s and containing some of the best rib vaulting in the country, was described by none other than Queen Elizabeth I as the "goodliest, fairest, most famous parish church in England." The church was built on the profits of wealthy merchants who wanted a place where they could pray for safe passage (and lots of prosperity) for their ships. *Open winter 8am to 5pm; summer 8am to 8pm. Tel. 0117 929 1487.*

Bristol's maritime heritage is marked by a number of attractions, three of which are located on the banks of the **Floating Harbour**, best reached by taking the ferry service which leaves from near the statue of Neptune at Quayhead, south of The Centre. The **Industrial Museum** contains models of ships and a mock-up of the cockpit used in the development of the *Concorde* at nearby Filton. *Open April to October Saturday to Wednesday 10am to 5pm; November to March Saturday and Sunday 10am to 5pm. Admission free. Tel. 0117 925 1470.* Take the ferry on to the *SS Great Britain*, the first propeller-driven ocean-going iron ship, designed by Isembard Brunel and completed in 1843. Built in Bristol (though her main route was between Liverpool and Melbourne) she was brought here from the Falkland Islands in 1968, having been abandoned there in 1886 after a storm. You can catch up on her history at the adjacent museum. *Open April to October 10am to 5.30pm; November to March 10am to 4:30pm. Admission adults £6.25, students and seniors £5.25, children £3.75. Tel. 0117 926 0680; www.ss-great-britain.com.*

If you're interested in maritime affairs, head off to the **Maritime Heritage Centre**, Wapping Wharf, which gives a detailed account of Bristol's shipbuilding and commercial maritime history. *Open winter daily 10am to 4:30pm; summer 10am to 5:30pm. Tel. 0117 926 0680.*

While in Bristol, check out **Clifton**, northwest of the University, once a separate spa town but now the city's most fashionable suburb. Its most striking natural feature is the 250-foot deep **Clifton Gorge**, through which the Avon flows on its journey to the Severn. Spanning it is the 700-foot long **Clifton Suspension Bridge**, completed in 1864 to a design by Brunel. The architect/engineer's original plan included Egyptian towers capped by sphinxes but the money ran out and these were never built. Close to the bridge on the Clifton side is a small observatory, originally a snuff mill built in 1829, with a **camera obscura** from which you can get 360 degree views of the surroundings. *Open summer daily 11am to 6pm; winter Monday to Friday noon to 3pm, Saturday and Sunday 11am to 4pm. Admission adults £1, children 75p.*

Also here is the famous **Bristol Zoo**, one of the best in England. *Open year-round daily 9am to 5:30pm (4:30pm in winter). Admission adults £8.20, seniors and students £7.20, children 3-13 £4.60. Tel. 0117 973 9851; www.bristolzoo.org.uk.*

EXCURSIONS & DAY TRIPS

A number of interesting attractions are within a short drive of Bristol: **Berkeley** (pronounced "Barclay") **Castle** on the main A38 about 20 miles north of Bristol dates back to Norman times, but more recently became a family home. Points of interest inside include the room where King Edward II was horrifically murdered. You can also see the dungeons, a medieval kitchen and the Great Hall, while the grounds contain an Elizabethan terraced garden and a butterfly farm. *Open April Tuesday to Sunday 2pm to 5pm; May, June and September Tuesday to Saturday 11am to 5pm, Sunday 2pm to 5pm; July and August Monday to Saturday 11am to 5pm, Sunday 2pm to 5pm. Admission adults £4, students and seniors £3.20, children £2. Tel. 01453 810332.*

Also worth a half-day excursion from Bristol is **Dyrham Park**, twelve miles east of the city on the A46, half-way between the M4 and the A420. This fine William and Mary mansion, built between 1692 and 1702 for William Blathwayt, William III's secretary of state for war, was furnished by Blathwayt in the Dutch style and has superb oak, cedar and walnut paneling and furnishings include pieces used by the diarist Samuel Pepys. Recently opened for the first time are the domestic offices, created in 1845 by Colonel Blathwayt, including Wet and Dry Larders, Victorian Kitchen, Bakehouse, Dairy and Tenents' Hall. The house stands on the site of a battle between Saxon and native British forces in 677, when the Britons were routed. The surrounding 270 acre deer park offers superb views across to the mountains of Wales. *Park open year-round daily noon to 5:30pm or dusk, house open March to November Friday to Tuesday noon to 5pm. Admission adults £7.50, children £3.80. Tel. 0117 937 2501.*

PRACTICAL INFORMATION

Bristol's main **tourist information center** is in *St. Nicholas Church, St. Nicholas Street, Tel. 0117 926 0767.* The city is well served by banks.

BATH

Bath has for many years been one of England's most visited tourist destinations. Quite apart from the Roman baths and the abbey, which are enough to warrant such attention in their own right, it's the amazing architecture of Bath – and the local, honey-colored Bath stone – that gives the town its enduring appeal. The elegant Regency terraces, crescents and Georgian public buildings, the pedestrianized commercial center with its fine boutiques, and back street tea and coffee shops all make this place well worth a visit.

The Romans, who had a thing about bathing, saw the possibilities here and built a bathing complex, with various hot and cold pools and a large pool, used mainly for recreation. After their departure, the bathing establishment declined, and the Saxons took over, making the city one of their most important centers. Saxon King Edgar, the first king of all England, was crowned in the abbey in 973.

There was a resurgence of bathing during Elizabethan times, but it wasn't 'till the eighteenth century when things really got moving. Bath became the place to be, with beautiful terraces and crescents built to house the aristocrats and wealthy merchants who wished to live here and enjoy the social scene cultivated by Beau Nash. Even later, Bath continued to attract some of the leading writers, poets and musicians of their day, including Jane Austen, who lived at 4 Sydney Place between 1801 and 1804, Thomas Hardy, Sir Walter Scott, Gainsborough, Handel, even Alistair Cooke. If you're into good food, this is your place: Bath is renowned for its excellent restaurants.

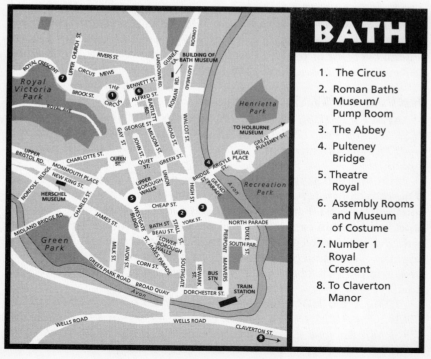

BATH

1. The Circus
2. Roman Baths Museum/ Pump Room
3. The Abbey
4. Pulteney Bridge
5. Theatre Royal
6. Assembly Rooms and Museum of Costume
7. Number 1 Royal Crescent
8. To Claverton Manor

ARRIVALS & DEPARTURES

By Car

From London, take the M4 to just past Swindon, where you link up with the A4 heading west. This will take you right into Bath.

By Bus

The city is well served by National Express buses from Victoria. *Call 0990 808080 for information.* The bus station is located in Manvers Street, very close to the center of town.

By Train

There's a through service from London Paddington to Bath's Spa Station, which is next to the bus station on Manvers Street. *Call 0345 484950 for information.* The journey time is around 95 minutes.

GETTING AROUND TOWN

Although Bath is a city of close to 100,000, its narrow streets and steep hills mean that driving and parking here is a nightmare, so it's advisable to park outside in one of the city's "Park and Ride" areas, where you have access to a frequent shuttle bus into the center – or else risk having your vehicle clamped and having to pay a huge retrieval fee to get the car back!

The best way of getting round the city is walking, and the tourist office can supply leaflets giving a range of self-guided tours. To get a good general overview of the city, **Guide Friday** operates single- and double-decker city tour buses, *Tel. 01225 464446.*

WHERE TO STAY

APSLEY HOUSE HOTEL, *141 Newbridge Hill, Bath BA1 3PT. Tel. 01225 336966, Fax 01225 425462. Rooms: 8. Rates: singles from £60, doubles from £75, four-poster room from £105. Dining room, bar, garden. All major credit cards accepted.*

Built in 1830 as the country residence for the Prime Minister, the Duke of Wellington, Apsley House is today a charming, welcoming small hotel with a relaxed atmosphere. Located on the outskirts of Bath, the hotel is still within easy reach of all the main attractions. The hotel has beautiful gardens, elegant public rooms and bedrooms graced by some original features and by antiques. If you decide to stay here, try to book a room at the back of the hotel to avoid noise from the busy Newbridge Road.

HOLLY LODGE, *8 Upper Oldfield Park, Bath BA2 3JZ. Tel. 01225 424042, Fax 01225 481138. Rooms: 7. Rates: single from £48, doubles from £79, four-poster from £85. Conservatory, garden, nearby leisure center with reduced rates for guests. All major credit cards accepted.*

Wonderful, loftily located yellow-painted Victorian B&B where no expense has been spared to create an ultra-relaxed, warm ambience. The bedrooms are all individually decorated and furnished (like one in the Egyptian style) and many have excellent views over Bath. The public rooms are extraordinarily posh and comfortable and, while there's no restaurant, the breakfast served here is of the highest quality.

QUEENSBERRY HOTEL, *Russell Street, Bath BA1 2QF. Tel. and Fax 01225 447928. Rooms: 29. Rates: singles from £100, doubles from £120. Two restaurants, bar, garden. All major credit cards accepted.*

Classy hotel in an elegant Regency townhouse built by one of the John Woods for yet another aristocrat – The Marquis of Queenberry. The largest bedrooms are to be found on the second floor – the drawing rooms of the original house – but all the rooms are exquisitely decorated and furnished with the best materials. The Olive Tree Restaurant has received many accolades for its cuisine, and the lovely garden is a great place to spend a warm summer's evening.

ROYAL CRESCENT, *16 Royal Crescent, Bath BA1 2LS. Tel. 01225 823333, Fax 01225 339401. Rooms: 34, plus 12 suites. Rates: double/twin from £190, deluxe double from £230, suites from £380. Restaurants, bar, garden, sauna, solarium, indoor pool, spa and treatment center. All major credit cards accepted.*

This has to be *the* place to stay in Bath. Located in the famous Royal Crescent, the hotel is lavishly decorated, with an entrance hall and public rooms that look much as they would have done in Beau Nash's day, and bedrooms that exude luxury and charm. A recently opened Bath House allows guests to enjoy a range of spa treatments, from exfoliation to yoga, and both the Brasserie and the Pimpernel Restaurant serve modern English cuisine with a gentle oriental touch. It's not the cheapest place in town, but if you're able to splash out, there's nowhere quite like it.

BATH SPA HOTEL, *Sydney Road, Bath BA2 6JF. Tel 0870 400 8222, Fax 01225 444006. Rooms: 98. Rates: singles from £160, doubles from £179. Bars, restaurants, indoor pool, sauna, gymnasium, tennis courts, beauty treatments, hairdressing salon. All major credit cards accepted.*

This magnificent, elegant building is set in a beautiful parkland setting overlooking the city of Bath. The bedrooms are decorated and furnished to an exceptional standard, and the public rooms include a sumptuous drawing room. There are two restaurants; the Alfresco, serving light meals and located in a colonnade overlooking the grounds; and the elegant Vellore, occupying a former ballroom.

DORIAN HOUSE, *1 Upper Oldfield Park, Bath BA2 3JX. Tel 01225 426336, Fax 01225 444699. Rooms: 8. Rates: singles from £42, doubles from £55. Bar. All major credit cards accepted.*

This pleasant Victorian house is just a brief walk from downtown

Bath, and boasts good views over the city and beyond. The high-quality accommodations include two elegant rooms with four-posters; all the bedrooms are well-equipped and non-smoking. The relaxing lounge, where there are plenty of books and magazines to browse, has a small 'honesty' bar. The prices here represent excellent value, especially given the proximity to Bath city center and all its attractions.

CLIFFE HOTEL, *Crowe Hill, Limpley Stoke, Bath BA3 6HY. Tel 01225 723226, Fax 01225 723871. Rooms: 11. Rates: singles from £75, doubles from £95. Bar, restaurant, outdoor pool. All major credit cards accepted.*

A bit of a surprise, this. Normally you'd expect Best Western places to be a good deal larger than this attractive, 11-room establishment in the village of Limpley Stoke, just off the B3108 south of Bath. It's a delightful place, full of charm and character, with fully equipped generally large rooms, some with four posters, and a large garden with outdoor pool. There's a decent restaurant overlooking the leafy garden and pool.

OLD MALT HOUSE, *Radford, Timsbury, Bath BA3 1QF. Tel 01761 470106, Fax 01761 472726. Rates: singles from £36, doubles from £72. Bar, restaurant. All major credit cards accepted.*

This small, quiet hotel a few miles from Bath city center was formerly the malt house of a local brewery, which gives it a rather unusual but very cozy atmosphere. There's an attractive bar area with wood burning stove and a restaurant with a number of traditional English options as well as some more eclectic ones. This is a good place to stay, especially if you don't need to spend all your time in Bath and want to explore the countryside around as well.

BATH LODGE HOTEL, *Norton St Philip, Bath BA3 6NH. Tel 01225 723040, Fax 01225 723737. Rooms: 8. Rates: singles from £50, doubles from £75. All major credit cards accepted.*

This highly unusual building, now a B&B establishment, looks like a small castle from outside, with turrets and battlements, stands in five acres of wooded grounds and is located around seven miles south of Bath city center. Built in 1806, the charm and character extends to the interior, and especially the bedrooms, where some of the turrets serve as circular shower rooms. To add to the atmosphere, some rooms have four-poster beds, and heraldic shields dotted around the place make you feel you're staying in a real castle. Dinner is available here at weekends.

CHERITON HOUSE, *9 Upper Oldfield Park, Bath BA2 3JZ. Tel 01225 429862, Fax 01225 428403. Rooms: 9. Rates: singles from £42, doubles from £62. All major credit cards accepted.*

Cheriton House is a lovely late Victorian town house, now a B&B, high on a hill overlooking Bath, just over half a mile from the city center. The recentl restored building has a spacious, comfortable lounge, and elegant, individually designed bedrooms, one of which is a four-poster.

WHERE TO EAT

CLOS DU ROY, *1 Seven Dials, Saw Close, Bath BA1 1EN. Tel. 01225 444450. Open daily noon to 2pm, 6pm to 10:30pm. Set lunch from £9.95, set dinner from £16.50 (both for two courses). All major credit cards accepted.*

There's a musical theme in this French restaurant, tucked away on the upper floor of a pedestrian precinct: pale yellow walls decorated with a medley of instruments and giant staves. It's not just the food here that's French: the proprietor, the chef and staff are too. The result is classic bistro fare – steak bearnaise – that kind of thing. And you can guess what the wine list is – something beginning with F?

GREEN STREET SEAFOOD CAFE, *6 Green Street, Bath BA1 2JY. Tel. 01225 448707. Open Tuesday to Saturday noon to 3pm, 6pm to 11pm. Main courses from £7.50 to £13. All major credit cards accepted.*

Where better to have a seafood restaurant, right above a fish market. This bright, relaxed restaurant relies on the freshly caught fodder for the broad variety of dishes on its menu, which is enhanced by a daily special etched on the blackboard. The service is efficient and unassuming, and the wine list – mostly white, as you'd expect – starts from £8.75 for a bottle of house.

HULLABALLOOS, *26 Broad Street, Bath. Tel. 01225 443323. Open Monday 6pm to 10.30pm; Tuesday to Saturday noon to 2pm, 6pm to 10:30pm. Set lunch £5.99, set dinner £14.50 (both two courses). All major credit cards accepted.*

Centrally located Bath restaurant that offers good, largely Mediterranean-style food at excellent prices. The restaurant operates a Bring-Your-Own-Bottle policy which, in addition to the already low prices, helps bring down the cost of a meal even more. Note that the BYOB policy refers only to wine; the restaurant does have a license to serve alcohol, so you can still have your G&T as an aperitif.

LETTONIE, *35 Kelston Road, BA1 3QH. Tel. 01225 446676. Open Tuesday to Saturday, noon to 2pm, 7pm to 9:30pm. Set lunch £15 to £25, set dinner £44. All major credit cards accepted.*

With its large rooms, high, ornate ceilings, and smattering of antiques, this lovely Georgian house is home to one of Bath's finest restaurants – and the only one with two-stars from Michelin. The food is French, with a touch of Latvian – like a starter of borscht terrine with shredded beef pirogi and sour cream. There's an extensive, international wine list.

OLIVE TREE *(at the Queensberry Hotel), Russell Street, Bath. Tel. 01225 447928. Open Monday to Saturday noon to 2pm, 7pm to 10pm (no Sunday lunch). Set lunch £12.50 and up, set dinner £24. Credit cards: MC, Visa.*

This stylish hotel has an equally stylish restaurant, located in bright and cheerful basement rooms, the bright Mediterranean colors mixing well with the traditional Georgian fittings. The cooking is contemporary, and there are some especially good seafood choices – the provencale fish soup was one of the best I've ever had, and the baked halibut comes with a warm oyster, shellfish and orange sauce – and there's a good mixture of light and heavy desserts. The wine list favors France, with some New World additions.

NO. 5 BISTRO, *5 Argyle Street, Bath. Tel 01225 444499. Open Monday to Saturday noon to 2:30pm, 6:30pm to 10:30pm (closed Monday lunch). Main courses from £6. All major credit cards accepted.*

There's a wonderful, authentic bistro atmosphere in this lively eatery on busy Argyle Street, with its bare floorboards, walls covered by posters and lots of candles. The restaurant can get very busy on Fridays and Saturdays. The wide ranging menu includes main courses like cod in an herb crust with citrus butter, filet steaks with mixed peppers and the like. There's a good value wine list, with house French starting from as low as £8.95.

MOODY GOOSE, *7a Kingsmead Square, Bath. Tel 01225 466688. Open Monday to Saturday noon to 2pm, 6pm to 9:30pm. Set lunch £10, set dinner £20. All major credit cards accepted.*

Three smallish interconnecting rooms form this rather formal basement restaurant, with French watercolors on the walls and lots of wicker chairs. The food is superb, with such delicacies as fresh sea bass in a creamy horseradish cream, and a light (if light is possible) chocolate torte for dessert. The well-chosen wine list starts with house wine at £11 a bottle.

ROYAL CRESCENT HOTEL: BRASSERIE & PIMPERNEL'S. *16 Royal Crescent, Bath BA1 2LS. Tel 01225 823333. Brasserie open daily 12:30pm to 2pm, 7pm to 9:30pm; Pimpernel's Tuesday to Saturday 7pm to 10pm. Set dinner (brasserie) £28, set dinner (Pimpernel's) £44. All major cerdit cards accepted.*

The two restaurants on this site vary widely in character, but not in the quality of the food prepared. Pimpernel's, in a small, intimate room in a basement, specializes in Anglo-French cooking, like bluefin tuna with wakame and orange miso. There's a good selection of accomplished desserts to complete the picture. The Brasserie's menu is more straightforward – dishes like lamb shank, cod steaks with mussels and the like. The wine list in both restaurants is extensive and well chosen, if not on the cheap side.

WOODS, *9-13 Alfred Street, Bath BA1 2QX. Tel 01225 314812, Open Monday to Saturday noon to 3pm, 6pm to 11pm. Set dinner (2 courses) from £12.25. Credit cards: MC, Visa.*

This very pleasant neighborhood-style brasserie is located in a terraced house opposite Bath's famous Assembly Rooms. What's best about the place is that it offers good, carefully cooked dishes – casseroles of various descriptions are a prominent feature here, at very reasonable prices. The desserts tend to veer to the traditional side, so you could conclude your meal with something like Bakewell Tart or a sponge cake. The house wine starts at £10 a bottle.

THE ROOTS OF BATH

*The name Bath of course derives from the **hot springs** – the only ones in Britain – that were first tapped by the Celtic people. According to local legend, little attention had been paid to them until a local British prince who suffered from a rare skin complaint passed it on to some pigs in his possession. As the pigs frolicked in the muddy water, he discovered that the condition disappeared. He applied some water to himself, and his own skin condition improved.*

SEEING THE SIGHTS

Two buildings form the main focus of any visit to Bath. At the **Roman Baths**, right in front of the abbey, you can take a self-guided tour with the assistance of an audio phone. You'll see the original **Great Bath**, once covered but now open air, surrounded by Victorian columns and pillars. The pool, used for recreation, is still lined with the original lead from 2000 years ago. You can also see the **Circular Bath**, where bathers cooled off; the **Norman King's Bath** and the **Temple of Minerva**, the Roman goddess of water, and watch the water percolate at a constant 46.5 degrees Centigrade. This water originally fell on the Mendip Hills some 10,000 years ago and sinks to a depth of several miles, and then is forced up by the heat of the earth through a fissure under the baths. The adjacent **Pump Room** was once the social hub of Bath, and now contains, inevitably, a tea room, restaurant and shop. *Open April to September daily 9am to 6pm (August 9am to 9:30pm); October to March daily 9.30am to 5pm. Admission adults £6.76, students and seniors £6, children 6-18 £4. Tel. 01225 477785; www.romanbaths.co.uk.*

Across Abbey Yard, the current **Bath Abbey**, which has just celebrated its 500th anniversary, is a rebuilding of a much earlier Norman church in the Perpendicular style by Bishop Oliver King, who claimed to have seen a vision of angels ascending and descending a ladder to heaven – a dream which has been incorporated into the building either side of the main west window. The most striking features of the interior are the graceful **fan vaulting** and a large number of **monuments** celebrating famous local people. To discover the ecclesiastical history of Bath, you can take a journey through **the Abbey Heritage Vaults** which tell the story of 1,600 years of Christianity here. *Open Easter to October Monday to Saturday*

9am to 6pm; November to Easter Monday to Saturday 9am to 4:30pm. Admission free (but donation invited). Admission to Vaults adults £2, children £1. Tel. 01225 422462; www.bathwells.anglican.org.

To the northeast of the Abbey, up Grand Parade, is **Pulteney Bridge**, one of only two bridges in the world (the other being the Ponte Vecchio in Florence) with shops incorporated into its structure.

From Abbey Yard, Westgate Street passes the **Theatre Royal**, opened in 1805 and still in operation, veers to the right as Barton Street, then traverses beautiful **Queen Square**, designed by the architect John Wood (1700-1754). Further on, follow Gay Street to **The Circus**, a circle of three-story houses designed by Wood and completed after his death by his son, also named John. One of the homes here, **number 17**, was the residence of master painter **Thomas Gainsborough** from 1760 to 1774. Just east of the Circus, on Bennett Street, the **Assembly Rooms**, designed by Wood the Younger, were another major social center in regency Bath. Inside, a well-presented **Museum of Costume** traces the development of clothes and fashion from the Stuart period to the latest designs from the catwalk. *Open year-round daily 10am to 5pm. Admission adults £3.90, students and seniors £3.50, children 6-16 £2.80. Tel 01225 477789; www.museumofcostume.co.uk.* To the left, Brock Street leads to the most famous of Bath's Crescents, the **Royal Crescent**, started by Wood the Younger in 1767 – consisting of thirty terraced homes set back from the road by a spacious lawn. Number 1 has been restored to reflect how it would have looked when originally built. *Open mid-February to October Tuesday to Sunday 10:30am to 5pm; November Tuesday to Sunday 10:30am to 4pm. Admission adults £4, students, seniors and children £3; www.bath-preservationtrust.org.uk.*

Bath possesses a clutch of excellent museums, scattered around the city. On Roman Road, see the **Building of Bath Museum**, whose mission speaks for itself. Further east, at the end of Great Pulteney Street, is the **Holburne Museum**, with displays of decorative and fine art, including furniture, silverware, porcelain and eighteenth century paintings. *Open mid-February to mid-December Monday to Saturday 11am to 5pm, Sunday 2:30pm to 5:30pm. Admission £3.50.* West of the city center, **No. 19 New King Street** was once the home of **Sir William Hershel**, the Astronomer Royal, who discovered Uranus in 1781. There's a small but fascinating museum here that includes a replica of the telescope with which Uranus was discovered, and various bits and pieces from Hershel's time here. *Open March to October daily 2pm to 5pm: November to February Saturday and Sunday 2pm to 5pm. Admission adults £2.50, children 4-16 £1.*

Just outside Bath, near the village of **Claverton** is the **American Museum**, located in the manor house where Winston Churchill made his maiden political speech. A series of rooms contain dioramas depicting life in North America from the time of the Pilgrims to the nineteenth century, as well as exhibits on such topics as industry, whaling and Native American culture. The grounds are notable for a replica of George Washington's garden. *Open April to October Tuesday to Sunday 2pm to 5pm; grounds only Monday to Friday, Saturday and Sunday 1pm to 6pm. Admission adults £5.50, seniors and students £5, children 5-16 £3. Tel. 01225 460503.*

NIGHTLIFE & ENTERTAINMENT

Bath's main cultural attraction is its magnificent **Theatre Royal**, *Saw Close, Tel. 01225 448844,* built in 1805 and refurbished in the 1980s. Drama and ballet are the mainstays here. In May/June, there's the **Bath International Festival**, two weeks of classical music, jazz and folk, literary and arts events featuring some of the biggest names in their particular fields. A two-weekly listings magazine, *Venue,* is the best source for finding out what's on.

Bath has a host of interesting pubs, like the **Coeur de Lion** *on Northumberland Place*, **The George**, *next to the canal in Mill Lane, Bathampton*, and the **Pig and Fiddle**, *Saracen Street, near Pulteney Bridge.*

EXCURSIONS & DAY TRIPS

Twenty miles southwest of Bath on the A39 is the tiny city of **Wells**, the centerpoint of which is its magnificent **cathedral**, begun in 1180. The cathedral's most spectacular feature is its **west front**, built around 1230, its niches filled with the statues of 300 saints and kings; it only received minor damage at the hands of the Puritans. Inside, the long gothic nave is punctuated by a **"scissor arch"** built in the 1330s to help support a newly built tower. Much of the cathedral's **stained glass** dates back to the 14th century, and there's a splendid 14th century **Lady Chapel** built in the Decorated style. Other notable features include the amazing **carvings** on the capitals in the south transept – including a man with a toothache – and in the opposite transept, there's an **astronomical clock** that dates from the 1390s, with jousting knights charging each other on the quarter-hour. Nearby, a doorway leads up a flight of ancient steps to the eight-sided **Chapter House**, with more ribbed vaulting.

After looking around the cathedral, walk along the **Cloisters** to the **Bishop's Palace**, constructed in the 13th century and moated because of a dispute between the church authorities and the town in the 14th century. Further along, check out **Vicar's Close**, one of the best preserved medieval streets in Europe. Cathedral clergy have been living in the cottages since the mid-fourteenth century, and still do!

Take a stroll past the lovely seventeenth and eighteenth century houses on the north side of the Green to the **Chancellor's House**, now a

museum with various items from the cathedral as well as geological exhibits from **Wookey Hole caves**, two miles away in the Mendip Hills. *Open Easter to October daily 10am to 5:30pm (July and August open until 8pm); November to Easter Wednesday to Sunday 11am to 4pm. Admission £2.50, students and seniors £1.50, children £1 Tel. 01749 673477.* The caves themselves, carved out of the Mendip limestone by the River Axe over millions of years, are a complex network of subterranean passages, pools and caverns, some of cathedral-like proportions. The caves abound in legend and folklore. Guides will point out the petrified remains of the "**Witch of Wookey**," who was giving local farmers a hard time until the Abbot of nearby Glastonbury sent a monk to dispose of her. He's said to have sprinkled her with holy water, the effect of which was to turn her to stone. Some credence was given to the legend when in 1912 geologists discovered an ancient Romano-British skeleton of a woman, complete with dagger, sacrificial knife and two goat skeletons. *Open summer daily 10am to 5pm, winter: call for details. Admission adults £7, children 4-16 £3.50, under 4s free. Tel. 01749 672243; www.wookey.co.uk.*

Six miles from Wookey on the A371 is the village of **Cheddar**, which gives its name to the world's most popular cheese, though there can be few places in the world where it is not manufactured today. A right turn here leads to two-mile-long **Cheddar Gorge**, a fissure in the limestone 450 feet deep in places, beneath which two complexes of **caves** have become major tourist attractions. There's little to choose between the two (and you needn't bother anyway because one ticket gives you access to both), but if giant stalagmites and stalagtites, underground waterfalls, enormous caverns, some enhanced with hi-tech light and laser, are your thing, this is the place for you. *Open Easter to September daily 10am to 5pm; October to Easter 10.30am to 4.30pm. Admission adults £6.50, children £3.95. Tel. 01934 742343.*

Keeping up the mystical feeling about this whole area is the town of **Glastonbury**, about six miles south of Wells. In fact it's located right in the middle of the so-called **Isle of Avalon**, rich in associations with King Arthur and the Knights of the Round Table. But it was a Christian tradition that gave rise to the town in its present form (see sidebar on next page).

Whatever views we hold about the Glastonbury legend, one thing is clear: there was a monastic foundation on the site as early as the fifth century, making it the oldest Christian foundation in England. It was later enlarged by Dunstan, later to become Archbishop of Canterbury, and became the wealthiest Benedictine Abbey in the land. The **ruins of the medieval abbey** can be seen hidden between high gray walls in the center of Glastonbury. With its spacious lawns, it's an attractive site, which even to this day attracts hordes of pilgrims, most especially at the **Glastonbury**

Festival on the last Saturday in June – not to be confused with the massive **Glastonbury Rock Festival** that takes place about the same time. The abbey site is given additional mystery by its association with **King Arthur** and **Queen Guinevere**, who are said to be buried beneath the abbey choir. *Open winter daily 9:30am to 6pm; summer daily 9am to 6pm. Admission adults £2.50, seniors and students £3, children £1. Tel. 01452 832267; www.glastonbury.co.uk.*

A number of ley lines (a ley line is a straight line drawn linking various points of religious/spiritual significance) converge on **Glastonbury Tor**, about a mile from the abbey. At 521 feet, it's quite a climb, but worth it for the superb view which, on a clear day, reaches as far as the Welsh hills. There's also the ruins of a fourteenth century church, St. Michael's, of which only the tower remains.

THE GLASTONBURY LEGEND

*According to legend, Jesus was brought here (but God only knows why) by his uncle, **Joseph of Arimathea** – hence the line in William Blake's famous **Glastonbury Hymn**, better known as **Jerusalem**, "And did those feet in ancient time/walk upon England's mountains green?" Further legend says that Joseph, who later supplied Jesus' tomb after the crucifixion, kept the **holy grail**, the chalice used at the Last Supper which had been filled with Jesus' blood at the crucifixion, and brought it and the **spear** used to wound Jesus to Glastonbury. He then founded an abbey and the conversion of England got under way. Another legend states that when Joseph thrust his staff into the ground here, it sprouted. Its descendants still grow at Glastonbury.*

NIGHTLIFE & ENTERTAINMENT

There are lots of wonderful pubs in Bath. Try the **Saracen's Head**, the city's oldest, *Broad Street*. The main arts venue in Bath is the prestigious **Theatre Royal**, *Barton Street, Tel. 01225 448844.*

SHOPPING

Bath has an excellent shopping center. Most of the main **chain stores** are located on Stall and Union Street; for more traditional stores, try Milsom Street. In and around the commercial heart of the city are dozens of narrow lanes and alleyways where you can find all kinds of interesting shops, galleries and places to eat.

If you're into **antiques**, the best place to browse is the **Bath Antiques Market**, *Guinea Lane, open on Wednesdays from 6:30am to 2:30pm*; another is the **Great Western Antique Centre**, *Bartlett Street*, with more than 100 stalls.

PRACTICAL INFORMATION

The main **tourist office** is just at *Abbey Chambers, Abbey Church Yard, Tel. 01225 477101.* The city is well served by banks; there's also an **American Express** office at *5, Bridge Street, Tel. 01225 444747.*

18. THE MIDLANDS

The English **midlands** is a region of stark contrasts, a land of large and generally ugly industrial cities separated by some of the most idyllic rural countryside in the country. This lush landscape is speckled with old market towns and attractive villages – some of which have changed little in centuries – and some grand stately homes. For most American visitors, the chief draws here are the market town of **Stratford-upon-Avon**, Shakespeare's home town, with a clutch of Bard-related attractions, including the National Shakespeare Theatre; the glorious **Cotswold Hills** with villages that seem to grow out of the landscape; and of course **Oxford**, university city of dreaming spires, nightmarish traffic, *Brideshead Revisted* and *Inspector Morse*.

Just a few miles away from Stratford, **Warwick**, with its medieval castle, and **Coventry**, whose modern cathedral replaced one that was destroyed during World War II, are both eminently visitable, while further north, Britain's second largest city, **Birmingham**, has a wealth of artistic and cultural attractions despite its bland reputation. To the west, the cathedral city of **Worcester** and the nearby **Malvern Hills**, the home territory of the composer Elgar, are the epitome of how every North American thinks England should be; cricket in the shadow of the cathedral tower, the River Severn lazily flowing by, and all surrounded by lush, patchwork quilt countryside, which reaches towards **Hereford** and the Welsh border country. Further north, **Stoke-on-Trent** is the hub of the **Potteries** region, while the pretty county of **Shropshire** attracts millions of visitors to its industrial theme park, **Ironbridge**.

THE COTSWOLDS

The limestone **Cotswold Hills** are one of the most beautiful corners of England, a region of rolling hills and deep valleys, pretty honey-colored stone villages that seem to grow out of the ground, fine churches and historic manor houses that exude timelessness and peace. This was and still is one of the great sheep-rearing areas of England, and it was the success of the local wool industry that provided the means by which the exquisite towns and villages came to be built.

ARRIVALS & DEPARTURES
By Car
Take the M4 from London, linking up with the A419 at Swindon north to Cirencester. From Cirencester, take the A417 north, following the signs for Cheltenham. An alternative route is to take the M40 from London to Oxford, followed by the A40 from Oxford to Cheltenham. Cheltenham is about 100 miles from London.

By Bus
National Express buses serve the Cotswold region out of London's Victoria Bus Station. If you're traveling by bus, it makes a lot of sense to make Cheltenham your base – there are ten buses a day from London, with a journey time of just under three hours. From Cheltenham, a plethora of smaller bus companies take you to the towns and villages of the Cotswolds. There is also a one-bus-a-day service from Victoria to Moreton-in-the-Marsh. *Call 01452 425543 for information about local bus services in the region.*

By Train
Again, your best bet is to use Cheltenham as a base, though there is also a through service from the capital to Moreton-in-the-Marsh. For both destinations, the London departure station is Paddington. The journey time from London is about 2 1/2 hours. *For all rail information, call 0345 484950.* Cheltenham's train station is a half-mile to the west of the city center. From Cheltenham there are regular trains to Gloucester, a ten minute ride.

GETTING AROUND
The best way to get around the region is by **car**. If you need to rent one, try **Budget**, *Prestbury Road, Cheltenham, Tel. 01242 235222*. Both Cheltenham and Gloucester are best seen on foot. The best source of information about the Cotswolds as a whole is the **Heart of England Tourist Board**, *Larkhill, Worcester WR5 2EZ, Tel. 01905 763436*.
If you're the energetic type, you may want to consider renting a **bicycle**. Rather than try to explore the whole region by pedal power in one day, I suggest renting a bike in Cheltenham, then loading it in the car, setting off for a particular destination and exploring the locality from there. **Crabtrees**, *50 Winchcombe Street, Tel. 01242 515291*, rent out bicycles for around £10 a day.

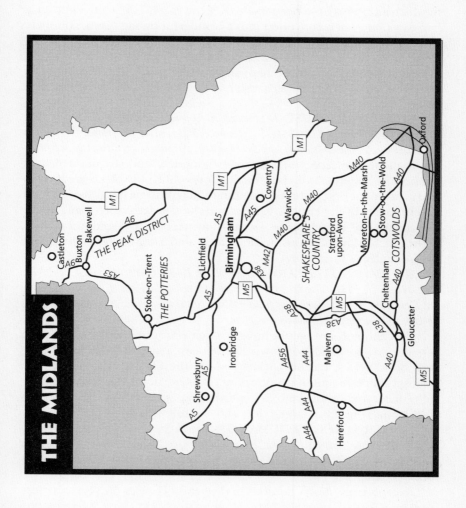

WHERE TO STAY

BARN HOUSE, *152 High Street, Broadway WR12 7AJ. Tel. and Fax 01386 858633. Rooms: 6. Rates: single from £25, double from £48, suite from £65. Note: no credit cards accepted.*

The nucleus of this charming B&B is a fifteenth century farmhouse, to which additions have been made over the years. The main addition, a barn, has now been converted into a wonderful public room, complete with tapestries, log fire, sumptuous furnishings and even a grand piano. The rooms are extremely comfortable and spacious; the only slight drawback being that two of them share a bathroom. That having been said, this hotel offers superb value – despite its size, there's even a swimming pool.

COTSWOLD HOUSE, *The Square, Chipping Campden GL55 6AN. Tel. 01386 840330, Fax 01386 840310. Rooms: 15. Rates: singles from £55, doubles from £120. Restaurants, bar, lounges, garden. All major credit cards accepted.*

Right in the center of Chipping Campden, and surrounded by a plethora of honey-colored houses, the Cotswold House offers great value and a host of period features, including a magnificent spiral staircase, an exceptionally pretty cottage garden and the Garden Restaurant, where the tinkling of grand piano ivories may accompany your meal. The bedrooms are lavishly furnished and decorated using the best fabrics and elegant antique furnishings.

HOTEL ON THE PARK, *38 Evesham Road, Cheltenham GL52 2AH. Tel. 01242 511526, Fax 01242 511526. Rooms: 12. Rates: singles from £76, doubles from £94, four-poster from £154. Restaurant, bar, lounges, library, garden. All major credit cards accepted.*

This three-story regency house, which overlooks an attractive park just minutes north of downtown Cheltenham, is a gem. With its neoclassical bookshelves, button back sofas and the like, it exudes a clubby atmosphere, redolent of bygone days. The bedrooms are similarly tastefully decorated, with canopies, plush drapes, antiques. The elegant restaurant, recently enlarged, has a strong following.

LOWER SLAUGHTER MANOR, *Lower Slaughter GL54 2HP. Tel. 01451 820456, Fax 01451 822150. Rooms: 16. Rates: singles from £150, doubles from £150. Restaurant, lounges, garden, indoor pool. All major credit cards accepted.*

Exceptional country hotel set in the heart of one of the region's most glorious villages, Lower Slaughter Manor dates back at least 350 years, but there has been a manor house on the site for the last 1,000. The bedrooms, divided between the main hotel and a converted coach house, are all tastefully decorated with period furniture and fittings, while the excellent restaurant specializes in French cuisine. Another plus is the grounds, where you can play tennis or just relax in the sunshine.

LYGON ARMS, *High Street, Broadway WR12 7DU. Tel. 01386 852255, Fax 01386 858611. Rooms: 63. Rates: singles from £143, doubles from £175, four-poster from £235. Restaurants, bar, lounges, games room, garden, indoor pool, tennis croquet, gym, sauna. All major credit cards accepted.*

The 16th century former coaching inn makes a number of plausible historical claims: it's said to have accommodated King Charles I and Oliver Cromwell (but not at the same time). No wonder, then that one of the rooms is known as the Charles I suite, with four-poster bed and dark wood paneling. If you're a bit spooked by such surroundings, you can opt instead for the 1970s wings, certainly comfortable, but without the creaky floorboards. Spooked or not, you'll enjoy a meal in the barrel-vaulted Great Hall, or you can opt (again) for something simpler in the brasserie. The hotel comes with an array of leisure facilities – but then that's probably what you'd expect at these prices.

MALT HOUSE HOTEL, *Broad Campden, Nr Chipping Campden GL55 6UU. Tel. 01386 840295, Fax 01386 841334. Rooms: 8. Rates: single from £89.50, doubles from £96.50, suite from £120. Restaurant, garden. All major credit cards accepted.*

Broad Campden is without doubt one of the most idyllic villages anywhere in England, let alone the Cotswolds. The hotel itself was the dwelling of the former village malster and is a gem, with lovely public rooms liberally sprinkled with Georgian antique furniture, lots of flowers and gold leaf in the lounge. The bedrooms, too are a dream – lush fabrics in deep colors and lots of authentic paneling – even in the bathroom! The excellent restaurant served modern British cuisine, using only the freshest ingredients, some of which come from the Malt House's own garden.

FOSSE MANOR, *Stow-on-the-Wold GL54 1JX. Tel 01451 830354, Fax 01451 832486. Rooms: 20. Rates: singles from £55, doubles from £98. Bar, restaurant, croquet, gold driving range, beauty salon. All major credit cards accepted.*

Ivy-clad Fosse Manor is a pleasing old manor house tucked away in the idyllic Cotswolds countryside about a mile south of Stow, on the A429. Its 20 bedrooms are tastefully decorated with a full range of modern, up-to-date facilities including TV; some have four-poster beds. There's a relaxing lounge, a bar where you can purchase snacks and light meals, and a fine restaurant. Other attractions here include croquet, a golf driving range and a beauty salon.

WHERE TO EAT

CHURCHILL ARMS, *Paxford, Chipping Campden. Tel. 01386 594000. Open daily noon to 2pm, 7pm to 9pm. Main courses from £6.50. Credit cards: MC, Visa.*

The Churchill Arms can get very crowded – especially at weekends when it tends to be invaded by hordes of London luvvies. But the excellent food, using fresh local produce, is great value and if you can't stand the intensity indoors, you can always get out into the beer garden.

DORMY HOUSE, *Willersey Hill, Broadway. Tel. 01386 852711. Open Monday to Friday 7:30am to 10:30am, 12:30pm to 2pm, 7pm to 9:30pm; Saturday 7pm to 9:30pm, Sunday 7pm to 9pm. Set dinner (weekdays) £30.50, set dinner (Sundays) £19. All major credit cards accepted.*

Set on a wooded hillside high above Broadway, with views of the Vale of Evesham, the Dormy House restaurant has an excellent reputation locally, with a mainly meat-focused menu, like loin of Welsh venison served with pithiviers of spinach and roast peppers with a peppered port sauce. The wine list is mostly French, with prices starting at £10.75.

LE PETIT BLANC, *Queen's Hotel, The Promenade, Cheltenham GL50 1NN. Tel. 01242 266800. Open daily noon to 3:30pm, 6pm to 11pm. Main courses £6.50 to £16.50. All major credit cards accepted.*

Le Petit Blanc occupies the ground floor of the Queen's Hotel, but is separate from it. The restaurant's interior is simple and modern, the food focusing on French provincial cooking with a hint of Asian. Because of the wide price range of dishes, this is a place where budget diners, and those who want to splash out a bit, can eat happily together. There's a good wine list, with house wines starting at £9.95.

LYGON ARMS, *Broadway, WR12 7DU. Tel. 01386 852255. Open daily 12:30pm to 2:15pm, 7:30pm to 9:15pm. Set lunch £25.50, set dinner £39.50. All major credit cards accepted.*

Even if you decide not to stay at this wonderful Cotswolds hotel (see above), you can do the next best thing and take a meal at its fine restaurant. In doing so, you'll be surrounded by just about everything that Olde Worlde England can throw at you: minstrel's gallery, barrel-vaulted ceilings, beams, suits of armor and the like. As well as all that, the food's very good too, if anything perhaps a little too rich; sometimes it seems as if all three courses have come on the one plate! Still, it's a great place to soak up the atmosphere.

SEEING THE SIGHTS

Gloucester

Start off your tour of the region with a visit to Gloucester, a working city with more than its fair share of ugly modern developments, though there are pockets of beauty. One such spot is the magnificent **cathedral**, standing sentinel over the town. The current building is not the first on the site; the Saxon abbey that originally stood here was replaced by the present building in the eleventh century. Originally a Benedictine foundation, the cathedral became a place of pilgrimage in the 1300s, when the body of murdered **King Edward II** was moved here, having been refused at Bristol and Malmesbury Abbey.

As pilgrimages increased, so did the cathedral's finances – enough to pay for major redevelopment into the perpendicular style in the fourteenth and fifteenth centuries, development which included the building of the massive 225-foot **tower**. Inside, you can still see parts of the original Norman building in the nave, particularly the vast pillars with their zigzag patterns, redolent of Durham. Further inside, check out the amazing 14th century **misericords** in the choir, and gaze up to the stupendous **east window**, finished in 1350 and the largest medieval window in the country. Below it to the left is the tomb of Edward II, in pretty good shape considering the time that has elapsed since his internment here. Before you leave, check out the **cloisters**, completed in 1367, remarkable for the fan vaulting, the first in the country, and an **exhibition** in the upstairs gallery above the north transept, which traces the development of the cathedral. *Open year-round Monday to Friday 7:30pm to 6pm, Saturday 7:30pm to 5pm, Sunday 7:30pm to 4pm. Admission free, but donations invited. Tel. 01452 528095.*

Gloucester's other attractions include the **Gloucester City Museum and Art Gallery**, in Brunswick Road, with exhibits on Gloucester's early history, 18th century furniture, and paintings by Gainsborough and Turner. There are also some dinosaur bones to keep the kids amused. *Open year-round Monday to Saturday 10am to 5pm, plus Sundays 10am to 4pm in July, August and September. Admission adults £2, students and seniors £1, under-18s free. Tel. 01452 524131.*

Also worth exploring in Gloucester are the restored **Victorian Docks**, home not only to offices and shops but to several museums, among them the **National Waterways Museum** in the Llanthony Warehouse. The museum tells the story of the development of Britain's canals with lots of hands-on exhibits, models, engines and photographs. *Open year-round daily 10am to 5pm. Admission adults £4.75, children 5-16, seniors and students £3.75. Tel. 01452 318054; www.nwm.org.uk.*

Gloucester's **tourist information office** is located at *28 Southgate Street, Tel. 01452 421188.*

Cheltenham

Gloucester's immediate neighbor – linked by the A40 – is Cheltenham, one of England's wealthiest towns, with wide leafy streets lined with elegant Georgian terraces and villas. Cheltenham, like its neighbor, Bath, was originally a **spa** town. In 1716 the first spa was discovered, and the town was put firmly on the map by a visit by King George III in 1788, and later on, the Duke of Wellington and Charles Dickens. Like Bath, Cheltenham soon became a place where wealthy members of society came to let their hair down, thereby gaining its reputation for snobbishness – a reputation that was enhanced with the arrival in town of British army officers from India, who claimed that the alkaline waters of Cheltenham were the only effective cure for their tropical ailments.

Start your tour of the town with a visit to the upmarket **Montpellier** area, full of antique shops and fashion boutiques. Make your way to the center of town along the flower-bedecked **Promenade**, flanked by large stores like Liberty's and the House of Fraser, and, behind them the Regent Arcade, an otherwise rather dull shopping mall but made noteworthy for the **Wishing Fish Clock**, a fanstastical clock designed by the children's author Kit Williams. It's a great draw for the kiddies, who love to stand by and watch as bubbles appear from the clock face and tiny animals from various doors. Cheltenham's **Art Gallery and Museum**, on Clarence Street, is well worth a visit for its collection of furniture and silver by designers from the Arts and Crafts Movement, including its most famous son, William Morris. There are exhibits on the social development of Cheltenham, plus oriental porcelain. *Open year-round Monday to Saturday 10am to 5:20pm. Admission free. Tel. 01242 237431; www.cheltenham.gov.uk/agm.*

For **tourist information** in Cheltenham, visit *77 The Promenade, Tel. 01242 522878.*

Winchcombe

About ten miles northeast of Cheltenham is the village of Winchcombe on the B4632. Here you can see **Sudely Castle and Gardens**, once the home of Katherine Parr and Lady Jane Grey. The treasures inside the castle include paintings by the likes of Rubens and Van Dyck, while outside, just as much a treasure, are the nine beautiful gardens. *Gardens open March to October daily 10:30am to 5:30pm; Castle April to October daily 11am to 5pm. Admission castle and gardens adult £6.20, students and seniors £5, children 5-15 £3.20. Admission gardens only adults £4.70, seniors and students £3.70, children £2.50. Tel. 01242 602308; www.stratford.co.uk/sudeley.*

Market Towns

The lovely countryside east of Winchcombe is dotted with peaceful picturesque villages with such delightful names as Temple Guiting and Upper and Lower Swell. Not such attractive names, but two of the loveliest villages in the area are **Upper and Lower Slaughter**, the latter with a tiny stream running down its main street and collection of honey-colored cottages clustered round. Just to the east of here is one of the Cotwolds' most popular spots – **Stow-On-The-Wold**, a beautiful small town whose market place still has its original stocks, and lined with antique, bric-a-brac and tea shops, all very quaint, quintessentially English. In fact the best thing you can do in this area is drive around at leisure, exploring the narrow country lanes, stopping every now again to take in a stunning view or sample the ambience of a local village. The good news is that the further north you drive, the countryside becomes even more picturesque.

North of Stow, on the A429, and bisected by the A44, is another market town – **Moreton-On-The Marsh**, and more of the same, though the layout is different. This time, a long wide main street lined with pubs, restaurants and more shopping therapy. It's a gorgeous place, great for just wandering (and maybe stopping off for a pint). Take the A44 west to possibly the Cotswolds' most visited village, **Broadway**, with a glut of pubs, hotels and tea shoppes – the legacy of its days as a staging post on the London to Worcester road. It's most definitely a tourist's delight, but despite the hordes of daytrippers you can still find peace and tranquillity here; just get off the A44 and follow the old main street east, to find more wisteria and rose-covered cottages, and, eventually, the **Broadway Tower**, offering panoramic views across, it's said, 13 counties. If you have kids along, amuse them by taking them to the adjacent **Broadway Tower Country Park**; there's a museum devoted to William Morris, who spent a lot of time here, an adventure playground and a red deer enclosure. *Open April to October daily 10am to 4:30pm. Admission adults £3.20, seniors and students £2.50, children 4-16 £2.20. Tel. 01386 852390.*

Broadway has its own **tourist information center** at *1 Cotswold Court, Tel. 01386 852937,* while Stow's is at *Hollis House, The Square, Tel. 01451 831082.*

Just a few miles to the east of Broadway is another much-visited Cotswold village – **Chipping Campden** – Chipping being an old English word for market. This was indeed a thriving market town in the middle ages, its prosperity built on the back of the wool industry. The result is some fine buildings, including the handsome **Church of St. James**, full of monuments to its wealthy benefactors. Though the demise of the wool industry led to more austere times, the town bounced back with the arrival of C.R. Ashbee, a Londoner with ideas way ahead of his time, who set about creating here a base for his **Guild of Handicrafts** movement, designed to preserve the traditional cottage industries that were being eroded by mass production.

Since that time, the town attracted silversmiths, jewelers, carpenters and various other craftspeople, and generated enough trade to keep them busy. Around Chipping Campden are a number of attractive smaller villages such as **Broad Campden**, **Hidcote Boyce** and **Ebrington**. Like I said before, this is a fantastic area to explore, not only for the villages, but for a host of manor houses, stately homes and gardens, many of which are open to the public.

Chipping Campden's **tourist office** is at *Woodstapler's Hall Museum, High Street, Tel. 01386 840101.*

SPORTS & RECREATION

Cheltenham is home to one of Britain's best known racecourses, located in the village of Prestbury, just north of the city, where the **Cheltenham Gold Cup** is held annually in March. *For race information, call 01242 513014.*

EXCURSIONS & DAY TRIPS

The **Heart of England Tourist Board**, *Tel. 01905 446680*, arranges tours of the region during the peak season.

STRATFORD-UPON-AVON

England's greatest draw for American visitors after London is **Stratford-Upon-Avon**, a fairly unremarkable country town, save for a clutch of attractive timber frame buildings and – of course - its connection with one **William Shakespeare**, who was born, baptized, educated and buried here.

Little is known about the Bard's early life, save that he was born and bred here, so much of the propaganda put out at the tourist sites must be taken with a pinch of salt – even the date of his birth, commonly celebrated on April 23rd. There was no register of births at the time, so baptismal records are the only source of information about his entry into the world. These indicate that he was baptised on April 25. Many take the view that his birth was assumed to be April 23, because it is St. George's Day, England's patron saint.

Although feted throughout the world, the typical English characteristic of playing down its success stories meant that it wasn't until 1769 that anything of any significance was done here to commemorate Shakespeare's contribution to national life. It was in that year that the acclaimed actor **David Garrick** organized the first of the Shakespeare birthday celebrations, an event which has been taking place every year since.

Because of the sheer volume of visitors, Stratford is an exceptionally busy place, especially in the peak summer season, when finding a room – let alone a space to park – can be a nightmare: this is one place where planning in advance certainly pays dividends.

ARRIVALS & DEPARTURES

By Car

From London take the M40 towards Birmingham as far as junction 15. Follow the signs for Stratford-upon-Avon, using the A46 – a total of just over 90 miles. Parking in Stratford can be horrendous, particularly during the peak season and on bank holiday weekends. There are large parking lots just outside the town center on Warwick Road (by the bus station) and on Arden Street.

By Bus

London's Victoria Bus Station serves the Stratford area around eight times a day, but a faster way to get to the town is to take a train to Coventry from London's Euston train station, then board a **Guide Friday** bus. The trip take about two hours in all, and there are around four departures a day. *Call 0207 387 7070 for details.* The main bus station is located just north of the town center, on the Warwick Road.

By Train

There's a direct train to Stratford from London's Paddington train station each morning – otherwise, it's a case of changing at Leamington Spa for the local service to Stratford. *For information, call National Rail Enquiries on 0345 484950.* The train station is located half a mile west of the town center, on Station Road.

GETTING AROUND TOWN

Walking is by far the best way to get around this compact little town, with the exception of Anne Hathaway's Cottage and Mary Arden's House. For both of these, catch a bus from Wood Street. *Call 01788 535555 for local bus information.*

Guide Friday, *Tel. 01789 294466,* runs guided bus tours of the town during the summer using open top buses. The main pick-up point is the tourist information center at Bridgefoot.

WHERE TO STAY

ALVESTON MANOR HOTEL, *Clopton Bridge, Stratford CV37 7HP. Tel. 01789 204581, Fax 01789 414095. Rooms: 110. Rates: singles from £120, doubles from £160. Restaurants, 24-hour rooms service, laundry, babysitting, free parking.*

This black and white timbered building has roots going back to well before the arrival of William the Conqueror, though the present building is largely Elizabethan. If it's a taste of the olde world you want then this is the place; slanting floors, beams, antique furnishings – or if you prefer something a bit more contemporary, there's a modern addition at the rear, connected to the manor by a covered walk. The rooms are all comfortable, and there's an excellent restaurant, the Tudor Room.

MOAT HOUSE, *Bridgefoot, Stratford CV37 6YR. Tel. 01789 414411, Fax 01789 298589. Rooms: 250. Rates: singles from £125, doubles from £145. Restaurants, pub, leisure facilities, including pool, sauna, laundry service, 24-hour room service. All major credit cards accepted.*

Large, modern hotel – part of a large British chain – standing in five acres of landscaped grounds on the banks of the River Avon, with a full range of facilities. The rooms are light, airy and spacious, and the Riverside Restaurant offers carvery-style meals.

FORTE POSTHOUSE, *Bridgefoot, Stratford CV37 7LT. Tel. 01789 266761, Toll free 800/225-5843 in US, Fax 01789 414547. Rooms: 50. Rates: singles from £80, doubles from £100. Restaurant, bar, free parking. All major credit cards accepted.*

Part of another British chain, this hotel is conveniently located close to Stratford's main attraction, and is just a ten minute walk to the RST. The bedrooms are modern, tastefully decorated, and come equipped with all the usual amenities, while the pleasant Swan's Nest restaurant is lined with eighteenth century paintings.

SALFORD HALL HOTEL, *Abbots Salford, Worcestershire WR11 5UT. Tel 01386 871300, fax 01386 871301. Rooms: rates: singles from £80, doubles from £110. Bar, restaurant. All major credit cards accepted.*

This beautiful Tudor mansion just off the A46 eight miles to the west of Stratford has been lovingly restored and is now one of the finest hotels in the area. You'll love the setting and the building itself, with its Tudor entrance and half-timber extension. The bedrooms are full of atmosphere and luxuriously appointed with up-to-date facilities, including mini-bars; some, inevitably, come with four-poster beds. The restaurant has established an excellent reputation locally.

SEQUOIA HOUSE HOTEL, *51-53 Shipston Road, Stratford-upon-Avon CV37 7LN. Tel 01789 268852, Fax 01789 414559. Rooms: 24. Rates: singles from £35, doubles from £65. Air-conditioned.*

The owners have gone to a lot of trouble to make this small hotel stand out above many of the rest. A light and spacious Victorian town house, the Sequoia House has 24 beautifully appointed bedrooms, all individually designed. There's a large lounge that's also tastefully furnished with antique furnishings, and an elegant dining room where hearty breakfasts are served. It's even air-conditioned – very unusual in the UK for a hotel of the size, and a sure sign of the owners' commitment to keep their guests comfortable and happy.

DUKES HOTEL, *Payton Street, Stratford-upon-Avon CV37 6UA. Tel 01789 269300, Fax 01789 414700. Rooms: 22. Rates: singles from £50, doubles from £69.50. Bar, restaurant, parking. All major credit cards accepted.*

Two restored Georgian villas linked together form this pleasant town center hotel that's close to all Stratford's attractions, including Shakespeare's Birthplace and the Royal Shakespeare Theatre. The bedrooms are comfortable and nicely decorated, and there's a bar and restaurant. The hotel also benefits from an extensive garden, which is especially pleasant in summer. Another major bonus here is that the hotel has its own parking lot; quite an advantage, especially in mid-season, when it's almost impossible to find a street parking place in the town.

CHARLECOTE PHEASANT COUNTRY HOTEL, *Charlecote, CV35 9EW. Tel 01789 470333, Fax 01789 470222. Rooms: 70. Rates: singles from £85, doubles from £110. Bar, carvery restaurant, heated pool. All major credit cards accepted.*

As Stratford just heaves with people in the summer, it's not a bad idea to stay just a ways out of the town. The Charlecote Pheasant Country Hotel is located four miles from Stratford, adjacent to Charlecote Manor and Deer Park. Originally converted from old farm buildings, after much enlargement it now boasts 70 rooms, all of which are pleasantly decorated and furnished, with all facilities. The hotel's bar attracts many locals as well as hotel residents, and the carvery restaurant offers a wide range of food options, buffet style. An added bonus is the swimming pool.

EAST BANK HOUSE, *19 Warwick Road, Stratford-upon-Avon CV37 6YW. Tel 01789 292758, Fax 01789 292758. Rooms: 10. Rates: singles from £32, doubles from £42. Credit cards: MC, Visa.*

Located on the main Warwick Road, this large Victorian home has 10 (no-smoking) comfortable bedrooms, eight of which have private facilities. The good thing about this place is that it's not only well situated for the sights and sounds of Stratford, but also for getting out of the town and exploring the countryside around – Warwick Castle, for example, is just a few miles up the road. There's no restaurant as such, but full breakfasts are served, and there are plenty of good restaurants within easy walking distance.

WHERE TO EAT

THE OPPOSITION, *13 Sheep Street, Stratford. Tel. 01789 269980. Open Monday to Saturday noon to 2pm, 5:30pm to 10:30pm; Sunday noon to 2pm, 6pm to 10pm. Main courses around £10. Credit cards: MC, Visa.*

Very popular with locals and tourists alike, this restaurant offers real value-for-money in a delightful sixteenth century building with bare brick walls, beamed ceilings and candlelit tables. The range of food varies from English specialities to spicier dishes with an eastern flavor, to French favorites. Because the place is so popular, it's essential to book in advance – the earlier the better.

RUSSON'S, *8 Church Street, Stratford. Tel. 01789 268822. Open Tuesday to Saturday 11:30am to 2pm, 5:30pm to 10pm. Main courses around £12/ 13. All major credit cards accepted.*

Delightful restaurant, possibly Stratford's best known, right in the center of town. It's particularly noted for its imaginative seafood choices, though the meat and vegetarian dishes are not to be sniffed at either.

There's a special pre-theater menu, which serves from the a la carte menu, but at lower prices.

ALADDIN'S INDIAN BRASSERIE, *4 Main Road, Tiddington, just outside Stratford. Tel 01789 294491. Open daily 5:30pm to midnight. Dinner from £10. All major credit cards accepted.*

Indian food is extremely popular in England, not surprisingly when it is cooked and presented as beautifully as it is here. The decor is rich and elegant, but not "over the top." The service is impeccably polite and friendly. Try their tandoori roasted king prawns with mild spices, cream and butter, and the selection of Indian ice creams – deliciously refreshing. There's a good wine list, or you could do what most Brits do when eating Indian – order a lager.

DESPORT'S, *13-14 Meer Street, Stratford. Tel 01789 269304. Open Tuesday to Saturday noon to 2pm, 6pm to 11pm. Set lunch £10.50, set dinner £14. All major credit cards accepted.*

This fairly new restaurant has already established a good reputation. Located in the eaves above Desport's Deli, the 16th century building's original features mix well with the bright yellow and blue the owners have chosen to decorate the place. The menu contains a fairly even mixture of nicely cooked and presented meat, fish and vegetarian dishes, English in essence with a touch of the Mediterranean.

MARLOWE'S, *18 High Street, Stratford. Tel 01789 204999. Open daily noon to 2:30pm, 5:30pm to 10:30pm (Sunday 7pm to 9pm). Set dinner £15. All major credit cards accepted.*

Marlowe's was originally an Elizabethan townhouse, and today it's full of original beams, brickwork and woodwork. There are two main dining rooms, separated by a pleasant atrium which is covered by canvas during the summer months and is a great place for a pre-meal cocktail. Among the dishes on offer are ravioli of smoked haddock and ricotta with spring onion (scallion) and butter sauce, or you may prefer the more traditional roasts that are usually available here. There's a good wine list, and the service is friendly and attentive.

THE GROSVENOR HOTEL, *Warwick Road, Stratford. Tel 01789 269213. Open noon to 2pm, 6pm to 9:30pm. Set dinner (2 courses) from £15. All major credit cards accepted.*

The Grosvenor Hotel is a rambling old Regency building, recently refurbished, and full of period features. The hotel's elegant Garden Restaurant is pleasantly decorated with hand painted murals and serves what is best described as international cuisine as well as some traditional English options, including roasts. There's an extensive wine list.

THE WHITE SWAN, *Rother Street, Stratford. Tel 01789 297022. Open noon to 2:30pm, 6pm to 9pm (10pm Saturdays). All major credit cards accepted.*

The White Swan is a lovely old half-timbered Tudor building that's very popular with tourists and locals alike. The restaurant serves what's best described as modern British cuisine, with such beguiling dishes as calf's liver with sage and rich balsamic jus on a bed of spinach and rosti. There's a wide choice of traditional desserts, as well as some more creative ones.

SEEING THE SIGHTS

A good place to start your visit here is **Shakespeare's Birthplace**, a half-timbered structure on Henley Street, where Will's parents John, a relatively prosperous glover who at one point became the town's mayor, and Mary (nee Arden) lived. The early sixteenth century house was

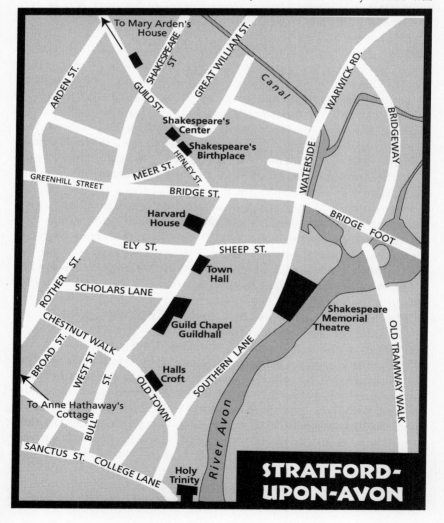

342 ENGLAND & WALES GUIDE

bought by public benefactors in 1847 and is now maintained by the **Shakespeare Birth Trust**. You enter the property though a modern **Shakespeare Centre**, with a museum illustrating the life and times of the Bard, along with the Trust's offices. You can opt to head straight for the cottage itself, with its fully equipped seventeenth century kitchen, living room, and the bedroom where Shakespeare was conceived and born (allegedly).

Unfortunately, the various points of interest in the house are very poorly marked – most likely in order to keep the 700,000-plus annual visitors moving. What is, however, very well marked indeed is the gift shop. *Open mid-March to mid-October, Monday to Saturday 9am to 5pm, Sunday 9:30am to 5pm; mid-October to mid-March Monday to Saturday 9:30am to 4pm, Sunday 10am to 4pm. Admission adults £4.90, 5s-16s £2.20. Tel. 01789 204016.*

A few hundred yards away in Old Town (the name of a street) is **Holy Trinity Church**, where Shakespeare is buried – not in Westminster Abbey, perhaps because of the epitaph "curst be he who moves my bones." A copy of the parish register records his baptism, as well as his burial in 1616. *Open Monday to Saturday 8:30am to 6pm, Sunday 2pm to 5pm. Admission adults 60p, 5s-16s and seniors 40p. Tel. 01789 266316.* Just down the street, and well worth a visit, is **Hall's Croft**, a delightful Tudor house where Shakespeare's daughter **Susanna** lived with her doctor husband, **John Hall**, who was well-liked in the town and had a thriving medical practice here. Displays relating to medical practices during Hall's time, along with some of the implements used, can be seen – sure to make you gasp in gratitude for the advances medical science has made. *Open mid-March to mid-October Monday to Saturday 8:30am to 6pm, Sunday 2pm to 5pm; mid-October to mid-March Monday to Saturday 10:30am to 4pm, Sunday 2pm to 5pm. Admission adults £3.30, students, seniors and 5s-16s, £1.60. Tel. 01789 292107.*

Two more important Shakespeare-related sites are located just outside of Stratford. The first, about two miles west of town in the village of **Shottery**, is the house where **Anne Hathaway** lived before her marriage to William Shakespeare. It's a pretty house, of wattle and daub construction, with plenty of low ceilings – people in Shakespeare's time were much shorter than they are today. Inside, it's been decorated in much the same way as it would have been in Anne's day – the kitchen with its collection of period utensils is particularly interesting. There's a lovely Elizabethan-style garden, which leads to the requisite gift shop where you can buy your Shakespeare souvenir mug. *Open mid-March to mid-October Monday to Saturday 9am to 5pm, Sunday 9:30am to 5pm; mid-October to mid-March Monday to Saturday 9:30am to 4pm, Sunday 10am to 4pm. Admission adults £3.90, students, seniors and children £1.60. tel 01789 204016.*

The other place of interest for Shakespeare buffs is the **House of Mary Arden**, the childhood home of Shakepeare's mother, just over three miles out of Stratford in the village of **Wilmcote**. Built in Tudor times as a farmhouse, it contains the kind of furniture that Shakespeare would have been familiar with, and in the outbuildings various farming implements illustrating the work of a country farm from Shakespeare's day to the present comprise **the Shakespeare Countryside Museum**. *Open mid-March to mid-October Monday to Saturday 9:30am to 5pm, Sunday 10am to 5pm; mid-October to mid-March Monday to Saturday 10am to 4pm, Sunday 10:30am to 4:30pm. Admission adults £4.40, students, seniors, children £2.20.*

SEE THE ROYAL SHAKESPEARE THEATRE IN ACTION!

*The best way to round off a day in Stratford, is, of course, a performance at the **Royal Shakespeare Theatre (RST)**, one of the two main bases (the other is the Barbican Centre in London) of the Royal Shakespeare Company. It's a disappointingly ugly, red brick building, but its setting, down by the Avon, is attractive and a great place to relax before a summer evening performance. The main auditorium seats 1,500, and the season runs from mid-March to December. Behind the main auditorium is the much smaller **Swan Theatre**, seating 450, much closer in design to a theater of Shakespeare's time than the RST. Rebuilt in the 1950s after a fire which destroyed the earlier Victorian Memorial Theatre, the Swan stages plays by Shakespeare and later playwrights.*

*   **Tours** of the complex and the **RSC Collection** of theatrical memorabilia can be arranged by calling 01789 403405. Tours depart Monday to Saturday at 1.30pm and 5.30pm, and on Sundays at noon, 1pm, 2pm and 3pm. The cost is £4 for adults, £3 for students, seniors and children aged 5-18. If you want a ticket for a **play**, call 01789 403403.*

Quite unrelated to Shakespeare, but well worth a trip out of town – it's about twelve miles west of Stratford – is the stunningly beautiful **Ragley Hall**, just south of **Alcester**, a 120-room Palladian mansion that was built in 1680. The home of the Marquis of Hertford, it has been painstakingly restored, right down to some of the original wallpaper patterns. The various items of furniture and works of art, including paintings by Sir Joshua Reynolds and the Dutch masters, on display are the result of centuries of collecting by the family. Check out the **Great Hall,** with its fine baroque plasterwork, and the grounds, laid out by none other than – you guessed it – Capability Brown. *Open April to September Tuesday to Thursday, Saturday and Sunday (and Bank Holiday Mondays)*

344 ENGLAND & WALES GUIDE

11am to 5pm (park open 10am to 6pm). Admission adults £4.50, seniors £4, children £3. Tel. 01789 762090.

NIGHTLIFE & ENTERTAINMENT

Stratford's nightlife – apart from seeing a play at the RST, see sidebar above – focuses on its many pubs, the best-known of which is **The Dirty Duck (Black Swan)**, *Waterside,* which attracts a fascinating (and often noisy) mix of residents, tourists and actors. Other pubs in Stratford include the quaintly named **Slug and Lettuce**, *38 Guild Street*, and the **Windmill Inn**, arguably the town's oldest hostelry, *on Church Street.*

PRACTICAL INFORMATION

All the major banks have offices in Stratford, as do **American Express**, *c/o The Tourist Information Centre, Bridgefoot, Tel. 01789 415856,* and **Thomas Cook**, *c/o HSBC Bank, 13 Chapel Street, Stratford, Tel. 01789 294688.* Stratford's main post office is on Henley Street.

Visitor information is provided by the **Heart of England Tourist Board**, *Woodside, Larkhill, Worcester WR5 2EF, Tel. 01905 763436,* and by Stratford's own tourism department, *Bridgefoot, Tel. 01789 293127; www.shakespeare-country.co.uk.*

WARWICK & COVENTRY

Just eight miles north of Stratford on the A429 is one of the region's other highlights. The ancient town of **Warwick** is an attractive city with a host of Tudor (and earlier) buildings that remained intact after a disastrous fire in 1694 which destroyed much of the rest of the town; there are also some delightful post-fire Georgian homes. The town's history goes back at least as far as 1088, when the son of William the Conqueror created the title Earl of Warwick, though the town authorities claim Ethelfreda, daughter of King Alfred the Great, as its founder. The other building the fire didn't ravage, and Warwick's main tourist attraction, is its magnificent castle.

Coventry, another 11 miles past Warwick, is well-known for its magnificent modern **Cathedral**.

ARRIVALS & DEPARTURES

By Car

Warwick is on the main A429 from Stratford.

By Bus

Stagecoach buses, *Tel. 01788 535555*, connect Warwick with Stratford and Coventry and stop in Market Place. National Express buses operate from Old Square.

By Train
There are train connections from Warwick Station (Station Road, north of the town center) to Birmingham, Coventry and London.

WHERE TO STAY

AYLESFORD HOTEL, *1 High Street, Warwick CV34 4AP. Tel. 01926 492817, Fax 01926 493817. Rooms 8. Rates: double from £75, family room from £90 (prices include breakfast). Restaurant. Credit cards: MC, Visa.*

Just a short walk from the castle and other town center attractions, this charming hotel has recently been refurbished to a high standard. Part of a local landmark, the Three Sisters, the tallest buildings in the area, it was built after the 1696 fire. The old cellar is now an very pleasant restaurant with bare brick walls, and bright and airy bedrooms.

WARWICK ARMS HOTEL, *17 High Street, Warwick CV34 4AT. Tel 01926 492759, Fax 01926 410587. Rooms: 35. Rates: singles from £55, doubles from £65. Bar, restaurant. All major credit cards accepted.*

This relaxed and friendly hotel right in the center of Warwick caters to a large number of business clients, but this does not detract from the overall comfortable ambience of one of Warwick's main hotels. The bedrooms comes in various shapes and sizes, but all are equipped to a good standard. Meanwhile, a full range of meals are served in the restaurant, both from an a la carte and a prix fixe menu.

LEOFRIC HOTEL, *Broadgate, Coventry CV1 1LZ. Tel 0500 636943, Fax 01773 880321. Rooms: 94. Rates: singles from £95, doubles from £105. Bar, restaurant. All major credit cards accepted.*

This large hotel right in the center of Coventry was built on the site of much devastation following the World War II bombings, in which many of Coventry's ancient buildings, including its cathedral, were destroyed. The Lefric was allegedly the first new hotel to be built in Britain following that war. Recently refurbished, it offers 94 comfortable rooms, a choice of bars and a brasserie restaurant. It's within yards of Coventry's main shopping area (in fact, it's part of it) and the modern Cathedral of St. Michael is a short walk.

WHERE TO EAT

FINDON'S, *7 Old Square, Warwick. Tel. 01926 411755. Open Monday to Friday lunch noon to 2pm, Monday to Saturday dinner 7pm to 9:30pm. Set lunch up to £15.95 (2 courses), set dinner (2 courses) £15.95. All major credit cards accepted.*

Stylish restaurant occupying an elegant Georgian house in the center of town. Tables are well-spaced with white tablecloths and fresh flowers, with classical jazz playing in the background. The beautifully cooked food has an English/French slant, with main course dishes like breast of duck with cherries and cinnamon, or cinnamon apple brioche with calvados ice cream for dessert. There's an extensive wine list, with the emphasis again on French.

THE HIPPOPOTAMUS, *48, Brook Street Warwick. Tel 01926 493504. Open daily noon to 2:30pm, 6:30pm to 9:30pm. Main courses from £6.95. All major credit cards accepted.*

Located right in the center of Warwick is this unusual and remarkable African/Caribbean/English restaurant. All meals are served with salads and accompaniments, including seasonal African vegetables, mango or iceberg salad or chaka-chaka rice. Main courses include Boerewurst, a traditional South African sausage served with Magongo or peri-peri sauce – or – not for the squeamish – crocodile tail in a cream and lemon sauce served with sweet potato gratin and African vegetables. There's a full range of exciting desserts and a reasonable wine list. Despite the name, I don't think hippopotamus is on the menu – though no doubt one would be a good investment.

ROYAL BENGAL, *172 Earlsdon Road, Coventry. Tel 024 7671 2345. Open Sunday to Thursday 6pm to midnight, Friday and Saturday 6pm to 1am. Set meals for two from £21.95. All major credit cards accepted.*

There are some fine Indian restaurants in Coventry and this is one of the best. Established in 1986, the Royal Bengal has built up a strong local following. There's a vast range of choices here; for simplicity, you may want to go for one of the set meals for two – the Indian Dinner set menu consists of popadoms, sheek kebab and chicken tikka, chick tikka masala, rogan josh vegetable curry, pilao rice, nan bread and coffee. If that doesn't make an iota of sense to you don't worry – the helpful staff will explain all. There's a bar where wines can be ordered, or you may wish to join in that venerable British tradition of drinking lager with your meal.

SEEING THE SIGHTS

Warwick Castle's roots date back at least as far as 914, when the mound on which it sits was claimed by Ethelfreda. Later on, when the Normans took over, a motte and bailey were constructed, but this was destroyed in 1264 by Simon de Montfort. The infamous Beauchamp family, who were the most illustrious medieval Earls of Warwick, rebuilt the castle in the mid-14th century, much of which survives. Later on, the castle was given to Sir Fulke Greville by James I, who set about spending £200,000 – a mind-boggling sum in those days – turning the existing castle buildings into an extravagant palace for himself.

Among the highlights of the castle are the **Ghost Tower**, reputed to be haunted by none other than Sir Fulke himself, and the magnificent **Great Hall**, restored to its former glory after a disastrous fire in the 1870s. The state rooms house fine collections of paintings, furniture, arms and armor, while down below, the gloomy dungeon recreates a vivid picture of the castle's turbulent past and the kind of punishments that were meted out to the Earl's prisoners. *Open April to October daily 10am to 6pm,; November to March daily 10am to 5pm. Admission adults £10.50, seniors £7.50, 4s-16s £6.25. Tel. 01926 406600; www.warwick-castle.co.uk.*

Just nineteen miles north of Stratford is the sprawling industrial city of **Coventry**, famed for its vast modern **Cathedral**, designed by Sir Basil Spence. It was completed in 1962 to replace its 14th century predecessor, which was destroyed during an enemy air raid in World War II. The ancient blackened ruins of the old cathedral of St. Michael next door, linked to the newer building by a vast porch, are a potent reminder of the futility of war. Among the points of interest in the new building are the **baptistry**, with its font of Tournai marble, the **Chapel of Reconciliation**, some fine modern stained glass windows, and a massive altar tapestry of *Christ in Glory*, designed by Graham Sutherland, reputedly the largest tapestry in the world.

The exterior is dominated by the massive bronze masterpiece, *St. Michael Slaying the Devil*, by Sir Jacob Epstein; higher up, the spire was lowered by helicopter. In the cathedral's undercroft is **The Spirit of Coventry**, an excellent three-dimensional holographic display, a contemporary Stations of the Cross that includes a bombed house. Here, the cathedral's treasures, many of which were saved from the old building, are on display. Perhaps the greatest treasure of all, however, is the crude **cross of nails** made from medieval nails found in the ruins of the old cathedral. The cross has been placed behind the behind the altar, inscribed with the evocative words, *"Father, Forgive."*

American visitors to Coventry will want to consider taking an excursion to the village of **Sulgrave**, whose **Manor House** was built by **Lawrence Washington**, one of George Washington's ancestors and a former Mayor of Northampton, in 1539. Colonel John Washington, George's great-grandfather, left England to settle in Virginia in 1656. In 1914, the house was purchased by a group of English Amerophiles in acknowledgment of the bond between the two countries. Over the years, the house has been restored to something like its original state, with lots of period furniture and an original portrait of George Washington by renowned Rhode Island artist Gilbert Stuart. In the summer, actors in period costume are present to answer your questions. *Open April to October Monday, Tuesday, Thursday, Friday 2pm to 5:30pm, Saturday and Sunday 10:30am to 1pm and*

*2pm to 5:30pm (March, November, December, closes 4.30pm. Admission £3. Tel.
01295 760205.*

ALTHORP HOUSE – DIANA'S FINAL RESTING PLACE

*If you're in this area during July and August you might even be tempted
to travel on another twenty miles or so to **Althorp House**, the last resting
place of the late Diana, Princess of Wales. The house (and the grounds,
where Diana is buried on an island in the middle of a lake) have been
besieged by such vast crowds that the only safe way to gain entry is by pre-
booking your ticket. Diana's family, the **Spencers**, have lived here since the
early 1500s. Inside the house, there's a wonderful collection of paintings by
artists of the caliber of Van Dyck, Gainsborough and Rubens, but,
inevitably, it's the lake that most people come to see. Open July 1 to August
31. Admission adults £10, seniors £7.50, 5s-17s £5. Pre-booking necessary.
Tel. 01604 770107; www.althorp-house.co.uk.*

PRACTICAL INFORMATION

Warwick's main post office is on Market Street; the **tourist information center** is on Jury Street, close to the junction with Castle Street,
Tel.01926 492212.

OXFORD

City of dreaming medieval spires, turrets, pinnacles (and maybe soon
a minaret or two), **Oxford** is a mecca for most tourists to England, and a
visit without it is like going to Rome without seeing the Colosseum,
Athens without the Acropolis. Today's city of around 120,000 is dominated by its 12th century **university**, one of the world's foremost places
of learning, with a cast list that includes such luminaries as Sir Walter
Raleigh, Sir Christopher Wren, John Wesley, William Penn, Margaret
Thatcher and Bill Clinton to name but a few.

This is a bustling modern industrial city too; cars and steel are
produced here, giving rise to a some rivalry summed up in the expression
"town vs. gown." In the city center, these two major elements seem to
merge in a hodgepodge of contemporary office buildings, high street
stores and venerable college institutions with their peaceful quadrangles,
or "quads." So when you arrive in Oxford, don't ask, "Where's the
University?" – it's all around you.

The city's origins go back to Saxon times, when it served as a defense against the marauding Danes. As time went on, its function as a market town was eclipsed by its new-found role as a center for learning.

Today, Oxford has 41 colleges and halls, most of which are worthy of a mention, but there's simply not time or space here, so I've concentrated on a handful, plus a few other attractions that will keep you busy.

ARRIVALS & DEPARTURES
By Car
Oxford is easy to get to from London. Take the A40 (Westway) out of town, then follow the M40 until you come to the A40 junction, from which signs clearly mark the way to Oxford city center. Parking is notoriously difficult in Oxford. Consider using one of the city's Park and Ride schemes. Parking itself is free, but the round trip bus journey costs £1.

By Bus
There's a frequent bus service from London's Victoria Bus Station operated by **City Link**, *Tel. 01865 785400*. Departures leave every fifteen minutes in the peak season, and the journey time takes just under two hours, depending on the traffic. The **Oxford Tune**, *Tel. 01865 772250*, is another company with frequent service to Victoria, as is **The Oxford Bus Company**, *Tel. 01865 785400*.

By Train
Trains from London's Paddington Station leave for Oxford regularly throughout the day. The journey times is just over an hour. *Call 01345 484950 for information.* The train station is west of the city center on Park End Street.

GETTING AROUND TOWN
By far the best way of getting around Oxford is on foot. **Guide Friday** runs regular bus tours of the city throughout the year (though they're much more frequent in summer – every 10 minutes). Buses leave from the train station. *Call 01865 790522.*

To get to places outside the city, use the local bus services – **City Link**, *Tel. 01865 785410*, and **Stagecoach**, *Tel. 01865 772200* or consider renting a car – Hertz has an office on Woodstock Road, *Tel. 01865 319972*.

Taxis can be hailed in the street, or picked up at either the train station or bus station. A trip to Blenheim will cost around £16.

WHERE TO STAY

BATH PLACE HOTEL, *4-5 Bath Place, Oxford OX1 3SU. Tel. 01865 791812, Fax 01865 791834. Rooms: 13. Rates: singles from £90, doubles from £95. Restaurant, bar. All major credit cards accepted.*

Originally a row of Jacobean weavers' cottages built onto the outside of the city wall, Bath Place is full of the kind of character and atmosphere you'd expect to find in such a venerable dwelling place, with lots of beams, wobbly floors and suchlike. The rooms are fairly small, but utterly charming and in keeping with the unique character of the place.

COTSWOLD HOUSE, *363 Banbury Road, Oxford OX2 7PL. Tel. and Fax 01865 310558. Rooms: 7. Rates: singles from £41, doubles from £65. Credit cards: MC, Visa.*

Just minutes from the city center, this very pleasant small, modern B&B in the north of Oxford has seven well-equipped and comfortable bedrooms. The atmosphere is extremely convivial and the owners go out of their way to offer advice on what to see and how to get there. The large breakfasts are very popular, and vegetarian options are available.

OLD PARSONAGE HOTEL, *1 Banbury Road, Oxford OX2 6NN. Tel. 01865 310210, Fax 01865 311262. Rooms: 30. Rates: singles from £125, doubles from £145. Restaurant, bars, roof garden. All major credit cards accepted.*

The Old Parsonage dates back to the 1660s, but was completely refurbished in 1991. The best way to describe it is as a country house right in the middle of a city. There are stone gables, tall chimneys and wisteria-covered walls. The public rooms exude a country club atmosphere, while the bedrooms are tastefully decorated and furnished with sumptuous marble bathrooms. The service is impeccable, and they'll even go so far as to arrange tours of the colleges for you.

THE RANDOLPH, *Beaumont Street, Oxford OX1 2LN. Tel. 01865 247481, Fax 01865 791678. Rooms: 110. Rates: singles from £140, doubles/twins from £170. Restaurant, bar. All major credit cards accepted.*

Oxford's largest city center hotel is a lavish affair, and therefore a bit on the pricey side. However, if you want to stay somewhere that truly reflects the atmosphere of the city, this is the place. Lining the main staircase are lancet arches and photographs from the Oxford Union. The rooms maintain the ambience – William Morris-designed curtains and wallpaper and the like. The public rooms are sumptuous, and the hotel features in PBS's *Inspector Morse* and in the film *Shadowlands*.

GABLES, *6 Cumnor Hill, Oxford OX2 9HA. Tel 01865 862153, Fax 01865 864054. Rooms: 6. Rates: single from £22, doubles from £44. Garden. Credit cards: MC, Visa.*

This delightful B&B is some way out of central Oxford, following the Botley Road (which later becomes Cumnor Hill). The owners take great pride in their premises and are constantly redecorating and refurbishing the premises so that the bedrooms – which come with TV and the usual facilities – always look and feel fresh and attractive. There's a lovely garden, with beautiful floral displays. It's a friendly place and the owners will do virtually anything for you; they've even managed to negotiate an arrangement with a local video store so that guests can hire films for the VCRs in their rooms. Breakfasts are excellent.

GALAXIE HOTEL, *180 Banbury Road, Oxford OX2 7BT. Tel 01865 515688, Fax 01865 556824. Rooms: 31. Rates: singles from £39, doubles from £72, family room from £81. Garden. Credit cards: MC, Visa.*

This attractive, ivy-covered building in Summertown is far enough out of central Oxford and the exorbitant prices of many of the hotels there, but near enough to access most of the city's attractions as well as the surrounding countryside. The bedrooms are individually decorated with the usual facilities available and are all non-smoking; there's a pleasant conservatory, where you have breakfast, and a nice garden with pond. Children are made very welcome here.

COTSWOLD LODGE, *66a Banbury Road, Oxford OX2 6JP. Tel 01865 512121, Fax 01865 512490. Rooms: 50. Rates: singles from £105, doubles from £125. Bar, restaurant. All major credit cards accepted.*

This old Victorian building (not to be confused with the nearby Cotswold House) is located about half a mile from downtown Oxford in a peaceful conservation area. The 50 bedrooms have all been recently refurbished to a high standard, and there's a cozy bar with log fires in the winter. The Cotswold Lodge also boasts a fine restaurant, with a selection of English and French dishes.

LINTON LODGE HOTEL, *913 Linton Road, Oxford OX2 6UJ. Tel 01865 553461, Fax 01865 310365. Rooms: 70. Rates: singles from £95, doubles from £115. Bar, restaurant, library. All major credit cards accepted.*

The country-house style Linton Lodge is located in a tree-lined street just under a mile north of Oxford city center, so within easy reach of all the city's major attractions. The country house atmosphere is exacerbated by the presence of an oak-paneled library; meanwhile the bedrooms all boast a full range of facilities, including TV and hostess trays. The restaurant offers both a la carte and carvery-style menus.

WESTON MANOR HOTEL, *Weston-on-the-Green OX6 8QL. Tel 01869 350621, Fax 01869 350901. Rooms: 34. Rates: singles from £90, doubles from £115. Bar, restaurant, pool, gardens. All major credit cards accepted.*

This splendid historic country house is a little ways (six miles) out of Oxford, but within easy reach of the city's attractions; it's just a mile away from Junction 9 of the M40 motorway with connections to London and the north. The public rooms are beautifully furnished, and the bedrooms are large and comfortable. One of the highlights here are the extensive, peaceful grounds – ideal for getting away and reading – or for popping into the pool for a swim on those hot summer days. The elegant oak-paneled restaurant serves traditional and modern English dishes, so expect lots of fresh local game.

WELCOME LODGE, *Junction 8a, M40 motorway OX33 1LT. Tel 01865 877000, Fax 01865 877016. Rooms: 40. Rates: all rooms from £45. No restaurant. All major credit cards accepted.*

If you're not too bothered about being in central Oxford yet want to stay somewhere that's accessible to the main attractions, and inexpensive as well, then this is the place. The Welcome Lodge chain has established a reputation for clean, comfortable, modern accommodations, and this one is no exception. There's no restaurant as such, but there are a number of eating options very close by.

WHERE TO EAT

AL-SHAMI, *25 Walton Crescent, Oxford. Tel. 01865 310066. Open daily, noon to midnight. Main courses £6 to £12. Credit cards: MC, Visa.*

If you enjoy Lebanese food, this is the place to come. Situated on a quiet crescent, the restaurant's interior is light and airy. There's an extensive selection of hors d'oeuvres, including Armenian spiced sausages, or lamb's brain salad, while for main courses you can choose from a variety of grilled meats. Pastries and desserts are very sweet, as you'd expect, and Lebanese house wine is available from £9.99 a bottle.

CHERWELL BOATHOUSE, *50 Bardwell Road, Oxford. Tel. 01865 552746. Open Tuesday to Saturday, noon to 2pm, 6pm to 10:30pm; Sunday lunch only noon to 2pm. Set lunch from £12.50 (weekdays), £19.50 (weekends); set dinner £20.50. All major credit cards accepted.*

The Cherwell Boathouse is just that: a former boathouse located at one of Oxford's main punting departure points. Despite its location it's an unpretentious kind of place, and this is reflected in the menu. Most offerings are fairly straightforward but immensely satisfying, dishes like sea bass with clack linguine in a tomatoey dressing to chicken with mushroom sauce. The wine list is extensive, with house wines starting at £8.50.

LEMON TREE, *268 Woodstock Road. Tel. 01865 311936. Open daily noon to 11pm. Set lunch from £12.50. All major credit cards accepted.*

Light and spacious restaurant done out in bright colors, with indoor palms, overhead fans and wicker chairs that make it feel like you're in the south of France. The menu is international: French chickens, Scottish beef and Cornish lamb abound. There are lots of tarts and pies in the dessert line-up, and the wine list starts with house French at £9.95.

LE PETIT BLANC, *71-71 Walton Street, Oxford. Tel. 01865 510999. Open daily for breakfast 11am to noon, lunch noon to 2:45pm, afternoon tea 3:30pm to 6pm, dinner 6pm to 10:45pm. Set lunch and dinner from £12.50. All major credit cards accepted.*

This original offshoot of famous chef Raymond Blanc's *Manoir aux Quatre Saisons* offers mostly French food at digestible prices. It's all there – from Caesar Salad to terrine de porc persille to lemon tart, and there's a well-chosen wine list to boot, with the house wine coming in at £9.95.

RESTAURANT ELIZABETH, *82 St Aldate's Oxford. Tel. 01865 242230. Open Tuesday to Saturday 12:30pm to 2:30pm, 6:30pm to 11pm; Sunday 12:30pm to 2:30pm, 7pm to 10:30pm. Set lunch £16. All major credit cards accepted.*

Lots of escargots, bouillabaisse, duck a l'orange and filet de boeuf maison at this traditional French restaurant in the heart of Oxford. The service is efficient and there's a pleasant ambience.

IL CORTILE, *4/5 Bath Place, Oxford. Tel 01865 791812. Open Tuesday to Saturday 12:30pm to 2:15pm, 7pm to 9:30pm. Set lunch 314.50. All major credit cards accepted.*

As to be expected from the name, this restaurant offers good Italian fare at reasonable prices. What's good about it is that, although you will find traditional Italian favorites here, the chef has introduced a more creative streak, so alongside various pizza and pasta dishes you'll find such alternatives as grilled sea bass on a bed of crispy risotto. The ice cream is worth a taste, too; it's all home-made and delicious! The wine list, naturally, has a strong Italian twist.

GEE'S, *61 Banbury Road, Oxford. Tel 01865 553540. Open Monday to Saturday noon to 2:30pm, 6pm to 11pm, Sunday noon to 11pm. Set lunch £9.75. All major credit cards accepted.*

Gee's was a florist's shop in an earlier life, hence the conservatory, still laden with leafy plants, and filled with closely packed tables and bamboo chairs, giving the place a unique atmosphere that seems to appeal to tourists and locals alike. As for the food? Well, it's best described as modern European, so you can expect choices like mussels steamed with coriander and pan-fried duck breast with smoked aubergine (eggplant) and polenta. There's a good wine list, with prices starting at around £10 a bottle for the house.

SEEING THE SIGHTS

As far as exploring the city goes, start from **Magdalene** (pronounced Maudlin) **Bridge** from where you'll enjoy a lovely across the city. As you look toward **The High**, Oxford's main street, on your right is **Magdalene College**, founded as long ago as 1458. It has a particularly impressive main

quadrangle, enclosed by ancient, vaulted, wisteria-clad cloisters. Among those who have studied here are characters as diverse as Oscar Wilde, Cardinal Wolsey and Dudley Moore. *Open October to June daily 2pm to 6pm; July to September daily noon to 6pm. Admission adults £2, children £1. Tel. 01865 276000.* At the foot of the Bridge you can rent one of Oxford's famous **punts** – a shallow bottomed boat that's manoeuvred and driven by a long pole. Once you've mastered the technique, it's a wonderful way to spend a leisurely summer's afternoon – especially if you've brought a bottle of bubbly as well. Expect to pay around £10 per hour for the privilege, plus £25 deposit, *Tel. 01865 761586.*

Keep walking until you reach the **University Church of St. Mary the Virgin**, its huge 14th century tower dwarfing the buildings around. The church itself is interesting in its own right – but the best thing to do here is to climb the **tower**, which affords spectacular views of the whole city. If you're hungry, there's a super new cafeteria to the rear. Just behind the church is the 17th century **Radcliffe Camera**, with one of the largest domes in Britain. It was built in the 1730s in the Italian baroque style by James Gibbs. The camera contains part of the **Bodleian Library**, a two million strong collection of books dating back to 1602. You can visit part of the library on a tour only; otherwise the public can only see the **Divinity School**, with a lovely room where various exhibits are held. *Open April to December Monday to Friday 10am to 4pm; January to March Saturday only (call for times). Tours Monday to Friday at 10:30am, 11:30am, 2pm, 3pm; Saturday at 10:30am, 11:30am. Admission £3.50. Tel. 01865 27700; www.lib.ox.ac.uk/olis.*

THE GENTLE ART OF PUNTING

It's a lovely way to spend a warm summer's afternoon – gently punting along the Isis (Oxford's name for the Thames), stopping perhaps in the shade of a large tree to nibble some cucumber sandwiches or take a swig of champagne. A punt is a flat-bottomed boat that's both navigated and propelled by means of a long pole that's pushed against the river bed. Punting is much more difficult than it first looks – beginners inevitably get the pole stuck in the mud of the river bed, then must quickly decide to drag the boat back or risk being stuck at the top of it! You can hire a punt at Magadalene Bridge, or better still – especially if it's busy there – at the Cherwell Boat House near Wolfson College which is off the Banbury Road. You'll be asked for a deposit (likely around £30) and will be charged about £10 an hour for the boat.

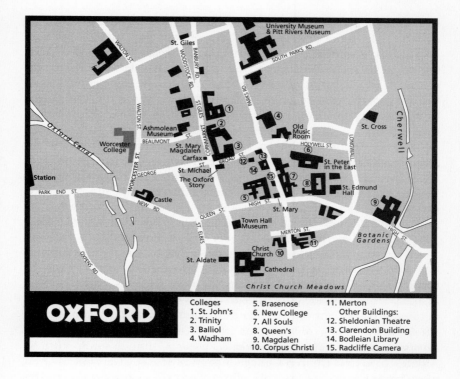

Colleges
1. St. John's
2. Trinity
3. Balliol
4. Wadham
5. Brasenose
6. New College
7. All Souls
8. Queen's
9. Magdalen
10. Corpus Christi
11. Merton
Other Buildings:
12. Sheldonian Theatre
13. Clarendon Building
14. Bodleian Library
15. Radcliffe Camera

OXFORD

Further back on Broad Street is the **Sheldonian Theatre**, where the university's graduation ceremonies are held. Designed by Christopher Wren, it was started in 1663. Inside there's an elaborately painted ceiling, while externally the vast stone pillars are topped by the heads of 18 Roman emperors, replacements of earlier heads that had been damaged by pollution. *Open mid-February to mid-November Monday to Saturday 10am to 12:30pm, 2pm to 4:30pm; mid-November to mid-February Monday to Saturday 10:30am to 3:30pm. Admission adults £1.50, children 5-16, £1. Tel. 01865 277299.*

Stay on Broad Street now for the **Oxford Story Exhibition**, which gives an overview with dioramas and reconstructions, including sounds and smells, of Oxford's 800-year history. Visitors tour the exhibit in small cars resembling medieval students' desks. *Open April to June, September and October daily 9:30am to 5pm; July and August daily 9am to 5:30pm; November to March Monday to Friday 10am to 4:30pm, Saturday and Sunday 10am to 5pm. Admission adults £5.50, children, seniors and students £4.50. Tel. 01865 790055.* On the right is **Balliol College**, dating back to 1263, and where, in 1555 and 1556, during the reign of Roman Catholic Queen Mary, Protestant church leaders, Archbishop of Canterbury Thomas Cranmer,

Bishops Latimer and Ridley were burned at the stake. You can still see the scorch marks in the wooden doors between the quadrangles. *Open daily 2pm to 5pm. Admission £1 (maximum eight in a group). Tel. 01865 277777.* Outside, a small cross on the road marks the spot of execution. Round the corner in St. Giles is **St. John's College**, founded in 1555, and with two Oxford superlatives – stunningly beautiful gardens, and the music made by its chapel choir – on par with the choir of King's College Cambridge. *Open daily 1pm to 5pm. Admission free. Tel. 01865 277300.*

Almost opposite, with an entrance on Beaumont Street, is the **Ashmolean Museum**, the oldest public museum in Britain, with a vast collection of artifacts from around the world, many brought back to Oxford after archaeological excavations conducted by the university. You can see Egyptian mummies, drawings by Michelangelo, and a host of important paintings. *Open Tuesday to Saturday 10am to 5pm, Sunday 2pm to 5pm. Admission free. Tel. 01865 278000; www.ashmol.ox.ac.uk.*

Head south from the Ashmolean down **Cornmarket**, Oxford's modern shopping drag, to **Carfax**, where four roads converge. Here is the **Carfax Tower** originally part of **St. Martin's Church**, where William Shakespeare was made godfather to baby William Davenant, who later became a playwright himself. You can climb the tower. *Open April to October daily 10am to 5:30pm; November to March daily 10am to 3:30pm. Admission adults £1.20, children 60p. No phone.* Continue south down St. Aldate's to **Christ Church College**, begun in 1525 by Cardinal Wolsey, when it was known as Cardinal College. The College possesses Oxford's largest quadrangle, and **Tom Tower** houses **Great Tom**, the 18,000-pound bell that rings every night at 9:05, marking the closure of the college gates. Among Christ College's other attractions are the 16th century **Great Hall**, with some fine paintings by artists such as Thomas Gainsborough and Joshua Reynolds. In the College's Canterbury Quadrangle, the **Christ Church Picture Gallery** features works by Veronese, Tintoretto and Van Dyck, as well as drawings by Michelangelo and Da Vinci. *Open year-round Monday to Saturday 9am to 6pm, Sunday 11:30pm to 6pm. Admission adults £3, seniors, students, children £2. Tel. 276150.*

The college's chapel also doubles up as the **Cathedral** for the Anglican Diocese of Oxford. It was begun in the twelfth century, and among its principle features are the great Norman **pillars** and the fifteenth century **fan vaulting** in the choir. Near the Lady Chapel you can see the shrine of **St. Frideswide**, a Saxon princess to whom the original priory's foundation is attributed.

South of the College, idyllic **Christ Church Meadow** stretches along the side of the Thames – wonderful for an early evening walk.

Other Museums Worth Visiting
MUSEUM OF THE HISTORY OF SCIENCE, *Broad Street. Open Tuesday to Saturday noon to 4pm. Admission free. Tel. 01865 277280; www.mhs.ox.ac.uk.*

This seventeenth century building that was the original home of the Ashmolean Museum now houses a motley collection of scientific knick-knacks, including clocks, microscopes, and even Einstein's blackboard.

PITT RIVERS MUSEUM, *Parks Road. Open Monday to Saturday 1pm to 4:30pm. Admission free. Tel. 01865 270927; www.prm.ox.ac.uk.*

A fascinating anthropological museum with all kinds of odds and ends testifying to the intricate weave that is humankind. There are voodo dolls, peace pipes, shrunken heads – in fact you could almost substitute a visit to the Chamber of Horrors with this.

UNIVERSITY MUSEUM, *Parks Road. Open daily noon to 5pm. Admission free. Tel. 01865 272950.*

This is Oxford's natural history museum with a vast collection of various stuffed (and unstuffed) animals, dinosaurs, fossils and the like. Kids will love it.

NIGHTLIFE & ENTERTAINMENT

There are dozens of lively pubs in Oxford. Among them, try the **Bullingdon Arms**, *162 Cowley Road*, where there's live jazz on Wednesday nights, and the **Head of the River**, *by Folly Bridge*.

Meanwhile, if it's theater you want, the **Oxford Playhouse**, *Beaumont Street, Tel. 01865 798600*, stages a mixture of serious plays and music, while the **Old Fire Station**, *George Street, Tel. 01865 794490*, is the place for mostly classical drama.

EXCURSIONS & DAY TRIPS

A day or two in Oxford wouldn't be complete without a visit to **Blenheim Palace**, about eight miles from Oxford just off the A44. The Palace's roots go back to 1704, when the Duke of Marlborough (Sir John Churchill) defeated the French at the Battle of Blenheim. The grateful **Queen Anne** rewarded him with the cash to build this massive pile, designed by eminent architect Sir John Vanbrugh on over 2,100 acres of land, which would be landscaped by none other than Capability Brown. The result was this magnificent palace, as opulent and luxurious as any in the world.

Outside, see the vast columns and upturned obelisks, and inside, you can't fail to go weak at the knees at the lavishness of the **Red Room**, where portraits of various dukes by eminent painters like Sir Joshua Reynolds and John Stringer Sargent decorate the walls. You'll be staggered at the huge, intricately carved silverwork and the priceless antique furniture. Some will go even weaker at the knees when they see the small room where Winston Churchill was born in 1874.

The grounds are worthy of a visit in their own right, especially at dusk when herds of sheep are let loose, natural mowers for the vast lawns. In the grounds are various family attractions, too – a miniature railroad, a butterfly house, play areas, and a lake where you can take a boat trip or even fish. If the kids are wearing you down, you can always put them in the Marlborough Maze. *House open mid-March to mid-October daily 10:30am to 5:30pm. Park open daily 9am to 5pm. Admission adults £8.50, children 5-15 £4.50, seniors £6.50. Tel. 01993 811325.* You may also want to make the pilgrimage two miles south of Woodstock on the A4095 to the village of Bladon, in whose small peaceful churchyard **Sir Winston Churchill** is buried in a simple, unassuming grave.

Cotswold Roaming, *Tel. 01865 250640*, offers guided bus tours to various destinations around Oxford, including Blenheim Palace and the Cotswolds.

PRACTICAL INFORMATION

The city is well served with post offices and banks, the majority of which are located in the Cornmarket area, and there's an **American Express** office at *5, Queen Street, Tel. 01865 240441*.

Most of the major **car rental** companies have branches in Oxford, including **Hertz**, *Woodstock Road, Tel. 01865 319972*.

Oxford's main **tourism office** is located at *The Old School, Gloucester Green, Oxford OX1 2DA, Tel. 01865 726871*. The city runs a website at *www.oxford.gov.uk* with details of many of the city's visitor attractions.

BIRMINGHAM

England's second largest city, **Birmingham** – known as "Brum" – was once, like Stratford, an unexceptional market town, until the Industrial Revolution – and in particular the arrival of canals – caused massive expansion. Today, with a population of around one million, multi-ethnic Birmingham, with its neighbor Wolverhampton, sprawls across a hundred square miles of territory to the west of Coventry.

Sneered at by the English (the local accent was dubbed the least loved of all the regional accents), Birmingham has undergone a radical transformation in recent years, thanks to a progressive policy by the city council. Many of the fine Victorian buildings in the city center have been restored, new pedestrian-only zones established, and a host of new buildings built. One of the best is the excellent **Symphony Hall**, home of the world-famous **Birmingham Symphony Orchestra**, now accompanies the ugly '60s monstrosities – like the hideous Bull Ring Shopping Centre and the vast, upturned pyramid-shaped library – in the heart of Brum. Even the city's arts scene has blossomed: the long-established repertory company, the **Birmingham Rep**, has a reputation as being one of the best companies in the nation, and the city managed to entice **Sadler's Wells Royal Ballet** out of London to a new base.

ARRIVALS & DEPARTURES

By Car

Birmingham is in many ways the hub of the British motorway network. The M40 from London takes you there direct. Getting around Birmingham takes a bit of extra concentration, with the various ring roads.

By Bus

National Express buses leave London's Victoria Bus Station at frequent intervals throughout the day, arriving at Birmingham's Digbeth Bus Station, just south of the city center – not the most salubrious of introductions to the city. The journey takes about three hours.

By Train

Birmingham is a hub for Britain's rail network too. Thirty trains a day leave London's Euston station for the city's massive New Street Station, a journey which takes around one hour and 40 minutes. Trains from Stratford or Warwick arrive at Snow Hill and Moor Street Stations respectively, just minutes from downtown.

ORIENTATION

Downtown Birmingham is surrounded by the **Inner Ring Road**. The vast majority of the places of interest lie within this area. The city's main shopping street, **Corporation Street**, meets the other main drag, **New Street** just by the main entrance to the vast Pallisades shopping center.

GETTING AROUND TOWN

For a city of its size, Birmingham is amazingly compact, and most of the sites listed here can easily be reached on foot. A one-day Daytripper ticket on the local buses and trains costs just £3.70. *For information about rail and bus services in and around Birmingham, call 0121 200 2700.*

WHERE TO STAY

NOVOTEL, *70 Broad Street, Birmingham B1 2HT. Tel. 0121 643 200, Fax 0121 643 9796. Rooms: 98. Rates single from £170, double from £195. Restaurants, air conditioning, indoor pool and leisure suite, beauty salon, parking. All major credit cards accepted.*

Modern, purpose-built hotel just a couple of minutes' walk from the Symphony Hall and five minutes from other downtown attractions, including the City Museum and Art Gallery. The rooms are spacious and comfortable, with TV, tea- and coffee-making facilities. The Garden Brasserie has established a good reputation locally or you can eat in the Bar.

THE PLOUGH AND HARROW, *135 Hagley Road, Birmingham. Tel. 0212 454 4111, Fax 0121 454 1868. Rooms 44. Rates: single from £105, doubles from £115. Singles off-peak £55, double off-peak £75. Restaurant, parking. All major credit cards accepted.*

Long established ivy-clad, characterful hotel a mile west of the city center in the salubrious suburb of Edgbaston. The bedrooms come in a variety of shapes and sizes, but all are tastefully decorated and comfortable, with TVs and tea- and coffee-making facilities. The restaurant has had an excellent reputation for many years.

TRAVELODGE, *230 Broad Street, Birmingham B15 1AY. Tel. 0121 644 5266. Rooms: 136. Rates: doubles from £49.95. No restaurant. Credit cards: MC, Visa.*

Part of a large chain of inexpensive but well-equipped and comfortable hotels, the Travelodge is exceptional value given its proximity to central Birmingham, about a fifteen minute walk away. Broad Street is full of restaurants, many offering ethnic cuisine. Naturally the furnishings are nothing to write home about, but at this rate, who cares? A number of family rooms are available, and a number of rooms are set aside for people with disabilities.

SWALLOW HOTEL, *12 Hagley Road, Birmingham B16 8SJ. Tel 0121 452 1144, Fax 0121 456 3442. Rooms: 98. Rates: singles from £130, doubles from £150. Two restaurants, bar, library, indoor pool, gym, solarium. All major credit cards accepted.*

This sumptuous hotel, located at one of Birmingham's busiest and less salubrious traffic roundabouts, was once a red brick office block, and now makes up for its grim surroundings with a plush, luxurious interior that includes marble floors, mirrors and wood paneling. The service is impeccable, and the bedrooms, whose decor is based on a floral theme, boast double-glazed windows which keep out the sound of the traffic below. The hotel boasts two fine restaurants: the award-winning Sir Edward Elgar, with grand piano and its own wine cellar, and Langtry's, more informal but equally good.

JARVIS PENNS HALL HOTEL & COUNTRY CLUB, *Penns Lane, Walmley, Sutton Coldfield B76 1LH. Tel 0121 351 3111, Fax 0121 313 1297. Rooms: 136. Rates: singles from £49.50, doubles from £90. Bar, restaurant, health club, indoor pool.*

Located about six miles east of central Birmingham in the leafy town of Sutton Coldfield, the Jarvis Hall is a modern low-rise establishment overlooking a lake in its own extensive grounds. The bedrooms are well equipped and comfortable, many with balconies overlooking the water. There's an excellent health club, which includes an indoor heated pool and solarium. The restaurant serves both a la carte and table d'hote menus. In all, this hotel represents one of the best deals in the area.

LYNDHURST HOTEL, *135 Kingsbury Road, Erdington, Birmingham B24 8QT. Tel 0121 373 5695, Fax 0121 5697. Rooms: 14. Rates: singles from £35, doubles from £49. Restaurant. All major credit cards accepted.*

There may not be much to differentiate the Lyndhurst from many of the other homes in this suburb of Birmingham, but inside it's a different story: the 14 bedrooms are all pleasantly furnished with facilities that include TVs and hostess trays. There's a very comfortable lounge and a restaurant, which serves English-style home cooked meals at very reasonable prices. The hotel is just half a mile from the junction of the M6 motorway, which means you have easy access to many places of interest in the region, as well as downtown Birmingham itself.

WHERE TO EAT

Despite its size, Birmingham long had a reputation for bland, insipid restaurants – except where ethnic cuisine was involved. Things have changed a lot in the last fifteen years, and the city's collective taste buds are coming to life. Many of the new establishments are located along Broad Street, and in the area round Hurst Street and Thorpe Street.

CHUNG YING GARDEN, *17 Thorpe Street, Birmingham B5 4AT. Tel. 0121 666 6622. Open daily noon to 11:30pm (10:30pm Sunday). Set dinner £14 to £20. All major credit cards accepted.*

One of Birmingham's best Chinese restaurants (and there are a lot of them!) the Chung Ying is a vast place, with seats for 250, and as many choices on the menu, so eating here is an experience in its own right. The cuisine is essentially Cantonese, so you can expect such delicacies as goose web with mushroom casserole, and ox tripe with pickled cabbage. The various fish dishes – like fried eel – may not be for the squeamish, but then I'm not squeamish.

LEFTBANK, *79 Broad Street, Birmingham B15 1AH. Tel. 0121 643 4464. Open Monday to Friday, lunch noon to 2pm, Monday to Saturday dinner 7pm to 10pm. Set lunch around £13. All major credit cards accepted.*

In my day, Broad Street was a gloomy thoroughfare full of boarded-up shops and bric-a-brac stores. Today it's home to a large number of excellent restaurants, among which Leftbank must be numbered among the best. Converted from an old bank, Leftbank (get the name?) has opulent decor and wafts with the sound of jazz as well as the smell of dishes like monkfish with a galette of eggplant and tomato tooped by silver smelts (known as sprats here) with an anchovy puree.

MAHARAJA, *23-25 Hurst Street, Birmingham B5 4AS. Tel. 0121 622 2641. Open Monday to Saturday noon to 2pm, 6pm to 11pm. Set lunch and dinner £12.50. All major credit cards accepted.*

You can't go to Birmingham without sampling one of the city's myriad Indian restaurants, and this is as good as any. Long established, and still tremendously popular, the Maharaja excels in authentic North Indian cooking, with dishes like tandoori mackerel and chicken samarkand regularly featuring among the daily specials. Best of all, it's extremely good value – value which thankfully extends to the wine list.

RESTAURANT GILMORE, *27 Warstone Lane, Hockley, Birmingham. Tel 0121 233 3655. Open Tuesday to Saturday noon to 2pm, 7pm to 9:30pm (closed for Saturday lunch). Set dinner from £21.50. All major credit cards accepted.*

Birmingham's jewelery quarter is not the most elegant collection of buildings – but it's amazing what you can do with an interior. Such is the case with this new restaurant, converted from an industrial building with strong colors and a relaxed, friendly ambience. The food's pretty good, too; dishes like seared tuna and foie gras with charred red onions, traditional desserts like bread and butter pudding and a creditable wine list with house red coming in at £10.50 a bottle. It's a bit of a trek from downtown Brum, but well worth it.

HYATT REGENCY HOTEL, *2 Bridge Street, Birmingham. Tel 0121 643 1234. Open Monday to Saturday noon to 2pm, 7pm to 9:45pm (closed for lunch Saturday). Set lunch £16.50, set dinner £19.50. All major credit cards accepted.*

Downtown Birmingham has undergone a bit of a renaissance over the past ten years, and this restaurant is a sumptuous symptom of it. Located in a quarter that ten years ago was grimy and run down, the building of the new Convention Centre (to which the Hyatt is linked) and Symphony Hall has led to a burgeoning of fine restaurants around here, including this one, where fresh British ingredients – Cotswold lamb, Cornish crab and the like – are given a creative twist by the chef. The dessert trolley is equally creative and there's a well-chosen wine list, where house starts at £10.95 a bottle.

SEEING THE SIGHTS

The city's most interesting buildings are located within a stone's throw of optimistically named Paradise Circus, an oval-shaped large traffic circle, over part of which the ugly concrete **Central Library** – one of Europe's largest, and notable for a large collection of Shakespeare-related material – has been built. Just to the west of here is the **Repertory Theatre** and **Symphony Hall**, built in 1990. A bit further down Broad Street is the unappealingly named **Gas Street Basin**. It definitely was an unappealing kind of place, a canal basin, until recently when many of the old buildings around it were restored, along with canal paths and lighting, so that it has become a fashionable place for restaurants and bars. Just east of the Library in Victoria Square is the **Town Hall**, a colonnaded concert hall completed in 1846 with a design based on the Roman temple in Nimes, France.

Just behind the fine Victorian Council House, in Chamberlain Square, is the **City Art Gallery and Museum**, the largest regional museum in England, with lots of pre-Raphaelite works, including pieces by Holman Hunt, Rosetti, and most famous of all, Burne-Jones. The fine collection of 18th to 21st century British art includes watercolors by Constable. The museum also houses a fine **Industrial Gallery**, relating Birmingham's history as one of Britain's major manufacturing centers, and galleries devoted to the silver and jewelry manufacture, for which the city is world famous, more local history displays, a natural history section, and a delightful Edwardian **tea room**, one of the best places in the city for a snack or light lunch. *Open Monday to Thursday and Saturday 10am to 5pm, Friday 10:30am to 5pm, Sunday 12:30pm to 5pm. No charge, but donations welcome. Tel. 0121 303 2834; www.birmingham.gov.uk.*

Take Colmore Row off Victoria Square to **St. Philip's Anglican Cathedral** – tiny by cathedral standards, but a fine example of English baroque architecture, and set in an attractive grassy square. The church, which became a cathedral in 1905, contains some fine stained glass by Burne-Jones, who was born and bred locally. The labyrinth of streets south of here leads to **Corporation Street**, Birmingham's main shopping drag, home to Rackham's, England's largest provincial department store, and to the High Street, with a host of chain stores. Just below the circular office block, known as the Rotunda, is The Pallisades, a vast indoor shopping mall, through which you cab gain access to **St. Martin's-in-the-Bull Ring**, Birmingham's parish church, a largely Victorian replacement of a much older building that once graced the site.

If you've bucks to spare, you won't want to miss the **Jewellery Quarter**, just north of the city center and established in the mid-1700s. There are more than 500 jewelry-related businesses here, many of which are open to visitors, and where you can often pick up bargains. If you decide to explore this area, don't miss the engrossing **Museum of the Jewellery Quarter**, 75-79 Vyse Street, housed in a redundant factory. Because much of the factory's original machinery was left intact, the museum has been able to effectively recreate the atmosphere of a jewelry production line. There's also a section devoted to the history of jewelry making in the city. *Open Monday to Friday, 10am to 4pm, Saturday 11am to 5pm (closed Sunday). Admission adults £2.50, seniors and students £2. Tel. 0121 554 3598.* Finally, while you're in the Jewellery Quarter, take a peek at **St. Paul's Church**, a handsome Georgian structure in St Paul's Square.

About 2 1/2 miles west of the city center, along leafy Bristol Road, are the Italianate red brick buildings of **Birmingham University**, founded in 1901 by city father Joseph Chamberlain, who is commemorated by the **Chamberlain Tower**, a lanky campanile tower that at 325 feet is almost as high as Big Ben. The University's own art gallery, the **Barber Institute** on the eastern side of the campus close to the Bristol Road, is home to a wonderful collection of European masters including works by Rubens, Rembrandt, Monet, Gauguin, Van Gogh and Bartolome Esteban Murillo's masterpiece, *The Marriage Feast at Cana. Open Monday to Saturday 10am to 5pm, Sunday 2pm to 5pm. Admission free. Tel. 0121 414 7333; www.barber.org.uk.*

NIGHTLIFE & ENTERTAINMENT

Birmingham has a number of theaters: the **Birmingham Rep** (see above) for serious plays; the **Alexandra Theater**, *Tel. 0121 643 1231,* for mainstream musical and drama productions; and the **Hippodrome**, *Tel. 0121 622 7486,* home of the Royal Ballet. The Birmingham Symphony

Orchestra plays at the **Symphony Hall**, *Tel. 0121 212 3333*, major rock and pop concerts are held outside the city center at the **National Exhibition Center**, *Tel. 0121 780 4133*.

In addition to the theaters, there are literally hundreds of **pubs** and **clubs**, among them the **Institute and Dance Factory**, *Digbeth High Street, Tel. 0121 643 7788*, with live music, and the **Glee Club**, *Hurst Street, Tel. 0121 693 2248*, for stand-up comedy.

PRACTICAL INFORMATION

The city is a major **banking** center, so changing your money will be no problem. Birmingham maintains several **tourist offices**, *www.birmingham.gov.uk*, the most central of which are located at:
• *2, City Arcade, just off New Street, Tel. 0121 643 2514*
• *Central Library, Chamberlain Square, Tel. 0121 236 5622*

WORCESTER

Just under 30 miles south west of Birmingham, just off the M5 and on the banks of the River Severn, is the ancient city of **Worcester** (pronounced "Wooster"), whose magnificently graceful **cathedral** dominates the jumble of ancient and medieval buildings – many of them half-timbered – below. In addition to the cathedral, Worcester is famous for the high quality bone china, known as **Royal Worcester**, which is manufactured here, and as being the location for one of the most decisive battles of the English Civil War. It was the **Battle of Worcester** in 1651 that resulted in the future King Charles II's exile to France.

ARRIVALS & DEPARTURES

By Car

From London take the M40 towards Birmingham. At the junction with the M42, take the M42 west as far as the M5 south. For Worcester, take junction 6.

By Bus

National Express buses leave for Worcester from London's Victoria Bus Station. The journey time is about 3 1/2 hours. *Call 0990 808080 for bus information.*

By Train

The journey to Worcester from London's Paddington Station takes almost 2 1/2 hours. *For information call 0345 484950.*

GETTING AROUND TOWN

Worcester is another city that's easily explorable on foot. You might consider taking a river cruise with **Bickerlines**, *Tel. 01905 670679.*

WHERE TO STAY

BURGAGE HOUSE, *College Precincts, Worcester WR1 2LG. Tel. 01905 25396, Fax 01905 25396. Rooms: 4. Rates: singles from £30, doubles from £48. No credit cards.*

This no-smoking guest house located in a beautiful Georgian townhouse adjacent to Worcester Cathedral is a real gem. The building retains many original features, including an elegant stone staircase and original carving. The bedrooms are comfortable, with tea- and coffee-making facilities and TV. There's a lovely dining room where you can enjoy a full English breakfast and dinner, if required.

THE GIFFORD HOTEL, *High Street, Worcester WR1 2QR. Tel. 01906 726262, Fax 01906 723458. Rooms: 103. Rates: singles from £75, doubles from £75. Restaurants, bars, parking. All major credit cards accepted.*

Popular, modern city center hotel that's convenient for all of Worcester's attractions. The rooms vary in size, but all come equipped with the standard TV and tea- and coffee-making facilities. A number of the hotel's larger rooms are suitable for families.

STAR HOTEL, *Foregate Street, Worcester WR1 1EA. Tel 01905 24308, Fax 01905 23440. Rooms: 45. Rates: singles from £65, doubles from £75. Bar, restaurant. Credit cards: MC, Visa.*

The Star is located right in the center of historic Worcester, adjacent to the Foregate train station and within easy walking distance of the cathedral and the city's other main attractions, including the shopping center and Royal Worcester Porcelain. Built in the 16th century, it has been extensively refurbished to a high standard, with large, comfortable rooms and a fine restaurant, where the emphasis is on British cuisine.

WHERE TO EAT

BROWN'S, *24 Quay Street, Worcester WR1 2JJ. Tel. 01905 25768. Open Tuesday to Friday and Sun for lunch 12:30pm to 1:45pm; Tuesday to Saturday for dinner 7:30pm to 9:45pm. Set lunch £18.50, set dinner £34.50. All major credit cards accepted.*

This lovely restaurant housed in an old mill overlooking the River Severn has become one of Worcester's most popular eating places. The ambience is pleasant enough; tables bedecked with pink tablecloths and fresh flowers, cream-painted brick walls and fresh flowers at every table. The food is Anglo-French – old favorites such as coq au vin, deviled kidneys and the like rub shoulders with more adventurous dishes like crab ravioli in crab bisque. The helpful but unfussy staff are all clad in aprons, giving the whole place an air of relaxed efficiency.

KING'S RESTAURANT, *Fownes Hotel, City walls Road, Worcester. Tel 01905 613151. Open daily 12:30pm to 2:30pm, 7pm to 9:30pm (no lunch Saturday). Set meals around £16. All major credit cards accepted.*

The King's Restaurant is part of the luxury Fownes Hotel, which was converted into a hotel from a glove factory during Victorian times. The fairly traditional restaurant serves classic English cuisine as well as a range of more exotic dishes, and served on Royal Worcester porcelain. There's a wide range of desserts, including traditional stodgy ones so beloved by the English, and a comprehensive wine list.

KING CHARLES II RESTAURANT, *29 New Street, Worcester. Tel 01905 22449. Open Monday to Saturday noon to 2pm, 6:30pm to 9:30pm. Set meals from £15. All major credit cards accepted.*

This wonderful half-timbered house simply oozes history. In fact it's the house where King Charles II went into hiding after the Battle of Worcester. The restaurant is formal – with silver service – but the atmosphere is relaxed and friendly. The menu is a mixture of British, French and Italian, as well as a choice of fish and vegetarian options.

SEEING THE SIGHTS

Worcester Cathedral, with its massive **central tower**, was founded in 680, though the current building dates predominantly from the twelfth to fourteenth centuries, with some typically over-elaborate Victorian restoration in places. The vast **crypt**, the largest in the country, is older however, dating from Norman times, as is the **Chapter House**. In the main body of the church, the **nave** is of interest for the change in style from the rounded Norman arches to the pointed early English ones, while the pillars are decorated with bunches of fruit, some beautifully carved, some only adequately so – the original stonemasons fell prey to the Black Death, leaving the work to their apprentices.

Another highlight of the cathedral is the tomb of the much despised "bad" **King John**, who was buried here in 1216. In keeping with his megelomanic mind, John left instructions that he should be buried between the tombs of **Saint Wulstan** and **Saint Oswald** – both of which were later removed anyway. Don't miss **Prince Arthur's Chantry**, built in 1504, a memorial built by Henry VII for his son Arthur. Arthur died on his honeymoon to Catherine of Aragon, meaning that the throne (and the girl) would pass to his younger brother Henry, who would become the notorious King Henry VIII.

The cathedral is the setting every three years of the **Three Choirs Festival**, arguably the best choral festival in the world. The Worcester

Choir, along with counterparts from Hereford and Gloucester, sing a wide range of traditional and modern pieces, including specially commissioned work.

While in Worcester, don't miss the **Royal Worcester Porcelain Factory** on Severn Street, where you can take a factory tour and see how bone china materials are made – and browse through the seconds. *Open Monday to Saturday 9am to 5pm, Sunday 11am to 5pm. Admission for tours: £5 (no children under 11 allowed on tours. Tours depart daily at 10:30am, 11:30am, 1:30pm, 2:30pm. Tel. 01905 611002.* Also here is the **Dyson Perrins Museum**, which contains a large collection of some rare Worcester pieces from 1751, when the factory was founded, to the present day. *Open Monday to Friday 9:30am to 5pm, Saturday 10am to 5pm. Admission £3.50.* Close by, on Sidbury, is the **Commandery**, a hodgepodge of fifteenth century half-timbered buildings that was Charles II's headquarters before the battle of Worcester in 1651. The interior, with its fine wood paneling, has a room with wall paintings going back as far as 1500, while the beamed Great Hall is the venue for a lively audio-visual presentation about the Civil War. *Open Monday to Saturday 10am to 5pm, Sunday 1:30pm to 5:30pm. Admission adults £3.70, children £2.60. Tel. 01905 361821.*

Friar Street is notable for some fine Elizabethan and Tudor buildings, among them the **Tudor House Museum of Local Life**, which offers a kaleidoscope of city life through World War II, as well as reconstructions of Victorian and Edwardian shops, offices and homes. *Open Monday to Wednesday, Friday and Saturday 10:30am to 5pm. Tel. 01905 722349.* The town's own **Museum and Art Gallery**, in the Tything, contains exhibits relating to the great River Severn and other items of local interest. There is an art gallery that's rather dominated by Victorian works, but redeemed by some first-rate touring exhibitions that come here. *Open Monday to Wednesday and Friday 9:30am to 6pm, Saturday 9:30am to 5pm. Admission free. Tel. 01905 25371.*

EXCURSIONS & DAY TRIPS

Just a few miles southwest of the city are the **Malvern Hills**, the small chain of gentle hills that rise to around 1,000 feet and were the inspiration for much of the composer **Edward Elgar's** work (see sidebar below). If you're a music buff, stop at the village of Lower Broadheath on the B4204 to see the **Elgar Birthplace Museum**, where you can visit the cottage in which the composer of the *Enigma Variations* was born. On display are photographs, music scores, and several letters. *Open May to September daily except Wednesday 10:30am to 6pm; October to mid-January and mid-February to April 1:30pm to 4:30pm.*

SIR EDGAR ELGAR, 1857-1934

*One of England's greatest-ever musicians, **Sir Edward Elgar** was largely self-taught. As a young boy he learned the ropes singing in the choir where his father was organist and browsing the scores in the Worcester music shop that his father owned. Later on, he taught himself to play the violin. Because of his humble roots and lack of formal musical training, Elgar always felt that the musical establishment was stacked against him, and indeed many of his early works were barely recognized beyond the locality.*

*It was only in 1899 that his musical reputation was assured when Richard Strauss acclaimed Elgar's **Enigma Variations** as a masterpiece. Future works included **The Dream of Gerontius**, written in 1900, and the **Pomp and Circumstance Marches**, written between 1901 and 1930 and still as popular as ever, especially at the atmospheric Last Night of the Proms held annually at London's Royal Albert Hall, which reaches its climax when the patriotic piece 'Rule Britannia' is sung by one of the great divas of the day accompanied by masses of music fans from Britain and around the world.*

Head back towards Worcester on the A44, then take the A4103 and the B4503 to **Great Malvern**, a spa town that was much favored by the Victorians. The spa water – known as Malvern Water – is bottled here and distributed all over the world – especially to British expat communities. There's something of an explanation of the curing properties of Malvern's water at the town's **Museum**, located in the Abbey gateway on Abbey Road. *Open Easter to October daily except Wednesday, 10:30am to 5pm. Admission 50p.* Malvern's main attraction, however, is its fine **Priory Church**, which dominates the hilly streets in the center of town. The Priory's origins are Norman, but it was much altered during the Perpendicular period. Of particular interest is the **stained glass**, particularly the window in the north transept, dating from the fifteenth century and a masterpiece.

In May, the town gets packed for the **Malvern Festival**, with its bifocal emphasis on music and drama. Originally devoted to the works of Edward Elgar and George Bernard Shaw, today the Festival offers a wide variety of contemporary music and drama, while the acclaimed Malvern Fringe Festival specializes in off-beat productions. For more information about the Festival, contact the **Malvern Tourist Office** in the Winter Gardens Complex on Grange Road, *Tel. 01684 892289.*

PRACTICAL INFORMATION

Worcester is home to the main offices of the **Heart of England Tourist Board**, *Woodside, Larkhill, Worcester WR5 2EF, Tel. 01905 763436*. The city has its own tourist office at *The Guildhall, High Street, Tel. 01905 726311*. The city website is located at *www.worcester.gov.uk.*

HEREFORD

Approximately thirty miles southwest of Worcester is the lovely and bustling county town of **Hereford**, in a pleasant setting on the **River Wye**. With evidence of Iron Age, Celtic and Roman settlements, it's clear that Hereford has been an important city for centuries. Later on, it became the capital of the ancient Anglo-Saxon kingdom of **Mercia** Today it's the hub of a rich agricultural area that produces much of the country's fruit, as well as giving birth to one of the best-known breeds of cattle, the white-faced Hereford.

Being fairly isolated, Hereford has managed to escape the ravages of the Industrial Revolution and remains a a fascinating place with a host of medieval buildings, of which the **cathedral** is by far the most impressive and the focus of most visitors' attention.

ARRIVALS & DEPARTURES

By Car

Hereford is 25 miles west of Worcester on the A4103.

By Bus

National Express, *Tel. 0990 808080*, offers three services a day from Victoria, while the local service from Worcester to Hereford is operated by **Midland Red West**, *Tel. 0345 125436* – a journey which takes around 1 1/2 hours.

By Train

There's a regular service from Hereford to London, via Worcester, *Tel. 0134 4849500*. The journey to Worcester takes around an hour, to London, about three hours.

GETTING AROUND

Explore the city on foot, or else rent a bike from **Coombes**, *94 Widemarsh Street, Tel. 01432 354373*.

WHERE TO STAY

THE MERTON HOTEL, *28 Commercial Road, Hereford HR1 2BD. Tel. 01432 265925, Fax 01432 354983. Rooms: 19 Rates: singles from £35, doubles from £45. Restaurant, leisure suite, shooting & fishing (by arrangement), parking. All major credit cards accepted.*

Privately-owned, good value hotel close to Hereford's bus station and just a block from the train staion. Although an old building, the rooms have been extensively modernized and are well-equipped; two of them have four-poster beds. The hotel also benefits from a pleasant restaurant area and a lounge bar where bar meals can be taken.

OAKLANDS, *Cross Collar, Llandinabo, Much Birch, Hereford HR2 8JA. Tel. 01981 540500. Rooms: 3. Rates: single from £30, double from £40. No credit cards accepted.*

Former Victorian staging post now serving as a small but very comfortable guest house, with pretty guest rooms and a pleasant dining room. Situated about half-way between Hereford and Ross-on-Wye, it's a lovely, peaceful place to escape the hurly-burly, yet within easy reach of Hereford.

THE GREEN DRAGON, *Broad Street, Hereford HR4 9BG. Tel 01432 272506, Fax 01432 352139. Rooms: 87. Rates: singles from £70, doubles from £80. Two bars, lounge, restaurant. All major credit cards accepted.*

This large city center hotel is run by the Trusthouse Forte group. It's convenient to all the major attractions of Hereford, including the Cathedral and the River Wye. Each of the rooms comes with a full range of facilities – TV and tea- and coffee-making facilities – and there is a large comfortable lounge and two bars.

WHERE TO EAT

ANCIENT CAMP INN, *Ruckhall, near Eaton Bishop, Hereford HR2 9QX. Tel. 01981 250449. Open Tuesday to Saturday for lunch and dinner. Lunch only Sundays. Set price dinner: £22.50. Credit cards: MC, Visa. From Hereford, take the A465, turn right to Belmont. The Inn is about 3 1/2 miles along the road.*

Lovely country riverside restaurant built in the grounds of an old fort high above the River Wye. The premises started life as a shop, then were used as a forge, then a cider house. With its original flagstone floors, oak beams and old cider tables, this is a charming place, relying on fresh local produce. The cooking is traditional English, with such mouth-watering options as loin of Gloucestershire Old Spot pork roasted with honey and accompanied by a sage and garlic sauce, and warm sticky lime pudding for dessert.

CAFE AT ALL SAINTS, *High Street, Hereford. Tel 01432 370415. Open Monday to Saturday noon to 2:30pm (take-outs until 5:30pm). No credit cards.* This wonderful unpretentious cafe located in a lovely medieval (working) church uses fresh and organic produce as the base for all its food. You can choose from items as simple as a sandwich to hot meals, such as goats' cheese gratin. The mouth-watering desserts include an excellent home made pecan pie. Drinks range from locally produced apple juice to beer and a selection of wines. As it opens for take-aways (take-outs) from 8:30am, it's a great place to put together a really special picnic lunch.

SEEING THE SIGHTS

While lacking the graciousness of many other cathedrals, **Hereford Cathedral** does, however have a unique charm. Built originally by the Normans, it is crowned by a rather squat red sandstone tower that was added in the fourteenth century, competing with the Norman west tower which collapsed in 1786, taking much of the nave with it. Despite the survival of a number of Norman pillars and arches at the east end of the building, subsequent restoration work has never quite succeeded in giving the cathedral a sense of unity. However, there's still a lot of interest here, including the **Bishop's throne**, dating from the fourteenth century; intricately carved **misericords** in the choir; and the fine, graceful **north transept**, constructed in the thirteenth century in the early English style.

On the opposite side of the building, the Norman **south transept** contains a sixteenth century *Adoration of the Magi*, and a **fireplace**, an extremely rare feature in an English church. Don't miss the amazingly detailed **Mappa Mundi**, dating from 1289, which depicts the world as flat with Jerusalem at its center. The Map became the focus of some controversy in the 1980s, when the finance-strapped Dean and Chapter proposed selling it to raise funds for the cathedral. The outcry this caused resulted in a successful campaign to raise cash to keep it here, and today it's housed in the cathedral **crypt**. The cathedral's other main attraction is the **Chained Library**, with 1,500 books, including an 8th century copy of the Gospels.

Hereford's other points of interest include the **City Museum and Art Gallery**, on Broad Street, with a variety of exhibits on local history, geology and Victorian art. Broad Street leads into High Town, the city's main street, with some lovely Georgian buildings, the **Butter Market**, and the three-story **Old House**, a fine Jacobean construction, with predominantly seventeenth century furnishings. Here too is **All Saints Church**, a thirteenth century edifice containing 300 chained books and some fine misericords. *Open Tuesday, Wednesday, Friday 10am to 6pm, Thursday,*

Saturday 10am to 5pm. Open Sundays in May to September only, 10am to 4pm. Admission free.

If you're interested in cider production (and remember that British cider is pretty potent stuff, especially "scrumpy," the rougher version) you have two choices: the **Cider Museum**, in Pomona Place just off Whitecross Road, with a reconstruction of an old farm cider house, cooper's workshop, and venerable cider cellars; and **Bulmer's**, the country's largest cider producer, with a factory nearby in Plough Lane, which offers factory tours and some tasting! *Open April to October daily 10am to 5:30pm; November to March Monday to Saturday 1pm to 5pm. Admission adults £2.40, children £1.90. Tel. 01432 354207.*

EXCURSIONS & DAY TRIPS

Bibliophiles may want to take the twenty-mile excursion along the A438 west to **Hay-On-Wye**, a small, unassuming town which has since the early 1960s become one of the country's main centres for **bookshops**, which seem to have just about taken over the whole town, including a former movie hall and a castle! If you enjoy browsing for books, there's no better place in Britain for doing so. Check out the **Richard Booth Tourist Information Centre**, *44 Lion Street, Telephone 01497 820322.* Call them for more details, including information about the various book festivals and fairs which are held here, including the **Hay Literary Festival**, at the end of May, when London's literary gliterati arrive here in droves.

From Hereford, it's only a further fifteen miles south along the A49 to **Ross-On-Wye**, the perfect base for exploring the **Forest of Dean**, with its 2,000 miles of walking trails though forests of oak, silver birch and ash and some well-marked bicycling trails. What makes the Forest particularly interesting and atmospheric – in addition to a clutch of picturesque villages like **St. Briavels** and **Coleford** – are the old, derelict industrial buildings that are littered throughout the Forest, remnants of the once-thriving coal mines and iron smelting works that have been here since Roman times. Close to the town of **Cinderford** is the **Beechenhurst Enclosure**, a great place for exploring nature trails and also the **Forest of Dean Sculpture Trail**, a pleasant walk that's lined with contemporary artwork.

PRACTICAL INFORMATION

Hereford's main **tourist information office** can be found at *1, King Street, Tel. 01432 268430.*

THE NORTH MIDLANDS

Get away from the motorways and the sprawling industrial towns of this region and you have some of the most beautiful countryside in England – all rolling hills, deep river valleys, and patchwork-quilt fields. There are some lovely towns and villages to explore, too – like **Shrewsbury**, with many well-preserved half-timbered buildings – and **Lichfield** with its fine cathedral. Even the industrial areas have their merits – **Stoke-on-Trent** is the center of the Potteries region, which produces some of the world's finest china, with a host of visitor centers where you can see how it all started, and **Ironbridge** is the country's largest industrial museum.

ARRIVALS & DEPARTURES

By Car

From London, take the M1 to junction 19, where you then join the M6 north westbound. The cathedral city of Lichfield is accessed by taking the A5 eastbound at junction 12. For Stoke and the Potteries, continue on the M6 as far as junction 15, then follow the signs. For Shrewsbury, come off the M6 at junction 10, taking the M54 and A5 westbound into the town.

By Bus

There is a direct bus service from London's Victoria Bus Station to Stoke, taking around three hours. Shrewsbury is also served by National Express from London; the journey time here is closer to four hours. Lichfield is served by buses from Birmingham. *Call 0990 808080 for information.*

By Train

There are direct services from London Euston to Stoke, taking about 2 1/2 hours. For Shrewsbury, take the Birmingham train from Euston and change there. The station is a five minute walk north of the town center. For Lichfield, take the Birmingham train from Euston, then transfer to the local cross-city service to Lichfield. *For all train enquiries, call 0134 484950.*

GETTING AROUND TOWN

Shrewsbury and Lichfield are best explored on foot. *For information on transportation bus around Shrewsbury, call 0345 056785.* There's a guided walking tour of Shrewsbury from May to September, strating at 2:30pm on weekdays, 11am on Sundays. A regular two-hourly bus service from Shrewsbury to Ironbridge is run by **Williamsons**, *Tel. 01743 231010.*

WHERE TO STAY

ALBRIGHT HUSSEY HOTEL, *Ellesmere Road, Shrewsbury SY4 3AF. Tel. 01939 290571. Rooms 14. Rates: singles from £73, doubles from £85, including breakfast. Restaurant, parking. All major credit cards accepted.*

This half-timbered luxury hotel was built in 1524 as a moated manor house and stands in four acres of landscaped grounds. An architectural gem, most of its original features remain intact. It's in fact an amazing combination of ancient and modern, where you might find yourself in an oak beamed room with jacuzzi! You can't help but wonder what Charles I's troops would have made of it all – the place served as a garrison for Royalist troops during the Civil War. Each of the rooms in both the older part of the hotel and the modern wing is beautifully furnished and decorated and the oak paneled restaurant is a wonderful setting for a sumptuous meal (see below).

ROWTON CASTLE HOTEL, *Halfway House, Shrewsbury SY5 9EP. Tel. 01743 884044. Rooms: 19. Rates: singles from £67.50, doubles from £85. Restaurants, parking. All major credit cards accepted.*

Yet another ancient house, now serving as a hotel, the Rowton Castle was constructed in the 1400s. It's located in 17 acres of landscaped grounds. The restaurant, again oak-paneled, is full of character, with a 17th century fireplace and numerous other original features, while the lounge, with its elegant French windows overlooks the parkland outside. This is another wonderful place to get a feel of old England.

ABBOT'S MEAD HOTEL, *9 St. Julian's Friars, Shrewsbury SY1 1XL. Tel. 01743 235281, Fax 017743 369133. Rooms: 14. Rates from £30 per person. Restaurant, bar. All major credit cards accepted.*

This small hotel is built on the site of the Greyfriars Monastery, between Shrewsbury's Town Walls and the River Severn and just around the corner from the Abbey. The rooms are well-appointed, with TV and hospitality tray. This hotel offers really excellent value, friendly service and a central location.

PRINCE RUPERT HOTEL, *Butcher Row, Shrewsbury SY1 1UQ. Tel 01743 499955, Fax 01743 357306. Rooms 70. Rates: singles from £75, doubles from £95. Bar, restaurant, sauna, gymnasium, jacuzzi, weight training room, beauty salon. All major credit cards accepted.*

Part of this town center hotel dates back to medieval times, evidenced in the exposed beams in many of the refurbished, well-equipped bedrooms and in the public areas. The bedrooms include four luxury suites, family rooms and rooms with four-posters – so everyone is catered for. Food is provided in two restaurant, the more formal Royalist restaurant and a bar bistro called Chambers. The hotel is conveniently located for all of downtown Shrewsbury's attractions.

THE LION, *Wyle Cop, Shrewsbury SY1 1UY. Tel 01743 353107, Fax 01743 352744. Rooms: 59. Rates: singles from £65, doubles from £85. Bar, restaurant. All major credit cards accepted.*

This old coaching inn can trace its origins way back to the 14th century. Since then, it has entertained a number of famous guests including none other than – you guessed it – Charles Dickens. The public areas are elegant and comfortable, and the bedrooms are equipped with all modern facilities with pleasant decor and furnishings.

WHERE TO EAT

SOL, *82 Wyle Cop, Shrewsbury. Tel. 01743 340560. Open Tuesday to Saturday noon to 1:45pm, 7pm to 9pm. Set lunch £19.50, set dinner from £27.50. All major credit cards accepted.*

You might be forgiven for thinking this was a Mexican or Central American restaurant, given its bright, rather flamboyant, decor, but you'd be wrong. This restaurant draws on the best of fresh English produce to produce a varied a la carte menu that emphasises world cooking – dishes like Thai-spiced smoked haddock fish cake, or guinea fowl with mushroom butter sauce. The desserts are impressive, as is the wine list, where house wines start at £9.95 a bottle.

ALBRIGHT HUSSEY HOTEL, *Ellesmere Road, Shrewsbury. Tel. 01939 290571. Open daily. Dinner around £25. All major credit cards accepted.*

The beamed oak-paneled dining room of this wonderful hotel is full of atmosphere, with pink tablecloths, elegant furniture and, above all, superb food. The cuisine is basically modern British and French, using lots of fresh regional and local produce. The restaurant is particularly good on fish dishes like sea bass, char-grilled tuna, but that's not to say the meat and vegetarian dishes aren't great too. Dining here is a real experience.

SEEING THE SIGHTS

Despite its grimy industrial landscapes and generally run-of-the-mill countryside, the county of **Staffordshire** immediately north of Birmingham, is, surprisingly, home to two of England's major tourist attractions. **Alton Towers**, about 15 miles east of Stoke, just off the B5032, a vast theme park that attracts more visitors than any other tourist site in Britain, and the **Potteries**, centered around Stoke-on-Trent, surely one of the ugliest cities in Britain. Here it is that such famous companies as Royal Doulton, Wedgwood and Spode have their main manufacturing centers.

These and many other factories in the area operate factory tours, along with opportunities to purchase some of their products at reduced prices. To find out which are open to visitors, check with the area's main

tourist office on Quadrant Road in Hanley, *Tel. 01782 236000; www.stoke.gov.uk*. As an alternative, and for an overall perspective of the industry, visit the **Museum of the Potteries**, Bethesda Road, Hanley, with the most extensive display of Staffordshire ceramics in the world, and displays on how the industry evolved in the area. *Open Monday to Saturday 10am to 5pm, Sunday 2pm to 5pm. Admission free. Tel. 01782 232323.*

Much more attractive is the small city of **Lichfield**, with its fine three-towered **cathedral** surrounded by a collection of pretty, half-timbered houses. The present buildings dates from the 1080s – though its origins go back a further 300 years, when the original cathedral was built to house the mortal remains of **St. Chad**.

Apart from the towers, the cathedral's most striking feature externally is the **west front**, decorated with more than 100 statues of saints, local kings and queens, some of them 13th century originals, the bulk added during the Victorian period to replace those destroyed by **Cromwell** during his Puritan rampage in the 1640s. Inside, to the south of the choir, a thirteenth century addition to the building contains a gallery from which the head of the cathedral's patron, St. Chad, was displayed to pilgrims, while the **Lady Chapel**, behind the high altar at the extreme east end of the church, contains some wonderful sixteenth century **stained glass** from the Cistercian monastery at Herkenrode in Belgium. The cathedral's greatest treasure, however, is the **Lichfield Gospels**, illuminated manuscripts containing the complete texts of the gospels of Matthew and Mark and part of Luke. The cathedral has a website at: *www.lichfield-cathedral.org.*

Lichfield was the birthplace of diarist **Dr. Samuel Johnson**, who was born in a house on Breadmarket Street, just a couple of hundred yards from the cathedral, next to the Market Place. The **Samuel Johnson Birthplace Museum** is full of Johnson memorabilia, including books and manuscripts. Opposite the Johnson house, Lichfield's parish church of **St. Mary**, erected in the twelfth century, is home to the **Lichfield Heritage and Treasury Exhibition**, which traces the city's history. *Open daily (except Sundays in November, December and January), 10:30am to 4:30pm. Admission adults £2, children £1 – joint ticket for Johnson Birthplace and Heritage Exhibition, adults £3.20, children £2.20. Tel. 01543 264972.*

Follow the A5 west of Lichfield to **Shropshire**, one of England's most unspoilt counties, dominated by **Shrewsbury** (pronounced "Shroosebry" or "shrosebry") located on a hairpin bend in the River Severn that offered superb defensive potential to the town, an important military base since Roman times . Later on, the Normans built a **stone castle** here, and after the sequestration of nearby Wales by King Edward I, the town underwent rapid expansion due to its proximity to the Welsh wool trade. Today, the town is an important commercial center, with a large number of well-preserved sixteenth and seventeenth century houses, and a great place to explore on foot, especially the maze of narrow streets in the center of town.

Start with a visit to the **Castle**, overlooking the river at Pride's Hill on the northern edge of downtown, with roots going back to the sixth century. The Normans saw the strategic importance of the site and built a stone castle, much of which was dismantled during the Civil War. Famous architect and engineer Thomas Telford went about rebuilding the structure in the late eighteenth century as a dwelling for Sir William Pulteney. The Castle is home to the **Shropshire Regimental Museum**, and is also the setting for the open-air Shakespeare Festival in July.

Head up Pride's Hill towards the heart of the old town to the **Square**, and to the left, a warren of narrow streets and alleyways lined with some wonderful Tudor and Jacobean buildings. Two churches in the vicinity are worth a visit: **St. Mary's**, dating from around 1200, has one of the tallest parish church spires in England and some interesting iron-framed stained glass. *Open Monday to Friday 10am to 5pm, Saturday 10am to 3pm. Admission free. Tel. 01743 358516.* Meanwhile, off Fish Street, **St. Alkmund's**, built in 1795 on the site of a much earlier church, also has some fine stained glass. South of the Square, **College Hill** is enhanced by the Georgian facade of **Clive House**, home of Lord Clive, the statesman-soldier who led British forces in the Battle of Plassey in 1757. The house was Clive's home when he served as Shrewsbury's MP. Inside, you can see rooms furnished in much the same way as they were in Clive's time; there are also displays of Staffordshire porcelain and an exhibit of Clive's life and times.

West of the Square, on Barker Street, is **Rowley's House**, a superb half-timbered dwelling built in 1590 linked to an early 1600s brick mansion, and now housing a fine **Museum**. As well as local history, the museum has a collection of Staffordshire pottery, costume displays, and relics discovered at the nearby Roman city of Wroxeter, including a third century silver mirror. There's also a reconstructed seventeenth century bedroom, complete with well-preserved wall paneling and a four poster bed. *Open Tuesday to Saturday 10am to 5pm, Sundays from Easter to October 1, 10am to 4pm. Admission free. Tel. 01743 361196.*

Head back to the Square and follow High Street and Wyle Cop, crossing the English Bridge to **Shrewsbury Abbey**, dating from about the same time as the castle – not surprising, as both buildings were the work of one and the same man, Roger de Montgomery. The abbey became an important and very powerful Benedictine monastery. It managed to avoid destruction during the Dissolution of the Monasteries and survived as the parish church for the eastern end of Shrewsbury. Among its most notable features are an original Norman doorway and, above it a 14th century window of heraldic glass. *Open Good Friday to October 31 9:30am to 5:30pm;*

November to Good Friday 10:30am to 3pm. Admission free, but donations welcome. The remains of the abbey's former outhouses have been converted into an excellent new heritage center, the **Shrewsbury Quest**, which depicts monastic life during medieval times by means of a reconstructed scriptorium, library and cloisters. As Shrewsbury is the home of the fictional Brother Cadfael, of BBC and PBS fame, the center's planners couldn't resist giving the whole place a Cadfael theme – visitors can take part in solving a Cadfael-style mystery through clues devilishly hidden. *Open April to October daily 10am to 6:30pm, November to March 10am to 4pm. Admission adults £4.50, seniors and students £3.80, children under 12 £2.95.*

About fifteen miles to the east of Shrewsbury, just off the A4380, is **Ironbridge Gorge**, a deep ravine carved out of the rock by the River Severn. The fast flowing waters meant that this was an important iron-smelting site, and although the industry has virtually disappeared, the whole area – six square miles of it – has been preserved as the **Ironbridge Gorge Museum**, probably the best industrial heritage museum in Britain.

The extensive Shropshire coalfields spawned an important iron-smelting industry using coke instead of charcoal, which in turn led to the development of the forging process that facilitated the production of large items in iron. The area around Ironbridge soon became the nation's leading manufacturer of heavy-duty ironware such as rails, wheels and engines – and of course, the massive girders for bridges, like the world's earliest iron bridge, designed by Abraham Darby and built here in 1779, giving the place its name.

It makes a good deal of sense to purchase a **museum passport ticket**, which allows unlimited access to all the component parts of the museum, which includes the **Severn warehouse**, where an audio-visual display traces the history of the gorge and the construction of the bridge; the **Museum of the River**; the **Museum of Iron**, where the manufacture of iron and steel is explained and where in the adjacent **Elton Gallery** you can see the original blast furnace built by Abraham Darby; **Rosehill House**, a cottage containing artifacts belonging to a former ironmaster. There are more museums east of the bridge in the village of Coalport, where the **Coalport China Museum** contains displays of Coalport ware, and, most stimulating of all, **Blists Hill Open Air Museum**, a reconstruction of a Victorian village, complete with candlemaker's, doctors surgery with frightening utensils, a pub, candy store, saw mill as well as wrought-iron works and furnaces. *Open daily 10am to 5pm. Admission passport ticket (which allows access to all the museums on the site) adults £10, students and seniors £9, children £6. For the price of each individual museum check the ironbridge website, or call 01952 432166; www.ironbridge.co.uk.*

PRACTICAL INFORMATION

Shrewsbury's **tourism office** is at *The Music Hall, The Square, Shrewsbury SY1 1LH, Tel. 01743 350761*; Lichfield's *at Donegal House, Bore Street, close to the Market Place.*

Both cities are well served by banks, and Lichfield also has an **American Express** office, at *27 Claremont Street, Tel. 01743 236387.*

19. EAST ANGLIA

East Anglia, the large protrusion that juts out into the North Sea just north of the Thames estuary, is a place where you can really feel you're off-the-beaten-path. Because it's on the way to nowhere, many visitors – like the Industrial Revolution – pass it by. In doing so, they're missing out on one of England's most attractive, unspoilt rural regions. Made up of the counties of Essex, Suffolk, Norfolk and Cambridgeshire it contains some of the nation's most endearing, if unspectacular, countryside, as well as dozens of pretty towns and villages – even the occasional windmill – and some of the nation's grandest village churches, evidence of the region's enormous wealth when the wool industry was flourishing.

The area is rich in stately homes, as evidenced by the wonderful **Holkham Hall** and the royal residence of **Sandringham**. The semi-circular coastline ranges from broody marshes in the south to some fine sandy, often isolated beaches and small seaside resorts – as well as a couple of larger ones – further north. A few miles inland, the **Norfolk Broads**, a chain of mostly man-made waterways and lakes, are a favorite holiday destination for Britons wanting to get away from it all.

This is not a region of large cities; the only large city, **Norwich**, with its ancient Norman cathedral and a host of other historical attractions, is a real gem, as is tiny **Ely**, whose cathedral looms high above the "**Fens**" – the flat, low lying landscape that's similar to parts of Holland. More famous still is the spacious, elegant university city of **Cambridge**, where many of England's most illustrious personages – such as Milton, Bacon, Newton and Byron received their education. This region also produced Oliver Cromwell, the Puritan leader who ousted King Charles I from the throne, John Wesley, and many of the original *Mayflower* passengers.

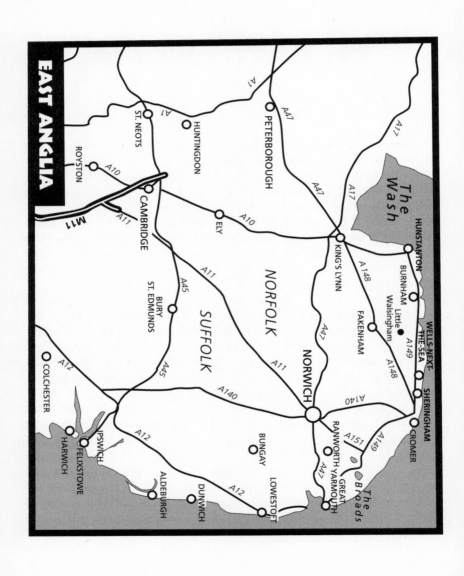

NORWICH

Norwich – pronounced Norritch – the largest city in East Anglia and the administrative center of the county of Norfolk, is dominated by the slender octagonal spire of its **cathedral**, most of which dates from the 11th century. It's an unusual place in that unlike many larger English cities it was virtually untouched by the Industrial Revolution, so many of its ancient buildings remain relatively intact. Although today it's a bustling community of nearly 250,000, in many ways it retains the feel of a small English cathedral city and is a great place to explore on foot.

The **Saxons** were the first to settle here. They found that the site, at the confluence of the rivers **Yare** and **Wensum** offered significant trading possibilities. Their successors, the **Normans**, also favored the site, and built two of the structures that remain the city's main attractions to this day – the **cathedral** and the **Castle**.

ARRIVALS & DEPARTURES
By Car
From London, take the M11 north to exit 9, where you connect with the A11 eat to Norwich. The total distance is just under 120 miles.

By Bus
National Express, *Tel. 0990 808080*, buses leave London's Victoria Bus Station. The journey time is about three hours, and the bus station about ten minutes' walk south of the city at All Saints' Green.

By Train
Norwich is served hourly by trains from London's Liverpool Street Station. The total journey time is just under three hours. *Call National Rail Enquiries at 0345 484950 for service and fare information.* The train station is a fifteen minute walk east of the city center.

GETTING AROUND TOWN
The compact city center can be explored comfortably on foot. *For information about the local public transportation system, call 01603 613613.*

WHERE TO STAY
THE POST HOUSE, *Ipswich Rd, Norwich NR4 6EP. Tel. 01603 506431, Fax 01603 506400. Rooms: 116. Rates from £80 per room. Restaurant, indoor pool, gym, sauna, free parking. All major credit cards accepted.*

Part of the Trusthouse Forte chain, the Posthouse is a large comfortable hotel, with fairly spacious if bland decor in both its public and private areas, a well-equipped health club with heated swimming pool, gym and sauna, and a restaurant whose speciality is traditional English fare. There's a pleasant bar, the Punch, decorated with early cartoons from *Punch* magazine, and a coffee shop decorated with farm tools to symbolize Norwich's links with the agricultural industry. Each of the 116 rooms comes with private bath/shower, tea- and coffee-making facilities and TV.

MAIDS HEAD, *Tombland, Norwich NR3 1LB, Tel. 01603 761111, Fax 01603 613688. 80 rooms. Rates singles from £85, doubles from £105. Restaurant/carvery. All major credit cards accepted.*

If it's real Olde Worlde stuff you want, then this is the place: the owners claim that this city center hotel, operating since 1272, is the oldest continuously operating hotel in Britain. That's easy to believe, since the hotel is located adjacent to the cathedral in the oldest part of the city. Though "recent" additions date back to the Georgian period, an older section dating back to Elizabethan times (including a room where it is alleged Queen Elizabeth I once slept) replaced an even earlier building. This first-rate hotel is beautifully maintained, with some nice touches, including daily newspapers in the rooms, and various traditional services that you rarely find nowadays, such as shoe cleaning and a full breakfast in bed. There's a popular Carvery restaurant, and a paneled Minstel Room where dinner is served.

BY APPOINTMENT, *25 St. George's Street, Norwich NR3 1AB. Tel and Fax 01603 630730. Rooms: 4. Rates: singles £65, doubles from. £85. Credit cards: MC, Visa.*

This very smart little establishment in Norwich's city center dates back to the 16th century and is full of charm and character. In addition to the narrow hallways and winding staircases it's notable for a series of small sitting rooms, liberally sprinkled with antiques; individually decorated, somewhat eccentric bedrooms also brimming with antiques – as well as modern conveniences such as trouser presses, hair dryers and TVs – and excellent cuisine.

THE OLD RECTORY, *103 Yarmouth Road, Thorpe St Andrew, Norwich NR7 0HF. Tel 01603 700772, Fax 01603 300772. Rooms: 9. Rates: singles from £60, doubles from £78. Restaurant/dining room, garden, outdoor pool. All major credit cards accepted.*

Although this former church rectory is only about two miles out of Norwich city center it has the feel of a rural retreat, with more than an acre of grounds. The house itself is Georgian, the creepers that engulf enhances that country feeling. Both the elegant drawing room and the dining room overlook the lovely garden where there's a heated pool. The rooms, some of which are located in the main building while others are in the coach house are exceptionally comfortable, with the usual amenities and some nice extras such as rather decadent bathrobes.

SPROWSTON MANOR HOTEL, *Sprowston Park, Wroxham Road, Norwich NR7 8RP. Tel 01603 410871, Fax 01603 423911. Rooms: 87. Rates: singles from £87, doubles from £93. Bar, restaurant, indoor pool, spa, sauna, solarium, beauty salon. All major credit cards accepted.*

Located about three miles from Norwich city center on the A1151 to the Norfolk Broads, the Sprowston Manor, part of the Best Western chain, is a great place to relax and pamper yourself with a full range of leisure and sporting facilities. To start with, the hotel is surrounded by 10 acres of parkland that's ideal for walks; this in turn is surrounded by an 18-hole golf course. The rooms are what you'd expect from a chain; a bit insipid but perfectly adequate. The big plus here is is a new indoor swimming pool, which has the bonus of a children's pool if you're traveling with kids, and a full leisure and fitness suite. It's convenient both for Norwich city and for touring the Broads and the north Norfolk coast.

WHERE TO EAT

ADLARD'S, *79 Upper St Giles Street, Norwich NR2 1AB. Tel. 01603 633522. Open Monday to Saturday 12:30pm to 1:45pm, 7:30pm to 10:30pm (lunch not served on Mondays). Set lunch £19, set dinner £33. All major credit cards accepted.*

City center restaurant specializing in modern British cuisine, in comfortable, elegant surroundings enhanced by some original paintings. The service is formal, without being rigid, offering such flavorsome dishes as herb-crusted braised neck filet of lamb cooked with olives in a dark sauce. There's a very good wine list, with house wines starting at £12.50 a bottle, and lunchtime is a real bargain.

MARCO'S, *17 Pottergate, Norwich NR2 1DS. Tel. 01603 624044. Open Tuesday to Saturday, noon to 2pm, 7pm to 10pm. Set lunch £15, main dinner courses around £16. All major credit cards accepted.*

Another pleasant city center establishment, this time serving excellent Italian food. Home-made pasta includes an excellent gnocchi with creamy tomato sauce, and fairly standard but sensitively-cooked meat or poultry main courses, such as chicken breast in lemon sauce, are offered. The excellent wine list focuses entirely on Italian products.

FEMI'S, *42 King Street, Norwich. Tel 01603 766010. Open Tuesday to Friday, noon to 1:30pm, Tuesday to Saturday 7pm to 10pm. Main courses from £8.50. All major credit cards accepted.*

This popular city center restaurant is located just a couple of hundred yards from the cathedral and about the same distance from the castle. It offers British eclectic cuisine; offerings like fish soup with noodles, marinated Thai-style chicken and the like. There's a wide range of tempting desserts.

BRUMMEL'S SEAFOOD RESTAURANT, 7 *Magdalen Street, Norwich. Tel 01603 625555. Open daily noon to 2pm, 6pm to 10pm. 2-course set meals (lunch and dinner) from £21.95, 3-course from £26.95. All major credit cards accepted.*

Very popular city center fish restaurant where the menu changes according to availability, and where they will mix and match the various sauces and preparations to suite your requirements. Among the more exotic choices here are cuttlefish in red wine and ink, and Jamaican red tilapia stuffed with cabbage and celeriac. There are meat dishes, too, and a good array of desserts, including the inevitable apple pie.

SEEING THE SIGHTS

Norwich Cathedral was begun in 1096 by Herbert de Losinga, a Norman, whose tomb is visible today next to the high altar. But the cathedral's most striking feature is its **spire** – at 315 feet the second tallest in England after Salisbury. Inside, the long **nave** with its huge Norman columns draws the eye to the high altar and up to the **vaulted ceiling**, where colorful bosses illustrate biblical stories, while the detailed medieval **misericords** in the choir and frescoes in the treasury are also worth a close inspection. In addition, check out the **Dispenser Reredos**, a fourteenth century painted panel in the **Chapel of St. Luke.** Just off the south aisle of the nave are the cathedral **cloisters**, started in 1297 and rare in that they are two-story. They also contain more bosses, again depicting scenes from the Bible.

Leaving the cathedral via the cloisters you can see the grave of World War I heroine **Edith Cavell**, who was killed by the Germans in 1915 after helping Allied prisoners escape from Belgium. Outside, the vast **Cathedral Close** is a lovely place to get a feel for medieval Norwich, with a cluster of medieval and Georgian houses, and a pathway that leads down to **Pulls Ferry**, an ancient water gate. *Open summer daily 7:30am to 7pm, winter 7:30am to 6pm. Admission free; suggested donation £3. Tel. 01603 764383; www.cathedral.org.uk.*

To the west of the cathedral, **Tombland**, whose name derives not from tombs but from the Saxon word for open space, is the site of the old **Saxon market**, though you would never guess it today. Turn left at the northern end to **Elm Hill**, a jumble of Tudor and Georgian houses in a pretty cobbled street – and a good place to get a nice cuppa tea. Heading south, you'll soon come to the 15th century **Church of St. Peter Hungate**, no longer functioning as a church but as a center for ecclesiastical art and furnishings as well as a brass rubbing center.

Head south on Bank Plain where standing high on a hill overlooking the city is the unmistakable **Norwich Castle**, another Norman construction, with decorated stone facing that makes it look a bit unusual. Though it served a military deterrent, its main function for many years was as a **prison**, a role in which it continued well into the nineteenth century. There are regular guided tours of the dungeons and battlements, as well as an interesting museum with displays on the city's history, and an art gallery devoted to the Norwich School of landscape painters. *Note: The Castle is closed until spring 2001 for major refurbishment. Call 01603 493625 for more information.*

The city's main focal point for 900 years, the **Marketplace**, once the location for more than forty hostelries, lies just west of the castle. Among the buildings to note here are the **Church of St. Peter Mancroft**, Norwich's finest parish church, with an elaborate fifteenth century tower; the rather severe **City Hall**, built in the 1930s; and the fifteenth century flint and stone **Guildhall**, which today houses the city's main **tourist office**. While you're here, check out the **Sir Garnett Wolseley pub**, the only one of the original forty or so that's left.

Other attractions in the city center include the fascinating **Bridewell Museum**, once the city jail and today dedicated to exhibits on local industry. *Open year-round Monday to Saturday 10am to 5pm. Admission adults £2, seniors and students £1.50, children £1. Tel. 01603 667228.* Just round the corner at 3, Bridewell Alley is the intriguing **Mustard Shop** – a reminder that Norwich has been – and still is – the UK's main producer of mustard. *Open Monday to Saturday 9:30 to 5pm.* About 250 yards further west, on Charing Cross, is the **Stranger's Hall**, a fourteenth century house built for a wealthy merchant that was lived in for many years by immigrant weavers – hence the name. Among the features are the Great Hall, dating from the fifteenth century, the walnut room and a Georgian dining room. There's also an extensive collection of costumes, including one of the best collections of underwear in the country. Marks and Spencer, from whom almost a third of all Brits buy their underwear, take note! *Open for guided tours only Wednesday & Saturday 11am, 1pm and 3pm. Admission adults £2.50, students and seniors £2, children £1.50. Call 01603 667229 in advance to book.*

A little way out of the main core of the city at 115, King Street is the **Dragon Hall**, built originally as a cloth showroom for a former city mayor and merchant. *Open April to October Monday to Saturday 10am to 4pm; November to March Monday to Friday 10am to 4pm. Tel. 01603 663922. Admission adults £1.50, students and seniors £1, children 50p; www.virgin.net/ dragon.hall/index.htm.* In the Great Hall you can see the medieval wooden dragon for which the place is named. Close by, check out **St. Julian's Church**, *open daily, 7am to 6pm, admission free*, whose adjacent monastic cell was the retreat of the fourteenth century "anchoress" and mystic, **Mother Julian**. Julian, a local woman, claimed to have had visions of Jesus which inspired her to write *Revelations of Divine Love*, the first book written by a woman in the English language, and still, centuries on, a bestseller. Further down King Street, disguised by its seventeenth century façade, is the **Music House**, the oldest domestic building in the city, dating from 1175. Unless you want to sign up for a local adult education course in, say flower arranging or creative writing, you won't get in.

About three miles out of town on its western outskirts, the **University of East Anglia**, established in the 1960s, is worth a visit, particularly for its unusual collection of paintings and sculptures displayed in the amazing **Sainsbury Center for Visual Arts**, designed by eminent architect Sir Norman Foster in 1977. On show are modern works by the likes of Picasso and Henry Moore alongside traditional tribal art from around the world. The Centre can be reached by taking bus #12, 14, 15, 23 26 or 27 from the city center (Castle Meadow).

NIGHTLIFE & ENTERTAINMENT

Norwich has some great **pubs**, including **The Plough** on *St. Benedicth's Street* and the **Red Lion** on *St. George Street*, both of which provide hearty, inexpensive meals.

The **Theatre Royal**, *Theatre Street, Tel. 01603 630000*, features productions by visiting repertory companies, as well as ballet and some concerts, while the **Norwich Arts Centre**, *St. Benedict's Street, Tel. 01603 660352*, features concerts, musicals, dance and cabaret.

SHOPPING

There's some great browsing to be had around **Elm Hill** and **Tombland**, with a number of antiques and antiquarian bookstores. One place not to miss is the **Antiques and Collectors' Centre**, *Tombland*, opposite the cathedral, with rooms full of antiques stalls and shops. Meanwhile, **St. Michael-at-Plea**, *Bank Plain*, is an old church converted into an antiques emporium.

PRACTICAL INFORMATION

The **Norwich Tourism Information Centre** is located at *The Guild Hall, Gaol Hill, Tel. 01603 666071; www.norwich.gov.uk*.

Norwich is a large city and branches of the main banks can be found, with the main post office, on Bank Plain. There's a also a branch of **Thomas Cook** at *15 St. Stephen's Street, Tel. 01603 621547*.

You're unlikely to need a car to explore the city itself, but one might come in very handy further afield. Both **Avis**, *Tel. 01603 416719*, and **Hertz**, *Tel. 01603 404010*, have offices at Norwich Airport, Cromer Road.

THE BROADS

To the east of Norwich, best accessed by the A47 out of the city, is a low-lying area known as the **Norfolk Broads**, a series of large stretches of water that were once thought to be natural lakes, but in reality are the result of wide-scale peat cutting during the middle ages – peat was a valuable commodity for fuel in those days, in an area relatively void of woodland. When North Sea levels rose in the fourteenth century, these peat pits became flooded, giving Norfolk one of the most important areas of **wetland** in Europe, and a habitat for all kinds of rare species of flora and fauna. Latterly, the Norfolk Broads have caught on among the English as a popular area for **boating holidays**, though the inevitable dangers of mass tourism – erosion and pollution particularly – brought their own problems. The Broads was afforded **National Park** status in 1988, and since then efforts have been made to protect the area's fragile ecosystem from further damage.

Today, there are over 120 miles of **navigable waterways** to explore, a very relaxing and restful way to see some of the country's best parish churches, interesting windmills, and idyllic out-of-the-way pubs, as well as to observe the area's bird life. One of the best churches is at **Ranworth**, four miles southeast of Wroxham. Known as "the cathedral of the broads," it contains a beautiful rood screen and the Sarum Antiphoner, an illuminated manuscript dating from the fifteenth century.

Renting a boat

If you're interested in renting a boat for a week or two on the Broads, check out both **Blakes**, based in Wroxham, Tel. 01603 782911, and **Hoseasons of Lowestoft**, Tel. 01502 501010. Prices usually start at around £550 a week for four people sharing a boat.

Renting a bicycle

You also might want to think about renting a bicycle; there's a complex network of paths and bike rental centers throughout the region. For more information, contact the **Broads Authority**, Tel. 01603 782281.

GREAT YARMOUTH & THE NORTH NORFOLK COAST

One of the places you can reach by boat – crossing the much larger and wider Breydon Water – or by car along the A47 from Norwich, is **Great Yarmouth**, a very popular if rather tacky seaside resort, with a long promenade backed by an endless array of amusement arcades, candy floss and seafood stalls and flanked by a large pier. But Yarmouth's history goes back much further than its seaside resort days. In the middle ages it was an important port, making good use of its strategic position on the coast, where it could monopolize trade heading inland for Norwich. By the nineteenth century it had become the leading herring producing port in Britain. When these stocks ran out in the 1960s, Great Yarmouth's saving grace was its proximity to the offshore gas and oil industry.

ARRIVALS & DEPARTURES
By Car
Great Yarmouth lies due east of Norwich on the A47.

By Bus
There are regular buses from Norwich to Great Yarmouth, run by Eastern Counties. The service takes around 45 minutes and costs £2.75.

By Train
Yarmouth is also connected to Norwich by a frequent train service. *For information, call 0345 484950.*

GETTING AROUND TOWN
Great Yarmouth is an eminently walkable kind of place. If you're going to be exploring the coast, though, you'll need a car. See above under Norwich *Practical Information* for details of car rental companies in the area.

WHERE TO STAY
DUKE'S HEAD, *Tuesday Market Place, King's Lynn PE30 1JS, Tel. 01533 774996. Rooms: 71. Rates: singles from £60, doubles from £90. Restaurants, bars. All major credit cards accepted.*

Wonderful, atmospheric and deceptively large (71 rooms) old hotel overlooking the Tuesday Market Place in the center of King's Lynn. The hotel, part of which dates from the 17th century, has beautifully appointed rooms and a large lounge where you can relax in front of an open fire in winter, or enjoy a traditional cream tea. Each of the rooms comes with bath and the usual facilities.

HOSTE ARMS, *The Green, Burnham Market PE31 8HD. Tel. 01328 738777, Fax 01328 730103. Rooms: 28, including four suites. Rates: singles from £52, doubles from £64, four posters from £74. Restaurants, bar, lounge. All major credit cards accepted.*

You can easily spot the lemon and white facade of the Hoste Arms among the period buildings fronting Burnham's village green. With lots of country pine furniture, bright red walls, lots of antiques and exposed brickwork, it's an attractive, cozy place, with several bars and a conservatory where you can get bistro-style meals at reasonable cost. The bedrooms too are well-apportioned and tastefully furnished, while outside you can while away those lazy summer afternoons in a lovely walled garden.

RUSSET HOUSE HOTEL, *53 Goodwins Road, King's Lynn PE30 5PE. Tel and Fax 01553 773098. Rooms: . rates: singles from £35, doubles from £48. Bar, restaurant. All major credit cards accepted.*

The Russet House is a lovely Victorian house about ten minutes (walk) from the town center of King's Lynn, with all its attractions and shopping facilities and the River Ouse. Among the amenities here are a pleasant, cozy bar where log fires roar in winter, an elegant dining room with long drapes and chandeliers and attractive bedrooms with all modern facilities. There's also a beautiful garden where you can relax and unwind. Top all that with friendly service and you have a very pleasant place to stay.

THE CROWN, *The Buttlands, Wells-next-the-Sea NR23 1EX. Rooms: 15. Rates: singles from £40, doubles from £60. Bars, restaurant. All major credit cards accepted.*

There's a haunting beauty about the north Norfolk coast and there's nowhere better to enjoy it than from The Crown at Wells. A former coaching inn, it boasts several cozy and atmospheric bars where inexpensive meals are readily available, and an excellent, highly acclaimed restaurant. The 15 bedrooms are similarly cozy and come with the usual facilities. It's a great place to come back to and relax after a long day exploring the beaches, marshes and country houses of this corner of Norfolk.

REGENCY DOLPHIN HOTEL, *Albert Square, Great Yarmouth NR30 3JH. Tel 01493 855070, Fax 01493 853798. Rooms: 49. Rates: singles from £30, doubles from £60. Bar, restaurant, pool.*

The recently refurbished Regency Dolphin is a traditional British seaside hotel located adjacent to Great Yarmouth's seafront. The rooms are all pretty the same, but they come with a full range of facilities, including hostess trays and TV. The hotel benefits from a heated outdoor pool, bars and a fine restaurant, the Boulevard. It can get very crowded and noisy in the summer.

WHERE TO EAT

ROCOCO, *11 Saturday Market Place, King's Lynn. Tel. 01553 771483. Open Tuesday to Saturday, noon to 1:30pm, 7pm to 10pm. Set dinner (2 courses) from £24.50. All major credit cards accepted.*

Strikingly modern restaurant with a pleasant relaxed ambience in one of the old houses on King's Lynn's ancient Saturday Market Place. The food is contemporary too; fresh local ingredients served in creative ways, such as roast loin of Norfolk lamb with rutabaga fondant and mustard spatzl. There's also a wide selection of traditional desserts to make the mouth water, again with a slightly unconventional touch, such as lemon tart on a citrus caramel sauce.

HOSTE ARMS HOTEL, *The Green, Burnham Market, near King's Lynn. Tel 01328 738777.*

This former coaching inn, built in the 16th century and about half-way between Burnham and Qells on the A149, has been converted into a delightful combination of small hotel, village pub serving a range of fines ales, and superb restaurant. The cuisine is best described as modern British, which means fresh local ingredients, creatively cooked with a hint of ethnicity (the proprietor boasts that these all come from within a 20 mile radius of the inn), creative desserts and an extensive and well-chosen wine list.

MORSTON HALL, *Morston, Holt, Blakeney NR25 7AA. Tel 01263 741041.*

This lovely 17th century country house hotel is located in a small coastal village surrounded by mature plantings and lawns. The four-course, no-choice menu is painstakingly prepared by the chef, and is best described as modern English, using the best local produce. The fish dishes are particularly good, and the wine list features special "wines of the month" to match the particular menu – and are available by the bottle or glass.

SEEING THE SIGHTS

Most holidaymakers and day-trippers head for the **seafront**, where the attractions begin with the **Sealife Centre**, an aquarium featuring sharks and hundreds of other glugging sea creatures. *Open daily 10am to 5pm, admission adults £5.75, children £3.95, Tel. 01493 330631; www.sealife.co.uk.* **The Marina**, *open daily 10am to 10pm,* is a sports complex with a swimming pool, aquaslide and wave machine that's just perfect on one of those cool, bracing days for which the east coast is famous. Best of all, there's the **Maritime Museum**, which traces Great Yarmouth's history as a port, as well as the development of the Broads. *Open summer only Monday to Friday and Sunday 10am to 4:30pm. Tel. 01493 842267.*

Because of its prosperity during the late middle ages, Great Yarmouth was able to produce some fine architecture, though many of its best buildings were destroyed or damaged by enemy bombing during WWII. Among what remains, the **Church of St. Nicholas**, begun 1101, is notable for an extremely wide nave – the widest, in fact, in Britain – and an attractive west front. Also close by is the **Hospital for Decayed Fishermen**, which despite the off-putting name is in reality a rather lovely 1702 building with a small courtyard flanked by Dutch gables. You can also see large stretches of the town's original medieval walls, including some of the defensive towers.

Also of interest are a couple of small museums. The **Tolhouse Museum** once served as the town courthouse and jail. *Open summer only Monday to Friday and Sunday 10am to 1pm and 2pm to 5pm. Admission adults £1.10, students and seniors 90pm, children 70p. Tel. 01493 858900.* At the **Elizabethan House Museum**, on South Quay, you step back into the past and into the lives of families who lived on Quayside over the centuries. Of special interest is the Conspiracy Room, where allegedly the trial and execution of King Charles I was plotted, and a special children's room with replica period toys. *Open mid-April to September Sunday to Friday 10am to 5pm, admission adults £2, students and seniors £1.50, children £1, Tel. 01493 8555746.* Another fascinating feature of the old town are the "**rows**" – narrow alleyways that linked the river with the shore, of which 69 survive to this day. You can explore some of them by taking one of English Heritage's **guided walking tours** that leave from the Old Merchant House in Row 117.

The North Norfolk Coast

Lonely and windswept for much of its length, it's not until you reach **Cromer**, about thirty miles north of Great Yarmouth on the A149, that things liven up a tad. Like Great Yarmouth, a significant port in medieval times, Cromer's contemporary wealth is derived from tourism, especially since the advent of the railroad in the 1880s, when a clutch of grand hotels were built, only one of which, the **Hotel de Paris**, survives. And of the fishing industry, only a handful of crab boats remain.

Four miles further along the coast is **Sheringham**, another popular seaside resort but considerably smaller. Just west of the town, the vast shingle barrier was built to prevent a repetition of the great flood of 1953 when over 1,000 souls perished. The **Cley Marshes**, just to the south of the barrier, was established in 1926 as the nation's first nature reserve and abounds in wading birds. The shingle barrier here ends at **Blakeney Point**, where colonies of seals and terns can be seen, though instead of walking across the shingle here you'd do better to take one of the **boat trips** that leaves from the quay in the town of Blakeney, a mile west, though you'll need to check the times very carefully – the port is only accessible from the sea for a couple of hours at high tide. Points to note in Blakeney include a rather pleasant high street and a **church** that boasts, in addition to its main tower, a second tower which doubled up as a lighthouse in earlier times.

The name **Wells-Next-The-Sea** is something of a misnomer these days – the town is about a mile from open water. In medieval times, however, it was a different story, and Wells was one of the pre-eminent ports of Tudor England. While you're here, explore the **Buttlands**, a broad rectangular Green flanked by oak and beech trees and some very pleasant Georgian houses. South of here, you can enjoy a stroll along the narrow lanes of the town center, including **Stathe Street**, the main street, at the end of which is the **Quay** – with a clutch of amusement machines – and the road to a very nice sandy beach, backed by woods, and brightly-colored beach huts. If you want to flirt with the water, be careful. At low tide the water can recede well over a mile and consequently comes in at a very fast pace, so don't get caught out!

A few miles west from here, along the A149, is **Holkham Hall**, an eighteenth century mansion built in the Palladian style by architect **William Kent**, who was commissioned by the Coke family, the Earls of Leicester, who still own it. Among its magnificent features are the **Marble Hall** and a 60-foot high **Great Hall**, brimming with gold and alabaster. Twelve further rooms are on show, containing the fabulous works of art that Thomas Coke brought back from his "grand tour" of Europe in the late 18th century, among them paintings by Gainsborough, Van Dyck and Rubens. The whole place is surrounded by **grounds** landscaped by Capability Brown in 1762, the main feature of which is an 80-foot high obelisk. There's a wonderful sandy beach here; just leave the estate by the north gate, and you'll find acres of dunes backed by pine trees with all the attendant bird life. *Open June to September, Sunday to Thursday 1pm to 5pm. Admission (house and bygones museum) adults £6, children £3. Tel. 01328 710227; www.holkham.co.uk.*

About five miles west of Little Walsingham (see sidebar on next page) is the village of **Burnham Thorpe**, birthplace of local hero and national icon **Horatio Nelson**, whose father was rector of the local parish church. Although Nelson had requested that he be buried in the parish church, he is in fact buried in St. Paul's Cathedral, London, though there are plenty of Nelson reminders here; both the lectern and the altar cross are made out of timbers from his flagship, the *Victory*, and there's a permanent exhibition in Nelson's honor in the south nave. The village **pub**, named, surprise, surprise, the **Lord Nelson** is the place where the admiral put on a party for the locals in 1793, and where you can still get a tot of "Nelson's Blood" rum.

It's about seven miles due west of here on the A149 to **Hunstanton**, another small Victorian resort that like so many others on this coast was originally a fishing village. There are some pleasant beaches, backed by cliffs, and various all-weather attractions, including another **Sea Life Centre** and a leisure center. West of Hunstanton, the coast dips to the south, forming the eastern edge of the vast estuary known as **The Wash**, whose main tributary, the **River Ouse** meets the sea at **King's Lynn**. At the

ENGLAND'S NAZARETH

*Just inland from the coast is the village of **Little Walsingham**, for centuries one of England's most important places of pilgrimage. It all started in 1061 when local woman Richeldis de Faverches claimed to have seen visions of the Virgin Mary, prompting here to build a **Holy House** in Mary's honor. Before long Augustinian and Franciscan monastic communities were established, and the place was frequented by kings and queens, each following tradition by covering the last mile or so on their knees – the **Slipper Chapel** marks the site where footwear was put aside for the final stretch of the journey. Though Henry VIII had come here as a pilgrim in 1511, it was he who was responsible for the shrine's destruction during the Dissolution. The shrine was rebuilt in the 1920s and is today an important pilgrimage place for Anglicans, Roman Catholics and Orthodox.*

*The main focus here is the over-the-top 1920s **Anglican shrine** in the center of the village, with its Holy House, well, statue of Our Lady of Walsingham and a myriad votive candles. Across the road the ruins of the original abbey remain, as does the sixteenth century **Shirehall Museum**, which tells the village's history, along with a well-preserved 1770 Georgian courtroom. Open April to September Monday to Saturday 10am to 5pm, Sunday 2pm to 5pm, October weekends only. Admission £1. Tel. 01328 821510. Walsingham's parish church, rebuilt after a fire in the 1970s, retains much of the original stonework.*

crossroads of the A10 and A149, King's Lynn is an old port town whose prosperity grew as a result of the import of Scandinavian fish, Baltic timber and French wine, and the export of wool and corn. This is still a busy port, dealing in a variety of products, including cars, and grain. Although King's Lynn lacks the wholesale charm of many other east coast towns, it does nevertheless possess several lovely buildings, including England's oldest guildhall, and a variety of Georgian townhouses and quayside warehouses.

The town possesses two market places, named after the day of the week they operate. The **Saturday Market Place**, the older of the two, contains the **Trinity Guildhall**, with a checkered stone front that covers buildings from four different periods, from the original 1421 Guildhall to the extension of 1895. The Guildhall is now the Civic Center for the borough of King's Lynn and is not generally accessible to the public, unless you're on civic business. You can, however, enter the attached **Old Goal House**, used as the town police station until 1954, and housing the **tourist office**, a fascinating museum on crime and punishment and, in the undercroft, the **Regalia Rooms**, which contain a collection of various treasures owned by the town, such as a 14th century chalice known as **King John's Cup**.

Other buildings of note in the town include, on the quayside, the **Hanseatic Warehouse**, dating from the late fifteenth century, its half-timbered upper floor jutting out over the cobbled street below, and, on King Street, **the St. George's Guildhall**, built in 1420 and the oldest surviving guildhall in the country. Used as a theater during Elizabethan times, it now houses an **arts center** administered by the National Trust, and is the focal point for the annual **King's Lynn Festival**, held in July. Further on is the **Tuesday Market Place**, considerably larger than Saturday's, big enough, in fact, to have hosted a huge sit-down meal for 600 to celebrate the end of the war with France in 1814. Among the buildings to look out for are the **Duke's Head Hotel**, dating from 1689, coincidentally the year of the Duke of Monmouth's ill-fated attempt to seize the crown – and the neo-classical **Corn Exchange** building.

The countryside around King's Lynn is rich in stately homes, among which are the neo-Jacobean **Sandringham House** on the B1439 off the A149, where the royal family spends Christmas – it's about ten miles north of the town. Bought in 1861 by Queen Victoria for her son, Edward, later to become Edward VII, the mansion's main purpose, it seems, was to keep the future king from being bored – with its shooting lodge in the grounds, a ballroom, billiards room and bowling alley. The grounds are rich in rhododendrons and azaleas, creating a blaze of color in the spring, while the old stables contain an **exhibition of royal memorabilia** – a must for all royal fanatics. The house and gardens are closed when the royals are in residence, though surprisingly the stables and surrounding woodlands remain open. *Open daily mid-April to October (closed mid-July to early August when the Royal family is in residence) house 11am to 4:45pm, museum 11am to 5pm. Admission adults £4, students and seniors £3, children £2. Tel. 01553 772675.*

Five miles east of here off the A148 is **Houghton Hall**, a lovely Palladian house that future King Edward VII rejected in favor of Sandringham. Built in the 1730s for Britain's first prime minister, **Sir Robert Walpole**, it contains a number of ornate state rooms, the most fabulous of which is the **Stone Hall**. Although much of the art collection that once hung here was sold off to Catherine the Great to pay off the debts of a pennyless earl, some beautiful items remain – like a collection of Sevres porcelain and an army of 20,000 model soldiers. *Open Easter to end of September Sundays, Thursday and Holiday Mondays 2pm to 5pm. Admission adults £5.5, concessions £3. Tel. 01485 528569.*

About ten miles west of here on the A149 is **Castle Rising**, its ruined twelfth century keep in pretty good condition, with much of the original decoration intact. It's located right in the middle of some much older earthworks. The village of Castle Rising contains some pretty seventeenth century almshouses, whose residents still attend church all dolled up in the traditional costume of pointed black hat and red cloaks – the colors of the original benefactor, the Earl of Northampton.

Finally, there's **Oxburgh Hall**, just off the A134 around twenty miles southeast of King's Lynn, built in 1482 by the Bedingfeld family, devout Catholics who remained so throughout the various periods of persecution that accompanied the Reformation. Approached by a tall ceremonial gatehouse, followed by the main gatehouse of the manor itself, it's the archetypal English manor house, enclosed by a moat dappled with water lilies. The interior, however, apart from some tapestries that were made by the imprisoned Mary, Queen of Scots, is disappointing. *Open April to October Saturday to Wednesday 1pm to 5pm. Admission £5.30, garden and estate only £2.60. Tel. 01366 328258.*

PRACTICAL INFORMATION

Most of the small towns described have post offices, but don't count on there being a bank. Rather, get your cash in Great Yarmouth, or one of the larger towns like Cromer.

Great Yarmouth's **tourism office** is located on the seafront at *Marine Parade, Tel. 01493 842195; www.great-yarmouth.gov.uk.* King's Lynn's **tourism office** is in the *Custom House, Tel. 01493 763044.*

CAMBRIDGE

The famous university city of Cambridge, one of the most beautiful cities in Britain, is quite a contrast from Oxford; although Cambridge is a busy market town, there's little industry here, and much of the city center is unscathed by modern development. The result is a mesmerizing mixture of elegant classical buildings, medieval churches, hidden courtyards and wide open spaces.

Cambridge University, one of world's great institutions of learning, is of course the city's main raison d'etre and many of the world's greatest minds have passed through its portals. Most of its older colleges were built round quadrangles, or quads – large courtyards, helping to give the city a spacious, open feel. Many of these quads are open to the public, although access during examination periods is often limited. The college buildings themselves, with the exception of the **chapels**, are generally out of bounds to the public, though there are exceptions, so it's worth checking with the tourism department. Perhaps the best way to get a feel of the city and its university and to see as much as possible without running into limited access is to take a walking tour with one of the city's **Blue Guides**, who leave at regular intervals from the city tourist office.

ARRIVALS & DEPARTURES

By Car
The M11 motorway from London takes you direct to Cambridge, a journey of around 50 miles.

By Bus
Buses from London's Victoria bus station leave for Cambridge every two hours during the summer (and less frequently out-of-season). *Call 0990 808080 for information.* The bus station is centrally located at Drummer Street.

By Train
London's Liverpool Street Station is the place to get trains to Cambridge, a journey that can take up to an hour and a half. *Call National Rail Enquiries on 0345 484950 for information.* Cambridge's train station is located on Station Road, fifteen minutes southeast of the city center.

GETTING AROUND TOWN

If you're driving into the city, note that cars have been banned from much of the city center. There are a number of Park and Ride parking lots, where the cost is £1. While it's a compact city, and walking is by far the best way to explore it, you can also get around by bus or taxi. **Stagecoach Cambus**, *Tel. 01223 423554*, the local bus operator, sells daily and weekly explorer tickets which give you unlimited travel within the city and in the countryside beyond. You can hail a taxi or call **Cabco**, *Tel. 01223 312444*.

This is a great city for cycling, and a number of companies vie for the rental trade, including **Geoff's**, *65 Devonshire Road, Tel. 01223 365629*, and **Mike's Bike**, *Mill Road, Tel. 01223 312591*. Prices range from about £5-7 per day to £8-20 per week. If you must rent a car, try **Avis**, *245 Mill Road, Tel. 01223 212551*.

A good way to get an overview of the city is to take a tour on a **Guide Friday** bus, *Tel. 01223 363444*. These start at the train station, but can be picked up at various strategic points throughout the city. Pick up your ticket on the bus, or at the Guide Friday office at the station.

WHERE TO STAY

UNIVERSITY ARMS HOTEL, *Regent Street, Cambridge. Tel. 01223 351241, Fax 01223 315256. Rooms: 115. Rates: singles from £90, doubles from £135. Restaurant. All major credit cards accepted.*
This large hotel is right in the center of town, and within easy reach

of all the main attractions. Rooms are comfortable, with many of those at the rear of the building having views over Parker's Piece, a green space that is dear to English cricket fans as the place where one of its most famous players, Jack Hobbs, learned the tricks of his trade. It's still used as a cricket ground, so don't be surprised if on a Sunday afternoon you occasionally hear the "thwack" of leather against willow accompanied by gentle applause. There are three bars, a restaurant serving traditional English cuisine (the hotel's English breakfasts are particularly good) and a large lounge where you can take afternoon tea.

ARUNDEL HOUSE, *53 Chesterton Road, Cambridge. Tel. 01223 367721, Fax 01223 367721. Rooms: 105. Rates: singles from £49, doubles from £65, family rooms from £90. English breakfast £3.95. All major credit cards accepted.*

Perhaps the best situated of all of Cambridge's hotels, the Arundel House overlooks the Cam and green meadows and is no more than a few minutes' walk from most of the city's main points of interest. Part of a Victorian terrace, its pleasantly furnished rooms all come with bath or shower, TV, dryer and beverage-making facilities. There's also an attractive Victorian-style conservatory, where you can take afternoon tea, or have dinner later on, while out back an old coaching inn has been converted into a conference center with more rooms.

THE GARDEN HOUSE, *Granta Place, Mill Lane, Cambridge CB2 1RT. Tel. 01223 259988, Fax 01223 316605. Rooms: 116. Rates: singles from £135, doubles from £165, deluxe double from £245, suite from £360. English breakfast £13.50. All major credit cards accepted.*

This may be a modern hotel, but it's slap bang between the riverbank and an old cobbled street in one of the oldest parts of the city, and is no more than a couple of minutes from most of the major sites. Best of all are the views – many of the guest rooms have balconies and views of the river, as do the extensive, 3-acre gardens and outdoor terraces, where afternoon tea and drinks are available in the summer. The bedrooms are well-furnished and come with all the usual facilities. There's also an extensive leisure center, which includes an indoor swimming pool, sauna and gym, and a pleasant restaurant, Le Jardin, which also overlooks the river.

HAMILTON HOTEL, *156 Chesterton Road, Cambridge CB4 1DA. Tel. 01223 365664, Fax 01223 314866. Rooms: 25. Rates: singles from £25, doubles from £45. Restaurant, parking. All major credit cards accepted.*

Small hotel about a mile northeast of the city center, just off the A1134 ring road. It looks fairly undistinguished from the outside, but offers comfortable and well-appointed accommodations, each room having the usual range of facilties including TV and tea- and coffee-making equipment – though not all rooms have en suite bathrooms, so make sure you specify that's what you want. There's a restaurant and bar where you can get snacks.

GONVILLE HOTEL, *Gonville Place, Cambridge CB1 1LY. Tel 01223 366611, Fax 01223 315470. Rooms: 65. Rates: singles from £86, doubles from £106. Bar, restaurant. All major credit cards accepted.*

This modern, mock-Georgian hotel is part of the Best Western chain and is conveniently located, within easy walking distance of Cambridge's main attractions – including most of the colleges – and overlooking the famous Parkers Piece. The 65 rooms are spacious and comfortable, though not particularly exciting.

THE DUXFORD LODGE HOTEL, *Ickleton Road, Duxford, near Cambridge CB2 4RU. Tel 01223 836444, Fax 01223 832271. Rooms: 15. Rates: singles from £75, doubles from £95. Bar, restaurant. All major credit cards accepted.*

This Victorian country house hotel is located about eight miles south of Cambridge, in the pretty village of Duxford. The village is close to the M11 motorway, which means that you're within easy reach of London, as well as the attractions of Cambridge itself, just a few minutes' drive away. The hotel boasts a comfortable bar and a fine restaurant serving English/ French style cuisine. Among the 15 pleasantly furnished bedrooms, a number have four-poster beds, and four rooms open out on to the extensive lawns.

POSTHOUSE CAMBRIDGE, *Lakeview, Bridge Road, Impington, Cambridge CB4 9PH. Tel 0870 400 9015, Fax 01223 233426. Rooms: 165. Rates: all rooms from £99 (single or double occupancy). Bar, restaurant, indoor pool, jacuzzi, sauna, gymnasium.*

The Posthouse, part of the Trusthouse Forte chain, is a spacious modern establishment located in a rural setting just a few miles from downtown Cambridge and its many attractions at the junction of the A14 and B1049. It's a large hotel, with 165 well-appointed, spacious rooms, with a number of suites, and some special rooms for people with disabilities. One of the hotel's main attractions is its health club, which boasts a large pool as well as sauna and gym. There's a nice courtyard garden, with a play area for children. The Junction restaurant offers a wide range of dishes.

OLD SCHOOL HOTEL, *9 Greenside, Waterbeach, Cambridge CB5 9HW. Tel 01223 861609, Fax 01223 441683. Rooms: 8. Rates: singles from £42, doubles from £60. Bar, restaurant, indoor pool. All major credit cards accepted.*

Attractively located right on the village green in the village of Waterbeach, just outside Cambridge (but easily accessible for the city), the Old School Hotel was just that in a former life – an early Victorian Parochial school. The rooms are spacious, pleasantly decorated and furnished and there's a lovely courtyard garden overlooked by a conservatory lounge. The hotel is located about half a mile from the main A10; just look out for the signs for Waterbeach village – once there, you can't miss the hotel.

CAMBRIDGE LODGE HOTEL, *Huntingdon Road, Cambridge CB3 0DQ. Tel 01223 352833, Fax 01223 355166. Rooms: 10. Rates: singles from £50, doubles from £62. Bar, restaurant. All major credit cards accepted.*

The Cambridge Lodge Hotel is a large, mock Tudor house set in a pleasant garden on the A1307 about a mile from the center of Cambridge. It offers comfortable, roomy bedrooms and a good restaurant specializing in English/French cuisine; the breakfasts here are particularly good. It's particularly good value, given its proximity to the major attractions – yet away from the hustle and bustle of the city center.

WHERE TO EAT

BROWN'S, *23 Trumpington Street. Tel. 01223 461665 (no reservations). All major credit cards accepted.*

Sumptous palace of a restaurant that was originally built as the emergency room of a former hospital. The high ceilings and fans, wicker chairs and pale yellow decor give it the feel of an imperial age, though it claims to be an American/French style brasserie. There's an extensive menu ranging from hot sandwiches and hamburgers to more exotic dishes like mushroom and guiness pie, while a large blackboard indicates the chef's daily specials.

MIDSUMMER HOUSE, *Midsummer Common, Cambridge. Tel. 01223 369299. Open Sunday and Tuesday to Friday, lunch noon to 2pm, Tuesday to Saturday dinner 7pm to 10pm. Set dinner (2 courses) £35.*

Spacious restaurant near to the River Cam, with a delightful lemon-colored conservatory offering views across to the Cam. The emphasis here is on continental cuisine, using fresh, imaginatively presented local ingredients. How about a filet of cod on a bed of eggplant caviare with oyster beignets and tapenade butter? Sounds great, but could someone tell me what beignets are? The wine list is extensive, focusing on France and the New World, with house wines starting at £12.95.

22 CHESTERTON ROAD, *22 Chesterton Road, Cambridge. Tel. 01223 323814. Open Tuesday to Saturday dinner only 7pm to 9.45pm. Set dinner £23.50. All major credit cards accepted.*

Smart, sophisticated restaurant located in an elegant town house close to the river to the west of Cambridge city center, giving it a warm domestic feel. The food is essentially English, but with some "modern" touches that reflect England's new ethnic and cultural diversity – a number of dishes, for example, combine traditional ingredients with just a hint of curry, like the monkfish with green curry and coconut sauce. The service is relaxed and unhurried and house wines start from as little as £9.25 a bottle.

BANGKOK CITY, *24 Green Street, Cambridge. Tel 01223 354382. Open daily (except Sunday lunch) noon to 3pm, 6pm to 11pm. Set 2-course dinner £22.95, 3-course £24.95. All major credit cards accepted.*

Bangkok City is a good Thai restaurant that's especially popular with university students, so expect a lively ambience. There's a wide variety of fish dishes, plus the usual mixture of curries and noodle choices; the rice here is particularly good. The service is friendly and attentive, and though the prices a cut above the norm for this kind of place, it's worth it.

LA MARGHERITA, *15 Magdalene Street, Cambridge. Tel 01223 315232. Open daily noon to 2:30pm, 6pm to 10pm. A la carte menu, prices starting at £6.50 for pasta dishes, from £11 for meat/fish. All major credit cards accepted.*

Excellent and atmospheric Italian restaurant in the center of Cambridge, with a wide variety of authentic pasta dishes, as well as veal, steaks and so on, all reasonably priced. In particular, try the tiramisu, which is out of this world! The service is friendly and efficient on the whole (try to avoid the peak student times).

HOT POT, *66 Chesterton Road, Cambridge. Tel 01223 366552. Open Tuesday to Sunday noon to 1:30pm, 6pm to 11pm (closed Sunday lunch). 2-course meal from £10.30. credit cards: MC, Visa.*

A very small (and therefore occasionally cramped) restaurant that specializes in Mongolian cooking. The house special is interesting: a metal stove is placed on your table. Water is heated, and you then dip the assortment of fish, meat and vegetables into it. If cooking your own dinner doesn't entice, you can opt for a wide range of kitchen-cooked meals, including lemon chicken and Szechuan pork. This is one of the less expensive city center eating places.

HOBBS PAVILION, *Park Terrace, Cambridge. Tel 01223 367480. Open Tuesday to Sunday, noon to 2:15pm and 7pm to 9:45pm. All major credit cards accepted.*

Named after a famous English cricketer, Hobbs Pavilion – a converted cricket pavilion overlooking Parkers Piece – specializes in pancakes and crepes (there's no evidence that these were a particular favorite of Hobbs, though), with a wide variety of fillings, sweet and savory. As well as the pancakes, there's a dessert list that includes some delicious ice cream choices, including ginger flavor – and even (but not for the faint-hearted) garlic flavor.

SEEING THE SIGHTS

Perhaps Cambridge's most famous college is **King's College**, on King's Parade, whose alumni have included the writer E. M. Forster and economist John Maynard Keynes, the bane of Mrs. Thatcher. Founded by

King Henry VI in 1441, Kings' most famous building is its magnificent **Chapel**, built in the late 1400s in the intricate perpendicular style popular at the time. Inside it's the graceful **fan vaulting** that grabs the attention, with brightly coloured bosses at the cross points. The huge **windows**, all 16th century except the great west window which is Victorian, allow in plenty of light to add to the feeling of spaciousness. The eye is also drawn to Rubens' *Adoration of the Magi* behind the high altar. You'll be intrigued by the **exhibition** in the northern side chapels that explains how the chapel was built. The College is also home to one of the finest church choirs in the world. Every Christmas Eve their *Festival of Nine Lessons and Carols* is broadcast on TV and radio throughout Britain and much of the world. During weekdays of term time, there's an opportunity to hear the choir sing (for free) at the regular 5:30pm service of Evensong.

Cambridge's oldest college, **Peterhouse**, on Trumpington Street, was founded in 1284 by Hugh de Balsham, Bishop of Ely. Very few of the original buildings remain – though parts of the dining hall are said to date back to the 1290s – but you can see the **hall**, restored in the 19th century, with stained glass windows by William Morris, and the attractive **chapel**, constructed in 1632.

Emmanuel College, on St. Andrew's Street, is of interest to Americans as being the college where **John Harvard**, founder of Harvard University, studied. Established in 1584, the college was a hotbed of

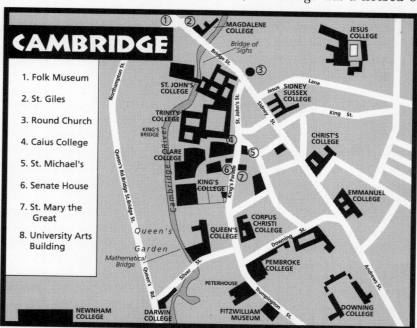

STUDYING IN CAMBRIDGE

The vast majority of Cambridge's students live in the individual colleges, just as they do at Oxford. Here they eat, drink (quite a lot) and have their "tutorials" – supervised sessions with their teachers where the work they have produced is discussed in detail. Lectures, examinations and the like are organized on a university basis. Today, a large proportion of Cambridge students come from overseas.

Puritan activity in its early years. Among the attractive buildings are a chapel and colonnade designed by Christopher Wren, whose work is very much in evidence throughout the city.

Meanwhile, **Queens' College**, on Queens' Lane, has to be one of the most attractive of all the colleges. Started in 1448, its plural title is derived from its dedication to not one but two queens, the wives of Henry VI and Edward IV. The peaceful **second cloister** is flanked by the sixteenth century half-timbered president's lodge. Among Queens' other attractions is the **Mathematical Bridge**, dating from the early 1900s and replacing an earlier bridge that was held together without nuts and bolts.

St. John's College, on St. John's Street, was established in 1511 by Lady Margaret Beaufort, Henry VII's mother, and covers the site of an ancient hospital. Although the Tudor gateway and the ancient courts are impressive, it's the famous **Bridge of Sighs**, modeled on the original in Venice, that grabs the attention. Spanning the River Cam, it links the more venerable part of the college with the mock Gothic **New Court**, built in 1825. The Bridge of Sighs itself is closed to visitors; the best view of it is had from nearby **Kitchen Bridge**.

Cambridge's largest college is **Trinity** (not to be confused with Trinity Hall), established by Henry VII in 1546, with 700 undergraduates; Sir Isaac Newton, Lord Tennyson and Prince Charles all studied here. Check out its 17th century "great court" where a large gatehouse contains **Great Tom**, a large clock whose chimes were familiarized in the race round the quadrangle in the movie *Chariots of Fire*. There's also a library designed by Christopher Wren, with its impressive colonnades.

The city's other attractions include the **Fitzwilliam Museum**, Trumpington Street, with an outstanding display of art and artifacts. Among the paintings on display are works by Titian, Rubens, Constable, Gainsborough and some French Impressionists. The museum also houses a collection of Egyptian antiquities, including mummies, a large display of Staffordshire pottery and a collection of armor. **Great St. Mary's**, known as the University Church, is also worth a visit. Though the present building "only" dates from 1478, it replaces an earlier structure built in the eleventh century, and has witnessed among its preachers such famous clergy as Archbishops Cranmer, Latimer and Ridley, all burned at the stake in Oxford.

NIGHTLIFE & ENTERTAINMENT

The city's main arts and entertainments center is **The Corn Exchange**, with a wide range of productions, from children's shows to ballet, *Tel. 01223 357851*. Meanwhile, the newly restored **Arts Theatre** is at *6 St. Edward's Passage, Tel. 01223 503333*. An international **Folk Music Festival** is held in the city in July, *Tel. 01223 358977*, as does the **Cambridge International Film Festival**. Check with the tourist information center for details.

A number of Cambridge's **pubs** serve inexpensive food in an authentic medieval atmosphere that can't be beaten. Try **The Eagle**, *Bene't Street, Tel. 01223 505020;* **The Pickeral Inn**, *Magdalene Street, Tel. 01223 355068;* or **The Anchor**, *located on the Cam between Granta Place and Silver Street, Tel. 01223 353554.*

SHOPPING

Cambridge is a shopper's paradise. The usual chain stores can be found in the **Grafton Centre** and **Lion's Yard** precincts. For more interesting shopping, check out the smaller stores around **Trinity Street**. Cambridge naturally hosts a large number of bookstores, among them **The Cambridge University Press store**, *1 Trinity Street*, and Heffer's, *20 Trinity Street*. For secondhand books, you need look no further than **The Bookshop**, *24 Magdalene Street*.

PRACTICAL INFORMATION

The main Cambridge **tourist information** office is in *Wheeler Street, Tel. 01223 322640; www.cambridge.gov.uk*. There are plenty of **banks** in downtown Cambridge, as well as an **American Express** office at *25 Sidney Street, Tel. 01223 461460.*

ELY

Ely, pronounced "Eelee," just fifteen miles northeast of Cambridge on the A10, is an ancient cathedral city with roots going back as far as the seventh century. Then it was that Saxon **Queen Ethelreda** built an abbey on what was essentially an island in the midst of thousands of acres of marshy wetlands known as the **Fens**, accessible only with the assistance of the "fenslodgers," expert navigators who would cross the marshy expanse with wide, ski-like footwear. During the reign of Hereward the Wake, **Eel Island** became the center of Anglo-Saxon opposition to the Normans, until it finally yielded to Norman power in 1071. It was then that the Normans decided to build a huge **cathedral** on the site, a true "cathedral of the Fens" that would be visible for miles around – a constant reminder to the Saxons of who was the boss.

Today's Ely, with a population of around 8,000, is, after Wells, the second smallest cathedral city in England, and retains much of its medieval charm. Its other claim to fame is that it was, for ten years, the home of **Oliver Cromwell**.

ARRIVALS & DEPARTURES
By Car
It's a short drive to Ely from Cambridge along the A10.

By Bus
Frequent buses from Cambridge's Drummer Street Bus Station stop at Market Street in Ely.

By Train
There are regular trains from Cambridge. They take just 15 minutes. Ely's train station is a half-mile south of the city center.

GETTING AROUND TOWN
Visiting the sights in this tiny city couldn't be easier – walking is the only method that makes any sense!

WHERE TO STAY
LAMB HOTEL, *2 Lynn Road, Ely CB7 4EJ. Tel. 01353 663574, fax 01353 662023. Rooms: 32. Rates: single off-peak rate £50, double off-peak rate £70 (standard rates £67 and £90 respectively). Restaurant, parking. All major credit cards accepted.*

This former coaching inn dates back as far as the 15th century when, known as the Holy Lambe, it served as a stopping-off point for pilgrims. The hotel is located right in the center of town, very close to the cathedral. The 32 comfortable rooms all have bath or shower, and four-poster beds are available. Rooms come with the inevitable tea- and coffee-making facilities. There's a restaurant where you can get traditional English cuisine, or bars where you can eat more informally.

OLD EGREMONT HOUSE, *31 Egremont Street, Ely CB6 1AE. Tel./ Fax 01353 663118. Rooms: 3. Rates: single £29, double/twin £44. No credit cards accepted.*

Very nice non-smoking bed and breakfast close to the cathedral, with a lovely view of the building from the garden. It's very small, with just three rooms, but they're all more than adequate. You can count on a warm welcome from the owner, Sheila Friend-Smith. The breakfasts are particularly good, using fresh local produce – in all, an excellent value.

NYTON HOTEL, *7 Barton Road, Ely CB7 4HZ. Tel 01353 662459, Fax 01353 666217. Rooms: 10. Rates: singles from £40, doubles from £65. Bar, restaurant. All major credit cards accepted.*

The family-run Nyton Hotel is set in pleasant, two-acre grounds and offers a variety of accommodations varying in size and style. All are comfortable and come with the full range of facilities. The public rooms include a bar, where informal meals are served, a delightful wood-paneled restaurant for more formal dining, and a large conservatory. The Nyton offers particularly good value, and is within easy reach of Ely's fabulous cathedral.

TRAVELODGE, *Witchford Road, Ely CB6 3NN. Tel./Fax 01353 668499. Rooms: 40. Rates: doubles from £39.50. All major credit cards accepted.*

Modern hotel, just outside Ely, but convenient for all the attractions. The decor and furnishings are what you'd expect from a large chain, but the rooms are all spacious and well-equipped. There's no restaurant on the premises itself, but the kids will be delighted to know that there's a Burger King very close by (not to mention British fast food chain Little Chef, which also has a restaurant here). All in all, excellent value, especially if you have children with you.

WHERE TO EAT

OLD FIRE ENGINE HOUSE, *25 St Mary's Street, Ely. Tel. 01353 662582. Open daily for lunch, 12:15pm to 2pm, Monday to Saturday for dinner 7:15pm to 9pm. Main courses around £13-15. Credit cards, MC, Visa.*

Long established, charming, rustic restaurant in a converted fire station close to the cathedral with bare wooden floors and scrubbed pine tables. A second dining room doubles up as an art gallery and has an open fire. The food focuses on traditional local ingredients such as baked pike, pigeon and hare and – if you can face it – eel pie – but what more appropriate in Ely. Traditional British sweets predominate, such as syllabubs and apple pie. There's a good wine list, and in the summer you can dine outside.

SEEING THE SIGHTS

From whichever angle you approach Ely, you won't fail to be impressed by the massive cathedral, towering above the local landscape. Begun in 1083, it seems out of all proportion to the tiny city around. If the external elevations are impressive, then just wait till you get inside! The **nave**, one of the longest in England, and flanked by massive Norman pillars, is topped by a striking **painted ceiling** depicting biblical scenes – fashioned by amateur artists, including the father of acclaimed Victorian composer Sir Charles Hubert Parry – in the nineteenth century.

At the **crossing**, where the nave meets the transepts, is the cathedral's most striking feature, and a masterpiece of medieval engineering and artistry – the **octagon**, known as the "lantern of the Fens." Built in 1322 to replace a central tower that had collapsed, it is essentially a medieval skylight, composed mainly of wood and stained glass weighing some 400 tons and unique in England. Further east lies the **choir**, rebuilt after the damage caused by the central tower's collapse, and then the **presbytery**, where once thousands of pilgrims came to venerate the relics of **St. Ethelreda**, the founder of the original monastic buildings. Another important feature of the building is its 14th century **Lady Chapel**, accessible from the north transept, and virtually detached from the main structure. Imagine how stunning the chapel must have looked before the Reformation, during which some 200 statues were defaced, mainly by having their heads lopped off. Fortunately, the beautiful **fan vaulting** was left intact. Also worth a look is the cathedral's marvelous collection of

THE FENS

The Fens, *which cover a vast area of countryside between Cambridge up to Boston, Lincolnshire, is one of the weirdest landscapes in England. Originally this low lying area was a virtually untraversable landscape of deep bogs, marshes, and small clay islands where small communities eked out a living cutting peat for fuel, marsh grass for thatch and survived by living off the fish (especially eel) and wild fowl that populated the area. Although there had been various attempts to drain the land during medieval times, it was only in the 1600s that serious attempts were made to dry out the area. At Wicken Fen, seven miles to the southeast of Ely, you can see one of the last remaining areas of undrained fenland, 600 acres or so that was donated to the National Trust by Victorian entymologists in 1899. The place is open daily, year-round, from dawn to dusk, and entry costs £3.*

stained glass dating from 1240 onwards, that can be seen in the **north triforium**. *Open Monday to Saturday 7am to 7pm, Sunday 7:30pm to 5pm. Admission £3. Tel. 01353 667735.*

Ely contains some of the oldest and best-preserved medieval domestic architecture in England, much of which is now part of the **King's School**, a private boarding school where cathedral choristers are trained. You can also see, adjacent to the cathedral's west front at 29 St. Mary's Street, the half-timbered former vicarage that was once the home of **Oliver Cromwell**. The "Lord Protector" lived here for ten years beginning in 1636, leading the parliamentary forces in their opposition to King Charles I. The house today contains an exhibition on the life and times of Cromwell, and is also the home of the **Ely tourist office**, *Tel. 01353 662062; www.ely.org.uk.*

20. THE NORTHWEST

Stretching in the south from the Roman city of **Chester** to the hilly **Scottish border** in the north, England's northwest is one of its most diverse regions. Two of the nation's largest cities are here: **Manchester**, an industrial metropolis that has undergone something of a resurgence in recent years and now has a vibrant arts and cultural scene – as well as the world's most successful soccer club – and the great port of **Liverpool**, for many years England's busiest commercial port and home town of the "Fab Four" – John, Paul, George and Ringo.

To the east of the region, the **Peak District** is an area of dramatic landscapes, pretty villages and magnificent stately homes, while on the Lancashire coast, England's most visited resort, brash and bawdy **Blackpool** is the place to see Brits at play. Between Blackpool and the Scottish border lies England's most stunning landscapes in the area much beloved by Bryron, Keats and Wordsworth – the **Lake District** – as well as the 75-mile long **Hadrian's Wall**, built by the Romans in the second century AD to fend off invasion by the Pict tribes from southern Scotland.

CHESTER

Chester was founded as a military camp by the **Romans** as early as the first century AD – the name Chester comes from the Latin "castra" meaning "camp." Situated on the **River Dee**, it also served as a port from Roman times, attaining its greatest prosperity in the twelfth and thirteenth centuries, until the river began to silt up and nearby Liverpool began to usurp its trade. Today, Chester is a thriving commercial and tourist center of about 100,000 residents, notable for its well-preserved, colonnaded **half-timbered buildings**, its fine **cathedral** and **castle**, and one of Britain's best **zoos**.

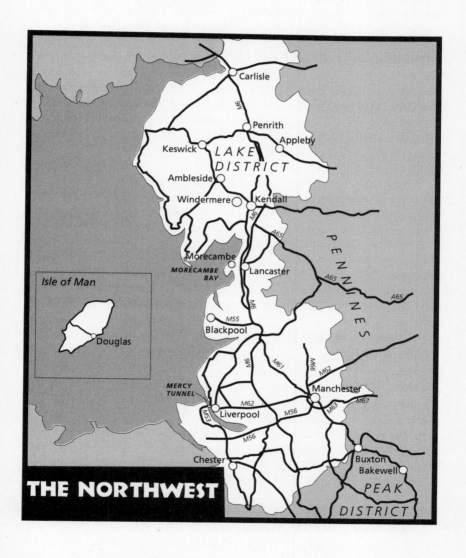

THE NORTHWEST

The city is at the heart of a rich agricultural region, with rolling green hills, a host of dairy farms and some beautifully preserved towns and villages, several of which come with their own medieval manor houses. Be aware that, as a major tourist destination, the city can get exceptionally busy during the peak summer months and bank holiday weekends; if you decide to stay here, make sure you book your hotel in advance.

ARRIVALS AND DEPARTURES

By Car

From London, take the M1 north to the junction with the M6 (junction 19). Take the M6 northwest as far as junction 10 with the M54. At junction 3 of the M54, take the A41 north direct to Chester. It's about 190 miles from London.

By Bus

There is a limited direct service from London's Victoria Bus Station to Chester. Otherwise, change at Birmingham, where regular National Express buses leave for Chester every couple of hours. The normal journey time is just under six hours. Chester's National Express terminal is north of the city walls at George Street.

By Train

A regular service for Chester leaves London Euston Station, taking just over three hours. *Call 0345 484950 for information.*

GETTING AROUND TOWN

Chester is built on a loop in the River Dee. The main sights of interest are located inside the ancient city walls, the focal point of the city being High Cross, from which roads radiate to the four main city gates. Chester is a walkable city, and in any case much of the city is closed to vehicular traffic for much of the day.

Chester City Transport, *Tel. 01244 347452*, can provide you with information about the city's buses. **Guide Friday** offer open-top bus tours of the city, *Tel. 01244 347457*. Bicycles can be rented from **Davies Cycles**, *2-12 Cuppion Street, Tel. 01244 319204*, for about £10 a day.

WHERE TO STAY

CHESTER GROSVENOR HOTEL, *Eastgate, Chester CH1 1LT. Tel. 01244 324024, Fax 01244 313246. Rooms: 85. Rates: singles from £152, doubles from £229. Restaurant, bars, sauna, gymnasium. All major credit cards accepted.*

This quintessentially English hotel is situated within the city's Roman walls and within easy reach of all the main city attractions. The five-story, part half-timbered building houses an intimate brasserie, and the more formal Arkle restaurant (see below). In addition to the usual public rooms there's even a Library, which gives the place the ambience of some London gentleman's club on Pall Mall. The rooms are exceptionally comfortable, and there's an extensive leisure suite. As part of the package, guests are also offered free membership of a country club, two miles from the hotel, with complimentary transport provided.

POSTHOUSE CHESTER, *Wrexham Road, Chester CH4 9DL. Tel. 0870 400 9019, Fax 01244 674100. Rooms: 145. Rates: singles from £85, doubles from £85 (includes full breakfast). Restaurant, bars, pool, tennis courts, gymnasium, sauna. All major credit cards accepted.*

Large, modern spacious hotel that's ideal for families with children, on account of the pool, children's play area and sports facilities – guaranteed to keep the little ones happy. There is a selection of well-equipped family rooms, the best of which are the newer "Millennium Rooms," so if you're going to have your family with you, ask for one of these when you book. Guests can also benefit from 24-hour room service and an all-day lounge menu.

ROWTON HALL COUNTRY HOUSE HOTEL, *Whitchurch Road, Rowton, Chester CH3 6AD. Tel. 01244 335262, Fax 01244 3355464. Rooms: 42. Rates: singles from £85, doubles from £85. Restaurants, indoor pool, tennis courts, sauna, solarium, gymnasium. All major credit cards accepted.*

An impressive ivy-clad 18th century house in several acres of mature grounds, just off the A41 heading southeast of Chester and within easy raech of the main attractions. The traditional-style rooms in the manor house are spacious and comfortable, or you can opt for more modern rooms in the new extension, which also houses the leisure center. There's a good restaurant, and bar meals are served throughout the day.

CRABWALL MANOR HOTEL, *Park Gate Road, Mollington, Chester, CH1 6NE. Tel 01224 851666, Fax 01224 851400. Rooms: 48. Rates: singles from £125, doubles from £150. Restaurant/dining room. Indoor pool, sauna, solarium, Jacuzzi spa, gym. All major cards accepted.*

If its history you're after then Crabwall Manor has it. The hotel dates back to the 17th century and was mentioned in William the Conqeror's Domesday Book. The striking appearance of its turret style frontage is truly inspiring. The hotel boasts spacious bedrooms and tastefully designed suites, all of which are equipped with TVs and the usual amenities. The hotel boasts a number of compact lounge areas, a billiards room and a restaurant situated in the conservatory.

MOLLINGTON BANASTRE HOTEL, *Parkgate Road, Mollington, Chester CH1 6NE. Tel 01224 851471, Fax 01244 851165. Rooms: 63. Rates: singles from £75, doubles from £95. Restaurant/dining room, indoor pool,* squash/racketball courts, croquet, sauna, solarium, Jacuzzi spa, hairdressing health and beauty salon. All major cards accepted.

Part of the Best Western chain, this hotel is well suited to its attractive grounds in which it is set. Its grounds hold an ornamental lake visible from inside the hotel. The hotel caters to both leisure and business customers boasting a well equipped leisure centre, two restaurants and a stylish bar. The bedrooms are well equipped with the usual expected amenities.

CHESTER MOAT HOUSE, *Trinity Street, Chester CH1 2B2. Tel 01244 899988, Fax 01244 316118. Rooms: 160. Rates: singles from £115, doubles from £135. Restaurant/dining room. Sauna, solarium, gym, Jacuzzi spa, steam room, beauty treatment room. All major cards accepted.*

Operated by the Moat House chain, this hotel's city center location mean it's close to all the city's major attractions. All the hotels rooms are well equipped with the all the expected facilities. The large public areas including its leisure area are located on the first floor. Meals are available from the hotel's strikingly decorated non-smoking restaurant.

QUEEN'S HOTEL, *City Road. Chester CH1 3AU. Tel. 01244 305000, Fax 01244 318483. Rooms: 128. Rates: singles from £60, doubles from £70. Restaurant/dining room. Croquet, live entertainment. All major cards accepted.*

This stylish 19th century hotel stands strikingly its a central location opposite the railway station. There are many features that make it elegant, in particular its central gallery staircase and its cheerfully designed bedrooms with all the modern up-to-the-minute facilities. This hotel also benefits from its own private garden.

WHERE TO EAT

ARKLE RESTAURANT, *Grosvenor Hotel (see above). Tel. 01244 324024. Open Tuesday to Saturday noon to 2:30pm, 7pm to 9:30pm. Set lunch from £25, set dinner from £40. All major credit cards accepted*

This is the place to come for a real slap-up meal. The restaurant, named after the famous racehorse Arkle, winner of the Grand National at Liverpool's Aintree racecourse, is a huge windowless room, with an enormous skylight and stone pillars. The atmosphere is slightly dated, with waiters in dinner jackets and tail and heavy silverware at the tables. The food is French and Italian influenced, with main courses like langoustine ravioli with sauce vierge. There's an extensive wine list.

GARDEN HOUSE, *1 Rufus Court, off Northgate Street. Tel. 01244 313251. All major credit cards accepted.*

Two-floor restaurant in the center of the city where you can get excellent meat and poultry, especially game, dishes using fresh local ingredients and vegetarian choices that have won awards. There's a very pleasant garden and patio for eating outside in the summer, and an extensive wine list.

SEEING THE SIGHTS

Chester is a walkable city, with most of its attractions within a few hundred yards of **The Cross**. Before you start out, it's not a bad idea to get an overview of the city. The best place for this is the **Chester Heritage Centre** on Bridge Street Row, which traces the city's history from Roman times to the present. It's an ideal place to start a tour of the city. *Open Monday to Saturday 11am to 5pm, Sunday noon to 5pm. Admission £1.50.*

Chester is best known for its beautiful half-timbered buildings, typified in **The Rows**, medieval double-decker rows of shops, one colonnaded tier at street level, the upper level forming long galleries with dozens of stores that line the four streets – Watergate, Northgate, Eastgate and Bridge streets – that converge in the center of town, at The Cross. Many have medieval crypts below them, and some even have Roman foundations.

Among the city's other attractions are **The Walls**, best accessed by climbing the steps by the **Eastgate Clock**, built to commemorate Queen Victoria's Diamond Jubilee in 1897. Take a walk along the two-mile long walls and you'll be rewarded with some superb views of the city, including the Dee, the cathedral and some Roman ruins. It's a particularly attractive thing to do on a sunny evening. Just off Market Square is **Chester Cathedral**, with origins going back to Roman times, though the current building dates from 1092. Originally a Benedictine abbey, it became a cathedral in 1541. Inside, you'll find some fine medieval **wood carvings** in the choir, well-preserved **medieval roof bosses** in the lady chapel, and the **south transept** with its range of side chapels. A number of original monastic buildings, including refectory, cloisters and chapter house, have survived relatively intact. Had the abbey not been converted to a cathedral for the Diocese of Chester in that year, those buildings may well have been lost when Henry VIII dissolved most of England's monastic foundations. The cathedral's most unusual feature is a recently completed freestanding **bell tower**. *Open daily 7am to 6:30pm. Admission free. Tel. 01244 324756; www.chestercathedral.org.uk.*

Chester also has a **Castle**, built by the Normans, who were as impressed by the city's strategic qualities as the Romans had been. The castle, which overlooks the Dee, lost its moats and battlements 200 years ago when civil and criminal courts, jail and barracks were constructed. The castle's main attraction is the simple uncluttered chapel of **St. Mary de Castro**. *Open Easter to September daily 10am to 6pm; October to Easter daily 10am to 4pm. Admission free.* Part of the castle has been given over to the **Cheshire Military Museum**. Just south of here, at the southeast corner of the walled town are the **Roman Gardens**, and across the road are the remains of a 7,000-seater Roman amphitheater, one of the largest in

Britain, though you'll need a very vivid imagination to visualize how it might have looked in Roman times. *Open Easter to September 10am to 6pm; October to Easter 10am to 1pm and 2pm to 4pm. Admission free.*

Chester is also famous for its beautifully landscaped **Zoo**, the second largest in Britain after London, sprawling over more than 100 acres. Founder and animal lover George Mottishead is said to have visited a zoo in nearby Manchester as a child and announced to his mother, "When I have a zoo it won't have any bars." So don't expect to be able to order a gin and tonic here. Highly respected for its conservation work and for its broad collection of animals, it includes many endangered species. The Zoo is located just off the A41. *Open daily 10am to 3:30pm (5:30pm in summer). Last admissions 1 1/2 housr before closing. Admission adults £9.50. 3s-15s £7, seniors £7. www.demon.co.uk/chesterzoo.*

NIGHTLIFE & ENTERTAINMENT

The **Alexander Jazz Theatre**, *Rufus Court, Tel. 01224 34005*, is a wine bar, coffee bar and tapas bat all rolled into one, with jazz the main item on the menu. There's also the **Gateway Theatre**, *Hamilton Place*, for plays and musicals.

Chester has dozens of pubs. The **Yates's Wine Lodge**, *Frodsham Street, Tel 01244 344813* (Yates is part of a national chain of pubs), has occasional live music, as does **Murphy's** on *Northgate Street.*

PRACTICAL INFORMATION

Chester's **tourist information** office is located at the *Town Hall, Northgate Street, Chester CH1 2HJ, Tel. 01244 402111; www.chestercc.gov.uk.* There are plenty of **banks** in the city center, as well as a branch of **American Express**, *23 St. Werburgh Street, near the cathedral*. The main **post office** is on *St. John's Street, just east of the Grosvenor Shopping Centre.*

LIVERPOOL

It's only half an hour's drive from Chester along the M53 and through the Mersey Tunnel to **Liverpool**, at one time England's prime transatlantic port and for a time the second city of the British Empire. It's a city that a lot of outsiders have been all too ready to put down over the years, with a rough and ready reputation. True, tremendous poverty and deprivation have existed here – and to some extend, still exist – but no one can deny the Liverpudlian spirit, nor the city's tremendous vibrancy. On top of all that I've always found it one of the most friendly cities anywhere.

Liverpool had been a small fishing port for centuries, and only came into its own as a major commercial port about 300 years ago, a process exacerbated by the silting up of Chester's River Dee and by the growth in the slave trade, where alcohol, firearms and textiles were exchanged for African slaves who were shipped to the Caribbean or America. The ships then loaded up with Caribbean rum, forming the slave triangle.

After the abolition of slavery in 1807, Liverpool found new ways of making money, becoming Europe's main port of embarkation for more than nine million **emigrants** between 1830 and 1930 mostly to America and Australia. At the same time, many **immigrants** arrived, principally Irish, following the disastrous potato famine of the 1840s, and Afro-Caribbeans. Liverpool was for a while also the main commercial and passenger departure port for the United States. The city's **decline** as a major port was due to a number of factors: the arrival of cheap airfares which led to the demise of the luxury liner business; and the loss of much business to ports in the south of England, much closer to continental Europe. With the decline of the shipping industry, and the closure of scores of manufacturing factories, Liverpool experienced high unemployment in the 1960s and '70s, and degrees of poverty unseen in other parts of the country

Like its big city neighbor Manchester, Liverpool has witnessed something of a **revival** in recent years, with many of its old warehouses converted into fashionable apartments in the **Albert Dock** area. The city still has plenty of problems, but there's an extraordinary community spirit here, best seen after the **Hillsborough Stadium** disaster, when 95 Liverpool soccer supporters lost their lives. Today, Liverpool makes an interesting if unusual place to visit, with its two vast **cathedrals**, various attractions linked with the **Beatles**, all natives of the city, and a bevy of **museums** and **galleries**, including the Tate Gallery.

ARRIVALS & DEPARTURES
By Car
From London, take the M1 north to the M6. Take the M6 northwest to junction 21a, where you join the M62 east. The M62 then takes you direct to Liverpool. Total journey time is normally around 3 1/2 hours.

By Bus
Liverpool is well served by buses from London Victoria, which arrive at Norton Street Coach Station. *Call 0990 808080 for information.*

By Train
There are both long-distance trains from London Euston direct to Liverpool's Lime Street Station, and also a regular (every half hour) local service from Manchester Piccadilly. *Call 0345 484950 for details.* Lime Street Station is right in the heart of the city, and a 10 minute walk to the Albert Dock.

ORIENTATION

Liverpool is a large city, but relatively easy to negotiate. Several of the main tourist attractions are in the **Albert Dock area**. From here, Hanover Street leads into the commercial heart of the city. **Hope Street**, with the two cathedrals, is half a mile to the east.

GETTING AROUND TOWN

In spite of its size, Liverpool is a city that's easily explored on foot. There's a complex network of bus services operated by **Merseytravel**, *Tel. 0151 236 7676*, who have a desk in the tourist information office in Clayton Square. You can purchase all-day bus tickets for £4.50. Most local buses leave from Queens Square. Taxis can be hailed in the street or by calling **Mersey Cabs**, *Tel. 0151 298 2222*.

For local travel information, including ferries and local bus services: *Tel. 0151 236 7676*.

WHERE TO STAY

LIVERPOOL MARRIOTT CITY CENTRE, *1 Queen Square, Liverpool L1 1RH. Tel. 0151 476 8000, Fax 0151 474 5000. Rooms: 146. Rates: singles from £110, doubles from £130. Air conditioning, restaurant, bars, indoor pool, sauna, solarium, gymnasium. All major credit cards accepted. Covered parking available.*

Large, modern, stylish hotel located in the newly redeveloped Queen Square area in the center of the city. The interior is swish and elegant, with marble floors and spacious public areas, and the bedrooms are large and pleasantly furnished. There's a full range of leisure facilities and a fancy restaurant. Having covered parking available is a definite bonus in a city where parking places are at a premium.

PREMIER LODGE, *45 Victoria Street, Liverpool L1 6JB. Tel. 0870 700 1422, Fax 0870 700 1423. Rooms: 39. Rates: singles, doubles from £46. All major cards accepted.*

Part of a nationwide chain, the Liverpool Premier Lodge couldn't be more central, and represents excellent value for a downtown establishment. The 39 rooms are pleasantly adequate, with TVs and the usual tea- and coffee-making facilities. There's no restaurant; but there are plenty of eating establishments within easy walking distance. This really is a great place to stay if you're on a strict budget, yet want somewhere that's convenient for all the city's main attractions.

LIVERPOOL MOAT HOUSE, *Paradise Street, Liverpool L1 8JD. Tel 0151 471 9988, Fax 0151 709 2706. Rooms: 263. Rates: singles from £115, doubles from £135. Restaurant/dining room. Indoor pool, sauna, solarium, gym, Jacuzzi spa, whirlpool steam room. All major cards accepted.*

Situated within walking distance of the Albert Dock and the various

Beatles attractions as well as the city's main shopping areas, the Liverpool Moat House boasts spacious, comfortable rooms with all the modern facilities you would expect. The hotel has an excellent variety of leisure and conference facilities making it a favorite with both business and leisure guests, and a good base to explore the history and culture of this fascinating city.

THE ROYAL HOTEL, *Marine Terrace, Waterloo, Liverpool L22 5PR. Tel 0151 928 2332, Fax 0151 949 0320. Rooms: 25. Rates; singles from £45, doubles from £65. Bar, restaurant. All major credit cards accepted.*

The Royal is located about six miles northwest of Liverpool city center, just off the A565 Liverpool to Southport Road. It's a lovely 1815 building, next to the Marine Gardens, and with excellent views towards north Wales. Despite the age of the building, the well-equipped rooms are bright and modern, as are the public rooms; some of the bedrooms have four-posters. There's a very pleasant, contemporary style restaurant, adjacent to which is a conservatory for soaking up that Liverpool sunshine!

BLENHEIM LODGE, *37 Aigburth Drive, Sefton Park, Liverpool L17 4JE. Tel 0151 727 7380, Fax 0151 727 5833. Rooms: 17. Rates: singles from £19.50, doubles from £33. Bar, dining room. Credit cards: MC, Visa.*

This large Victorian house on the edge of the suburb of Sefton Park was once the home of Stuart Sutcliffe of Beatles' fame, and represents excellent value, although if you want your own private bathroom, you'll have to make that clear when you book. The bedrooms are modern and there's a pleasant bar, and a dining room where delicious full English breakfasts (and other, more simple choices) are served. The hotel is situated just off the A561.

WHERE TO EAT

BECHER'S BROOK, *29a Hope Street, Liverpool L1 9BQ. Tel. 0151 707 0005. Open Monday to Friday noon to 4pm, Monday to Saturday 5pm to 10pm. Main courses £12.50 and up. All major credit cards accepted.*

Named after the famous fence at Aintree Racecourse, Becher's Brook (pronounced "Beecher's") is located in an end-of-terrace Georgian house in Hope Street, the road that links the city's two cathedrals. With whitewashed brick walls and bare pine floorboards, the decor is simple. The menu is classically based but with eclectic, especially Japanese, influences. How about roasted lobster on a smoked haddock and crab brandade with Japanese salad? The wine list offers a wide range of choice.

TAI PAN, *W.H. Lung Building, Great Howards Street. Tel. 0151 207 3888. Open daily noon to 11pm. Main courses £6 to £11. All major credit cards accepted.*

Wonderful, popular Chinese eatery situated above an Asian supermarket in the city center. The menu is extensive, and the dishes authentic Cantonese, like aromatic crispy duck. The dim sum is particularly tasty. The house wines startat around £8.50 a bottle.

FAR EAST, *27-35 Berry Street, Liverpool. Tel 0151 709 3141. Open daily noon to 11pm. Set lunch from £6, set dinner from £15. All major credit cards accepted.*

Liverpool's once vibrant Chinatown is alas no more – or at least, there's not much left of it. One of the remaining vestiges of Chinatown is the long-established Far East restaurant, where you can find offerings like cod fillets with stir-fried vegetables or crispy roast duck. Desserts leave something to be desired. On the liquid front, tea flows as freely as the Yangtse River; wine is available too, from about £9 a bottle.

ZIBA, *15-19 Berry Street, Liverpool L1 9DF. Tel 0151 708 8870. Open daily noon to 2:30pm, 6pm to 10pm (closed Sunday evening). Set lunch and dinner from £10.50 (2 courses). All major credit cards accepted.*

This edge-of-Chinatown eatery was once a car showroom – now it's a pleasant, two level dining room that is drawing ever increasing crowds. The cuisine is best described as "modern British," so you can expect guinea fowl terrine with foie gras running through it, accompanied by beetroot and orange, layered in a cylindrical shape. There are lots of tarts and sorbets for dessert, an eclectic wine list with house wines starting at around £10, and oodles of atmosphere.

SEEING THE SIGHTS

Head towards Liverpool's main train station, **Lime Street**, a good place to start a tour of the city due to its close proximity to many of the attractions. Opposite the station, for example, is **St. George's Hall**, a vast Greek Revival building that was built on the proceeds of Liverpool's maritime prosperity. This was Liverpool's main concert venue for a long period, and contains one of the largest Willis organs is Europe, played in recitals in July. Otherwise, the hall is only open to the public for three weeks in August, when the floor, covered with 30,000 Minton tiles, is revealed – and for the occasional craft fair. Just north of here on William Brown Street is the **Liverpool Museum** and Planetarium with exhibits of glassware, china, silver and antiques which at one time graced the mansions of Liverpool's wealthy shipping magnates during the city's heyday. *Open year-round Monday to Saturday 10am to 5pm, Sunday 2pm to 5pm. Admission by NMGM Standard 8 pass, which allows you into eight of Liverpool's main attractions. Cost adults £3, children under 16 and seniors £1.50.*

Further along William Brown Street is the **Walker Gallery**, one of England's best provincial galleries, with works by Turner, Constable, Degas, Cezanne right through to David Hockney. There are also pieces by

George Stubbs, a local animal artist. *Open Monday to Saturday 10am to 5pm, Sunday noon to 5pm. Admission as Liverpool Museum (above). Tel. 0151 207 0001.* From Lime Street Station turn south to Renshaw Street and Berry Street to the city's monstrous **Anglican Cathedral**. Started in 1903 but only completed in 1978, England's largest cathedral and the world's fifth largest was built in the Gothic style of local sandstone. Inside, you can gape at the world's tallest **gothic arches** and its highest and heaviest **bells**. The 330-foot **tower**, which is open to visitors, offers splendid **views** of the city and surrounding countryside as far as the Welsh hills. *Open daily 8am to 6pm. Free, but donations welcome. Tower admission £1. Tel. 0151 709 6271.*

Liverpool has long been a city noted for its religious rivalry, with large Catholic and Protestant populations. It's appropriate, then, that the Anglican Cathedral is linked to the Roman Catholic cathedral of **Christ the King** by Hope Street. Built in 1962 on the site of an old workhouse, and affectionately known as "Paddy's Wigwam" on account of its circular shape and its largely Irish congregation, it was originally intended that the building would vie in size with St. Peter's Rome, but those plans were dropped due to lack of finance. It's an amazing contrast to the Anglican building. *Open daily. Admission free.*

From here, head west along Mount Pleasant Street to Ranelagh Street, passing the grotesque Clayton Square Shopping Centre, and along Hanover Street, where, on the right, the **Bluecoat Chambers** – accessed in School Lane – a former Anglican boarding school built in 1717 now houses a **modern art gallery** with an excellent cafe and bookstore. Keep going along Hanover Street to the **Albert Dock**, the heart of Liverpool's revitalized docks area.

The Albert, an important part of Liverpool's immense docks complex until its demise early in the twentieth century, was rescued by planners who saw its potential as a tourist attraction, turned many of its old warehouses into speciality shops and the four-story **Maritime Museum**, with displays on Liverpool's history as a port, and especially on its role as the point of departure for countless **emigrants**. There are models of boats and ships of all descriptions and an 1854 Liverpool street scene, while a powerful new addition traces the development of the slave trade, including the reconstruction of a slave ship, complete with authentic Afro-Caribbean voices reading from the slaves diaries. *Dock open daily 10am to 5:30pm. Free. www.merseyworld.com; Maritime Museum open daily 10am to 5pm. Admission NMGM pass (see above) Tel. 0151 478 4499.*

Just across the dock outside is the **Museum of Liverpool Life**, a fascinating glimpse into Liverpudlian life. It focuses on the many factors, positive and negative, that have made the city what it is today, particularly the economic hardship, poverty and the resilience of its people (known as **Scousers** by outsiders). There are sections on the role of the trade

THE BEATLES

*Liverpool has been synonymous with music ever since the late 1950s, but while bands come and go, none is every likely to have the same impact as did **The Beatles**, and many visitors come to Liverpool just to check out their haunts.*

*The best known of these is the **Cavern Club**, on Matthew Street west of Central Station. Sadly the club is closed, covered by the ugly Cavern Walks Shopping centre. Also on Matthew Street is the **Beatles Shop** which possesses the largest range of Beatles memorabilia in the world. If you're a real Beatles groupie, the best time to be here is the late August Bank Holiday (the last Monday in that month) for the **Matthew Street Festival**.*

*You're better off, however, going to either the static **Beatles Story**, in the Albert Dock, which follows the Beatles' progress from their earliest efforts at the Cavern right through to John's untimely death in New York City. Here's also an exhibition of Lennon photos commemorating the singer/songwriter's life, and you can buy maps giving self-guided tours which take in such famous places as **Strawberry Fields** and **Penny Lane**. Open daily 10am to 6pm. Last admission 5pm. Cost £7.95 adult, £5.45 concessions/ children, £19 family ticket (2 adults, 2 kids). Tel. 0151 709 1963.*

*The normally very staid National Trust has just opened the **Paul McCartney House**, at 20 Forthlin Road, the 1950s council house that was Paul's home from 1955, when he was 13, to 1963, the time the Beatles became an entity. The group used to meet here to practise and to compose songs. The house has been restored with authentic furnishings and fittings to resemble how it was when Paul lived there. Open April to October, Wednesday to Saturday; November to mid-December Saturday only. Admission £5.10, child £2.60. Tel. 0151 486 4006.*

*Your best bet, however, has to do the two-hour **Magical Mystery Tour**, which leaves the Albert Dock daily at 2:20pm. The double-decker bus is staffed by guides who offer pithy anecdotes, and visits such places as the terraced streets where the lads lived, Strawberry Fields and Penny Lane. Cost £10.95 for the tour without the exhibition, £15 with the exhibition (same for all ages).*

unions, women's issues, the arts in the city, and the riots that took place here in the mid-1980s. And, of course, the city's two famous soccer clubs, Liverpool FC and Everton. *Open daily 10am to 5pm. Admission by NMGM pass (see above). Tel. 0151 478 4080.*

There's been a deliberate policy by the British government in recent years to move the focus of art and culture away from London to the provinces. There's evidence next door with the new **Tate Gallery Liverpool**, a showcase for twentieth and twenty-first century art in some superb, well-lit galleries. There's also an excellent café and a shop brimming with books, posters and postcards. *Open year-round Tuesday to Sunday, 10am to 6pm. Admission free, though there may be a charge during exhibitions.*

A little further north, at **Pier Head**, you can take a round trip on the frequent **ferry service**, *Tel. 0151 630 1030*, over to the town of **Birkenhead** – made famous by the 1960's hit song *Ferry Across the Mersey* by Gerry and the Pacemakers. From the ferry, you'll get a great view of the Liverpool skyline, including the twin towers of the Liver Insurance Building, crowned by the mythical **Liver Birds** (pronounced Lie-ver), said to have given the city its name.

NIGHTLIFE & ENTERTAINMENT

One of Britain's best orchestras, the **Royal Liverpool Philharmonic**, plays at the **Philharmonic Hall**, *36 Hope Street, Tel. 0151 709 3789*, while major musical productions, including ballet and opera are held at the **Liverpool Empire**, *Lime Street, Tel. 0151 709 1555*. Major pop concerts are held at the **Royal Court**, *Roe Street, Tel. 0151 709 4321*. For serious theater, check out what's on at the **Everyman Theatre**, *5-9 Hope Street, Tel. 0151 709 4776*.

Liverpool has a vast number of pubs and bars, among which **The Philharmonic**, *36 Hope Street*, and the more traditional **Black Horse**, *21 Berry Street*, stand out. For the latest information, get a copy of the free monthly *In Touch* listings magazine.

SPORTS & RECREATION

Liverpool is home to two of Britain's best known soccer clubs, **Liverpool**, based at the 50,000-capacity **Anfield Stadium**, *Tel. 0151 260 6677*, and **Everton**, with a ground at **Goodison Park**, *Tel. 0151 330 2300*. Both teams play in the top-notch English Premiership.

Liverpool is also famous for **Aintree Race Course**, *Tel. 0151 523 2600*, where Britain's best-known horse race, the **Grand National**, has been held annually in March or April almost every year since 1839.

PRACTICAL INFORMATION

The city's main **visitor information center** is located at the *Merseyside Welcome Centre, Clayton Street Shopping Centre, Liverpool L1 1QR, Tel. 0151 708 8838*. There's another office at the *Atlantic Pavilion, Albert Dock, Liverpool L3 4AE, Tel. 0151 708 8838; www.liverpool.gov.uk.*

The city is very well served with banks and post offices. There's also an **American Express** office at *54 Lord Street, Tel. 0151 708 9202*.

MANCHESTER

Mark Twain was very rude about **Manchester**. Very rude. He once said, "I would like to live in Manchester, England. The transition between Manchester and death would be unnoticeable." Of course, he said plenty of rude things about American cities too!

Things have changed since Twain's day, and Manchester is now an exciting, vibrant city with cultural and entertainment facilities second only to London's. The city's history goes back to Roman times, when a small camp was built here. The original village grew only slowly through the Saxon and Norman periods, when it was an insignificant market town. By the mid-1300s, a flourishing wool trade began to develop in the area, the first indication perhaps of the major growth in textiles that Manchester was to become famous for.

It was much later, after the start of the Industrial Revolution, when Manchester really came into its own, particularly with mechanization in the **cotton industry** and the construction of the world's first cotton mill powered by steam in 1783. Within 50 years, a major new canal, the **Manchester Ship Canal**, turned the city into a port capable of selling its own goods overseas, without having to rely on Liverpool. Meanwhile, the railways brought Manchester's produced goods to the domestic market.

Manchester soon began to expand beyond all recognition, with a rapid increase in population, and the construction of row upon row of tiny "jerry-built" homes that even today feature in one of the nation's best-loved sitcoms – *Coronation Street* – set in Weatherfield, a fictional suburb of neighboring Salford. The poor conditions and low pay experienced by the vast majority of the workers helped make Manchester a major center for political change. Events like the 1819 **Peterloo Massacre**, when eleven protesting workers were killed, fueled the anger of the masses against the wealthy factory owners. It was here in Manchester that the **Chartist Movement**, campaigning for universal suffrage, originated. Manchester was also a hotbed for the **Anti-Corn Law League**, a radical movement opposed to the tough trade tariffs.

Manchester has taken decades to shake off its old-fashioned "cloth cap" image of a city of soot-covered buildings and women in curlers chatting to neighbors from their front doorway, but at last it has succeeded, thanks to some major injections of government cash and some progressive thinking by the city council. There was a serious setback for the city in 1996 when an IRA bomb detonated in the city center, injuring hundreds of people and causing untold damage. The city however, has responded well, with the restoration of many of the older buildings, the construction of new concert halls and sports facilities, and a burgeoning of the arts and entertainment scene, so that today Manchester is one of the nation's liveliest cities. The city's coup de grace is its successful bid to stage the 2002 **Commonwealth Games**, for which a new 70,000-seat stadium is being constructed.

ARRIVALS & DEPARTURES

By Air

Manchester has a major international **airport** of its own about 10 miles south of the city. Known as Manchester Ringway, it is a hub for flights from all over the UK and Europe. British Airway, Continental and Delta operate direct flights to the US from here, while Air Canada serves the city from Toronto.

By Car

From London, take the M1 north to the junction with the M6, which you leave at junction 21a for the M62 east. Follow the signs for Manchester city center.

By Bus

Buses from London (Victoria) leave regularly for Manchester's Chorlton Street Bus Station. *Call 0990 808080 for information.*

By Train

Manchester's Piccadilly Station is very well served by trains from London Euston, with a journey time of around 2 1/2 hours. *Call 0345 484950.*

GETTING AROUND TOWN

Most but not all of Manchester's main attractions are within walking distance of Piccadilly Gardens, the city's main square, which also happens to be the main departure point for local bus services. These local buses are run by **GMPTE**, *Tel. 0161 228 7811*. There's also a tram system in Manchester, which links some of the city's main attractions and hotels. It's called **Metrolink**, *Tel. 0161 205 2000*. Taxis – black cabs in particular – are abundant, and can be hailed anywhere.

For information about a number of **walking tours** of Manchester city center given by the Blue Guides, contact the tourism office, *Tel. 0161 234 3157*.

WHERE TO STAY

ALBANY HOTEL, *21 Albany Road, Chorlton-cum-Hardy, Manchester M21 0AY. Tel. 0161 881 6774, Fax 0161 862 9405. Rooms: 17. Rates: singles from £39.50, doubles from £69.50. Restaurant, bar, parking. All major credit cards accepted.*

Small, early Victorian hotel a few miles out of Manchester city center, just off the A6010. The hotel has an excellent reputation for its friendly hospitality and service, and the bedrooms are all attractively appointed in period style, in keeping with the age of the house. The elegant restaurant serves traditional English cuisine.

COMFORT INN, *Hyde Road, Birch Street, West Gorton, Manchester M12 5NT. Tel. 0161 220 8700, Fax 0161 220 8848. Rooms:90. Rates: singles and doubles from £47.75. Restaurant, bar, gymnasium, parking. All major credit cards accepted.*

Part of a large chain, the Comfort Inn is a great place to stay if you want to keep your spending in check and don't mind being a little bit out of the main downtown area! Located about three miles from Manchester's city center on the A57, the rooms are modest yet well-equipped, with full en-suite and tea- and coffee-making facilities. The hotel is also notable for its friendly and helpful staff. Great value.

EXPRESS BY HOLIDAY INN, *Waterfront Quay, Salford Quays, Manchester M5 2XW. Tel. 0161 868 1000, Fax 0161 868 1068. Rooms: 120. Rates: all rooms from £36.50 (includes continental breakfast). All major credit cards accepted.*

Another modern purpose-built hotel that offers very inexpensive accommodations, just a couple of miles of downtown Manchester, between neighboring Salford's new Lowry Art Centre and Old Trafford, home of Manchester United and Lancashire Country Cricket Club. The rooms are as you'd expect; comfortable and functional; family rooms are available. There's no restaurant, but there are plenty of eating places within easy reach.

LE MERIDIEN VICTORIA AND ALBERT, *Water Street, Manchester M3 4JQ. Rooms: 156. Rates: singles from £94.50, doubles from £165 (includes full breakfast). Brasserie, restaurant, leisure facilities 2 minutes walk away. All major credit cards accepted.*

A large, modern hotel created from former warehouses on the banks of Manchester's River Irwell, and just opposite the Granada TV Studios, one of the city's main attractions. The rooms are comfortable, and named after Granada TV productions (like Britain's favorite soap, *Coronation Street*, and *The Adventures of Sherlock Holmes* with Jeremy Brett) with pictures to match. Exposed brick wall, iron pillars and wooden beams add to the warehousey atmosphere. The brasserie is open all day.

PALACE HOTEL, *Oxford Street, Manchester M60 7HA. Tel 0161 288 1111, Fax 0161 288 2222. Rooms: 252. Rates: rooms from £111. Bars, restaurant. All major credit cards accepted.*

This large city center hotel was originally built in 1890 as the headquarters for one of Britain's leading insurance companies, the Refuge. The Gothic landmark building, within easy walking reach of all the major attractions in the city, is full of typical architectural and decorative style of the period; lots of ornate tiles, paneling and plaster-work. The hotel was recently refurbished at great expense and boasts more than 250 bedrooms, all decorated and furnished to a high standard. The public rooms include an impressive ballroom, bars, and a fine restaurant.

THISTLEWOOD HOTEL, *Urmston, Manchester M32 9EF. Tel 0161 865 3611, Fax 0161 866 8133. Rooms: 9. Rate: singles from £32, doubles from £46. Lounge, dining room. Credit cards: MC, Visa.*

If you don't mind staying a few miles out of the city center (but within easy reach of the motorway network), then this may be the place for you; it certainly represents good value. It's located in the quiet residential suburb of Urmston, not far from the famous Old Trafford football ground (home of the world's largest soccer club, Manchester United), and the vast new Trafford Park shopping mall. The rooms are comfortable and well-equipped, with a lounge for guests and plenty of parking space.

WILLOW BANK HOTEL, *340 Wilmslow Road, Fallowfield, Manchester M14 6AF. Tel 0161 224 0461, Fax 0161 257 2561. Rooms: 117. Rates: singles from £50, doubles from £70. Bar, restaurant. All major credit cards accepted.*

The Willow Bank is a modern hotel, conveniently situated just three miles from downtown Manchester and within easy reach of the motorway. The hotel has recently had an extensive refurbishment; the well-equipped rooms are all decorated and furnished to a high standard. This is another hotel that represents extremely good value – especially if you don't mind being a little bit away from the bustling (and very noisy) city center.

KEMPTON HOUSE HOTEL, *400 Wilbraham Road, Chorlton-cum-Hardy, Manchester M21 0UK. Tel. and Fax 0161 881 8766. Rates: singles from £25, doubles from £34. Bar, breakfast room. Credit cards: MC, Visa.*

This small, family-run B&B facility located in the pleasant suburb of Chorlton-cum-Hardy, about five miles from Manchester city center, offers excellent value for money. The bedrooms are adequately furnished and come with tea- and coffee-making equipment. Note, however, that not all rooms have en suite shower or bath, so specify when you book that that's what you want; otherwise, you might end up sharing. This hotel is also notable for its excellent breakfasts, enough to convert you to English breakfasts forever.

WHERE TO EAT

CROWNE PLAZA MIDLAND, FRENCH RESTAURANT, *Peter Street, Manchester. Tel. 0161 236 3333. Open Monday to Saturday 6:30pm to 10:30pm (11pm on Fridays and Saturdays). Set dinner £38. All major credit cards accepted.*

Major city center hotel with all the atmosphere of one of the grand Edwardian hotels. The elegant ambience extends to the restaurant – a huge oval room with high ceilings and ornate plasterwork. Expect to find all the classics of French cuisine here, with some creative additions. There's a good wine list, and house wine comes in at £13.50.

KOREANA, *King's House, 40a King Street West, Manchester M3 2WY. Tel. 0161 832 4330. Open Monday to Friday noon to 2:30pm, 6:30pm to 10:30pm, Saturday 6:30pm to 10:30pm only. Set lunch £5.50 and up, dinner £13.50 and up. All major credit cards accepted.*

Popular Korean restaurant that's been around a long time. The room itself is pleasant – a wood-paneled basement – and the service impeccable. What's more it offers tremendous value – and for just £13.50 you can put together your own 3-course meal. All the Korean classics are available, as well as some less conventional concoctions. The low prices extend to the wine list; house wine is offered at just £7.95 a bottle.

MASH AND AIR, *40 Chorlton Street, Manchester M1 3HW. Tel. 0161 661 6161. Open Air Tuesday to Saturday 6:30pm to 11pm; Mash Monday to Saturday noon to 3pm, 5pm to 11pm (12.30am Saturday). Meals Air main courses from £14, Mash main courses from £7. All major credit cards accepted.*

Interesting concept: Mash bar on the first floor; Mash brasserie on the second; and Air restaurant at the top. The brasserie's focus is on Italian, with scrumptious pizzas from the wood-fired oven among other a la carte items; Air is the smarter of the two, serving an a la carte menu that's strong on fish and poultry – pan-fried cod with polenta, for example. There's an extensive wine list, and house wine starts at around £13 a bottle.

SIMPLY HEATHCOTES, *Jacksons Row, Manchester. Tel. 0161 835 3536. Open daily 11:45am to 2:30pm, 5:30pm to 11pm (9:30pm on Sunday). Set lunch and dinner from £14. All major credit cards accepted.*

This former register office is now a big, bright, noisy and colorful eatery serving lively creative versions of some classic main courses, like thin filet steak with ale sauce and horseradish risotto. There are a number of vegetarian options, and, among the desserts, the bread and butter pudding is particularly delicious. There's an extensive wine list, with house wine starting at £11.50.

YANG SING, *3 Charlotte Street, Manchester. Tel. 0161 236 2200. Open daily noon to 11pm. Set lunch and dinner from £15. All major credit cards accepted.*

After a fire at its premises in Princess Street in 1999, Yang Sing moved here. Whether the move is permanent or temporary remains to be seen. The food is of course Chinese, with a full range of dim sum until late afternoon, and an extensive selection of old favorites as well as daily specials. What's especially nice about this place is the fact that so many Chinese can be seen eating here – always a good sign. There's a good wine list, with house wines coming in at just under £10.

MOSS NOOK, *Ringway Road, Manchester M22 5DW. Tel 0161 437 4778. Open Tuesday to Friday noon to 1:30pm, 7pm to 9:30pm (closed Saturday lunch). Set dinner from £15.50. All major credit cards accepted.*

Not far from the airport, this place, but it could be another world, with its long, heavy drapes and dark red upholstery. The food's good – choices come from a small but carefully thought-out menu, so honey-glazed duckling with a plum sauce and tournedos rossini figure prominently. The desserts are excellent, and the mainly French wine list starts at £9.95 a bouteille.

SEEING THE SIGHTS

The best place to start a tour of the city center is **Albert Square**, which memorializes Queen Victoria's beloved husband. One side of it is completely taken up by the immense Victorian **Town Hall**, built in 1867, and a real statement about how the city saw itself at that period in history. Particularly interesting is the vast **Great Hall**, with a hammer-beam roof and murals painted in the 1850s by Pre-Rapaelite artist Ford Madox Brown. Guided tours are available of the building. *For information, call 0161 234 1750.* Adjacent to the Town Hall is the **Central Library**, once the largest municipal library in the world, and built in 1930 to emphasize the city's commitment to education.

Behind the Library, on Mosley Street, is the **City Art Gallery**, with a wonderful collection of pre-Raphaelite work, including pieces by Madox Brown, Holman Hunt and Burne-Jones. Other work on display includes pieces by Gainsborough, Turner, Cannaletto and George Stubbs. *Open Monday, 11am to 5:30pm, Tuesday to Saturday 10am to 5:30pm, Sunday 2pm to 5:30pm. Admission free. Tel. 0161 236 5244.* Also near the Station, on Peter Street, is the **Free Trade Hall**, the home of the city's world-famous **Halle Orchestra** before it moved to the new Bridgewater Hall (see below) in 1996. The building, constructed on the site of the Peterloo Massacre, has just been converted into a luxury hotel.

Two buildings on Lower Mosley Street south of the Free Trade Hall bear witness to the city's ambitious rebuilding program. The **G-Mex Centre**, formerly a train station, is now a major exhibition center, while the **Bridgewater Hall**, constructed in 1996, claims to have the nation's best acoustics and is home to Manchester's **Halle Orchestra**. The hall is constructed on special state-of-the-art pilings that cut out external noise.

From here, take Liverpool Road to Lower Byrom Street and a cluster of out-of-the-ordinary visitor attractions. Most popular is the **Granada Studios Tour**. Granada, the ITV region that covers the northwest of England and one of the largest TV companies in Britain, makes some of the nation's popular programs. *The Adventures of Sherlock Holmes*, with Jeremy Brett, for example, was made here, as is the forty-year-old soap *Coronation Street*, still the most watched show on British TV. The studios include a reconstruction of Downing Street, the Baker Street of Sherlock Holmes, and Coronation Street itself, where you can sup a pint in the soap's pub, the *Rovers' Return*. *Open Mid-April to September daily 9:45am to 6pm, last admission 4pm; October to mid-April Monday to Friday 9:45am to 4:30pm, weekends 9:45am to 5:30pm, last admission 3pm. Admission charge £14.99. Tel. 0161 832 4999.*

'CORONATION STREET'

Britain's – and the world's – longest-running TV soap, ITV's **Coronation Street***, celebrated its 40th anniversary in 2000. Based in fictional Weatherfield, a suburb of Manchester, the soap follows the lives of the families and individuals who live in a terraced, working class street. Most of the actors have become household names, and a handful have been with the series since it began in 1960. Today the soap is still regularly at the top of the TV ratings, with more than 12 million viewers on the four nights it's on – Monday, Wednesday, Friday and Sunday. The show is also popular in 40 other nations, including Canada. You can visit the set of "The Street" as part of the Granada Studios Tour (see above).*

Close by the **Castlefield Visitor Centre** is a 7-acre **urban heritage park** that covers the site of an old Roman fort. You can see a reconstruction of the gate to the Roman fort, while the **Museum of Science and Industry** traces the city's industrial past in a series of displays which include the world's oldest passenger railroad station. Walk – if you dare - through a Victorian sewer and check out a bevy of working steam mill engines. *Open Monday to Friday 10am to 4pm, Saturday and Sunday noon to 4pm. Admission £6. Tel. 0161 834 4026.*

Follow Lower Byrom Street and Gartside Street north to Bridge Street to the excellent **People's History Museum**, which follows the plight of working people through the time of the Industrial Revolution to the present. You can trace the background to the Peterloo Massacre here, and there's a lovely collection of artifacts, including union banners, children's toys, photographs, kitchen equipment and tools that illustrate how working people lived during the toughest economic times. *Open Tuesday to Sunday 11am to 4:30pm. Admission £1. Tel. 0161 839 6061.*

Just off Deansgate, with its shops and offices, including the upmarket **Kendal Milne** department store, is St. Anne's Street, which in turn leads to **St. Anne's Square**, an attractive oasis of trees, with some fine shops and boutiques and the elegant **St. Anne's Church**, built in 1712. The church contains, among other things, the painting *The Descent from the Cross* by Annibale Carraci. It's also the place where essayist Thomas de Quincey was baptized. Close by is the **Manchester Royal Exchange**, formerly a cotton market that at one time could hold up to 7,000 traders. The building underwent considerable damage after the 1996 IRA bombing, but has since been restored, as has the **Royal Exchange Theatre**, one of the nation's foremost repertory theaters. *For information about current productions, call 0161 833 2833.*

Follow Victoria Street north to **Manchester Cathedral**, mainly Perpendicular in style, a parish church until it was elevated to the status of cathedral in 1847. It's unusually wide for its length and contains a host of interesting features, including some fine 16th century choir stalls, a 'brass' of warden Huntingdon who died in 1458 that's in excellent condition (a brass is a usually medieval brass panel, dedicated as a memorial to an individual), and an octagonal chapter house dating from the 1480s. *Open year-round daily 8am to 6pm. Tel. 0161 833 2220.*

Head back along Deansgate to the **John Rylands Library**, built in the 1890s in a heavy Gothic style by Enriquetta Ryland to hold the theological works collected by her husband. Among the million or so volumes on the premises are bibles in more than 300 languages, various historical documents and some ancient manuscripts. Here also is the **Grafton portrait**, which may be one of the more accurate likenesses of William Shakespeare. *Open Monday to Friday 10am to 5:30pm, Saturday 10am to 1pm. Admission free. Tel. 0161 834 5343.*

Birmingham University has its Barber Institute, and, not to be outdone, Manchester University has the **Whitworth Art Gallery**, in the suburb of Moss Side. The light and spacious interior of this Victorian red brick building contains an internationally acclaimed collection of British watercolors, the largest wallpaper and textile collection in the country outside London, and a new mezzanine floor for contemporary sculpture. *Open Monday to Saturday, 10am to 5pm, Sunday 2pm to 5pm. Admission free. Tel. 0161 275 7450; www.man.ac.uk/WAG.*

NIGHTLIFE & ENTERTAINMENT

Manchester has a vibrant entertainment and cultural scene. Symphony concerts by Manchester's own **Halle Orchestra** and by visiting orchestras are held at **The Bridgewater Hall**, *Lower Mosley Street, Tel. 0161*

907 9000, while the **Royal Northern College of Music**, *124 Oxford Road, Tel. 0161 273 4504*, also offers a varied program of classical music. Rock and pop concerts by major celebrities are held at the **G-Mex Centre**, also in *Lower Mosley Street, Tel. 0161 832 9000*, and at **Labatt's Apollo**, some way out of the city center at *Ardwick Green, Tel. 0161 242 2525*.

If you prefer theater, check what's on at the **Royal Exchange**, *Tel. 0161 833 9833*, and at the **Library Theatre**, *St. Peter's Square, Tel. 0161 236 7110*, while opera buffs need look no further than **The Opera House**, *Quay Street, Tel. 0161 242 2509*, which also hosts concerts and recitals.

In addition to its theaters and concerts halls, Manchester boasts a vibrant club scene. For rock, reggae and R&B, one of the best venues is **Band on the Wall**, *25 Swan Street, Tel. 0161 832 6625*, which has live music most night of the week. Meanwhile, **Manchester Board Walk**, *Little Peter Street, Tel. 0161 228 3555*, and **The Venue**, *17 Whitworth Street, Tel. 0161 236 0026*, are other, similar venues. With literally hundreds of pubs and a growing number of cafe-bars dotted around the city, it's almost a question of exploring for yourself; there are raucous, studenty type pubs, such as the **Lass O' Gowrie**, *Charles Street*, which has its own microbrewery, **The Circus** pub at *86 Portland Street*, Manchester's smallest.

For food, try **The Mark Addy**, *on the corner of Bridge and Stanley streets*; they offer an overwhelming choice of cheeses and pates. Manchester's gay village is centered on Canal Street, where there are around 30 gay venues, from the contemporary **Manto Bar**, *Number 46*, to more traditional gay pubs like the **New Union**. A guide to gay goings-on in Manchester is available from many of these vanues, or by calling the **Lesbian and Gay Switchboard**, *Tel. 0161 274 3999*.

SHOPPING

Manchester is one of England's leading shopping centers, with a number of large department stores as well as a host of smaller specialist shops that could easily keep you occupied all day. Most Mancunians (that is, people from Manchester!) do their shopping downtown in the vast but dreary **Arndale Centre**, which has just received a major (and much needed) facelift in the wake of the IRA bomb blast in 1996. All the major high street stores are there, as well as a large market area.

Between the Centre and Piccadilly Plaza are **Debenham's** and **Lewis's**, two massive department stores, while another upmarket department store, **Kendal Milne**, can be found on Deansgate. The nation's largest **Marks and Spencer's** store is on Market Street, while for smaller shops and boutiques, check out the area around **St. Anne's Square**.

SPORTS & RECREATION

The world's largest soccer club, **Manchester United**, is based at the 60,000-capacity **Old Trafford Ground** in the city, *Tel. 0161 872 0199*, while rivals **Manchester City**, recently promoted to the English Premiership League, play at their **Maine Road Ground**, *Tel. 0161 224 5000*, though they expect to move shortly to the new 50,000-capacity Commonwealth Games Stadium.

Manchester is also home to one of the world's largest indoor sports facilities - the **NYNEX** indoor stadium at the old Victoria Station, *Tel. 0161 930 8000*.

PRACTICAL INFORMATION

Manchester's main **tourism office** is at the *Town Hall Extension, Lloyd Street, Manchester M60 2LA, Tel. 0161 234 3157*. There's also an information desk in the arrivals hall at Manchester Airport, *Tel. 0161 436 3344*. The city is very well served by banks and post offices, and the **American Express** office is situated at *10-12 St. Mary's Gate, Tel. 0161 833 0121*.

THE PEAK DISTRICT

The **Pennine mountains**, often referred to as the "backbone" of England, are at their most picturesque in the **Peak District**, a 540-square mile national park about 25 miles southeast of Manchester. Although few of the peaks reach more than 2,000 feet in height, it's the combination of hilly landscapes, delightful towns such as **Buxton** – the best place to make your base – and **Bakewell**, and glorious country estates such as **Chatsworth** that make this region so special. The roads throughout the area are generally good, but even in the summer months bad weather such as torrential rain and fog can descend very quickly, so check the weather forecast before you set out.

It's a great area for outdoor activities such as caving, walking, and hiking, so make sure you're well-prepared. Many trails criss-cross the area, the best-known of which is the **High Peak Trail**, a seventeen mile path (a former railroad track) from Cromford to Dowlow. For information on this, and just about everything else, contact the **Peak District National Park Office**, *Tel. 01629 814321*.

ARRIVALS & DEPARTURES

By Car

From London follow the M1 north as far as exit 24, where the A6 takes you directly to Buxton.

By Bus

There are regular, two-hourly services to Buxton from Manchester's Chorlton Street Bus Station, *Tel. 0161 228 7811*, or alternatively, the Manchester to Derby **Transpeak** service also offers a two-hourly service to most Peak District towns. Local services in the Peak District are operated by **Derbyshire Bus Line**, *Tel. 01332 292200*.

By Train

There is no direct service to this area from London. However, you can take the train from Euston to Manchester, then link up with the half-hourly local service to Buxton, which takes just under an hour. Buxton's train station is on Station Road, just north of the town center. *Call 0345 484950 for more information.*

ORIENTATION

The 555 square miles of the Peak District is sandwiched between the industrial cities of Manchester and Sheffield, though you'd never think it. The landscape in the southern part of the region, with its dry stone walls, tends to be gentler and greener than that in the north. The larger Peak towns tend to be in the southern half of the region.

GETTING AROUND

Buxton, Bakewell and individual towns and villages mentioned in this section can easily be explored on foot. For driving in between them, and for exploring the highways and byways of this beautiful area, a car is essential. For local bus information in the Peak District, call **Derbyshire Bus Line**, *Tel. 01332 292200*, who operate a comprehensive bus service throughout the region.

WHERE TO STAY

PALACE HOTEL, *Palace Road, Buxton SK17 6AG. Tel. 01298 22001, Fax 01298 72131. Rooms: 122. Rates: singles from £99, doubles from £116 (includes full breakfast). Restaurant, indoor pool, croquet, putting, sauna, gymnasium. All major credit cards accepted.*

Large Victorian hotel, adjacent to Buxton's train station, and dating from the time when people came to Buxton for the spa. The building offers fine views over the town and surrounding hills, and there are a number of elegant public rooms, including bars, and a library lounge. The comfortable rooms are equipped with all the usual facilities, and many of them enjoy wonderful views.

THE OLD MANSE, *6 Clifton Road, Silverlands, Buxton SK17 6QL. Tel. 01298 25638. Rooms: 8. Rates: singles from £22, doubles from £44. All major credit cards accepted.*

Large semi-detached house that formerly belonged to a local minister and now offers good value accommodations in comfortable, well-equipped rooms. The public areas include a cozy sitting room and a bar/dining room where breakfast is served. Note that four of the rooms use shared facilities, so make sure you specify you want en suite when booking.

BUXTON VIEW GUEST HOUSE, *74 Corbar Road, Buxton SK17 6RJ. Rooms: 5. Rates: singles from £20, doubles from £40. No credit cards.*

This very pleasant small guest house is located in a quiet part of Buxton within easy reach of all the main attractions. The rooms are specious and well-appointed and there's a large comfortable lounge overlooking the garden, and a conservatory where meals are provided. All the rooms have either bath or shower ensuite.

WHERE TO EAT

RENAISSANCE RESTAURANT, *Bath Street, Bakewell. Tel. 01629 812687. Open for lunch Tuesday to Sunday; for dinner Tuesday to Saturday. Dinner from £21.55.*

Quiet, pleasant restaurant in a tastefully converted former barn overlooking a small walled garden. The cuisine is mainly French, with main courses such as paupiette of turbot with wild mushrooms and Normandy sauce. There's a good wine list, where the emphasis is again mainly French.

SEEING THE SIGHTS

The "capital" of the Peak District is **Buxton**, a handsome spa town located on the A6, which, at 1,000 feet above sea level is one of the highest communities in Britain. It was the Romans who first discovered the place. They arrived in 79 AD and made a bee-line for the **mineral springs**, which produce water from up to 5,000 feet below ground at a constant temperature of 82 degrees Farenheit. They were thought to cure a variety of ills. When spas again became popular in the eighteenth century, Buxton, like Bath, began to prosper, and although the place is not on the same scale as Bath, there are distinct parallels in what happened here.

Like Bath, Buxton has its own **Crescent**, St. Ann's Hotel, located on the northwest side of Slopes Park, built in 1780 by architect John Carr for the fifth Duke of Devonshire, owner of nearby Chatsworth House. The building looks rather tatty following the closure of the hotel some years ago, but a multi-million pound government grant should make a big difference. The **thermal baths** at the end of the street were closed in 1972, leaving only a Perrier-owned bottling plant and **St. Ann's Well**, on the

Crescent, where the locals still come to fill bottles. If you've come to Buxton to check all about microbes, then don't miss a visit to the **Micrarium**, housed in the former Pump Room.

Just to the left of the Crescent is Buxton's **Opera House**, a rather flamboyant structure built in 1903, where in the last two weeks of July the **Buxton Opera Festival** is held. If you don't want to see a concert, you can take a guided tour of the Opera House on Saturdays at 1pm. The Slopes Park, behind the Micrarium, leads to the **Buxton Museum and Art Gallery**, Terrace Road, with an interesting collection comprising various fossilized remains from the Peak District, the jaw bones of lions dating from the Neolithic period and various human-made implements. A display upstairs traces the history of the area from Neolithic times, and there's also a collection of Blue John stone, a semi-precious rock found only in this area. *Open Tuesday to Friday 9:30am to 5:30pm, Saturday 9:30am to 5pm. Admission £1. Tel. 01298 24658.*

Buxton's other main attraction is **Poole's Cavern** on the A53, a huge underground cave below Buxton Country Park that's named after a fifteenth century robber. There is evidence that the cave was inhabited by humans during prehistoric times. The chambers contain the requisite but impressive stalagtite and stalagmite formations. From the mouth of the cave, you can walk through the Grinlow Woods to **Solomon's Temple**, a folly built during Victorian times which offers outstanding views across Buxton and the countryside around. *Open March to October daily 10am to 5pm. Admission £4.50. Tel. 01298 26978; www.poolescavern.co.uk.*

A number of small towns in the vicinity of Buxton offer pleasant detours. These include **Bakewell**, famous in Britain as being the birthplace of the **Bakewell tart**, invented by accident in 1860 when a young cook messed up a recipe for strawberry tart. The town, which straddles the **River Wye**, has an interesting parish church, where you can see some fine sixteenth century tombs – and the ninth century **Saxon cross** outside is certainly worth a look. Otherwise, head up the hill to the **Bakewell Old House Museum**, Cunningham Place, a yeoman's Tudor house once owned by Richards Arkwright, and containing various tools and artifacts from Bakewell's past. *Open April to October 2pm to 5pm. Admission adults £1.80, children 80p.*

Bakewell holds on to a number of weird and wonderful customs, particularly in the late spring, with the tradition of **well-dressing**. Local wells and spring are dressed with beautiful floral designs, some with biblical themes, to celebrate their life-giving properties. The original of the festival is lost in the mists of history.

Another town worth visiting is **Castleton**, ten miles northeast of Buxton in the Hope Valley on the A625, where a complex of limestone caverns attract visitors from many nations. The town can trace its history back to the early 1100s, about which time **Peveril Castle**, on a crag overlooking the town, was built. Now ruined, the castle offers excellent views of the town and beyond. The castle is protected on its western side by a deep gorge, which formed when a cave collapsed many centuries ago. *Access from Market Place. Open April to October daily 10am to 6pm; November to March Wednesday to Sunday 10am to 4pm. Admission £2. Tel. 01433 620613.*

Here, **Peak Cavern** once provided shelter for a rope-making factory and for a tiny village. Far more interesting is **Speedwell Cavern**, a fifteen minute walk away, which you have to enter by boat through a half-mile long tunnel, blasted by lead miners in the nineteenth century. The cavern you reach at the end, at around 600 feet underground, is the deepest public access cave in Britain. The chamber contains the "bottomless pit," a pool where miners used to dump the debris left over from their work. Needless to say, it never filled up – despite having 40,000 tons of rubble toppled down it. *Open April to October daily 10am to 5pm; November to March weekends only 10am to 5pm. Admission £4. Tel. 01433 620285.*

If you rapidly find yourself turning into a cavern explorer, you may want to check out the **Treak Cliff Cavern**, just along the hill from Speedwell, and, fifteen minutes further on again, the **Blue John Cavern**. Whatever you do, make sure you leave time to explore one of England's greatest stately homes: **Chatsworth House**, four miles northeast of Bakewell, approached through some wonderful landscaped grounds speckled with sheep and deer. It's on the B6102, off the A6.

The House was built in the seventeenth century by the First Duke of Devonshire, whose family still owns it. This Palladian-style "**Palace of the Peaks**" contains such striking rooms as the **Blue Drawing Room**, where two of the most famous portraits in England hang: *Georgiana, Duchess of Devonshire and Her Baby*, by Sir Joshua Reynolds, and John Singer Sargent's *Acheson Sisters*. Check out the **Dining Room**, in the north wing, with the table set as it was for a visit of George V and Queen Mary in 1933, and with a number of Van Dycks gracing the walls. There's also a **Sculpture Gallery**, where among other things you can see a Rembrandt. Outside, the house is surrounded by extensive formal gardens, and the vast park designed in the 1750s by Capability Brown with further work by Joseph Paxton. He it was who built the **Emperor Fountain**, originally the world's highest gravity-fed water jet. The grounds also contain attractions for children including a farmyard with milking demonstrations and a petting area. *House open daily 11am to 5:30 (last entry 4.30pm); garden daily 11am to 6pm (last entry 5pm). Admission house and gardens adults £6.75, students and seniors £5.50, children £3. Admission gardens only adults £3.85, students and seniors £3, children £1.75. Tel. 01246 565300; www.chatsworth-house.co.uk.*

SPORTS & RECREATION

Hiking is the most popular activity in this region, and the region is crisscrossed with marked paths. Information on walking trails isn pro-vided by the information centers listed below under *Practical Information.*

EXCURSIONS & DAY TRIPS

Blackpool

After a brief sojourn in Chester, Manchester or Liverpool, most visitors head straight up the M6 motorway for the Lake District, but, for a bit of a break on the way, and a chance to see Brits at play, there's no better place than brash, breezy **Blackpool**, a Victorian seaside resort that's still the most popular holiday destination for more than 16 million annually. The resort, which had hitherto been an insignificant coastal village, came to life with the advent of the railroad in the 1840s, which brought hordes of visitors from the huge industrial cities nearby. The resort, which sprawls for about six miles along Morecambe Bay, is dominated by the 519-foot iron-made **Tower** that looks a bit like a smaller version of the Eiffel Tower. For a spectacular view over the town and surrounding countryside, enter the **Tower World** theme park, where you can also visit an Edwardian ballroom and a circus. *Open from Easter daily from 10am. Admission adults £10, children £5.*

Further south, and best reached by taking a **tram ride** along the Promenade, is Blackpool's other main attraction, the **Pleasure Beach**, with various white-knuckle rides including, at nearly 90 mph, the world's fastest roller-coaster. *Call 0870 444 5566 for information.* The town was wise to build the Sandcastle swimming pool complex opposite; for several years the resort's beaches have failed to meet the minimum European standards for hygiene and at a constant 84 Farenheit it's a great place to escape from the biting winds outside. Other attractions here include the **Sea Life Centre**, with the usual creatures glugging their way round large tanks, and the **Louis Tussaud's Waxworks**, opposite Central Pier, with wax effigies of historical and contemporary figures, like Pierce Brosnan and Arnold Schwarzenneger, and a Chamber of Horrors. *Open daily from 10am. Adults £4, 5s-16s £2, seniors £3. Tel. 01253 625953.*

In the late season, the whole seafront comes ablaze with color with the **Blackpool Illuminations**, one of the most dazzling displays of lights anywhere in the world. For more information about what's going on in the town, contact the **tourist office** at *1, Clifton Street, Tel. 01253 21623.*

PRACTICAL INFORMATION

The **Peak District National Park** head office *at Baslow Road, Bakewell, Derbyshire DE45 1AE, Tel. 01629 814321,* will be pleased to provide information about the area, as will the local **tourism offices** at Buxton, *The Crescent, Buxton SK17 6BQ, Tel. 01298 25106;* and at Bakewell, *Old Market Hall, Bridge Street, Bakewell DE4 1DS, Tel. 01629 813227.* Both Buxton and Bakewell have branches of the main high street banks, and both are also well served by post offices.

It's only about thirty miles across by thirty in length, but the **Lake District** manages to pack into that small area no fewer than sixteen major lakes and some of England's highest peaks, wide glacier-shaped valleys and waterfalls – an irresistible combination that has attracted and inspired countless writers and poets over the centuries, including Worthsworth, Coleridge and Keats. Man's contribution is a smattering of picturesque stone-built villages and a handful of larger towns, as well as clearing many of the thickly-forested uplands for farming. This is, scenically at least, by far England's most attractive corner. The trouble is, everyone else knows it, and so it can get extremely busy anytime from Easter to September. To avoid disappointment, book in advance.

ARRIVALS & DEPARTURES FOR THE LAKE DISTRICT
By Car
From London, take the M1 to its junction with the M6. Take the M6 north, passing Blackpool and Lancaster, until you see the signs for the Lake District. For the southern lakes area, it's best to hook up with the A590/A591 to Kendal; continue up the M6 to the A66 if it's Penrith, Keswick and the northern lakes that you want.

By Bus
The region is well served by buses from London Victoria, especially in the summer. The journey time to Kendal is around 7 1/2 hours – depending on the traffic, which can be pretty awful at weekends – and another hour or so to Keswick. There are also regular services to the region from both Manchester and Liverpool. *Call 0990 808080 for information.*

By Train
The southern part of the region is served by trains from London's Euston station. Look for trains heading for Carlisle, Glasgow or Edinburgh, but check with the timetable that they stop in **Oxendale**, where you'll need

to change to the local service to Kendal and Windermere. If you're headed further north, stay on the main line train to Penrith Station, where you can access the **Cumberland Bus** service to Keswick.

LAKE DISTRICT TRAVEL INFORMATION

*The **Cumbrian Tourist Board**, Ashleigh, Holly Road, Windermere LA23 2AQ, Tel. 015394 44444, covers the whole region. See each individual town below for local offices. The main towns are well served by High Street banks but there are no American Express offices in the region. Instead, try **Thomas Cook**, 49 Stricklandgate, Kendal, Tel. 01539 724259.*

KENDAL

To all intents and purposes the gateway to the Lake District is **Kendal**, well marked from the M6, and about 70 miles north of Manchester. At one time it was an important textile center – even before the Industrial Revolution. These days it's a bustling kind of place with a gurgling stream and lots of pretty stone houses tucked away on either side of Highgate and Stricklandgate in the "**ginnels**" – narrow winding streets dating from medieval times.

For various arrivals information, see *Arrivals & Departures for the Lake District,* above.

GETTING AROUND TOWN

Kendal is easily walkable. You can, however, rent a car for traveling further afield from **Avis**, *Station Road, Tel. 01539 733582.*

WHERE TO STAY

Other than Holmfield, your options are limited here; Windermere (see below) offers more lodging and dining choices.

HOLMFIELD, *41 Kendal Green, Kendal LA9 5PP. Tel. and Fax 01539 720790. Rooms: 3. Rates: single from £24, double from £44. Lounge, garden, outdoor pool. Credit cards not accepted.*

This lovely Edwardian house just 10 minutes from the center of Kendal with all its attractions is a wonderful place to spend a relaxing few days. Stay here for the lovely bright lounge and breakfast room (the breakfasts are a delight here), heated swimming pool (summer only, it's far too cold at any other time) and pleasant bedrooms (though facilities are shared).

LANE HEAD COUNTRY HOUSE HOTEL, *Helsington, Kendal LA9 5RJ. Tel 01539 731283, Fax 01539 721023. Rooms: 6. Rates: singles from £41, doubles from £75. Restaurant. All major credit cards accepted.*

The Lane Head is a former manor house, built in the 17th century, and with a number of its original features intact, enjoys extensive views over the pretty Kent Valley. The bedrooms are tastefully decorated and well-equipped, the public rooms spacious. There's a high-standard restaurant which opens up on to a sun terrace. This is one of the better-value places to stay in the area.

CASTLE GREEN HOTEL, *Kendal LA9 6RG. Tel 01539 734000, Fax 01539 735522. Rooms: 100. Rates: singles from £65, doubles from £75. Bar, restaurant, indoor pool, tennis courts, solarium, gymnasium, steam room, yoga, beauty salon. All major credit cards accepted.*

The Castle Green Hotel is nicely positioned, offering extensive views of the distant hills and a peaceful, relaxed ambience. The rooms are generally large, well-furnished and come with the full range of facilities; some have far reaching views. There's a fine restaurant, The Greenhouse, and guests are very well provided for with leisure facilities; you can even brush up on your yoga!

HIGHER HOUSE FARM, *Oxenholme Lane, Natland, Kendal LA9 7QH. Tel 015395 61177, Fax 015395 61520. Rooms: 3. Rates: rooms from £49. Dining room. No credit cards.*

Higher House is a delightful old farmhouse built in the 1600s, and offers lots of character. Because it's small (there are only three guest rooms), you can expect a really warm welcome; breakfast is served at a communal table in the dining room. The non-smoking bedrooms are individually styled, and have up-to-date amenities. The orchard and gardens command lovely views of the fells. Note: children under 12 are not accepted.

WHERE TO EAT

OLD VICARAGE, *Church Road, Witherslack LA11 6RS. Tel 015395 52381. Open Sunday 12:30pm to 1pm, Monday to Saturday 7pm to 9pm. Mains courses from £13.50. All major credit cards accepted.*

Really cozy, attractively furnished and long-established restaurant located in a former Georgian rectory just off the A590. The cusine here can best be described as Anglo-French, using fresh local ingredients like Mansergh Hall lamb and Morecambe bay flukes. There's a range of traditional – generally heavy – desserts, like dark chocolate tart and steamed sponges. The wine list veers towards Italy, with house wines starting from £9.

AYNSOME MANOR, *Cartmel LA11 6HH. Tel 015395 36653. Open Sunday lunch 1pm (one sitting) Monday to Saturday 7pm to 8:30pm (closed Sunday dinner). Set dinner from £16.50. All major credit cards accepted.*

This jacket and tie establishment is a bit of a trek from Kendal, but worth the effort. It's an old Georgian house, now a comfortable hotel, with magnificent ceilings and white-painted paneled walls. As you can guess from the "jacket and tie" request, it's one of those rare traditional places, with dishes like rack of lamb with mint jelly on the main course list, and a good selection of carefully prepared desserts. House wines here start at £10.50 a bottle.

SEEING THE SIGHTS

Stop by the **Market**, Market Place, though the old market hall is now an indoor shopping center. However, open air stalls do operate here on Wednesdays and Saturdays. When you're wandering around the town pick up a slab of **Kendal Mintcake**, a lethal-looking lump of sugar and peppermint oil that is supposed to give walkers and hikers that little bit of extra energy need to climb the nearby hills – or weigh them down.

Kendal has three **museums**, two of which are housed in the Georgian **Abbot's Hall**. In the hall itself, which has been lovingly restored to its 1760s prime, there's an interesting collection of portraits by local painter **George Romney**, along with pieces by Ruskin and Turner and a collection of period furniture made by Gillows of Lancaster. The hall's former stable block houses the **Museum of Lakeland Life and Industry**, with absorbing exhibits on the art of rural crafts – blacksmiths, wheelwrights, weavers and the like – with further displays on local architecture and customs. There's a special room devoted to Arthur Ransome, author of the children's favorite *Swallows and Amazons* and another devoted to John Cunliffe, writer of the British children's TV favorite, *Postman Pat* (not forgetting his cat). *Open year-round daily 10:30am to 4pm. Admission adults £3, seniors £2.80, students and children £1.50. Tel. 01539 722464; www.abbothall.org.uk.*

Opposite the train station, housed in an old wool warehouse is the **Kendal Museum**, founded as far back as 1796, which traces the natural history and archaeology of the area. There are a number of displays on the life of local man Alfred Wainwright (1907-1991), a former town treasurer, who set about putting together a series of 47 walking guides around the Lake District, all handwritten and accompanied by sketches. *Open April to October daily 10.30am to 5pm; November to March daily 10:30am to 5pm. Admission £3. Tel. 01539 721374; www.kendalmuseum.co.uk.*

Just two miles south of Kendal, off the A591, is **Sizergh Castle**, a large manor house, which owes its title "castle" to its 14th century **pele tower** – a defensive feature of many northern homes when they were used as a refuge during the cross border raids during the middle ages. The house was modified somewhat during Elizabethan times, when much of the paneling was added, along with some elaborate carved ceilings. Throughout the castle, family portraits hang on the walls, and there is some lovely furniture, including a bedstead made from a former pew in Kendal parish church. *Open April to October Sunday to Thursday 1:30pm to 5:30pm. Admission adults £4.60, children £2.30. Garden only, £2.30. Tel. 015395 60070.*

Just two miles south of here is the 16th century **Levens Hall**, built by James Bellingham, and notable for its fine 1694 **topiary garden**, where you can see yew tees shaped like pyramids and the like. Like its neighbor, Sizergh, Levens Hall is built around a much earlier pele tower, and it also has some fine plasterwork, paneling, and furniture. *Open April to mid-October Sunday to Thursday garden 10am to 5pm, house noon to 5pm. Admission adults £5.50, children £2.80. Garden only adults £4, children £2.10; www.levenshall.co.uk.*

PRACTICAL INFORMATION

Kendal's **tourist information office** is at the *Town Hall, Highgate, Tel. 01539 725758.*

WINDERMERE

The town of **Windermere**, the main center for touring this part of the Lake District, was non-existent until the arrival of the railroad in 1847, though the lake itself had already achieved fame as the result of its connection with **William Wordsworth** and the other romantic poets. Although it's a mile from the Lake, the town expanded rapidly, soon encroaching on the neighboring (and much older) lakeside town of **Bowness-On-Windermere**.

ARRIVALS & DEPARTURES

By Car

It's just ten miles from Kendal along the A591 to Windermere.

By Bus

There are two buses a day from Manchester to Windermere, and one a day from London Victoria. The bus station is in Station Precinct in Windermere.

By Train

Windermere has its own train station (next to the bus station, above) with connections via Oxenholme to London Euston.

GETTING AROUND

Winderemere itself is easily walkable. You can hire bicycles from **Blazing Saddles**, *Quarry Rigg, Lake Road, Windermere, Tel. 015394 447100*, for up to £15 a day.

WHERE TO STAY

STORRS HALL HOTEL, *Storrs Park, Bowness-on-Windermere LA23 3LG. Tel. 015394 47111, Fax 015394 47555. Rooms: 18. Rates: singles from £125, doubles from £215 (both include full breakfast). Four-poster beds available. Restaurant, bars, private fishing, sailing, water-skiing. All major credit cards accepted.*

Beautifully restored Georgian mansion located on a peninsula of Lake Windermere, with fantastic views to three sides. The revamped bedrooms are stunning, and are lavishly furnished with fine arts and antiques. The public areas are luxurious, too, with wonderful deep-cushioned sofas. The staff are helpful and friendly atmosphere is very relaxed. It's not exactly cheap, but a wonderful place to relax and unwind, enjoy a bit of fishing and sailing, especially if you've just spent a few days in London.

THE OLD COURT HOUSE, *Lake Road, Bowness-on-Windermere LA23 3AP. Tel. 015394 45096. Rooms: 6. Rates: singles from £25, doubles from £40. Parking. All major credit cards accepted.*

Bowness's former police station and courthouse, dating from the Victorian period, has been transformed into a this lovely small hotel. Many of the original features remain, and several of the rooms have four-poster beds. There's no restaurant, but there is a bright cheerful breakfast room where the full English breakfast is superb. This is a no-smoking hotel, and children under 7 are not accepted.

QUEEN'S HEAD HOTEL, *Main Street, Hawkshead LA22 0NS. Tel. 015394 36271, Fax 015394 36722. Rooms: 13. Rates: singles from £50, doubles from £75. Restaurant, bar. All major credit cards accepted.*

Pretty 17th century inn with low, oak-beamed ceilings and open log fires, and lots of old-fashioned furniture. The rooms have all been refurbished of late and are attractively furnished, some with four-poster beds. Three of the bedrooms are situated in the adjacent cottage, but all are of the same high standard.

THE SWAN, *Grasmere LA22 9RF. Tel. 0970 400 8132, Fax 015394 35741. Rooms: 38. Rates: singles from £72, doubles from £144 (prices include full breakfast). Restaurant. All major credit cards accepted.*

Located on the outskirts of Grasmere, The Swan is mentioned in Wordsworth's poem *The Waggoner*. This 300-year-old hotel has 38 comfortable rooms, many of which have lovely views of the surrounding fells.

Fresh flowers decorate the cozy lounges, one of which contains a chair that belonged to William Wordsworth. There's an excellent restaurant, or you can take meals in the more informal Cygnet lounge.

2 CAMBRIDGE VILLAS, *Church Street, Ambleside LA22 9DL. Tel 015394 321142. Rooms: 5. Rates: rooms from £32. Dining room. No credit cards.*

This is a small five-bedroom guest house located close to Ambleside town center, and within easy reach of all the major sights and attractions. Although the rooms are a bit on the small side, they come with a full range of facilities, except, in some cases, individual bathrooms. However, just specify that's what you want and there should be no problem. There's a pleasant lounge on the second floor (don't forget to call it the first floor here) and a dining room where you'll be served substantial breakfasts to set you up for a full day's walking.

WHERE TO EAT

WHITE MOSS HOUSE, *Rydal Water, Grasmere. Tel. 015394 35516. Open Monday to Saturday – one sitting at 8pm. Set dinner £28. Credit cards: MC, Visa.*

The house was once owned by none other than William Wordsworth himself. The dinners are served at bare wooden tables in a small dining room and follow a regular pattern: soup to start, followed by a fish combo, a main course composed of local produce, such as Cumbrian venison, traditional English desserts like bread and butter pudding or jam roly poly – great if you like heavy, stodgy stuff – and a selection of cheeses. There's a good wine list, with a number of vintages, and house wine starts at £10.50.

JERICHOS, *Birch Street, Windermere. Tel. 015394 42522. Open Tuesday to Sunday 6:45pm to 10pm. Main courses from £10. Credit cards: MC, Visa.*

Located just off Windermere's shopping district, Jericho's distinctive interior, with its purple decor, striking floral arrangements and open-view kitchen, has become a firm favorite with locals and visitors alike. There's a French influence to the main courses here, and plenty of traditional desserts – rice pudding, sponges, lots of custard and so on. The service is good, and the wine list chosen mainly from the New World, with house wines at £10.75 a bottle.

HOLBECK GHYLL, *Holbeck Lane, Windermere. Tel. 015394 32375. Open daily noon to 2pm, 7pm to 9pm. Set lunch from £10 for one course, set dinner from £32. All major credit cards accepted.*

This nineteenth century former hunting lodge is now a pleasing country hotel, with lovely views over lake Windermere. There are two restaurants: one oak-paneled with bare wooden tables, the other with French windows leading out to a terrace for outdoor dining. The emphasis is continental, mainly French, with a touch of Italian, best exemplified in a handful of exotic pasta dishes. There's a wide range of delicious desserts to choose from, and the wine list, as you'd expect, is mostly French. House wines start from £13.95.

MILLER HOWE, *Rayrigg Road, Bowness-on-Windermere. Tel. 015394 42536. Open daily 1pm and 8pm sittings. Set lunch from £10 for two courses, set dinner £35. All major credit cards accepted.*

Small whitewashed Edwardian hotel whose excellent restaurant is a magnet for miles around – not only on account of the superb views, but for the food itself, which is essentially British with a creative streak – like sirloin steak in an onion marmalade for a main course. The desserts are pretty traditional; a particularly sticky toffee pudding is a great favorite. The staff are friendly and attentive, and the wine list again focuses mainly on the New World, though the house wines are a bit steep, coming in at £16.50.

SEEING THE SIGHTS

Windermere is very much the transportation hub of the southern lake region, but Bowness has more charm. To be honest, the two of them are so close – linked by the W1/599 bus which runs every 20 minutes in the summer – that it doesn't really make much difference where you decide to stay. Just be aware of the fact that during the summer they become totally congested with vacationers, so that it's absolutely essential to book a hotel room in advance.

In Bowness, check out the **Windermere Steamboat Museum**, on Rayrigg Road, a wonderful collection of historic steam- and motor-powered water craft. Among the attractions is *The Dolly*, built in 1850, and touted as one of the two oldest mechanically-driven boats in the world. She's in pretty good condition – all the more remarkable as she spent 65 years in the mud at the bottom of Ullswater. Among other exhibits of note are Beatrix Potter's rowing boat and a dinghy belonging to Arthur Ransome. *Open mid-March to October daily 10am to 5pm. Admission adults £3.25, children under 16, £2. Tel. 015394 45565; www.steamboat.co.uk.*

Children will be bowled over by the **World of Beatrix Potter Museum** in Bowness, where some of the author's best-loved characters are presented in 3-D. You can buy Potter souvenirs here, and there's a tea shop. *Open April to September 10am to 5:30pm; rest of year 10am to 4:30pm. Admission adults £3.25, children £2. Tel. 015394 88444.* Grown-up Potter fans might prefer to visit the author's home, **Hill Top**, on the other side of the lake in **Near Sawrey** (for ferry information see below). For a spectacular 360 degree view which takes in the lake, and on a clear day reaches as far as the Yorkshire fells to the east, follow the signs near the Windermere Hotel for **Orrest Head**. Note: because of the volume of visitors to Hill Top, visits are strictly timed. *Hill Top open March to May Sunday to Wednesday 11am to 4:30pm; June to August Sunday to Wednesday 11am to 4:30pm; September and October Sunday to Wednesday 11am to 4:30pm. Admission adults £4, children £2. Tel. 015394 36269.*

Boats & Ferries

The ferry to **Sawrey**, on the other side of the lake, takes just a few minutes, and departs every 20 minutes in the peak summer months. Alternatively, you might want to head out on to the lake in a rented rowing boat; these can be rented at the pier. Meanwhile, **Windermere Lake Cruises** operate attractive steamboats to lakeside, hourly.

LAKE WINDERMERE

*Eleven miles may not seem a great length for a lake – especially by American standards – but it makes **Lake Windermere** the longest lake in England. It's not very wide either, just a mile and a half, but at 200 feet it's pretty deep, the reason being that it's in a rocky gorge between steep wooded hills. Even though by English standards it's large, you can imagine that it gets very crowded, especially in the summer, when scores of pleasure craft, water sports facilities and ferries vie to make use of the space. It's a good place to fish, too; char, a kind of lake trout being the favorite catch*

From Windermere it's just three miles to **Brockhole**, and the **Lake District National Park Visitor Centre**, set in a lovely lakeside mansion with gardens sloping down to the water. As well as general **tourist information** on transport, accommodations, and an excellent bookshop where you can get stocked up on the requisite maps and guides, there are exhibits on the ecology of the Lake District. Activities at the Centre also include lectures, guided walks and demonstrations of traditional lakeland practices such as dry stone walling – and of course, the inevitable cafe.

A few miles north of here at the top of Lake Windermere is the small town of **Ambleside**, whose greyish-green buildings seem almost to grow out of the landscape. It's a popular tourist center, with several B&Bs, cafes, and a market which takes place on Wednesdays, when it can get even more congested than usual. About a mile south of the center is the small "suburb" of **Waterhead**, with plenty of rowboats for rent, and attractions that include the grass-covered outline of a second century Roman Fort and St. Mary's parish church, where a mural depicts the ancient ceremony of rush bearing. Perched on a stone bridge spanning the fast-flowing Stock Ghyll is a picturesque 17th century **cottage** that has been requisitioned by the National Trust and now houses a shop and information center.

Many people, of course, come to Ambleside for the walking. For a relatively short walk that takes in **Rydal Mount**, where the poet **William Wordsworth** lived from 1813 until his death in 1850, simply follow the A591 north of Ambleside. Wordsworth was already an accomplished poet when he moved here. Inside, you can see the study where he worked, and the 4 1/2 acre garden planted by the man himself. The whole area around Rydal Mount and **Dove Cottage**, Wordsworth's home before 1808, gave great inspiration to the poet, as you will see when you walk the paths. One of his favorite places, **Dora's Field**, below Rydal Mount next to the Church of St. Mary (where he rented a pew) is enhanced in the spring by a stunning show of daffodils, planted by none other than the man himself. *Rydal Mount open March to October daily 9:30am to 5pm; November to February daily, except Tuesday, 10am to 4pm.*

A further 1 1/2 miles northwest of Rydal Mount is **Dove Cottage**, where the poet lived from 1799 to 1808. The cottage, formerly an inn, was first opened to the public in 1891 and contains much of Wordsworth's own furniture and memorabilia. Other famous poets came here too: Wordsworth nursed his friend Coleridge back to health after an illness, and later on Thomas deQuincey bought it. The cottage, the headquarters for the **Centre for British Romanticism**, traces the contribution made by Wordsworth and the other lake poets with some original manuscripts. There's a cafe and restaurant. *Open daily 9:30am to 5:30pm. Tel. 015394 35544; www.dovecott.demon.co.uk.*

Head north of Dove Cottage to the pretty village of **Grasmere**, situated on a small lake fringed by woods. The maze of narrow streets contains a motley collection of shops, restaurants and galleries. Wordsworth, his wife Mary, his sister Dorothy and beloved daughter Dora are all buried in the churchyard of **Grasmere Parish Church**. Coming out of the churchyard, stop at the **Gingerbread Shop**, once the village schoolhouse – where you can buy wonderful gingerbread made from a recipe that's kept locked up in a bank safe. For a lovely view over the village, follow the sign-posted track on the western side of the lake to Loughrigg Terrace.

Some seven miles south of Grasmere on the A593 is the lovely lakeside town of **Coniston**, overlooked by the 2,600-foot **Old Man of Coniston**. You can reach the summit by taking tracks up from the village past the Sun pub. For most people it takes about two hours. Seasoned walkers may wish to continue to **Swirl How** and **Wetherlam**, then return to the village – a seven mile hike in all.

Coniston is not as large a lake as Windermere –it's only five miles long – but it became famous for two reasons; first, as the setting for *Swallows and Amazons,* **Arthur Ransome's** children's classic of the '30s and as the place where **Donald Campbell** set a new water speed world record of 260 mph back in the '50s. Sadly, Campbell was later killed when in 1967 he set out to improve on the record; his body was never found.

On the eastern shore of Coniston Water is **Brantwood**, the home of Victorian artist and social reformer **John Ruskin** (1819-1900). The large white Victorian house he built is situated on extensive grounds of 250 acres, and contains Ruskin memorabilia, such as his mahogany desk, his own paintings and drawings, and a bath chair he used in his latter days. As well as his own art, Ruskin managed to collect some fine pieces by other artists, including Turner. You can drive here easily from Coniston, but for a more memorable experience, go to Coniston Pier and take either the Coniston Launch or the *Gondola,* a nineteenth century steam yacht. *Brantwood open mid-March to mid-November daily 11am to 5:30pm; rest of year Wednesday to Sunday 11am to 4:30pm. Admission adults £4, children £1; grounds only, £1; www.brantwood.org.uk.*

Halfway between Coniston Water and Lake Windermere lies **Hawkshead**, a village with narrow cobbled streets and pretty gray stone cottages. Once a thriving wool marketing center, the resulting prosperity meant that the town could afford a grammar school. Wordsworth was a student at the **Hawkshead Grammar School** from 1779 to 1787, and you can see a desk into which he carved his name. While you're here, take a peep at **St. Mary's Church**, where the poet was baptised. Imagine the young Wordsworth staring at the 26 psalms and biblical quotations painted on the walls during the 17th and 18th centuries. *Open Easter to October Monday to Saturday 10am to 12:30pm and 1:30pm to 5pm, Sunday 1pm to 5pm. Admission adults £2, children 50p.*

On the village's Main Street is the **Beatrix Potter Gallery**. Potter's husband, a solicitor, rented rooms in Hawkshead for his practice, and these have been maintained for you to visit! The rooms are full of original Potter illustrations, and exhibits her work as a naturalist and conservationist. Note: this is another place where visits are timed, due to the sheer volume of people. *Open April to October Sunday to Thursday 10:30am to 4:30pm. Admission adults £3, children £1.50. Tel. 015394 36355.*

For something a little different, visit the **Grizedale Forest**, between Windermere and Coniston Water. There's no bus there, but bikes can be rented from the camp site in Hawkshead, from where you can cycle the four miles to the **Grizedale Forest Centre** (you can also rent a bike here if you haven't already). From the Centre head off on foot or by bike along the **Silurian Way**, a ten-mile path linking around fifty stone and wood **sculptures** scattered among the trees. Since 1977, artists have been invited to come here to create sculptures in response to the natural surroundings, using natural materials only. Some of the resultant pieces are quite startling. Make a day of it, and bring a picnic.

SPORTS & RECREATION

Information on walking trails is available at the tourist information center in Windermere. Meanwhile, the **Lakeland Leaisure Company**, *Lake Road, Tel. 015394 44786*, runs paragliding courses as well as guided cycling tours.

PRACTICAL INFORMATION

Windermere's **tourism office** is on *Victoria Street, Tel. 015394 46499*. There's another one in Bowness, but it's only open Fridays to Sundays, *Tel. 015394 44786*. The town's main post office is on Crescent Road.

LAKE DISTRICT WRITERS

I wandered lonely as a cloud
That floats on high o'er vales and hills
When all at once I saw a crowd,
A host, of golden daffodils.
– William Wordsworth: "I wandered lonely as a child."

The Lake District has attracted many writers over the centuries of whom **William Wordsworth** *is probably the best known. Wordsworth was born at nearby Cockermouth in 1770, attended school at Hawkshead, then spent time at Cambridge and in Somerset before returning to the Lakes in 1799, settling at Grasmere with his sister Dorothy. His* **Guide to the Lakes** *is still a useful traveling tool. Fellow poets* **Samuel Taylor Coleridge** *and* **Robert Southey** *spent a good deal of time with Wordsworth, forming a group that later became known as the* **Lake Poets***. They were joined by* **Thomas de Quincey***, who became a close family friend of the Worsworths, buying Dove Cottage from them in 1809. De Quincey is best known for his* **Confessions of an English Opium Eater***.*

Later on, the Worsdworths made Rydal Mount their home, during which period William Wordsworth became Poet Laureate. He died in 1850, and was buried inside St. Oswald's churchyard in Grasmere

Other writers who made the Lake District their home have included **John Ruskin***, who made his home at Brantwood, near Coniston, and the children's writers* **Arthur Ransome** *and* **Beatrix Potter***.*

KESWICK

The further north you go in the Lake District, so the scenery becomes more dramatic. Keswick is a good base for exploring this part of the region, especially beautiful **Borrowdale** – the starting point for walking routes to some of the Lake District's highest peaks – such as **Skiddaw** and **Blencathra**.

ARRIVALS & DEPARTURES

By Car

From Kendal, take the A591 to Keswick.

By Bus

There's a daily service from London to Keswick via Birmingham. **Stagecoach**, *Tel. 01946 63222*, operates a regular service between Kendal and Keswick.

By Train

There's no train station in Keswick itself. The nearest one is at **Penrith**, from which three buses a day head for Keswick, *Tel. 01434 381200*.

GETTING AROUND

Keswick itself is small, and easily explorable **on foot**. For attractions further afield, you can rent a car from the **Keswick Motor Company**, *Lake Road, Tel. 01768 72064* or, for the more energetic, rent a bike from **Keswick Mountain Bikes**, *Tel. 01768 75202*.

WHERE TO STAY

DALEGARTH HOUSE COUNTRY HOTEL, *Portinscale, Keswick CA12 5RQ. Tel. 017687 72817, Fax 017687 72817. Rooms: 10. Rates: singles from £30, doubles from £60. Restaurant, bar, parking. Credit cards: MC, Visa.*

A delightful large house peacefully located in the lakeside village of Portinscale, just north of Keswick. The bedrooms, which are all furnished and decorated to a high standard, come in a variety of styles. There are two large lounges, one of which doubles up as a bar, and an elegant restaurant with a full a la carte menu. This is a no-smoking hotel, and children under 5 years old are not accepted. From Keswick take the A66 to Postinscale. The hotel is about 100 yards past the Farmers Arms pub – on the left.

LYZZICK HALL COUNTRY HOUSE HOTEL, *Under Skiddaw, Keswick CA12 4PY. Tel. 01768772277, Fax 01768772278. Rooms: 29. Rates: singles from £45, doubles from £90 (prices include full breakfast). Restaurant, bar, indoor pool, sauna. All major credit cards accepted.*

This fine country house nestles in the foothills of Skiddaw, England's second highest peak, and has spectacular views across Derwentwater. Surrounded by extensive gardens, the rooms are nicely decorated and there are two spacious lounges and a restaurant with an extensive a la carte menu.

KESWICK COUNTRY HOUSE HOTEL, *Station Road, Keswick. Tel. 0176872020, Fax 0176871300. Rooms: 74. Rates: singles from £88, doubles from £120 (prices include full breakfast). Restaurant, putting green, snooker (like pool) table, croquet. All major credit cards accepted.*

Delightful Victorian country house hotel, much enlarged from the days when part of it it served as a railroad station. The hotel has been tastefully modernized throughout, and many of the bedrooms have wonderful views. The hotel is surrounded by 4 1/2 acres of lovely grounds, and is just a short stroll across Fitz Park to the town's main market place. The conservatory that links the main hotel to the old railway station is a wonderful place to enjoy afternoon tea or after-dinner drinks.

DERWENT COTTAGE, *Portinscale, Keswick CA12 5RF. Tel 017687 74838. Rooms: 6. Rates: rooms from £53. Bar, restaurant. Credit cards: MC, Visa.*

Derwent cottage is located in its own attractive gardens a few miles out of the center of Keswick, but within easy reach of the amenities there. The six bedrooms are comfortably furnished and you can benefit from a couple of cozy lounges and an intimate bar. One of the big pluses here is the delightful home cooking; the Cumbrian breakfasts are particularly good. As with a number of the smaller hotels and B&Bs around here, children under 12 are not allowed; neither is smoking.

WHERE TO EAT

SWINSIDE LODGE, *Grange Road, Keswick. Tel. 017687 72948. Open daily 7:30pm to 8pm (one sitting). Set dinner from £28. Credit cards: MC, Visa.*

Small hotel in a pretty setting above Derwent Water. The menu is pre-set, so you take what you get (except for the dessert, where there are four or five choices). The meal begins with a complimentary sherry, then it's four courses, with an optional fifth course of cheese. The premises are unlicensed, so if you want wine with your meal, it's a case of bringing your own.

DALE HEAD HALL LAKESIDE HOTEL, *Thirlmere, Keswick CA12 4TN. Tel 01768772478. Open 7:30pm to 8pm. Set dinner (5-courses) £30. All major credit cards accepted.*

Part of this lovely lakeside hotel dates as far back as the 16th century, and in the dining room too there are some original oak beams and wood paneling, adding to the atmosphere. The menu here is British but with French influences, so duck and pheasant breast are wrapped in puff pastry with a wild mushroom farce, juniper and gin sauce. If that's not enough to get you tipsy, there's a good wine list, which is arranged, unusually, according to color and taste rather than by region.

SEEING THE SIGHTS

Keswick, pronounced "Kezzick," on **Derwent Water**, an important wool trading center, was granted its royal charter in 1276. Then, in the 1500s graphite was discovered and led to a complete change of emphasis for the town. You might want to take a peep at the **Cumberland Pencil Museum**, which not only traces the development of a pencil-making industry in Keswick, but explores the other applications for which graphite was used, such as moldings for cannonballs. *Open daily 9:30 to 4pm. Tel. 0178773626.* Meanwhile the **Keswick Museum and Art Gallery**, in Fitz Park, contains manuscripts by Wordsworth, a Lake District diorama, fossils and the like. *Open April to October daily 10am to 4pm. Admission adults £1, children 50p. Tel. 01787 73263.*

Another site worth visiting close by is the **Castlerigg Stone Circle** – 39 chunks of Borrowdale volcanic stone forming a circle 100 feet in diameter, with another ten blocks forming a rectangle inside the main circle. Scholars believe that the main function of the circle was astronomical; whatever it is, few can fail to be inspired by the setting. To get there, follow the rail path for half a mile from the end of Station Road, turn right on to a minor road and keep going for another mile.

Derwent Water itself is a glorious lake. If you walk to the shore from Keswick town center, follow the **Friar's Crag** path for about 15 minutes. Friar's Crag is a peninsula in the lake, with wonderful views across the water to the surrounding mountains, including the famous **Jaws of Borrowdale**. An even better way to see the lake is to take a short cruise from the wooden jetty. The boats leave the pier hourly from April to November – or if you really want tranquillity, you can also rent a rowboat here.

Seven miles south of Keswick, **Seatoller** is a small village with a couple of restaurants, a smattering of cottages and another lake District Park Information Centre. It's the starting point for a number of walks in the stunningly beautiful **Borrowdale Valley**. From here, you can see England's tallest mountain, **Scafell Pike**, at 3,210 feet, which you can access from the village of **Seathwaite**, a mile or two south of Seatoller. However, you may choose a less fatiguing walk by traveling southwest round the mountain to **Wasdale Head**, situated at the head of **Wast Water**, England's deepest lake. Also here is 400-year-old **St. Olaf's Church**, reputedly the smallest in England. The church holds just 39 people. The memorials outside are dedicated to the victims of climbing accidents in the area, and are testament to how dangerous the mountains can be.

SPORTS & RECREATION

Local permits for fishing in Derwentwater are available from **Field & Stream**, *79 Main Street, Keswick, Tel. 017867 74396.*

Meanwhile if you're into water sports, **Derwentwater Marina**, *Portinscale, Keswick, Tel. 017896 72912*, offer instruction in windsurfing, sailing, canoeing and rowing.

PRACTICAL INFORMATION

Keswick's **tourism information center** is at *Moot Hall, Market Square, Tel. 017687 72645.*

PENRITH

The further north you go, the more dramatic the scenery gets. It's especially noticeable on the journey from Kendal to **Penrith**, which takes you through the bleak and desolate **Shap Fells**, a moorland plateau well over 1,000 feet above sea level. Penrith was once the capital of the kingdom of Cumbria way back in the 9th and 10th centuries.

ARRIVALS & DEPARTURES

By Car

From Keswick, take the A66 east to Penrith.

WHERE TO STAY

THE GEORGE, *Devonshire Street, Penrith CA11 7SU. Tel 01768 862696. Rooms: 34. Rates: singles from £45, doubles from £70. Bar, restaurant. Free use of local pool and gymnasium. All major credit cards accepted.*

This old, long-established town center hotel has recently been up-graded. Consequently the bedrooms are decorated and furnished to a very high standard. The public rooms and bar are more old-fashioned and in keeping with the traditional style of the building – which is popular with locals as well as visitors. The bedrooms come with the full range of facilities, and open parking is available.

BRANDELHOW GUEST HOUSE, *1 Portland Place, Penrith CA11 7QN. Tel 01768 864470. Rooms: 5. Rates: singles from £20, doubles from £32. Dining room.*

Small, cozy B&B located in a terrace close to Penrith town center. The bedrooms vary in size, but are pleasantly decorated and furnished with tea- and coffee-making facilities and TV. Not all have baths/showers, however, so when booking specify exactly what you want. Sumptuous breakfasts are served in a pleasant dining room. Open parking is available.

WHERE TO EAT

YANWATH GATE INN, *Yanwath, Penrith. Tel 01768 862386. Open Monday to Saturday noon to 2:15pm, 6:30pm to 9:30pm, Sunday 6:30pm to 9pm. Main courses from £6. All major credit cards accepted.*

Located a couple of miles south of Penrith on the B5320, the village of Yanwath is home to this attractive, 300 year-old hostelry which attracts a mixture of locals and tourists alike. The cuisine is traditional, with old favorites like roast beef and Yorkshire pudding and a host of mouth-watering desserts, again mostly on the traditional side. The service is particularly friendly and welcoming.

A BIT ON THE SIDE, *Brunswick Square, Penrith. Tel 01768 892526. Open Tuesday to Friday and Sunday noon to 2pm (no lunch Tuesday), 7pm to 9pm. Main courses around £11. All major credit cards accepted.*

This small, friendly restaurant is located in the center of Penrith and has woken up local taste buds with a variety of imaginative and creative lunch and dinner choices, including such delights as roasted gray mullet and sun-dried tomato and cheese tortelloni. The desserts are equally impressive, and there's a good wine list.

SEEING THE SIGHTS

Penrith is a pleasing market town with a 14th century **Castle**, built to defend the town against the Scots, and a fine **museum**, which served as a school for 300 years from the 1670s to 1970. It houses the town's **information center**, where you can get a leaflet describing the **town trail walk**, which takes you along sites of interest, including the plague stone on King Street, the place where food was left for those suffering from the Black Death, and the Castle.

Rather than spend a lot of time in Penrith, head off along the A66 and A592 to **Ullswater**, with one of the most spectacular setting of any lake in the Lake District, overlooked to the west by **Helvellyn**, at 3,118 feet one of England's tallest mountains. Stay on the A592 for the best views, as far as the villages of **Glenridding** and **Patterdale** at the southern end, where you can enjoy lakeside walks and rent rowboats. There are a number of hikes from here – but because of the terrain and the unpredictable weather patterns, these should only be undertaken by experienced walkers. Stay on the A592 for **Aira Force**, a series of waterfalls that cascade through a narrow ravine into Ullswater. There's a small parking lot by the roadside, and from there it's a 25-minute (signposted) trek to the Falls – but well worth it.

Towards the Border

The area between the Lake District and the Scottish border is a land of stark hills, bleak moorlands, small villages and the vast Solway Firth estuary. The main city here and Cumbria's capital is **Carlisle**, but apart from a pretty disappointing cathedral, there's little to see here. Inland from the coast are the remnants of **Hadrian's Wall**, but the best parts of the wall are across the Northumberland border and are described in Chapter 22, *The Northeast*.

PRACTICAL INFORMATION

The Penrith **tourist information center** is located in the *Penrith Museum, Middlegate, Tel. 01768 867466.*

THE ISLE OF MAN

*It's highly unlikely that you'll want to visit the **Isle Of Man**, an offshore island that's equidistant from England, Scotland and Ireland, and which has become a major tax haven for Brits over the years – although the island is exceptionally beautiful in parts, with mountains, lakes, sandy beaches and towering cliffs. The island has its own Parliament (The Tynwald) and legal system. The main town and capital, **Douglas**, doubles up as a seaside resort with a full range of seasidey facilities as well a whiff (and only a whiff) of culture.*

*If you want to visit the island, **The Isle of Man Steam Packet Company**, Tel. 01624 661661, runs one sailing a day in winter, and from five to ten sailings a day in the peak summer season, from Heysham, near Morecambe in Lancashire. Ferries also run (four to seven a week in summer, one a week in winter) from Liverpool. The main tourism office is located in the Douglas Sea Terminal Building, Tel. 01624 686766; www.isle-of-man.com.*

21. YORKSHIRE

Yorkshire people are very proud of their county, England's largest by far. In fact, many Yorkshire folk say that the best thing to come out of neighboring Lancashire is the M62, the main motorway that leads into Yorkshire. As you'd expect with its size, Yorkshire offers a tremendous variety of scenery, from the rugged **coast** between Whitby and Scarborough, to the windswept **North York Moors**, just a few miles inland. To the west, the rolling **Yorkshire Dales** offer endless opportunities for walking and exploring, while further south the landscape of the **Vale of York** is closer to the kind of countryside you'd find in the south of the country.

Yorkshire's piece de resistance is the wonderful, intriguing, ancient city of **York**, with one of Europe's most beautiful cathedrals and roots going back to Roman times. Not far away, the great industrial cities of **Leeds** and **Bradford** with their large ethnic populations offer a different cultural experience, a wealth of excellent restaurants, museums and parks. The whole county is dotted with picturesque towns and villages, stunning churches and peaceful ruined abbeys. "Ee bah gum," as a Yorkie might put it, "there's nowt like it."

YORK

The city of **York**, which gives its name to England's largest county, is one of the highlights of any tour of England. This city of 100,000 was named *Eboracum* in Roman times, when it was an important military center. Later on the Saxons established a small settlement here and brought Christianity to the place when, on Christmas Eve, 627, the local Northumbrian King Edwin was baptized in a tiny wooden church. Later on, the Vikings claimed the city as their capital in England, naming it Jorvic; relics of their period in the driving seat are in evidence all over the city. During the Norman period, the foundations of the massive **Minster** church, the city's greatest treasure, were laid.

York was spared much of the destruction wrought by the Industrial Revolution, which changed the face of so many ancient English cities, meaning that much of its medieval and regency architecture remained relatively intact. Today, the heart of medieval York is a maze of narrow streets and narrow alleys, or "snickleways," seen at its best in the **"Shambles**," a medieval street that was once full of butcher's shops, now replaced by trendy boutiques and souvenir emporia.

Perhaps the best way to get a general overview of York is to take a walk around the **city walls**, erected in the 14th century to replace the original earthen ramparts built by the Vikings to keep out raiders, and extensively restored since then. There's a narrow path along the top, which passes over a number of fortified gates, known here as "bars" – **Monk's Bar** on Goodramgate, **Bootham Bar** in Exhibition Square, **Micklegate Bar** and **Walmgate Bar** among the best examples.

ARRIVALS & DEPARTURES

By Car

The main route from London to York is the M1, from which you take the A64 for the last twenty miles of the journey.

By Train

GNER (Great North Eastern Railways) operate a fast, 125 mph service from London's King's Cross direct to York, with a journey time of about two hours. *Call 0345 484950 for more information.* York's train station is situated just west of the city center over the Lendal Bridge.

By Bus

National Express buses run from London's Victoria Bus Station direct to York, taking just under five hours. *Call 0990 808080 for information.* A plethora of bus companies operate the various inter-town routes throughout the region.

GETTING AROUND TOWN

York's own main bus operator is **Rider York**, *Tel. 01904 435600.* Bicycles can be hired from **Bob Trotter's**, *13 Lord Mayor's Walk, Tel. 01904 622868*, which is about ten minutes' from the train station.

While in York, you might want to partake of a **ghost tour** – the place is just made for them. Two companies offering ghoulish guided tours are **The Ghost Trail of York**, *Tel. 01904 633276*, which starts at 7:30pm every night at the front door of the Minster (adults £3, 4s-14s £2) or **The Ghost Hunt of York**, from the Shambles and also at 7:30pm, *Tel. 01904 608700;*

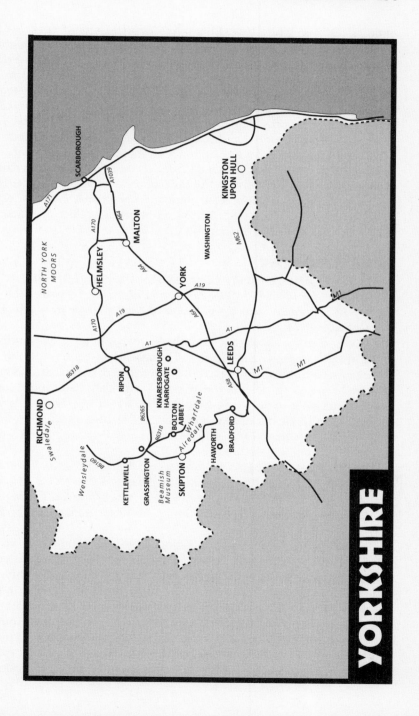

same prices. The **White Rose Line** operates boat tours of York, leaving from Lendal Bridge. The one-hour guided trips sail regularly throughout the day from February to November, *Tel. 01904 623752*. **Guide Friday** buses offer regular tours of York on open top buses, leaving from the tourist center at the *De Grey Rooms, Exhibition Square, Tel. 01904 640896*. Guided walking tours also leave from the same place at 10:15am and 2:15 in the summer months. The tour, led by a member of the official York Association of Voluntary Guides, is free, but a gratuity is expected.

This is an easily walkable city, but with so many places of interest in the vicinity, renting a car is not a bad idea if you're using York as a base. Parking, however, is very tough. All the major car rental companies have offices in York. In addition, local company **Leedhams**, *1 Rougier Street, York YO1 6HX, Tel. 01904 625222*, has a brand new fleet of Vauxhalls (GMs) for pickup or delivery.

WHERE TO STAY

DEAN COURT HOTEL, *Duncombe Place, York YO1 2EF. Tel. 01904 625082 or toll-free in US 800/528-1234, Fax 01904 620305. Rooms: 40. Rates: singles from £80, doubles from £100. Restaurant, coffee lounge, free parking. All credit cards accepted.*

The best thing about this 40-room Victorian hotel is its wonderful location right opposite the Minster. Though it had been in decline for some years, the rooms have been refurbished to high standards, and many of them have superb views of the Minster – especially inspiring at night, when it's floodlit. You won't be able to park at the hotel, it's in a pedestrianized area. but valet parking is available. There's a coffee lounge and a restaurant that serves mostly traditional English cuisine with a smattering of international dishes.

MIDDLETHORPE HALL, *Bishopthorpe Road YO23 2GB. Tel. 01904 641241, Fax 01904 620176. Rooms: 31. Rates: singles from £99; double/twin from £145; deluxe double/twin from £160; four-poster from £225; suites from £185. English breakfast: £12.50. Restaurants, health spa, gardens, free parking. Credit cards: MC, Visa.*

This stately William and Mary house built in 1699, right on the outskirts of York near the famous racecourse, had fallen into some disrepair until it was bought by Historic House Hotels and completely refurbished. The place has a feel of a country manor house (which indeed it was), with lots of antiques, an elegant drawing room and even a library. Some of the rooms are located in a gorgeous courtyard setting. Another very nice touch is the fresh flowers that adorn the rooms and public places. There's also a fine, wood-paneled restaurant serving classic Anglo-French cuisine, including fresh vegetables grown in the hotel garden.

JUDGE'S LODGING, *9 Lendal, York YO1 2AQ. Tel. 01904 638733. Rooms: 13. Rates: singles from £75, doubles from £100. Restaurants. All major credit cards accepted.*

This charming, elegant hotel was once a private home belonging to a Dr. Wintringham. Later on it was used as a lodging house for judges who had traveled up north from London's Inns of Court. You pass through a pretty front yard to enter a reception area with an outstanding circular wooden staircase – the only one of its kind in Britain. The bedrooms, some of which have four-poster beds, are cozy and comfortable, and the main salon on the ground floor is a quaint, slightly eccentric mixture of Queen Mother pastels, gilded mirrors and over-ripe chairs. There are two dining rooms, both of which are intimate.

MOUNT ROYALE, *The Mount, York YO2 1GU. Tel 01904 628856, Fax 01904 611171. Rooms: 17, plus 6 suites. Rates: singles from £85, doubles from £95. Bar, restaurant, outdoor pool. All major credit cards accepted.*

One of York's most prestigious hotels, the Mount Royale has been run by the same family for more than 30 years. Although perhaps not in pristine shape, this grand old William IV period building is noted for its elegant public and private rooms, and excellent service. Among the hotel's points of interest are an amazingly over-the-top Italian bed in Room 15, and a garden room with private patio. There's a lovely garden and an excellent restaurant serving a mixture of modern and traditional food. For the really brave hearted, there's an outdoor swimming pool – thank goodness it's heated.

GRASMEAD HOUSE HOTEL, *1 Scarcroft Hill, York, YO24 1DF. Tel and Fax 01904 629996. Rooms: 6. Rates: rooms start at £65; family rooms from £87. Bar. All major credit cards accepted.*

This delightful small hotel's six bedrooms all come with four-posters – some pretty ancient – so you can't escape them. The rooms are a bit on the small side, but there's a cozy lounge that's full of character with more antiques, including an old-fashioned gramophone player and bar. It's a short walk from the hotel to the center of the city.

HOLMWOOD HOUSE, *114 Holgate Road, York YO24 4BB. Tel 01904 626183, Fax 01904 670899. Rooms: 14. Rates: singles from £45, doubles from £55, triple £85. Restaurant. All major credit cards accepted.*

This highly popular, fairly central small hotel, just a few minutes' walk from the train station and main attractions, is notable for a number of things, including some bedrooms with views of the Minster, and one bedroom with a spa bath (which gets booked up well in advance). It's a cozy place, with lashings of country-style decor and a dining room where breakfast is served.

THE GRANGE, *1, Clifton, York YO30 6AA. Tel 01904 644744, Fax 01904 612453. Rooms: 30. Rates: singles from £99, doubles from £120. Bar, three restaurants. All major credit cards accepted.*

One of York's classier establishments, The Grange has hosted a number of big name celebrities, including Shirley Bassey. The entrance hall, with its pink columns, leads to a spiral staircase, which in turn leads to the bedrooms, all individually decorated and furnished to a high standard. The hotel, unusually, boasts three restaurants – in the basement there's an informal brasserie; a more formal restaurant, The Ivy, with an impressive marquee trompe l'oeuil; and a seafood bar.

AMBASSADOR HOTEL, *123 The Mount, York YO24 1DU. Tel 01904 641316, Fax 01904 640259. Rooms: 25. Rates: all rooms start at £85. Bar, restaurant. All major credit cards accepted.*

The Ambassador is an elegant Georgian building located a few miles from downtown York, near the famous racecourse. The ambience is peaceful and relaxed and the rooms come in a variety of shapes and sizes, many of them overlooking the secluded grounds to the rear of the property and all with a full range of facilities. There's an elegant restaurant, Gray's.

HUDSON'S, *60 Bootham, York YO30 7BZ. Tel 01904 621267, Fax 01904 654719. Rooms: 25. Rates: singles from £70, doubles from £90. Bar, restaurant. All major credit cards accepted.*

Hudson's is centrally located, convenient to all York's attractions. The older part of the hotel is comprised of two Victorian houses, tastefully converted, where the bedrooms tend to be more traditional, and a modern mews development with purpose-built bedrooms. There's a pleasant dining room, and a bistro with some original flagstone floors and fairly conservative menu.

YORK MOAT HOUSE, *North Street, York YO1 6JF. Tel 01904 459988, Fax 01904 641793. Rooms: 200. Rates: singles from £120, doubles from £140. Bar, restaurant, solarium, sauna, beauty salon. All major credit cards accepted.*

Massive by York standards, the multi-story Moat House is part of a large and successful British chain of hotels. Located in a wonderful setting on the River Ouse, the hotel is within easy walking distance of all York's major sites. What's more, parking is available, so important in such a busy, bustling city center where finding a parking space is well nigh impossible. The rooms are large and comfortable, and there's a large restaurant, as well as an extensive fitness and leisure suite and a beauty salon. The prices are a bit on the steep side, yet when you take into account the city center location and the facilities the hotel has to offer, maybe it's not such a surprise.

WHERE TO EAT

MELTON'S, *7 Scarcroft Road. Tel. 01904 634341. Open Monday 5:30pm to 10pm; Tuesday to Saturday noon to 2pm, 5:30pm to 10pm; Sunday noon to 2pm. Set lunch £15 (3 courses); dinner £19.50 (3 courses). Credit cards: MC, Visa.*

One of the best-known restaurants in York, Melton's is a lively yet unassuming place with an open kitchen and local art decorating the salmony-pink walls. The food is good – the chef, Michael Hjort, worked for a time with the Roux brothers – and it shows. The main focus here in on English, Continental and seafood dishes, with one of Melton's boozy trifles a particularly good way to finish.

MIDDLETHORP HALL, *Bishopthorpe Road, York. Tel. 01904 634341. Open daily 12:30pm to 1:45pm, 7pm to 9:45pm. Set lunch £14.50, dinner £32. All major credit cards accepted.*

Jackets and ties are on the menu at this classic restaurant located in one of York's best hotels, a 17th century country house restored and maintained by Historic House Hotels. Just as you'd expect, the menu in the wood-paneled dining room here focuses on classic dishes using the best, usually local produce, like filet of lamb in a red wine sauce, poached oysters and the like. The wine list starts with house French at £13. This is a great place to come for a special occasion – such as your arrival in York!

19 GRAPE LANE, *19 Grape Lane. Tel. 01904 636366. Open Tuesday to Friday noon to 2pm, 6pm to 9pm; Saturday noon to 2pm, 6pm to 10pm. Set lunch (2 courses) £9, dinner (3 courses) £19. Credit cards: MC, Visa.*

Housed in a 14th century building in the center of town, this very busy yet unpretentious restaurant is prized by locals who come here for a variety of modern English dishes. As well as the a la carte menu, there are daily specials which often offer the best value. Special offers available include a novel "Beat the Clock" dinner option; the time you order a three course meal between 6pm and 8pm is the price you pay for your main course!

YORK PAVILION HOTEL, *45 Main Street, Fulford, York. Tel 01904 622099. Open noon to 2pm, 6:30pm to 9:30pm. Dinner from £25. All major credit cards accepted.*

This attractive Georgian hotel a short distance from downtown York is notable for its brasserie restaurant, where the menu changes regularly, and where daily specials (influenced by market availability) are notched up on a board. The cuisine, best described as modern British, used fresh produce imaginatively presented, like monkfish on mashed potato with a hint of lemon, with seared Parma ham and a gazpacho dressing. The vegetable accompaniment is similarly fresh, and not overcooked as in so many establishments. There's an extensive wine list.

SPURRIERGATE CENTRE, *Spurriergate, York. Tel 01904 629393. Open all day, but not for dinner. No credit cards.*

This disarmingly attractive cafeteria is located on the edge of downtown York in the former (now deconsecrated church) of St. Michael's, complete with shrines and wall tablets liberally sprinkled throughout. It's a favorite place for morning coffee and afternoon tea, including delicious scones, but lunches are good and wholesome too. A good bet for a lunchtime snack or something a bit more filling as you continue your explorations of this fascinating city.

PIERRE VICTOIRE, *2 Lendal, York. Tel 01904 655222. Open daily noon to 2:30pm, 5pm to 10:30pm. Three course dinner (with wine) around £25. Credit cards: MC, Visa.*

This ever-popular Edinburgh-based chain has built its reputation on serving excellent French-style cuisine at affordable pries, both at lunchtimes, when the fare tends to be a little less elaborate – and amazingly inexpensive – and at dinner, when the dishes tend to be a little more adventurous. Still, at £20-25 for a three course meal with wine, you can't go far wrong. Because of the excellent value on offer here, it tends to get very busy, particularly with a young student crowd.

SEEING THE SIGHTS

Wherever you are in York, you just can't miss **York Minster**, the largest Gothic church in England, which looms over the city and the surrounding countryside. The Minster's origins can be traced back to the 7th century, though the present building dates largely from the 13th century. Inside, what first hits you on entry is the sheer size of the place – it's more than 530 feet long, 249 feet wide at the transepts and 90 feet from floor to ceiling – no wonder it took 250 years to complete.

Because of the time it took to build the Minster, various architectural styles are in evidence – the **transepts,** for example, which are constructed in the Early English style of the 1200s; the **nave** in the later Decorated style (1300s); and the **chancel** in the Perpendicular style of the late 1300s to 1400s. You can't fail to be impressed by the medieval **stained glass**, most notably the **Great West Window** of 1388, known as the "Heart of Yorkshire." Externally, the most striking feature is the three lofty **towers**, the central one soaring to a height of almost 200 feet. It's a tough climb, but well worth it for the view. The **chapter house** is also worth seeing. Built in the 1270s, it's unusual in that it has no central supporting pillar. Best of all are the foundations. Excavation work in the '60s discovered fragments not only of an earlier Norman cathedral, but an Anglo-Saxon and Viking cemetery, along with evidence of an original Roman basilica. Watch out for the spooks; a number of visitors claim to have witnessed

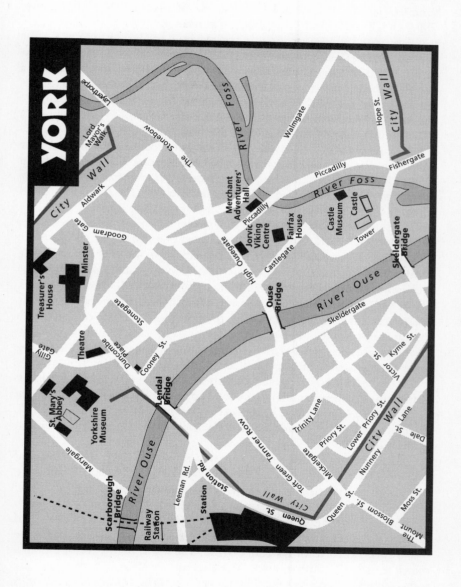

legions of Roman soldiers walking through the foundations! *Open Monday to Saturday 7am to 6pm, Sunday open after 1pm (unless you are attending a service.) Admission to foundations: adults £2, seniors & students £1.50; children 5-15, £1. Chapter House 70p, 5-15s, 30p; Central Tower £2.50, 5-15s, £1, crypt 70p/30p. Tel. 01904 639347; www.yorkminster.org.*

A former 18th century debtor's prison built on the site of York Castle, the fascinating **Castle Museum** at 2, Coffee Yard, off Stonegate, contains a number of interesting exhibits, including a detailed re-creation of a cobbled Victorian street, a neoclassical Georgian dining room, and a sitting room set in 1953, complete with TV to watch the Queen's coronation. But pride of place here goes to the **Coppergate helmet**, a 1,200 year-old Anglo-Saxon helmet that was found during some excavations taking place in the city. Also on display are costumes, armor, and the cell where the notorious highwayman, Dick Turpin, spent his last night alive before his execution. *Open summer daily 9:30am to 5pm, winter 9:30am to 4:30pm. Admission adults £4.95, seniors, students & 5s-16s, £3.50. Tel. 01904 653611.*

Most of the Viking city of **Jorvic** lies several feet below the street level of modern-day York, and excavations always seem to be taking place somewhere. This authentic Viking site, known as the **Jorvic-Viking Center**, and located on Coppergate, has been painstakingly restored by archaeologists to create a typical Viking street on an October day in 948. "Time cars" whisk you back in history, first to 1067, when the Viking city was overrun by the Normans, then further back to 948. You can visit a Viking family home, and down to the river to see ship chandlers at work. And the sights are accompanied by the sounds (and smells) of the Viking city. At the end of the tour, a detailed exhibit shows visitors thousands of artifacts discovered. Be warned: this is York's most popular tourist attraction and there are likely to be long lines. *Open November to March 9am to 3:30pm, April to October daily 9am to 5:30pm. Admission adults £5.65, seniors and students £5, children £4.25. Tel. 01904 643211; www.jorvik-viking-centre.co.uk.*

York was for many years a major railway center. The **National Railway Museum**, in Leeman Road, is a refurbished steam locomotive depot and is now the world's largest **train museum** and a delight for all rail enthusiasts. Among the displays are some of the greats of the steam locomotion era; the *Agenoria*, dating from 1829 and a contemporary of George Stephenson's famous *Rocket*, and the *Mallard*, which holds the world speed record for a steam engine (126 mph) that was more than a match for the 125 mph inter-city trains of today. Also on display here are some passenger coaches used by Queen Victoria. *Open year-round daily 10am to 6pm. Admission adults £6.50, seniors and children up to 16 free, concessions/students £4. Tel. 01904 621261; www.nmsi.ac.uk.*

Housed in the gardens of ruined **St. Mary's Abbey**, which dates from 1089, the **Yorkshire Museum** specializes in the natural and archaeological history of Yorkshire, particularly the Roman, Anglo-Saxon and Viking eras. The highlight of the museum is the 15th century **Middleham Jewel**, a pendant containing a large sapphire, and which is considered to be the best piece of Gothic jewelry found in England this century. The kids will definitely find the display about Roman culinary habits to their taste, even if you don't! *Open year-round daily 10am to 5pm. Admission adults £4.25, seniors, students & 5s-15s £2.70. Tel. 01904 629745.*

There are literally scores of places to explore in York, but for something a little different, head for to **Fairfax House**, in Castlegate, an elegant Georgian town house that's now a museum of decorative arts. It was originally built in 1762 for the ninth Viscount Fairfax of Emley. Of particular note are the marble dining room and the grand salon with its crystal chandeliers. The house was extensively restored during the 1980s and now boasts a superb collection of Georgian furniture. *Open late February to early January Monday to Thursday & Saturday 11am to 4:30pm; Sunday 1:30pm to 4:30pm. Admission adults £4, seniors & students £3.50, children 5-16, £1.50. Tel. 01904 655543.*

EXCURSIONS & DAY TRIPS

Twenty miles west of York on the A59 lies the elegant spa town of **Harrogate**, which became one of the nation's leading inland resorts during the 18th century. Following the demise of spa resorts, Harrogate reinvented itself as a major convention center, building a vast new complex that attracts huge numbers of conference delegates and other visitors to the town. Harrogate remains an attractive town of pleasant Regency terraces and impressive green spaces. You can trace the town's history as a spa town with a visit to the **Royal Pump Room Museum**, built over the foul-smelling sulphur well that started the spa ball rolling in 1842. If you're feeling a bit flustered or stressed, you can visit the **Royal Baths Assembly Rooms**, for a relaxing Turkish bath or a sauna in the exotic, tiled chambers that date from 1897.

Just three miles east of Harrogate on the A59 is **Knaresborough**, an attractive old town in its own right, with its own medieval castle, market square and river. But it's best known for **Mother Shipton's cave**, a ten minute walk south of downtown, reputed to be the birthplace of Mother Shipton, a 16th century prophetess who is said to have predicted, among other things, the Great Fire of London. *Open daily 9:30am to 5pm. Admission adults £4.55, seniors & students £4.25, 5s-17s £3.45. Tel. 01423 864600.*

Nine miles northwest of Knaresborough, signposted off the A6265, is the gorgeous 18th century water garden and deer park known as

Studley Royal, replete with the stunning ruins of **Fountains Abbey**, a Cistercian monastery founded in 1132 on the banks of the River Skell. Although it most definitely is a ruin, many of the original buildings survive, and it's easier here than perhaps anywhere else in England to imagine how monastic life might have been. Among the best preserved buildings are the lay brothers' refectory and dormitory and the graceful 15th century Perpendicular style tower. The National Trust, which owns the property, operates free guided tours around the complex, or you can guide yourself round using one of the leaflets available at the entrance. This really is one of the most peacefully picturesque and romantic sites in England and well worth a visit. *Open April to September daily 10am to 7pm, October to March daily 10am to 5pm. Admission adults £4:30, children £2.10. Tel. 01765 608888; www.fountainsabbey.org.uk.*

Just a few miles northeast of here off the B6325 is the ancient city of **Ripon** with an attractive 13th century cathedral, built on the site of earlier structures, including a Saxon church whose remains can be seen in the crypt. Nearby, don't miss **Newby Hall**, an early 18th century house that contains some of the finest interior decorative art of its time in western Europe, largely the work of Robert Adam, one room having been designed round a collection of priceless Gobelin tapestries. The grounds contain a number of ancient roses and rare shrubs and a sunken garden, as well as a range of additional attractions including a narrow-gauge steam railway and river excursions. *Open April to September Tuesday to Sunday and bank Holiday Mondays, gardens 11am to 5pm, house noon to 5pm. Tel. 01423 322583; www.newbyhall.co.uk.*

NIGHTLIFE & ENTERTAINMENT

York is brimming with pubs, many of which can trace their roots back to medieval times. The oldest, reputedly, is **The Black Swan**, *Peasholme Green*. Also good is the riverside **King's Arms**, *King's Staithe*, though because of its setting it can get very crowded in summer. Another interesting old pub is **The Spread Eagle**, *Walmgate*, where the bar food is also very good.

The focal point of York's cultural life is the **Theatre Royal**, *St. Leonard's Place, Tel. 01904 623568*, a handsome old building that hosts all kinds of productions from classic plays to musicals and pantomimes.

York also hosts a number of annual festivals that bring many additional visitors to the city. These include a **Viking Festival** in February, which includes re-enactments of Viking vs. Anglo-Saxon confrontations, and the four-yearly **York Mystery Plays**, next due to take place in the summer of 2004. *For information on these and other festivals, call the Tourist Information Office, Tel. 01904 621756.*

SHOPPING

York is a great place for browsing bookstores, new and secondhand. Most of these are congregated around Petergate and Stonegate. Oxford-based **Blackwell's**, *32 Stonegate, Tel. 01904 624531*, is hard to beat for new titles, while for secondhand books, maps and prints, head for **Minster Gate Bookshop**, *8 Minster Gate, Tel. 01904 621812.*

If antiques are your weakness, head over to the **York Antiques Centre**, *2 Lendal*, a collection of 34 shops spread over two floors, with all manner of goodies to weigh down your luggage.

PRACTICAL INFORMATION

The regional tourist board is the **Yorkshire and Humberside Tourist Board**, *312, Tadcaster Road, York YO2 2HF*. York's own **main tourist** information center is located at *De Grey Rooms, Exhibition Square, York YO1 2HB, Tel. 01904 621756*. The city runs an excellent, visitor-friendly website at *www.york.gov.uk.*

York abounds in **banks** and **post offices**, so you'll have no problem changing money. The main post office is at Lendal, while the main branches of the banks are located around St. Helen's Square.

LEEDS, BRADFORD & WEST YORKSHIRE

This part of Yorkshire is synonymous with the wool industry, which brought great prosperity to the region for centuries. In addition to wool, the textile, chemical and engineering industries did well here, but have left their mark in a number of ugly townscapes – though the flip side is that their prosperity paid for some excellent civic buildings, many of which survive to this day. Chief among the cities that prospered is **Leeds**, currently experiencing something of a rejuvenation, as well as **Bradford**, Wakefield, Huddersfield and Halifax.

North of the Calder Valley and south of the Aire is the gaunt landscape made famous by the **Bronte sisters**, centering on **Haworth**, where the old parsonage in which the sisters lived is now a museum dedicated to their work. But it's best to get out of the town and explore the countryside around to get a feel for the vistas made famous in *Wuthering Heights* and other novels.

ARRIVALS & DEPARTURES

By Car

The M1 from London gets you direct to Leeds in about two hours. Bradford is just a short (20 minutes) drive away along the A647.

By Bus

There are regular, direct buses to Leeds and Bradford from London's Victoria Bus Station. *For information, call 0990 808080.*

By Train

Trains from London's Euston Station take around 2 1/2 hours to get to Leeds. *Call 0345 484950 for information.*

GETTING AROUND

In Leeds and Bradford, **Metro buses**, *Tel. 0113 245 7676*, serve the conurbation and reach out into the surrounding countryside, including the Dales. Leeds Central Bus Station, for local services, is located on St. Peter's Street, while long distance coaches arrive at the terminal on Wellington Street. In Bradford, the travel interchange is on Croft Street.

WHERE TO STAY

Leeds

42 THE CALLS, *42 The Calls, Leeds LS2 7EW. Tel. 0113 244 0099, Fax 0113 234 4100. Rooms: 41. Rates: singles from £98, doubles from £128. Restaurant (see below). Brasserie. Leisure facilities. Fishing! All major credit cards accepted.*

This state-of-the-art conversion of a former warehouse into one of Leed's plushest hotels took a good deal of guts. but it seems to have paid off. Each of the 41 rooms retains original features such as brickwork and exposed beams, and comes with state-of-the-art facilities from CD players and TVs to low-flush loos and power showers. There's a very pleasant lobby lounge, and 24-hour room service is available.

ARAGON HOTEL, *250 Stainbeck Lane, Leeds LS7 2PS. Tel 0113 275 9306, Fax 0113 275 7166. Rooms: 12. Rates: singles from £40, doubles from £50. Bar, restaurant. Credit cards: MC, Visa.*

Located in a leafy suburb in the north of Leeds, a few miles from the city center. The Aragon is a small relaxing hotel with 12 nicely furnished and well-equipped rooms, a small and intimate bar, separate guests' lounge and dining room.

HALEY'S HOTEL, *Shire Oak Road, Headingley, Leeds LS6 2DE. Tel 0113 278 4446, fax 0113 275 3342. Rooms: 29. Rates: singles from £90, doubles from £125. Bar, restaurant. All major credit cards accepted.*

Haley's Hotel is set in located in a tree-lined cul-de-sac in the suburb of Headingley, famous (in England, at least) as the home of Yorkshire Cricket Club. The hotel is comprised of two late Victorian houses; the bedrooms are spacious and decorated and furnished to a good standard with antiques – and in some cases, four-poster beds. The public areas are equally roomy, and there's a restaurant featuring modern British cuisine.

Bradford

QUALITY VICTORIA HOTEL, *Bridge Street, Bradford BD1 1JX. Tel. 01274 728706, Fax 01274 736358. Rooms: 63. Rates: Singles from £83, doubles from £98. Restaurant, free parking, leisure suite. All major credit cards accepted.*

In the unlikely event that you'll want to stay any length of time in Bradford, this is the place to come. A former railway hotel, it was built in 1875 and has recently been stylishly renovated, with elegant public rooms. The 63 rooms all come with bath, TV and comfortable fittings. You may choose to eat at Vic and Bert's, which, despite the name, offers stylish eating and an eclectic grill menu, or prefer to explore some of Bradford's wonderful Asian eateries, many of which are within easy walking distance of the hotel.

APPERLEY MANOR, *Apperley Lane, Apperley Bridge, Bradford BD10 0PQ. Tel 0113 250 5626, Fax 0113 250 0075. Rooms: 13. Rates: singles from £59, doubles from £69. Bar, restaurant. All major credit cards accepted.*

This pleasant, friendly manor house hotel is conveniently located between Leeds and Bradford, just a couple of miles from the international airport. The 13 rooms are spacious and well-appointed, with modern facilities; some family rooms are available. There are two restaurants, including a newly opened brasserie.

WHERE TO EAT

If you adore Indian food as much as I do, then there's no better place to come – and the great thing about eating curry and similar dishes is that a full meal can be so inexpensive. Both Leeds and Bradford have a wide range of restaurants, many serving ethnic, primarily Asian, food.

Bradford, in particular, is often referred to as the "**curry capital**" of Britain. If you're staying there, it's well worth sampling one of the many curry houses the city has to offer, many of which, like **The Kashmir**, Britain's oldest curry house, and the **Taj Mahal**, can be found on Morley Street. Both serve excellent curries, from very mild to extremely hot, and a variety of authentic tandoori dishes that are superb, especially when washed down with Indian or Pakistani beer.

Bradford

THE KASHMIR, *27 Morley Street, Bradford. Tel 01274 726513. Open daily 11am to 3pm. Curries around £4. No alcohol license – bring your own! Credit cards: MC, Visa.*

Established as long ago as 1958, the Kashmir is Britain's longest-established Indian restaurant, and so must take some of the blame – or crdeit – for a major change in the British diet. Curry is now the nation's most popular dish, having replaced roast beef (and hamburgers) years ago. The immensely popular Kashmir still churns out old favorites and at very competitive prices. There's a large selection of desserts, and a wine list – though you may prefer to indulge in the quaint old (post-1958) British habit of accompanying your curry with a pint of lager.

NAWAAB. *32 Manor Road, Bradford. Tel 01274 720371. Open Monday to Friday noon to 2pm, 6pm to midnight, Saturday 6pm to midnight, Sunday 1pm to midnight. Credit cards: MC, Visa.*

Authentic Indian restaurant with a choice of dishes as long as the President's Valentine's list. Choose from well-known favorites like Lamb Tikka Masala or go for the more exotic: Shahi Safeid Korma is a unique dish first introduced by the same king who built the Taj Mahal. The king insisted eveything in the palace had to be white; hence the dish comprises a mild white sauce, of yogurt, garlic and onion puree, with almonds and double cream. Chicken breast is prepared with mild herbs and spices. Sounds delicious? It's only £7.95. There's a good choice of Indian desserts and wine (and lager) is available. On Sundays a special buffet lunch is served – an overwhelming array of choices for little more than a fiver (£5).

Leeds

LEODIS BRASSERIE, *Victoria Mills, Sovereign Street, Leeds. Tel 0113 242 1010. Open Monday to Friday noon to 2pm, 6pm to 10pm (11pm Fridays and Saturdays). Three-course set dinner £14.95. All major credit cards accepted.*

Converted from a former factory, Leodi's is a wonderful waterfront brasserie with great atmosphere and a commendable choice of seasonal menus, including a wealth of vegetarian options. The cuisine and the decor is contemporary, the service outstanding, and there's a good (if a little pricey) wine list.

AKMAL'S TANDOORI BISTRO, *235 Woodhouse Lane, Hyde Park, Leeds. Tel 0113 242 4600.*

Wonderful tandoori restaurant with efficient, friendly service. The meals somehow manage to be both light (for a curry) yet immensely satisfying. The restaurant may leave a lot to be desired on the decor front, and it's popular with university and college students, so expect lots of noise, especially on a Friday and Saturday night when it stays open to the (very) small hours.

POOL COURT AT 42, *44 The Calls, Leeds LS2 7EW. Tel. 0113 234 3232. Open Monday to Friday, noon to 2pm, 6:30pm to 10:30pm. Saturday lunch only noon to 2pm. Dinner around £35. All major credit cards accepted.*

Attached to the hotel, this upmarket, three rosette-winning eating place serves contemporary French and English food, with a hint of Mediterranean. It's a pleasant, modern space, and the menu includes a number of vegetarian options, as well as some excellent fish and poultry choices. Next door, the **Brasserie** is a slightly less expensive option, though the food is of the same high quality as that in the formal restaurant.

SHEAR'S YARD, *The Calls, Leeds. Tel 0113 244 4144. Open Monday to Saturday noon to 2:30pm, 6pm to 10pm (10:30 Thursday, Friday, Saturday). Closed Sunday Dinner around £22. All major credit cards accepted.*

Shear's Yard, as you might guess from this establishment's name, is a converted sheep shearing shed now converted into a pleasant and atmospheric restaurant in the upmarket Calls area of Leeds. It's a lively place, especially at weekends, and the food is excellent, covering the gamut of European cuisine from tapas to rack of lamb with rosemary. There's a good wine list, with house wines starting at around £10 a bottle. In the summer, you can dine al fresco on the terrace. There's occasionally live jazz.

RASCASSE, *Canal Wharf, Water Lane, Leeds. Tel 0113 244 6611. Open Monday to Saturday, noon to 2pm, 6:30pm to 1opm (no lunch Saturday). Set 3-course dinner from £17. All major credit cards accepted.*

Another of Leed's burgeoning collection of upmarket eateries, Rascasse is located canal-side. When you enter, first impressions are that you're on a ship, with the polished wooden floors and a curved staircase leading up to a bar. To complete the picture there are beautiful floral displays and some high-tech furniture. And the food? Well, it's best described as Anglo-European; freshly produced meats and vegetarian dishes accompanied by backed up by tapenades, gazpacho sauces and the like. There's a great dessert trolley, and the eclectic wine list offers a wide range of international choices, with house wines starting at about £11.

FOUTH FLOOR CAFE AT HARVEY NICHOLS *107 Briggate, Leeds. Tel 0113 204 8000. Open: store hours. Dinner around £25. All major credit cards accepted.*

Located in the chic department store whose London branch was nirvana for the girls in the hit TV comedy *Absolutely Fabulous*, the store's upmarket emphasis is maintained in the cafe, where as well as some delicious gourmet sandwiches and an array of mouth-watering cakes and desserts, you can enjoy beautifully prepared hot meals such as fresh cod with a wild mushroom and herb crust. An added bonus here is the stunning views over the rooftops of Leeds. If you're out shopping and feel a bit peckish, there's nowhere better!

SEEING THE SIGHTS
Leeds

Leeds has undergone quite a transformation in recent years, after decades of decline. Much of this has been due to government investment and incentives, which have brought to the city chic stores such as Harvey Nicholls, of *Absolutely Fabulous* fame, and a wealth of outdoor cafes and high class restaurants. Another newcomer is the **Royal Armouries**, transferred here from their former base in the Tower of London.

Leeds is a green city, despite some rather grimy suburbs, and there are a number of city parks that make it a pleasant spot in the summer. Leeds stands on the River Aire, an important trading route in ancient times. Though the river and the warehouses and factory buildings on its banks were left to deteriorate for many years, a series of "urban regeneration" projects in the past decade has meant that the river and its surrounds is again a major attraction. **Granary Wharf**, in the Canal Basin, *www.granarywharf.co.uk*, for example, has a number of design, arts and crafts shops, as well as musical events and a regular festival market on Saturdays and Sundays. Further east at **The Calls**, a number of new restaurants, cafes and a hotel have sprouted along the cobbled streets and quayside.

The Tetley company of tea fame also brews beer in profusion, and Tetley's Bitter is still one of the nation's favorites. Tetley's **Brewery Wharf**, on The Waterfront, celebrates the history and traditions of the English public house in a series of exhibits, and you can also partake of a guided brewery tour – with free tastings. *Open April to September, Tuesday to Sunday 10:30am to 5:30pm; October to March Wednesday to Sunday 10am to 4:30pm. Admission £5 (brewery tour extra). Tel. 0113 242 0666.*

The prosperity that came to the city in Victorian times is best evidenced in the fine arcade and civic buildings, including the **Town Hall**, a huge building built in 1853 in the classical style. Designed by local architect Cuthbert Broderick, it is widely recognized as one of the finest public buildings in Britain.

Just across the road from the Town Hall are two of the city's main attractions. The **City Art Gallery** contains a notable collection of painting and sculpture, particular emphasis given to 20th century British art, including works by Holman Hunt, Lowry and Spencer, and sculpture by Henry Moore, who studied art at Leeds College of Art and whose name lives on in the adjacent **Henry Moore Institute**, given over to temporary exhibitions of modern sculpture. *Open Monday to Saturday 10am to 5pm (Wednesday until 8pm), Sundays 1pm to 5pm. Admission free. Tel. 0113 247 8254.*

Next door is the **Leeds City Museum**, with a mixture of exhibits ranging from natural history and geology and ethnology – Leeds has a vast Asian population – and flora and fauna. Pride of place in the museum, however, goes to the "Leeds Mummy," Natsef Amun, the Keeper of the Bulls which has been in the city's possession for more than 200 years. *Same hours as City Art Gallery; free.*

In the late 1990s, the decision was taken to move the bulk of the **Royal Armouries Exhibition** from its home of centuries in the Tower of London to Leeds. Though the thinking behind the scheme puzzled all but the most ardent inhabitant of Leeds, the result has been the development of a huge, 13-acre site in the dockland area in a purpose-built, state-of-the-art building, that's full of hands-on exhibits and interactive displays to entrance the kids, computer simulations, and even the occasional live demonstration. With five themed galleries tracing the development of weaponry through the ages, this is highly recommended. *Located at Armouries Drive, just off the M1 motorway. Open year round November to March 10:30am to 4:30pm, April to October 10:30am to 5:30pm. Admission adults £4.90, seniors & students £3.90, under 4s free. Tel. 0990 1066 66; www.armouries.org.uk.*

Two other buildings close to Leeds warrant a closer inspection. The first of these, **Harewood** (pronounced Harwood) **House**, about seven miles north of the city on the A61, and reachable by bus from the city's main bus station, is the spectacular neoclassical home of the Queen's cousin the Earl of Harewood. The house was built in 1759 by architect John Carr of York, and contains some impressive Robert Adam interiors, as well as some exquisite Chippendale (a local boy) furniture. The attractive grounds contains woods and a lake, as well as child-friendly attractions such as an adventure playground and a butterfly house. *Grounds and bird garden open march to October 10am to 4:30pm; House open April to October 11am to 4pm. Admission adult £7.25, seniors £6.50, students & children £5. Tel. 0113 218 1010.*

Four miles east of Leeds off the A63, and again accessible from Leeds Central Bus Station at regular intervals, is **Temple Newsam**, dating from Elizabethan and Jacobean times. Its main claim to fame is that it was the birthplace, in 1545, of **Darnley**, who would later become the (ill-fated) husband of **Mary, Queen of Scots**. The house is now owned by Leeds City, and contains a vast collection of furniture, paintings and ceramics. Outside, you'll want to visit the massive park, originally laid out by landscape architect Capability Brown in 1762, and containing walled rose gardens, greenhouses and some glorious woodland walks. *Open November, December & March Tuesday to Saturday 10am to 4pm, Sunday noon to 4pm; April to October Tuesday to Saturday 10am to 5pm, Sunday 1pm to 5pm. Admission adults £2, seniors & students £1, children 50p. Tel. 0113 264 7321.*

Bradford

Just nine miles west of Leeds on the A647 is another major industrial center, **Bradford**, which owed its prosperity, like so many other towns in this part of the world, to the **wool industry**, established here as early as the 16th century. But, in common with those other towns, inflation and recession have taken their toll over the years – though more recently, like neighboring Leeds, an injection of government cash has meant that it has been able to spruce itself up a bit. Hilly Bradford is also notable for its vast

Asian population – and today there are more mosques and temples here than churches. Though there have been ethnic flare-ups in the past, particularly following the publication of Salman Rushie's *Satanic Verses,* generally the city is a peaceful place that prides itself on its good race relations.

Despite the gloom, Bradford does its best to welcome visitors, who are rewarded with a number of attractions; some of the grand civic buildings of the Victorian era survive, chiefly the 1851 **St. George's Hall**, and the **Wool Exchange** (1864) on Market Street. But most come to Bradford for its museums, of which the best known is the **National Museum of Photography, Film and Television**, though, like the Armouries in Leeds, it's a bit of puzzle to work out why it's here. The museum opened in 1983 and is dedicated to the history of photography and film. It contains dozens of interactive models, photographic machinery and artifacts from primitive television cameras to TV props. There's also an IMAX screen, and the Pictureville cinema that shows mainly repertory films. *Open year-round Tuesday to Sunday (and bank Holiday Mondays) 10am to 6pm. Admission free. Tel. 01274 2220030; www.nmpft.org.uk.*

Don't miss the **Industrial Museum and Horses at Work**, about three miles northeast of the city center on the A658 at Moorside Mills, which outlines the development of the city's woollen industry with exhibits such as workers' homes from the 1870s and a mill owner's home from the 19th century as well. It occupies a former spinning mill. The horses in question are the huge and beautiful shire horses which can be seen pulling horse trams as well as giving rides. *Open year-round Tuesday to Saturday 10am to 5pm, Sunday noon to 5pm. Admission free. Tel. 01274 631756.*

Four miles north of Bradford (follow the signs from the A650) is the former model factory community of **Saltaire**, typical of a number of similar communities set up by anthropologist-industrial magnates in the 19th century – perhaps the most famous of which is Bournville, in Birmingham, owned by the Cadbury family – or Lowell in Massachusetts. Row upon row of terraced houses for the workers were combined with hospitals, libraries, schools and leisure facilities. Saltaire is remarkable in that it was fashioned in Italianate style; today, its former mills and homes have been converted into shops, restaurants and galleries. While you're here, don't miss the permanent exhibition of 400 works by local artist made good **David Hockney**. These are featured in the **1853 gallery** in Salt's Mill.

NIGHTLIFE & ENTERTAINMENT

Among Leeds' best pubs are the **Victoria**, *Great George Street,* and **Whitelock's**, *Turks Head Yard, off Briggate.* Both serve excellent pub grub.

Close by is the **Grand Theatre**, *46 New Briggate, Tel. 0113 244 0971*, which is the home of England's first major provincial opera company, **Opera North**. Leeds' other main auditorium is the **West Yorkshire Playhouse**, *Playhouse Square, Quarry Hill, Tel. 0113 244 2111,* an ultra-modern facility where a wide range of productions are held.

SHOPPING

For some elegant shopping, visit **Harvey Nichol's** store, *Briggate in Leeds* – the only one in Britain outside of London. And you shouldn't miss a visit to **Kirkgate Market**, *Vicar Lane in Leeds*, a wonderful Edwardian structure. There are more top-notch stores in the Victoria Quarter, Briggate, and in the restored **Corn Exchange**, *Call Lane*.

PRACTICAL INFORMATION

Leeds' main **tourist office** is located *at Leeds City Station, Leeds LS1 1PL, Tel. 0113 242 5242*. There's an excellent city website with lots of tourist information at *www.leeds.gov.uk*.

Bradford's **tourist information office** can be found at *the Central Library, Prince's Way BD1 1NN, Tel. 01274 753768*. That city's website is at *www.bradford.gov.uk*.

Leeds and Bradford are both major cities, with more than their share of banks and post offices. There is a plethora of bus companies that serve this region.

HAWORTH & BRONTE COUNTRY

Haworth is, after Stratford-upon-Avon, the most celebrated literary shrine in England, thanks to its close associations with the **Brontes**, the three daughters of the local parson, who were responsible for some of the best known works of English literature: Emily, with *Wuthering Heights* in 1847, Charlotte, with *Jane Eyre*, also in 1847, and Anne, who penned the *Tenant of Wildfell Hall* in 1848.

ARRIVALS & DEPARTURES
By Car

The A6144 from Bradford takes you directly to Haworth.

By Bus

There are frequent buses from Bradford to Haworth – after all, it's only ten miles away.

By Train

This is by far the most enjoyable way to get to Haworth. Take a train from Leeds (or Bradford) to Keighley, then change on to the **Keighley and Worth Valley Steam Railway**. The frequency of trains on this route fluctuates with the season (there are for example eight a day in high season and only one a day in mid-winter) so check with the company first. *Their number is 01535 645214.*

GETTING AROUND TOWN

Haworth is easy to get around on foot, the main attractions being located around a triangle formed by North Street, West Lane and Main Street, and along the length of Main Street, where most of the commercial outlets are found.

WHERE TO STAY

APOTHECARY GUEST HOUSE, *86 Main Street, Haworth. Tel. 01535 643642. Rooms: 7. Rates: rooms from £40.*

Right at the top of Main Street, near the Bronte parsonage, is this 17th century house which offers seven comfortable rooms, all with shower. The only meal that's served is breakfast – a hearty affair – but there are plenty of cafes, tearooms and pubs close by, including the Black Bull, Branwell's (the only brother of the Bronte sisters) favorite haunt.

OLD WHITE LION, *6 West Lane, Haworth BD22 8DU. Tel. 01535 642313, Fax 01535 646222. Rooms: 15. Rates: singles from £46, doubles from £62 (including breakfast). Restaurants. Credit cards: MC, Visa.*

Wherever you see an English village church you're never very far from a hostelry, and this is so true here. The Old White Lion is adjacent to the church where the Rev. Patrick Bronte used to be the Vicar. It's a quaint old place that's sprinkled with antiques and other paraphernalia; the 15 rooms, each with bath, are comfortable, and there's a full-service restaurant on the premises.

THREE SISTERS HOTEL, *Brow Top Road, Haworth BD22 9PH. Tel 01535 643458, Fax 01535 646842. Rooms: 9. Rates: singles from £33, doubles from £45. Bar, restaurant. Credit cards: MC, Visa.*

The Three Sisters, named of course after the Bronte siblings, was converted into a hotel and inn from a Victorian farmhouse. The bedrooms are spacious and pleasantly furnished, and you can enjoy freshly prepared meals in either the bar or the restaurant. From the hotel there are excellent views over Haworth and the beautiful countryside around. The best thing about this place, is of course, the price.

WHERE TO EAT

WEAVERS, *15 West Lane, Haworth. Tel. 01535 643822. Open Tuesday to Saturday eves only. Dinner around £22.50. Credit cards: MC, Visa.*

Very popular family-run restaurant and guest house converted from a row of old cottages that now serves traditional local dishes such as Whitby Fisherman's Pie, Yorkshire pudding, and various local stews – try the lamb. There are daily specials, including fish, and the local Gressingham duck is a good bet. There's a special tourist dinner menu, but you must get here before 7pm to qualify for this.

SEEING THE SIGHTS

Haworth is not an unattractive village, with its stone-built homes and location on the edge of the Yorkshire moors from which the sisters gained so much of their inspiration. Climb the steep, cobbled **Main Street**, little changed since the mid 19th century, for several places of note, including the **Black Bull** pub, where Branwell, the Brontes' only brother, drank himself to death, the **Post Office**, from which the sisters mailed their manuscripts to London, and the **Church of St. Michael**, below which Charlotte and Emily are buried in the family vault – Anne is buried in the coastal town of Scarborough.

The parsonage where they lived from 1820, after their father was appointed local Vicar, is now the **Bronte Parsonage Museum**, which contains some original furniture owned by the family, personal belongings, pictures, portraits painted by Branwell, a trained artist, and books. On a pleasant day (or perhaps, more evocatively on a gloomy, moody day) you can take the marked path to the **Bronte waterfall**, often described in Emily's and Charlotte's writings. The walk takes an hour or so, so take good shoes and protective clothing – you know from the sisters' books how unpredictable the weather can be round here.

PRACTICAL INFORMATION

Haworth's **tourism office** is at *2-4 West Lane, Tel. 01535 642234*, where you can get information on the Brontes and on some of the walks in the area. The town's post office and branches of the main banks are on Main Street.

THE YORKSHIRE DALES

With some of the most beautiful scenery in England, the **Yorkshire Dales**, meandering river valleys that tumble down south and east from the Pennines, are perfect walking country. You'll encounter some fascinating relics of the past here, such as **Bolton Priory**, a monastic ruin that captivated Wordsworth. Stone villages centuries old seem to grow out of the soil, bubbling brooks gurgle down to the nearest river. The whole area is criss-crossed with tracks and pathways, so that walking is not arduous – though you'll always have to keep an eye on the weather. If you're planning to stay in the area, it makes sense to use the attractive market town **Skipton** as your base.

ARRIVALS & DEPARTURES

By Bus

Keighley and District buses operate regular services from Bradford to Keighley, and from Keighley to Skipton (#71 and #72).

By Car

The A650 and A629 links Bradford with Skipton, via Keighley.

By Train

There are direct trains to Skipton from Leeds and Bradford. The station is about a half-mile out of town on the Swadford Road.

WHERE TO STAY

CONISTON HALL LODGE, *Coniston Cold, Skipton BD23 4EB. Tel 01756 748080, Fax 01756 749487. Rooms: 40. Rates: all rooms from £40. Bar, restaurant. All major credit cards accepted.*

Coniston Hall Lodge is located on a vast 1,200-acre estate with a 24-acre lake where guests can try their hand at trout fishing. The bedrooms are modern and tastefully decorated. Many of them come with king size beds, not a common occurrence in England, and with a full range of facilities, including TV and tea- and coffee-making facilities. Meals can be taken in Macleod's Bar or in the adjacent Buttery

LOW SKIBEDEN FARMHOUSE, *Skibeden Road, Skipton BD23 6AB. Tel 01756 793849, Fax 01756 793804. Rooms: 5. Rates: singles from £25, doubles from £40. Private fishing, falconry, archery. All major credit cards accepted.*

This lovely old stone farmhouse B&B is located on the outskirts of Skipton, high above the town, just off the A65. The bedrooms are comfortable and well-equipped, the service friendly and helpful, the breakfasts enormous! Various sporting activities are offered at the hotel, including, unusually, falconry and clay pigeon shooting. This B&B represents excellent value.

UNICORN HOTEL, *Devonshire Place, Keighley Road, Skipton BD23 2LP. Tel 01756 794146, Fax 01756 793376. Rooms: 9. Rates: singles from £40, doubles from £51. Restaurant. All major credit cards accepted.*

The Unicorn is located right in the center of Skipton above a row of stores and opposite the bus station. There's a small but pleasant lounge and the nine bedrooms are comfortably furnished with all in-room amenities, including TV. This is an excellent place to come if you want to sample good Yorkshire home cooking.

THE OLD BREWERY GUEST HOUSE, *29 The Green, Richmond. Tel. 01748 822460, Fax 01748 825561. Rooms: 5. Rates double from £44. Credit cards: MC, Visa.*

Situated on a quiet green just below the Castle, and just a few minutes' walk away from the town center, the Old Brewery is one of Richmond's best-kept secrets. The rooms aren't particularly large, but they ooze charm, there's a cozy lounge and a small, award-winning patio garden to while away those balmy summer evenings (both of them). You can order evening meals, but you may prefer to sample pubs and restaurants in the town center. Breakfast, included in the price, comes with home-made muffins.

LANGCLIFFE COUNTRY HOUSE, *Kettlewell BD23 5RJ. Tel. 01756 760243. Rooms: 8. Rates double from £100 including 4-course dinner.*

It may be hard to find, but this small, relaxing country house hotel is well worth the effort: a warm welcome, superb views across Wharfedale, eight charming pine-furnished rooms, and home-made food – stews, pies and the like - served in the conservatory. To find the place, look for the King's Head pub and follow the road opposite marked "for access only." If it's peace and quiet you're after, this is the place for you.

WHERE TO EAT

LE CAVEAU, *86 High Street, Skipton. Tel 01756 794274. Open Tuesday to Saturday noon to 1:45pm, 7pm to 9:30pm. main courses from £7. All major credit cards accepted.*

This cellar restaurant with its stone vaulted ceilings once served as a jail. Today's diners need not worry though; after a meal here, you may not *want* to leave! The cuisine is generally English/French, so expect rack of lamb with minty breadcrumb coating, Toulouse sausage served with bubble and squeak. There's a good choice of desserts and house wine starts at about £8.95.

LA PIAZZA, *5 Albert Street, Skipton. Tel 01756 796216. Open Tuesday to Friday 5pm to 10:30pm, Saturday 10:30am to 10:30pm. Pasta dishes from £5.95. Main courses from £8.95. Credit cards: MC, Visa.*

Attractive Italian restaurant offering authentic Italian food and wine in a relaxed atmosphere. The menu includes a fairly unadventurous range of dishes for starters, such as avocado with shrimp; the main course lists such choices as filet steak with black pepper brandy and cream sauce. There's also a wide range of pastas to choose from. This is basically good Italian home cooking at reasonable prices.

EASTWOODS FISH RESTAURANT, *Keighley Road, Skipton. Tel 01756 795458. Open Monday to Friday noon to 2pm, 5pm to 10:30pm; Saturday 11:30am to 10:30pm, Sunday 3:30pm to 10pm. Credit cards: MC, Visa.*

Everyone should try a traditional fish restaurant when in Yorkshire; after all, Yorkshire folk proudly proclaim that the nation's best fish and chips comes from their fair county! Eastwoods fits the bill. A modern building, its menu contains a variety of seafood choices as well as the traditional fish and chips (usually cod or plaice – a flatfish) so beloved of the Brits. You might also try their delicious Yorkshire fishcake, made to their own recipe.

ANGEL INN, *Hetton. Tel. 01756 730263. Open Sunday lunch noon to 2pm; Monday to Saturday 6pm to 9pm. Set lunch £20, set dinner £30. All major credit cards accepted.*

This attractive, out-of-the-way all-oak-beams and open fires stone pub is located in the small hamlet of Hetton, about five miles north of Skipton just off the B6265. But be warned! The place gets extremely busy, especially at weekends: you can book in advance, or take a chance with the restaurant's "first come, first served" policy. The restaurant specializes in fresh local produce often cooked with a southern European hint. The fish is particularly good, particularly the locally caught baked sea bass and the salmon, which comes with horseradish mashed potato. There's an extensive, and inexpensive, wine list.

OLD HALL INN, *Threshfield. Tel. 01756 752441. Open Monday to Saturday 11am to 3pm, 6pm to 11pm. Sunday noon to 3pm, 7pm to 10:30pm. Credit cards: MC, Visa.*

Another quaint, off-the-beaten-path establishment, this time in the hamlet of Threshfield, a mile west of Grassington. It's a pretty, atmospheric country pub with flagstone floors, with a superb original menu which offers a mixture of traditional dishes with more adventurous choices such as haddock with a tapernade crust and various ethnic curries. There's a good wine list, with house wine at around £9 a bottle.

SEEING THE SIGHTS

Airedale

Airedale is another of the Yorkshire Dales that warrants attention. Its main focus is **Skipton**, a bustling market town. Pride of place here goes to the well-preserved **Skipton Castle**, built by the Normans in 1090, and unaltered until the 17th century. The Castle stands at the top of the busy

High Street, and inside you can see such delights as the original banqueting house, kitchens, the bedchamber and privy. You can also explore the spooky dungeon and climb the battlements. *Open October to early-February Monday to Saturday 10am to 6pm, Sunday noon to 6pm. Admission adults £4.20, seniors and students £3.60, children 5-17 £2.10, under 5s free. Tel. 01756 792442; www.skiptoncastle.co.uk.*

Wharfedale

Around 12 miles north of Haworth, in **Wharfedale**, lies **Bolton Abbey**, the remnants of a large Augustinian monastic foundation on a bend in the River Wharfe, and is today part of the estate of the Duke and Duchess of Devonshire. You can wander round the 13th century ruins or take a peek at the priory, which is still used today as the parish church. Among devotees of Bolton Priory were J.M.W. Turner, who painted it, and John Ruskin, the Victorian art critic, who described it as being the most beautiful of all the English ruins.

Close to the Priory, surrounded by disarmingly pretty woods, is **The Strid**, the name given to a narrow crack in the rocks through which the River Wharf tumbles furiously. Further on, the medieval hunting lodge known as **Barden Tower** is also a ruin, and can be visited. *Open year-round. Admission vehicles £3, occupants free. Tel. 01756 710533.* Ten miles north of Skipton on the B6265 is the small stone village of **Grassington**, through which the **Dales Way** footpath passes. There's a particularly attractive cobbled marketplace, surrounded by a good number of eating places, guest houses, pubs and cafes. The place gets very busy in the summer.

The National Park Centre is a good starting point for a day out in the Dales. As well as the usual guide books, maps and bus timetables, there are organized tours with guides who will explain the local flora, fauna and geology. Or you may prefer to use **Kettlewell**, six miles north of Grassington, as a base. It's the largest settlement in Upper Wharfedale, with plenty of facilities.

Wensleydale

Head north from Kettlewell on the B6160, then turn left onto the A684, keeping an eye open after five miles for signs to **Askrigg**, an attractive enough Wensleydale village, but one easily forgotten, save for its association with *All Creatures Great and Small*, James Herriot's books based on the life of a country vet, which became a successful TV series and was shown on PBS. The episodes were filmed in and around the village, when it was known as **Darrowby**. Five miles west, still on the A684, is **Hawes,** said to be the highest market town in England. The place really buzzes on Tuesdays – market day – when farmers and locals crowd into town for the weekly market.

Hawes is also an important center for other local industries, chief among which is cheesemaking – crumbly Wensleydale cheese is made here. You can find out more about the cheese making process at the **Wensleydale Creamery Visitor Centre**, on the edge of the town. The **Cheese Museum**, which explains how Wensleydale cheese came to be, has a viewing gallery, where you can watch the cheese being made – don't forget to sample some before you leave. *Open summer 9am to 5:30pm, winter 9:30am to 4:30pm. Admission £2.50. Tel. 01969 667664.* www.wensleydale-creamery.co.uk

Hawes' old train station contains the **Dales Countryside Museum**, in the National Park Information Centre, which focuses on the traditional industries of the area and gives an idea of how people here lived in the past. There's a rope-making shop.

About twenty miles to the east of here, just off the A1, is the attractive town of **Richmond**. The town grew up around the massive **Castle** built by the Normans in the late 1000s to quell the locals. The castle's vast 100-foot high keep towers above the River Swale, affording excellent views over the surrounding countryside. Considering its age, it's exceptionally well preserved, still possessing its curtain wall and chapel, and a partially-restored **medieval hall**, complete with 14th century grafitti. From the Castle, there's a very pleasant walk along the banks of the River Swale to **Easby Abbey**, a medieval foundation that was sacked during the reformation. *Richmond Castle open April to September daily 10am to 6pm, October 10am to 5pm, November to March 10am to 1pm, 2pm to 4pm. Admission adults £2.50, seniors & students £2, children £1.30. Tel. 01748 822493.*

Richmond is certainly a pleasant place for passing a few hours, with a maze of narrow Georgian streets and terraces to explore, and a huge cobbled **market place**, said to be the largest of its kind in the country. On **Friars Wynd**, you can visit the miniscule Georgian **Theatre Royal**, the oldest theater in England still in use, and unchanged since the days of David Garrick, who performed here in the 18th century. With its original gallery boxes and old wooden seats, it's a real gem, all the more remarkable for the detail. Outside of performance times, you can tour the backstage area and visit the small **museum** that contains unique painted scenery dating from the early 1800s. *Call 01748 823021 for museum opening times and tours information; www.georgiantheatre.com.*

PRACTICAL INFORMATION

Skipton has a full range of services, including banks and a post office. The same is true of Richmond. Most of the smaller towns mentioned, however, do not, so make sure you take this into account before setting out. The Skipton **tourist information office** is located at *9 Sheep Street, Tel.*

01756 792809. As well as information about Skipton itself, they can provide details of walking paths and cycle routes across the Dales.

THE NORTH YORKSHIRE COAST

The at-times spectacular **north Yorkshire coast** stretches from the old fishing port of **Bridlington**, 40 miles east of York, to the border with Tyne and Wear. With some fine sandy beaches, rocky coves and picturesque fishing villages, it's a great place for exploration, although you'll not find it particularly comfortable for swimming – the temperature of the North Sea rarely rises above 55 degrees Farenheit, even in mid-summer.

There are several interesting seaside resorts, where you will delight in watching the British at play – resorts like **Scarborough** and Filey, which have specially designated bathing areas with lifeguards. The jewel of this stretch of the coast is **Whitby**, where the River Esk tumbles down a ravine creating a very pretty harbor that's also home to a thriving fishing fleet.

ARRIVALS & DEPARTURES
By Car
The main A64 leads from Leeds, Bradford and York to Scarborough. The A64 also connects with the A1, if you're arriving here from the south. From Scarborough take the A171 north to Whitby.

By Bus
From Leeds and York the **Yorkshire Coastliner** service operates frequent services to Scarborough, *Tel. 01653 692556,* and Whitby. Scarborough and Whitby are connected by the regular **Tees & District** bus service, #93 and #93a, stopping off at Robin Hood's Bay, *Tel. 01947 602146.*

By Train
There's a regular service throughout the day from York and Leeds to Scarborough. Scarborough's train station is located fairly close to the center on Valley Bridge Road.

GETTING AROUND
Both Scarborough and Whitby are easily explorable on foot, though some climbing may be involved.

The pickup point for local buses in Scarborough is the train station and Westborough pedestrian mall. In Scarborough, taxis can be hailed in the street, outside the Scarborough train station, or by calling **Station**

Taxis, *Tel. 01723 361 366366.* In Whitby, the main rank is also by the train station – or call **Harrison Cabs,** *Tel. 01947 600606.*

WHERE TO STAY

Scarborough boasts dozens of hotels and guest houses of all grades. A number of the more elegant hotels are located along the Regency Esplanade. If, however, you want to save a buck or two, and mingle with real Brits on their "hols" (holidays) try one of the smaller hotels and guest houses.

THE CROWN, *Regency Esplanade, Scarborough. Tel 01723 373491, fax 01723 362271. Rooms: 83. Rates: singles from £43, doubles from £66. Bar, restaurant. All major credit cards accepted.*

One of Scarborough's larger hotels, with 78 rooms, all with bath, the Crown is the focal point of the Regency Esplanade, with views across South Bay and towards the castle. It was built to accommodate some of the wealthier visitors to the resort in the 18th century, and after a period of neglect, it has now been restored to something close to its former glory. The rooms, many of which have sea views, are nicely furnished and decorated, and there's a fine restaurant and several bars. If you're booking in advance, you might want to take advantage of the special weekend packages that the hotel offers.

THE BLACK SWAN, *Market Place, Helmsley. Tel. 0870 4008112. Rooms: 45. Rates singles from £120, doubles from £145. Free parking, night porter, all major credit cards accepted.*

This medium-sized establishment that dates originally from the 16th century, when it served as a coaching inn, is on the edge of the market square in Helmsley. Clad in ivy, it's a pretty place that has been extensively restored and refurbished to offer 44 comfortable rooms. At the rear, there's an old walled garden where you can while away lazy summer afternoons playing that most British of sports, croquet. There's also a fine restaurant which serves traditional British food, using fresh local ingredients, and a bar.

SEACLIFFE HOTEL, *North Promenade, West Cliff, Whitby YO21 3JX. Tel and fax 01947 603139. Rooms: 20. Rates: singles from £30, doubles from £60. All major credit cards accepted.*

This small, pleasant hotel is located on the North Promenade at Whitby, close to all the major sights and attractions, including Whitby Abbey and the town museum. The hotel, which has been run by the same family for several years, boasts 20 tastefully decorated and well-equipped rooms, some of which have sea views. There's a good restaurant, which excels in fresh, locally caught seafood, as well as steaks and vegetarian dishes.

WHERE TO EAT

FEVERSHAL ARMS HOTEL, *1 High Street, Helmsley. Tel 01439 770766. Open daily noon to 2pm, 7pm to 9:30pm. Dinner from £15. Credit cards: MC, Visa.*

An excellent restaurant with a distinctive, seductive atmosphere, lots of mahogany furniture and even some Goya prints on the walls. The cuisine is a mixture of English, French and Spanish, England represented by a delicious broccoli and Stilton soup, Spain by a wide selection of tapas and France with an out-of-this world moules mariniere. The wine reflects this ethnic diversity. The whole place is to undergo a complete refurbishment in late 2000. Plans include a lavish new bistro due to open early in 2001.

WREA HEAD COUNTRY HOTEL, *Scalby, Scarborough. Tel 01723 378211. Open noon to 2pm, 7pm to 9pm. Lunch from £12.95, dinner from £25. All major credit cards accepted.*

This country house hotel has established a good local reputation for its cuisine, with an elegant dining room and an imaginative menu that includes noisettes of lamb with apricot and olive stuffing, and a wide choice of traditional and more contemporary desserts. The hotel is signposted from the A171 as you travel north from downtown Scarborough

THE MAGPIE CAFE, *14 Pier Road, Whitby. Tel 01947 602058. Open daily 11:30am to 9pm. Two course meal from £10. All major credit cards accepted.*

The Magpie, popular as much with locals as with visitors, has been run by the same family for nearly 40 years. Specializing in fresh local fish, including locally caught crab and lobster, the non-smoking Magpie is pleasantly located, with tables overlooking the Abbey and harbor. The service is both friendly and welcoming. There are some good, generally traditional desserts, and wines are available by the bottle or glass.

SEEING THE SIGHTS

Whitby is a glorious place, row after row of red-tiled buildings rising up a steep cliff, atop which is perched the stark ruins of **Whitby Abbey**, which dates right back to the 7th century. In the 1800s, Whitby became a prosperous whaling port, its ships setting sail for the icy waters off Greenland from the mid-18th century, led by locals such as William Scoresby, inventor of the crow's nest, to whom Melville refers in his famous whaling novel, *Moby Dick*. Further wealth came to the town through shipbuilding – it was from Whitby that James Cook, later Captain Cook – sailed in 1747, and all four of his subsequent vessels were built here. The result of all this wealth was some very fine town houses, many of which still survive on the **west side** of the river, while the **Old Town**, on the east side, is choc-a-bloc in summer with visitors exploring the narrow alleyways and souvenir shops.

Captain Cook is commemorated in the **Captain Cook Memorial Museum**, in an 18th century house that once belonged to shipowner John Walker. Cook lived as an apprentice here from 1746 to 1749. Items on show include mementos of his various voyages of discovery, such as maps, drawings and a diary. *Open March weekends only 11am to 3pm, April to October daily 9:45 to 5pm. Admission adults £2.80, seniors & students £2:30, children £2. Tel. 01947 601900.*

Founded by St. Hilda in 657, the ruins of **Whitby Abbey** stand sentinel over the town. Among the ecclesiastical celebrities who lived here was the monk Caedmon, a contemporary of Bede, and possibly the first identifiable poet of the English language. Though it was sacked by the Vikings in the ninth century, the abbey was restored in the 11th century and then enlarged in the 13th. *Open April to September daily 10am to 6pm, October daily 10am to 5pm, November to March 10am to 4pm. Admission adults £1.70, seniors & students £1.30, children 90p. Tel. 01947 603568.*

It's a stiff climb (199 steps) from the end of Church Street to the **Church of St. Mary**, but it's worth the effort. A maritime church if there ever was one, it has a ship's deck roof, triple–decker pulpit and enclosed galleries. Although the origins of the church go back to the 12th century, most of the building seen today is the result of Victorian renovations. You might want to explore the atmospheric churchyard, full of the tombs of old sailors, and offering excellent views of the town and harbor below. **Bram Stoker** visited the place and set part of *Dracula* here.

You'll likely be disappointed to hear that **Robin Hood's Bay**, about seven miles down the coast from Whitby on the B1447, has no connections whatsoever to the famous outlaw of Sherwood Forest. This tiny fishing village, with a smattering of shops and cottages, is built along a ravine where a stream flows into the North Sea. It's a popular spot and can get obscenely crowded in the summer, when cars are banned from the center and drivers have to use the parking lots at the top of the village. There's a beach, but like many others along this coast, it's not really suitable for swimming – the water's freezing even in the summer. Contraband was landed by smugglers here and whisked away through a maze of secret passages under the cottages.

The largest resort on this stretch on the coast, **Scarborough**, was also once a small fishing village, until the 17th century discovery of a mineral spring on the foreshore and the establishment of a spa. By the late 1700s, when **seaside bathing**, inspired by George III in Weymouth, became fashionable, Scarborough really took off. Bathing machines, mobile cabins that were wheeled down to the water's edge, cluttered the beach,

IN SEARCH OF ROBIN HOOD

*Mythology or fact? Did **Robin Hood** really exist? No-one really knows, but the legend of the man who robbed from the rich to give to the poor lives on, especially in the county of **Nottinghamshire**, south of Yorkshire, where according to tradition, Robin and his Lincoln-green-clad merrie men (not to forget the lovely Maid Marian) lived deep in **Sherwood Forest**. And the wicked Sheriff of Nottingham? Well, Nottingham does have a castle, but it depends on your historical perspective as to whether individual sheriffs were wicked or not.*

*The earliest reference to Robin comes in Langland's **Piers Plowman** of 1377. In it, Robin is regarded as fictional – a nobleman who unlike many of his peers had a strong sympathy for the underclass and a strong dislike for corrupt clerics and bad policemen (i.e. the sheriff). There's no real mention of his robbing from the rich to give to the poor – sorry! And it seems that popular characters like Marian and Friar Tuck were later embellishments. So there, Hollywood.*

while a plethora of hotels and guest houses were built to accommodate the multitudes.

Scarborough's attractive location, spread out on tall cliffs overlooking a sandy bay, with a huge rocky promontory capped by an ancient **castle** at one end, make it a favorite with British holidaymakers to this day. Families flock to the cafes, ice cream kiosks, tacky souvenir shops, seafood stalls and bingo establishments on the north side of town, while the more sedate residential suburbs to the south are notable for their elegant Victorian villas, lush gardens and clifftop walks.

A visit to **Scarborough Castle**, built by the Normans on the site of a Roman signalling station, and consisting of a three-story keep and a 13th century barbican, is rewarded with some spectacular views across the bay and town. The medieval **Church of St. Mary,** in Castle Road, contains the tomb of Anne Bronte, the third of the famous Bronte sisters, who was brought here in the errant belief that the sea air might save her. *Castle open April to October daily 10am to 6pm, November to March daily 10am to 4pm; admission £1.50. Tel. 01723 372451.*

A popular new attraction for children is the **Scarborough Millennium**, in Harbourside, which traces the history of the resort back to its early days as the Viking settlkement of Skarthaborg. *Open May to September 10am to 10pm; for off-season opening times and prices call 01723 501000.*

At the other end of town, in The Crescent, **Wood End**, was holiday home of the Sitwell family. Writers Edith, Osbert and Sacheverell spent their summers here. Inside, there's a collection of their works, as well as paintings and portraits of the family. The building also houses a **Museum of Natural History**. *Open May to September Tuesday to Sunday 10am to 5pm; October to April Friday to Sunday 10am to 4pm. Admission free. Tel. 01723 367326.*

One of the main attractions for children is the **Sea Life Centre**, Scalby Mills, North Bay, where glugging guppies and severe sharks can be seen in an attractively laid-out displays. *Open June to September daily 10am to 9pm; October to May daily 10am to 5pm. Admission £6. Tel. 01723 376125.*

NIGHTLIFE & ENTERTAINMENT

Both Scarborough and Whitby have plenty of lively pubs. In Whitby, try the **Angel Hotel**, with live music, just like the **Tap and Sile**, *opposite the train station.*

In Scarborough, the **Stephen Joseph Theatre** has the distinction of hosting world premieres of plays by local playwright Alan Ayckbourn, as well as works by other dramatists. *It's located next to the train station, Tel. 01723 37054.*

EXCURSIONS & DAY TRIPS

For sheer, dramatic, desolate beauty, there's nowhere better than the **North York Moors**. Around thirty miles north of the city of York, this 553-square mile stretch of relatively barren, remote and windswept moorland extends from the Cleveland Hills to the east right down to the North Sea coast. It was once dense forest, but much of this was changed with the establishment of monastic settlements at **Riveaulx** and nearby **Fountains Abbey**, when large tracts of woodland were felled to make way for arable farming. The rolling, heather-clad hills are given extra poignancy with a sprinkling of ancient burial sites, and in the valleys a collection of isolated stone-built villages adds additional charm.

From Whitby, the main routes leading to the North York Moors are the A171 and the A169, from Scarborough the A170, which links up with the A169 at Pickering. From York, take the A64 northeast to the Moors.

The town of **Helmsley**, on the southern edge of the moors, marks the start point of the **Cleveland Way**, a 110-mile long distance walking path that extends across the moors to the coast and then south along the coast to the resort of Filey. Helmsley's main attraction is a wide marketplace surrounded by pleasant pubs, cafes and shops. There's also a ruined castle. From Helmsley it's only a couple of miles along the B1257– about an hour and a quarter's walk – to the stunning ruins of **Rievaulx** (pronounced Reevo) Abbey, located in a parkland setting on the banks of the River Rye. Like other monastic foundations in the area, it owed its substantial prosperity to the wool trade. Among the remnants of the original monastic buildings are the **Chapter House**, which contains a shrine to the original abbot of Rievaulx, William, cloisters and various other buildings. *Open April to September daily 10am to 6pm (9:30am to 7pm in July and August), October 10am to 5pm, November to march 10am to 4pm. Admission adults £3.40, seniors & students £2.60, children £1.70. Tel. 01439 798228.*

Possibly Yorkshire's most impressive man-made attraction after York Minster, **Castle Howard** is located in the Howardian Hills just west of the village of **Malton**. Designed by eminent architect Sir John Vanbrugh, who also designed Blenheim Palace, the opulent Baroque style residence was begun in 1699 for the Earl of Carlisle, Charles Howard, whose descendants still live here. More recently it became the principal location in the filming of the hit TV series *Brideshead Revisited*. The impressive facade is topped by an 80-foot high gilded dome, and among the architectural features inside are a 192-foot long gallery and a chapel that contains stanied glass by the renowned artist Sir Edward Burne-Jones.

The opulence of the architecture is matched by that of the furnishings; massive tapestries, porcelain and sculptures, together with a collection of paintings by such eminent artists as Rubens, Reynolds, Gainsborough and Holbein. Outside, the landscaped grounds, too, are memorable, with lakes, bridges, obelisks, two rose gardens, the Temple of the Four Winds, designed by Vanbrugh himself, and a family mausoleum designed by another well-known British architect, Nicholas Hawksmoor. *Open mid-March to early November 10am to 4:30pm. Fully inclusive price for grounds, gardens and Castle adults £7.50, seniors & students £6.75, children 4-16 £4.50; www.castlehoward.co.uk.*

PRACTICAL INFORMATION

Scarborough's **tourist information office** is located *at Pavilion House, Valley Bridge Road, Scarborough, Tel. 01723 373333*, opposite the train station, while Whitby's is at *New Quay Road, Tel. 01947 602674*, also opposite the train station.

22. THE NORTHEAST

England's most remote region is also one of its most attractive, not only for the wealth of beguiling historical buildings – including some of the country's most spectacular castles and one of its most inspiring cathedrals – but for a magical, moody landscape that ranges from lonely windswept moors of the **Northumbria National Park**, speckled by isolated stone villages and crossed by the ancient Roman **Hadrian's Wall**, to a long coastline alternating between rocky promontories topped by historic ruined fortresses and long, sandy beaches backed by acres of dunes. This was the cradle of Christianity in northern England, begetting a host of saints and ascetics, drawn and inspired by its raw beauty. The region also boasts some of the nation's most spectacular medieval buildings – **Bamburgh Castle**, on the coast south of Berwick, and **Alnwick Castle**, the "Windsor of the North" and home of the powerful Percy family for centuries – and one of the most magnificent **cathedrals** in Europe at **Durham**. Just a dozen miles away is the region's powerhouse, the great city of **Newcastle**, a major industrial, commercial and cultural center.

Much of the southern half of this region formed part of one of the world's largest coal mining areas. Though the demise of the coal industry is well documented, many of the associated manufacturing and chemical industries continue to this day, so that the landscape can vary tremendously from the sublime to the hideous. Further north along the coast and inland it's a different story; the industrial revolution hardly reached here, and the legacy is an unspoilt, dramatic, atmospheric and utterly beautiful landscape that can still truly claim to be "far from the madding crowd."

ARRIVALS & DEPARTURES

While I've given separate travel directions for the destinations in this chapter, bear in mind that the directions are the same for all: each place is accessible directly from the **A1**, which straddles the region from south

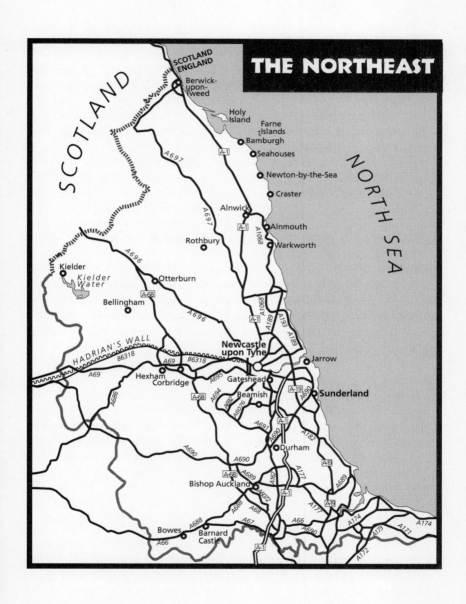

to north on its way from London to Edinburgh, and from the main London to Edinburgh rail line, which runs virtually parallel to the A1.

By Car

Despite the distance from London, getting here is much more straightforward than getting to most other English regions. Either take the A1 north out of London, which will take you all the way to **Durham**, **Newcastle** and **Berwick-upon-Tweed** (note that while sections of this road are of motorway standard, most of it is not). Alternatively, you could take the M1 motorway north from London, which links up with the A1 just north of Leeds. The M1 too can be very busy, but you're more likely to arrive at your destination quicker by using this route.

For **Hexham** and **Hadrian's Wall** take the A69 west at Newcastle, and for the **coast**, take the B6345 east from the A1, then the BB1339 and the B1340 north. **Lindisfarne** is just four miles off the A1; watch for the signs just north of Fenwick. Getting off the beaten path and exploring the roads and lanes of this remote part of England can be a very rewarding experience. An *Ordnance Survey* map of the region will serve you well.

By Bus

National Express serves the northeast from London Victoria Bus Station. Service to **Durham** takes about 5 hours, about another 15 minutes to **Newcastle**, and another 2 1/2 hours to **Berwick**. *Call 0990 808080 for information*. For local bus information in and around Newcastle call **Nexus**, *Tel. 0191 232 5325*.

By Train

There's an excellent, fast service from London's King Cross station to Durham, Newcastle, Alnmouth and Berwick, run by GNER (Great Northeastern Railway). Trains take about 3 hours to **Durham**, 3 hours 15 minutes to **Newcastle**, and 3 hours 45 minutes to **Berwick**. Some trains also stop at **Alnmouth**. From Newcastle train station, there are local services to **Hexham**. *Call 0345 484950 for information.*

DURHAM

It's small – population about 20,000 – but **Durham** boasts not only one of the **finest medieval cathedrals** in Europe but also one of the most dramatic settings of any city in England, perched on a rocky crag that's virtually an island, thanks to the meandering River Wear. Though it was the Saxons who first settled here – seeing no doubt the advantages of the high rocky headland for military purposes – and established a tiny church dedicated to **St. Cuthbert**, it was the Normans who really got things moving. They constructed the massive **Durham Castle**, then turned to building the even more enormous cathedral in the 1090s.

For centuries, Durham's **"prince bishops,"** who had been given extensive powers by William the Conqueror, wielded temporal as well as spiritual power over the citizens of the northeast, establishing their own court system, their own coins, and so on – it wasn't until 1836 that these powers were restored to the monarchy. As well as its ecclesiastical connections, the city is also notable for its **university** – not as ancient as Oxford or Cambridge, but which dominates this relatively small community in the same way that Oxbridge does. Though Durham like much of the northeast has more than its fair share of economic and social problems, it's a fine city that's easily explorable on foot, and with a host of excellent restaurants and pubs to provide refreshment.

ARRIVALS & DEPARTURES
By Car
Either take the A1 north out of London, which will take you all the way to Durham (note that while sections of this road are of motorway standard, most of it is not). Alternatively, you could take the M1 motorway north from London, which links up with the A1 just north of Leeds. The M1 too can be very busy, but you're more likely to arrive at your destination quicker by using this route.

By Bus
National Express serves the northeast from London Victoria Bus Station. Services to Durham take about 5 hours. *Call 0990 808080 for information.*

By Train
There's an excellent, fast service from London's King Cross station to Durham, run by GNER (Great Northeastern Railway). Trains take about 3 hours to Durham. The train station is a 10 minute walk north of the cathedral.

ORIENTATION
Durham's cathedral and castle are situated on a high rocky outcrop surrounded on three sides by the **River Wear**.

GETTING AROUND TOWN
Durham is a small walkable city, though be prepared for some stiff climbs. For getting to Beamish and other locations outside you might

want to grab a taxi. **Pratt's**, *Tel. 0191 386 0700*, do the job as well as anyone. Or you could rent a car from **M & S Ford**, *Tel. 0191 386 1155*.

WHERE TO STAY

SWALLOW ROYAL COUNTY HOTEL, *Old Elvet, Durham DH1 3JN. Tel. 0191 386 5282, Fax 0191 386 0704. Rooms: 151. Rates: single from £99, double/twin from £135. Two restaurants, leisure club. All major credit cards accepted.*

Large hotel that retains much of its historical character and charm in a location that is central for all attractions, overlooking the River Wear. The rooms are generally spacious, some of them coming with four-poster beds, while the oak staircase, the hotel's most notable feature, comes originally from Loch Leven Castle, Scotland, where Mary, Queen of Scots was held prisoner. The hotel also boasts an excellent restaurant (see below), an indoor heated swimming pool, sauna and health club.

THREE TUNS HOTEL, *New Elvet, Durham DH1 3AQ. Tel. 0191 386 4326, Fax 0191 386 1406. Rooms: 50. Rates: single from £65, double from £75. Traditional hotel. Restaurant. All major credit cards accepted.*

A former 16th century coaching inn that has been recently refurbished and is located right in the heart of Durham City, within easy reach of all the major attractions. It's a fairly traditional hotel, with large, comfortable rooms, and guests can use the leisure facilities at the nearby Royal County Hotel, just a minute's walk away.

THE UNIVERSITY OF DURHAM, *The Commercial Office, Old Shire Hall, Durham DH1 2HP. Tel. 0191 374 3454, Fax 0191 374 7393. Rooms: 160. Rates: single from £20.50, double from £41.*

Durham University's halls of residence double up during the school vacations as comfortable and conveniently located accommodations, complete with bars and good food. Self-catering options are also available, and special activity and study holidays are available. The vast majority of the rooms are singles, and most involve the use of shared bathroom facilities, but if you don't mind that, this represents excellent value.

HALLGARTH MANOR HOTEL, *Pittington, Durham DH6 1AB. Tel 0191 371 1188, Fax 0191 372 1249. Rooms: 23. Rates: singles from £40, doubles from £60. Bar, restaurant. All major credit cards accepted.*

This attractive hotel is located in the peaceful village of Pittington, about three miles from the center of Durham, with all its attractions, including the magnificent cathedral. The hotel is tastefully decorated throughout, and there's a particularly nice lounge and bar overlooking a pretty garden. The rooms are all well-equipped, furnished and decorated to a high standard, and there's a good restaurant with an extensive a la carte menu as well as daily specials. The hotel is located to the northeast of Durham, just off the A690.

GEORGIAN TOWN HOUSE, *10 Crossgate, Durham DH1 4PS. Tel and Fax 0191 386 8070. Rooms: 6. Rates: singles from £45, doubles from £60. No credit cards.*

Lovely, welcoming Georgian town house B&B at the top end of a pretty cobbled street in old Durham, with views of the Norman cathedral and castle. The building retains many of its original fittings and is full of character and charm. The bedrooms are all nicely furnished and decorated; all are well-equipped, with bath/shower, and some have views of the cathedral. This place represents excellent value considering its prime location.

LUMLEY CASTLE HOTEL, *Chester-le-Street, near Durham DH3 4NX. Tel 0191 389 1111, Fax 0191 387 1437. Rooms: 65. Rates: courtyard annex rooms from £95 per room, main building from £115 per room. Bar, restaurant, library, jacuzzi. All major credit cards accepted.*

Located three miles west of Beamish, this is a real castle, complete with its original dungeons and a host of extras that make it an experience not to be missed. To start with, there's a wonderful library/bar, with over 3,000 volumes to browse. There's also an excellent restaurant, The Black Knight, where fresh local produce is used imaginatively and where the menu includes a number of local specialties. The bedrooms are lavishly furnished and decorated, with a full range of facilities, and come in a variety of shapes, sizes and styles; some even have their own jacuzzis, and there is a number with four-poster beds. It's not particularly cheap to stay here, but it's well worth the money.

WHERE TO EAT

BISTRO 21, *Aykley Heads House, Aykley Heads, Durham DH1 5TS. Tel. 0191 384 4354. Open Monday to Saturday noon to 2:30, 6pm to 10:30pm. Set lunch £12 to £14, main courses from £10 to £13.50. All major credit cards accepted.*

A former farmhouse near Durham's main police station is the unlikely setting for this sophisticated restaurant, part of an upmarket chain. The farmhouse has been lovingly restored, with farming implements, dried flowers and other paraphernalia giving it a unique atmosphere, while the food is a mixture of traditional English and Mediterranean, with a blackboard of daily specials.

PIERRE VICTOIRE, *40-42 Saddler Street, Durham. Tel 0191 386 4923. Open Monday to Saturday 10:30am to 2:30pm, 5:30pm to 10:30pm. Main courses from £6.90. Two course set lunch £4.90, dinner £9.95 All major credit cards accepted.*

Pierre Victoire is part of an Edinburgh-based chain of restaurants that comes as close as any to captivating the ambience and style of an authentic French bistro. Popular, especially with students and at weekends, the

Durham version may be a bit cramped and a bit noisy, but is full of life and atmosphere. What's best about this chain is the phenomenally low prices. With main courses such as roast breast a maigret duck served on red plum and port wine sauce at just £10.90, and a selection of desserts at just £3, you can hardly go wrong here. There's a decent and inexpensive (mainly French) wine list too.

SWALLOW ROYAL COUNTY HOTEL, *Old Elvet, Durham DH1 3JN. Tel 0191 386 6821. Open daily 12:30pm to 2:15pm, 7pm to 10:15pm (9:15pm Sundays). Three course dinner £33. All major credit cards accepted.*

One of Durham's best hotels, the Royal County has long had an excellent reputation for its cuisine. That reputation holds true today. Both the impressive a la carte and set menus feature a combination of modern and classic English dishes, from medallions of venison, to salmon cooked Asian-style. The dessert menu is equally impressive, with a similar mixture of traditional English favorites like apple pie to contemporary creations.

RAMSIDE HALL HOTEL, *Carrville, Durham DH1 1TD. Tel 0191 386 5282. Open daily noon to 2pm, 7pm to 9:30pm. Four course dinner £24. All major credit cards accepted.*

This central Durham hotel boasts no fewer then three eating areas – a recently expended Restaurant, with choices such as roast breast of duck with vanilla pods served with orange segments and a grand marnier sauce, a grill room specializing in Aberdeen steaks cooked on the charcoal grill, and a carvery, with a range of seafoods, cold meats, salads and the house specialty – standing leg of roast beef. There is an extensive wine list, with house wines starting at £10.

EMILIO'S, *96 Elvet Bridge, Durham. Tel 0191 384 0096. Open Monday to Saturday 11:30am to 2:30pm, 5:30pm to 10:30pm, Sunday 6pm to 10:30pm. Main courses from £7. All major credit cards accepted.*

What really sets this Italian eating place in central Durham apart is its location inside the 11th century chapel of St. Andrew. Popular, especially at weekends, the restaurant boasts views of Durham Cathedral; in the summer, it's open throughout the day as a continental-style pavement cafe. The menu here is nothing out of the ordinary – the usual range of pasta, pizzas, with a risotto or three thrown in – a full complement of desserts and a (mainly Italian) wine list. But it's all good, reliable stuff, and moderately priced.

SEEING THE SIGHTS

The main attraction in Durham is undoubtedly the great **cathedral**, located right in the center of the city at Palace Green. It's a massive building, not only in its dimensions, but in the feeling of strength and solidarity it manages to create, with its huge rounded arches and massive pillars etched with zigzag patterns typical of the Norman period, all so different from the more graceful early English, Decorated and Perpendicular style of church architecture that superseded it. This was also the first cathedral in the whole of Europe to be given a **stone** – not wooden – **roof**, an amazing feat at the time.

Visitors to the cathedral enter through the **northwest porch**, where they are greeted by a 12th century bronze **Sanctuary Knocker**, shaped like the head of an awesome mythological beast. The Knocker is so-called because in the middle ages criminals who grabbed the ring inside the animal's mouth could claim sanctuary for up to 35 days – records indicate that many hundreds did invoke their right in this way.

It's hard not to have a lump in the throat in the vast, almost overpowering **nave**, characterized by enormous pillars. In the distance, separated from the nave by a Victorian choir screen is the **choir**, where dark-stained 17th century stalls are dominated by the spectacular **Bishop's throne**, built in the 14th century by the militaristic Bishop Hatfield and still the highest in Christendom. Further east, the 13th century **Chapel of the Nine Altars** stands out from its surroundings because of the more intricate early English style employed in its use. Close by is what medieval pilgrims would travel hundreds, even thousands of miles to see for its supposed healing powers: the **Shrine of St. Cuthbert**, one of the great early English saints, surrounded by columns of marble. The remains of Cuthbert himself are buried beneath a simple stone slab, in accordance with his wishes.

At the opposite end of the church, in the **Galilee Chapel**, is the final resting place of the 8th century Northumbrian monk known to the world as the **Venerable Bede**, celebrated as England's first historian on account of his history of the English people (the book is titled *History of the English Church and People*). Bede died at Jarrow in 735, and was moved to Durham in 1020.

Opposite the main entrance, an old wooden doorway leads to the cathedral **cloisters**, where the monks used to spend their leisure time. Much of the original monastic buildings that formed this vast religious complex are long gone, but the **undercroft** of the monks' dormitory now houses the cathedral **Treasury**, where all kinds of ecclesiastical paraphernalia are on show – from illuminated manuscripts, clergy regalia to fragments of St. Cuthbert's coffin and communion vessels. Also down here is a pleasant cafe, and the cathedral shop. *Cathedral open May to September Monday to Saturday 9:30am to 8pm, Sunday 12:30pm to 8pm; October to April Monday to Saturday 9:30am to 6pm, Sunday 12:30pm to 5pm. Admission: free (but donations welcome). Treasures of St Cuthbert Exhibition open Monday to Saturday 10am to 4:30pm, Sunday 2pm to 4:30pm. Admission* *adults £1.50, students and seniors £1, children 50p. Tel. 0191 3864266; www.durhamcathedral.co.uk.*

It's just a short walk from the cathedral across the Green to **Durham Castle**, commanding a strategically important position overlooking the River Wear. Built by the Normans, for centuries it served as home to a succession of prince-bishops who presided over large chunks of northern England from within – as well as keeping the fearsome Scots at bay. The castle hardly looks medieval now – various refurbishments by the bishops saw to that, as well as further changes made when the castle was handed over to the university after the power of the prince-bishops was curtailed early in the 19th century. The castle keep now serves as a hall of residence for students, which in turn doubles up as relatively inexpensive accommodations for tourists in the long vacations. Because of its status as a residence, the castle is only open as part of a guided tour, during which you can visit the 15th century kitchen, and check out the enormous hanging staircase. *Open mid-March to September Monday to Saturday 10am to 12:30pm, 2pm to 4pm, Sundays 10am to noon, 2pm to 4pm; October to mid-March Monday, Wednesday, Saturday, Sunday 2pm to 4pm. Admission adults £3, children £2. Tel. 0191 374 3800.*

Among the city's other attractions are the **Durham Light Infantry Museum**, at Aykley Heads on the A691, with military exhibits including uniforms, weapons and insignia, as well as a Durham At War exhibit and the Durham Art Gallery. *Open April to October daily 10am to 5pm; November to March daily 10am to 4pm. Admission adults £2.50, children £1.25. Tel. 0191 384 2214.* Also worth visiting is the **Oriental Museum**, on Elvet Hill two miles to the south of the city center, with a superb display of Chinese ceramics as well as artifacts from Egypt, India, Tibet and Japan. *Open year-round Monday to Friday 10am to 5pm, Saturday and Sunday noon to 5pm. Admission adults £1.50, children 75p. Tel. 0191 374 7911.* Meanwhile, the **Botanic Gardens**, not far from the Oriental Museum, with a selection of hothouses, a cafe, and 120-acre tract of woodland. *Open daily 9am to 4pm. Admission free.*

However, you may prefer to give all these a miss, and take a stroll along the banks of the **River Wear**. A charming **footpath** runs all the way round the crag on which the cathedral and castle are located, affording – especially from some of the bridges which span it – some glorious views of the city and up towards the vast medieval buildings on the summit. Among the bridges are **Framwellgate Bridge**, which originated in the 12th century but which has since (many times) been extended. **Prebends Footbridge**, an 18th century structure, is another excellent vantage point, as J.M. W. Turner found when he painted a scene from here. The lane leading back to the cathedral is lined with some attractive Georgian houses, several of which are used by the university. Among them, the former Church of St. Mary-le-Bow now houses the **Durham Heritage Center**, with a variety of displays and dioramas, as well as a section of brass rubbings. *Open April and May Saturday, Sunday and Bank Holiday Mondays 2pm to 4:30pm; June and September daily 2pm to 4:30pm; July and August daily 11am to 4:30pm. Admission adults £1, children 30p. Tel. 0191 386 8719.*

NIGHTLIFE & ENTERTAINMENT

There are a number of great pubs in and around Durham – far too many to list here; for a start, try the **Swan and Three Cygnets** *west of Elvet Bridge*. Some offer entertainment, such as the **Travellers Rest** *on Gilesgate*. For more serious entertainment – theater, cinema and the like – punters tend to go into Newcastle.

EXCURSIONS & DAY TRIPS

The area around Durham was one of the most prolific **coal-producing** areas in the United Kingdom, with, at the beginning of the twentieth century, nearly 200,000 miners producing over 40 million tons of the black stuff. The result was a landscape heavily scarred with collieries and the associated "slag heaps." The decline of the coal industry down to just a handful of pits today resulted in widespread unemployment and economic hardship for thousands, and left many of the old colliery villages depressed and lacking purpose.

You can get a feel for the coal mining industry and the culture that went with it at the open-air **Beamish Museum**, about ten miles north of Durham on the A693. The 260-acre site includes a reconstruction of a colliery village as it was in 1913, complete with church, cottages and mine; a train station with goods yard; a reconstructed 1920s High Street, complete with pub, grocery, garage and dentist's surgery; and a manor house and farm with several local breeds like the famous Durham Shorthorn cattle. Many of the costumed guides used to work in mining or associated industries, like the former miner who will take you down the drift mine. *Open April to October daily 10am to 5pm (last entry 3pm); November to March Tuesday to Thursday, Saturday and Sunday 10am to 4pm (last entry 3pm). Admission summer adults £10, 5s-16s £6, students and seniors £7. Admission winter: all categories £3.*

Just six miles east of the Beamish Museum is a must for all US visitors, **Washington Old Hall** – the ancestral home **of George Washington**, first President of the United States. Washington's direct ancestors, the de Wessyngtons, lived here from the 12th to the 13th centuries and other members of the family continued to live here until the early 17th century, when the house was rebuilt in the Jacobean style. The house is most notable for its 18th century wood paneling and a variety of Washington exhibits. The property is now owned by the National Trust. *Open April to October Sunday to Wednesday 11am to 5pm. Admission £2.80. Tel. 0191 416 6879.*

Head south of Durham on the A1, then take the A688 at junction 61 for the town of **Bishop Auckland**, the country seat of the Bishops of Durham for nearly 700 years, and their official home for the past hundred. The **Auckland Palace** of today dates mainly from the 16th century, having been remodelled extensively by successive bishops, including Bishop Cosin, who in the 17th century transformed a dilapidated 12th century banqueting hall into a stunning marble and limestone **chapel**, with stained glass windows depicting the lives of early northern saints like Bede, Aidan and Cuthbert. The Castle stands in nearly 800 acres of grounds. *Open May to mid-July Friday and Sunday 2pm to 5pm; mid-July to August Sunday to Friday 2pm to 5pm; September Friday and Sunday 2pm to 5pm. Admission adults £3, 12s-16s £2, under 12s free, seniors £2. Tel. 01388 601627; www.auckland-castle.co.uk.*

Another seven miles to the southwest on the A688 is **Raby Castle**, most of which dates from the 14th century, when it was a stronghold of the powerful Neville family. It was Charles Neville who in 1569 conceived a cunning plan to replace England's Queen Elizabeth I with Mary, Queen of Scots. The plan of course, failed, and the Neville estates were confiscated, passing to the Vane family in 1626. The second owner, **Sir Henry Vane**, was a leading Puritan, and became the governor of the state of Massachusetts in 1636, though his tenure was short-lived. The Castle's interior is lavishly decorated and furnished, and the well-preserved **medieval kitchens**, the Palladian **library** and the octagonal **drawing room** are particularly worth a look, as is the vast **Baron's Hall** on the second floor. The grounds contain a 200-acre deer park, as well as a delightful walled garden. *Open May and September, Wednesday and Sunday castle 1pm to 5pm, grounds 11am to 5:30pm; June to August Sunday to Friday, castle 1pm to 5pm, grounds 11am to 5:30pm. Admission adults £3, children and seniors £2. Tel. 01833 660202.*

Another seven miles to the southwest on the A67 lie the remains of 11th century **Barnard Castle**, whose ruins jut out from a precipice overlooking the River Tees and the small town that bears the same name. For many years, the castle was the home of the **Balliols**, an Anglo-Scottish family, whose family name again turns up in the famous Oxford college. Parts of the 14th century **Great Hall** remain, as does a 13th century circular tower – not to be confused with the later Round Tower – which was built by Bernard Balliol. The castle's current ruined status is due to the fact that much of its stone was plundered by the Vane family to repair nearby Raby Hall (see above). *Open April to September daily 10am to 6pm; October daily 10am to 5pm; November to March Wednesday to Sunday 10am to*

1pm and 2pm to 4pm. Admission adults £2:30, students and seniors £1.70, children £1.20 (under 5s free). Tel. 01833 638212.

The town itself is attractive, the most notable feature being the **Market Cross**, or butter market hall, at the confluence of Throngate, Newgate and Market Place. Nearby is the **King's Head Inn**, where Charles Dickens stayed when researching *Nicholas Nickelby*, a story which focuses on the abuse of physical and emotional children in local boarding schools.

Barnard Castle is also home to the **Bowes Museum**, a French-style chateau, just over a quarter-mile east of Market Place. Started in 1869, its raison d'etre was to hold the amazing art collection of John and Josephine Bowes, Victorian philanthropists who collected much of their treasures in Paris. The collection includes not only paintings by Goya, Canaletto and El Greco, but furniture, tapestries, ceramic and general paraphernalia, including an 18th century mechanical, musical silver swan that performs a fish-catching ritual twice daily. *Open year-round daily 11am to 5pm. Admission adults £3.90, students, seniors and children £2.90. Tel. 01833 690606.*

The high moorland village of **Bowes**, four miles to the west of Barnard Castle also on the A67, is dominated by the massive 12th century stone keep of **Bowes Castle**, built on the site of a Roman fort. You can still see the house on which Dickens modeled Dotheby's Hall in *Nicholas Nickelby*, while the last building in the main street once housed the boarding school whose headmaster, William Shaw, is the character on whom Dickens based his wicked Wackford Squeers.

PRACTICAL INFORMATION

Durham's main **tourism office** is at *Market Place, Tel. 0191 384 3720.* The main post office and branch of **Thomas Cook's** are on Market Place.

NEWCASTLE

The northeast's largest city by far, **Newcastle** – or, to use its full name Newcastle-upon-Tyne – was originally settled in Roman times, but only really came into its own during the Elizabethan period, when it was a major **coal exporting** center. Later, it became famous for **shipbuilding**, which, together with a number of other industries, prompted phenomenal growth. With the decline of shipbuilding and of the city's manufacturing base, Newcastle suffered terrible economic decline, and is only now beginning to recover, thanks largely to the spirit of its people, known throughout Britain as "**Geordies**" – much loved for the gritty determination, but not, perhaps, for the **Geordie accent** that is virtually indecipherable to most British ears, let alone American ones.

Much of the city's earlier prosperity is evident in a swath of Victorian neoclassical streets, such as **Grey Street**, once dubbed "the finest street in Europe," and by the **River Tyne** on the Quayside, with a clutch of 17th century houses adjoining vast warehouses that have been converted into trendy restaurants and bars. The city's most famous landmark, the **Tyne Bridge**, erected in 1929, is notable for its gentle, curved proportions, while the nearby remains of a **Norman castle** are a reminder of the city's strategic importance.

ARRIVALS & DEPARTURES

By Car

The A1 from London bypasses within a couple of miles of Newcastle city center.

By Bus

National Express serves Newcastle from London Victoria Bus Station, with a journey time of 5 hours 15 minutes to Newcastle. *Call 0990 808080 for information.*

By Train

There's an excellent, fast and reliable service from London's King Cross station to Newcastle, run by GNER (Great Northeastern Railway). Trains take about 3 hours 15 minutes to Newcastle.

GETTING AROUND TOWN

Newcastle is a huge city, but all the major attractions are within a smallish area to the east and northeast of the train station, so walking is your best bet. Driving is really a no-no; the road network is confusing, the traffic heavy at times, and parking is difficult.

For local bus information in and around Newcastle call **Nexus**, *Tel. 0191 232 5325.* The city also has an underground train service, the **Metro**. You can get a Daysaver ticket for use on buses and trains for just £3.60.

If you want to rent a car here, try:
• **Avis**, *7 George Street, Newcastle-upon-Tyne, Tel. 0191 232 5283*
• **Hertz**, *Newcastle Airport, Tel. 0191 286 6748*

WHERE TO STAY

THE COPTHORNE, *The Close, Quayside, Newcastle-upon-Tyne NE1 3RT Tel. 0191 222 0333, Fax 0191 230 1111. Rooms: 156. Rates: single from £145, double from £170. Restaurants, solarium, gymnasium, indoor pool. All major credit cards accepted.*

Among the glut of new hotels that have opened in recent years in Newcastle, this is probably the most luxurious. It's located right on

Newcastle's historic quayside, and all the comfortable, if somewhat bland, bedrooms overlook the River Tyne, as do the bars, restaurants and leisure club. It's close to the city's main attractions and to the train station. There also a whole floor of "Conoisseur" rooms with their own exclusive lounge.

CHASLEY HOTEL, *Newgate Street, Newcastle-upon-Tyne NE1 5SX. Tel 0191 232 5025, Fax 0191 232 8428. Rooms: 93. Rates: singles from £95, doubles from £105. Bar, restaurant. All major credit cards accepted.*

Very pleasant hotel located right in the heart of downtown Newcastle. Many of the bedrooms have been refurbished recently, and all come with TV and the usual amenities. Half the hotel's rooms are reserved for non-smokers. One of the highlights of this hotel is a rooftop restaurant, affording views over the city. Another major plus is that the hotel offers secure car parking, so no worries about having to find a parking place in what is a very busy, bustling city center.

MALMAISON, *Quayside, Newcastle-upon-Tyne NE1 3DX. Tel 0191 245 5000, Fax 0191 245 4545. Rooms: 116. Rates: all rooms (single or double occupancy) from £105. Bar, restaurant, sauna, solarium, gymnasium. All major credit cards accepted.*

The Malmaison Hotel, converted into a modern hotel from a much older property, is located in the revitalized riverside area of Newcastle, close to a number of excellent restaurant and bars, as well as the city's major attractions. The bedrooms are bright and airy, with desks, music systems and modems, as well as the usual in-room facilities. There's a bright cheerful brasserie, where you can get meals throughout the day, and a leisure suite that offers sauna and gymnasium.

WHERE TO EAT

COURTNEY'S, *5-7 The Side, Newcastle. Tel. 0191 232 5537. Open Monday to Friday noon to 2pm, 6pm to 10:30pm, Saturday 6pm to 10:30pm. Set lunch £10.95, dinner main courses from £12 up. All major credit cards accepted.*

This atmospheric converted quayside restaurant in the older part of Newcastle specializes in fairly straightforward dishes using fresh local produce, with a flutter of more exotic touches such as roasted halloumi cheese. It's also a good place for inexpensive set lunches, and surprise, surprise, it's air-conditioned, though goodness knows why in this climate.

21 QUEEN STREET, *21 Queen Street, Newcastle. Tel. 0191 222 0755. Open Monday to Friday noon to 2pm, 7pm to 10:30pm, Saturday 7pm to 10:30pm. Set lunch £14.50, main courses £18.50 and up. All major credit cards accepted.*

One of the region's best restaurants – good food, friendly, unhurried service and pleasant surroundings down by the quayside. The food is an innovative cosmopolitan mixture of dishes, some originating in the

506 ENGLAND & WALES GUIDE

northeast, like ham knuckle with flavored mashed potato, and some French, Italian and Asian. There's an excellent wine list.

METROPOLITAN, *35 Grey Street, Newcastle. Tel. 0191 230 2306. Open Monday to Saturday noon to 3pm, 6pm to 10:45pm. Set lunch £8.95, dinner main courses from £3 and up. All major credit cards accepted.*

Once a branch of the Bank of England, this large downtown restaurant serves its food – from early morning coffee to late evening dinners – in a tall, elegant room that was once the main banking hall, and is now decorated with art-deco mirrors and colorful walls. The bistro-style food has a strong French influence, as well as some traditional British and northeastern dishes done with flair and imagination. The wine list is well-chosen, and set lunches and early-bird specials are available.

FISHERMAN'S LODGE, *Jesmond Dene, Jesmond, Newcastle. Tel 0191 281 3281. Open Monday to Saturday noon to 2pm, 7pm to 10:45pm. Three-course dinner from £34. All major credit cards accepted.*

The Fisherman's Lodge is located is a peaceful parkland setting in Jesmond, a couple of miles to the north of downtown Newcastle-upon-Tyne. As indicated by the name, this restaurant specializes in fresh seafood, ranging from fairly straightforward choices like salt cod with garlic fishcakes to lobster (though the price of lobster in the UK will send a shiver down the spine of most North Americans). Meat dishes are also available, such as braised lamb shank with garlic mash and a rosemary sauce. There's an extensive dessert menu, and house wines come in at around £10 a bottle.

SEEING THE SIGHTS

Castle Garth Keep, next to Newcastle Cathedral on St. Nicholas Street, is the "new" castle from which the city gets its name. The present structure, which replaced an even earlier wooden construction, dates from 1168. There are some fascinating exhibits on Newcastle's history, and some excellent views. *Open Tuesday to Sunday 9:30am to 5:30pm (to 4:30pm from October to March). Admission £1.50.*

Newcastle boasts one of Britain's best regional art galleries, the **Laing**, on Higham Place, with a collection of pre-Raphaelites, some fascinating paintings by local artist John Martin, and an exhibition entitled 'Art on Tyneside,' which traces the history of art and craft in the region. *Open Monday to Saturday 10am to 5pm, Sunday 2pm to 5pm. Admission free. Tel. 0191 232 7734.*

The city center boasts a number of large department stores and specialist shops, but many British shoppers prefer to visit the massive **Metro Center** in neighboring **Gateshead**, for many years the largest out-of-town shopping center in Britain, and still packing 'em in. Close by, alongside the A1, is the **"Angel of the North,"** a huge, rusty metal statue erected in 1998 that looks more like a glider standing on its tail. The statute is supposed to symbolize the spirit of the north. Gateshead itself, not the most attractive town in the universe, is also the location for a new art museum, not open yet at press time, to be housed in a converted warehouse overlooking the Tyne.

Mention the town of **Jarrow** to Brits and they'll immediately think of the **"Jarrow Crusade,"** a protest march from here to London by unemployed workers during the 1930s Depression. But Jarrow is also notable for its connection to the early – some say the earliest – English historian, the **Venerable Bede**, who was a monk when Jarrow was a leading religious and academic center, and wrote his *History of the English Church and People* here in 731, though the community's roots go way back to 681, when a Saxon church was built. Today, the site has been turned into a major historical and cultural attraction known as **Bede's World**, with 11-acre farm featuring reconstructed Saxon farm buildings and rare breeds such as Iron Age pigs; a modern museum explaining life in Anglo-Saxon times, and St. Paul's Church itself, in continuous use for some 1,300 years and featuring some of the oldest stained glass in Europe. *April to October Tuesday to Saturday 10am to 5:30pm, Sunday 2:30pm to 5:30pm; November to March Tuesday to Saturday 11am to 4:30pm, Sunday 2:30pm to 5:30pm. Admission adults £4.50, children £2.50. Tel. 0191 489 2106.*

NIGHTLIFE & ENTERTAINMENT

Newcastle has a lively entertainment scheme, much of which is focused on the **Bigg Market** area which can get quite rowdy, especially on weekends, and around the **Quay** area, where there is a variety of clubs and pubs catering for all tastes. Try: **The Cooperage**, *32 The Close, Quayside;* **Blackie Boy**, *Bigg Market*; and **Forth Hotel**, *Pink Lane.*

On a more sober note, the **Theatre Royal**, *100 Grey Street, Tel. 0191 232 0997*, is a wonderful old theater where you can see top-notch productions from the West End – the Royal Shakespeare Company performs here regularly.

PRACTICAL INFORMATION

Newcastle's **tourism office** is located at the *Central Library, Princess Square, Tel. 0191 261 0610,* with another office conveniently located at the train station. The main post office is on Collingwood Street near the train station. and there's a branch of **Thomas Cook** on *New Bridge, Tel. 0191 261 2163.*

HEXHAM & HADRIAN'S WALL

The 73-mile long **Hadrian's Wall** marked the northern boundary of the Roman Empire, stretching from **Wallsend** (Wall's End) near Newcastle in the east to **Bowness-on-Solway** in the west. Its construction followed successive invasions of southern Britain by Julius Caesar in 55 and 54 BC. In 83AD the Roman governor, Agricola, attempted to push further north, but his army was depleted by a transfer of several thousand soldiers to the Danube. The remaining legions withdrew to the Stanegate, an ancient road between Carlisle and Corbridge. The best place to use as your base when exploring the Wall area is **Hexham**, a busy market town with its impressive **Abbey**, which forms one side of the main square.

ARRIVALS & DEPARTURES

By Car

The almighty automobile really is the only way to see the wall properly – unless you're on a guided tour. Both Avis and Hertz have branches in Newcastle:
• **Avis**, *7 George Street, Newcastle-upon-Tyne, Tel. 0191 232 5283*
• **Hertz**, *Newcastle Airport, Tel. 0191 286 6748*

By Bus

Bus #685 from Newcastle to Carlisle, on the west coast, stops at Hexham.

By Train

Hexham is on the main Newcastle-to-Carlisle railway line.

GETTING AROUND TOWN

Hexham can easily be explored on foot. To get to the Wall, head out of the town on the A69 that runs parallel to the Wall for much of its length. Sections of the Wall that are open to the public are well signposted. There is a bus (#682) that operates in the summer months only and runs between Hexham and Haltwhistle along the B6318, which runs very close to the Wall and stops at the main sites. Call **Northumbria Buses**, *Tel. 0191 212 300,* for details.

WHERE TO STAY

LANGLEY CASTLE HOTEL, *Langley on Tyne, Hexham NE47 5LU. Tel. 01434 688888. Rooms: 14. Rates: singles from £75, doubles from £105, four-posters from £155. Restaurants, bars, garden. All major credit cards accepted.*

This is a fantastic place to stay! It's actually 14th century castle, built by Sir Thomas de Lucy, a veteran of the Battle of Crecy. Later on, after years of neglect, the castle fell into ruin, until Victorian Cadwaller Bates restored it. There's so much to admire about this place it would be easy to write pages about it. Best of all are the lavishly decorated bedrooms, replete with Gothic arches, mullioned windows, fireplaces and all modern conveniences including, in some cases, four-poster beds and personal saunas. The public rooms, such as the drawing room and the dining room, are the height of elegance, with original features mingling with luxuriant decor to stunning effect. When you take all this into account, it's really not expensive at all.

LORD CREWE ARMS HOTEL, *Blanchard, Consett, County Durham DH8 9SP. Tel. 01434 675251, Fax 01434 675337. Rooms: 20. Rates: singles from £80, double from £110. Restaurant. All major credit cards accepted.*

Unusual place in the off-the-beaten-path hamlet of Blanchard, ten miles south of Hexham off the B6306. Once used to provide guest accommodations for Blanchard Abbey, today's guests are intrigued by a fascinating array of medieval features, such as a priest's hole and and vaulted crypt with bar. The 20 rooms are well furnished and many have oak-beamed ceilings, including one said to be haunted by the ghost of a young girl. The serene atmosphere of the hotel is maintained in the dining room, where dishes using fresh local produce such as pheasant abound.

DE VERE SLALEY HALL, *Slaley, Hexham NE47, 0BY. Tel 01434 673350, Fax 01434 673050. Rooms: 139. Rates: singles from £95, doubles from £150. Bars, restaurant, indoor pool, sauna, solarium, gymnasium, jacuzzi, hot air ballooning, clay shooting. All major credit cards accepted.*

This wonderful, elegant hotel, part of the deluxe De Vere chain, is located in over 1,000 acres just off the A68. There are two championship golf courses and a wealth of sports facilities. from a well-equipped leisure suite to archery and clay pigeon shooting. The rooms are beautifully appointed and air-conditioned, and the fairways Brasserie has earned a good reputation locally for the quality of its cuisine. When you consider what's on offer here, the prices don't seem so bad.

DENE HOUSE, *Juniper, Hexham NE46 1SJ. Tel and Fax 01434 673413. Rooms: 3. Rates: single from £20, doubles from £40. No credit cards accepted.*

You'll love this small, cozy former farmhouse, situated in the village of Juniper just outside Hexham off the B6306. The house is surrounded by meadow and gardens. There's a lounge where log fires burn in winter and a very pleasant sun lounge. The bedrooms are spacious, with pine, cottage-style furniture. The farmhouse-style kitchen is the venue for some sumptuous breakfasts.

PRIORFIELD, *Hippingstones Lane, Corbridge NE45 5JP. Tel./Fax 01434 633179. Rooms: 2. Rates: single from £28, doubles from £45. No credit cards accepted.*

Corbridge is just a few miles from Hexham just off the A69, and within easy reach of Hadrian's Wall and other local attractions. Priorfield is a delightful Edwardian house in a secluded location not far from Corbridge's bustling town center. The owners have a penchant for interior design that is evident in the decor and furnishings throughout the house. Both rooms have tea- and coffee-making facilities; one of them boasting a whirlpool bath. Breakfast is taken en famille around one large table in the dining room.

WHERE TO EAT

THE ANGEL INN, *Main Street, Corbridge NE45 5LA. Tel 01434 632119. Open daily 7pm to 9pm (lunchtime bar food available). Dinner around £16.95. All major credit cards accepted.*

The Angel is Corbridge's oldest pub, hence it's full of character and charm. It's a good place to stop off for a lunchtime snack before spending an afternoon exploring nearby Hadrian's Wall, or come here for a full meal in the evening, where the menu includes many traditional English and Northumbrian favorites. Or maybe just spend an hour or two supping a pint with the locals.

HEXHAM ROYAL HOTEL, RESTAURANT AND PRIESTPOPPLE BRASSERIE, *Tel. 01434 602270. Open Tuesday to Saturday, noon to 2:30pm, 5:30pm to 9:30pm. Set 2 course lunch £6.99, set dinner (before 7pm) from £7.99. All major credit cards accepted.*

This hotel is a former Georgian coaching inn, full of elegance and charm. The elegance and charm extends to both the brasserie restaurant on the ground floor, and the more formal hotel restaurant upstairs. Whichever you choose, you can be assured of excellent value in a menu that's best described as modern British with a twang of French; whole quail on a bed of endive dressed with walnut oil and sherry vinegar, to that good old British staple, roast beef and Yorkshire pudding. The wine list is excellent and well-priced; house wines start as low as £7.50.

SEEING THE SIGHTS

Hexham

Much of the **Hexham Abbey** dates from the 12th century, but there has been a Christian place of worship on the site for over 1,300 years. You enter by a door in the south transept, where there's a first century **tomb** honoring Flavinus, a standard-bearer in the Roman cavalry. Close by, you can climb the 35 worn steps that form the **canons' night stair**, where in medieval times canons would make their way from the church to their dormitory (Canons in this sense are priests based at a cathedral, abbey or monastic foundation). Very few of these are in existence, having been destroyed during the Dissolution of the Monasteries. Below the main floor, the **crypt** is a Saxon construction using old Roman stones. The church's reliquaries were once on show here for pilgrims passing through. At the end of the nave, there's a superb 16th century **Rood Screen**, with the portraits of local bishops. *Open May to September daily 9:30am to 7pm; October to April daily 9am to 5pm. Tel. 01434 602031.*

Outside, Hexham's **market place** has been the site of a weekly market for nearly 800 years, held on Tuesdays. Across from the Abbey, the **Old Gaol**, dating from 1330, houses the town's **information office** as well as the **Border History Museum**, with models, drawings, and weapons, a Border house interior and a reconstructed blacksmith's shop. *Open Easter to October daily 10am to 4:30pm; February, November Saturday to Tuesday 10am to 4:30pm. Tel. 01434 652349.*

Hadrian's Wall

Much of Hadrian's Wall disappeared long ago, but some fine stretches remain, mainly concentrated in the area around **Chollerford**, three miles north of the market town of **Hexham**, and **Haltwhistle**, sixteen miles west. Between **Housesteads** and **Steel Rigg**, in particular, the Wall is well preserved, as its clings to the Whin Sill, a rocky ridge towering above the inhospitable Northumbrian landscape. At this point, a path round along the top of the ridge affords wonderful views and the opportunity to visit several notable archaeological sites and a museum, including the remains of **Housesteads Fort** and **Vindolanda**.

Take the A6079 north of Hexham to the B6318, which runs west to east almost parallel to the wall. Just west of the junction, **Chesters Roman Fort** protected the point where the wall crossed the North Tyne River. Inside the site is a collection of intriguing artifacts, including altars, milestones, statues, and even handcuffs. The bathhouse close to the river is one of the best preserved in Britain. *Open November to March daily 10am to 4pm; April to October daily 10am to 6pm. Admission adults £2.80, 5s-15s £1.40, seniors and students £1.40. Tel. 01434 681379.*

Further west, and marked from the B6318, is the well-preserved **Housesteads Roman Fort**, one of the most frequently visited sections of the Wall. There's a small **museum**, from which you can walk over to the south gate, alongside which are the remains of the civilian settlement that grew up around here when the place was populated with more than 1,000 soldiers. You can see the cubicles of the soldiers' barracks, the remains of the commanding officer's courtyard, granaries and gateways. You can avoid entering the museum and paying the admission fee if it's just a beautiful walk you want. The hike west past **Crag Lough** offers some

WHY HADRIAN'S WALL?

*The **Emperor Hadrian**, who visited the country in 122 AD, followed a simple policy: he wanted the Roman Empire to live at peace, with stable frontiers, defined in most cases by geographical features – rivers, mountain ranges and the like. No visitor to the north of England would dispute that the area was inhospitable, but there was no specific geographical barrier to maintain control over incursions from the "barbarians" from the northern tribes. So Hadrian decided to build a wall – not a barrier in itself, but a link for patrols who could then push out into hostile territory and deal with any insurgence, and exercise some control over who came into the Roman jurisdiction.*

*The wall would be punctuated with **milecastles**, serving as gates and small barracks, and **observation turrets** – two between each pair of milecastles. Later, a series of **forts** was added to the wall at six to nine mile intervals. Hadrian ordered the building of the wall that bears his name, but in reality the construction work was supervized by the Governor of Britain, Nepos. The work took nearly nine years to complete, and was undertaken by soldiers from three legions – the second legion, based at Caerleon in Wales, the sixth legion, from York, and the 20th, all the way from Chester – plus locally conscripted labor – all under the guidance of a host of engineers, surveyors, masons and carpenters. The wall was around 73 miles long and was built in the east of local sandstone and further west of turf, later replaced by stone. At the start of its construction it was built ten feet thick, a width that was later reduced to eight feet or less to speed up construction. No one knows how high it was, though it's believed that it must have attained at least 21 feet – and, surprisingly, for part of its life it was whitewashed!*

spectacular views of the Wall as its snakes its way across the crags and promontories in the distance. *Same opening times and admission charges as Chesters. Tel. 01434 344525.*

Three miles further west along the B6318 is the great **Vindolanda garrison**, which actually predates the Wall. Containing the remains of no fewer than eight successive Roman forts and civilian settlements, the excavations that have taken place here have given archaeologists a great deal of information about how such military garrisons operated. The excavations at Vindolanda include homes, an administrative building, commander's house and gates, and there's a fully re-created section to give visitors an inkling of what the Wall would have looked like in Roman times. There's a **cafe** and a **museum**, with a vast collection of Roman leather items – shoes, belts, and other exhibits that feature daily life in the fort – with demonstrations by blacksmiths, pottery and, in a reconstructed **Roman kitchen**, cooking demonstrations. Perhaps the most fascinating section deals with the several hundred **writing tablets** that were discovered here over a period of twenty years from 1973. The subjects they cover include such topics as filing systems, children's schoolwork, soldiers' requests for more beer – even birthday invitations. *Same opening times as Chesters. Admission charges adults £3.80, children £2.80, seniors and students £3.20. Tel. 01434 344277; www.vindolanda.com.*

Eight miles further west, close to the village of **Greenhead**, is the **Roman Army Museum**, located at the garrison fort of **Carvoran**, where full-size models, authentic Roman graffiti found on the walls of an excavated barracks, and ongoing excavations make this a fascinating stop. No less fascinating is the shop, where you can buy a Roman ruler (where a foot equals 11.5 inches) and Roman cookbooks.

Open March to October daily 10am to 6pm; February and November Saturday and Sunday 10am to 4pm. Admission adults £3, students and seniors £2.60, children £2.10. Tel. 016977 47485. Note: You can purchase a joint ticket for Vindolana and the Roman Army Museum for: adults £5.60, seniors and students £4.70, children 32.80.

Corbridge, four miles to the east of Hexham, is an affluent medium-sized town with attractive yellow stone houses, and a number of excellent shops, restaurants and pubs. Among the attractions here is the **Vicar's Pele**, a 700 year-old fortified tower used as a refuge against marauding Scots. Just to the west of Corbridge proper are the remains of another Roman garrison – **Corstopitum** – begun 40 years before the Wall was started and occupied longer than any other fort on the Wall. It was strategically placed, at the meeting place of east-west and north-south Roman roads. There's a **museum**, with a large selection of military artifacts and outside, the remains of granaries, temples, homes and military buildings. *Open Easter to October daily 10am to 6pm; November to March daily 10am to 4pm. Admission adults £3, children £2. Tel. 01434 632079.*

EXCURSIONS & DAY TRIPS

Escorted Tours Limited, *Tel. 0191 536 4393,* runs whole day and half-day tours of the region. Some of the itineraries cover Hadrian's Wall. They are based near Sunderland, and can arrange pick-up in Newcastle or Durham.

PRACTICAL INFORMATION

The Hexham **tourist office** is located at *Hallgate, Tel. 01434 605225.* Hexham has branches of all the main banks and a post office. It makes a good deal of sense to stock up with cash here, as there's nowhere else to do so around the Wall.

THE NORTHUMBERLAND NATIONAL PARK

Between Hadrian's Wall to the south, the Cheviot Hills to the north and the coastal plain is the vast tract of bleak, remote, windswept, rugged terrain that has been designated as **Northumberland National Park**. In addition to the barren uplands where thousands of sheep graze are several large tracts of man-made forest, most notably **Kielder Forest**, the largest man-made coniferous plantation in Europe, a number of river valleys, including Coquetdale, Tynedale and Reddsale, and several reservoirs and lakes, the largest of which is **Kielder Water**, a reservoir that has also become a major **water sports center**. This is the land of the **Border Reivers** – outlaws who, between the thirteenth and sixteenth centuries, took advantage of the area's remoteness to engage in endless acts of cross-border rustling, smuggling and general bad behavior. Evidence of their activities can be seen in a host of fortified farmhouses, called **bastles**, and **peels** – defensive towers that litter the landscape.

This is preeminently walking country, and there are several walking trails straddling the landscape, most obviously the **Pennine Way**, which enters the National Park at Hadrian's Wall, then passes through the pleasant town of Bellingham en route to the Cheviot (at 2764 feet, the region's highest mountain), before continuing on across the Scottish border to Kirk Yetholm.

WHERE TO STAY

RIVERDALE HALL HOTEL, *Bellingham, Northumberland NE48 2JT. Tel. 01434 220254, Fax 01434 220457. Rooms: 20. Rates: single from £80, double from £110. Restaurant, indoor pool, sauna, fishing. All major credit cards accepted.*

Spacious country hotel run by the same family for 21 years, in extensive grounds with a wide range of facilities including indoor swimming pool, sauna and free trout and salmon fishing. The twenty rooms are all nicely furnished and come with tea- and coffee-making facilities, and there's an excellent restaurant that has won a number of awards. In addition to the rooms, the hotel has four self-catering apartments. It's convenient for Hadrian's Wall, Kielder Water and the Pennine Way.

WHITTON FARMHOUSE HOTEL, *Whitton, Rithbury NE65 7RL. Tel./Fax 01669 620811. Rooms: 3. Rates: singles from £26, doubles from £52. Pony-trekking stables. All major credit cards accepted.*

A friendly country hotel that overlooks the Northumberland National Park and the River Coquet valley. All the ground floor rooms have en suite bathrooms, and meals, all home-made, are taken in an unusual barn-like restaurant. Services available include riding from the hotel's own stables.

WHERE TO EAT

RIVERDALE HALL HOTEL, *Bellingham. Tel 01434 220254. Open. Three course dinner from £17. All major credit cards accepted.*

This menu at this popular and sometimes quite noisy family restaurant is hardly ambitious. Firm favorites with the British like prawn (shrimp) cocktail as a starter, and peppered steak with chips for a main course, figure prominently, but what they do here they do very well.

SEEING THE SIGHTS

Bellingham (pronounced bellinjum), a pleasant enough, remote town on the eastern fringes of the National Park on the B6320, is notable mainly for its medieval **parish church of St. Cuthbert**, rare in that it has a stone vaulted roof – its purpose being to prevent the church being burned down by the Border Reivers. On Front Street you can visit the **Heritage Center** with exhibits on this violent phase in local history and more general information about the local life and culture. West of Bellingham, narrow country lanes fan out towards Keilder Water and Forest, offering some panoramic scenery, and a chance to check out some of the bastle houses, the best of which is the late 16th century **Black Middens Bastle House**, to all intents and purposes a fairly ordinary ruined stone farmhouse until, on closer inspection, you can see how thick the walls are, that the main door and living area are on the upper floor, and narrow upper floor windows. There are several more of these bastles along the Tarset Valley. Be mindful that this remote area has very little in the way of facilities, so it's best to stock up on food and drink and make any telephone calls you need to make before leaving Bellingham.

Take the Stannersburn road west from Bellingham, until you reach **Kielder Water** itself, with its several visitor and waterside activity centers. The **Visitor Centre** at **Tower Knowe** is worth a quick stop; there's a decent enough **cafe**, and you can immerse yourself in the history of the valley and how the reservoir was formed. Four miles west again, the small community of **Leaplish** with its **waterside park** is the focal point for much of the lake's watersports activity, and as well as aquatic sports on offer, you can also rent bikes, go pony trekking, swim in the pool, fish, or go for a cruise. **Kielder Water Cruises**, *Tel. 01434 240398,* operate 75-minute rides around the lake from April to Septembeer from 11am to 3:30pm. *Open April to October daily 10am to 4pm; May to September daily 10am to 5pm. Cost adults £4. Tel. 01434 250312.*

At the northern tip of the reservoir is **Kielder Castle**, not really a castle at all but a hunting lodge built by the Duke of Northumberland in 1775. It now serves as an information and exhibition center for the Forestry Commission, whose Border Forest Park surrounds it. *Open April to October daily 10am to 5pm; August daily 10am to 6pm; January to Easter and October to December Saturday and Sunday 11am to 4pm. Tel. 01434 250209.* From the castle, you can explore a number of well-marked **footpaths** into the forest, or maybe you'd prefer to rent a bike – **Kielder Bikes** has a rental facility here.

Right on the eastern tip of the National Park on the B6341 west of Alnwick, on the River Coquet, stands the attractive resort town of **Rothbury**. Here you'll find a fine, wide and tree-lined main street enhanced by some elegant buildings and interesting shops, as well as the **Rothbury Cross**, put up as late as 1902. On Church Street, the **National Park Visitor Centre**, *Tel. 01669 620887,* has information on local hiking trails, several of which start off in the Simonside Hills parking lot, two miles west of the town center.

Rothbury's best known feature, though, a couple of miles out of town also on the B6341 west of Alnwick, is **Cragside**, a large Tudor-style country house – a bit out of place in the Northumbrian landscape – built by the first Lord Armstrong in 1890. The architect Norman Shaw designed the house, whose interior contains some William Morris **stained glass** as well as furnishings belonging to Armstrong, and a Renaissance-style **marble chimney** piece in the drawing room. The proximity to the house of the fast-flowing Debdon Burn gave the avid innovator Lord Armstrong the opportunity to seek ways of harnessing its power to fuel several domestic appliances – the dumbwaiter in the kitchen being one of them – and eventually to provide electricity for the house itself. Thus, in 1880, Cragside became the first house in the world to be powered by **hydro-elecricity**. The remnants of the original system can be seen in the 660-acre grounds – which are particularly attractive when the hundreds of rhododendrons are in bloom.

Open April to October Tuesday to Sunday 1pm to 5:30pm house, 10:30am to 7pm grounds; November to mid-December Tuesday, Saturday and Sunday 10:30am to 4pm. Admission £5.80. Tel. 01669 620333.

THE NORTHUMBERLAND COAST

There's only one word to describe the Northumbrian coast – magical! Stretching 50 miles from **Warkworth** in the south to **Berwick-upon-Tweed** and the Scottish border in the north, it's a wonderful combination of rocky coves washed by the North Sea surf; long deserted sandy beaches, dunes, estuaries; ruined and intact castles and abbeys, including **Lindisfarne Abbey**, the cradle of Christianity in northern England, and **Alnwick Castle**, known as the "Windsor of the north." It's the sort of place where you can walk for miles without seeing another soul, your only company gulls, fulmars and kittiwakes.

ARRIVALS & DEPARTURES

By Car

The A1 runs parallel to the coast, which can be accessed at a number of points.

By Bus

Services along this remote stretch of coast are few and far between. A Northumbria bus links Alnwick with Berwick three times a day, but that's about it.

By Train

There's an excellent service from London King's Cross to Alnmouth (less frequent stops) and Berwick (frequent stops). The journey time to Berwick is about four fours.

GETTING AROUND

Getting around by bus or train are non-starters; you really need a car. The main car rental companies aren't represented in Berwick or Alnwick, the two main centers, but you could try a local company, **Semple's**, *Tel. 01289 330707,* in Berwick.

WHERE TO STAY

WHITE SWAN HOTEL, *Bondgate Within, Alnwick, Northumberland NE66 1TD. Tel. 01665 602109, Fax 01665 510400. Rooms: 58. Rates: single from £80, double from £110. Restaurant, bars.*

Restored by the great Victorian architect Salvin, White Swan Hotel offers good value for the money. The rooms are lavishly decorated, and there's a good restaurant on the premises featuring local fare (see below).

MARSHALL MEADOWS, *Berwick-upon-Tweed TD15 1UT. Tel. 01289 331133, Fax 331438. Rooms: 19. Rates: singles from £75, double from £85. Restaurant, bar. Credit cards: MC, Visa.*

This large Georgian country house that prides itself on being "the most northerly hotel in England" is located just off the A1, a ten minute drive north of Berwick. Despite its proximity to the road, it's a relatively peaceful location, just yards from the sea (and the main London to Edinburgh rail line) and surrounded by farmland populated mainly by sheep. It offers 25 delightful en suite rooms, a handsome, elegant sitting room, lounge bar and restaurant, open to non-residents, specializing in local produce, including game. The 15-acre grounds, with their mature shrubs and wide lawns, are a delight.

THE KING'S ARMS, *Hide Hill, Berwick-upon-Tweed. Tel. 01289 307454. Rooms: 36. Rates: single from £60, double from £90. Restaurant, cafe. All major credit cards accepted.*

This centrally located hotel is handy for exploring the town walls and Berwick's other attractions. Located on Hide Hill, it was formerly a coaching inn – and another lodging place that Charles Dickens somehow found his way to. The rooms are comfortable if not luxurious, and there's a decent full-service restaurant and a separate pizzeria on the ground floor, as well as a very pleasant garden where you can eat and drink al fresco in the summer.

WAREN HOUSE HOTEL, *Waren Mill, Belford, Northumberland NE70 7EE. Tel. 01668 214581. Rooms: 10. Rates: single from £85, double from £115 Restaurant. All major credit cards accepted.*

Set on Budle Bay, a peaceful inlet between Bamburgh and Holy Island that's also a wildlife refuge, Waren House, set in six acres of mature gardens and woodland, dates from Georgian times when it was a private country house. The rooms are nicely furnished and decorated, each reflecting a different style. The restaurant, with views of Holy Island, is outstanding, and as well as local meat and game dishes, there are some excellent seafood options.

VICTORIA HOTEL, *Front Street, Bamburgh NE69 7BP. Tel 01668 214431, Fax 01668 214404. Rooms: 29. Rates: singles from £32, doubles from £70. Bar, restaurant, games room. All major credit cards accepted.*

This recently revamped hotel is located in right in the center of the beautiful village of Bambrugh, just off the A1 about ten miles south of Berwick, overlooking the village green and very close to the magnificent, massive castle. The hotel boasts 29 comfortable and well-equipped rooms, some with four poster-beds; a bar, brasserie and a children's play area and games room.

IVY COTTAGE, *1 Croft Gardens, Cornhill-on-Tweed TD12 4SY. Tel./ Fax 01890 820667. Rooms: 2. Rates: rooms from £46. No credit cards accepted.*

This modern, welcoming family home in the village of Crookham west of Berwick-upon-Tweed (and very close to the Scottish border) has two letting bedrooms, both furnished with antiques, stylishly decorated and with full amenities. Dinner is available by arrangement with the owners; sumptuous breakfasts that will set you up for the rest of the day are prepared in a farmhouse-style kitchen.

THE OLD VICARAGE, *Church Road, Tweedmouth, Berwick-upon-Tweed TD15 2AN. Tel 01289 306909. Rooms: 7. Rates: singles from £17, doubles from £34. No credit cards accepted.*

This 19th century former clergyman's house is located in the town of Tweedmouth, just across the River Tweed from Berwick-upon-Tweed proper. Tastefully furnished and decorated and with many period features, it boasts a number of antiques, adding to the quaint atmosphere. The rooms come in a variety of sizes, some of them very large indeed. A comfortable lounge is the source of a variety of books and magazines, and you're welcome to pick up snacks and beverages from the fridge. The large dining room is the setting for delicious breakfasts.

WHERE TO EAT

FUNNYWAYT'MEKALIVIN, *41 Bridge Street, Berwick, Tel. 01289 308827. Open by arrangement only. Main courses around £15. Credit cards: MC, Visa.*

This small, highly individual restaurant in a 17th century building, close to the River Tweed and the Elizabethan walls, is virtually a one-woman show run by the owner and chef, Elizabeth Middlemiss. The food is excellent – local, Northumbrian produce with a French twist.

WAREN HOUSE HOTEL, *Waren Mill, Belford (south of Berwick, just off the A1). Tel. 01668 214581. Open daily 7pm to 10pm. Main courses around £18. Set 5-course meal £25. All major credit cards accepted.*

The Waren House Hotel's restaurant prides itself on using only the freshest local produce, preferring to term its cooking "Modern Northumbrian" rather than modern British or whatever. Meals are taken in a lovely, elegant dining room, with pale yellow walls, oil paintings and antiques. Among the choices for main courses are sauteed pigeon breast cooked in a gin and juniper sauce, and poached rainbow trout wrapped by a cream dill sauce, while ginger cheesecake will set you off nicely. There's a good wine list.

OLD SHIP HOTEL, *Seahouses NE68 7RD. Tel 01665 720200. Open daily noon to 2pm, 7pm to 9pm. Dinner from £16. All major credit cards accepted.*

This small hotel is located very close to the harbor in the slightly down-at-heel resort of Seahouses. As well as a hotel it also serves as a popular watering-hole for the locals. The restaurant, which serves traditional English cuisine, with an emphasis on freshly caught fish, is lined with lots of nautical memorabilia. Not only is the seafood good here; you can enjoy excellent fresh meat dishes, including several roast options. There's also a popular saloon bar where you can enjoy an aperitif (with the locals) before eating.

WHITE SWAN HOTEL, *Bondgate Within, Alnwick, Northumberland NE66 1TD. Tel. 01665 602109, Fax 01665 510400. Rooms: 58. Rates: single from £80, double from £110. Restaurant, bars.*

The restaurant in this hotel has paneling and furnishings bought from the salvage of the *Olympic,* sister ship of the more famous *Titanic.* Expect fine classic Northumbrian fare, such as Kilder game pie and cranachan, a creamy dessert made with local rum, raspberries and oatmeal.

SEEING THE SIGHTS

To explore the coast, start at **Warkworth**, about twenty miles north of Newcastle and clearly marked from the A1. The town's greatest asset is its **castle**, perched on a grassy hill at the end of the main street. Built largely in the 14th century and the home of the Percy family for 200 years, the castle's most striking feature is its **three-story keep**, with polygonal turrets and high central tower. *Open April to September daily 10am to 6pm; October to March 10am to 4pm. Admission adults £2.40, seniors and students £1.80, children £1.20. Tel. 01665 711423.* From here, Castle Street leads down to the Norman **church of St. Laurence**, with some fine ribbed-vaulting and an attractive setting, particularly in spring when the daffodils are out.

It's just three miles north from here on the A1068 to the mainly Victorian seaside town of **Alnmouth** (pronounced Allanmouth), set on a hill overlooking the attractive sandy estuary of the Aln. It was a thriving port until 1806, when a freak storm changed the course of the river, making the original harbor defunct. Alnmouth's attempt to reinvent itself as a holiday resort was only mildly successful, though with its wide beach and acres of dunes, it's an attractive place from which to bathe, so long as you can stand the cold North Sea waters.

The main event round here is Alnmouth's sister town – or maybe it should be mother town – of **Alnwick** (pronounced "Annick"), about four miles inland just off the A1. Quite apart from its main attraction, the vast **castle** owned by the Percy family since 1309, the town has much more to commend it, including some lovely Georgian houses, cobbled streets, some fine shops and a weekly market that's been going strong for 700 years, as well as plenty of banks and a post office.

Alnwick Castle is often known as "The Windsor of the North," not least for its size – it has over 150 rooms – and grandeur. The first occupant, Henry de Percy, purchased the original Norman keep and adapted it into a fortified residence. Over the years, the castle has undergone many changes, especially in the eighteenth century when the grounds were landscaped by none other than Capability Brown. Although the castle looks rather squat and cumbersome from the outside, the interior is quite different and palatial. Only a small part of the building is open to view, but among the highlights are a galleried library, Venetian mosaic floors, Meissen dinner services, huge marble statues and armor. The Percy family held sway over much of northern England for centuries. *Open year-round daily 11am to 5pm (house from noon). Admission adults £6.25, seniors and students £5.25, children 5-15 £3.50. Family ticket (2 adults, 2 children): £15. Tel. 01665 510777.*

Heading back to the coast again, it's six miles north, signposted off the B1339, to the tiny fishing village of **Craster**, famous for its smoked kippers which can be bought from **Robson's factory** almost opposite the **Jolly Fisherman** pub, where you can get good bar food, including excellent locally caught crab sandwiches. From the village, you can walk the clearly marked footpath to the romantic ruins of 14th century **Dunstanburgh Castle**, standing on a lonely promontory about one and a half miles north of the village and built as part of England's defense against the Scots. The castle's main feature is its huge **keep**, which can be seen for miles around. The stunning location, with the sea crashing below, inspired 19th century artist J.M.W. Turner to paint it several times, and more recently the castle featured in the 1990 film rendition of *Hamlet* with Mel Gibson. *Open April to September daily 10am to 6pm; October daily 10am*

CRASTER KIPPERS

*Kippers may not be as popular in Britain as they once were, but these specially smoked herring can be found on the breakfast menus of most of the better hotels. Craster has been synonymous with kippers for more than 150 years. Although the production process has become much more mechanized in recent years, no longer employing the "herring lassies" to split and clean the fish, it's basically the same: The raw herring are cleaned, salted and then hung on tentersticks and placed high up in the chimney of the 130 year-old smokehouses. They then cure for up to 16 hours above fires composed of white wood shavings covered with oak sawdust. You can trace the process process at **Robson's factory**, where you can also purchase kippers to send home or to enjoy as tomorrow's breakfast, accompanied by just a dab of fresh butter.*

to 4pm; November to March Wednesday to Sunday 10am to 4pm. Admission adults £1.80, children 90p, seniors and students £1.40. Tel. 01665 576231.

If you're in a walking mood, continue north along the coast, along beautiful sandy beaches to the picturesque tiny village of **Low Newton-by-the-Sea**, with a three sided square of tiny fishermen's cottages and pub facing out to sea.

Twelve miles north of Craster on the B1340 is the somewhat down-at-heel seaside town of **Seahouses**, but with an attractive harbor from where Billy Shiels, the self-styled Farne Island Boatman, operates boat trips to the windswept **Farne Islands**, just a few miles off the coast. The Farnes are a collection of rocks, some of which are only visible at high tide, but which are home to a vast number of seabirds, including puffins, terns, kittiwakes and guillemots as well as gray seal colonies. Only two of the islands are open for visitors – a move designed by the islands owners, the National Trust, to protect the birds. These are **Inner Farne**, where there's also a miniscule chapel built to honor local hero Saint Cuthbert, who spent much of his time here, and **Staple Island**. To see the islands, contact **Billy Shiels Farne Island Boat Trips**, *The Harbour, Seahouses, Tel. 01665 720308.*

It's a lovely, exhilarating walk along the beach from Seahouses to the pretty village of **Bamburgh** (if you're driving it's also on the B1340) dominated by the massive, spectacular pile that is **Bamburgh Castle**, set high on a rocky crag overlooking the sea and visible for miles around. The defensive potential of the site was first recognized by the Celts, but it was the under the rule of the Anglo-Saxons that it became the capital of their kingdom of Northumbria, and also the resting place of the head and hand of **St. Oswald**. Much later, the castle came into the hands of the Armstrong family, who replaced the medieval ruins with the castellated mansion that now sits atop the crag, complete with a massive **Great Hall** with teak ceilings and a stunning collection of Faberge stone animal carvings. Down in the dingy basement of the keep, which retains its Norman architecture and atmosphere, suites of armor are displayed. *Open April to October daily 11am to 5pm. Admission adults £4, 6-16s £1.50, seniors £3. Tel. 01668 214515.*

Bamburgh village, with a smattering of pubs and restaurants, is also home to the **Grace Darling Museum**, opposite the 13th century parish church of St. Aidan. The museum is a celebration of the life of the woman who, with her lighthouse keeper father William, rowed through tumultuous seas in September 1838 to rescue nine passengers from the stricken steamship *Forfarshire*, which had been dashed against the rocks. Grace received national acclaim for her efforts, though it didn't do her much good – she died of tuberculosis in 1842 – aged just 26. *Open Easter to September daily 10am to 5pm.*

You'll need to get back on to the A1 in order to reach **Lindisfarne**, or **Holy Island** as it's more commonly known. One of the northeast's most popular tourist destinations, access to the island is by driving (walking, cycling or horseriding) across a narrow causeway that for about five hours of the day is covered with water. Note: It's impossible to cross to the island between the two hours before high tide and the 3 1/2 hours after. Tide tables are printed in local newspapers and displayed at the start of the causeway. Make *absolutely sure* that you check the tide table at one of the local tourist offices or at the beginning of the causeway before crossing.

After all the hype, first impressions of Lindisfarne can be quite disappointing. Just a mile wide by one and a half long, it's flat, virtually treeless and the village is nothing to write home about. But Lindisfarne, especially during the off-season, has a habit of growing on you.

It was here that newly-converted Christian King Oswald of Northumbria invited a monk called Aidan to set up a religious foundation. The monastery grew quickly in size and in reputation and became the main center for evangelizing northern England, as well as an acclaimed center of education and art, some of which can be seen in the **museum**, adjacent to the parish church of St. Mary. Other, more famous artifacts, such as the beautiful **Lindisfarne Gospels**, are now on show in the British Library in London, though after public pressure they are likely to be returned to their native region within the near future – at least for some of the time.

The most famous religious leader here, **Cuthbert**, preferred the total isolation of life in a hermit's cell on Inner Farne (see above) and only stayed here two years, before returning to the cell where he died in 687. After his death, his body was brought back to Lindisfarne, which, after his canonization, became a place of **pilgrimage** until 875, when the body was transferred to Durham Cathedral when it seemed that the island might be attacked by marauding Danes. Despite the attempt by a group of Benedictine monks from Durham to revive the monastery in 1082, it never really gained the momentum that it had had during its earlier years.

You can visit the evocative remains of pink stone **Lindisfarne Priory**, which date from the later Benedictine period and whose stones have been worn down by centuries of exposure to the elements. You can see clearly the Romanesque arches of the nave and the patterned main doorway. Adjacent to the Priory is the church of **St. Mary the Virgin**, built in the 13th century, and a more recent building which houses the **museum**, with exhibits relating to the growth of Chrisrtianity in Northumbria. *Priory and museum open April to September daily 10am to 6pm; October to March daily 10am to 4pm. Admission adults £2.80, seniors £2.10, children £1.40. Tel. 01289 389200.* Note: These times obviously cannot account for the tide – again, make sure you check the tide times before you set out to avoid disappointment.

On a warm day – a rare thing up here – it's a very pleasant walk past the village and along the shore to **Lindisfarne Castle**, another defensive stronghold against the Scots, built in the 16th century. By the late 1800s it had fallen into such disrepair that it was snapped up for peanuts by the editor of *Country Life* magazine Edward Hudson, who engaged celebrated architect Edwin Lutyens to turn it into a holiday retreat. Lutyens did a spectacular job retaining the medieval atmosphere of the castle with huge fireplaces, bare stone walls and rounded columns, with a wonderful walled garden created by Gertrude Jekyll. The castle is today owned by the National Trust. *Open April to October daily except Friday 1pm to 5pm. Admission £4. Tel. 01289 389244.*

As well as a number of decent pubs on the island, there's also a **mead factory**, where visitors can enjoy some mead tasting at **Lindisfarne Ltd**, *St. Aidan's Winery, Tel. 01289 389230.*

As Lindisfarne is a very small island (population of just 200) with limited access because of the tides, very few people choose to actually stay here. Should you want a bite to eat or a pint, or you decide you do want to stay here, try **The Crown and Anchor**, *Tel. 01289215*. The pub offers comfortable B&B accommodation for around £20 per person per night.

It's just eleven miles north of here on the A1 to England's northernmost town, **Berwick-Upon-Tweed** which changed hands between the Scots and the English no fewer than thirteen times between 1174 and 1482, when it was finally handed over to the English and in whose hands it has remained ever since. Berwick had once been one of the most prosperous towns in Scotland, backed up by the fertile farming territory of the Tweed Valley – mainly in Scotland – and by a thriving port. When the English finally took over the town in 1482, they cut it off from its fertile hinterland and it became little more than a garrison, strengthened in the late 1500s – at a time when the Scots were again forging links with the French – by the construction of extensive **fortified walls**, which remain incredibly well preserved to this day. No wonder; no more than twenty feet high, they are amazingly thick, with grass dykes beyond the walls themselves providing an additional line of defense. The walls took eleven years to build and cost £128,000 – a princely sum in those days – more, in fact, than Queen Elizabeth I had paid for all her other fortifications put together. Ironically, the French attack never materialized and within forty years, England and Scotland were united.

You can walk around a large portion of the walls, which afford some lovely vistas of the town, with its elegant Georgian houses and distinctive red and orange tiled roofs, especially along **Quay Walls**, where some of the town's wealthier residents built homes. Also worth a look in town is the **Town Hall**, at the foot of Marygate, topped by a spire and a bell, with an original jailhouse that now houses the Cell Block Museum. From here, walk along Church Street to **Holy Trinity Church**, unusual in that it is a Church of England parish built during the Commonwealth (Puritan) period. The fact that it has no tower is said to be due to Cromwell's belief that they were sacrilegious.

Opposite the church are the imposing **Barracks**, built in the early 18th century and used as such until 1964, when the King's Own Borderers Regiment moved out. Today, they house an interesting **regimental museum**, and an exhibition of the life of British infantrymen from the 16th to 19th centuries. The barracks is also home to the excellent **Borough Museum**, with dioramas, local artifacts and models, and, upstairs, the superb (for a town of its size) **art gallery**, whose nucleus came from a gift from the Scottish shipping magnate and philanthropist William Burrell. Among the works on show is a sketch by Degas, Chinese bronzes, and a church plate. *Open April to September daily 10am to 6pm; October daily 10am to 6pm; November to March Wednesday to Sunday 10am to 4pm. Admission adults £2.60, seniors £2, children 5-16 £1.30. Tel. 01289 304493.*

PRACTICAL INFORMATION

Berwick's **tourist office** is on *Marygate, Tel. 01289 330733*, as is the main post office. The town's banks are located at the foot of Marygate on Hide Hill. There's a **tourist information office** in Alnwick at *The Shambles, Tel. 01665 510665.*

23. WALES

Wales is a small country within a country – for like England, Scotland and Northern Ireland it forms part of the United Kingdom. When you visit Wales, you'll be amazed at the variety of scenery in a land that's just one sixth the area of England with only one sixteenth the population of its neighbor. It's an enchanting land of mountain and meadow, moorland and beach, lake and forest, great rivers and cascading waterfalls. Its man-made features – except for some of the ugly refineries and factories in the south of the country – by and large enhance the landscape; glorious churches and cathedrals, pretty villages and best of all mighty, majestic, magnificent castles. From the **Snowdonia National Park** in the north, with Wales' highest peak (it's also 300 feet higher than England's tallest), to the stunning **Pembrokeshire coast**, to the cosmopolitan cities of the south, Wales has something for everyone.

Wales is a peaceful, tranquil land today, but it hasn't always been so. The Welsh people, with their Celtic roots and culture, were violently oppressed by their Anglo-Saxon and Norman neighbors. Edward I of England did eventually unite the two countries, but not without a great struggle from the Welsh people who were far from anxious to give over their beautiful land.

Seven centuries have passed; times have changed and by and large the English and Welsh get on pretty well, with one legal system, and education and health systems shared by both (as distinct from Scotland, which has its own legal and educational systems). Though an upsurge of Welsh nationalism in the 1960s and '70s saw a number of cottages belonging to absentee English owners burnt to the ground, this has been the exception to the rule and most Welsh have been keen to maintain close ties with England, as evidenced by past referenda.

The most recent referendum on **devolved government** for Wales, however, gave the nationalists something to shout about. Although the majority in favor of devolution was not large (and certainly nowhere near as large as in Scotland on the same issue), it was enough to see the

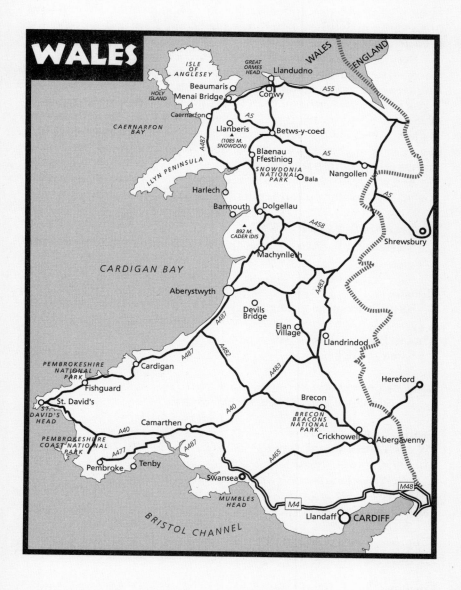

establishment of a **Welsh Assembly**, the result of which has been the devolution to this Assembly in Cardiff of powers formerly held by the Westminster government in London. The result thus far has been an upsurge of confidence, epitomized by the new waterfront developments in Cardiff and Swansea, brand new public buildings and a deepening pride in the Welsh culture.

Despite the overbearing nature of the beast next door, Wales has managed to retain a very real and unique identity, not least in the Welsh language, the most vibrant and widely spoken of the Celtic tongues. Welsh is being spoken by more and more people all the time, and in parts of the north and on the island of Angelsey is spoken in preference to English. Welsh culture is maintained in the fine tradition of song and dance, seen in abundance at the annual **National Eisteddfodd** and at various other cultural festivals.

As I've already said, Wales is not large, not much bigger than some English regions, so you can get to most destinations in a day.

PLANNING YOUR TRIP

See Chapter 6, *Planning Your Trip*, for references to England in this section.

Climate
Virtually identical to England.

What to Pack
Same as England.

Entry Requirements
No additional entry requirements needed.

Tourist Boards for Wales
• **Wales Tourist Board**, *Dept RJ3, PO Box 1, Cardiff CF1 2XN, Tel. 01222/ 499909; www.wtb.co.uk*
• **North Wales Tourism**, *77 Conway Rd, Colwyn Bay LL29 7LN, Tel. 01492/ 531731 or 0800/834820; www.nwt.co.uk*
• **Mid-Wales Tourism**, *The Station, Machynlleth SY20 8TG, Tel. 01654/ 702653 or 0800/273747; www.mid-wales-tourism.co.uk*
• **Tourism South & West Wales**, *Charter Court, Phoenix Way, Enterprise Park, Swansea SA7 9DB, Tel. 01792/781212 or 0800/243731*

Customs
Same applies as in England.

s appear in both English and
Welsh.

Hitchhiking
Same applies as in England.

Hotels
Same applies as in England.

DO'S & DON'T'S IN WALES

The Welsh are a proud people, friendly and welcoming. However, there are a couple of simple do's and don'ts that you'll need to bear in mind:

Do remember that for many centuries mainly Celtic Wales was independent from England.

Don't refer to a Welsh person as English. They will probably be too polite to say anything about it, but will nonetheless not appreciate it.

Don't refer to the Queen as Queen of England. She's Queen of Wales and the rest of the UK, too!

BASIC INFORMATION
See Chapter 7, *Basic Information*, for references to England in this section.

Bank Holidays
Same as England's. March 1 (**St. David's Day**) is Wales' national day and is sometimes observed, though it's not an official holiday.

Banks
The same major banks operate in Wales as in England.

Cost of Living
The cost of living is slightly cheaper in Wales than in most of England, but it's barely noticeable.

Currency
Same as England's.

Electricity
Same as England.

Gay Travelers
Attitudes in the larger Welsh cities are the same as in England, and Cardiff in particular has a lively gay scene. Rural areas may be a little less tolerant.

Health & Safety
The National Health Service is uniform throughout Britain (supposedly).

Crime
Same basic rules apply as in England. Be particularly careful in the cities.

Road Safety
Same as England

Queuing
The Welsh love to queue too!

Newspapers
Welsh editions of the main London newspapers are widely available. US papers can be purchased in Cardiff and Swansea.

Postal Services
Same as England. The stamps may look a little different – the Queen's head is accompanied by a small dragon!

Religion
Presbyterianism is strong, as is the Baptist Church. The Church of Wales is an offshoot of the Church of England. Place of worship of other faiths – Judaism, Islam, etc – are largely confined to the larger centers of population.

Sundays
In some parts of Wales, particularly the rural north and Angelsey, religious sorts have insisted that shops and pubs close all day.

Taxes
Same as England. The Welsh Assembly did not gain tax-raising powers.

Telephones

Same as England.

Time

The same as England: Wales follows GMT (Greenwich Mean Time) in winter, BST (British Summer Time) in summer.

Tipping

Same as England.

TV

All the general UK channels are available here, though with some Welsh language content. **Channel S4C** is a Welsh-only channel (i.e., broadcast in Welsh).

Water

Same as England.

Weights & Measures

Same as England.

South Wales extends from the border with England to the spectacular coastline of Pembrokeshire. It's a varied region that includes Wales' two largest cities: the capital, **Cardiff**, a lively, stately, cosmopolitan place with wide avenues and sweeping lawns, and industrial **Swansea**, the gateway to the Gower Peninsula.

North and west of Cardiff are the industrial valleys where coal has been mined for centuries, and, by contrast, the unspoilt **Brecon Beacons National Park**, a pretty region of hills and lake. To the west is the **Pembrokeshire Coast National Park**, with mile after mile of glorious sandy beaches, rugged headlands and towering cliffs.

CARDIFF

The capital city of Wales has come into its own of late, particularly with the urban regeneration around the docklands area, and the setting up in 1999 of the new **Welsh Assembly**, based in the city. The city's roots go back to Roman times, when a small settlement was established here, just to the east of the River Taff. When the Romans deserted Britain, the site was left deserted too, right up until the Normans arrived and built a motte (tower) and bailey castle, remnants of which can still be seen in the grounds of the current **Cardiff Castle**. But Cardiff never really took off until the mid-1800s, when the coal mining industry developed, and Cardiff became the main port for exporting the black stuff. The prosperity continued (though there was always great poverty here) until the slump of the 1930s, and then World War II, which wreaked havoc on the city.

Since the demise of the coal mining industry in the '80s and '90s, Cardiff has been trying to reinvent itself, with remarkable success. Vast areas of the city have been rebuilt, the headquarters of the new Welsh Assembly are firmly rooted here, there's a burgeoning arts scene and the city is fairly booming once again.

ARRIVALS & DEPARTURES

By Car

Getting from London to Cardiff by car is very easy. Simply take the M4 west. It will take you all the way, crossing the spectacular Severn Bridge as you approach Wales.

By Bus

There's a frequent National Express service to Cardiff from London's Victoria Bus Station. *Call 0990 808080 for information.*

By Train

Cardiff is on the main line from London to Swansea. Trains leave from Paddington Station every hour. Cardiff Queen Street Station is located a short walk to the east of the St. David's Centre.

ORIENTATION

Cardiff's main attractions, including the main shopping and commercial district, are all little more than a stone's throw from the Castle. The regenerated docklands area is further afield, but easily walkable – though it is served by plenty of buses from the center.

GETTING AROUND TOWN

Walking is the best way to get around the city; much of the city center is pedestrianized and restricted to vehicular traffic in any case. The local buses are operated by **Cardiff Bus**, who have an office in Wood Street by the bus terminal, *Tel. 029 20396521*, where you can get a good map of local transportation services. The Cardiff Buses offer a Day Out bus ticket with which you have unlimited use of the buses in the central area.

If you insist on using a car, try **Avis**, *14 Tudor Street, Tel. 029 2034 2111*, or **Budget**, *Penarth Road, Tel. 029 2066 4499*. Bicycling is another option, especially if you want to make use of the **Welsh National Cycle Route** that runs the entire length of the country. You can rent bikes for around £10 a day from **Taff Trail Cycle Hire**, *Cathedral Road, Tel. 029 20398362*.

THE WELSH NATIONAL CYCLE ROUTE

"Sustrans" (short for sustainable transport) is a national UK organization that has the laudable aim of creating 6,500 miles of cycle paths throughout the nation, linking most of the major cities and towns. Half the proposed network will use traffic-free routes, such as old disused railroad lines and canalside paths. Some stretches of the system are already open – including **Lon Las Cymru**, *the Welsh National Cycle Route, opened in 1995, and which stretches north-south across the country from Angelsey to Cardiff. Maps of the route are available from the various regional tourist boards listed in Chapter 6, "Planning Your Trip."*

WHERE TO STAY

CARDIFF MARRIOTT, MILL LANE, *Cardiff CF1 1EZ. Tel. 029 2039 9944, Fax 029 20395578. Rooms: 182. Rates: singles from £90, doubles from £120. Restaurant, coffee shop, leisure facilities, pool. All major credit cards accepted.*

This high-rise hotel is right in the center of Cardiff and close to the St. David's Centre and the main shopping and commercial district. Needless to say, the hotel offers splendid views over the city and beyond from most of its comfortably furnished bedrooms – as you'd expect from the Marriott chain – and comes with a full range of leisure facilities, including sauna and indoor swimming pool. The staff is helpful and friendly.

QUALITY HOTEL, *Merthyr Road, Tongwynlaid, Cardiff CF15 7LD. Tel. 029 2052 9988, Fax 029 2052 9977. Rooms: 95. Rates: singles from £83, doubles from £108. Restaurant, bar, indoor pool, leisure suite. All major credit cards accepted.*

This well-equipped modern hotel is conveniently located where the M4 meets the A4054 into Cardiff, so it's useful not only for getting in to explore the city's major sights, but for the surrounding places of interest. The reception area is bright and spacious, and the bedrooms comfortable, with tea- and coffee-making facilities. There's plenty of parking, and a leisure suite with sauna, solarium and gymnasium.

SANDRINGHAM HOTEL, *21 St Mary Street, Cardiff CF10 1PL. Tel 029 2023 2161, Fax 029 2038 3998. Rooms: 28. Rates: singles from £45, doubles from £55. Bar, restaurant. All major credit cards accepted.*

The Sandringham is conveniently located right in the center of lively Cardiff, close to all the attractions, including the castle and the St. David's Centre. The modern rooms are well-equipped, and on the ground floor there's an upmarket restaurant and bar: Cafe Jazz, which is the source of excellent a la carte and set-price meals. This is an especially attractive place to stay if you like like jazz, which is played here several nights a week.

WHERE TO EAT

LE CASSOULET, *5 Romilly Crescent, Canton, Cardiff. Tel. 029 20221905, Fax 029 20221905. Open Tuesday to Saturday, noon to 2:30pm, 6pm to 10pm. Main courses around £15. All major credit cards accepted.*

This long-standing bistro has been one of Cardiff's best eating places for years. The emphasis here is on French provincial cooking, particularly from the southwest region, so you can expect to find dishes like cassoulet toulousain and lamb shank cooked in straw on the menu. There's a clear connection with the city of Toulouse, right down to a photograph of the Toulouse rugby team and a wine list with a definite southwestern twist. The house champagne by the glass is a particular bargain.

CHIKAKO'S JAPANESE RESTAURANT, *10-11 Mill Lane, Cardiff. Tel. 029 20665279, Fax 029 20665279. Open daily for dinner only. Main courses around £10. All major credit cards accepted.*

This Japanese restaurant in Cardiff's city center offers excellent, good value authentic Japanese food in pleasant, welcoming surroundings. Particularly impressive are the sashimi and sushi, while those of a nervous disposition and not inclined to opt for raw fish might consider the various choices of the tempura and teriyaki ilk.

LE GALLOIS, *6-8 Romilly Crescent, Cardiff, Tel. 029 20341264, Fax 029 20237911. Open Tuesday to Saturday, noon to 2:30pm, 6pm to 10pm. Three course meal around £25. All major credit cards accepted.*

This restaurant, a recent winner of the Automobile Association Restaurant of the Year for Wales Award, has been wowing diners in the Cardiff area since it opened a few years ago. The name of the restaurant gives away its distinct French emphasis, but a closer inspection of the menu shows this to be a little misleading; it's perhaps best described as Modern British. Among the offerings are such yummy choices as salt marsh lamb with fondant potatoes and roasted provencale vegetables (maybe there is a French influence after all). The fish and seafood dishes are all meticulously cooked, and the desserts are every bit as mouth-watering as the main courses.

ARMLESS DRAGON, *97 Wyeverne Road, Cardiff CF2 4BG. Tel. 029 2038 2357. Open Tuesday to Friday noon to 2:15pm, 7pm to 10:15pm (closed Saturday lunch). Main courses from £9. All major credit cards accepted.*

Corny the name may be, but this well-established bistro provides for some serious eating. Essentially it's two terraced houses knocked together. Inside, the green and terracotta walls along with fresh flowers at each table give a pleasing effect. The menu includes lots of steak dishes, duck, chicken and roast wild rabbit. There's a good wine list, with house wines starting at a very affordable £7.90 a bottle.

SEEING THE SIGHTS

Start your tour of Cardiff with a visit to **Cardiff Castle**, in Bute Park, close to the main shopping center. The Castle contains fragments of the original Roman walls and a Norman keep, but it was radically transformed in Victorian times by the architect William Burges (1827-1881), working for the third Lord Bute, who created an interior that is, to say the least, over the top – with an **Arab Room** and **Fairytale Nursery**, both of which, along with the **Banqueting Hall**, are included on the regular guided tours. *Open March to October daily 9:30am to 6pm, November to February 9:30am to 4:30pm. Tours operate in summer every twenty minutes. Admission £4.80. Tel. 029 20878100.*

THE CARDIFF CARD

*You might want to consider getting a **Cardiff Card**, which allows unlimited travel on local buses and free entry to a number of city attractions, including the Castle. It costs £12 for 48 hours. You can purchase them from the tourist information office at Cardiff Central Station, Tel. 029 2022 7281.*

Just to the east of the Castle, in **Cathay's Park**, is the Cardiff Civic Centre, a collection of pleasant turn-of-the-(twentieth)-century buildings in a parkland setting. The site comprises law courts, the city hall, government offices, the university and **The National Museum of Wales**, which traces the history and development of Wales from prehistoric times to the present. Among the displays that will delight the kids and young at heart are the skeleton of a washed-up whale and animatronic mammoths. There's a superb collection of paintings, including works by Renoir, Monet and Degas. *Open year-round Tuesday to Sunday 10am to 5pm. Admission adults £4.25, children £2.50. Tel. 029 20397951.*

South of Cathay's Park is the vast **St. David's Centre**, a vast complex that houses a wide range of shops, a post office, and the excellent St.

David's Hall, which has outstanding acoustics for the classical, rock, and jazz concerts that take place there.

While you're in Cardiff, take a look at the **docklands** area, a couple of miles south of the city center, certainly walkable but also accessible with the #8 bus. Once notorious for its slums, the area has now been transformed with a new promenade with sculptures, a clutch of new museums, public buildings and housing, and the **Welsh Industrial and Maritime Museum** with an array of exhibits about Wales' industrial and maritime heritage. A separate building (but part of the museum) at 126 Bute Street contains the reconstructed interiors of old houses and shops. *Open year-round Tuesday to Saturday 10am to 5pm, Sunday 2:30pm to 5pm only. Admission adults £1.25. Tel. 029 20481919.*

Also on the waterfront is **Techniquest**, a hands-on science museum and technology center, which also contains a planetarium. *Open year-round Monday to Friday 9:30am to 4:30pm, weekends 10:30am to 5pm. Admission adults £4.75, children £3.50. Tel. 029 2047 5475.*

To get an overview of what's going on in the docklands area, check out the nearby **Cardiff Bay Visitors' Centre**. It's open the same hours as Techniquest and admission is free.

Just outside Cardiff is the leafy suburb of Llandaff, where you'll find **Llandaff Cathedral**, which dates from the 1130s and was heavily restored during Victorian times. It then took a major hit during World War II and had to be restored again. With its two main towers, one dating from the 15th century, the other Victorian, it's not an unattractive building, but its most captivating feature is not its architecture but the statue of *Christ in Majesty* by Jacob Epstein. There's also some work by Burne-Jones in the St. Dyfrig's Chapel.

To get to Llandaff Cathedral from Cardiff city center: cross the River Taff at Cardiff Bridge, and you'll soon come to Cathedral Road on your right. From Cathedral Road, you can either walk the two miles to the cathedral, or catch the #133 bus from the bus stop on the left hand side of the road.

NIGHTLIFE & ENTERTAINMENT

St. David's Hall, *St. David's Centre, Tel. 029 20878444*, hosts the gamut of musical productions, from rock to classical, except, that is for opera; the **New Theatre**, *Park Place, Tel. 029 20878889*, is the home of the **Welsh National Opera**, probably the most adventurous of Britain's opera outfits. Meanwhile, there's serious theater at the **Sherman**, *Senghennydd Road, Tel. 029 20230451*. The **Cardiff International Arena**, *Mary Ann Street, Tel. 029 20224488*, is a vast new auditorium that hosts concerts of the Shirley Bassey (a local girl) variety.

There are, as you'd expect, plenty of pubs and clubs in Cardiff; try **The Wellington**, *Mill Lane*, and **The Old Arcade**, *Church Street*.

SPORTS & RECREATION

The Cardiff City football team has long ceased to be a major force in British soccer. Rather, this is rugby territory. A brand new 75,000-seater stadium to be used for national rugby games (and even the English FA Cup soccer final during the rebuilding of London's Wembley Stadium) has just been completed. For more information about events here, contact **Millennium Stadium**, *Castle Street/Westgate Street, Cardiff, Tel. 029 2039 0111.*

SHOPPING

The city's bustling new shopping malls are complemented by some lovely Victorian arcades containing smaller stores selling everything from designer clothes to lighting.

Queen Street, Cardiff's largely pedestrian-only main shopping drag, runs east to west through the city center. It contains a huge variety of shops, including everything from large branches of all the major UK retailers through to small exclusive boutiques and specialist stores. At the Newport Road end of the street, the new **Capitol Centre** provides two floors of stores, while further down Queen Street is the entrance to the **St. David's Centre**, another indoor mall where large branches of UK retail giants Boots, Marks and Spencer and Debenhams can be found.

Further west is another indoor shopping center, **Queens West**, with branches of Laura Ashley and a number of smaller retail outlets. At its western end, near the Castle, Queen Street runs into **Duke Street**. South of here, a warren of smaller streets and shopping arcades, many of them dating from the Edwardian period, offer a number of small specialist shops and stores, from designer boutiques to specialist record stores.

EXCURSIONS & DAY TRIPS

At **St. Fagan's**, four miles west of Llandaff, is the excellent **Museum of Welsh Life** which, as the name implies, traces the history of the Welsh people. Set on 100 acres of parkland, the site contains cottages, row houses and farmhouses illustrating the development. To get to St. Fagan's by car, take the A4232 west from Cardiff city center. After about four miles, look out for signs to the Museum. Alternatively, you could take bus #32 from Cardiff's Central Bus Station, Central Square. *Open July to September daily 10am to 6pm; October to June daily 10am to 5pm. Admission: £5.25.*

About ten miles north of Cardiff – accessible by train or bus #71 from Cardiff – is the town of **Caerphilly**, famous, apart from its cheese, for a lovely medieval **castle** with moat. Built in the late 13th century by Gilbert de Clare, a Norman, to thwart attack by the Welsh Prince Llewellyn, the castle is accessed over a causeway that leads to the keep. Like Cardiff Castle, this one had also fallen into a state of disrepair and was rebuilt by the Bute family, ever keen to make their mark. *Open Easter to October daily 9:30am to 6pm; November to Easter Monday to Friday 9:30am to 4pm, Sunday 11am to 4pm. Admission adults £2.40, children £1.90.*

PRACTICAL INFORMATION

Branches of all the main banks can be found in the main commercial district, and a main post office in the St. David's Centre. Cardiff has a branch of **American Express**, *3 Queen Street, Tel. 029 20668858.* The city's **main tourist information center** is at *Cardiff Central Station, Tel. 029 2022 7281.*

ABERGAVENNY

Abergavenny is an attractive market town on the edge of the **Brecon Beacons National Park**, and makes a good base for touring the **Black Mountains**. It's an ancient town – even before the Romans arrived and established a fort there had been a Neolithic settlement here, but like so many other places hereabouts, it was the construction of a **castle** here in 1090 that put the place on the map.

ARRIVALS & DEPARTURES

By Car

From Cardiff, take the M4 towards Newport. Then take the A49 north to Abergavenny.

By Bus

To get to Abergavenny from London, you'll need to change at Hereford. The town is connected to Cardiff and Brecon by services operated by Stagecoach Red & White, *Tel. 01633 266336.*

By Train

There are regular services to Cardiff from Abergavenny. For London, you'll need to change at Newport.

GETTING AROUND TOWN

Walking is the best way to see Abergavenny.

WHERE TO STAY

LLANWENARTH HOUSE, *Govilon, Abergavenny NP7 9SF. Tel. 01873 830289, Fax 01873 832199. Rooms: 4. Rates: single from £58, double from £79. No credit cards accepted.*

This gloriously peaceful country house retreat dates back to the 16th century and is full of charm, character and warmth – all the more so for the various family photographs and animal prints that bedeck the walls of the elegant dining room and drawing room. Both these rooms have original fireplaces and antiques, along with wide French windows that offer wonderful views of the nearby Sugar Loaf Peak. Then there's the staircase, a beautiful regency affair topped by a lantern dome. The bedrooms are roomy, with high ceilings, more antiques, and fireplaces. The room that particularly took my fancy was the Main Room, which has an enormous gilt French empire bed.

BEAR HOTEL, *Crickhowell NP8 1BW. Tel. 01873 810408, Fax 01873 811696. Rooms: 28. Rates: singles from £60, doubles from £80. Restaurant, bar. All major credit cards accepted.*

Right in the middle of the attractive town of Crickhowell is this ancient and atmospheric coaching inn, where you're made to feel very welcome not only by the staff but by the locals who congregate in the characterful, charming bar, bedecked with various mementoes from the days when this was a staging post for coaches from London. There's a fine restaurant with lots of fresh local produce, or you can order good value food from the bar. The comfortable bedrooms have lots of character – some of the rooms are located in a converted stable yard.

WHERE TO EAT

WALNUT TREE INN, *Abergavenny, Tel. 01873 852797. Open daily lunch (bistro only) noon to 2pm; dinner 7pm to 10pm. Main courses around £18. All major credit cards. accepted.*

It's noisy and cramped, the tables are close together and sometimes wobble a bit, but for 30 years people have been coming in droves from miles around to sample the unique culinary delights of The Walnut Tree. So what's the attraction? Unquestionably the food, a unique blend of Italian with a dash of Welsh is how it's perhaps best described; thus for spaghetti alla vongole we have spaghetti with fresh local cockles, tagliolini using local crab. There are a number of other, even more unusual dishes: hare agrodolce, roast woodcock, and Welsh lamb with borlotti beans and polenta. The same Italian/Welsh themes extends to the desserts; for each course there's an enormous choice of at least 15 in each category. As you'd expect, the wine list focuses on Italy (thankfully not Wales), with house reds coming in at around £9 a bottle.

SEEING THE SIGHTS

The **castle**, built in 1090, has a depressingly grisly history: in 1176, Norman knight William de Braose invited the local Welsh chiefs to a Christmas meal. Before they could get to the roast turkey and stuffing, they were all slaughtered by de Braose's men. Days later, the Welsh hit back in retaliation and virtually destroyed the castle. There's not much of it left now except a keep that was fancifully restored by the Victorians, but there is a **museum of local history**, which among other things, contains a Welsh Kitchen exhibit with old fashioned implements on display, and a 1950s grocer's store.

Heading out of Abergavenny on the A40 northwest is **Crickhowell**, a pleasant town on the banks of the River Usk, with a ruined castle. Further along, on the A479, is **Tretower Court**, a fortified medieval manor house adjacent to the ruins of a Norman castle. *Open March to October daily 10am to 6pm. Admission £2.50. Tel. 01874 7730279.*

To the southwest of Abergavenny is the village of **Blaenavon**, in one of the valleys that were once the home of a vast, thriving coal mining industry – of which the Rhonnda Valley, immortalized in the film *How Green Was My Valley* – is the best known. Here, inside a real mine that closed more than 20 years ago, is the **Big Pit Mining Museum**. Former miners take you down 250 feet to the pit floor down an old mine shaft. You can see the coal face, the original miners' bathhouses and a blacksmith's workshop. Note: this is not a place to visit if you're claustrophobic. *Open March to November daily 9:30am to 5pm. Admission adults £5.50, children £3.75. Tours take one hour. Tel. 01495 790311.*

PRACTICAL INFORMATION

Abergavenny's **tourist information office** is located in *Swan Meadow, Tel. 01873 857599.*

BRECON

Brecon is a lovely old market town, with a host of fine regency buildings and some pleasant walks by the river. The town makes a fine base for exploring the **Brecon Beacons National Park** (see below under *Seeing the Sights*).

ARRIVALS & DEPARTURES

By Car

From London, take the M4 to Newport, then the A4024 to Brecon.

By Bus

Stagecoach Red & White operate services linking Brecon to Cardiff, Abergavenny and Hereford, *Tel. 01633 266336.* National Express also operates a regular service to Cardiff, which then links with services to other parts of Britain, *Tel. 0990 808080.*

By Train

The nearest train station is at Abergavenny, 20 miles away.

WHERE TO STAY & EAT

BEST WESTERN CASTLE OF BRECON HOTEL, *Castle Square, Brecon LD3 9DB. Tel. 01874 624611, Fax 01874 623737. Rooms: 42. Rates: singles from £45, doubles from £59. Restaurant, two bars. All major credit cards accepted.*

The Castle of Brecon Hotel stands adjacent to the imposing ruins of Brecon Castle, with wonderful views of the Usk Valley and Brecon Beacons National Park. The public rooms include two bars, an additional lounge and a large restaurant. The bedrooms are comfortable enough, with TV and tea- and coffee-making facilities and some of them enjoy nice views over the valley. Parking is available. The great thing about this hotel is the low price.

LLANGOED HALL, *Llyswen, Brecon LD3 0YP. Tel. 01874 754525, Fax 01874 754545. Rooms: 23. Rates: singles from £155, doubles from £185. Restaurants, leisure facilities. All major credit cards accepted.*

This top-notch establishment was founded in 1990 by Sir Bernard Ashley, widower of the late Laura Ashley, and soon became one of the most prestigious places to stay in Wales. The Hall is located in the beautiful Wye Valley on the A470 seven miles northeast of Brecon. The elegant public rooms are festooned with antique and fine furniture and of course Laura Ashley fabrics are all over the place. The bedrooms are sumptuous and many of them have superb views towards the Black Mountains, and there's an excellent restaurant.

SEEING THE SIGHTS

The town has a number of interesting attractions in its own right, chiefly the **cathedral**, fragments of whose Norman construction remain in the walls and nave; most of the what you can see today dates from the 13th and 14th centuries. In the Cathedral Close there's a **heritage centre** with exhibits about the cathedral – past and present. *Admission is free, but a donation of £1 is requested. Tel. 01874 625222.* The **Brecknock Museum** contains a fascinating collection of Welsh lovespoons, a reconstructed Welsh kitchen and a dugout canoe found in a nearby lake. There's also a complete Victorian courtroom. *Open year-round Monday to Saturday 10am to 5pm. Admission 50p. Tel. 01874 624121.* If you're interested in military matters, you might like to visit the **South Wales Borderers' Museum**, which traces the history of the local regiment, *Tel. 01874 613310.*

The Brecon Beacons National Park
This 520-square-mile stretch of rolling hills, windswept moors and deep wooded valleys is about 16 miles from north to south and 45 miles from east to west. The landscape isn't as dramatic as Snowdonia, to the north, but the park is outstandingly beautiful in its own right, and surprisingly green. Though much of the park is in private hands, and given over to sheep farming, much of the region is accessible to the public, making it a great place for walking or pony trekking..

The best place to get information on the Park and its many trails and myriad activities is the National Park Visitor Centre, just west of the A470 at Libanus, five miles southwest of Brecon, where you can get a fine view of **Pen-y-fan**, at 2,900 feet, the highest point in the park and, for that matter, in the whole of south Wales. If you're intending to go hiking take extreme care – even on a warm, calm, summer's day the weather can suddenly turn very nasty. *For information, call 01874 623366.*

LOVESPOONS
In the 17th to 19th centuries many young men in rural Wales would spend hours every evening carving ornamental wooden spoons, known as "love spoons." They would then be presented as tokens to the girls or women they were courting. If the gift was accepted it was a signal that the courtship would lead to marriage; if not, the young man would start making another love spoon. Love spoons can be seen in museums and in homes all over Wales; there's a particularly good collection in the Brecknock Museum in Brecon (see above).

NIGHTLIFE & ENTERTAINMENT
The pubs I'd recommend here are the **Boar's Head**, *Ship Street*, and **Sarah Siddons**, *The Bulwark*.

SWANSEA

Swansea is Wales' second largest city after Cardiff, a sprawling industrial conurbation of close to 200,000 inhabitants. It's not the prettiest of places, though there are some excellent attractions, including a maritime museum in the revitalized maritime quarter. It's also the birthplace of poet **Dylan Thomas**, 1914-1953.

ARRIVALS & DEPARTURES

By Car

The M4 continues past Cardiff to Swansea, which is about 40 miles west of the capital.

By Bus

There's a regular, hourly bus service from Swansea to Cardiff. The journey time is just under an hour. *Call 01792 580580 for information.*

By Train

There are through trains to Swansea from London Paddington. *Call 0345 484950 for details.*

WHERE TO STAY

POSTHOUSE SWANSEA, *The Kingsway Circle, Swansea SA1 5LS. Tel. 0870 400 9078, Fax 01792 456044. Rooms: 99. Rates: singles from £70, doubles from £90. Restaurant, bar, indoor pool, leisure suite. All major credit cards accepted.*

Despite its size, Swansea isn't exactly brimming with hotels, though the recent Marina developments may be changing all that. From what there is, this is one of the best and certainly one of the most convenient for the city's attractions. Located right in the center of the city, the Posthouse offers pleasant, functional bedrooms with TV, tea- and coffee-making facilities and two restaurants, including the Mongolian Barbecue, and a leisure spa with pool, sauna, solarium and gymnasium.

BEAUMONT HOTEL, *72-73 Walter Road, Swansea SA1 4QA. Tel 01792 643956, Fax 01792 643044. Rooms: 17. Rates: singles from £40, doubles from £59.*

Another pleasant, family-run hotel, the Beaumont is within easy reach of Swansea city center with its extensive shopping facilities, and also of the spectacular, windswept Gower peninsula. The hotel, including bedrooms and public areas, has recently been refurbished to a high standard; bedrooms are comfortable and well-equipped, some of them with four-poster beds. There's also a very pleasant dining area, a conservatory, where good home cooking is available.

WHERE TO EAT

LA BRASERIA, *28 Wind Street, Swansea SA1 1DZ. Tel 01792 469683. Open Monday to Saturday noon to 2:30pm, 7pm to 11:30pm. Set lunch from £6.75 (two courses). All major credit cards accepted.*

Value is the word at this lively, occasionally noisy brasserie, where first courses include poached scallops and a delicious fish soup, the main courses ranging from red mullet to steaks. Simplicity is the other byword here; most items tend to be chargrilled. There's a wide range of desserts, some of them a bit on the heavy side, and wines are available by the glass from as little as £2.

HANSON'S, *Pilot House Wharf, Trawler Road, Swansea Marina, Swansea SA1 1UN. Tel 01792 466200. Open daily noon to 2:30pm, 6:30pm to 10pm (closed for dinner Sundays). Credit cards: MC, Visa.*

Located above a fishing tackle shop at the end of the Swansea Marina, Hanson's is an attractive place, filled with maritime memorabilia. Fish figures prominently on the menu, as you'd expect in this location, all good, fresh stuff, but there are also meat and poultry options and some vegetarian choices. Desserts are fairly traditional – my favorite, bread-and-butter pudding takes pride of place here – and house wine starts at about £9.

SEEING THE SIGHTS

Even Swansea has a **castle**! Dating from the 14th century, it's now a ruin, but a pretty one at that. Oliver Cromwell was the main culprit; he "slighted" it in 1647. *Open year-round. Admission free.*

Swansea's **Maritime Quarter** is definitely a must-see. What was a run-down docks area has been transformed into a major tourist attraction, including the **Swansea Museum**, on Victoria Road, which covers local archaeology. *Open year-round Tuesday to Sunday 10am to 5pm. Admission free. Tel. 01792 653763.* Next to the new Marina, the **Swansea Maritime and Industrial Museum** traces the city's development. There's original machinery from a woollen mill that still works, a 'Gilbern Invader,' an early sports car with fiberglass body and a Ford V6 engine made nearby, and upstairs a collection of boats, including a coracle. A steam tug and a lightship are moored nearby in the marina. Close by, just off Somerset Place, is the **Dylan Thomas Centre**, opened by President Jimmy Carter in 1995. It houses a theater, various exhibition galleries, a restaurant, and, most appropriately perhaps given the author's propensity for booze, a bar. *Open Tuesday to Sunday 10:30am to 4:30pm. Admission free. Tel. 01792 463980.*

Swansea's other fascination for me is its **Covered Market**, which sells a wealth of fresh foods, including local cockles from Penclawdd on the

Gower Peninsula, and Welsh laver bread, made from seaweed and totally delicious. The Market has been here since 1830. *Open from Monday to Saturday, 8:30am to 5:30pm.*

NIGHTLIFE & ENTERTAINMENT

The pubs I'd recommend in Swansea are the **The No Sign Bar**, *56 Wynd Street*; **The Adam and Eve**, *High Street*; and **Dylan's Tavern**.

PRACTICAL INFORMATION

Swansea's **tourist information center** on *Singleton Street, Tel. 01792 468321.* The main post office is on The Kingsway, and there are banks in adundance.

TENBY

Tenby is a very attractive seaside town with a cluster of Georgian houses and a harbor flanked on either side by sandy beaches.

ARRIVALS & DEPARTURES

By Car

From Swansea, take the M40 west to the A48, then the A477 west to Tenby. The total distance is just over 50 miles.

By Train

There are through trains from Swansea to Tenby, which operates every day except Sunday. The journey takes about 1 1/2 hours.

WHERE TO STAY

ATLANTIC HOTEL, *The Esplanade SA70 7DU. Tel 01834 842881, fax 01834 842881. Rooms: 42. Rates: singles from £60, doubles from £84. Bar, restaurant, indoor pool, solarium, steam room. All major credit cards accepted.*

As the address implies, the Atlantic is situated on Tenby's main seafront, overlooking the beach and Isle of Caldy. The bedrooms are all very pleasantly furnished and decorated and come with a full range of up-to-date facilities. There's a cocktail bar, an excellent bistro restaurant and a well-equipped leisure facility, with indoor pool and steam room.

ESPLANADE HOTEL, *The Esplanade, Tenby SA70 7DU. Tel and fax 01834 842760. Rooms: 15. Rates: rooms from £40. Bar. All major credit cards accepted.*

Located just outside the old town walls, this delightful hotel overlooks sandy South Beach and Caldey island offshore. Several of the bedrooms, many of which have been recently refurbished, boast excellent sea views, and the public areas are comfortably furnished and decorated in open-plan style. The hotel is closed from November to February.

WHERE TO EAT

PENALLY ABBEY COUNTRY HOUSE, *Penally, Tenby SA70 7PY. Tel 01834 843033. Open 7pm to 8:45pm. Three-course dinner around £30. All major credit cards accepted.*

This country house hotel just outside Tenby has an elegant dining room with a menu that emphasises fresh local produce, including seafood and particularly beef and lamb. There's a good choice of desserts and a good wine list.

SEEING THE SIGHTS

The town still has its medieval walls, within which is a warren of narrow streets full of shops, pubs and restaurants. On Quay Hill, check out the Tudor **Merchant's House**. It dates back to the 15th century and illustrates the life of a merchant during this period. *Open April to October daily except Wednesday and Saturday, 10am to 5pm, Sunday 1pm to 5pm. Admission £1.80. Tel. 01834 842279.*

Like so many other towns in this part of the world, Tenby has a castle, wonderfully located overlooking the sea, and affording lovely views across the bay. Close by on Castle Hill is the **Tenby Museum**, which is a treasure trove of local historical information, *Tel. 01834 842809.*

PRACTICAL INFORMATION

The **tourist information center** is located in *The Croft, Tel. 01834 842404.*

PEMBROKE

Pembroke is a relatively small country town whose history goes back well over 900 years. Its chief attraction is its magnificent castle, which dates originally from 1093, though the current buildings date from a century later, when Anglo-Saxons and Normans set about subjugating the Welsh.

Your best bet if visiting here is to stay in nearby Tenby (see *Where to Stay* above).

ARRIVALS & DEPARTURES

By Car

Pembroke is 14 miles west of Tenby on the A477.

By Bus

Bus #333 operated by First Cymru, *Tel. 01792 580580*, connects Pembroke with Tenby and Swansea.

By Train

Pembroke is on the branch line that connects with Tenby.

GETTING AROUND TOWN

Walking is far and away the best means of getting around this town.

WHERE TO EAT

LEFT BANK, *63 Main Street, Pembroke SA71 4DA. Tel 01646 622333. Open Tuesday to Saturday noon to 2:30pm, 7pm to 9:30pm. Set lunch and dinner (two courses) from £19. Credit cards: MC, Visa.*

As you'd expect with the name, Parisian street scenes decorate the walls of this small restaurant, where fresh local ingredients are given a slightly Gallic twist. Choose from a selection of tasty soups, and for the main course, go for beef with parsnips or maybe the salmon fish cake with curry sauce. There's a good wine list, with house wines coming in at £9.95 a bottle.

SEEING THE SIGHTS

The **castle** is the main attraction here. This Norman edifice retains its massive original walls, punctuated by towers connected by passages. They enclose an area of grass and a parade ground, as well as a cylindrical keep that offers superb views to the town and beyond. Its survival is testament to the solidity of its construction; during the Civil War of 1642-1649, this Royalist stronghold was besieged by Parliamentary forces, but to no avail, such was its strength. Eventually the occupants had to be starved out. This is the site of the birth, in 1457, of Henry Tudor, later to become Henry VII. *Open April to September daily 9:30am to 6pm; November to March 9:30am to 4pm. Admission adults £3, children £2. Tel. 01646 681510.*

Across the road from the castle at Westgate Hill is the **Museum of the Home**, which has a fine collection of domestic implements, including cooking gear from times past and a fascinating collection of toys and games, including the first snakes and ladders board. *Open May to September, Monday to Thursday, 11am to 5pm. Admission adults £1.20, children 90p.*

NIGHTLIFE & ENTERTAINMENT

Good pubs include **The King's Arms**, *Main Street*, which also serves excellent pub food; and **The Old Cross Saws**, *Main Street.*

SPORTS & RECREATION

For you horseriding fans, try the **Pemrokeshire Riding Centre**, *Pennybridge Farm, Hundleton, near Pembroke, Tel. 01646 682513.*

PRACTICAL INFORMATION

At the **tourist information center**, *Commons Road, Tel. 01646 622388,* you can get a good walking guide of the town.

ST. DAVID'S

St. David's is in reality a small village of about 1,500 inhabitants, but earns its title "city" from the presence of its beautiful 12th century cathedral – the most recent occupant of the site – there has been a church here since the sixth century.

ARRIVALS & DEPARTURES

By Car

From Pembroke, take the A477 and A4706 to Haverfordwest, then the A487 to St David's.

By Bus

There are frequent buses from Haverford west.

GETTING AROUND TOWN

Walking is the best way to explore this small city. Otherwise, you can rent a bicycle from Voyages of Discovery, *Tel. 01437 721911,* on the town square for about £10 a day.

WHERE TO STAY

WARPOOL COURT HOTEL, *St. David's SA62 6BN. Tel. 01437 720300, Fax 01437 720676. Rooms: 25. Rates: singles from £61, doubles from £120. Restaurant, indoor pool, leisure suite. All major credit cards accepted.*

The Warpool Court Hotel was originally the choir school of St. David's Cathedral, and is full of charm and character, with many period features. The public rooms are spacious and comfortable, but best of all are the glorious landscaped grounds with views out to sea – just perfect for a leisurely stroll or for reading a book in peace. The bedrooms are nicely decorated and furnished, there's an excellent restaurant – if a bit on the pricey side – and a leisure suite with pool, sauna and gymnasium. If you're the sporty type, there are tennis courts, and a bonus for parents is the special children's play area.

WHERE TO EAT

MORGAN'S BRASSERIE, *20 Nun Street, St David's. Tel.: 01437 720508, Fax 01437 720508. Open Monday to Saturday, noon to 2pm, 7pm to 9:30pm. Main courses around £15. All major credit cards accepted.*

Opened in 1993, this bright, pleasant, modern brasserie has white-washed walls festooned with modern art and is a striking contrast to all the olde worlde stuff outside. But once you get tucked in at your table and take a peek at the menu you realize that maybe it's not so modern after all: when it comes to the menu, it's fairly traditional fare, with items like confit of duck and filet steak with red wine sauce, all using fresh local produce. The desserts are fairly traditional too, but are nicely presented.

SEEING THE SIGHTS

The **Cathedral of St. David** is dedicated to Wales' patron saint, who established a monastic community here some 14 centuries ago, close to where he was born. To this day, his relics are kept inside the cathedral. In medieval times it was a great place of pilgrimage. Indeed, the Church decided that two visits to St. David's was the equivalent of a visit to Rome. The most interesting aspect of the building in some ways is its location down in a hollow. The reason for this was to protect it from being seen and pillaged by Vikings, who were frequent visitors to these shores.

From the outside, the building is not particularly outstanding, but a look inside rewards you with a variety of absorbing sights: **St. David's Shrine** in the north choir aisle; **Bishop Vaughan's Chapel**, with its fine fan vaulting; the beautiful carving on the choir stalls and a carved oak ceiling in the Norman **nave**. It's a wonder (some would say a miracle) that the building hasn't toppled over; the floor slopes one meter upwards and the pillars are way out of kilt, the result of subsidence and an earthquake in 1248. *Open daily from 8am. Admission free, but donation of £2 is suggested. Tel. 01437 720517.*

Across the stream are the remains of the 14th century **Bishop's Palace**, used as a residence until the 16th century. These days it's the spectacular location for outdoor plays. *Open Easter to October daily 9:30am to 6:30pm; November to Easter 9:30am to 4pm. Admission adults £1.70, children £1.20. Tel. 01437 720517.*

Almost a mile to the south of the cathedral is the site of St. David's birth, next to a bay – **St. Non's Bay** – that was named after his mother. When David was born, it's said that a spring appeared. This is still a place of pilgrimage for many; there are ruins of a 13th century chapel dedicated to St. Non, a modern chapel and a retreat house.

Between St. David's and Fishguard, 16 miles to the northeast, is a wonderful unspoilt stretch of coast that's just perfect for walking, starting with Whitesand Bay, a wide sandy beach that's a mecca for surfers. Just off St. David's Head is **Ramsey Island**, owned and maintained by the Royal Society for the Protection of Birds. Cruises round the island are run by **Ramsey Island Pleasure Cruises**, *Tel. 01437 720285,* leaving from the village of St. Justinian, three miles from St. David's. Further north east is the coastal village of **Porthgain**, with the wonderful **Sloop Inn** – one of the best pubs around.

NIGHTLIFE & ENTERTAINMENT

Your best bet for enjoying a pint in St. David's is **The Farmer's Arms**, *Goat Street*, with excellent bar food and a terrace for sitting out in the summer.

SPORTS & RECREATION

As I've already said, there's some great walking to be had round here, especially along the coastal path that extends for 189 miles round the Welsh coast. For information and the best routes, contact the national park visiting center (see below under *Practical Information*).

If you're into scuba diving, St. David's has its own **Scuba Diving Centre**, *Caerfai Bay Road, Tel. 01437 721788*, while **TYF Adventure Days**, *1 High Street, Tel. 01437 721611*, is the place to go if you're interested in canoeing, surfing or kayaking. Boat trips around the coast are offered by **Thousand Island Expeditions**, *Tel. 01437 721611*. Boats depart from nearby Whitesand Bay.

PRACTICAL INFORMATION

The **Pembrokeshire National Park Visitor Centre**, *High Street, Tel. 01437 720392*, offers extensive information on local attractions, walks. Nearby is the city's post office.

FISHGUARD

There's not a great deal to entice you to **Fishguard** – unless you're heading across the sea to Ireland in one of the ferries that operate from the port – but it's not an unattractive place.

ARRIVALS & DEPARTURES

By Car
Fishguard is located 16 miles northeast of St. David's on the A487.

By Bus
An hourly service to Haverfordwest is operated by Richards, *Tel. 01239 820751*, who also have services to St. David's.

By Train
Fishguard's train station is at the end of a line that connects with the main line to London. *Call 0345 484950 for information.*

Ferries
Fishguard is connected to Rosslare, Republic of Ireland by a ferry operated by **Stena Line**, *Tel. 0990 707070.*

WHERE TO STAY

ERW-LON FARM, *Pontfaen, Fishguard SA65 9TS. Tel 01348 881297. Rooms: 3. Rates: single from £20, doubles from £40. No credit cards.*
You can expect a warm welcome and plenty of good home cooking at this Welsh farmhouse that stands well above the beautiful Gwaun Valley, with far-reaching views. The three bedrooms are nicely proportioned and comfortable, with tea- and coffee-making facilities, and there's also a separate lounge for guests.

CARTREF HOTEL, *15-19 High Street, Fishguard SA65 9AW. Tel 01348 872430, Fax 01348 873664. Rooms: 10. Rates: singles from £32, doubles from £49. Bar, restaurant. All major credit cards accepted.*
This small, friendly hotel is conveniently located close to Fishguard town center and within easy reach of the ferry. The rooms are nicely made up and include TVs and tea- and coffee-making facilities. Family rooms are available.

WHERE TO EAT

THREE MAIN STREET, *3 Main Street, Fishguard SA65 9HG. Tel 01348 874275. Open Tuesday to Saturday noon to 2pm, 7pm to 9pm. Set dinner from 321. No credit cards accepted.*
In a place with the name of Fishguard, you'd expect to find at least one decent seafood restaurant, and here it is. Set in a lovely Georgian house, it's an elegant yet relaxed kind of place, where the best local ingredients, from the free-range eggs to freshly caught fish, are used. But the menu is by no means confined to fish; they do a wonderful confit of duck, and the spring lamb on a mound of spring green is out of this world. The desserts

include a mixture of light and heavier fare, and house wine begins at £10.50 a bottle.

SEEING THE SIGHTS

The main focus of life in the town is located on a hill above Goodwick, where the train station and harbor are located. To the east of the town center is Fishguard's picturesque **old harbor**, the location for the filming of *Under Milk Wood*, which brought Elizabeth Taylor and Richard Burton to the town.

In **St. Mary's Town Hall** there's a massive tapestry telling the story of the invasion of Britain in 1940. *Open year-round daily Monday to Saturday 10am to 5pm, Sunday 2pm to 5pm. Admission £1.20. Tel. 01348 874997.*

NIGHTLIFE & ENTERTAINMENT

Interesting pubs in Fishguard are **The Royal Oak**, *The Square*, which contains lots of World War II memorabilia, and **The Fishguard Arms**, *Main Street*.

PRACTICAL INFORMATION

Fishguard's **tourist information center** is in the *Town Hall, Market Square, Tel. 01348 873484.*

The peaceful central part of Wales is a land of green fields, rolling hills, farms, forests and lakes, along with some lovely unspoilt market towns and a host of picturesque villages. The gently undulating terrain in the south of the region gives way to the towering hills and mountains of Snowdonia in the north, while the long coastline is punctuated by rocky headlands and wide, sandy estuaries, with some excellent beaches to boot. If you really want to get far away from the crowds, it's hard to beat mid-Wales.

LLANDRINDOD WELLS

Llandribdod Wells is known to locals as Llandod. It's an old spa town 700 feet above sea level that has managed to retain much of its Victorian charm, though there's evidence that the site was occupied by the Romans many centuries before. The Victorian legacy is a fussy hodgepodge of towers and turrets, balustrades, cupolas – but somehow it works here. Although the town was a spa as early as 1670, it was not until the coming of the railroad in the 19th century that the place really began to take off.

ARRIVALS & DEPARTURES

By Car
Llandrindod Wells is about 68 miles north of Cardiff, on the A470.

By Train
Llandrindod has a station on the Shrewsbury to Swansea rail line, known as the Heart of Wales Line. Approximately five trains a day stop here. You can connect with the main London intercity line at either of these destinations. *Call 0345 484950 for information.*

By Bus
There are direct bus services to Cardiff and to Hereford, just over the English border. Both have connections to London. *For local bus service information, call 01597 851226.*

SEEING THE SIGHTS

In **Memorial Gardens**, you can visit a museum that traces the development of Llandod as a spa and explains in detail some of the "cures" practised by the Victorians. *Open May to October every day except Wednesday and Sunday, 10am to 12:30pm, 2pm to 4:30pm. Rest of year open Saturday 10am to 12:30pm only. Admission free. Tel. 01597 824513.*

In **Rock Park**, you can visit the town's restored **Pump Room**, where visitors used to "take the waters" in the hope that they would cure them of some ailment or another. You can "take the water" outside the Pump Room, but inside it serves tea and refreshments.

Between Llandrindod Wells and Aberystwyth is the **Elan Valley**, known as the "Lake District of Wales." The lakes, all seven miles of them, were actually man-made in the 1890s, when local rivers were dammed up to store water for the fast-growing city of Birmingham, 75 miles away. From Llandrindod, you need to take the A4081 and A470 to **Rhyader**, the best base for exploring the lakes region.

NIGHTLIFE & ENTERTAINMENT

If you're thirsty after a day of are sightseeing, head to the **The Llanerch**, *Waterloo Road.*

PRACTICAL INFORMATION

The town's **tourist information center** is in the *Old Town Hall, Memorial Gardens, Tel. 01597 822600.*

LLANGOLLEN INTERNATIONAL EISTEDDFOD

*The annual **Eisteddfod** is a celebration of Welsh culture held annually at Llangollen. All over Wales local **eisteddfodau** ("sittings") are held in schools, chapels and local halls, where local musicians, dancers, actors, artists and writers compete to reach the next stage of the in the two categories of **Awdl** (a form of ancient Welsh poetry) and **Pryddest** (free verse). The national competition reaches its climax in the first week of August, when the whole proceedings is presided over by the Gorsedd of Bards in their traditional druid robes.*

ABERYSTWYTH

Aberystwyth, half-way along Cardigan Bay, is a lively, attractive small town of 9,000, but with enough major attractions to make it feel like a place ten times its size. It's primarily a seaside resort – and a popular one at that – with a pleasant beach below a rugged headland and a small harbor where you can watch the boats coming in. It's also a university town; the university houses the **National Library of Wales**, open to visitors. It's also a great base for exploring the gorgeous countryside around.

ARRIVALS & DEPARTURES

By Car

From Cardiff, take the A470 north to Llangurig, then the A44 west to Aberystwyth.

By Bus

There's one National Express bus a day from London Victoria to Aberystwyth, a journey that takes around 7 1/2 hours. From Cardiff there's a direct service three times a day operated by Arriva Cymru, *Tel. 01970 617951.*

By Train

Aberystwyth is on the Cambrian rail line which runs from Shrewsbury, with trains every couple of hours. There are through trains from London to Shrewsbury. The train station is located on Alexandra Road.

GETTING AROUND TOWN

Aberystwyth has a compact town center that can easily be negotiated on foot. Or you might want to join the hordes of university students by renting a bicycle. Try **On Your Bike**, *Tel. 01970 626996, Old Police Yard, Queen's Road.*

WHERE TO STAY

CONRAH HOTEL, *Ffosrhydygaled, Chancery, Aberystwyth SY23 4DF. Tel. 01970 617941, Fax 01970 624546. Rooms: 20. Rates: singles from £78, doubles from £125. Restaurant, bar, lounges, garden, sauna, swimming pool. All major credit cards accepted.*

This farmhouse hotel, located a few miles south of Aberystwyth on the A487, was built in the 18th century, though parts of it may be earlier. The house was significantly upgraded in Victorian times but suffered a serious blaze in 1911, and was rebuilt all over again. As you'd expect from a large house of this period, there's an abundance of wood paneling, plasterwork and stained glass; the pleasant lounges and dining rooms offer lovely views of the Merionnydd Hills.

The rooms are fairly large and comfortable, with TV, hairdryers and all the other features you'd expect in a hotel of this type. Particularly attractive is the bar, with light bamboo decor and lots of parlor palms. Slightly cheaper rooms are available in the adjacent coach house.

RICHMOND HOTEL, *44 Marine Terrace, Aberystwyth SY23 2BX. Tel 01970 612201, Fax 01970 626706. Rooms: 15. Rates: singles from, Doubles from. Bar, restaurant. All major credit cards accepted.*

As the address implies, this hotel is located right on the promenade/ boardwalk in Aberystwyth, with far-reaching views both from the public rooms and from many of the bedrooms, all of which are comfortably furnished and well-equipped. There's a large bar, and a dining room with an a la carte menu.

WHERE TO EAT

CONRAH HOTEL, *Ffosrhydygaled, Chancery, Aberystwyth SY23 4DF. Tel 01970 617941. Open noon to 2pm, 7pm to 9pm. Three course meal from £27. All major credit cards accepted.*

Nice country house hotel (see above) with fantastic views of the Cambrian Mountains and with a good restaurant serving meals using the freshest local ingredients. The beef is particularly good, and the mouth-watering array of desserts include a mixture of old favorites and more contemporary choices.

BELLE VUE ROYALE HOTEL, *Marine Terrace, Aberystwyth SY23 2BA. Tel 01970 617558. Open 12:30pm to 2pm, 6:30pm to 8:30pm. Dinner around £18. All major credit cards accepted.*

This small family-run hotel is right on Aberystwyth's seafront. There's a good, solid menu with plenty of local specialties, including rack of Welsh lamb and Welsh beef steaks. There's a good choice of desserts and a decent wine list, the hosue wines coming in under £9.

SEEING THE SIGHTS

Aberystwyth's **castle**, above south beach at the southern end of town, was begun in 1277 and extended in 1282 by Edward I in his aim of subjugating the Welsh. However, it was taken in 1404 by the Welsh rebel leader **Owain Glyndwr**, then two and a half centuries later destroyed by Oliver Cromwell. Today it's yet one more romantic ruin with fine views across the bay and out to sea. At the far end of the Marine Terrace is the **cliff railway**, the longest of its kind in Britain, running from the Promenade to the top of Constitution Hill, a climb of 430 feet. At the top is the **Great Aberystwyth Camera Obscura**, its 14-inch lens giving you a look not only at the town below, but beyond, including 26 mountain peaks. *Trains: Easter to October 10am to 6pm. Fee: adults £2, children £1. Entrance to Camera Obscura free. Tel. 01970 617642.*

North of the town center, the **university campus** contains a theater, concert hall and arts center, as well as the imposing **Welsh National Library**, with more than five million books and various ancient manuscripts on show. *Open Monday to Friday 9:30am to 6pm, Saturday 9:30am to 5pm. Free. Tel. 01970 623800.*

Other attractions in Aberystwyth include the **Ceredigion Museum** in the old Coliseum Theatre on Terrace Road, restored to its Edwardian glory in the 1980s. The museum contains displays relating to the main occupations of people of the region: agriculture, lead mining and seafaring. *Open Monday to Saturday 10am to 5pm. Admission free. Tel. 01970 617911.*

From Aberystwyth train station you can also take the narrow-gauge **Vale of Rheidol Railway** on the twelve-mile journey to **Devil's Bridge**, where the River Theidol and the River Mynach converge in a series of spectacular falls, as their gurgling waters are squeezed through a gap between two cliffs. The lowest of the three bridges here is known as the Devil's Bridge because legend has it that the devil himself built it, though God knows why. There are actually three bridges here, the oldest of which is more than 800 years old. The steam trains ply the route twice a day from Easter to October, four times a day in July and August, but the timetable is rather complicated, so I advise you to call the Railway when planning your trip or when you arrive, *Tel. 01970 625819.*

NIGHTLIFE & ENTERTAINMENT

A number of hotels put on live entertainment during the summer months. Decent pubs include the **Castle Hotel**, *Castle Terrace*, and **Rummers Wine Bar**, *by the river on Bridge Street*. To see what's happening on campus: *Tel. 01970 623800*.

PRACTICAL INFORMATION

The **tourism office** is *on Terrace Road, at the junction with Bath Street,* *Tel. 01970 612125*. Aberystwyth has branches of all the main banks.

MACHYNLLETH

Machynlleth is a pleasant country town with a long wide main street lined with buildings in a variety of architectural styles. The town is best known for its association with **Owain Glyndwr**, the last native Welsh leader, who established a Welsh parliament here in the early 1400s. More recently, the town has been known as a center for green living, the result of the presence of a Centre for Alternative Technology on the edge of town.

ARRIVALS & DEPARTURES

By Car

Machynlleth is on the A487 about 17 miles from Aberystwyth.

By Bus

There's a regular bus service from Aberystwyth to Machynlleth, operated by Arriva Cymru, *Tel. 01970 617951*.

By Train

Machynlleth is on the Shrewsbury to Aberystwyth train line.

GETTING AROUND

Macynlleth is easily explored on foot. Cycles can be rented from **Greenstiles**, *Tel. 01654 703543*.

WHERE TO STAY

MAENLLWYD, *Newtown Road, Machynlleth SY20 8EY. Tel and Fax 01654 702928. Rooms: 8. Rates: singles from £25, doubles from £40. All majore credit cards accepted.*

Located on the outskirts of Machynlleth, within easy reach of the local golf course and the town center, this attractive Victorian house offers a warm welcome. Surrounded by lawns and gardens, the bedrooms are comfortable with all modern conveniences, there's a large comfortable lounge, and plenty of parking space.

WYNNSTAY HOTEL, *Maengwyn Street, Machynlleth SY20 8AE. Tel 01654 702941, Fax 01654 703884. Rooms: 23. Rates: singles from £45, doubles from £70. Bar, restaurant. All major credit cards accepted.*

The historic Wynnstay is located right in the center of Machynlleth, close to the shops and attractions. The bedrooms are comfortable, with a full range of facilities; some have four-poster beds. The bars are popular with the locals, and you can get good bar food here. For those in search of a "proper" meal, there's a more formal restaurant with an extensive prix fixe menu.

WHERE TO EAT

YNYSHIR HALL, *Eglwysfach, Machynlleth SY20 8TA. Tel 01654 781209. Open daily 12:30pm to 1:30pm, 7pm to 8:30pm. Three-course dinner (3 choices for each course) £37. All major credit cards accepted.*

This lovely white Georgian mansion is the setting for a fine, elegant restaurant with a strong Mediterranean ambience, with hand-painted menus and a host of other thoughtful trimmings. The menu is likely to include such delights as roast monkfish with fennel and a wide range of deserts, including pears poached in wine. There's an extensive wine list, focusing, as you'd expect, on French.

SEEING THE SIGHTS

Among the attractions here are the **Glyndwr Parliament House**, with displays relating to life in medieval Wales and an exhibition about **Owain Glyndwr**, the last native Welsh leader. More impressive, though, is Celtica, a large exhibition center in the park behind the shops, that traces the history of the Celtic people, not only in Wales, but throughout Europe. The main focus of the center is an imaginative multimedia presentation showing life in an ancient Celtic settlement, and a meeting with a Druid. The center also houses a bookshop and restaurant. *Open year-round daily 10am to 6pm. Admission £4.65, children £3.50. Tel. 01654 702702.*

PRACTICAL INFORMATION

The **tourist information center** is in the *Owain Glyndwr Centre, Tel. 01654 702401.*

DOLGELLAU

Dolgellau (pronounced Dol-gethlee) is a pleasant market town with a cluster of dark stone buildings and a couple of old coaching inns. It makes a great base for walks on nearby **Cadair Idris**, the second highest peak in the **Snowdonia National Park**.

ARRIVALS & DEPARTURES

By Car

The most pleasant way of getting to Dolgellau from Machynlleth is to take coastal A493, where you'll be rewarded with some spectacular views.

By Bus

From Aberystwyth, Arriva Cymru bus # 32 serves Dolgellau seven times a day.

GETTING AROUND TOWN

This is a small town, and the only sensible way to get around is on foot.

WHERE TO STAY & EAT

TY ISAF, Llanfachreth, Dolgellau LL40 2EA. Tel. 01341 423261. Rooms: 3. Rates: single from £37, double from £54. Lounge, study, garden. No credit cards accepted.

This small guest house located in a picturesque valley just outside Dolgellau is a great get-away-from-it-all place. The house is actually a Welsh longhouse, with lots of character, including a lounge with inglenook fireplace and a dining room with original oak beams. The rooms are very comfortable, with cottagey furniture, more beams and, of course, views. The food in the restaurant is exquisite; lots of fresh local produce and some local recipes to boot. When you take a look out of the window, you may notice two very odd shapes outside: these are Math and Mathonwy, two llamas that were introduced here by the owners back in 1996.

SEEING THE SIGHTS

Back in the 15th century the town was a stronghold of Owain Glyndwr, and his parliament was held here for a while. The town has strong liunks with the Quaker Movement, and in the main Eldon Square, above the tourist information center, you can visit the **Museum of the Quakers**, with exhibits relating to the growth of Quakerism and the emigration of so many of them to America. *Open summer daily 10am to 6pm, winter 10am to 4pm. Admission to Quaker Museum free.*

The town was also for many years an important center for the wool industry. Later on, it became a gold prospecting town; good-quality gold was discovered nearby in the 1800s and Dolgellau gold is still used to make royal wedding rings. From Dolgellau you can get the courtesy bus for the hour and a half journey to **Gwynfynydd Gold Mine**, well to the north of the town amid dense forests. The bus leaves from the **Welsh Gold Visitor Centre** in Dolgellau. *Open April to Octoiber 9:30am to 4pm. Admission £10. Tel. 01341 423332.*

South of the town looms **Cader Idris**, at 2,947 feet the second highest mountain in Snowdonia. You can get information on trails up the mountain from the tourist information center.

NIGHLIFE & ENTERTAINMENT

The **George III** pub, *Penmaenpool,* just outside Dolgellau, has a good selection of bar food.

PRACTICAL INFORMATION

The **National Park Information Centre** is in *Eldon Square, Tel. 01341 422888.*

BARMOUTH

Barmouth is a traditional and popular seaside town located on the northern side of the pretty Mawddach Estuary.

ARRIVALS & DEPARTURES

By Car

Barmouth is just 10 miles west of Dolgellau on the A496.

By Bus

There is a regular bus service between Barmouth and Dolgellau.

WHERE TO STAY

WAVECREST HOTEL, *8 Marine Parade, Barmouth LL42 1NA. Tel./ Fax 01341 280330. Rooms: 9. Rates: singles from £23, doubles from £40. Bar, restaurant. Credit cards: MC, Visa.*

This small hotel is right on the seafront at Barmouth with views from many of its rooms across Cardigan Bay to the Cader Idris mountains. The bedrooms are attractively furnished and decorated with a full range of facilities; there's a bar with an extensive selection of malt whiskies on offer, and a fine restaurant where fresh local produce is used.

BRYN MELYN HOTEL, *Panorama Road, Barmouth LL42 1DQ. Tel 01341 280556, Fax 01341 280342. Rooms: 9. Rates: singles from £29, doubles from ££44. Bar, restaurant. All major credit cards accepted.*

Situated in extensive grounds overlooking the Mawddach estuary, the Bryn Melyn is a family-run establishment with nine comfortable well-equipped rooms and a very pleasant conservatory, done out with cane furniture. You can also benefit from a pleasant lounge and a small restaurant where good home cooking is available.

WHERE TO EAT

TY'R GRAIG CASTLE HOTEL, *Llanaber Road, Barmouth LL42 1YN. Tel 01341 280470.*

This unusual property, just outside of Barmouth on the A496, was built by a gunsmith in Victorian times in the shape of a double-barrelled shotgun. Today, it's the location for a very pleasant restaurant serving British/European cuisine, and using the best local produce. The wide range of dishes available includes traditional favorites with a contemporary twist – such as medallions of local beef with tomato couscous. There's a good wine list.

SEEING THE SIGHTS

The **Mawddach Estuary** is a great place to relax and enjoy the sea air for a while. There's a long stretch of sandy beach flanked by a Promenade, and a cluster of hotels. Barmouth has been a popular resort for some time, and has attracted more than its fair share of gliterati over the years: **Alfred, Lord Tennyson** was one such visitor. He wrote part of his *In Memoriam* here. **Percy Bysse** and **Mary Shelley** stayed here in 1812 and **Charles Darwin** worked on the *Origin of Species* from a house in the front. **John Ruskin** was another frequent visitor.

PRACTICAL INFORMATION

Barmouth's **tourist information center** is located on *Station Road, Tel. 01341 280787.*

WELSHPOOL

The best – maybe the only – reason for coming to Welshpool is to visit **Powis Castle**, one of the most impressive medieval fortresses in Wales.

ARRIVALS & DEPARTURES

By Car

Welshpool is just south of the A458, some 50 miles east of Barmouth.

By Train
Welshpool is on the Shrewsbury to Aberystwyth train line. The journey to Shrewsbury takes about half an hour.

GETTING AROUND TOWN
This is another small town, so walking is the way to go.

WHERE TO STAY
ROYAL OAK HOTEL, *Welshpool, SY21 7DG. Tel 01938 552217, fax 01938 556652. Rooms: 24. Rates: singles from £45, doubles from £75. All major credit cards accepted.*

This pleasant, traditional hotel in this old market town is more than 350 years old and has been taken over by the Best Western chain. The bedrooms are all well-equipped and pleasantly decorated, and there are several bars and a cafe/restaurant where full meals are served throughout the day and evening.

GUNGROG HOUSE, *Rhallt, Welshpool SY21 9HS. Tel 01938 553381, Fax 01938 554612. Rooms: 3. Rates: single from £40, doubles from £50. No credit cards.*

Located about two miles out of Welshpool, off the A458, the non-smoking Gungrog House is an attractive 16th century building affording superb views over the Severn Valley and Powis Castle. There are three attractive bedrooms, a pleasantly furnished lounge and some additional holiday cottages for let in the grounds.

WHERE TO EAT
GOLFA HOTEL, *Llanfair Road, Welshpool SY21 9AF. Tel 01938 553399. Open noon to 2pm, 7pm to 9pm. Dinner from £18. All major credit cards accepted.*

The Golfa Hotel was converted from one of the original farmhouses of the Powis Castle estate. The pleasant restaurant serves what is best described as modern British cooking with a strong French influence, and using the freshest local ingredients. There's a good sweets trolley and a wine list where house wines start at around £10.

SEEING THE SIGHTS
As I said above, the main reason to come to Welshpool is to visit the majestic **Powis Castle**. Built in the 13th century and continuously occupied ever since, it's notable for its sturdy red walls and battlements and some lovely terraced gardens, enclosed by vast yew hedges atop wide lawns and Elizabethan gardens. The opulent castle contains paintings by Gainsborough and Reynolds, a collection of Greek vases, a 16th century

Italian antique table inlaid with marble, and a host of treasures, mainly Indian art, brought back by Clive of India. There's a wonderful tea room and a shop. *Open April to October Wednesday to Sunday (plus Tuesday in July and August), gardens 11am to 6pm, castle noon to 5pm. Admission adults £7.50, children £3.75. Tel. 01938 554336.*

A few miles to the south, the village of Berriew is home to the **Andrew Logan Museum of Sculpture**. Logan is one of Britain's top sculptors and this fine (if a bit tongue-in-cheek) collection is well worth a visit if you like that sort of thing. *Open May to October weekends 2pm to 6pm; July and August Wednesday to Sunday 2pm to 6pm; November, December Sundays oinly. Admission £2. Tel. 01686 640689.*

PRACTICAL INFORMATION

Welshpool's **tourist information center** is in the *Vicarage Gardens car park, Tel. 01938 552043.*

This is easily Wales' most spectacular region. It has a dramatic landscape of mountains, lakes, rivers, moorlands and a rugged coastline with a host of man-made features that enhance, rather than detract, from its beauty: the Menai Straits Bridge to Anglesey, Harlech Castle and Carnarvon Castle, to name but a few. The region is dominated by the towering mass of **Mount Snowdon**, at 3,560 feet the tallest mountain in England and Wales. Snowdon gives its name to the 840 square miles of **Snowdonia National Park**, one of the last great places in England and Wales to truly get away from it all. However, it's not always peaceful. In recent years it has become one of the most popular places anywhere for walkers who arrive in droves, especially during the summer months.

To the north, the sandy coast is home to a bevy of seaside resorts, **Llandudno** and **Colwyn Bay** being the chief among them, as well as **Anglesey**, where Welsh is spoken more frequently than English, and the beautiful **Llyn Peninsula** jutting out into the Irish Sea.

PORTHMADOG

Porthmadog, the gateway to the beautiful Llyn pensinsula, is a small seaside town with a harbor that was originally built to transport slate from nearby Blaenau Ffestiniog. It's an attractive little place, popular in the summer. There are some lovely beaches around.

ARRIVALS & DEPARTURES

By Car

Porthmadog is on the main A487, which links Aberystwyth and Caernarfon.

By Bus

Express Motors, out of Caernarfon, operate a regular service every hour from Caernarfon to Porthmadog. *Call 01286 674570 for information.*

By Train

There are trains from Portmadog to Shrewsbury, changing at Machynlleth.

GETTING AROUND TOWN

This is another small town, so walking is the way to go.

WHERE TO STAY

HOTEL PORTMEIRION, *Portmeirion, Penrhyndeudraeth LL48 6ET. Tel. 01766 770000, Fax 01766 771331. Rooms: 29, suites 11. Rates: singles from £85, doubles from £105, suite from £125. Restaurant, bar, lounges, library, gardens, outdoor pool, tennis. All major credit cards accepted.*

If you're a fan of the cult TV series *The Prisoner*, you'll know exactly what to expect here: a model Italian village (allegedly modeled on Portofino), with narrow lanes, whitewashed and pastel shaded cottages, cupolas and bell tower. The main villa houses some lovely public rooms, including a restaurant with marble pillars, and some of the bedrooms, though most people choose to stay in the various rooms and cottages scattered throughout the landscaped grounds – all of which are luxuriously furnished, some of which come with stunning views. If you want somewhere different to stay, and don't mind hordes of day-trippers gaping at you, this is the place for you.

CASTLE COTTAGE, *Penllech, Harlech LL46 2YL. Tel. and Fax 01766 780479. Rooms: 6. Rates: singles from £27, doubles from £58. Restaurant, lounge. Credit cards: MC, Visa.*

One of the oldest buildings in Harlech, this 16th century castle has, shall we say, a bit of a pig theme about it: the place is full of porky paraphernalia, such as clocks, pictures, figurines, piggy banks and so on – and even the rooms are named after breeds of pigs. Once you've got over the initial shock of it all, you'll discover that the rooms are a bit on the small side, but are nicely decorated and furnished. The best are on the top floor, where the sloping ceilings and fine views to the castle and beyond add to the atmosphere. The restaurant is a lovely space with beamed ceilings, and, yes, expect to find ham and pork on the menu.

WHERE TO EAT

THE HOTEL PORTMEIRION, *Portmeirion, Penrhyndeudraeth. Tel.: 01766 770000. Open daily noon to 2pm, 6pm to 10pm. Main courses around £18. All major credit cards accepted.*

The glorious setting of the hotel has to be seen to be believed. Your visit to the highly acclaimed restaurant is rewarded with superb views over the Traeth Bach estuary. The old Victorian villa was converted into a hotel in 1926, and the restaurant added four years later. The menu's emphasis is modern Welsh, with a hint of Mediterranean – perhaps not surprising in such a Mediterranean outpost. The menu is not overburdened with too many choices; in fact these are generally limited to a very sensible five – all using fresh local ingredients. There's a sensible dessert list (by sensible I mean not heavy) and a wine list that mirrors the menu in choice and emphasis.

SEEING THE SIGHTS

You approach the town by a mile-long embankment known as the **Cob** (for which there is a small toll charge). From the town quay, the oldest and most famous of the Welsh narrow-gauge railway lines runs along the Cob up though a beautiful wooded valley and mountains to Baleau Ffestiniog. *For information about train services, call 01766 512340.*

Just east of Porthmadoc is the remarkable village of **Portmeiron**, a fantasy Italian village said to be modeled on Portofono. It was constructed in 1926 by the architect Clough Williams-Ellis (1883-1978), and there's a hotel, town hall and cottages that are let to guests. The village became particularly famous when it was used for the filing of the cult television series *The Prisoner*, starring Patrick MacGoohan. It truly is an exceptional, relaxing place, and has entertained many famous celebrities over the years. Close by, at **Tremadog** is the site of the birth of **T.E Lawrence**, better known as Lawrence of Arabia, who spent most of his later years in Dorset.

South of here, on the B4573, is one of Wales' most spectacular castles – **Harlech**, built in the 13th century and totally dominating the tiny coastal town below it. The castle was the scene in 1468 of a heroic defense by Welsh leader Dadydd ap Eynion, who later survived an eight year siege during the Wars of the Roses, and was the last fortification in Wales to fall in the 17th century Civil War. *Open late March to October 9:30am to 6:30pm; reest of year Monday to Saturday 9:30am to 4pm. Admission £3.50. Tel. 01766 780552.*

PRACTICAL INFORMATION

The **tourist information center** is on *High Street, Tel. 01766 512981.*

BETWS-Y-COED

This small resort town is a good base for exploring **Snowdonia National Park**.

ARRIVALS & DEPARTURES

By Car

The A470 links Betws-y-Coed to Llandudno in the north, Blaenau Ffestiniog further south.

By Bus

Buses leave regularly from Llandudno for Betws-y-Coed.

By Train

Betws-y-coed is served by seven trains a day trains from Llandudno, with a journey time of 35 minutes.

GETTING AROUND TOWN

Betws-y-Coed can be seen on foot, but this is a great area for walking, and the information center (see below) has information on various hiking trails in the vicinity. Bicycling is another option, and **Beics Betws**, *Tan Lan, Tel. 01690 710766*, who rent out mountain bikes, are a mine of information as to what routes to take.

WHERE TO STAY

THE FERNS, *Holyhead Road, Bewts-y-Coed LL24 0AN. Tel. and Fax 01690 710587. Rooms: 9. Rates: single from £25, doubles from £42. Credit cards: MC, Visa.*

Not particularly inspiring from the outside, and not particularly inspiring from the inside, for that matter, The Ferns does, however, have a lot going for it: a comfortable, cozy, unpretentious ambience, with comfortable bedrooms (though the rooms at the front can be a bit on the noisy side). Best of all is the atmosphere: on arrival you're treated like long-lost relatives by the owners, who from that moment on will go out of their way to make your stay a pleasant and happy one – whether it's packed lunches, flasks of tea or coffee – or just advice on the best places to walk. Not surprisingly there's a good hearty breakfast (but no evening meals are served – there are places locally).

GLYNTWROG HOUSE, *Betws-y-Coed LL24 0SG. Tel 01690 710930, Fax 01690 710512. Rooms: rates (per person per night): from £22. Credit cards: MC, Visa.*

Located just outside the village (but within 10 minutes' walking distance) in six acres of tranquil woodland with wonderful views of the

Conwy Valley, this small, welcoming B&B offers comfortable, cozy accommodations and excellent home-cooked food. You can opt for the B&B only; dinner costs an additional £10 per person.

SUMMER HILL NON-SMOKERS' GUEST HOUSE, *Coed Cynhelir Road, Beyws-y-Coed LL24 0BL. Tel./Fax 01690 710306. Rooms: Rates (per person per night) from £17.50. Lounge, restaurant. All major credit cards accepted.*

Surrounded by peaceful gardens, and overlooking the river, Summer Hills boasts seven extremely comfortable rooms, a residents' lounge and a wood-paneled dining room where good, hearty home-cooked meals are served (breakfast included, dinner extra). The Guest House is just 150 yards from shops and cafes.

WHERE TO EAT

TAN-Y-FOEL, *Capel Garmon, Betws-y-Coed. Tel. 01690 710507. Open for dinner only, 6:30pm to 9:30pm. Set dinner £33. All major credit cards accepted.*

Chef Janet Pitman's appearance on BBC2 TV in 1999 clearly hasn't gone to her head: the fine dining tradition that she established here continues, and meticulously cooked fresh produce is the order of the day. Though her signature dish may be Celtic pancakes with Carmarthen ham, pork and sage and apple puree, the menu in the beautiful country manor house restaurant – decorated with bright modern colors – reflects much broader tastes, particularly Italian, hence the loin of pork with apple puree, Parma ham, potato cakes and apple wine gravy. The desserts are equally tempting, ranging from a selection of fresh fruits, to a Welsh cheese plate with celery.

THE WHITE HORSE, *Capel Garmon, Betws-y-Coed LL26 ORW. Tel 01690 710271. Open Wednesday, Thursday, Sunday 7pm to 9:30pm, Friday, Saturday 7pm to 9:30pm. Main courses from £9.95. All major credit cards accepted.*

This 16th century inn right in the heart of Snowdonia offers superb views. The inn is noted for its cozy Cottage restaurant, where the Chef's Special – Welsh lamb in red wine with garlic, tomatoes and rosemary – is a great favorite, as is the filet steak in Stilton cream sauce. Bar meals are also available seven days a week and there's a good wine list.

SEEING THE SIGHTS

This small mountain resort – an ideal base for exploring the **Snowdonia National Park** – is best known for the picturesque **Swallow Falls**, just to its west, where the River Llugwy cascades down a wooden valley. The rivers Llugwy and Conwy converge at Betws-y-coed, which has some lovely views of Snowdonia, and a clutch of hotels, restaurants and a number of excellent craft shops. Spanning the Conwy is an ornate iron bridge built by Thomas Telford, and erected in 1815.

SNOWDONIA NATIONAL PARK

The Snowdonia National Park offers some of the most beautiful and dramatic landscapes in Britain – over 800 square miles of mountains, deep valleys, lakes, rivers and wide expanses of moorland. The Park gets its name, of course from the 3,560-foot Mount Snowdon, not tall by American or Canadian standards but easily the highest peak in England and Wales. It's located in the southwestern corner of the Park.

At its foot, from the town of Llanberis, you can get the Snowdon Mountain Railway with staggering views as you ascend the mountain – views which on a clear day extend towards Ireland, and south to the mountains of Merionethshire and Harlech Castle. Check the weather forecast, though – the mountain can suddenly be enveloped in swirling mist. The park is popular with hikers, climbers and simple holidaymakers, staying perhaps for a few days in one of the string of small seaside resorts that line the northern coast – all wanting to explore (often it seems, all at once) the highways and byways of this oasis of tranquillity, by car or by bus – or even by train.

Apart from the raw beauty of the place, what attracts many to this area is that it is one of the few places in England and Wales where you can get a real sense of isolation and solitude. Therein lies the problem; as its popularity as a walking, climbing and sightseeing destination increases, so the environmental pressures increase; there's already concern that Mount Snowdon itself is being worn down by hikers and climbers. Of course, summer is easily the busiest time here, but both spring and fall have a beauty of their own; spring with broad swaths of wild flowers, the bright green of new grass; autumn with its foliage, haunting mists and an almost tangible – and mystical – silence.

NIGHTLIFE & ENTERTAINMENT

Good pubs in town are at the **Cross Keys Hotel**, *High Street*, and **Pont-y-Pair Hotel**, *High Street*.

SPORTS & RECREATION

If you'd like to go pony trekking, try **Ty Coch Farm**, just outside of Betws, *Tel. 01690 760248.*

PRACTICAL INFORMATION

The **Snowdonia National Park Visitor Centre** is at *Royal Oak Stables, just past the train station, Tel. 01690 710426.*

LLANBERIS

This small village at the foot of **Mount Snowdon** is another important center for visitors to Snowdonia National Park. Its location is spectacular – straddled between two lakes at the foot of the **Llanberis Pass**, a steep-sided gorge that cuts through the mountains in the park.

ARRIVALS & DEPARTURES

By Car

Llanberis is located about eight miles south east of Caernarfon, just off the A4086.

By Bus

There are regular bus services from Llanberis to Caernarfon and, in the high season, to Llandudno.

GETTING AROUND TOWN

There's only really one street in Llanberis – High Street – so everything is within easy walking distance.

WHERE TO STAY

ROYAL VICTORIA HOTEL, *Llanberis LL55 4TY. Tel 01286 870253, Fax 01286 870149. Rooms: 111. Rates: singles from £29.50, doubles from £59. Bar, restaurant. All major credit cards accepted.*

The Royal Victoria is located close to the foot of Mount Snowdon, almost opposite the Snowdon Mountain Railway on the A4086. Well established and popular, the hotel is surrounded by attractive grounds. The public rooms are large and spacious and there's a large restaurant with conservatory overlooking the nearby Peris and Padarn lakes. The hotel's bedrooms have recently been refurbished to a high standard.

PLAS COCH GUEST HOUSE, *High Street, Llanberis LL55 4HB. Tel 01286 872122, Fax 01286 872648. Rooms: 7. Rates: singles from £20, doubles from £32. No credit cards.*

This solid-looking stone house is set in attractive grounds and is close to the Snowdon Railway and other local amenities. The bedrooms are comfortable, with period furnishings, tea- and coffee-making facilities and are non-smoking. There's a cozy guests' lounge.

WHERE TO EAT

Y BISTRO, *43-45 High Street, Llanberis LL55 4EU. Tel 01286 871278. Open Monday to Saturday 7:30pm to 9.45pm. Closed Mondays and Tuesdays in winter. Set dinner from £20. Credit cards: MC, Visa.*

This pleasant restaurant is in fact three dining rooms, occupying what used to be a corner shop. The food is excellent; hearty, well-prepared fresh local fare, such as baked filet of trout and a delicious seafood risotto cake. The dessert list is equally enticing, but fairly traditional, and maybe a bit on the heavy side – unless your a devotee of suet. The wine list starts at £9 a bottle.

SEEING THE SIGHTS

There are a number of hiking trails from the top of the the the **Llanberis Pass**, a steep-sided gorge that cuts through the mountains in the park, but the terrain is dangerous, particularly in bad weather. Prospective hikers must take every precaution before heading out.

Llanberis is also the point of embarkation for the **Snowdon Mountain Railway**, a rack-and-pinion affair which climbs within 70 feet of the top of England and Wales' highest mountain. Some of the track is amazingly steep, but that doesn't seem to deter the thousands of visitors who come here every year. If, weather permitting, you get to the top, you'll be rewarded with stunning views not only of Wales, but of much of England, and as far distant as the Wicklow mountains in Ireland. *Open March to October. Tel. 01286 870223. Round trip fare £16.*

Across the lake in Padarn Country Park is the **Welsh Slate Museum**, part of the old Dinorwig Slate Quarry, where you can see demonstrations of how slat is split into roof tiles. *Open April to September 9:30am to 5:30pm. Admission £3.50. Tel. 01286 870630.*

NIGHTLIFE & ENTERTAINMENT

Check out the pub at **The Heights Hotel**, *High Street.*

SPORTS & RECREATION

Pony trekking is available at the **Dolbadarn Centre**, *Dolbadarn Hotel, Tel. 01286 870277.*

Kayaking, canoeing, climbing, abseiling and other activities are offered by the **Padarn Watersports Centre**, *Llyn Padarn, Tel. 01286 870556.*

PRACTICAL INFORMATION

The Llanberis **tourist information center** is located *opposite the post office, on High Street, Tel. 01286 870765.*

CAERNARFON

Caernarfon is one of Wales's most impressive castles, and played an important part in Welsh history.

ARRIVALS & DEPARTURES

By Car

From Porthmadog and the south, take the A487; from the east, take the A5 to the junction with the A487. Turn left on to the A487 heading southwest for approximately seven miles.

By Bus

Caernarfon is eleven miles from Bangor, which has regular bus connections to London with National Express, *Tel. 0990 808080.*

By Train

Bangor also has direct train connections to London (Euston). From Bangor, you can get bus 5 or 5A to Caernarfon, with a journey time of about 25 minutes.

GETTING AROUND TOWN

The best way to see Caernarfon is on foot.

WHERE TO STAY

CAER MENAI, *15 Church Street, Caernarfon LL55 1SW. Tel and Fax 01286 672612. Rooms: 7 Rates: singles from £26, doubles from £38. No credit cards.*

This small friendly guest house is located within the town walls and within easy reach of all Caernarfon's amenities. The rooms are bright, with tea- and coffee-making facilities and TV, and the property's back garden is backed by the original town walls.

SEIONT MANOR, *Llanrug, Caernarfon LL55 2AQ. Tel 01286 673366, Fax 01286 672840. Rooms: 28. Rates: singles from £95, doubles from £140. Bar, restaurant, indoor pool, private fishing, sauna, solarium, gymnasium. All major credit cards accepted.*

This attractive hotel, converted from various rural buildings, is located in peaceful countryside about 2 1/2 miles eat of Caernarfon on the A4086. The 28 bedrooms are individually designed with all modern facilities. There are comfortable country-house style public rooms and an excellent leisure suite, comprising pool, sauna and gymnasium. The restaurant serves good food with a local/regional twist.

WHERE TO EAT

TY'N RHOS COUNTRY HOTEL & RESTAURANT, *Llanddeiniolen, Caernarfon. Tel. 01248 670489. Open daily. Main courses around £16. All major credit cards accepted.*

The Ty'n Rhos is one of those special places where an idyllic location and superb food combine to create a really magical dining experience. The converted farmhouse is situated in a peaceful location with views to the Isle of Anglesey. The chef uses only the best local produce, some of which is grown right there on the farm. You really can't beat Welsh lamb, so a particularly good main course choice is rack of lamb with rosemary and red wine; there's a good selection of desserts or you could opt for the selection of Welsh cheeses accompanied by traditional homemade oatcakes. The staff are friendly and efficient.

THE BLACK BOY INN, *North-Gate Street, Caernarfon LL55 1RW. Tel 01286 673023. Open daily noon to 2pm, 6:30pm to 9pm. Main courses from 310. Credit cards: MC, Visa.*

This attractive atmospheric inn is located within the walls of Caernarfon Castle, and dates back as far as the 15th century. The food is essentially traditional home-cooked steaks and seafood – not particularly imaginative, but who needs imagination when you've got such fantastic views around. There's a good choice of (filling) desserts, and plenty of wines to choose from.

SEEING THE SIGHTS

Caernarfon Castle is one of Wales' most majestic fortresses, standing sentinel over the peaceful River Seiont below, its strong, polygonal towers patterned with bands of colored stone. Yet Caernarfon's history is far from peaceful. Built by England's **King Edward I** as a sign of his determination to subdue the Welsh tribes, the virtually impregnable fortress saw many attempted sieges, but none to any avail.

But Edward wanted more than just to quell any Welsh uprising; he wanted to win the hearts and minds of the people – so he thought up a clever plan. The Welsh chieftains had made it clear that they would never accept a foreign prince, so Edward promised to propose a ruler who would speak no English. In 1284, Edward sent his pregnant wife, Eleanor of Castille, to Caernarfon, so that she could give birth there. She did, allowing Edward to present the baby to the Welsh chieftains as one who had been born on Welsh soil, spoke no English and whose first words would be spoken in Welsh. Hence the **first Prince of Wales** was created. The tradition continues to this day; in 1969 Queen Elizabeth II presented her eldest son, Charles, as prince of the Welsh people; a position he retains to this day. *Open March to October daily 9:30am to 6:30pm; October* *to March Monday to Saturday 9:30am to 4pm, Sunday 11am to 4pm. Admission £5. Tel. 01286 677617.*

Caernarfon's other attractions include St. Mary's Garrison Church, of medieval construction and built into the city walls, and, just outside the city, the Roman Fortress of Segontium, where you can see various items discovered on the site of this large Roman fort. *Open March, April and October Monday to Saturday 9:30am to 5:30pm, Sunday 2pm to 5pm; May to September Monday to Saturday 9:30am to 6pm, Sunday 2pm to 6pm; November to February Monday to Saturday 9:30am to 4pm, Sunday 2pm to 4pm. Admission £1.50. Tel. 01286 675625.*

NIGHTLIFE & ENTERTAINMENT

Try The Liverpool Arms, *on the Quay.*

PRACTICAL INFORMATION

Caernarfon has a small **airport** on *Dinas Dinlle Beach Road*, where you can take short aircraft flights over Snowdon and Anglesey. *Call 01296 830800 for details.* The **tourist information center** for Caerarfon is at *Oriel Pendeitsh,* opposite the entrance to the castle, *Tel. 01286 710426.*

THE LONGEST PLACE NAME

Half-way between Bangor on the mainland and Angelsey's holyhead is a small, insignificant village by the name of – Llanfairpwllgwyngyllgogerychwyrndrobwllllantysiliogogogoch. With 58 characters, it's by far the longest place name in Britain, but is it original? No! It was dreamed up by a bright spark in Victorian times to pull the tourists in. Many do indeed stop at the station here to take a look at the platform sign and, of course to buy a platform ticket. And the meaning? Yes, it has one: "St. Mary's Church in the hollow of the white hazel near a rapid whirlpool and the Church of St Tysilio near the red cave." So there!

BEAUMARIS

Beaumaris is on the offshore island of Anglesey, which is linked to the mainland by the Britannia road and rail bridge and by Thomas Telford's amazing chain suspension bridge, built in 1826 over the Menai Straits. Beaumaris is a surprisingly elegant town of Georgian houses, older cottages and a potpourri of interesting shops and stores.

The town's roots go back to 1295. Then it was that Edward I started work on the castle, built, like all of the others in his iron ring of fortresses, to keep the Welsh under control.

ARRIVALS & DEPARTURES

By Car

Take the A55 from Conwy to the Menai Bridge, then follow the signs for Beaumaris.

By Bus

There's a regular bus service from Bangor (with train and bus connections to London) to Beaumaris.

By Train

The nearest train station to Beaumaris is at Bangor, which is on the main line to London and has connections to other parts of the country. From Bangor there's a regular, hourly (#57) bus to Beaumaris, with a journey time of around half an hour.

WHERE TO STAY

OLDE BULL'S HEAD, *Castle Street, Beaumaris LL58 8AP. Tel. 01248 810329, Fax 01248 811294. Rooms: 16. Rates: singles from £53, doubles from £83. Restaurants, bar, lounge. All major credit cards accepted.*

This old coaching inn dates back to the 15th century, and has a wealth of fascinating period features: creaky floors, beams and a massive courtyard gate on one hinge. The inn has had some intriguing guests, too, among them diarist Dr. Samuel Johnson and Charles Dickens (who seemed to like staying anywhere there was a good bar). The rooms are all named after characters in Dickens' novels and are nicely decorated and furnished with reproduction furniture. A nice touch here is that early suppers are provided for children; seeing as children under seven aren't allowed in the restaurant evenings, that's not so surprising. See the description of the brasserie and restaurant below.

WHERE TO EAT

OLDE BULL'S HEAD, *Castle Street, Beaumaris. Tel. 01248 810329. Open daily noon to 2:30pm, Monday to Saturday 7pm to 10pm. Main courses around £17. All major credit cards accepted.*

A brand-new brasserie has recently open at the Olde Bull's Head below the attractive oak-beamed restaurant – all part of a comprehensive renovation program. Despite the changes, the food, which relies heavily on fresh local ingredients such as crab and lamb with a red currant and rosemary sauce, is exquisitely cooked and beautifully presented. Desserts are fairly traditional, the service friendly and welcoming and the wine list is predominantly French.

SEEING THE SIGHTS

The **castle**, the last and largest of all Edward I's endeavors, was built in 1295 and is spectacularly located at the western approach to the Menai Straits. *Open April to October daily 9:30am to 6:30pm; November to March Monday to Saturday 9:30am to 4pm, Sunday 11am to 4pm. Admission £2.50. Tel. 01248 810361.*

The old **courthouse**, right opposite the castle, was built in 1614, with an interesting plaque that demonstrates that the public's perception of the legal profession hasn't changed very much over the centuries; two men are pulling a cow, one by the horns, the other by the tail, while a lawyer sits in the middle, milking. Close by at 1 Castle Street is the **Museum and Memorabilia of Childhood**, a fascinating mixture of toy trains, cars, music boxes, piggy banks, magic lanterns, dolls and the like. *Open March to October Monday to Saturday 10am to 5:30pm, Sunday noon to 5pm.*

BEAUMARIS' ART FESTIVAL
*There's an **arts festival** in Beaumaris, held annually in late May/ early June, and featuring concerts, recitals, plays and dance, with the whole town as a backdrop. Call 01248 713177 for information.*

PRACTICAL INFORMATION

There's no tourist office in Beaumaris. Visitors can get call the **Isle of Anglesey Tourist Board**, *Llangefni, Angelsey LL77 7JW, Tel. 01248 750057,* for information about Beaumaris.

CONWY

Conwy is a fine example of a Welsh medieval town, with an impressive castle featuring incredibly thick walls, and interesting period architecture throughout.

ARRIVALS & DEPARTURES
By Car

Conwy is on the main A55 which conncts Chester to Angelsey, and at the northern end of the A470 from Betws-y-Coed.

By Bus

There are frequent bus services from Conwy to both Llandudno and Bangor.

By Train
Llandudno Junction Station is a short walk from the center of Conwy and has connections to London.

GETTING AROUND TOWN
Conwy is a compact little town and is best explored on foot.

WHERE TO STAY
BERTHLWYD HALL, *Conway LL32 8DQ. Tel. 01492 592409, Fax 572290. Rooms: 5. Rates: single from £40, doubles from £60, four-poster from £80. Bar, garden, nearby swimming pool for use of guests. Credit cards: MC, Visa.*

This Victorian country house, approached rather unceremoniously through a trailer park, is about two miles from the center of Conwy. It has a wonderful cordial atmosphere that quickly puts you at ease. Inside there are lots of typically Victorian period features; wood paneling, stained glass, fireplaces and the like, and particularly a lovely galleried entrance hall. The rooms are bright and spacious, and furnished with antiques.

WHERE TO EAT
ALFREDO'S, *The Square, Conwy. Tel 01492 592381. Open daily 6pm to 10pm. Main courses around £7. Credit cards: MC, Visa.*

It doesn't take a lot of guessing to work out that this is an Italian restaurant, conveniently located right in the center of town. Along with the restaurant's pleasant ambience, there's an extensive menu which includes, as you'd expect, lots of pasta and pizza dishes, and a range of meat (especially veal) options. There's a good choice of desserts, and a wine list which, of course, focuses on Italian.

SEEING THE SIGHTS
The focal point of this lovely medieval town is again the **castle**, on the River Conwy's west bank, built (again) by Edward I – strong and sturdy, with towering turrets and massively thick walls. One of the best ways to approach the castle is across the suspension bridge built by Telford in 1825. The town has a large number of medieval buildings; the atmosphere is enhanced by the presence of well-preserved walls enclosing the old town. Certain stretches of the wall can be walked, offering stunning views across the rooftops of the old town to the castle and estuary beyond.

Just south of Conwy off the A470 is **Bidnant Garden**, an 87-acre garden that was set out in 1875, and contains a host of rhododendrons, azaleas and camellias. The result, particularly in the spring, is magnificent. There are also rockeries, terraces, rose gardens and a pinetum. *Open March to October daily 10am to 5pm. Admission £5. Tel. 01492 650460.*

PRACTICAL INFORMATION
The town's **tourist information center** is in the *Conwy Castle Visitrs' Centre, Tel. 01492 592248*. The post office is at the western end of High Street.

LLANDUDNO
Llandudno is a very popular seaside resort town, with an authentic Victorian feel about the place.

ARRIVALS & DEPARTURES
By Car
Llandudno is just off the main A55 from Chester, with connections to the M6.

By Bus
Llandudno has direct services to London with National Express, *Tel. 0990 808080*.

By Train
There are direct trains, *Tel. 0345 484950*, from Llandudno to London Euston, with a journey time of about 3 1/2 hours.

GETTING AROUND TOWN
The center of Llandudno is compact and easily negotiable on foot.

WHERE TO STAY
BODYSGALLEN HALL HOTEL, *Llandudno LL30 1RS. Tel 01492 584466, Fax 01492 582519. Rooms: 35. Rates: singles from £104, doubles from £140. Bar, restaurant, indoor pool, tennis courts, sauna, solarium, gymnasium, beauty salon, steam room. All major credit cards accepted.*

This exceptional hotel is located on the A470 just outside Llandudno on a 220-acre parkland estate, with views to Conwy Castle and Snowdonia. Many of the lavishly decorated and furnished public rooms are wood paneled, and on the walls you will even find Old Masters! The bedrooms, some of which are in converted cottages, are similarly luxuriously appointed. There's a superb restaurant, and an extensive range of leisure facilities.

THE LIGHTHOUSE, *Marine Drive, Great Ormes Head, Llandudno LL30 2XD. Tel 01492 876819, Fax 01492 876668. Rooms: 3. Rates: singles from £60, doubles from £110. Credit cards: MC, Visa.*

This amazing building, which was functioning as a lighthouse until the 1980s, was built in the style of a mini-castle. Now a guest house, it has lashings of character, from the wood paneled walls of the entrance hall to the antique-furnished guest rooms, which have superb sea views and are thoughtfully supplied with binoculars. There's a beautiful breakfast room that's full of character; for other meals, Llandudno town center is just a couple of miles away.

STRATFORD HOTEL, *8 Craig-y-Don Parade, The Promenade, Llandudno LL30 1BG. Rooms: 10. Rates: singles from £21, doubles from £38. All major credit cards accepted.*

This small seaside hotel is located on the promenade, just a short walk away from Llandudno's shops and theater. The bedrooms, some of which have canopied beds, are comfortable, and come with TV and tea- and coffee-making facilities. There's a small bar, and a patio that overlooks the water. This place is popular with British holidaymakers, and, though it lacks the refinement of the two other establishments listed, you just can't argue with the price.

WHERE TO EAT

MARTIN'S "RESTAURANT WITH ROOMS", *11 Mostyn Avenue, Craig Y Don, Llandudno. Tel. 01492 870070. Open Tuesday to Saturday. Set dinner (two courses) from £17.95. All major credit cards accepted.*

Martin James, the "Martin" in the restaurant's title, has created a really special neighborhood restaurant close to Llandudno seafront. It's situated in an attractive Edwardian townhouse, fresh flowers adorning the tables and reflecting Martin's care for his establishment. That care extends to the food, too. Martin makes his own bread; the menu is creative and makes good use of the best local ingredients, like steamed halibut with a smoked haddock and creamy crab mousse. The desserts are equally appealing, and as you'd expect, the wine list has been carefully chosen. In addition to the excellent food, the service is warm and friendly, but not overbearing.

BISTRO 9, *Old Road Llandudno LL30 2HA. Tel/Fax 01492 875424. Open Tuesday to Saturday noon to 1:45pm, Monday to Saturday 7pm to 9:30pm . Main courses from £9. All major credit cards accepted.*

The burgundy walls of this friendly bistro, just a few minutes' walk away from Llandudno's pier and promenade, add to the feeling of informality and warmth, as do the quaint old pine benches, tables and bar which come from a former chapel. Particularly good are the goat's cheese parcels roasted in tapanade and served with salad, followed by fresh cod in basil and tomato sauce. Desserts include toasted almond meringue roulade filled with raspberries and cream. There's a good wine list, with a bottle of house wine starting at £9.25.

SEEING THE SIGHTS

Wales' best-known seaside resort has an air of genteel decay, but is all the more charming for it, with lots of Victorian buildings in a good state of preservation and a typical **Victorian Pier** that's slightly eccentric. What's more, there are very few of the brash, noisy amusement arcades that disfigure so many other British resorts. You can stroll along a wide **Promenade**, shop in the neighboring streets or take a trip on the town's cable car to the **Great Orme**, a headland that offers wonderful views of the resort and beyond.

Apart from the seafront, with its obvious charms, Llandudno's best attraction is the **Alice in Wonderland Centre**, at 4 Trinity Road. Llandudno was the summer home of Dr. Liddell, father of Alice, Lewis Carroll's model for *Alice in Wonderland*. In the center, various enchanting displays bring pages from the book to life. Children (and one or two adults, I suspect) will love it! *Open Easter to October daily 10am to 5pm; November to Easter Monday to Saturday 10am to 5pm. Admission £2.95. Tel. 01492 860082.*

NIGHTLIFE & ENTERTAINMENT

Llandudno boasts one of Wales' largest theaters, the **North Wales Theatre**, *on the Promenade, Tel. 01492 872000.*

The King's Head, *Old Road*, next to the Great Corme tramway station, and **The Cottage Loaf**, *Gloddaeth Street,* are both worthy pubs.

PRACTICAL INFORMATION

There's a **tourist information center** at *1 Chapel Street, Tel. 01492 876413.* All the major banks are represented in the town; there's a branch of **Thomas Cook**, *Mostyn Street.*

INDEX

THINGS CHANGE!

Phone numbers, prices, addresses, quality of food, etc, all change. If you come across any new information, we'd appreciate hearing from you. No item is too small! Drop us an e-mail note at: Jopenroad@aol.com, or write us at:

England & Wales Guide
Open Road Publishing, P.O. Box 284
Cold Spring Harbor, NY 11724